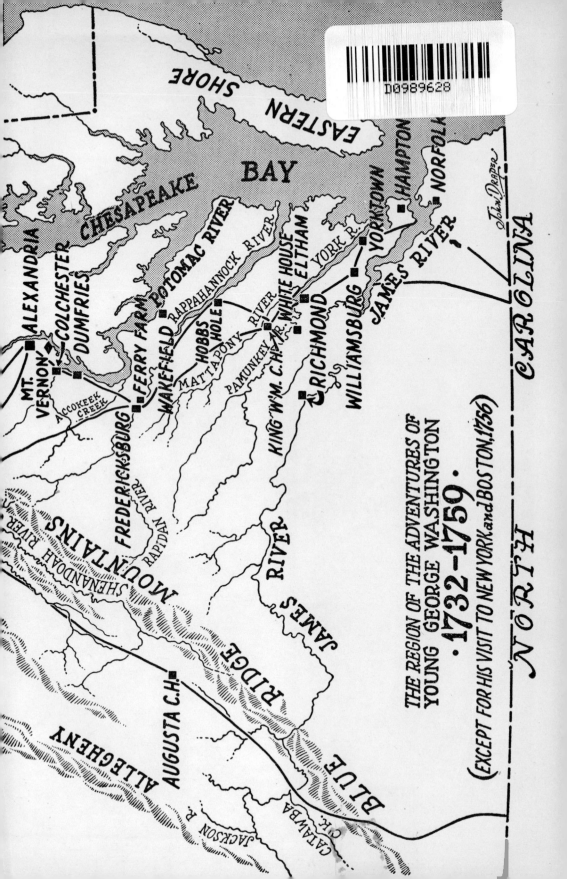

THE REGION OF THE ADVENTURES OF
YOUNG GEORGE WASHINGTON
·1732-1759·
(EXCEPT FOR HIS VISIT TO NEW YORK and BOSTON, 1756)

John Draper

CHESAPEAKE BAY

EASTERN SHORE

NORTH CAROLINA

BLUE RIDGE MOUNTAINS

ALLEGHENY

SHENANDOAH RIVER

FREDERICKSBURG

RAPIDAN RIVER

ALEXANDRIA
MT. VERNON
COLCHESTER
DUMFRIES
ACCOKEEK CREEK
FERRY FARM
WAKEFIELD
POTOMAC RIVER
RAPPAHANNOCK RIVER
HOBBS HOLE
MATTAPONY RIVER
PAMUNKEY RIVER
KING WM. C.H.
WHITE HOUSE
ELTHAM
YORK R.
RICHMOND
WILLIAMSBURG
YORKTOWN
HAMPTON
NORFOLK
JAMES RIVER
JAMES RIVER

AUGUSTA C.H.
JACKSON R.
CATAWBA CK.

D0989628

GEORGE WASHINGTON

BOOKS BY DOUGLAS SOUTHALL FREEMAN

———

George Washington
Lee's Lieutenants
The South to Posterity
R. E. Lee

———

Charles Scribner's Sons

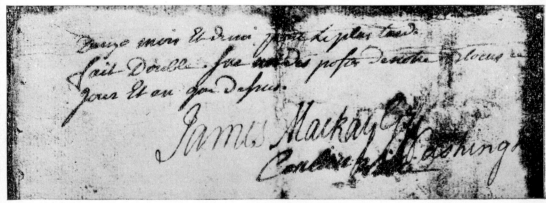

THE CAPITULATION OF FORT NECESSITY, JULY 3, 1754

This document, preserved in the archives of the District of Montreal, is rain-blotted and in several places is erased and corrected. It is signed by Washington, by James Mackay, commander of the British Independent Company, and by the French commander of the attacking force, Coulon de Villiers. Shown here are part of Page One and the signatures on Page Three.

GEORGE WASHINGTON

A BIOGRAPHY

By

Douglas Southall Freeman

VOLUME TWO

YOUNG
WASHINGTON

LONDON
EYRE AND SPOTTISWOODE

A

CONTENTS

APPENDICES

ILLUSTRATIONS

MAPS

GEORGE WASHINGTON

CHAPTER I

RESENTMENT, REGRET, INVITATION
(NOVEMBER, 1754–MARCH 14, 1755)

GEORGE WASHINGTON's resignation as Colonel of the Virginia Regiment in November, 1754, did not destroy his ambition for a military career. He quit the service because he felt that Governor Dinwiddie had humiliated him personally and had deprived him of public honors by dividing the troops into Independent Companies. Instead of his former position as Colonel, George would have had that of provincial Captain only, outranked, as he wrathfully put it, by "every Captain, bearing the King's commission, every half-pay officer, or other, appearing with such a commission." [1] He would not endure that, but he still wanted to learn more of "the military art," and he began to ask himself and his influential friends if there might not be some way by which he could serve in the campaign of 1755 as a volunteer. Especially was he disposed to this when he heard that the next march on Fort DuQuesne was to be under the direction of an experienced British General, and not under Colonel Innes or Governor Sharpe, neither of whom he esteemed as a soldier. [2]

Whatever the prospect of new military service as a volunteer, George had his own fortune to advance. His mother was still at Ferry Farm, though under the will of Augustine the property was to be George's when the son became of age. None of the other tracts belonging to the retired young Colonel had on it a suitable residence. For a man not yet twenty-three he was well to do, but he had no home of his own. He wanted an establishment, he could afford one, and he had now a prospect of leasing the property he most desired, Mount Vernon. His sister-in-law, Nancy Fairfax Washington, widow of Maj. Lawrence Washington, had married Col. George Lee, only son of the third Richard Lee, on the 16th of December, 1752, less than six months after the death of her first companion. [3] She was now rearing a second family

---

[1] See *supra*, Vol. I, p. 440.   [2] Cf. 1 *G. W.*, 107.   [3] *Lee of Virginia*, 140.

and was residing on her husband's estate, Mount Pleasant, Westmoreland County. As Mrs. Lee had no personal use for the house George loved, he undertook to lease it from Colonel Lee.

It did not prove an easy transaction, because the poorly-written will of Major Washington raised no less than three disputable questions. One concerned the scope of Mrs. Washington's life-interest; the second was whether she was entitled to half of Lawrence's household goods free of liability for his debts; a third had to do with the rights of any children by her second marriage. Still other questions, of wide ramification, were created by the death in 1754 of Lawrence's only surviving child, Sarah.[4] There was no denying the fact that on the payment of £100 sterling to Mrs. Lee, the personal property of Sarah and her right to half the slaves of the estate would pass to Lawrence's brothers; but the contention of Colonel Lee was that Lawrence's debts were a prime charge against Sarah's part of the estate and not against Mrs. Lee's share. John Mercer gave the Washington brothers an opinion that upheld their contention in full; Edmund Pendleton contended, in support of Colonel Lee's position, that the debts were chargeable against Sarah's estate and, after that, among the legatees in proportion to the value of their respective bequests under the will.[5]

Because of the close ties between the Fairfaxes and Washingtons, it was imperative that opposing views be reconciled, if possible, on the advice of counsel and without the odium of a suit. Full agreement could not be reached amicably, but a devise of the slaves was accepted according to a form drafted by John Mercer for the executors and the legatees.[6] In the presence of a number of kinsfolk and friends on Dec. 10, 1754, the Negroes were divided into two groups, each of which was worth a total of about £750, exclusive of sixteen infants and small children. The transaction was made a matter of record by this document:

Memorandum: The division of the slaves of the late Lawrence Washington, Esq., as made pursuant to the last will and testament of the said Lawrence

[4] The precise date has never been determined. Washington himself in time forgot even the year and, writing a genealogical sketch in 1792 (32 *G. W.*, 28) entered it as "175—." In the accounts of Lawrence's executors for 1759 is payment for "velvet cap for Miss Washington" (*Fairfax Wills,* C, 1, p. 14). This entry might be interpreted to mean that the heiress was then alive but, in all likelihood, the cap was for Jane, two-year-old daughter of John Augustine Washington, some of whose orders occasionally appear on the books of the estate. The document about to be quoted in the text leaves no doubt that Sarah was dead by Dec. 10, 1754.

[5] Copies of the two opinions, December, 1754, are in 1 *Papers of G. W.,* 95, 96; LC.

[6] *Ledger A,* folios 7, 18 and 19. George charged his brother Samuel with 5 s. 4½ d. on each of Mercer's two fees.

is hereunto annexed: and that moiety of the said slaves the use of which by the will of the aforesaid was devised to the widow of the said Lawrence during her life, George Lee, Esq., of Westmoreland County, who intermarried with the said widow, doth hereby acknowledge to have received. The other moiety which by the death of the said Lawrence's daughter Sarah, is to descend according to the true intent of the will to the several devisees therein mentioned: they also acknowledge to have received as per this division, and agree on both sides to abide thereby in pursuance of the Testator's direction, true meaning and intention. In witness whereof they have set their hands and seals this 10th day of December, 1754.

> George Lee
> Ann Lee
> Auge Washington
> G. Washington.[7]

Col. William Fairfax, George William Fairfax, and several other witnesses signed this paper as if it were a souvenir of a happy occasion.[8] In one sense it was precisely that, because it probably facilitated the lease of Mount Vernon. Colonel and Mrs. Lee agreed, Dec. 17, 1754, that George might have the use of the estate and of the eighteen resident slaves at a fixed annual rental of 15,000 lbs. of tobacco per annum, or the equivalent in current money of Virginia at the rate of 12s, 6d. per hundredweight of tobacco. The agreement ran for the term of Ann Lee's life interest and stipulated that if any of the slaves died, a deduction of 500, 800 or 1000 lbs. of tobacco should be made in the annual rental, according to the value of the labor of the individual. Use of the "water grist mill" on the property was included. If the rent was not paid within five months after the due date, which was December 25, Colonel Lee and his wife could levy by distress or could take over the estate and the slaves. The lease was to begin when signed.[9]

Before he was twenty-three, George thus became tenant and master of Mount Vernon, at a rental not more than double his annual net compensation as District Adjutant. As it chanced, he was having some difficulty in collecting that salary, which he did not think he had forfeited while receiving pay as a Colonel on active duty. A letter to Governor Dinwiddie, asking for arrearages, brought a brief and coldly

[7] Photostat VHS, after the original owned by George A. Plimpton. This document almost certainly is in the autograph of George Washington.

[8] Bryan Fairfax specified that he witnessed Augustine Washington's signature, which circumstance may indicate that Augustine was not present when the others signed. It is possible that Bryan Fairfax had carried the "Memorandum" to him for his acceptance.

[9] *Fairfax Deeds.* C, 1, p. 822.

polite answer that the account could not be settled at the time, but that "when the Council meets, I shall let them know your demand, and if they agree with me it will be paid." [10] In this George could read unmistakably that the Scotch Governor still was angry over his resignation, but the letter left no doubt the money would be in his hands before long. It could be supplemented easily with sufficient other income to cover the lease of Mount Vernon and thereby to keep the rent from being a charge on the crops of 1755 and later. Whatever could be grown on the estate would be net profit, after taxes were paid and the slaves were fed and clothed.

To the arrangement of these business affairs and to the completion of some unavoidable journeys George devoted most of his time in the last days of 1754. He went to Frederick County in the final week of November [11] and he had planned to visit William Byrd III at Westover, James River, during the Christmas holidays, but an accident kept him on the Potomac. [12] In that pleasant neighborhood, apparently, he spent the season of celebration among the Fairfaxes and the Carlyles, with no livelier diversion than that of cards, at which his three-day winnings were 14 s, 3 d. [13] After New Year's, there was some visiting to Col. John Baylor of Newmarket, Caroline County, whom Washington esteemed highly, [14] and to Col. John Spotswood of New Post, Spotsylvania County, son of Gov. Alexander Spotswood. [15] On George's return to Mount Vernon, his instinct for order and his disposition to put first things first led him to buy slaves, to make provision for his livestock, and to

[10] Dinwiddie to Washington, Dec. 20, 1754; 1 *Din.*, 435–36.

[11] *Ledger A*, folio 17.

[12] Washington to William Byrd, April 20, 1755; 1 *G. W.*, 113–14. Of the accident, George gave no detail: "I had enjoyed much satisfaction in the thought [of a visit] when an unexpected accident put it entirely out of my power . . ." The only suggestion in Washington's accounts of any medical expenses is the payment on Nov. 11, 1754, of 5 s. to Doctor Halkerston (*Ledger A*, folio 17). As Halkerston practiced for a time in Fredericksburg (*Blanton*, 361), the charge may have been an account of treatment George required for some accident that occurred while he was returning from Williamsburg after resigning his commission. Related entries indicate he was in the vicinity of Fredericksburg at that time. Concerning the proposed visit to Westover, it would be romantic to think that Washington was seeking the hand of one of the daughters of the brilliant William Byrd II, father of William Byrd III, but, unfortunately for romance, all these young ladies were older than George and were married. See 32 *V* 37, where a typographical error makes it appear that Anne Byrd, who married Charles Carter of Cleve, was born in 1735. The correct year was 1725. See 31 *V* 34.

[13] *Ledger A*, folio 18.

[14] George was at Colonel Baylor's Jan. 9, 1755 (*Ledger A*, folio 18). For Baylor, twenty-seven years George's senior and County Lieutenant of Orange, see 24 *V* 373. He was father of Lt. Col. George Baylor who appears in Volume IV of this work.

[15] See R. A. Brock, ed. *Official Letters of Alexander Spotswood*, v. I, p. xiv. Washington's host was the same John Spotswood whose youthful letter in the *Virginia Gazette* was quoted *supra*, Vol. I, p. 117. New Post often was confused with Newport, a nearby Waller home. See 8 *W* (1) p. 79; 9 *W* (1) p. 64; 11 *W* (1) p. 2; 4 *W* (2) p. 84; 26 *V* 33.

acquire some of the needed furniture for the house. He did not undertake any large repairs.[16] As George had little experience in housekeeping and had kind and sympathetic neighbors, it is likely that he consulted often the family at Belvoir and, in particular, the charming Sally Cary Fairfax. His feelings for her may not have undergone any change of which he was conscious, but he certainly admired her as much as it was proper to regard the wife of a close friend. In the company at Belvoir, he later was to confess, he spent the happiest days of his life.[17]

During these months of pleasantness, John Carlyle was acting for Lawrence's other executors and was keeping the accounts required by the court. The final appraisal of the personal estate was £1729 in Fairfax and £666 in Frederick.[18] Of this amount, £399 came from the principal sale of personal property in Fairfax. The slaves there and in Frederick represented £1518; stock and tools brought £246.[19] George's previous purchases of £55 from the estate were not increased.[20] Effects removed by Colonel Lee and charged against Ann Lee's account amounted to £126.[21] A suit for breach of trust that Lawrence in his will had directed his executors to prosecute against Gersham Keys was duly followed through the courts and, in time, was won.[22]

George's small share in the settlement of Lawrence's affairs, his interest in Belvoir, and his numerous activities on his own plantation did not occupy all his thought. He had developed his mind and his interests to the state where he could find measurable satisfaction in doing thoroughly whatever he had to do; but he had too deep a devotion to arms, even after his unhappy experience over his commission, to ignore events subsequent to his resignation.

Much of interest had occurred during the autumn and winter; still more was in prospect. Both Governor Dinwiddie of Virginia and Governor Sharpe of Maryland were resolved to press the campaign against the French in 1755 and to recover the territory and the prestige the English had lost the previous year. Although George did not now share

---

[16] See *Ledger A*, folios 18 and 19.
[17] 36 *G. W.*, 263.
[20] See Vol. I, p. 266.
[18] *Fairfax Wills*, B, 1, p. 117.
[19] *Ibid*.
[21] *Fairfax Wills*, B, 1, p. 117.
[22] *Fairfax Wills*, C, 1, p. 14 ff. The sum initially paid by Keys July 26, 1756, "per judgment" was £186, 12 s., 6 d., but certain payments were deferred by court order and subsequently were made to the estate (1 *Hamilton*, 231). Keys—the name often spelled Key and occasionally Keyes—resided "on the west bank of the Shenandoah, above the Blue Ridge Gap which was then (as it is now) generally called for him." (Fairfax Harrison in 32 *V* 313 n.). The nature of Keys's "breach of trust" may be suggested in 1 *Papers of G. W.*, 28; LC.

the councils of his Governor or of the neighboring executive who was acting Commander-in-Chief, the young master of Mount Vernon might have learned, had he inquired, that agreed plans for the operations of the spring and summer had five essential aspects: First, the Colonies must have the leadership of officers and troops "from home"; second, the Colonies themselves must supply soldiers of their own and provisions for them and for the forces from England; third, colonials and redcoats should seek the assistance of all the Indians who could be won to their side; fourth, to prevent hunger and loss of time when the season for active fighting began, a large store of provisions must be accumulated in advance and must be transported as far toward the Ohio as practicable; fifth, for the proper storage and custody of these rations, a fort was to be constructed at Wills Creek.

The last of these tasks was of necessity the first to be performed. About the time George was riding back from Williamsburg after resigning in November, Governor Sharpe had gone to Wills Creek,[23] where a Company of Maryland volunteers was stationed along with the remnant of the Virginia Regiment. Sharpe had been shocked by the conditions he found at the outpost. Few provisions had been accumulated; a fort nearing completion was small and manifestly inadequate.[24] The Governor had ordered a much larger fort erected on a different site, and, with Dinwiddie, had sought to establish a sound commissary system there.[25] In the arrangements for supply, the experience of 1754 was not forgotten.[26] A less bad road, shorter by thirty miles, was laid out between Winchester and Wills Creek.[27] Over this road, wagons slowly but regularly carried flour and salt meat to the fort,[28] where one of two newly-appointed commissaries was supposed to be on regular duty.[29] Many disappointments were encountered. Farmers were reluctant to have their animals used as pack horses;[30] wheeled vehicles were so scarce that attempts had to be made to construct some in Northern Virginia;[31] few provisions could be purchased in that immediate re-

[23] Md. Gazette, Nov. 14, 1754.   [24] 1 Din., 372, 405, 408, 430.

[25] 1 Sharpe 136, 201; Lowdermilk, 83, 90 ff. In the course of this work, Dinwiddie's relations with Innes had been strained twice (1 Din., 397, 422), but had been repaired. The Governor had solicited vainly a commission for Innes as a Major on the regular establishment so that, if anything happened to Sharpe, a successor would be at hand (ibid., 404, 409).

[26] Cf. 1 Din., 425.

[27] 1 Din., 427. For details of this route, see infra, p. 32.

[28] 1 Din., 415, 418–19.

[29] Ibid., 418 ff, 432, 436, 439. One of these commissaries, Major Charles Dick, was denied repayment of funds he advanced personally (1 Hamilton, 87). For references to him and to his interesting collection of books, see 18 W (1), p. 112.

[30] 1 Din., 489.   [31] 1 Din., 480.

gion;[32] the cost of carriage was excessive—20 s. for each barrel of beef delivered at Wills Creek.[33] Where distances were great and communication insecure, no assurance could be had that dealers would accept contracts for provisions or would make delivery when they had agreed to do so.[34] In spite of all these difficulties, Dinwiddie was to be able to say, before the beginning of spring, that he had provided rations at Wills Creek sufficient, he thought, to feed 3000 men or more for almost eight months.[35]

This was to be achieved by, and only by, the unstinted use of £20,000 of royal coin and credit[36] because, in another essential of preparation, that of colonial joint effort, Dinwiddie and Sharpe were able to achieve little during the winter of 1754–55. Governor Dinwiddie, on the 8th of November, had called on the other provincial executives to procure from the legislative assemblies supplies of men or money or both,[37] though he had felt sure the lawmakers could not be aroused from their "lethargic indolence," their "supine and unaccountable obstinacy."[38] About the middle of November he had exploded: "It's a monstrous thing to think of the supineness and backwardness of our neighboring Colonies in granting supplies. South Carolina, Pennsylvania or the Jerseys have granted none."[39] The refusal of Pennsylvania to vote money or to furnish money was resented particularly. That Colony was regarded by some as the most important in America;[40] but its Assembly declined to support the campaign on the ground that all the French forts were beyond its boundaries.[41] South Carolina similarly was on the black books of Dinwiddie, both because he disliked Governor Glen and because he was required by the home government to supply South Carolina with £1000 of funds from the Virginia export tax of 2 s. per hogshead of tobacco. This money was to be used for

---

[32] Ibid., 461.

[33] Sir John St. Clair to Maj. Gen. Edward Braddock, Feb. 9, 1755; Pargellis, 61.

[34] A typical case, that of Dinwiddie's efforts to procure 600,000 lbs. of flour, may be traced in 6 Penn. Col. Rec., 294 ff.

[35] 1 Din., 528.

[36] Ibid.

[37] 1 Din., 392 ff.

[38] Ibid., 366. Cf. ibid., 371.

[39] 1 Din., 405–06. The painful process of extracting money from the reluctant assemblies may be traced in 1 Sharpe, 158, 161; in 1 Din., 496, 512, 521, 526; and in 2 ibid., 3, 26. An admirable summary will be found in Baker-Crothers, 78. For details of North Carolina's aid and the limited circulation of her "Proclamation money," see 5 N. C. Col. Rec., 312, 571; 1 Din., 508. Maryland's contribution is explained in 1 Sharpe, 196, 215, 242, 243, 244; Md. Gazette, Aug. 15, 1755.

[40] Cf. Calvert in 31 Md. Arch., 476.

[41] 6 Penn. Col. Rec., 233. For Pennsylvania's subsequent contribution of the road from Shippensburg to the Youghiogheny, see infra, p. 30, 45.

the construction of a frontier defence against Indian attack.[42] In disgust over the divided counsel, the selfishness and the apparent indifference of the Colonies, Dinwiddie renewed his recommendation of a direct tax by Parliament on the Americans.[43]

Recruitment, too, presented many obstacles to the Virginia executive during the months his most active former officer, Colonel Washington, was occupying his energies on the Mount Vernon estate. The Governor in October, 1754, had set his mark at 2000 men, and in November had made vigorous appeals for volunteers; but he soon had to lower his goal to 1000, and, before many weeks, could say only that he hoped by February, 1755, to have a force of 800.[44] The cost of each recruit was high,[45] so high, in fact, that Dinwiddie wished for a law that would permit him to draft one in ten of all the militia.[46] Disillusioning though his experience was with the unmartial Virginians,[47] Dinwiddie had not cast off his ambition to lead them in the field. He still had hoped to receive command of them, with authority to fill in blank commissions from the King,[48] but he had instructed the Virginia agent in London, James Abercromby, not to press for this if it did not seem proper to do so.[49]

What the provincials needed to offset their weakness, Governor Dinwiddie believed the Southern Indians and the British regulars could and would supply. His faith in these two of the five essentials of the campaign of 1755 never waned. Although Governor Glen openly resented what he considered to be Virginia's interference with the Catawbas and the Cherokees of South Carolina,[50] Dinwiddie continued to solicit their help in accordance with what he told Glen were "orders from home," [51] and he confidently assumed that he had great influence with these savages. They would come in large numbers to Virginia the next spring, he believed, if Glen did not deter them.[52] These hopes were built, in

---

[42] See the Virginia protest in 17 *V* 273. Cf. *ibid.,* 383 and 1 *Din.,* 494–95. Strictly speaking, this grant of £1000 was from a credit of £10,000 that included the receipts from the "two-shilling tax." Governor Glen in April, 1755, sought to procure from Dinwiddie an additional £3000 for this fort (2 *Din.,* 24–26). Subsequently, South Carolina made a grant of £4000 for the Ohio expedition of 1755.

[43] 1 *Din.,* 493.

[44] 1 *Din.,* 392, 402, 403, 412 ff, 420, 429, 437, 447.

[45] *Ibid.,* 447.   [46] *Ibid.,* 367.

[47] "No more pacific people than the Virginians existed in the colonies—save the Quakers—if the military qualities are to be measured by actual experience with war." Osgood, *op. cit.,* v. 4, p. 225.

[48] 1 *Din.,* 365, 372, 373, 376.   [49] Letter of Nov. 16, 1754; 1 *Din.,* 410.

[50] 1 *Din.,* 364, 377–78.   [51] *Ibid.,* 378.

[52] For Dinwiddie's various reports on the coöperation of these Indians and for his appeals to them, see 1 *Din.,* 364, 368, 375, 377–78, 391, 400, 428, 484–85, 514, 524.

part, on the assumed sympathy of the Catawbas and Cherokees with the English, and in part on the pleasure that members of these tribes had expressed after visiting Williamsburg, where they had received presents and entertainment at the Governor's hands.[53] In like optimism, Dinwiddie anticipated better relations with some of the Northern Indians [54] and he hoped to complete a formal alliance between them and the Southern natives, in support of the English, at a conference to be held at Winchester in April, 1755.[55] The Governor's faith in the Indians was not shared by all his contemporaries. Charles Thomson of Philadelphia, for example, was looking eagerly to the union of all the Colonies because, among other gains, it would assure safety from "the insults of our haughty aspiring neighbors, the French," and no less because it would make "our security independent of the fickle humor of our Indian allies." [56]

Indian alliances, colonial recruits, the begrudging supply of stinted funds by suspicious assemblies, the tedious upbuilding of the store of provisions at Wills Creek—all these preparations looked to the arrival of disciplined regulars from England. Well-trained troops, led by professional soldiers, would be the core of the column that would advance irresistibly to the Ohio and drive away or destroy the French. This was the conviction of Dinwiddie. He had believed for months that two Regiments from England, with proper engineers and ordnance, were necessary for the recovery of the "Beautiful River" [57] and he had been persistent in his appeals to the home government for such a force.[58] He had warned the Lords of Trade: ". . . without two Regiments of men from Britain, we shall not be able effectually to defeat the unjust invasion of the French." [59] By Dec. 12, 1754, he had received confirmation of his hopes [60] that the troops would be sent—that transports had been taken in October and that Capt. Augustine Keppel would convoy them with a fifty-gun ship.[61] Shortly after hearing this good news, Dinwiddie learned also that two additional Regiments were to be raised in New England and were to be led by Gov. William Shirley of Massa-

---

[53] 1 *Din.*, 364.   [54] *Ibid.*, 472.   [55] *Ibid.*, 469.
[56] Letter to Joseph Shippen, Philadelphia, Jan. 31, 1755; *Shippen Papers*, 32.
[57] See Vol. I, p. 422 ff.
[58] 1 *Din.*, 364–65, 401, 402–04, 407, 409. See *ibid.*, 433, for an effort by Dinwiddie to have cannon balls, "iron shot," of a diameter of 3½ inches cast by Col. John Spotswood.
[59] Letter of Nov. 16, 1754; 1 *Din.*, 401.   [60] See *supra*, Vol. I, p. 437.
[61] 1 *Din.*, 422; 1 *Sharpe*, 146. Dinwiddie styled Keppel "Commodore," but that was the officer's courtesy title as senior officer of a mixed squadron of warships and merchantmen. Keppel did not become a Commodore by commission until after the declaration of war with Spain in 1762.

chusetts and Sir William Pepperell, the first native American ever to
be made a baronet.[62]

As this information was printed in the *Virginia Gazette*,[63] George
soon saw it at Mount Vernon. He felt a new stirring of his military
ambition, and he admitted that he would like to share in the campaign,[64] but he took no step to recover his commission or to volunteer
for service. Almost every subsequent issue of the newspaper whetted
his appetite for honors. He had just returned from a visit to Colonel
Baylor's plantation and probably to Ferry Farm [65] when word came
that a distinguished British officer had reached Williamsburg from
England—Sir John St. Clair, baronet of Scotland and former Major of
the 22nd Foot, who had been assigned as Deputy Quartermaster
General of forces in America with local rank as Lieutenant Colonel.[66]
Later that month George doubtless heard that Sir John had made a
favorable impression on Dinwiddie,[67] had contracted promptly for
100 pack horses,[68] and then, after arranging hospital facilities at
Hampton,[69] had proceeded to Winchester in the conviction that the
transport of supplies from Alexandria to Wills Creek would be
formidable and expensive and should be studied with much care.[70]
George probably learned in February that St. Clair most heartily had
damned the road from Winchester to Wills Creek as the worst he ever
had traveled.[71] At that outpost, which now was styled Fort Cumberland, St. Clair had reviewed the Independent Companies and had discharged more than forty of the men as unfit for service.[72] The Deputy
Quartermaster General manifestly was a positive officer who knew his
own mind.

While the colonials were beginning to discover what manner of
person St. Clair really was, they received information that the two
promised Regiments [73] were en route and that they were commanded

---

[62] 1 *Din.*, 438. The *Md. Gazette* of Jan. 2 and 9, 1755, contained the London dispatches of
Oct. 8 and 12, 1754, with specific mention of Shirley and of Pepperell.

[63] 1 *Din.*, 438.   [64] See *infra*, p. 14.

[65] The reason for stating he may have stopped to see his mother on his way back to Mount
Vernon from Newmarket is that on Jan. 13–15, 1754, he won small sums at cards and billiards
from men who lived in the neighborhood of Ferry Farm. See *Ledger A*, folio 19.

[66] For his career, see 9 *Penn. Mag.*, 1–14; and for London reports, Oct. 17, 1754, of his
assignment, see *Md. Gazette*, Jan. 2, 1755. St. Clair reached Hampton Jan. 9, 1755 (St. Clair's
dispatches in *Pargellis*, 58–59), and proceeded immediately to Williamsburg. An incorrect date
is given in 1 *Din.*, 453, 458.

[67] *Cf.* 1 *Din.*, 461, 465, 468.   [68] St. Clair in *Pargellis*, 59.

[69] *Ibid.*   [70] St. Clair in *Pargellis*, 60–61.

[71] *Ibid.*, 61–62.   [72] 1 *Sharpe*, 201.

[73] For early news from the *London Gazette* of Oct. 1, 1754, of the selection of these two
Regiments, see *Md. Gazette*, Jan. 2, 1755.

by Col. Sir Peter Halkett and Col. Thomas Dunbar. During the last week in February, George ascertained that on the night of the 19th–20th, Commodore Keppel's flagship, *Centurion,* had dropped anchor off Hampton along with *Syren* and *Norwich,* on which last vessel was Maj. Gen. Edward Braddock, His Majesty's Commander-in-Chief of the forces in North America.[74] It was reported soon that General Braddock had arrived in advance of any of his troops and that he had gone forthwith to Williamsburg,[75] where he was in prolonged private conference with Governor Dinwiddie and with Sir John St. Clair.

The *Virginia Gazette* announced also that the General was accompanied by "Captain Orme, Aide-de-Camp and Mr. Shirley, secretary." [76] George read and envied. These young men were doing exactly what he wanted to do: they were in close daily relationship with an experienced soldier of long service from whom they could learn much of the "military arts" that fascinated George. Soon the young Virginian identified "Mr. Shirley" as William Shirley, son of the Governor of Massachusetts. A little later George found that Braddock was to have another Aide-de-Camp, Roger Morris, who bore the surname and might be a kinsman of the Governor of Pennsylvania.[77] If they could serve with Braddock as members of his "military family," why should not a Virginian, also? George did not solicit appointment directly, but he took pains to write a letter of congratulations to Braddock on the General's arrival in America, and thereby he let His Excellency know there was such a person as George Washington.[78]

Braddock remained in Williamsburg, hard at work. Newspapers and returning travelers told of vigorous recruiting to fill out the expected British Regiments,[79] and of the organization of Virginia Companies of rangers, carpenters and light horse, to be commanded by officers of Braddock's selection.[80] In addition George, of course, heard gossip of Braddock, Keppel and St. Clair, because three such notables could not

[74] For the arrival of the squadron see *Va. Gazette,* Feb. 28, 1755; 1 *Din.,* 511, and Sargent, *op. cit.,* 283. This last source is the journal of Lieut. (usually styled Capt.) Robert Orme, and for ready identification is cited hereafter as *Orme,* with the page reference to Sargent.

[75] *Va. Gazette,* Feb. 28, 1755. For the various drafts and final form of Braddock's instructions, see *Pargellis,* 34 ff, 45 ff, Sargent, *op. cit.,* 393 ff, and 2 *Penn. Arch.,* 203 ff. Keppel's instructions appear in *Pargellis,* 48 ff.

[76] Issue of Feb. 28, 1755.

[77] These young men are sketched, *infra,* as of mid-April, 1754, when George met them. So far as is known, Captain Morris was not a kinsman of Governor Morris.

[78] In 1 *G. W.,* 108, is George's remark that he had sent such a letter which unfortunately has disappeared.

[79] This special recruiting had been started in January. See *Va. Gazette,* Feb. 28, 1755.

[80] Braddock to Sir Thomas Robinson, Williamsburg, Mch. 18, 1755; P.R.O., C.O. 5; 46, p. 1–10, Braddock in *Pargellis,* 78; 1 *Din.,* 515.

come to the quiet Virginia capital and not create chatter. Never had there been such planning, such talk of ships and soldiers, such contracts —for 200 hired wagons, among other things, and 2500 horses.[81] In comparison with George's expedition of 1754, the scale of everything was trebled or quadrupled; promises made by the colonials were in proportion. Proud Virginians and their Scotch Governor, in particular, did not intend to let it appear that they lacked the facilities to do anything their King and his Commander-in-Chief demanded of them.

To the young master of Mount Vernon, the resigned Virginia Colonel, all this was at once far off and at the same time familiar. He knew what the preparations involved and forecast, but he was not a part of them. Interested, he was detached. A veteran of the frontier, he was a bystander. He had resigned because a regular Captain could give orders to him, a colonial officer three grades higher. Now his humiliation was confirmed and his action was justified. The King's "pleasure" was made known. Provincials and regulars were informed "that all troops serving by commission signed by us, or by our General commanding in chief in North America shall take rank before all troops which may serve by commission from any of the Governors, Lieutenant or Deputy Governors, or President, for the time being, of our provinces in North America."

As printed, the order was even more bluntly specific: "And it is our further pleasure that the General and field officers of the provincial troops"—that would have included George—"shall have no rank with the General and field officers who serve by commission from us; but that all Captains and other inferior officers who are, or may be, employed in North America are on all detachments, courts martial or other duty, wherein they may be joined with officers serving by commission from the Governors, Lieutenant or Deputy Governors, or President for the time being of the said Provinces, to command and take post of the said provincial officers of the like rank, though the commissions of the said provincial officers of the like rank, should be of elder date." [82]

That was not as clear as it professed to be concerning the command a colonial Colonel might exercise over a regular Captain. There might, indeed, be contradiction between the opening reference to "all troops" serving by royal commission and the closing clauses on the command

[81] All these, Braddock wrote Sir Thomas Robinson, June 5, P.R.O., C.O. 5; 46, p. 35–41, were pledged before St. Clair left Williamsburg.

[82] Royal Orders of Nov. 12, 1754; facsimile in 1 *Hamilton*, opposite p. 56.

royal company officers were to have over "provincial officers of the like rank." [83] However that might be interpreted, George was out of the service and out of the controversy . . . until the 14th of March, 1755, when this letter was delivered to him:

Sir: The General having been informed that you expressed some desire to make the campaign, but that you declined it upon the disagreeableness that you thought might arise from the regulation of command, has ordered me to acquaint you that he will be very glad of your company in his family by which all inconveniences of that kind will be obviated.

I shall think myself very happy to form an acquaintance with a person so universally esteemed and shall use every opportunity of assuring you how much I am

Sir
Your most obedient servant
Robert Orme aid de camp

Williamsburg, Mch. 2,
     1755 [84]

[83] See Col. F. T. Nichols in 4 *W* (3), p. 135.
[84] 1 *Hamilton,* 57–58.

CHAPTER II

AN OFFER WEIGHED AND ACCEPTED

(MARCH 14–MAY 10, 1755)

GEORGE HAD to admit that Orme had been informed correctly regarding his state of mind: he wanted to share in the campaign; he was unwilling to be subordinate to regular officers of a rank lower than he had held in the service of Virginia. His interest in the expedition had risen after he had learned that it was to be headed by a senior officer who had fought in the War of the Austrian Succession.

The opportunity of joining Braddock's staff came, unfortunately, at a time when George's military ambitions clashed with his personal economy. The lease and partial equipment of Mount Vernon had involved considerable expense; he had no manager of his property; [1] if he followed his impulse and went again to the Ohio he might lose heavily at the very time he otherwise might profit. The impulse persisted; so did the doubt.

Balancing gain and sacrifice, he at length decided to postpone a final answer until he had met Braddock and had talked with the General. In an awkward but completely candid reply to Orme's letter, George told of his desire and difficulties and went on: "I shall do myself the pleasure of waiting upon his Excellency as soon as I hear of his arrival at Alexandria, (and would sooner, was I certain where) till which I shall decline saying further on this head; begging you'll be kind enough to assure him that I shall always retain a grateful sense of the favor he was kindly pleased to offer me . . ." [2]

George did not have long to wait. Approximately at the date he was

---

[1] 1 *G. W.,* 110. Concerning Braddock's offer, George wrote five letters that have survived the years—two to Captain Orme, one to Speaker Robinson, one to William Byrd III, and one to Carter Burwell, Chairman of the Military Committee of the House of Burgesses. These appear in succession in 1 *G. W.,* 107–16. They are written in the pompous, sometimes obscure style that George then thought elegant; but if they are read together and are analyzed, they will be found remarkable in their self-revelation. Seldom was a man, even a young man, so frank in the reasons he gave for a specific action.

[2] Letter of Mch. 15, 1754; 1 *G. W.,* 108.

writing to Orme, the last of the transports from Ireland arrived at Hampton, Virginia, with the rear Companies and stores of Braddock's command.[3] The men were in good health and were ordered to proceed on the same vessels to Alexandria, whither Braddock himself took ship with Keppel and Dinwiddie. On the 26th of March these celebrities disembarked at the proud new town.[4] The next day, in a manner strictly military and precise, Braddock published the camp regulations, which included the penalty of death for desertion, and announced the names of his Major of Brigade,[5] his Provost Marshal and his aides, Orme and Morris.[6]

Braddock and his "military family" received immediately the best welcome, the finest quarters and the choicest food and drink the Fairfaxes, the Carlyles and the other families of the Alexandria neighborhood could offer. In this circle of his intimates, it was as natural as it was easy for George to be presented to the General. Edward Braddock was then about sixty years of age, stout and short of body. Son of a Lieutenant Colonel of the Coldstream Guards, who had served as Major General, the younger Braddock had been in the British army forty-five years at the time George Washington first saw him. During that long period Braddock had learned completely the routine of army life and administration, but he had seen little of fighting. In September, 1746, though he had been sent to join the forces preparing for the descent on L'Orient, he had been denied a part in the actual operation. The next spring he had gone to Holland with the troops that had supported William of Orange in the effort to raise the siege of Bergen-op-Zoom.[7] Then, for a time, Braddock had been on garrison duty at Breda.

He was ordered home temporarily in December, 1748, and thereafter

3 The dates are not recorded precisely but they were approximately March 10–15. See 2 Din., 4.

4 Orme, 290–91. Departure from Williamsburg, according to Orme (op. cit., 290), was on March 21, though Dinwiddie wrote on the 17th that he and Braddock expected to leave the next day. Dates given in Orme's journal frequently are at variance with those reported by other officers of the expedition.

5 This officer usually was appointed only when troops were in camp or were brigaded in an Army. He was to the Brigade what the Adjutant General was to the Army; he received and distributed orders, saw that the rosters and records were in order, apportioned guard duty equitably, and arranged for proper rotation of the order of march. See Thomas Simes, Military Dictionary, heading Brigade Major.

6 Captain Morris probably had arrived on one of the transports after Braddock had landed. For the regulations of the camp, see Orme, 291 ff. The formal orders concerning aides appear in Lowdermilk, v. This pagination with Roman numerals after Lowdermilk, p. 496, includes the whole of Braddock's Orderly Books, Feb. 26–June 17, 1755, copied from the originals in LC. See also Orderly Book of the 44th Regiment, Mch. 28, 1755. This MS, also in LC, was kept by Ensign Daniel Disney and is cited hereafter as Halkett's Orderly Book. It is unpaged but chronological.

7 See 17 Gentleman's Mag. (1747), p. 250, 328, 346, 401, 409, 410, 439.

heard no fire more martial than that of the evening gun at Gibraltar, where he had served with the 14th Foot. To that Regiment he had transferred from the Coldstream Guards in 1753, and had been promoted from Lieutenant Colonel to Colonel. His commission as Major General bore date of Mch. 29, 1754, which meant that when he received Washington at Alexandria he had held for one year only a rank above that of Colonel. In manners, he was direct and frequently blunt; in wit, he was clumsy.[8] Quick to wrath, he was scarcely less quick in accepting as friends the individuals, especially the clever young officers to whom he was attracted. This much, George saw within a few days; beyond this, at the outset, he did not go in appraisal of a man who temporarily awed the colonials because he personified the exalted command of the envied "military establishment."

If George was half-blinded by the prestige of the first General he ever had seen, Braddock decided quickly that the tall young Virginian was worth attaching to his family. Washington subsequently thought that the interest shown in having him become an aide was due to his knowledge of the Indians and of the country in which the expedition was to operate;[9] but, whatever its origin, the feeling of Braddock was one of quick appreciation. He offered George a Captain's commission by brevet and had it explained carefully this was the highest position he had authority to fill.[10] In turn, George described his perplexity over entering the service in any capacity, and he asked whether, if he did join the staff, he could devote to his own affairs the time that would elapse before Braddock was ready to establish headquarters at Wills Creek.[11] When Braddock readily agreed to this, George thanked him and said he would give an early answer to the offer.[12] It was in most particulars as much an affair of business as the lease of Mount Vernon had been.

An interview with the General was not all. George must have made several visits to the camp and to the quarters of the younger officers,

---

[8] The only surviving example of his wit is in the remark he is supposed to have made at the Carlyle House to a young Negro maid named Penny: "You are only a penny now but I hope on my return you will be two pence" (3 *Penn. Mag.*, 13).

[9] Cf. Washington to John Robinson, April 20, 1755: "General Braddock . . . I suppose, imagined that the small knowledge I have had an opportunity of acquiring of the Country, Indians, &c. worthy of his notice and therefore thought I might become useful to him in the progress of this expedition." (1 *G. W.*, 112–13.)

[10] 1 *G. W.*, 114; 29 *ibid.*, 41.   [11] 1 *G. W.*, 111.

[12] This, at least, appeared to be a reasonable inference from part of the opening sentence of the letter of April 2, to Orme: "The arrival of a good deal of company . . . prevents me the pleasure of waiting upon you today; therefore I beg you'll be kind enough to make my compliments and excuse to the General." (*ibid.*, 109).

or else he must often have met them socially, because he soon was on friendly, bantering terms with Orme and William Shirley.[13] From their first meeting, George found Orme attractive and suave, a man of society, reared in the army, but possessed of little knowledge of business and, in particular, of business in America.[14] The General's secretary, Shirley, was much more than the son of a Governor. He had "goodness, clear understanding, fine judgment and kindness of heart."[15] Of Capt. Roger Morris, Washington apparently saw less at the time than of the others at headquarters. Morris then was twenty-seven, had been ten years in the army, was able and ready of tongue and was popular with the ladies.[16]

When George left the company of these young officers, it always was with the feeling that if he joined Braddock he would be associated with pleasant men not much older than himself. Deliberately and carefully he debated whether he should and could accept the invitation to be one of them. Pride and previous utterance led him to exclude even the possibility of accepting a Captain's commission by brevet. The essential question was whether he could afford to serve as a volunteer aide. He reasoned that if he went with Braddock he was certain to sustain loss by absence from Mount Vernon, but that, as he would eat at the General's table and would not have to maintain an establishment of his own, the direct cost would not be heavy. Besides, if he followed his inclination to share in the campaign, he would have the satisfying knowledge that he would be serving his country without reward. Weighing all the arguments, he decided about the 1st of April that he would accept, if he could perform the duty the General expected of him without too great or too prolonged neglect of his private affairs. He must have, for one thing, assurance of a leave of absence should operations be suspended. For another, he would like to be free to retire at the close of the year's fighting if he wished to do so.[17]

In this resolution, George prepared to ride to Alexandria on the 2nd of April and to undertake to gain the General's approval of his terms. Shortly before he was to leave, his mother arrived at Mount Vernon. She had heard he was planning to join Braddock's expedition and she

[13] Cf. 1 G. W., 111.

[14] William Shirley [Jr] to Robert H. Morris, May 23, 1755; 1 Hamilton, 64.

[15] R. H. Morris to William Shirley, Sr., [July n.d.] 1755; 6 Penn. Col. Rec., 496.

[16] Sargent, op. cit., 369 n; 18 W (1), p. 6; DAB. In the final phase of the campaign, Robert Dobson, senior Captain of the 48th, served as fourth Aide-de-Camp. See Sargent, op. cit., 211; 2 Shirley, 321; Pargellis, 119–20; and infra, p. 78

[17] 1 G. W., 110–11.

had hurried to the Potomac in an effort to dissuade him. Her attitude toward him had not changed perceptibly since the time she had forbidden his going to sea. He was of age, to be sure, but she insisted that he respect her wishes.[18] George by 1755 was unhappily familiar with this attitude. He stayed away from her as much as he could, and he showed no desire to have her reside on his newly leased estate; but now he bade her welcome, listened to her with the consideration he always showed her, and then he went on with his plans. Already there was a barrier between them. In some money matters and in the spirit of command they may have been too much alike; in other respects they were too dissimilar.

George postponed his visit to Alexandria in order to be both a host and a dutiful son; but he excused himself from her for a time and wrote Orme a letter in which he apologized for his failure to wait on the General that day. He clumsily continued: "I find myself much embarrassed with my affairs, having no person to whom I can confide, to entrust the management with. Yet, under these disadvantages and circumstances, I am determined to do myself the honor of accompanying you with this proviso only, that the General will be kind enough to permit my return as soon as the . . ."[19] or grand affair is over (if desired). Or, if there should be any space of inaction long enough to admit of a visit (for otherwise I could by no means obtain my own consent, whatever private losses I might sustain) to indulge me therein and I need not add how much I should be obliged by joining at Wills Creek only, for this the General has kindly promised. These things, Sir, however unwarrantable they may appear at first sight, I hope will not be taken amiss when it is considered how unprepared I am at present to quit a family,[20] an estate scarcely settled, and in the utmost confusion." Then George added a few trivial, friendly sentences which showed clearly enough that his heart already was with the young men at Braddock's headquarters.[21]

The General, who had been sick in Alexandria,[22] was to depart the next day for Annapolis to attend a conference of the Governors.[23] George consequently must have been pleased to receive a prompt reply which showed that Orme had laid his letter before Braddock, who had

---

[18] Cf. *infra*, p. 107.

[19] This word was erased in the revision Washington made of this letter late in life.

[20] Employment of this term to describe a household was as good eighteenth-century usage as the same word was when applied to a military officer's staff.

[21] 1 *G. W.*, 111.

[22] 1 *G. W.*, 109-10.

[23] 1 *Sharpe*, 189; *Orme*, 297.

accepted promptly the conditions young Washington had felt he should impose. The language of Orme's answer scarcely could have been more cordial: "The General orders me to give you his compliments, and to assure you his wishes are to make it agreeable to yourself and consistent with your affairs, and, therefore, he desires you will settle your business at home, as to join him at Wills Creek if more convenient to you; and, whenever you find it necessary to return, he begs you will look upon yourself as entirely master, and judge what is proper to be done." [24] This reassured George as a man of business and doubtless deepened his belief that Braddock, at bottom, was kindhearted and generous.

The bargain struck, George took pains to let his friends know he was to serve as a volunteer, without pay. To the most powerful member of the House of Burgesses, Speaker and Treasurer Robinson, he wrote: ". . . if there is any merit in going out upon such terms as I do, I was unwilling to lose [25] it among my friends, who I did not doubt might be made to believe I had some advantageous offers that engaged my services, when in reality, it is very far from it; for I expect to be a considerable loser in my private affairs by going." [26] To William Byrd he said: ". . . if I can gain any credit, or if I am entitled to the least countenance and esteem, it must be from serving my country with a free, voluntary will; for I can very truly say, I have no expectation of reward but the hope of meriting the love of my country and friendly regard of my acquaintances . . ." [27] Reputation and distinction were part of his supreme ambition.

In this contented, almost complacent state of mind, George began to arrange his affairs for an absence that might be prolonged. He concluded he could not do better than to have his brother "Jack" come to Mount Vernon and act as manager. "Jack"—more formally John Augustine—was then only twenty years of age,[28] but he was industrious and of course was what few proprietors ever admitted an overseer could be, completely to be trusted in all money matters.[29]

Meantime, though George continued to reside on the estate, he frequently visited the camp at Alexandria, where he found much that was interesting and no less that was ugly. Apparently he did not learn until

[24] 2 *Sparks,* 71. Sparks assigned no date to this letter and did not state where it was written.
[25] The text reads "loose."
[26] 1 G. W., 112.   [27] 1 G. W., 114.
[28] He was born Jan. 24, 1736. See *supra,* Vol. I, p. 53.
[29] The date and terms of "Jack's" agreement to come to Mount Vernon do not appear. George wrote, May 6, 1755, as if "Jack" had by that time given evidence of satisfactory direction of affairs at Mount Vernon (1 G. W., 120).

months later that the two Regiments, Halkett's 44th and Dunbar's 48th, had a bad name because, under different commanders, they had run away from the field of Preston Pans when they had faced the "young Pretender."[30] They were said, also, to have been filled with drafts of the most worthless men in some of the Irish Regiments, men who became disgusted and resentful when they found they had been banished, so to say, to America.[31] Braddock himself, at the time of their encampment in Alexandria, never had abused or disparaged them en masse but he was keeping them under severe and ceaseless discipline. Besides threatening death for deserters, even though they returned to duty,[32] the General had ordered that any men found drunk in camp should be denied their rations.[33] In spite of this, there was much drinking in the Regiments[34] and as much consorting with loose females as there were such persons around the camp. More than the allowable number of washerwomen had been brought over from England in order to provide for a hospital. As some of these undertook to demand higher wages, Braddock ordered that all those who would not work for 6 *d.* a day and provisions should be excluded from camp.[35] When Braddock read the reports on the New York Independent Companies, which had displeased St. Clair, they, too, fell under his disfavor.[36] As for the provincials, they scarcely were trusted at all by their General. New volunteers from Virginia were being incorporated principally into the two Regiments of the regular establishments. George Washington's veterans and the recruits of the Virginia Regiment were divided between Halkett and Dunbar, both of whose commands subsequently were termed Brigades.[37]

George's interest soon was turned from the men to the officers and especially to Braddock, because the General came back to Alexandria from Annapolis about the 9th of April[38]—and not in the best of his

[30] *Gentleman's Mag.,* August, 1755, p. 378. Washington's reference to this, Nov. 18, 1755 (1 *G. W.,* 235), sounds as if he might just have read the item. An admirable article by Francis T. Nichols on the organization of Braddock's army will be found in 4 *W* (3), p. 125 ff.

[31] 1 *Walpole Memoirs,* 390. *Cf.* London dispatch of Oct. 29, 1754, in *Md. Gazette* of Jan. 9, 1755.   [32] See *supra,* p. 15.

[33] *Lowdermilk,* xvii.   [34] *Orme,* 297.

[35] Orders of April 7, 1755; *Lowdermilk,* xvii–xviii. Many small details of organization and administration, not regarded as an essential part of the biography of Washington, will be found in *Halkett's Orderly Book,* Apr. 2 ff, 1755.

[36] 2 *Din.,* 14.

[37] Stephen's, La Peyroney's and Cocke's, with one of the Companies of rangers, were assigned Halkett's 44th; Waggener's, Hog's and Polson's Companies, with one of rangers and one of "artificers" (originally styled carpenters), went to Dunbar's 48th. See *Lowdermilk,* xv, xxxii–xxxiii.

[38] He left the Maryland capital April 7 (*Orme,* 297; 1 *Sharpe,* 189).

moods. He had gone to Maryland to confer with Governor Sharpe and with Governor Shirley. When the Massachusetts executive did not arrive as expected, Braddock became "a little impatient," as Sharpe mildly put it, and after a few days left with the implied notice that if Shirley wanted to talk of military affairs, the gentleman from New England could betake himself to Alexandria.[39]

Braddock by this time had seen enough of conditions in America to develop his characteristic likes and dislikes. Some of these were his own and some were accepted uncritically from St. Clair. Of Dinwiddie's zeal and efforts, the testy Braddock had good opinion;[40] most of the colonials he eyed with suspicious if not with active animosity. Among the instructions he had brought to America [41] was one to the effect that he should assist the Governors in endeavoring "to prevail upon the Assemblies" to make financial contribution to the campaign, but he had faced a resistance that had infuriated him even before he went on his vain mission to Annapolis. Almost from the first, he had denounced the refusal of Pennsylvania to do anything for the common cause, except to build a road from Shippensburg westward. Reports that the Pennsylvania Assembly declined to put an embargo on the shipment of provisions to Canada [42] fired him to rebuke "such pusillanimous and improper behavior" and led him to threaten to quarter his troops in the Quaker Colony the next winter.[43] Before he had been in Virginia a month, he had written Sir Thomas Robinson: "I am almost in despair of the [Assemblies'] complying with [the appeal for funds], from the jealousy of the people and the disunion of the several Colonies, as well among themselves as with one another." [44] St. Clair's censure of the "sloth and ignorance" of the Virginians, especially of those in the Shenandoah Valley,[45] doubtless would have been extended by Braddock to the population of the entire continent.

The delays and indifference of the provincials were most provokingly shown, Braddock thought, in their failure to offer adequate transport at reasonable price [46] for the journey over the mountains and to the Ohio. The General had never seen the Alleghenies. As a professional

---

[39] 1 *Sharpe*, 189, 194, 230.

[40] *Pargellis*, 81.

[41] Sargent, *op. cit.*, 395.

[42] *Cf.* 1 *Din.*, 473; *Shippen Papers*, 34.

[43] Braddock to Governor Morris, Feb. 28, 1755; 6 *Penn. Col. Rec.*, 307.

[44] Letter of Mch. 18, 1755; P.R.O., C.O. 5; 46, p. 1–10.

[45] *Pargellis*, 64.

[46] The King was being charged 10 s. per day for a four-horse wagon and team and 2 s. for a pack horse (*Pargellis*, 120). Orders against employment or impressment of wagons by officers, otherwise than on specific authorization, appear in *Halkett's Orderly Book*, Apr. 11, 1755.

soldier, he was not disposed to take the opinion of any person, other than of another trained soldier, concerning the obstacle the range presented. Sir John St. Clair consequently was the man to whom he listened, but the Deputy Quartermaster General was not himself accurately informed. At the end of January, St. Clair had gone from Fredericksburg to Winchester and thence to a point about two miles West of the South Branch of the Potomac. "I had," he later reported, "a full view of the mountains on each side of the Potomac above Wills Creek, and from what I could see, there is a road easily to be made across the country to the mouth of Savage River, which will be gaining thirty miles . . ." [47]

With that observation, having no officers for reconnaissance,[48] St. Clair had been content, and on that basis he advised Braddock.

From unhappy remembrance of Washington's experience, Dinwiddie believed that transportation of ordnance and supplies across the mountains would be back-breaking and time-consuming, "but," he said almost apologetically, "those better acquainted with these things than I am, seem to make light of it." [49] Had the Governor insisted on this point of view in talking to Braddock, there would have been small likelihood that his opinion would have found acceptance with the General. George, of course, could have named grades and distances and mountains [50] to refute St. Clair, but, as yet, he was not on a footing that permitted him to criticize a report of a Deputy Quartermaster General. Braddock, therefore, was warned merely by St. Clair that the road from Winchester to Wills Creek still was abominable and had to be improved.[51] Beyond Wills Creek, he was assured, the barrier was not excessively difficult.

The General's own particular task was to see that all his subordinates worked together to assure an early start from Wills Creek. Concerning this, Braddock was not optimistic.

"It is doubtful," he said, "whether there will be grass on the other side of the Allegheny Mountains before the latter end of April, which is indeed as soon as it will probably be in my power to get there." [52] That was restrained and semi-official. Privately he was more positive

---

[47] St. Clair to Braddock, Feb. 9, 1755; *Pargellis*, 62. For a reconnaissance by St. Clair and Forbes to determine the practicability of clearing the Potomac as a line of supply, see *Penn. Gaz.*, Feb. 11, 1755.

[48] 6 *Penn. Col. Rec.*, 300.

[49] To Sir Thomas Robinson, Mch. 17, 1755; 1 *Din.*, 525. Cf. *ibid.*, 514.

[50] Cf. 1 *G. W.*, 116.   [51] *Pargellis*, 61.

[52] Letter of Mch. 17, 1755 to Robert Napier; *Pargellis*, 78.

and increasingly vehement. On his visit to Annapolis, he had learned that no provision had been made for wagons on the Maryland side of the Potomac. This negligence provoked an explosion which frightened Governor Sharpe into pledging 100 vehicles,[53] but Braddock had not been placated. Nor was his temper improved, after he returned to Alexandria, by the admission of the authorities that no boats had been assembled to transport to Rock Creek a body of troops who, he had been assured, could march on Maryland soil, via Frederick, to Wills Creek.[54] The column finally received help from Keppel and got under way[55] while six Companies of Colonel Halkett's Regiment were marching toward Winchester by the usual Virginia route.[56]

Braddock himself remained in Alexandria to receive the tardy provincial executives.[57] The three from the Northern Colonies proceeded by way of Annapolis, where Sharpe joined them, and together they reached Alexandria on the 14th of April. Secret conferences began at once with Braddock, Keppel and Dinwiddie.[58] Among such dignitaries, young Washington of course had no place, but during the time the Governors were in town he was introduced to them. The man who most impressed him was the ablest of the five, Gov. William Shirley of Massachusetts. With more enthusiasm than he ever had shown for a public official, George wrote of Shirley, "[His] character and appearance has perfectly charmed me, as I think every word and every action discovers the gentleman and great politician."[59]

Concerning the results of the council in which Shirley had a notable part, George soon learned substantially all there was to know. Secrecy was not a virtue of military planning at so great a distance from the French. Without being inquisitive, George ascertained that Braddock's plan had been drafted in Britain, chiefly by the Duke of Cumberland, and was covered by instructions and by letters.[60] These provided for attack at three points that formed a concave arc from the Ohio at Fort

[53] Orme, 297.

[54] Orme, 299; Lowdermilk, xviii, xxii; Halkett's Orderly Book, Apr. 6 ff, 1755.

[55] "Seaman's" journal in Sargent, op. cit. (cited hereafter as Seaman, Sargent), p. 367.

[56] Orme, 296, 298; 2 Din., 12; Lowdermilk, xix. Details of the troops sent forward from the 44th will be found in Hackett's Orderly Book, Apr. 8 ff, 1755.

[57] If his letter of Mch. 10, 1755 to Governor Morris (6 Penn. Col. Rec., 332), was typical of those he wrote the other executives, Braddock himself was in part to blame, because he had called for a meeting at Annapolis without fixing a date.

[58] Orme, 300; 1 Sharpe, 203. The tradition is that the council was held at the Carlyle House, 18 W (1) p. 6.

[59] To William Fairfax, Apr. 23, 1755; 1 G. W., 116.

[60] For the instructions, etc., see Sargent, op cit., 393; 6 N. Y. Col. Docs., 920–22; Pargellis, 36 ff.

DuQuesne to Lake Champlain. First, Braddock was to march from Wills Creek to the junction of the Allegheny and the Monongahela. If, as expected, he made short work of Fort DuQuesne, he was to look to Fort Niagara, near the western end of Lake Ontario and on Niagara River, about 200 miles North and slightly East [61] of the first objective on the Ohio.

Fort Niagara, the river of the same name and the portage between Lake Ontario and Lake Erie constituted perhaps the most important part of the defences the French were developing between the St. Lawrence and the Mississippi. Destruction of this link of the tightening chain was to be the immediate task of the two Regiments that were to be raised in America for Shirley and Pepperell,[62] but Braddock, tramping 200 miles through the wilderness, was to be "in at the kill." With Niagara wrested from the French, the enemy would no longer have means of sending forward valuable presents with which to buy Indian aid against the English.[63]

For attacking Niagara, an excellent point of departure was offered at Oswego, which was 125 miles to the eastward, near the mouth of the Oswego River on the southern shore of Lake Ontario and not far from its southeastern end. The English had constructed there in 1726–27 a fort that later had fallen into disrepair, but this defence could be renewed and could be used to shelter men who would build vessels on Ontario "for asserting His Majesty's right to that lake." [64] Two Independent Companies in New York and two of those raised for Pepperell's Regiment were thought to be a sufficient force to restore and to guard Fort Oswego.[65]

The southern end of Lake Champlain was to be the objective of the third principal attack.[66] There, at Crown Point, the French in 1731 had reared Fort Frédéric, from which they could threaten the whole Valley of the Hudson. Conceivably, by advancing southward, they might sever New England from the other Colonies. To prevent even the possibility of this advance, Crown Point must fly the British flag again. William Johnson, the Indian agent, was the man to undertake the expedition.[67]

---

[61] Actually N, 12° E. The maps in James Truslow Adams, ed., *Atlas of American History*, Plates 42 and 44, are useful for quick refreshment of memory of these famous positions.

[62] See *supra*, p. 9–10.

[63] Cf. "Sketch for Operations," *Pargellis*, 46–47.

[64] Minutes of Governors' council, 6 *Penn. Col. Rec.*, 366.

[65] *Ibid.*

[66] It has been customary to regard the advance to Oswego not as a separate operation but as a preliminary of the campaign against Fort Niagara.

[67] Minutes of Governors' council, *loc. cit.*

In addition—and as a secret not recorded in the minutes of the council—a plan was formulated for an attack on Nova Scotia.[68] To this, probably, George gave little heed because he was intrigued by the nearer operations. Had he drawn a sketch of them, the design would have made his strong heart beat faster. It was a plan to appeal to a young soldier because, if its daring was rewarded, it would crush the enemy and terminate in speedy triumph the war with France. Washington had yet to discover how readily even experienced soldiers may be tempted to let their imagination outmarch their armies and their ambition disdain the limitations of their resources. The Virginian had lost his small battles with mud and mountains and haggling farmers who would risk a war to save a wagon. Would these commanders from home show him where he had erred and how he might have won?

Besides learning of this elaborate plan, Washington heard, also, of the Governors' other deliberations with Braddock—how they regretfully had told the General the Colonies would not provide a common fund for the support of the campaign, and how they had agreed that William Johnson should have direction of all dealings with the Indians.[69] The Governors also had pledged their Colonies to provide a fund for presents to friendly savages and they had promised to make arrangements for garrisoning Fort DuQuesne when Braddock had captured it and had moved on toward Fort Niagara.[70]

George listened; George pondered; in the remembrance of the hunger of his men the previous year, he felt that transportation was the problem of all problems for a successful advance. In his opinion, the mountains would be crossed with minimum difficulty by a large train of pack horses.[71] Braddock was a believer in wheeled transport rather than in pack animals; but he increasingly was disturbed by the difficulty and expense of procuring wagons and he was not encouraged by anything the Governors had said on this subject at their council with him. In some manner, also, he had misunderstood what was told him about

---

68 Cf. *Pargellis*, 47.

69 See his instructions, *Orme*, 303 ff. Braddock expressed deep displeasure at the Colonies' unwillingness to contribute adequately to the common defence and he recommended that the ministry find some means of compelling them to do so. See Braddock to Newcastle, Apr. 12, 1755; Br. Mus. Add. MS, 32854, f. 184.

70 6 *Penn. Col. Rec.*, 365–68; 1 *Sharpe*, 203; Dinwiddie to John Hanbury, May 3, 1755. Br. Mus. Add. MS, 32824, f. 378. Dinwiddie confided proudly that if he had not procured money and credit from home, the expedition could not have been undertaken because of the failure of the Colonies to vote funds.

71 ". . . retrench the wagons and increase the number of bat horses which is what I recommended at first . . ."—Washington to John Augustine Washington, June 14, 1755 (1 *G. W.*, 140). Strictly speaking a "bat horse" carried the baggage of an officer, but the term was used carelessly to cover animals of both types of burden. The proper inclusive word, sumpter, was not employed.

the distance over the mountains to Fort DuQuesne. He thought he had to traverse fifteen miles of rough country. When he learned that he had ahead of him between sixty and seventy miles of mountain and hill he became peevishly sensitive to everything that delayed an early start on the long and toilsome road. His letters home were a continual grumble. After the adjournment of the council of Governors he wrote: "I have been greatly disappointed by the neglect and supineness of the Assemblies of those provinces with which I am concerned; they promised great matters and have done nothing [,] whereby instead of forwarding they have obstructed the service. When I get to Wills Creek I will send you . . . what other information or intelligence I shall get there, it being impracticable to get any here, the people of this part of the country laying it down for a maxim, never to speak truth upon any account." [72]

Non-fulfillment of colonials' promises to supply wagons shaped Braddock's next move. He had been induced to send part of the troops through Maryland because he had the assurance that the farmers of that Colony would not rent their wagons for use outside its bounds but would supply vehicles on the Maryland side of the Potomac.[73] Now that Braddock was ready to have the artillery follow the infantry toward the frontier, he found that the wagons promised by Sharpe were not available for the guns.[74] Angrily the General sent an express to St. Clair, who had gone to Winchester and was expecting, when he had repaired the road, to proceed to Wills Creek.[75] After a few days, Braddock impatiently decided to ride to Frederick and to see for himself what could be done there to get wagons. By the 21st he was in the Maryland town.[76]

George remained behind to finish his business. In Alexandria, recently so crowded, the only troops were fifty sick and the guards and attendants.[77] The little town itself had felt immense pride in the presence of five Governors, a General and a Commodore—"a happy

---

[72] Braddock to Robert Napier, Apr. 19, 1755; *Pargellis,* 84. See also Edward Shippen to his father, Mch. 19, 1755; *Shippen Papers,* 35.

[73] *Ibid.,* 82.

[74] *Orme,* 307. For the dispatch, April 17, of thirty men of Halkett's Regiment to guard eleven wagons of powder from Alexandria to Wills Creek, see *Halkett's Orderly Book,* Apr. 16, 1755.

[75] Actually (*Pargellis,* 93), St. Clair reached Wills Creek April 16, which was about the date Braddock dispatched the express.   [76] *Seaman,* Sargent, 369.

[77] Journal of "Mrs. [Charlotte] Browne" in 32 V 307, edited by Fairfax Harrison, and written by a widow, identified only as respects her married name, who went with her brother, a commissary officer, to Wills Creek. So far as is known, this is the only preserved narrative by any of the women who accompanied the expedition.

presage," George hoped, for the expedition and for the place itself.[78] Social life never had been so gay there. Some of the ladies had sought to win the General's heart by gratifying his stomach; some perhaps had engaged in mild coquetry.[79] George had little time now in which to console the ladies who had lost their social lion. Instead, the new master of Mount Vernon had to attend to accounts and supplies and had to collect both bills and horses before he set out to join the General. A debt he sought to have the Colony pay him was one for £50 due morally, if not technically, for the personal effects he had lost at Fort Necessity.[80] As a careful manager, George felt, also, that he should visit his Bullskin farm in Frederick County in the company of his brother "Jack," who was to manage that property as well as the plantation on Little Hunting Creek while the older brother was absent.

George's final letter was to his neighbor and friend, Col. William Fairfax. It dealt in part with private business and in part with military affairs: "I cannot think of quitting Fairfax [County] without embracing this last opportunity of bidding you farewell. I this day set out for Wills Creek where I expect to meet the General and to stay, I fear too long, as our march must be regulated by the movements of the train, which I am sorry to say, I think will be tedious in advancing [,] very tedious indeed, as answerable to the expectation I have long conceived, though few believed." [81] In anticipation of long journeys and hard travel, George started, April 23, with four horses [82] but he took with him comparatively little money,[83] light baggage and a single pair of boots.[84] Misadventure came quickly. On the way to the Valley of the Shenandoah, one of George's horses was killed by over riding or by accident. Three others were disabled. When he reached Bullskin April 27 or 28, he was embarrassingly lacking in mounts and was fearful he might be delayed some days in procuring new animals.[85]

As arrangements for the farm did not take long, George soon had idle hours, which he knew would be longer and longer if on the frontier, as in 1754, he received no letters. He had, also, pleasant memories of the ladies of Belvoir and of the other homes in the neighborhood,

[78] Letter to William Fairfax, Apr. 23, 1755; 1 *G. W.*, 116.
[79] Cf. Washington to Mrs. George William Fairfax, May 14, 1755; 1 *G. W.*, 122–23.
[80] Letters to John Robinson and Carter Burwell, Apr. 20, 1755; 1 *G. W.*, 112–13, 114–16.
[81] Apr. 23, 1755; 1 *G. W.*, 116.
[82] 1 *G. W.*, 117.   [83] *Ibid.*, 119.
[84] 1 *G. W.*, 122, 123. It is not certain whether "Jack" accompanied George or met him at Bullskin. The probability is strong that they made the journey together.
[85] 1 *G. W.*, 117; cf. *ibid.*, 119. For subsequent injury to some of Washington's mounts, in 1756, see *infra*, 159, 161.

and he may probably have had already a half slumbering, half conscious affection for Sally Fairfax, the wife of his friend George William Fairfax. If George could induce her to exchange letters, he would have news from home and, perhaps, have also a not unpleasant fluttering of the heart. This was not a literay enterprise for which George's ponderous imitation of an "elegant style" was suited, but it was one he was determined to undertake. He wrote:

> Bullskin, April 30, 1755
> Dear Madam: In order to engage your correspondence, I think it expedient just to deserve it; which I shall endeavor to do by embracing the earliest, and every opportunity of writing to you.
>
> It will be needless to expatiate on the pleasures that communication of this kind will afford me, as it shall suffice to say; a correspondence with my friends is the greatest satisfaction I expect to enjoy in the course of this campaign, and that none of my friends are able to convey more real delight than you can to whom I stand indebted for so many obligations.

There followed a brief account of the misfortune he had with his horses and then—

> I must beg my compliments to Miss Hannah, Miss Dent, and any others that think me worthy of their enquiries. I am Madam Your most obedient Servant [86]

Beyond this, George did not adventure in the initiation of correspondence while he was at Bullskin, either because he realized how hard was the labor of inditing a letter to a lady, or else because he got horses sooner than he expected and, on May 1, started out to join Braddock in Frederick. A long, roundabout ride it was, and one that fatigued even George,[87] but it carried him to the Maryland village—a place of abundance [88]—just in time to catch Braddock before that officer was departing in disgust and wrath over conditions that in some respects duplicated and in others exceeded those George had to endure the previous year.

The General had arrived at Frederick on the 21st with his aides and his secretary; St. Clair had reached the settlement the same day.[89] They found few cattle accumulated for the troops and no wagons ready for

---

[86] 1 G. W., 117–118.   [87] 1 G. W., 119.
[88] Seaman, Sargent, 368.
[89] Ibid. St. Clair may have come in response to Braddock's express, supra, p. 26.

the journey to Wills Creek.[90] Some of the accumulated provisions gave
off so vile an odor that, in the polite language of an English reporter,
"he must have suffered very greatly from hunger who could have eaten
[them]." [91] Braddock, complaining of the cost of everything,[92] was
forced at heavy expense to send into the country around Frederick to
purchase beeves; and he was compelled to threaten dire things unless
the Justices of the Peace procured wagons for the movement of stores
and ammunition to Fort Cumberland.[93]

At length twenty-five wagons were delivered, but twenty-five only,
and some of them not fit for the road. Braddock almost went mad.
The expedition was at an end, he swore; he could not go on. There-
upon in the mild word of a guest, he "exclaimed" against ministers in
England who sent troops into a country destitute of transportation.
He must have not less than 150 wagons and must have them speedily!

The visitor who toned down Braddock's raucous damnation of the
ministry was a soft-spoken man of forty-nine, regarded as one of the
ablest as well as suavest of Philadelphia leaders. He was Benjamin
Franklin, of whom George must previously have heard though he had
no personal acquaintance. Franklin had come to Frederick in an effort
to assuage the wrath of Braddock and of St. Clair against Pennsylvania
and he believed he had removed some of their prejudices. Now, in
desperation, the General appealed to Franklin: would he undertake to
contract in Pennsylvania for 150 wagons and 1500 horses to be delivered by May 10 at Fort Cumberland? Franklin patriotically agreed
to make the effort, whereupon Braddock cheerfully advanced £800
from the army chest for the initial expenses [94] which, for this particular
reason, were to be even heavier than those the commander already had
denounced: The Pennsylvanians would wish to attend their teams in
person or to have one of their servants act as wagoner. That would
make the cost of wagon, four horses and driver 15 s. a day. Horses,
unattended, might be had for the prevailing figure, 2 s. per diem.[95]

Even at these figures, Franklin needed more than the appeal of

90 *Orme*, 308.
91 *Gentleman's Mag.*, August, 1755, p. 378.
92 *Cf.* Braddock to Sir Thomas Robinson, Apr. 19, 1755: "The contingent expense attending
the present service in America will be much greater than I persuaded myself . . . among the
innumberable causes are the number of horses, wagons, boats, vessels necessary for transportation
of artillery, baggage, etc., and the excessive price of labor." (P.R.O., C.O. 5; 46, p. 24.)
93 *Orme*, 307–08.
94 *Orme*, 308; Franklin, *Autobiography* (Bigelow ed.), 264.
95 See Franklin's advertisement in *Penn. Gazette,* Apr. 26, 1755; reproduced in 2 *Penn. Arch.,*
294 and in *Autobiography* (ed. cit.), 265.

patriotic duty to procure wagons from Pennsylvania Quakers and from Germans who knew nothing and cared nothing about a Gracious Majesty's dominion beyond the mountains. As it chanced, Sir John St. Clair a few days previously had created amazement and fear in the hearts of certain Pennsylvanians who had been named by Governor Morris to open a road from Shippensburg [96] to some designated point on Braddock's line of advance, so that the supply of the army subsequently could be based on Philadelphia. The road commissioners, on meeting St. Clair at Fort Cumberland, April 16, had received the full blast of his accumulated resentments against their government and their people. He refused to look at their sketch of the route of the proposed road, and he abused the Colony for its delay in starting the work. The more he talked, the madder he became until, after saying the Pennsylvanians would be to blame for the death of the men who would be killed by the reënforced French, he announced the army would march into Cumberland County at the end of nine days. He would make the residents build the road, he would kill the cattle, he would carry away the horses and he would burn the houses. If, later, the French defeated the English because of the delays of the people of the Province, he would pass through "and treat the inhabitants as a parcel of traitors." When he exhausted his own threats, he told the commissioners to go, if they pleased, to the General. Braddock, he said, would give them ten bad words for every one he had used. The Pennsylvanians made the best defence they could, but the Quartermaster remained fiercely inflexible. As the commissioners reported it, he roared that "our delays were unpardonable; he would do our duty himself and never trust to us, but we should dearly pay for it; to every sentence he solemnly swore, and desired we might believe him to be in earnest." [97]

Franklin doubtless knew of this tirade and realized that all Pennsylvania would hear of it soon. He observed, also, that St. Clair wore a uniform resembling that of the Hussars, the light cavalry used for pillaging and for foraging in central Europe,[98] whence many of the

[96] Seventy-two miles Northeast of Cumberland, Md., and almost on the line between Cumberland and Franklin Counties.

[97] George Croghan et al. to Governor Morris, Apr. 16, 1755; 6 Penn. Col. Rec., 368–69.

[98] Hussars originally were Hungarian, but their light equipment and their successful operations led to the establishment of similar units in the cavalry of most European countries. When troops of this type were incorporated in the English establishment, they became known as Light Dragoons. Contemporary military works echo the reputation Hussars had won in central Europe. Thus in A Complete System of the Military Art (ed. 1780): "They are resolute partisans, and are far better in an invasion or hasty expedition, than in a set battle." In Duane's Military Dictionary (ed. 1810): "[Hussars] never encamp . . . they always lie in the woods, outhouses, or villages, in the front of the army."

residents of Pennsylvania had come. It occurred to Franklin that if he could present St. Clair to the Germans as a Hussar, they would be much more disposed to rent the teams which they might think the Quartermaster General would take anyway. So, in a handbill printed for distribution in Lancaster, York and Cumberland Counties, Franklin told the farmers "it was proposed to send an armed force immediately into these counties, to seize as many of the best carriages and horses as should be wanted, and compel as many persons into the service as would be necessary to drive and take care of them." Franklin added that he thought the progress of soldiers through the Counties "especially considering the temper they are in, and their resentment against us, would be attended with many and great inconveniences to the inhabitants." To avert calamity, he "more willingly undertook" to see what could be done "by fair and equitable means." He described the service desired and the price offered, and he concluded by saying that if he did not procure the necessary vehicles in fourteen days, he had to notify the General, "and I suppose Sir John St. Clair, the Hussar, with a body of soldiers, will immediately enter the Province for the purpose aforesaid . . ." [99]

Besides hearing of this episode, George learned in Frederick that Braddock and St. Clair were engaged in a war of words with Maryland. In urging the English troops to move through that Colony to Wills Creek, so that farmers' wagons would not be hauled beyond the boundary, the authorities, perhaps even Governor Sharpe himself, had led Braddock to believe that a road existed, or would be constructed immediately, from Frederick to Wills Creek.[100] Some of the Virginians knew this would be a slow and awkward line of advance when actual conditions were taken into account. They were of opinion that Braddock was being imposed upon and they frankly were jealous because the troops had been moved northward across the Potomac. George now was told that no road through Maryland had been cut and that the column had to recross the Potomac, and proceed by part of the Virginia route that would have been followed if the troops had moved directly from Alexandria to Winchester.[101]

On the morning of the 2nd of May, the day after his arrival at Frederick, George started with the General on the march back to Virginia via Swearengen's Ferry on the Potomac.[102] Tired as Wash-

[99] Handbill reprinted in 2 *Penn. Arch.*, 295–96.
[100] *Orme*, 308; 1 *G. W.*, 118, 121–22. [101] *Ibid.*
[102] 1 *Sharpe*, 205, 208, where the name is spelled van Swerengen.

ington must have been as a result of his long ride on the 1st, he was delighted to observe how the Marylanders were being made to pay in humbled pride for misleading Braddock concerning their roads. ". . . I believe," George said, "the imposition has too evidently appeared for the imposters to subject us to the same inconveniences again."[103] In another letter he wrote, almost gleefully: "I . . . proceeded with the General by way of Winchester . . . which gave him a good opportunity to see the absurdity of the route, and of damning it very heartily. Colonel Dunbar's Regiment was also obliged to cross over . . . and . . . take the new road up, which gave me infinite satisfaction."[104] That satisfaction did not extend to the road from Winchester to Wills Creek. Although the route had been changed and improved, it still climbed mountains or clung too hazardously to the stream beds. On one low stretch of three miles, the trail crossed the same run twenty times.[105] "There is," the widow Browne indignantly asserted later, "no describing the badness of the roads."[106]

George did not have to test the truth of this immediately. Braddock, reaching Winchester May 3, lingered unwillingly there because he had been led to believe, from what Dinwiddie had told him at Williamsburg, that Indian Chiefs would meet him in the Valley town and would join in a council designed to strengthen alliances against the French. The General found no Indians at the rendezvous and heard that none had been there.[107] As excessively hot weather was added to disappointment,[108] Braddock probably was boiling inwardly and outwardly, but, of course, he was unwilling to stir until he was convinced that no Indians were on the road to attend the council. George, for his part, was bored. His sole business in the town continued to be that of finding horses to replace those lost when he came from Mount Vernon. To procure the wherewithal, he wrote and dispatched a request to Lord Fairfax at Greenway Court for the loan of £40 or £50.[109]

After his Lordship promptly sent him £40,[110] George sought some acceptable mounts and, for many idle hours, he amused himself as best he could. He had a friendly welcome from Braddock and the staff but he had, as yet, no duties. "I find," he told John Augustine, "there is no probability of marching the Army from Wills Creek till the latter end of this month, or the first of next; so that you may imagine time

---

103 1 *G. W.,* 118.
104 *Ibid.,* 121–22.
105 *Seaman,* Sargent, 371.
106 32 *V* 316.
107 *Orme,* 309.
108 *Seaman,* Sargent, 371.
109 1 *G. W.,* 119.
110 *Ledger A,* folio 21.

will hang heavy upon my hands." [111] To his mother he wrote briefly
in the same strain, though more formally. "Honored Madame," he
began, "I came to this place last Saturday . . ." Then he repeated the
substance of what he had written his brother. "I am very happy in the
General's family, and I am treated with a complaisant freedom which
is quite agreeable; so that I have no occasion to doubt the satisfaction
I proposed in making this campaign." He concluded as ceremoniously
as he had begun and with strange stiffness: "As we have met with
nothing worth relating I shall only beg my love to my brothers and
sisters; [112] and compliments to friends. I am, Honored Madame, your
most dutiful and obedient son." [113]

The next day, May 7, Braddock left Winchester for Wills Creek in
the conviction that longer waiting for the Indians would be time
wasted. With his staff and the Virginia Troop of light horse, he reached
Cresap's on the 8th [114] and spent the night there. A wet day assured a
muddy morrow; consequently all hands rested on the 9th; [115] but on
the 10th they were astir. Dunbar's Regiment started early; later Braddock climbed into his chariot [116] and gave the nod. Off rolled the
vehicle. George, Orme, and the others attended at a slow trot; the
Virginia Troop acted as guard and escort.

The ride was a pleasant one, close by the riverside [117] through the
greenery of early May and without the plague of dust. Shortly after
noon, not far from Wills Creek, George and his companions passed the
48th Regiment on the road. The men gazed at the fat gentleman in
the carriage; the drums beat the Grenadiers' March; the provincials
marveled: A new style of war had come to the wilderness. [118] Between
1 and 2 P.M., the cavalcade reached its destination. Seventeen guns
barked a salute.

George had not seen previously the new and larger stockade, the
eastern end of which stood about 200 yards from Wills Creek and ap-

111 Letter of May 6; 1 *G. W.*, 120.
112 He always referred to his sisters-in-law as his sisters.
113 Letter of May 6, 1755; 1 *G. W.*, 120–21. This is the earliest of Washington's extant
letters to his mother.
114 *Seaman,* Sargent, 373. Braddock promptly formed a dislike of Cresap. See Bailey,
Cresap, 97. En route, May 7, Halkett detached a party to assist the Quartermaster in "pressing
all the able horses he meets." *Halkett's Orderly Book,* May 7, 1755.
115 *Seaman,* Sargent, 373.
116 So said Sargent, *op. cit.,* 194, doubtless on the ground that as the chariot subsequently
was at Wills Creek, Braddock rode thither in it. This is probable, but "Seaman's" account of
Braddock's passing of the 48th Regiment did not mention any vehicle.
117 *Seaman,* Sargent, 373.
118 *Ibid.*

proximately 400 yards from the Potomac.[119] With a total length of 400 feet and a width of about 160, Fort Cumberland now was a formidable-looking structure, but so crudely was it put together that daylight could be seen between almost any adjoining logs of the huts At the eastern end of the enclosure were two trenches down which men might go to fetch water from Wills Creek, but nowhere inside the stockade was there then a well.[120] To a woman who came soon afterward, it was "the most desolate place" she ever had seen.[121] St. Clair already had grumbled: "I cannot learn what could induce people ever to think of making a fort or a deposit for provisions at Wills Creek: It covers no country, nor has it the communication open behind it either by land or water . . ." [122]

To George, though the stockade was new, the setting was familiar, even to the extent that it suggested long delay, similar to that of 1754, before any advance could begin. He anticipated days of comparative idleness while wagons and supplies were accumulated; [123] but this time there were differences from his earlier experiences at the outpost. Sir Peter Halkett was encamped there now with six Companies of the 44th, two Independent Companies and the Virginia troops; [124] soon after George arrived, Dunbar's Regiment reached the Creek. Never had George seen comparably so many soldiers at the fort, or so many supplies.[125] That was the principal difference. The next, of course, was the contrast between a professional commander and staff and the extemporized, inexperienced organization George had known under Fry and later under Innes. A third difference was symbolized by twelve words written in the orderly book of headquarters that day, May 10, 1755: "Mr. Washington is appointed aid de camp to His Excellency General Braddock." [126]

That meant new honor, new authority, new opportunity and perhaps a new vocation. George saw all this clearly and judged it proudly but

---

[119] *Ibid.* The fort proper was at the western end of the stockade, and transversely from bastion to bastion had an axis of about 140 feet. In each bastion were four guns. See the sketch in *Lowdermilk*, 92. For negotiations over the garrisoning of Fort Cumberland, see *Md. Gazette*, Feb. 6. 1756; 2 *Penn. Arch.*, 276; *Journ. H.B.*, 1752–58, p. 267; Dinwiddie to Sharpe, June 2, 1755, N.Y.P.L. Emmett Coll., 13444; 1 *Sharpe*, 218; Dinwiddie to Lords of Trade, June 18, 1755; *Sparks Transcripts*, VSL, No. 24.

[120] *Lowdermilk*, 90; Mrs. Browne's journal in 32 *V* 316.

[121] Mrs. Browne *loc. cit.*

[122] St. Clair to Braddock, Feb. 9, 1755; *Pargellis*, 62.

[123] 1 *G. W.*, 121 ff.

[124] *Orme*, 309. For the advance of these troops to Wills Creek, see 2 *Din.*, 12; *Orme*, 297, 298; *Pargellis*, 93; Braddock's *Orderly Book* in *Lowdermilk*, xvii, xix; *Halkett's Orderly Book*, May 7 ff, particularly May 18.

[125] Cf. *Pargellis*, 120. [126] *Lowdermilk*, xxx.

coldly and calmly, in terms of the effect on his career. He wrote John Augustine: "The General has appointed me one of his aids de Camps, in which character I shall serve this campaign agreeably enough, as I am thereby freed from all commands but his, and give orders to all, which must be implicitly obeyed. I have now a good opportunity, and shall not neglect it, of forming an acquaintance, which may be serviceable hereafter, if I can find it worth while pushing my fortune in the military way." [127]

Worth while?

[127] Letter of May 14, 1755, which, George noted, "was not sent." A similar letter of that date, addressed to "Austin" and likewise "not sent," somewhat more moderately appraised the opportunity: "I shall spend my time very agreeably this campaign, though not advantageously; as I conceive a little experience will be my chief reward." (1 G. W., 125).

CHAPTER III

THE CHALLENGE OF THE MOUNTAINS
(MAY 10–JUNE 20, 1755)

GEORGE'S DUTIES as aide to General Braddock scarcely accorded at the outset with the distinction the young Virginian attached to the post. His principal regular assignment was to see that the headquarters orderly book was written up carefully.[1] Further, in common with all other officers, George was supposed to wait on the General at the morning levee, held daily between 10 and 11 o'clock.[2] Then and always, Washington received the fullest consideration of Braddock, who soon formed attachment for him[3] and gave him patronage any of the Southern Governors would have coveted: in the hands of his new assistant the General placed several blank commissions for Ensigns, and authorized him to fill them out in the name of young men he approved.[4]

This pleasing evidence of Braddock's goodwill was appreciated, but the selection of a few Ensigns for these commissions,[5] and the discharge of his trivial routine duties occupied only a small part of George's time. He had leisure for letters to members of his family and to the household at Belvoir. In a teasing note to Sally Fairfax, he professed to have discovered that a lady who had received particular attention from Braddock during a review at Alexandria owed her preferment to the cake and potted woodcocks she had sent the General.[6]

This letter and virtually all the others George wrote during the first days at Wills Creek contained a warning to impatient friends that the expedition might be delayed for several weeks.[7] Himself systematic

---

[1] Cf. *Lowdermilk*, ii.

[2] *Ibid.*, xxxi.

[3] 1 *G. W.*, 125; Orme to Washington, Aug. 25, 1755; 1 *Hamilton*, 83.

[4] 29 *G. W.*, 41. These Ensigns were to serve without pay in the two Regiments until vacancies occurred (Braddock to Robert Napier, Apr. 19, 1755; *Pargellis*, 82–83).

[5] One of them, as already noted, went to a son of Anthony Strother, who lived next to Ferry Farm (1 *Hamilton*, 69).

[6] 1 *G. W.*, 122–23.   [7] *Ibid.*, 121–25.

and unhappily familiar with all the bafflement of the frontier, George doubtless saw before many days what some of his comrades-in-arms already had observed—that something besides horses and wagons was lacking. Beneath the show of strict conformity to military standards, and of blunt, open dealing on the part of the General,[8] there was much slowness, inefficiency, stupidity, lack of resourcefulness and some laziness. As one officer subsequently wrote, Braddock "was a man of sense and good natured too, though warm and a little uncouth in his manner —and peevish—withal very indolent and seemed glad for anybody to take business off his hands, which may be one reason why he was so grossly imposed upon by his favorite, who really directed everything and may justly be said to have commanded the expedition and the army." [9]

This favorite was George's friend, Robert Orme. Even before the troops had left Alexandria, there had been jealous talk "of young men" having excessive influence with Braddock, "and of others whose rank and age and character entitled them to respect being in disgrace and kept at a distance." [10] William Shirley, the secretary at headquarters, was aware of Orme's influence with Braddock and was pleased that if Braddock had to be influenced by anyone it should be, as he put it, by "so honest and capable a man." At the same time, Shirley was concerned over Orme's inexperience and Braddock's incompetence. "We have," said Shirley, "a General most judiciously chosen for being disqualified for the service he is employed in, in almost every respect." Shirley added: "It is a joke to suppose that secondary officers can make amends for the defects of the first; the mainspring must be the mover— the others in many cases can do no more than follow and correct a little its motions. As to these, I don't think we have much to boast. Some are insolent, others capable, but rather aiming at showing their own abilities than making a proper use of them." [11]

Young Washington discreetly refrained from writing about any of this, but in the still-sensitive memory of the difficulties of transportation in 1754, he wondered whether it would be possible for Braddock to get the artillery over the mountains. If that could be done, George believed the military task beyond the ridges could be discharged with

---

8 Cf. Orme in 1 *Hamilton*, 83–84.
9 Anon. letter of July 25, 1755 on Braddock's campaign; *Pargellis*, 119.
10 D. Dulany, *News Letter of 1755* in 3 *Penn. Mag.*, 13.
11 William Shirley to Gov. Robert Hunter Morris, May 23, 1755; 1 *Hamilton*, 64–65; 2 *Penn. Arch.*, 317.

THE DAILY MARCHES OF BRADDOCK'S ARMY

For a Virginia colonial soldier who had crossed the mountains and had encountered the French and Indians in 1754, even the early stages of Braddock's campaign the next year were a sickening experience.

Inherited pride in British arms turned fast to misgiving, then to disgust and soon to dismay. Stage by stage as the troops moved westward and northwestward, Washington could see that the officers of the regular army had no conception of the nature of the warfare with which they were to be met. They professed such confidence in the disciplined skill of their men and they

showed so much open contempt for their adversary that it was futile to explain to them how the Indians and French would offer no target and would find the British line a perfect mark for their fire.

Washington said all that he thought a volunteer aide should, and at other times he kept silent. Some of his fellow-Virginians talked without restraint to all who would listen. Their account of the cunning cruelty of stealthy Indians reached and alarmed the British in the ranks. Prediction of calamity, though scorned by officers, made every advance a strain and every camp a night-

(Continued on third page following)

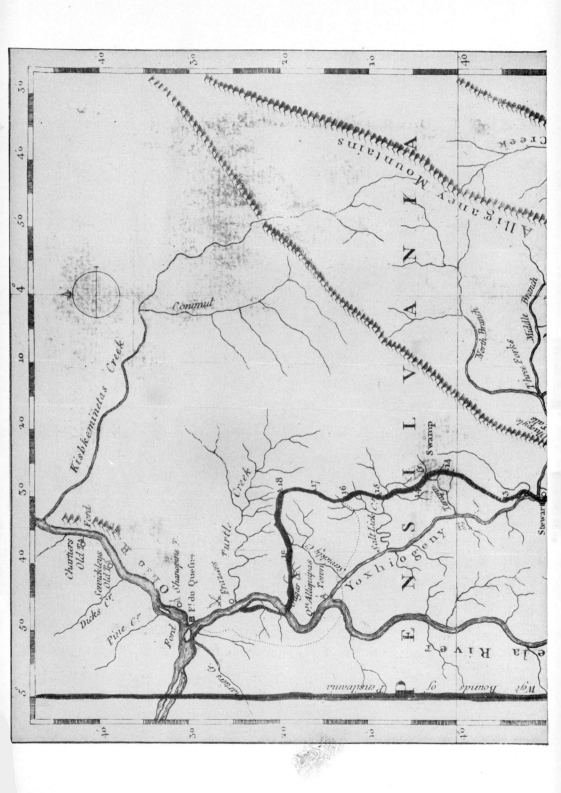

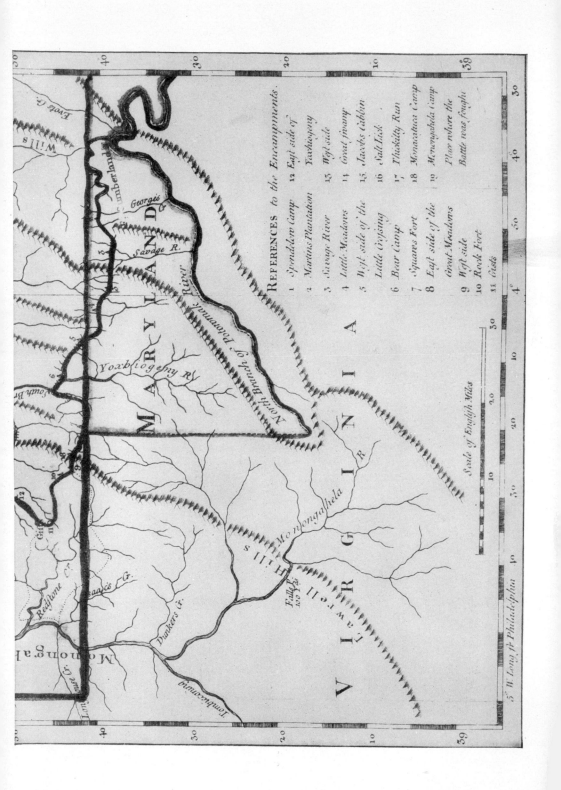

REFERENCES to the Encampments.

1 Spendelow Camp
2 Martins Plantation
3 Savage River
4 Little Meadows
5 West side of the Little Crossing
6 Bear Camp
7 Squaws Fort
8 East side of the Great Meadows
9 West side
10 Rock Fort
11 Gists
12 East side of Yoxhiogeny
13 West side
14 Great Swamp
15 Jacobs Cabbin
16 Salt Lick
17 Thickety Run
18 Monacatuca Camp
19 Monongahela Camp
Place where the Battle was fought

Scale of English Miles

Sr W. Long, P^t Philadelphia

mare for men who never before had seen wild, all-enveloping forests.

Daily marches were short but full of "pangs and fears." Lieut. Robert Orme, Braddock's principal aide, kept a record of distances and doubtless learned from the colonials the names of some of the places where the army halted. Other names may have been of his own selection. Nineteen they were in number from the day the column left Fort Cumberland until the army was close to the Monongahela on the 8th of July.

When it all was over and Orme had recovered from his wound, he prepared a journal not unlike those Washington had written, and he had maps drawn with care to illustrate the order of march, the arrangement of the camps and the disposition of the troops on the afternoon of July 9. As far as can be ascertained, most of these maps were accurate. Some of them contain data not procurable elsewhere. The one reproduced on the two preceding pages passed in time into the collection known as the "King's Maps," now in the British Museum. They tell the tale of a tragedy from which Washington was one of the few to emerge with credit and new reputation.

ease and honor. ". . . I fancy," he said, "the French will be obliged to draw their force from the Ohio to repel the attacks in the North . . ." [12] At the same time, he had regretfully to confide to his brother that the attempted crossing must wait on the slow assembly of wagons and on the accumulation of sufficient forage, which had to be hauled from Philadelphia.[13]

George noticed, too, that a second concern of the General, as he chafed at Wills Creek, was that of assistance from the Indians. About 100 savages—men, women and children—were encamped at Fort Cumberland when George arrived. [14] Among them were Monaka-toocha, White Thunder and probably a few others whom George knew, but these were not being treated with the wisdom and the tact that an understanding of the temperament of the savage would have dictated. During the day, the Indian women, as well as the men, were allowed to visit the British camp,[15] where soldiers long separated from the other sex saw them and sought to win their favor by giving them liquor or money. Braddock immediately prohibited all such gifts,[16] and on the 12th of May made an effort of the familiar sort to ingratiate himself with the natives. All his officers assembled at headquarters to share in ceremonies at 11 o'clock. Wampum was tendered. In the speech of the General the might of England was boasted; friends were assured good treatment; all others were put on notice that if they did not join the British, they would be counted as enemies. Unfortunately, the mistake made the previous year in failing to supply George's expedition had been repeated: the presents intended for the savages had not been sent forward. All that Braddock could do at the moment was to offer "drams around" and to explain that the gifts would arrive in a few days.[17] The Indians went off quietly and without grumbling, but George and the others who knew anything about the natives must have realized that the council had not been a success.

Besides the certainty of delay and the uncertainty of Indian allegiance, a third difficulty developed under George's eyes during the first days at Wills Creek. The weather was becoming warmer; some days were hot; thunderstorms already were occurring.[18] As a result of high tem-

---

[12] Letter of May 14, 1755, to John Carlyle; 1 G. W., 122.
[13] Washington to J. A. Washington, May 14, 1755; 1 G. W., 123.
[14] *Seaman*, Sargent, 373.
[15] *Seaman*, Sargent, 374. Dinwiddie subsequently maintained that the warriors of the Six Nations were absent because they were assisting Shirley and Johnson (2 *Din.*, 224).
[16] *Lowdermilk*, xxxii.   [17] *Seaman*, Sargent, 375; *Va. Gazette*, May 23, 1755.
[18] *Seaman*, Sargent, 375, 376.

perature and of poor packing, much salt meat spoiled.[19] That which remained sound was unpalatable to troops who had been compelled to
subsist on similar meat and on poor bread during the whole of their
advance to Fort Cumberland. It was almost imperative that they have
fresh provisions to keep them healthy, and that they be not fed salt
meat, even if it were good, until the march over the mountains began.
Braddock at once set up a public market, which he reasoned that farmers
around the fort would be glad to stock.[20] The death penalty was threatened against soldiers or camp-followers if they stopped or interfered
with anyone who was bringing provisions or forage to the market.[21]
Higher prices were offered for fresh meat, with the assurance that
none fit for consumption need be sold below that figure; but, of course,
in that frontier country, offerings were so far below the requirements of
the camp [22] that the idea of a market was almost ludicrous.

Although Braddock advanced some gold for the encouragement of
his feeble trade,[23] the few provisions brought to the fort were sold to
officers and men who wished at their own expense to supplement their
ration. Carriage and the pay of wagoners were charges that had to be
met promptly in cash from the headquarters chest if the Pennsylvania
farmers were to be encouraged to rent their vehicles and teams in answer to Benjamin Franklin's appeal.[24] Braddock's funds for these purposes were running low because of the high prices demanded for everything. He had now to replenish his stock of money and, on the 15th of
May, he gave George written instructions to proceed to Hampton and
to get £4000 from the Paymaster of the expedition, John Hunter. If
that official could not raise the entire sum in two days, the aide was to
bring back all that Hunter could supply.[25]

Speed was enjoined. Washington left Fort Cumberland the day he
received his orders and on the 16th he reached Winchester. There he
procured an express and directed the man to proceed to Hampton and
to deliver earnest instructions to Hunter to bring all the money he
could collect to Williamsburg, whither George would come as soon as
he could. In added caution George wrote also to another Hampton
businessman.[26] Then, instead of proceeding by way of Neville's Ordi-

[19] On the 12th and 15th of May, forty-four casks of beef were condemmed (*ibid.*, 375, 377).
[20] *Orme*, 311.
[21] *Lowdermilk*, xxxiii.　　　　　[22] *Orme*, 311.
[23] *Ibid.*　　　　　[24] See *supra*, p. 31.
[25] Braddock's instructions are in 1 *Hamilton*, 60–61. See also 1 *G. W.*, 125.
[26] 1 *G. W.*, 126. For the doubt concerning this "Mr. Belfour," see n. 43, *infra*.

nary to Fredericksburg, George took the familiar road over the Blue Ridge to Fairfax in order to get a fresh horse at Mount Vernon or at Belvoir.[27] When he reached the pleasant plantations on the tidal stretches of the Potomac, he found that his own neighbors had been called upon to supply some of the draft animals needed for the expedition to the Ohio. A team of George William Fairfax's, together with his servant Simpson, had been taken almost literally from the plow and had been carried off.[28] George's own mounts, of course, had been so reduced by the accidents of his ride to Bullskin in April [29] that he had none in reserve. After a day's search and delay, he had to accept the tender of Sally Fairfax's riding horse,[30] on which he started toward Williamsburg. As he felt the necessity of maximum speed, after losing time in Fairfax, he did not stop to visit his mother at Ferry Farm.[31]

His ride was hard and exhausting, through a country suffering from an extreme drought.[32] At Claiborne's Ferry on the 22nd, it looked as if George were to encounter failure as well as fatigue. The express he had dispatched from Winchester met him at the crossing, on the return journey to the Valley, and delivered a message from Dinwiddie. It was phrased, as George later wrote, "in the most expressive terms," [33] to the effect that John Hunter had gone North for money and would not return for a fortnight or longer. The Governor wished Washington to know that certain disappointment awaited him.[34] George accepted the message as correct, but he had orders to proceed and he concluded immediately that he should go on to Williamsburg at least. As the express was riding directly back to Winchester, George gave him a letter to Orme. This explained what had happened and what George intended to do, and it contained a request for further instructions if Dinwiddie's prediction was fulfilled.[35]

In Williamsburg, which he reached that evening, George received a surprise. Colonel Hunter's assistant or substitute was there, had most of the required £4000, and expressed confidence that with the help

27 It is entirely probable, of course, that by calling on Hunter to meet him in Williamsburg, George reasoned he could follow the longer route and have a day at Mount Vernon to look over the plantation, without losing any more time than would have been consumed in riding all the way to Hampton.

28 William Fairfax to Washington, June 28, 1755; 1 Hamilton, 67; Washington to G. W. Fairfax, June 7, 1 G. W., 135. Apparently, the team consisted of two horses.

29 See supra, p. 27.

30 1 G. W., 129.   31 1 G. W., 136.

32 1 G. W., 127. This drought extended northward into Pennsylvania where, as late as June 6, it was severe (6 Penn. Col. Rec., 422–23).

33 1 G. W., 127.

34 Ibid.   35 1 G. W., 126–27.

of the Governor and of others he would complete the sum the next day. Much relieved, Washington sent another report to Orme [36] and then sought out some of his friends in the General Assembly, which had been in session since the 1st of May. Much legislation had been under consideration, though the main purpose of the session was the now-familiar one of finding a new supply of funds for the defence of the Colony. Almost all the money the lawmakers had voted previously had been expended by the beginning of the second week in May; the Assembly, in Dinwiddie's judgment, was "very backward" in providing more.[37]

Of all this, and of the Burgesses' side of the case, George doubtless heard in the tavern and from his friend John Carlyle, who had fallen sick on a visit to the town [38] but had not lost, even temporarily, his interest in public affairs. That very day, as it chanced, the Committee of Propositions and Grievances had submitted to the House of Burgesses a bill for the division of Fairfax County.[39] As no material opposition was known to exist, the passage of the bill could be expected. That would mean two more representatives from the area included in Fairfax as then bounded. John Carlyle explained this to George, stated that one of the Fairfax members might not run again, and asked how George would like to be a Burgess. Washington thought Carlyle was in a jesting mood and therefore he did not commit himself. The subject was dropped when the gentleman from Alexandria observed somewhat mysteriously that "they" might elect the young soldier from the old county or the new without his knowing anything about it.[40] George tucked this away in his memory, as he had a habit of doing in matters that concerned his ambition or his advancement, and, bidding Carlyle good-bye, he went about the business that had brought him to Williamsburg.

The next morning, May 23, while the acting paymaster was scouring Williamsburg for specie to complete the £4000, George went shopping in the town where, happily, stocks had been replenished since the middle of January when not a hat or a stocking could be purchased in the capital or in Yorktown.[41] George was able to get a couple of

---

[36] This probably went by the special express set up under Dinwiddie's proclamation published in the *Va. Gazette* of May 9, 1755. Messengers were identified by a "badge being a copper plate on which a greyhound is engraved" (*Ibid.*).
[37] 2 *Din.*, 35.
[38] 1 *G. W.*, 136.   [39] 3 *Journ. H. B.*, 1752–58, p. 265.
[40] Washington to J. A. Washington, May 28, 1755; 1 *G. W.*, 130.
[41] 1 *Din.*, 461.

toothbrushes, three pairs of gloves, four pairs of thread stockings, and various needed small articles.[42] He found shortly, to his great satisfaction, that along with these personal effects, he would have the full £4000 to carry back to Wills Creek. Hunter's substitute had succeeded in procuring what he had lacked when he arrived from Hampton. The mission of Washington had not failed.[43] On the afternoon of the 23rd, he started toward Winchester and halted for the night at Chiswell's Ordinary,[44] on the first leg of what proved a protracted and dull journey, because Mrs. Fairfax's horse became lame and could not carry a load. George consequently had to pick up such animals as he could at intervals of fifteen or twenty miles.[45] Again, as on the downward journey, he did not feel he could take even an hour for a halt at his mother's home.[46]

From Winchester to Wills Creek, the country was so much exposed that arrangements had been made in advance for the Virginia Troop of light horse to meet Washington there and to escort the treasure to Fort Cumberland. To George's disgust, they were not in Winchester when he dismounted. "I should have received greater relief from the fatigues of my journey," he grumbled, "and my time would have been spent much more agreeably, had I halted below, rather than at this vile post; but I little imagined I should have to wait for a guard who should have waited for me, if either must have waited at all." [47] He had no alternative to remaining at Winchester until a guard of militia could be assembled. This he expected to take two days, for the reason, he said, that "you may with almost equal success, attempt to raise the dead to life again, as the force of this County." [48]

While George chafed, he pondered ambitiously what John Carlyle had said to him about becoming a candidate for the House of Burgesses. Washington frankly desired the position but, in his pride, he did not wish to be a candidate and to be defeated. The day after he reached Winchester he wrote "Jack" about it and asked his brother to ascertain, if possible, what were the sentiments of the bantering Carlyle and other leading men of the County. Characteristically, George went on: "I

42 *Ledger A,* folio 21.

43 It is to be regretted that Colonel Hunter's diligent agent is not readily identified. George wrote of him simply as "Mr. Belfour" (1 *G. W.,* 126). James Balfour was a merchant of Hampton, with whose firm, Balfour and Barraud, an account of Washington's appears in *Ledger A.* The association of this Balfour with Hunter appears probable but has not been established.

44 1 *G. W.,* 127.

45 1 *G. W.,* 129.   46 1 *G. W.,* 136.

47 Letter to J. A. Washington, May 28, 1755; 1 *G. W.,* 129–30.

48 *Ibid.,* 128–29.

know your good sense can furnish you with means enough without letting it proceed immediately from me. If you do anything in this, pray let me know by the first opportunity how you have succeeded in it, and how those gentlemen stand affected; if they seem inclinable to promote my interest, and things should be drawing to a crisis, you then may declare my intentions and beg their assistance. If on the contrary you find them more inclined to favor some other, I would have the affair entirely dropped. Parson Green's and Captain Mc-Carty's interests [49] in this would be of consequence; and I should be glad if you could sound their pulse upon the occasion. Conduct the whole till you are satisfied of the sentiments of those I have mentioned, with an air of indifference and unconcern; after that you may regulate your conduct accordingly." [50] The result was not encouraging. George decided to defer to a more favorable time the fulfilment of his developing ambition to be a Burgess.

Meanwhile, George had to get back to Wills Creek and had to possess a sufficient number of good horses to keep him in the saddle. So, on the 28th, while he was doing what he could to speed the muster of a guard, he bestirred himself for another mount and succeeded in finding a large bay horse. He had to pay slightly more than £10, but with this additional strong creature he fortified himself against emergency.[51] Somewhat surprisingly, too, he procured his escort without prolonged search by the militia officers and, probably on the afternoon of the 28th, he set out with them and Braddock's £4000. The "eight men," he later wrote, "were two days assembling; but I believe they would not have been more than as many seconds dispersing if I had been attacked." [52] As no French or Indians descended on the cavalcade, George reached Wills Creek with the money on the 30th of May, the fifteenth day after his departure for Williamsburg.[53] He had made excellent time and found himself at the journey's end in "tolerable health," as he put it, though he was somewhat worn.[54]

Much had happened during his absence. All the troops intended for the expedition had arrived or soon would. The artillery had experienced much trouble in reaching Fort Cumberland because of the usual shortage of wagons and teams. Had not Lieutenant Colonel Gage impressed vehicles and horses as he went forward, he might never have reached

---

[49] Rev. Charles Green and Daniel McCarty, for whom see Vol. I, p. 204.
[50] 1 G. W., 130–31.   [51] Ledger A, folio 22.
[52] Letter of June 7, 1755; 1 G. W., 139.   [53] 1 G. W., 131–32.
[54] Washington to Mrs. John Carlyle, June 7, 1755; 1 G. W., 137.

Wills Creek.[55] The last contingent known to be on the road, Dobbs's North Carolina Company, tramped into quarters the day of George's return.[56] There then were in the camp the two British Regiments of 700 men each, three Independent Companies, and one North Carolina, one Maryland and nine Virginia Companies, together with sixty regulars of the artillery train and thirty seamen accustomed to the use of block and tackle in moving heavy guns.[57] The Maryland Company had made a favorable impression on St. Clair,[58] in spite of the fact that recruits from the Colony for the regulars had included some convicts [59] and a number of servants who had scurried to the colors in the hope of terminating their indenture.[60] The Virginia troops had been well drilled by Ensign Allen of the regulars,[61] but, in the judgment of Orme, "their languid, spiritless and unsoldierlike appearance, considered with the lowness and ignorance of most of their officers, gave little hope of their future good behavior." [62]

George found, further, that the Governor of Virginia now had lost standing with the General and shared in Braddock's eyes the undependability of the soldiers of the Old Dominion. One of Dinwiddie's contractors had failed to deliver cattle he had promised; Michael Cresap had repeated his father's performance of 1754 and had not sent to Wills Creek an adequate supply of flour; Thomas Cresap had attempted to sell pickled meat so bad that it was condemned and buried.[63] In wrath and desperation, Braddock had been compelled to return wagons all the way to Winchester for provisions and had been forced to dispatch 300 pack horses to the Conococheague for flour.[64] Only the 150 vehicles promised by Franklin and about 500 of the desired 1500 pack animals had been delivered in specific and punctual performance of contracts.[65] Grateful for what Franklin had done, Braddock had written Governor Morris: "You will . . . be informed of the situation I am in by the folly of Mr. Dinwiddie and the roguery of the Assembly, and unless the road of communication from your province is opened and some contracts made in consequence of the power I have given I must in-

[55] Orme, 312. The dates of the arrival of the various units are given in Seaman, Sargent, 377, 378, 379, 380, 381. See also Pargellis, 93.

[56] Seaman, Sargent, 380.

[57] Ibid., 380.

[58] Pargellis, 62.

[59] 1 Sharpe, 204.

[60] 1 Sharpe, 211.

[61] Orme, 298. Allen was appointed, about the 8th of April, in Orme's words, to make the Virginians "as like soldiers as it was possible."

[62] Orme, 312.

[63] Orme, 313–315.

[64] Ibid., 313.

[65] Ibid., 321; Md. Gazette, June 19, 1755. Cf. Seaman, Sargent, 380.

evitably be starved . . . Cresap . . . has behaved in such a manner that if he had been a French Commis[sary?] he could not have acted more for their interest. In short, in every instance but in my contract for the Pennsylvania wagons, I have been deceived and met with nothing but lies and villainy." [66]

Little had been accomplished with the Indians during the absence of George. The soldiers had found some of the Indian girls not unattractive and altogether obliging, with the result that patrols had to be organized to scour the woods where assignations were being held.[67] George's friend White Thunder had a daughter, Bright Lightning, who had become quite the belle of the camp. Stern and still sterner penalties had been imposed on soldiers who gave or sold liquor to the Indians. Most of the savages were offended by the severity of the camp regulations; the troops, in turn, were demoralized by the presence of native women. Drunkenness, theft and gambling were increasing.[68] Official councils had been held with the Chiefs, and promises had been made by them; but, in reality, no service as scouts or warriors had been assured except by Monakatoocha and a few other unshakable friends of the English.[69]

All these disappointments and defeats had affected the temper of some of the seniors at headquarters. Braddock had given St. Clair what the young staff officers called a "set down" for the severity of the language the Quartermaster had used toward the Pennsylvanians.[70] The General had not exemplified the moderation he demanded of his subordinates and, in hot wrath, he told one of Governor Morris's agents that he would not march one foot North until he had assurance of a good road to the Youghiogheny.[71] Actually, before George's return from Williamsburg, Braddock had fixed his order of march,[72] had

[66] Letter of May 24, 1755; 6 Penn. Col. Rec., 400.

[67] Halkett's Orderly Book, May 21, 1755. The penalty was fifty lashes, immediately administered. As a reward for diligent performance of this duty, the pickets were allowed daily a gill of rum, mixed with three of water (ibid.).

[68] Lowdermilk, xl, xli; Halkett's Orderly Book, May 23, 26, June 6, 11, 1755. The last of these orders provided for the immediate hanging, without trial, of detected thieves.

[69] Orme, 309; Lowdermilk, 124, xxxv, xxxviii, xxxix; Seaman, Sargent, 378, 379, 380.

[70] William Shirley to Governor Morris, May 21, 1755; 2 Penn. Arch., 317.

[71] Richard Peters to James Burd, May 27, 1755; Shippen Papers, 39; Orme, 315–16. The negotiations for this road and the reports of progress in opening it will be found in 6 Penn. Col. Rec., 302, 329, 334, 368, 373, 380, 395, 425, 433 ff. Although it had been assumed that the terminus of this road had been fixed early at Turkey Foot on the Youghiogheny, Governor Morris's letter of July 3, 1755 (Shippen Papers, 41), shows that a final decision had not been reached at that date concerning the point at which the road from Shippensburg was to join Braddock's Road. For Indian marauders along this road, see Richard Peters to unnamed correspondent, July 17, 1755; P.R.O., C.O. 5: 16, 155.

[72] Orme, 321 ff.

promised *6d* per day extra pay to soldiers assigned to work on the grade over the mountains,[73] and had designated Major Chapman to move with 500 men [74] to the Little Meadows, in order to improve the trail, to construct a small fort and to establish an advanced store of provisions.[75]

Erection of this little work was the only action Braddock took toward the establishment of an advance base. In every other respect he proposed to move his men, his artillery and his wagons directly to the Ohio from Fort Cumberland, which thus became his general base. This projected march from Wills Creek to Fort DuQuesne was of necessity in six stages:

1. From Fort Cumberland westward to the Great Crossing of the Youghiogheny, a distance of about thirty miles through Maryland and Southern Pennsylvania, across Wills Mountain [76] and the main barrier of the Allegheny Range at an elevation of approximately 3000 feet.[77]

2. From the Great Crossing northwestward to Great Meadows and the site of Fort Necessity, a stretch of not more than fifteen miles, but over the forbidding grades of Laurel Hill, at a maximum elevation of about 2400 feet.

3. From Fort Necessity northwestward and northward to the crest and along the higher sweeps of Chestnut Ridge, at 1800 to 2200 feet, until the vicinity of the Jumonville Camp was reached, a distance of about eight miles.

4. From Jumonville Camp North along Chestnut Ridge and thence downgrade to Stewart's Crossing of the Youghiogheny, a total of twelve miles.

5. From Stewart's Crossing to the Monongahela in the vicinity of the Narrows of Turtle Creek—thirty-four miles of rolling country, 1200 to 1300 feet above sea level.

6. From the Monongahela and the Narrows to Fort DuQuesne itself, eleven to thirteen miles according to the choice of routes, at an elevation from 800 to 1200 feet.

[73] *Lowdermilk,* xlii; *Halkett's Orderly Book,* May 28, 1755. Sergeants were to receive a shilling daily.

[74] The "Seaman" (Sargent, 380), gave the number as 600.

[75] 1 *G. W.,* 131–32.

[76] This elevation, an outcropping of the Allegheny, has borne various names through the years. The one employed here is that used by Alfred P. James on the map of "the Upper Ohio" in the *Atlas of American History,* Plate 57.

[77] Braddock's route entered Pennsylvania about twelve miles Southeast of Fort Necessity near the present Addison, Somerset Co., Penn. Needless to say, the various elevations had not been determined in 1755. The great concern of the engineers was not elevation but grade. The figures used in the text are those of the United States Geological Survey.

The total distance to be covered in these six stages thus was about 110 miles, the greater part of it through rough, heavily wooded country. Dependence, to repeat, was to be upon the main base at Fort Cumberland; the column had to be self-sustaining because the country itself would supply nothing.

The first march of Chapman's advanced force, the first challenge of the mountains by the British regulars, was under way when George rode into camp on the 30th of May. Before Chapman had started, 300 men had spent three days in filling the gullies, clearing away the brush and reducing the grades, but they could not provide easy passage for the heavy vehicles. British officers were appalled by the difficulties presented on this first stretch of a long, long road. Said Orme: ". . . Major Chapman marched . . . at daybreak, and it was night before the whole baggage had got over a mountain about two miles from the camp. The ascent and descent were almost a perpendicular rock; three wagons were entirely destroyed . . . and many more were extremely shattered." [78] Such warnings as George and the frontiersmen had felt themselves free to give Braddock had failed to prepare the General for these realities of the road. Braddock himself reconnoitred and concluded that he could not get his howitzers up the steep grades, but he could find no other expedient than that of detailing more men to shovel earth and stone out of the way.[79]

Then fortune changed as rapidly as the weather did in those Maryland mountains. Lieutenant Spendelowe [80] of the naval detachment went out with some other officers on the 2nd of June, while soldiers languidly were digging on the defiant road. After some time he left his companions and, unattended, made his way along the east bank of Wills Creek. About 2 o'clock he came back with a report that he had skirted the ridge West of the fort and, without encountering heavy grades, had reached the old trail. By employing this route and passing through the Narrows, the road was lengthened two miles only and the terrific pull was avoided altogether.[81] As the country previously had been reconnoitred with what was assumed to be care,[82] Lieutenant Spendelowe's report scarcely seemed credible, but it was confirmed by examination of the ground. Everything else forthwith was stopped in

---

[78] *Orme*, 323.   [79] *Orme*, 324.

[80] The name is variously spelled. Next to Spendelowe, which appears on official returns, the form apparently most favored was Spendlow.

[81] *Seaman*, Sargent, 381; *Orme* 324; 1 *G. W.*, 132; *Lowdermilk*, 136–37.

[82] *Orme*, 324.

order that a new road might be cut. Spendelowe became overnight a figure of much reputation and enlarged authority.[83]

While this was being done, concern and irritation increased still further in the camp—concern because a form of bloody flux had shown itself among the soldiers more widely,[84] and irritation because Braddock had lost all patience and no longer could argue anything without wrath. Consideration and every quality of moderation were thrown away.[85] Convinced more than ever of slothfulness, rascality and lack of truth among the provincials, the General would concede no virtue to any of them otherwise than to admit that Franklin had kept the contract to deliver 150 wagons. Braddock often renewed his arraignment of the Virginians and the Marylanders before George, who would defend them against sweeping allegations. "Instead of blaming the individuals as he ought," young Washington wrote indignantly of his commander, "he charges all his disappointments to a public supineness, and looks upon the country, I believe, as void of both honor and honesty." [86] George's resentment would have been even greater had he seen the dispatches the General was sending the home government during these days of waiting: The Virginians were "very indifferent men"; there was "want of honesty and inclination to forward the service"; the promises of the people of Virginia and of Maryland were "not to be depended on"—and so, endlessly.[87] As for Indian support, which Governor Dinwiddie still thought the expedition would receive on the Ohio from the Cherokees,[88] Braddock would not quite throw away all hope, but he believed that Dinwiddie most inexcusably had pursued the wrong policy and had misled him.[89]

Bickering increased with idleness and as a result of the explosions of the General. Jealousy of Orme was aggravated when he was admitted to the council of war. Col. Peter Halkett, who especially disliked Orme, swore that if he ever succeeded to the command he would dismiss the General's favorite the very next day.[90] Orme, for his part, did not

---

[83] *Ibid.*, and *Seaman*, Sargent, 382–83, *Halkett's Orderly Book*, June 12, 1755. Spendelowe was given a free hand with the naval detachment and with a small party assigned him.

[84] 1 *G. W.*, 139.

[85] Perhaps his fullest general indictment of the Colonies, from South Carolina northward, was in a letter of June 5, 1755, to Newcastle, Br. Mus. Add. MS 32855, f. 336.

[86] Washington to William Fairfax, June 7, 1755; 1 *G. W.*, 133.

[87] Cf. Braddock to Robert Napier, June 8, 1755; *Pargellis*, 84–85.

[88] 2 *Din.*, 55.

[89] *Orme*, 314; Dinwiddie to Sir Thomas Robinson, June 5, 1755; P.R.O., C.O. 5: 46, p. 35–41.

[90] Anon. letter of July 25, 1755; *Pargellis*, 122; *cf.* Dulany's *News Letter* of 1755; 3 *Penn. Mag.*, 20.

consider his position one to be envied. He subsequently confided to George, "I saw myself a slave, constantly engaged in keeping peace." [91] Washington had a somewhat similar, though a less conspicuous duty.

In addition, while the army waited for Spendelowe's road to be completed, George made another clumsy attempt to get the Carlyle and Fairfax sisters-in-law to correspond with him,[92] and he discharged a number of somewhat unpleasant chores. The horses taken from Belvoir were sought in vain;[93] a curious request from his mother had to be answered. She had asked him in a letter delivered by one of their friends to provide her with a "Dutch man," doubtless as a farmer, and to send her some butter, probably because the drought had reduced her own supply. "[I] am sorry," George patiently wrote back, "it is not in my power to supply you with a Dutch man, or the butter as you desire, for we are quite out of that part of the country where either are to be, as there are few or no inhabitants where we now lie encamped, and butter cannot be had here to supply the wants of the camp." She had informed him, also, that she intended to go to Mount Vernon during his absence. "I hope," he replied, "you will spend the chief part of your time at Mount Vernon, as you say, where I am certain everything will be ordered as much for your satisfaction as possible, in the situation we are in." [94] Had he been of different temperament he might have laughed grimly at the thought of being able to supply his mother with fresh butter from the very edge of the wilderness. Being the young man he was, he replied formally, with his "Honored Madam" in opening, and his concluding "Dear Madam, your most affectionate and dutiful son." [95]

These letters of June 7 were the last he was able to write at that time from Wills Creek, because, by that date the new road was open and the first Brigade was ready to start. Although the day was one of thunderstorm and rain,[96] Halkett's men, with their wagons and two field-pieces, marched over Spendelowe's road with far less difficulty than would have been encountered on the steep old trail. By nightfall, Halkett was within a mile of the junction of the new and the customary route.[97] The next day Lt. Col. Ralph Burton started with the Independent Companies, the artillery, the wagons laden with ammuni-

---

[91] Letter of Nov. 10, 1755; 1 *Hamilton*, 125.
[92] 1 *G. W.*, 137–38.   [93] 1 *G. W.*, 135. See *supra*, p. 40.
[94] Letter of June 7, 1755; 1 *G. W.*, 135–36.
[95] *Ibid*.   [96] *Seaman*, Sargent, 382.
[97] 1 *G. W.*, 132; *Orme*, 326; *Lowdermilk*, xlvi; *Seaman*, Sargent, 382. For the composition of Halkett's Brigade, 984 effectives, see *Orme*, 327.

tion [98] and those with provisions.[99] Moderate loads proved too heavy
for feeble horses on a new road that doubtless had been softened by
the rain of the previous day. Burton's progress was slow. Dunbar, commanding the final units, had to wait until the 10th before the way was
clear.[100] Braddock and his headquarters moved that day, also, and
halted for the night at what then was called Grove Camp, subsequently
termed Spendelowe's, near the junction of the new route with the old.[101]
There, on the 10th, Lieutenant Colonel Burton reported formally to
Braddock that he had taken two days to move the train of artillery and
the wagons five miles, and he reminded the General that the road over
which they had passed at so slow a pace was better than they could
expect farther on. The horses available simply could not haul the
loads they had.[102]

Braddock's first response was to call together all his officers and to
explain the plight of the column. He asked that they send back to
Wills Creek all unnecessary baggage. If, he went on, any of the officers
had extra horses which they would release for the army's use, the
generosity of these gentlemen would not be forgotten. To this appeal,
of course, George and the other members of the General's staff immediately responded. Braddock himself was not backward. From the
"family" of the commander, twenty horses were provided. Line officers
contributed almost eighty.

Nearly 100 animals thus were turned over to the wagonmasters for
use as pack horses [103] but these manifestly were not a sufficient reenforcement to keep wheels turning westward and northward. More had
to be done. At a council of the General and his field officers on the
11th, a decision was reached to send back two of the six-pounders, which
weighed from 1300 to 1500 pounds each,[104] four cohorns [105] and some
ordnance stores. This decision would give twenty additional wagons
among which to spread the load, but unfortunately, it was found that
the wagons of the regular establishment, brought from England, had
too much weight of their own and carried shafts too wide for the light

98 In the military parlance of the day, the "train of artillery" was the inclusive term for the
guns, the ordnance supplies and the ammunition vehicles.

99 *Orme,* 326; Gordon in *Pargellis,* 104; 1 *G. W.,* 132. There is a difference of one day,
possibly of two, in some of the accounts of this advance and of the council that followed.

100 *Orme,* 326.   101 1 *G. W.,* 132.

102 *Orme,* 331.   103 *Orme,* 331.

104 The weight of the standard Saker 6-pdr. was 1300 but other makes sometimes were
heavier.

105 The standard 4.6 in. cohorn weighed about eighty-six pounds, according to the table in
Duane's *Military Dictionary.*

American horse. The return of these wagons to Fort Cumberland left the expedition with small net gain in vehicles.[106] Besides, the "King's wagons" had been fitted and used to carry powder. The colonial wagons had to be protected against the weather when it was decided to use them for the explosive. Two days—the 11th after the hour of the council of war and the whole of the 12th—were devoted to preparing the vehicles and shifting the powder.[107]

Then the column started again. George watched, counselled, and in the memory of his own difficulty in crossing the mountains, became convinced that success demanded a further reduction of transport. More particularly there had to be an increase in the number of pack animals at the front,[108] even though it was manifest that the inferior creatures supplied for the expedition could carry only half the load that would be borne by strong horses.[109]

Washington was unhappily accurate in his forecast. The first "division" marched about five miles on the 13th and went into camp, but the second "division" did not cover that distance until 11 A.M. of the 14th. Men and horses were so worn that Braddock had to order a day's rest at that camp, known as Martin's Plantation.[110] George, like the others, shared the day of idleness, but he did not get refreshment. Instead he developed fever and sharp pains in his head,[111] symptoms that might mean typhoid fever or the bloody flux, or, as he hoped, merely a brief indisposition. He resolved to keep steadily on with the General and to ignore his malady, but he found he could not remain in his saddle. Much as he disliked it, he had to get permission to ride in one of the wagons while the column passed through the dense woods known as the "Shades of Death," [112] beyond which were the Little Meadows.[113]

There George found Sir John St. Clair with Chapman's advance force that had left Wills Creek on the 29th of May under orders to improve the road, to construct a small fortification, and to prepare a store of provisions. As St. Clair had to get fifty wagons over the road, which had received no care whatever since the previous year, he did not reach the Little Meadows until June 5. He was ashamed to have spent eight days in covering twenty miles, but he blamed his slow advance on the

106 *Orme*, 331–32.
108 1 *G. W.*, 140.
110 *Orme*, 333.

107 *Orme*, 331–32.
109 *Orme*, 332.
111 1 *G. W.*, 141.

112 *Orme*, 335. See also *Lowdermilk*, 144, 145. For the tactical arrangements to assure security of march, see *Halkett's Orderly Book*, June 13, 1755.
113 Braddock almost certainly was with the first "division" at this time and, if so, he and his "family" arrived at Little Meadows on the 16th of June. See *Orme*, 335.

size of his train and on the fact that the road was "either rocky or full of bogs." [114] Sir John was more than ever depressed by the expense of hiring vehicles, which he estimated at £40,000 sterling,[115] and he was convinced that Braddock could not get to Fort DuQuesne until more wagons and supplies were at hand and the road from Shippensburg was opened.[116] Of this the Quartermaster had decided to say nothing to Braddock until he saw the country beyond the mountains.[117] In unwonted silence he proceeded with his men to fell timber and to encircle the camp with an abattis.[118]

Braddock did not wait for counsel. He sought it. His troops had started from Wills Creek on June 7, after waiting four days for the completion of Spendelowe's road. It was now June 16. This meant that with the added two miles of the new road, twenty-two miles had been covered in ten days, or little more than two miles daily—an impossibly slow march for an army that had to reach the Ohio before the known approach of the British would lead the French to reenforce the garrison of Fort DuQuesne. For the first time now the probability of meeting increased opposition, as a result of slow approach, became a serious consideration in the General's planning.

Unaware of Braddock's reasoning, but conscious of the drag of the advance, George received a summons to the commander's tent. The young Virginian still was sick, weakened and in pain; but he had vigor and a clear head for the question the General put to him: What should be done next? George had heard the undependable reports that large French forces were on their way to strengthen the weak garrison at the fort. He believed they would move forward but he did not think they could arrive quickly because he assumed that the drought which was drying up the streams of Western Maryland and Southern Pennsylvania extended to French Creek [119] down which the enemy would be compelled to send supplies until the Allegheny was reached at Venango. Shallow water meant slow progress. George argued that if Braddock would push on with a chosen detachment, supported by artillery, Fort DuQuesne could be taken from its few defenders before French reenforcements arrived. While a lightly equipped English column was moving rapidly forward, the wagons could follow slowly and in safety because the advanced force would be between the

114 St. Clair to Robert Napier, June 13, 1755; *Pargellis,* 95.
115 *Ibid.,* 94.   116 *Ibid.*
117 *Ibid.,* 94–95.   118 *Penn. Gazette,* July 24, 1755.
119 George here styled it Buffalo River.

trains and the enemy.[120] Such was the suggestion of Washington. It was so detailed and was presented so quickly when Braddock inquired that it must have been matured earlier in the mind of the Virginian.

The next day, June 17, sicker than before, George probably heard that Braddock was talking of the plan he had suggested to the General on the 16th. St. Clair knew of it; [121] so did Sir Peter Halkett and Colonel Dunbar.[122] Apparently, none of these had any intimation that the design was not the General's but the young aide's. George, of course, was exceedingly proud [123] and too discreet to boast that the army now was to proceed as he, an uncommissioned provincial, had recommended. That had to remain a secret until it could be confided, under seal, to the family on the Potomac.

As preparations were made to organize the advanced detachment, George had to steel himself to proceed with it. The last day's journey in the jolting wagon had been almost intolerable; [124] his pain was ceaseless; [125] at intervals he may have been delirious; [126] but, of course, he wanted to go on. He soon learned that St. Clair had started with 400 men to clear the road, that Braddock was increasing the number of horses in the teams, that thirty-five days' provisions would be carried on pack animals, and that the advanced force would have to contend with no more than thirty wagons.[127] When the troops actually took the road,[128] George felt what he subsequently described as "the most infinite delight," though he was very ill at the time.[129] The column seemed precisely the right one for the task—slightly more than 1300 of the best men under Sir Peter Halkett,[130] four howitzers, four twelve-pounders and two six-pounders,[131] their ammunition, one hundred rounds per man of ball and powder, a load of Indian presents—and all this is in scarcely more than the designated thirty wagons and a manage-

---

[120] 1 G. W., 143.

[121] Pargellis, 102.

[122] Pargellis, 109.

[123] 1 G. W., 143.

[124] 1 G. W., 141–42.

[125] Ibid., 141.

[126] 29 G. W., 42. The fact that Washington wrote in 1783 of this delirium but said nothing of it in his letter of June 28, 1755, makes a qualified statement necessary.

[127] Orme, 336.

[128] Dunbar, in Pargellis, 109, and Halkett's Orderly Book stated that orders were for Gage to move on the 18th and for the remainder of the advanced column to start on the 19th. Orme (loc. cit., 336) and Washington (1 G. W., 143) gave the date of the first movement as the 19th. Although other troops supplemented Halkett's, his Orderly Book was continued, fortunately, on this advance by Ensign Disney. It supplements Orme invaluably.

[129] 1 G. W., 144.

[130] St. Clair's roadmaking force of 400 is included. Later reenforcements, sent forward with supplies, raised the total force on July 9 to 1459. See infra, p. 86, n. 160. Orders specified that the detachments from the two Regiments, chosen to be a part of the advanced force, were to be taken "out of those landed from Ireland" (Halkett's Orderly Book, June 17, 1755).

[131] These last were with St. Clair.

able number of pack animals.[132] If the guns were too heavy and too numerous, George was not qualified to say more about them than that they manifestly would be difficult to get over the mountains. Everything else seemed ideal: A fortunate company was about to sweep on to the Ohio and to plant the flag of England on the parapet of Fort DuQuesne.

Pain and fever did not yield to patriotic impulse. They racked and burned and left George almost prostrate on the 19th. Braddock knew of the aide's illness and unhappiness and considerately notified the young Virginian that when he was strong enough to go forward a wagon would be at his command.[133] Later that same day, George received written orders through his new friend Roger Morris to this effect:

Dear Washington:

I am desired by the General to let you know that he marches tomorrow and the next day but that he shall halt at the Meadows two or three days. It is the desire of every particular in this family and the General's positive commands to you not to stir but by the advice of the person under whose care you are till you are better which we all hope will be very soon . . . [134]

There was more, about doctors, but this was enough: George was forbidden to go on! Although he had of course to obey, he appealed to the General for one concession: Would Braddock promise that he would be brought to the front before the fort was reached? The commander gave word of honor but coupled with the promise the surgeon's warning that if George persisted in going forward immediately he would be risking his life.[135] Grimly and reluctantly George had to yield and had to stay behind on the 20th at Little Meadows . . . while the drums beat and his comrades rode away.[136]

132 *Orme*, 336.
133 William Findlay, quoting Washington, in 14 *Niles Register*, 179.
134 1 *Hamilton*, 66.
135 1 *G. W.*, 142.
136 The early paragraphs of Washington's letter to "Jack," June 28, 1755 (1 *G. W.*, 141 ff), create the impression that he was left behind on June 22, but Morris's statement that the date of Braddock's departure was June 20 is confirmed by George's statement on the 28th (1 *G. W.*, 144) that he had then been six days with Dunbar, who was two days behind Braddock (*ibid.*, 142). If George was left in camp on the 20th, and Dunbar arrived on the 22nd, the chronology fits together. It does not on any other assumption.

CHAPTER IV

A Desperate Gamble to Share a Battle
(June 20–July 8, 1755)

To THE wretchedness of George's pain and fever there now was added the feeling of separation from the scene of action, and of loneliness besides. John Alton, a white servant, had attended George on the expedition and had been always a reminder of home; but now John, too, was ill of the same malady with which George was afflicted [1] and was quartered elsewhere. In John's place George had to hire a nurse at 1s a day. [2] Definite relief of mind consequently was afforded on the 22nd by the arrival of Colonel Dunbar and his command, though, as it proved, the Colonel was bristling with resentments. Dunbar felt that he had been affronted by Orme and deceived by the General. Not long previously, in the company of Braddock and of the aide Dunbar had dwelt on the methods of some of the distinguished officers under whom he had served.

"Stuff," the irreverent Orme had said; "you might as well talk of your Grandmother."

"Sir," Dunbar had answered indignantly, "if she was alive, she would have more sense, more good manners, and know as much of military matters as you do."

Braddock had broken in: "Gentlemen, you are both warm."

"General," the regimental commander had answered, "you see the provocation I got."

There, for the moment, the matter had been halted but it had not been forgotten by the Colonel. [3] He felt even more keenly the handicap put on him by the organization of the advanced column. Braddock had assured Dunbar, before starting with the light force, that Halkett

---

[1] 1 G. W., 145.
[2] Ledger A, folio 22. William Findlay wrote in 1818, loc. cit., that Washington stated after 1789 that Braddock left a Sergeant to look after him. This may have been the case but, as the interval between the event and the statement is sixty-three years, the facts may have become confused. [3] Pargellis, 121–22.

was to keep not more than one day's march ahead and was to communicate with Dunbar by agreed signals if either needed the other. As soon as Braddock had set out with Halkett for Fort DuQuesne, Dunbar discovered that the General had taken the best wagon horses and many spare animals and had left him only a sufficient number to move two-thirds of the wagons at a given time with full teams of four.[4] Dunbar had no possible way of forwarding all the wagons except to use his horses for as many vehicles as he could on a given day, and then to send back the animals for the other wagons, with the result that three days were required to complete a single day's march.[5] The distance between the fast-moving men at the front and Dunbar's heavily burdened force was certain to be increased hourly.

Because of these circumstances, Dunbar had a bitterness he was destined to keep fresh [6] and he scarcely could have shown affectionate concern for a sick member of his commander's "family," but with Dunbar was Doctor Murdock, a surgeon whom George had been told he could trust.[7] Braddock, moreover, had sent back positive command that George should be given Doctor James's powders, a patent medicine subsequently both praised and disparaged.[8] The prescribed treatment was administered. To the restless young patient on the wilderness road to the Ohio, Doctor James's powders seemed, in George's own words, "the most excellent medicine in the world, for it gave me immediate ease . . ." [9] Almost from that date the fever diminished.

As George's fever fell, his interest in the movement of the troops ahead of him rose higher than ever. His desire to rejoin them became more intense every time an express or a returning drover brought news from the front. Indian and French scouts were harassing Braddock's column; they had captured Monakatoocha and had tied him to a tree from which, fortunately, he was rescued unhurt.[10] Other Indians had penetrated close to Fort Cumberland and into Frederick County, Virginia, and had scalped and slain white families.[11]

A nearer concern to George was the surprising and humiliating slowness of the advance of Braddock's men. "Instead of pushing on with

4 Dunbar to Robert Napier, July 24, 1755; 1 Pargellis, 109.
5 1 G. W., 144; Pargellis, 113.
6 Cf. Robert H. Morris to William Shirley, Sept. 5, 1755; 2 Penn. Arch., 401. See also William Findlay in 14 Niles Register, 179.
7 1 Hamilton, 66.
8 Its chief constituents were phosphate of lime and oxide of antimony, a compound that closely resembled the pulvis antimonialis of the later British Pharmacopœia. See DNB, James, Robert.
9 1 G. W., 141.   10 1 Sharpe, 234; Orme, 337.
11 Seaman, Sargent, 383; 1 Sharpe, 232, 234, 236; 2 Din., 85–86.

vigor, without regarding a little rough road," George wrote indignantly, "they were halting to level every mole hill [12] and to erect bridges over every brook; by which means we were four days getting twelve miles . . ." [13] George may or may not have known that, in addition, Braddock had received a visit from a mysterious frontiersman, known as Captain Jack, who had offered his services and those of a small company of experienced scouts in reconnoitring the country where Indians were most apt to be lurking. Braddock had been content to reply that he had troops on whom he could depend.[14]

If George heard of this it must have deepened an uneasiness he had felt for days. He believed with all his heart, and as a matter of course, that the expedition would reach the Ohio. As a guest of General Braddock and a provincial District Adjutant, he had at all times to be cautious in his criticism of British tactics, even of frontier tactics of Indian warfare; but he had been candid, if tactful. He wrote of himself years afterward that he "used every proper occasion till he was taken sick . . . to impress the General and the principal officers around him, with the necessity of opposing the nature of . . . defence to the mode of attack which, more than probably, [Braddock] would experience from the *Canadian* French and their Indians . . ." [15] George realized that he had not made any impression on men who had absolute faith in British discipline and fire power, and now, if he heard that a company of experienced Indian fighters had been rebuffed, he must have wondered . . .

By the 26th, George was sufficiently improved to proceed in a covered wagon to the familiar Great Crossing of the Youghiogheny [16] but there he had to remain because the physician did not think he had regained sufficient strength to cover on horseback or in a vehicle the twenty-five miles that now separated him from the advanced force.[17] Washington hoped on the 28th that he could go forward the next day, and on the 29th he felt confident he could start on the 30th. Rain and the veto of the doctor defeated him again.[18] Eagerly and yearningly he wrote Orme: "My fevers are very moderate and I hope are near a crisis; when I shall have nothing to encounter but excessive weakness and the difficulty in getting to you, which I would not fail in doing

[12] George wrote "Mold hill."
[13] Letter of June 28, 1755 to J. A. Washington; 1 *G. W.*, 144.
[14] 4 Hazard's *His. Reg.*, 416; 5 *ibid.*, 191. All the stories of "Captain Jack" have a vagueness that creates historical doubts.
[15] 29 *G. W.*, 41–42.   [16] 1 *G. W.*, 146.
[17] *Ibid.*, 144, 146.   [18] *Ibid.*, 146.

ere you reach DuQuesne for £500." Then he added for his own reassurance, "but I have no doubt of doing this as the General has given
me his word and honor in the most solemn manner." He asked for
news of the march and had to end almost abruptly because of weakness. ". . . oblige me in the above request," he pleaded, "and advise
the most effectual means for me to join you." [19]

Impatience could not bridge wilderness streams, dissipate loneliness,
nor ease the grade of mountain roads. John Alton continued sick,
though George now was able to dismiss his nurse after eight days'
service; [20] there were few letters of any sort from home, in spite of
George's effort to have communications forwarded from Wills Creek.[21]
He was sarcastic and almost bitter in writing "Jack" of this: "You may
thank my friends for the letters I have received, which has not been
one from any mortal since I left Fairfax, except yourself and Mr.
Dalton." [22]

As it was in the rear, so it was in front. Communication was slow.
George saw Dunbar hampered by overnumerous wagons and too few
horses and he began to doubt whether the rear division ever could
overtake Braddock. It might be possible, George thought, for Dunbar
to reach Great Meadows, but, as Washington confided to his brother,
"I believe shortly [Colonel Dunbar] will not be able to stir at all." [23]
He added: ". . . there has been vile management in regard to horses." [24]
Some of the animals that Braddock's wagon masters [25] had thought
unfit for the journey over the mountain dropped in their traces as they
struggled with the heavy loads Dunbar's drivers had to impose. Not
until July 1–2 could the first of Dunbar's wagons be dragged despairingly to a camp between the Great Crossing of the Youghiogheny and
the site of George's battle of the previous July. Dunbar all the while
was pleading with Braddock to assign him more horses so that he could
shorten the gap between front and rear. "I again and again set forth
my situation to him," Dunbar later wrote of Braddock, and continued:
"He once told me he sent me a wagon and eleven horses, the first I
saw and such as could be of little service. Again he wrote he sent me

19 Letter of June 30, 1755; 1 *G. W.*, 146–47. The full text of the closing sentence is stiffly
formal: "I am too weak to add more than my compliments to the General, family, &c., and
again to desire that you will . . ." and then as quoted.
20 *Ledger A,* folio 22.
21 Cf. Washington to James Innes, July 2, 1755; 1 *G. W.*, 147.
22 Letter of June 28, 1755; 1 *G. W.*, 145. "Mr. Dalton" was John Dalton of Alexandria, who
will appear again in these pages.
23 1 *G. W.*, 144–45, 146.   24 *Ibid.,* 144–45.
25 For their appointment and duties, see *Orme,* 314, 334.

forty horses. Though unloaded, there were but sixteen could come, they were so wore down." [26] This was Dunbar's plight when, probably on the 1st of July, a messenger arrived from the front with orders from Braddock to forward some beeves and 100 pack horses loaded with flour to replace a supply that had been damaged by heavy rains.[27] A Captain and 100 men were to escort the convoy.[28] Adam Stephen forthwith was designated.

Doubtless by the bearer of this order, George and the other officers at Dunbar's camp were given news of Braddock's advance to the beginning of the march of June 30. Progress had been as slow as George had apprehended. The men had felt that their numbers were too small for the work they had to do. Poor food caused grumbling. Still more complaint was made because the men had nothing to drink but water. Braddock had forded the Great Crossing of the Youghiogheny on the 24th of June and that day had passed an abandoned camp of hostile Indians whose French companions had left scurrilous messages on trees that had been stripped of bark. The next day, Braddock's advanced column had marched to a point three miles beyond the Great Meadows in the direction of Gist's settlement. Here had come ugly warning of the presence of Indian allies of the French: Three Englishmen who had slipped through the sentinels had been shot and scalped early on the morning of the 25th. Braddock's response was the offer of £5 reward for every Indian scalp taken by soldier or camp-follower.[29] The badness of the road had reduced Braddock's march of the 26th to four miles. Camp had been made that evening on a site from which French and Indians so recently had slipped away that their fires still were burning. Thereafter, four days of ugly, uneventful struggle with road and river had carried Braddock and his men by nightfall of June 30 no farther than one mile beyond Stewart's crossing of the Youghiogheny North of Gist's.[30]

Beyond that lay country George knew well. He had covered most of the forty miles to the site of the French fort at the junction of the

---

[26] Dunbar to Robert Napier, July 24, 1755; *Pargellis*, 110. As here repunctuated, Dunbar's sentences are believed to convey his meaning; but if the quotation is of special importance, the student should consult the original in Pargellis's faithful text.

[27] The order was dispatched June 30. If an early start was made, the mounted messenger should have reached Dunbar's camp on the 1st of July or, less probably, on the night of June 30–July 1.   [28] *Orme*, 345.

[29] *Halkett's Orderly Book*, June 26 [?], 1755.

[30] That is, close to the present-day Connellsville (Sargent, *op. cit.*, 344 n). The detailed contemporary sources on the advances of these days are *Halkett's Orderly Book*, particularly June 29–30, and *Orme*, 340–45.

Allegheny and the Monongahela, and he could count the marches that had to be made to Jacobs Creek and to Turtle Creek, parallel to the northerly course of the Youghiogheny and then of the Monongahela after it received the waters of its main tributary. On the assumption that Braddock had been across the last ford of the Youghiogheny on the 30th, George could reason that by July 2, the General might be within thirty, perhaps within twenty-five miles of Fort DuQuesne. If Washington was to have his coveted part in the great ceremony of raising the British flag over the ruins of the French defences, he must conquer weakness and must get forward speedily. It would be unendurable if he—the only officer in the expedition who had visited the site of Fort DuQuesne before the French reared their parapets—should not be there when the enemy was driven away. Ever since that April day of the previous year, when Ensign Ward had arrived at Cresap's with the report of the loss of the fort on the Ohio,[31] George had been looking and laboring for the time when he could ride triumphantly back: he must and he would, but he did not attempt to go with Adam Stephen and the guard of 100 men for the train of pack-horses that carried the flour from Dunbar's camp to Braddock's force.[32] George still was far too weak for the long rides on horseback.

The next time wagons started for the front, George climbed feebly into one of them and set his jaws for the torture of continuous jolting over the road to Gist's and then across the Youghiogheny. His first journey carried him past the Great Meadows where, almost a year previously, to the very day, he had been compelled to capitulate.[33] Then he traveled close to the scene of the skirmish with Jumonville, a skirmish that seemed trivial in terms of the force George now was to see Braddock hurl against the French. Northward, George passed Gist's settlement, whence he had retreated in 1754: the way was reversed now! Over the Youghiogheny George went next, and after that

---

31 See Vol. I, p. 350–51.

32 This is obvious from the fact that Orme reported (*op. cit.,* 350) the arrival of the pack animals on the 5th of July. Adam Stephen subsequently gave the date as July 6. He was of opinion that the enemy probably let him go on, as a means of luring Braddock forward, but of this there is no evidence from French sources. See Stephen to Henry Bouquet, Br. Mus. Add. MS, 21643. See also Stephen in the *Hardwicke Papers* (cited hereafter as *Stephen-Hardwicke*), Br. Mus. Add. MS, 21643, f. 127.

33 It may actually have been the first anniversary of the fight, July 3, or of the evacuation, July 4, of Fort Necessity. From the camp between the Great Crossing and the Meadows, the distance to the front was approximately fifty miles. Ten miles a day would have been excellent progress even for a well-horsed small convoy. As George's arrival was on the 8th, he must therefore have been on road five days. His departure from Dunbar's camp consequently was July 3 or July 4.

along a new stretch of road, about a mile in length, that Braddock had cut, as George subsequently learned, on the 1st of July.[34] Farther on, at Jacobs Cabins, George passed Braddock's camp site of the 2nd of July. Beyond that was a swamp where the work of St. Clair's men was visible in drainage and in a firmer road.

Jolting, jolting ceaselessly, the vehicle carried George to Jacobs Creek, where there were evidences of another English encampment for a night.[35] Thence the marks of footprints and of wagons led to Thicketty Run, one of the branches of Sewickley Creek.[36] Through country less mountainous and with forests of white oak not so dense as behind him,[37] George followed a trail, almost fresh, to the bank of the south fork of Turkey Creek,[38] but there he saw that the army had approached a precipice and had turned West along a ridge that led toward the Monongahela.[39] Following this new route, Washington on the 8th had his reward for the pain of his journey. In his wagon, he reached the army and that night encamped with it, about two miles from the east bank of the Monongahela,[40] and by the shortest route, not more than twelve miles [41] from Fort DuQuesne.[42]

George found, as always, a hearty welcome at headquarters that were busy with important decisions after a march that had been arduous but not costly in life. Three or four men in rear of the troops had been picked off on the 6th. In the confusion that followed, Monakatoocha's son had been mistaken for a French Indian and had been killed by British fire.[43] After that, existing strict orders for vigilance on the march and in camp and in the control of fires were made sterner.[44] Indians with the expedition—a mere handful in number—had been unwilling for days to reconnoitre, but on the 4th, two of them had been persuaded to scout the country in front of the column. Unknown to

[34] Orme, 345.

[35] July 3; Orme, 346; Halkett's Orderly Book, July 3–4, 1755.

[36] July 4; Orme, 349; Halkett's Orderly Book, July 3–4, 1755. The line of advance, in terms of later place names, is given in 2 Olden Times, 544 and in 2 Frontier Forts, 176 ff.

[37] Orme, 349.

[38] Often called the Brush Fork of Turkey Creek and, still later, Brush or Rush Creek.

[39] This was the valley of Long Run, West of Irwin and South of Stewart (Sargent, op. cit., 352; Orme, 351–52). The United States Geological Survey sheets for Greensburg and Pittsburgh are particularly useful in a study of the ground.

[40] Sargent, op. cit., 352; 1 G. W., 147. Gordon, in Pargellis, 105, gave the distance from the river as "a short mile."

[41] Washington thought it ten miles, 29 G. W., 42.

[42] The site of the camp traditionally is that of Braddock's Spring (Lowdermilk, 147).

[43] Orme, 350. The body of the boy was interred on the evening of July 5 (Halkett's Orderly Book, July 5, 1755).

[44] Halkett's Orderly Book, July 3–7, 1755. As far as can be ascertained, in limited knowledge of the activity of the enemy, these precautions appear to have been adequate.

these savages, Christopher Gist had gone out alone the same day. All three men had returned on the 6th. The Indians had displayed a scalp they said they had taken from a French officer they had killed when they had caught him while he was shooting near Fort DuQuesne. Gist narrowly had saved his own scalp, because he had been seen and pursued by two Indians whom he eluded metaphorically by a hair. The intelligence reports of the white guide and of the Indians were substantially the same. Gist had noticed smoke rising between the English camp and the French defences; the two friendly natives had seen some boats under the fort and one coming down the river. Little activity had been noticed; few men appeared to be afield to observe or to harass the advancing British.[45]

In the council of Braddock, a proposal had been made by Sir John St. Clair on the 3rd that the advanced force halt and wait for Colonel Dunbar to close the rear. This had been voted down on the grounds, among others, that long delay would consume much food and would give the French time to increase their numbers and to strengthen all their positions.[46] On the day of George's arrival, St. Clair had remarked that it might be well to send a detachment under cover of darkness to invest the fort, but he had not made representation on this point to Braddock and, after discussion with others, had admitted that it might be better to march onward for another day and then to undertake a night advance.[47]

Everything that regulations and European practice demanded for the protection of troops in proximity to the enemy had been done, step by step, as the army had approached.[48] The only question left to be decided now was that of final approach to the French fort. About four miles North of the ground where the army camped on the evening George reached the front, July 8, the Monongahela ran from Southeast to Northwest for some 2000 yards. Parallel to this was a similar stretch of Turtle Creek. The distance between the two streams was slightly more than two miles. This ground was termed the Narrows. At the upper end of the area, Turtle Creek turned at right angles to its former course and ran to the Southwest until it joined the Monongahela.

[45] *Orme,* 349. Careful directions for the march of July 7 appear in *Halkett's Orderly Book.*
[46] For the detailed considerations, see *Orme,* 347–48. St. Clair reported later that his plan "was rejected with great indignation" and he stated that he had wished "to have been recalled, finding I could be of little use, being never listened to" (*Pargellis,* 102, 103).
[47] *Orme,* 352.
[48] See the various orders as summarized in *Orme,* 345 ff.

The descent to the creek at the northwest end of the Narrows was steep; so was the opposite ascent on the side nearer Fort DuQuesne. Close to the Monongahela a difficult road ran through the Narrows.[49] Braddock's information from his guides was that much work had to be done to make this trail passable.[50] Labor and danger both could be avoided, the guides said, by taking advantage of the turns and fords of the Monongahela. It would be possible to cross to the west bank of the river near the mouth of Crooked Run, North of the camp. Then the army could march a couple of miles down the left side of the Monongahela and pass over another shallow ford, back to the right bank of the stream. Thence there was unobstructed advance to Fort DuQuesne.[51]

The gain in time, safety and convenience seemed beyond dispute. Braddock directed that the march be made accordingly. Colonel Gage must move before daybreak with 400 men [52] and two six-pounders and must take post on good ground beyond the second ford in order to cover the passage of the other forces. St. Clair must follow at 4 A.M. to prepare a road. At 5 o'clock the column would start with the wagons and the artillery.[53]

Some, at least, of these details of the plan George heard, and then he went to sleep for the night. He had arrived in time: One more day's march, that of the 9th, and then . . . Fort DuQuesne and "the land in the Fork," which he had said, when first he had seen it, "I think extremely well situated for a fort" . . .[54] He had come back to share in taking it . . . and in holding it!

[49] *Pargellis*, 103, 105.
[50] *Orme*, 352. The Narrows and the road through them appear to have been confused in Orme's mind.
[51] *Ibid*.
[52] These figures are not certain. See n. 3 on the next page.
[53] *Orme*, 352–53.
[54] See *supra*, Vol. I, p. 288.

CHAPTER V

MONONGAHELA

(JULY 9-31, 1755)

IT IS NOT in the heart of man, aroused from deep sleep at 2 o'clock in the morning, to have cheer or conscious, pulsing courage; but when the British camp began to stir at that hour on the 9th of July, 1755, there was confidence as well as expectancy in the minds of those who knew the plan for crossing the Monongahela and marching on Fort Du-Quesne. "The British gentlemen," one provincial officer wrote afterward, "were confident they would never be attacked and would have laid any odds that they never should [be] until they came before the fort—yea some went further and were of the opinion that we should hear the explosion of the French fort blown up and destroyed before we approached it." [1] Careful officers realized, of course, that the advance of the column might be disputed at one ford or the other. Even soldiers of cautious mind felt that if the troops, the artillery and the wagons could get across the Monongahela unresisted, the remainder of the campaign would be easy.

George's responsibility was neither for strategy nor for tactics but for being mounted and afield on the day of all days in his life of twenty-three years. His fever and his pain were gone; but they had left him with his muscles so weakened that he did not know whether he could endure the jolt of a fast-moving horse. He determined to try it, and, to lessen his ordeal, he procured cushions and tied them into his saddle. While George was making his arrangements,[2] Lieutenant Colonel Gage started with about 350 men [3] and two six-pounder cannon to cross the fords and then to take position beyond the second of them in order to

---

[1] *Stephen-Hardwicke*, loc. cit.   [2] Cf. 29 *G. W.*, 42.

[3] The exact strength of this advanced party is variously given. Orme, *op. cit.*, 352-53, stated that it was to consist of two Companies of grenadiers, plus 160 troops of the line, Gates's New York Company (100 enlisted men), and the men in charge of the six-pounders—a total of 460, less the day's absentees. A figure of 300 was given by the engineer, Harry Gordon, in a letter of July 23, 1755, to an unnamed correspondent. This document, containing perhaps the clearest account of the day's events, is printed in *Pargellis*, 104-09.

cover the advance of the army.[4] At 4 o'clock, Sir John St. Clair followed the same route with 250 carpenters and pioneers and their wagons.[5] An hour later Braddock's main force took the road. Directly under his charge were the remaining troops, about 750 all told,[6] most of the vehicles, the pack animals, the cattle to be slaughtered for food, and the greater part of the artillery—four twelve-pounders on traveling carriages with limbers, four eight-inch howitzers similarly equipped, and three cohorn mortars.[7]

Starting this mixed column was such slow work that watches pointed to 8 o'clock when Braddock reached the first crossing. As George splashed through the upper ford on his horse, he noticed how low the water was because of the drought that had parched Pennsylvania, Maryland and Virginia.[8] At the level then prevailing, passage of the river was easy. When it had been completed, Braddock formed his line of march and set off, in the footprints of Gage's and St. Clair's men, down a road that had been cut roughly parallel to the stream.[9] The General, George and the others had proceeded a mile only when a messenger brought fine news: Colonel Gage presented his compliments to His Excellency and begged to report that he had completed the second crossing without encountering opposition, and had taken position as ordered, on the right bank where his guns commanded the lower ford.[10] En route to the first shallow, Gage had flushed thirty Indians, who had made off.[11] At the second crossing the men of the advance guard had noticed that the water still was muddy, as if there had been recent passing, and they had seen many footprints on the river bank.[12] If these particulars were reported to Braddock, no importance was attached to them.

The march along the left bank continued without incident until, at length, the head of the column halted at a point slightly downstream from the mouth of Turtle Creek, which flowed into the Monongahela from the opposite side. As George and his companions looked, they saw on the other bank a sandy [13] bluff about twelve feet high through

---

[4] Orme to Sharpe, July 18, 1755; 1 *Sharpe*, 253. Substantially the same letter was addressed by Orme to several colonial officials. See Pargellis, "Braddock's Defeat," 41 *A.H.R.*, 255, n 4. These letters and Orme's journal are among the basic sources on the campaign; but, to repeat, Orme was not accurate concerning dates, numbers and hours.

[5] 1 *Sharpe*, 253; *Orme*, 353.

[6] Based on the assumption that the entire force was 1459. See *infra*, p. 86, n. 160.

[7] *Pargellis*, 97; unknown French writer in 20 *Penn. Mag.*, 409–11; 3 *Col. MMS rel. à la Nouvelle-France*, 544.

[8] 29 *G. W.*, 42. See *supra*, p. 40.

[9] *Orme*, 353.

[10] *Orme*, 354.

[11] *Seaman*, Sargent, 384.

[12] Dulany's News Letter, 3 *Penn. Mag.*, 17.

[13] *Pargellis*, 108.

which St. Clair's men busily were cutting an incline at the point chosen for the passage of the troops.[14] The situation was precisely as the messenger had reported: both the advanced parties were safely across the river at the place where a vigilant and courageous enemy might have repelled them. "Men hugged themselves with joy," one observer wrote, "at our good luck in having surmounted our greatest difficulties."[15] Braddock proceeded, in spite of this clear advantage, to do what his English and German seniors had said an officer should do in a like situation: he ordered all the vehicles drawn up properly on the bank and he posted pickets on the higher ground behind him.[16] Then he, his staff and his line officers had opportunity of examining the country ahead of them as far as it was visible from their position. George had never been on the left bank of the Monongahela, but he had some exciting memories of the side to which he was looking. Almost directly across the river from him was Frazier's trading post and gun shop to which he had come with Christopher Gist and their small party, on the 22nd of November, 1753, while he was carrying the message of Dinwiddie to Fort Le Boeuf.[17] It had been to Frazier's, too, that he and Gist had returned at the end of December, that same year, after their desperate struggle with the ice of the Allegheny.[18] Only nineteen months previously that had been . . . and now the wintry landscape had all turned to verdure . . . and the river bank was crowded with the coats and the cannon of the King.

Downstream from Frazier's, behind the low bluff, the advance of the army was to be through rising ground for a mile or more. Near the river was a fringe of heavy underbrush that extended northward for about 400 yards.[19] Beyond that elevation could be seen both northward and to the West. There, too, was a forest of large trees less densely set than in many parts of the country through which the expedition had passed.[20] If the landscape was cut by any deep ravines or watercourses, these were not visible.

Inspection was as deliberate as the prospect was beautiful. Completion of the passageway through the bluff occupied St. Clair's men until

[14] *Orme*, 354.
[15] Gordon in *Pargellis*, 106.
[16] *Orme*, 354.
[17] See *supra*, Vol. I, p. 286.
[18] *Ibid.*
[19] On this, the language of Sinclair (*Pargellis*, 103) and of Orme (*op. cit.*, 355) is not altogether clear. The underbrush, which both of them styled "underwood," might have extended downstream, instead of back from the stream, for a quarter of a mile, but the interpretation given in the text seems more probable.
[20] *Orme*, 355; *Pargellis*, 103, 117. The elevation at the highest point of this ground is about 340 feet above that of the opposite bank.

almost 2 P.M. When the incline at last was ready, Braddock sent Captain Morris [21] to order Gage and St. Clair to start down the ridge with their detachments and to open a road as they advanced. They were instructed to march until 3 o'clock, with the inference that the entire column would then be across the river sand would be ready to bivouac for the final advance the next day on Fort DuQuesne. The distance from the proposed halting place to the junction of the rivers would not be more than seven miles, no farther than the troops easily could move between suns in a country that presented no great natural obstacle.[22]

Officers on the left bank soon could see Gage's and St. Clair's men leave their posts and disappear. After the last of the advanced parties had cleared the other side of the ford, Braddock gave the word for his column to cross. It was easily and flawlessly done—in George's eyes the most thrilling sight of his entire life.[23] As the men came up the incline from the river, they took their place in the line of march, which now was complete. In front, mounting the ridge, were the guides and a few of Stewart's Company of Virginia light horse. Behind them was the engineer who was marking the route and blazing the trees that had to be felled to provide a roadway. His task was not difficult. The woods were so open that a vehicle could be driven almost anywhere among the trees. Besides, orders were to prepare a twelve-foot road—no wider. All that was needed now, in the judgment of the responsible officers, was room enough for the guns and the wagons. The men could look after themselves.[24]

As the engineer stopped at intervals and hacked the bark, Gage's covering party followed in files four deep. On the flanks were the grenadier Companies, spread in parties of twenty men, each under a Sergeant. Next were the carpenters and pioneers, and then the two six pounders with the ammunition wagon and a guard. Together, these men were the advanced force. Closing on them now was Lieutenant Colonel Burton with the vanguard, most of the wagons and part of the guns. The rearguard, with the remainder of the cannon, was under Col. Sir Peter Halkett.[25] If the proper intervals were being observed, everything was in the best style of the regular establishment. Braddock would not have been ashamed to have organized such a

[21] *Pargellis,* 103. [22] *Orme,* 385.
[23] 2 *Sparks,* 469. [24] *Pargellis,* 103, 117.
[25] *Pargellis,* 106; *Orme,* 355; *Seaman,* Sargent, 385. Full details of the line of march, not required for the present narrative, will be found in the familiar sketches by Patrick Mackellar, reproduced between p. 81 and p. 82.

FROM THE LAST CAMP TO THE SLAUGHTER

Nearly all the sketches made contemporaneously to illustrate the Battle of the Monongahela were based on those of Patrick MacKellar, already mentioned as senior British engineer who accompanied Braddock's expedition. The rough design on the opposite page, after the original in the Clements Library of the University of Michigan, may owe something to MacKellar, but it contains many obvious inaccuracies and it includes a crude outline, distinctly off scale, of the camp of July 8.

In spite of its errors, the sketch is interesting because it gives an idea of what the officers considered to be obstacles along "the Narrows" South of Turtle Creek.

Still again, this sketch bears out the evidence on MacKellar's first map that the attack was opened at a time when the rearguard barely had cleared the lower ford. As appears in MacKellar's second drawing, the column was closed after the van became engaged. The two drawings are shown between p. 81 and p. 82.

It will be observed, too, from his note "g" that the unidentified author of the sketch shared the belief the attack on Braddock's forces had been made by Indians, and inferentially, by Indians only. No scale is attached to the original. Natural objects and distances represented in this reproduction are so inaccurate—omitting for example the Youghiogheny—that a scale scarcely can be applied. One of two and a half miles to an inch is approximately correct on part of the sketch.

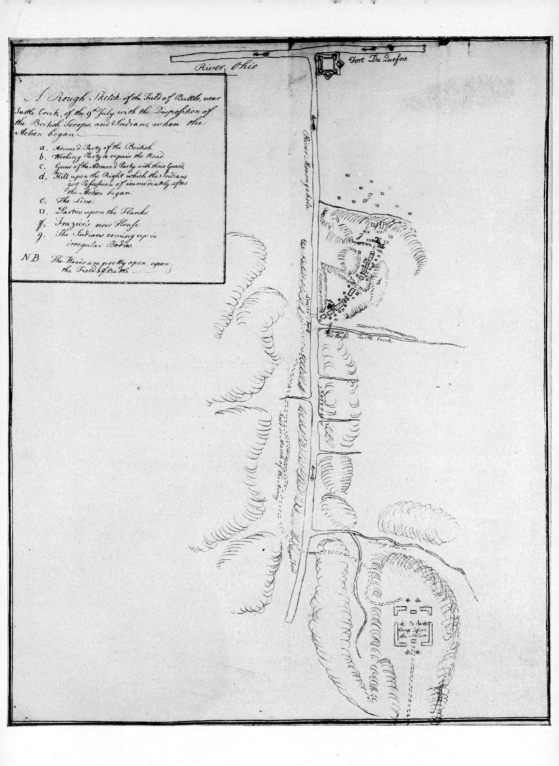

River Ohio

Fort Du Quesne

A Rough Sketch of the Field of Battle, near
Turtle Creek, of the 9th July with the Disposition of
the British Troops, and Indians, when the
Action began

a. Advanced Party of the British.
b. Working Party to repair the Road.
c. Guns of the Advanced Party with their Guard.
d. Hill upon the Right which the Indians
   got Possession of immediately after
   the Action began.
e. The Line.
□. Parties upon the Flanks.
f. Frazier's new House
g. The Indians coming up in
   irregular Bodies.

N.B. The Woods are pretty open, upon
     the Field of Battle

River Monongahela

Turtle Creek

1755	By Sum brought forward	411	16	1½
	By Cash to my Bro. John supposed to be as they were 5 dubloons	21	13	4
May 28	By a large Bay Horse of Saml. McRoberts	10	—	6
29	By Thomas for a Bell	0	5	9
	By Ditto gave		11	6
	By Ropes &c.		5	—
June 1	By shoeing my Horse		1	3
2	By Captain Ormes Servant		1	3
3	By Cresaps acct.	2	16	10
4	By Mr. Shirley's Servant		1	3
8	By John Alton		10	—
	By making a black Stock		4	—
	By Cash gave to		5	—
13	By Washing		10	3
	By Thos. Thomas	2	10½
17	By Col. Burtons Servant	2	10½
27	By Cleaning my Pistols		3	1½
July 2	By 8 days attendance of a Nurse in my Sickness	8	
4	By Milk		5	9
	By 3 pair Hopples		9	—
21	By Mr. Hawthorn for a Mattrass	1	2	6½
22	By Washing		5	9
	By Thomas Thomas for a Horse ...	2	1	6
	By Joseph Bunnian - Batman		5	9
	By Smith for Shoeing my Horse		1	3
23	By Expences at McCrackensNS		5	9
24	By Jos. Oliver		5	9
	By Expences at Winchester		2	6
	By Ditto at Edward Thompsons ..		5	9
27	By Water Mellons		1	3
31	By 40 Bushels of Oats	2	—	—
Augt. 1	By Mr. Posey	4	6	8
	By my Brothers Servt. 1/3 By Bishy in Ireland 9.6/3		7	6
	By Mr. Dalton for Paying Bell & Meads acct.	4	6	8
	By Sum carried Over	£466	12	3½

TRAGEDY BETWEEN TWO LINES OF A LEDGER

By running the eye down the left-hand column in the illustration on the opposite page, one observes a gap of seventeen days in Washington's expenditures between July 4 and July 21.

They were seventeen of the most exciting days the young colonial had experienced in his life of twenty-three years. This folio from Washington's "Ledger A" shows that on the 2nd of July he paid off and presumably dismissed the nurse who had attended him through the eight worst days of an attack of bloody flux. The young officer still could not subsist entirely on such food as well men ate, and, on the 4th, he paid for milk which he probably had been drinking in considerable quantity during his illness. He purchased, also, three pair of hobbles or fetters for the legs of horses which were apt to stray or to attract the eye of a footsore man of easy conscience.

After that entry, Washington had nothing to put into his ledger—or at least he remembered no expenditure—until Braddock was dead and the beaten army was arriving at Fort Cumberland. Then, on the 21st, Washington bought a mattress, perhaps for one of his wounded comrades.

Much history had been crowded between two lines of a ledger which, it will be observed, Washington did not "write up" daily. Sometimes the entries for an entire month or more were made with the same pen and presumably at the same time. The original of "Ledger A" is in the Library of Congress.

march in Flanders or to have had it made while even His Royal Highness, the Duke of Cumberland, was observing it.

As the rear of the column cleared the curve in the road near Frazier's trading post and started northwestward, George rode forward with the General and the staff. All were in high spirits. Gage was then about three-quarters of a mile beyond the ford;[26] from his front to the last man of the rearguard, the distance was about 1900 yards. Whether this was too great a length of column for advance in the enemy's country or too compact a column for maneuver in the event of attack, no officer troubled himself to consider. It scarcely mattered. If the French had intended to resist the British, they would have done so in the early morning, and at the fords, not beyond on the direct way to the fort.

Half-past two o'clock and close to 1500 men confidently in motion; then, suddenly, the sound of firing from the front, the roll of a volley, more of scattered, heavy fire, another volley! George was stiff in the saddle at the first crash. So was every officer. The troops tightened their grip on their muskets and looked toward their Captains. Braddock listened intently: the fire, he thought, was that of hostile parties heavily engaged. Halt the column; let one of the young aides go forward and find out what was happening.[27]

Harry Gordon, the engineer, had ridden ahead of the advanced guard to find the guides, and he had been looking for them when they had hurried back and had reported the enemy close at hand. As the engineer peered through the open forest ahead of him, he had seen about 300 men, French and Indians, approaching on the run. Most of them were stripped; all were ready for action. At their head was an officer who wore a piece of decorative armor at his neck.[28] He, too, was looking vigilantly ahead, but he had not yet discovered the British.[29]

26 1 *Sharpe*, 268.
27 The aide sent to the front probably was Shirley.   28 A gorget.
29 Gordon, Washington and others insisted that the attacking force did not exceed 300 men (cf. *Pargellis,* 106; 1 *G. W.*, 147, 151), but this figure was too low. Included in the column of attack were seventy-two French, 146 Canadians and 637 Indians, a total of 855, according to the Relation depuis le Départ des Trouppes de Québec; Arch. de Guerre, photostat, Canadian Arch., Ottawa. Cf. Sargent, *op. cit.,* 223, with notice of other estimates. The Relation du Combat, *loc. cit.,* gives the number as 133 French, 100 Canadians and 600 savages, total 833. Relation de la Bataille du Fort duQuesne, Paris, Aff. Etra. Mém. et Docts., France, 535, p. 110, spoke of "200 youths of great zeal, and at most 600 savages . . ." Gipson, *op. cit.,* 91, counted 108 regulars, including officers, and 146 Canadian militia. For another early French estimate of 250 Canadians and 650 Indians, see Relation de l'action . . . de 9e Juillet . . . *Cumberland Papers,* Box 46–28; Windsor Castle. Cf., also, *Penn. Gazette,* Jan. 8, 1756. The *Gentleman's Mag.*, August, 1755, p. 378, asserted that the French employed 1500 regulars, 600 irregulars and a "considerable number of Indians," but in its September issue, p. 426, the publication stated, on the mistaken assurance of private letters, that "no French troops were present."

A little later, when the French commander had caught a glimpse of the grenadiers, he had motioned with his arms to right and to left. His men then had divided and had begun to encircle the head and the flanks of the British column.[30]

The hideous Indian warwhoop swelled through the woods and froze the blood of the soldiers who never before had heard that sound. Farther from the front but within earshot, the yell of an invisible enemy was enough to make ignorant men think they had marched into a den of demons.[31] After their first instant of startled fright, the grenadiers delivered a volley and then loaded and fired again. Some of their bullets brought down the conspicuous French officers and a number of Indians.[32] The reply of the attacking force was strong enough to swell the volume of fire the column heard,[33] but the redmen and their white comrades did not intend to form line of battle and exchange volleys with the British in the woods. Before most of the English soldiers saw a single rifleman, the French and Indians disappeared, quickly and mysteriously. The hair-raising whoops continued. Down both flanks the fire spread. Soon it began to strike the British from the high ground on the right of the halted column.[34] All except one of the English flanking parties ran in;[35] one Company of grenadiers and one of carpenters were in danger of being cut off.[36] Almost before the officers could shout their commands, the whole of the advanced force fell back fifty or sixty yards.

There by pleas and threats and by riding among the bewildered troops, the Captains and Lieutenants were able to restore a confused line,[37] but it was for a few minutes only. Bulking above the heads of the crouching troops, the mounted leaders were ideal targets for the

---

[30] *Pargellis,* 106; *Seaman,* Sargent, 387.

[31] 29 *G. W.,* 42. Cf. Relation du Combat, *loc. cit.:* "les cris des Sauvages, dont les bois retentissoient, porterent l'épouvante dans les coeurs des ennemis."

[32] According to a French report in *Penn. Gazette,* Jan. 8, 1756, the number was fifteen Indians and four Canadians, as well as the commander of the force, Daniel Liénard Beaujeu, and two junior officers.

[33] For the heaviness of the fire see the contemporary account in 11 *Penn. Mag.,* 94.

[34] *Pargellis,* 116. Contemporary British and colonial writers did not always convey the same meaning when they spoke of "right" and "left" in the battle of the Monongahela. Officers near the front often used the terms with reference to the head of the column as it was at the moment of attack. Right to them was the northern flank of a front that was facing roughly westward. Later in the action, when the entire column was halted, some of the participants thought of the front as extending from West to East with the front to the North. So considered, the advanced guard was the left flank-element and the rearguard the right. In the present narrative "the right" and "the left" are employed as those flanks were until the battle front shifted. Notice then is given that "right" spreads East and "left" is toward the West.

[35] *Orme,* 355.

[36] *Seaman,* Sargent, 385.   [37] *Pargellis,* 106.

invisible marksmen. Down the officers tumbled from their steeds, dead or wounded. Most of those who escaped with their lives lost their horses.[38] Colonel Gage kept his saddle, but he found few subordinates to help him rally men who had no idea how to fight an enemy they could not see. Occasionally, through the thickening smoke, a soldier might get a momentary glimpse of a red face that appeared from behind a large tree. Sometimes, too, if a Briton happened to look in the proper direction at the right moment, he observed a smoke-puff from the ground where an Indian lay hidden in the grass.[39] That was all, except for the rattle of muskets, the whoop, and the thud of the body of man after man.

Now Sir John St. Clair rode up to ascertain what was happening—and got the information in the form of a bullet through his body. He managed to save himself from falling and, though losing blood fast, he returned to his own command and called on Polson's carpenters and on Peyroney's rangers—both of them Virginia commands—to cover the two six-pounders [40] which, with their teams and ammunition-wagon, were between St. Clair's men and his wagons.[41]

In rear of what had been the right flank of the marching column the fire was heavier every minute. Surviving officers who could see anything beyond the smoke-cloud realized soon that the Indians and the Canadians were firing from the hillside to the North of the road that had been cut through the forest.[42] Riflemen concealed there could cross fire with that of savages who had slipped down Gage's left, between the road and the river.[43] With front and both flanks thus enveloped, the British now were within a half-moon [44] of yelling adversaries. The accurate fire of the enemy already was sweeping the whole of the ground occupied by Gage and more and more, every minute, of that held by St. Clair.

Suddenly the rumor spread that the French and Indians were attacking the baggage train.[45] Stunned men under triple fire from an unseen foe did not stop to ask whether the rumor had probability. They concluded instantly that if the enemy was closing on their rear, they soon would be surrounded, scalped, massacred. With one impulse, Gage's

---

[38] Franklin, *Autobiography* (Bigelow ed.), 272.   [39] 29 *G. W.*, 42; *Stephen-Hardwicke.*
[40] *Pargellis,* 103. This is St. Clair's own account. As printed, Peyroney's name is Periwee, but there can be no doubt of the identification.
[41] See "F" in Mackellar's first sketch following p. 81.
[42] The crest of this hill has now (1948) an elevation of 1240 feet.
[43] *Pargellis,* 106.
[44] *Ibid.,* 116.   [45] *Pargellis,* 106.

men ran eastward, carried St. Clair's workers along, abandoned the two six-pounders—and at a distance of 300 yards stumbled into the uncertain files of Burton's vanguard which, by Braddock's order, had been advancing to their support up the twelve-foot road.[46]

Burton and his officers had halted their men because of the fire from the side of the hill to the North. Already these troops of the van were disturbed and confused, as Gage's and St. Clair's soldiers had been, by the viciousness of fire from invisible, whooping Indians; but the commanders had succeeded partially in getting some of them to form a line, facing North, for an assault on the hill. At the time, the three twelve-pounders with Burton's command were being placed South of the road to deal with the enemy on the side nearer the Monongahela.[47] Burton, in a word, was drawing a confused line along the road, from West to East. With his front to the North, his rear would be exposed to attack from the South if the cannon there could not be used to drive off the enemy. Gage and St. Clair had been perpendicular to the road, with the front to the West. When, therefore, the men of their advanced parties ran back eastward through the woods and reached the vanguard, the new left flank of Burton was rolled up. The line, if it could be so styled, was temporarily a capital T laid on its side, with the top to the West. Then, in their dismay, the remnant of Gage's and of St. Clair's troops began quickly to pull in, so to say, the two sides of the top of the bar until, in a matter of minutes, the front was like a half-opened umbrella lying in the road with the tip pointing toward Fort DuQuesne.

Tactically, this opening second phase of the battle would have been a difficult one to correct had like confusion of ranks and direction occurred on a drillfield through the blunder of an incompetent Colonel. As it was, under that persistent fire—from the North, from the West and from the South—the situation was completely beyond the control of the few officers who remained on horseback.[48]

Now Braddock rode up, attended by George.[49] The General had waited only a few minutes at the point where he had heard the first

---

[46] *Pargellis*, 107; 1 Sharpe, 253. Gage or one of his friends anonymously insisted that Burton's men already were "in confusion." See *Penn. Gazette,* Sept. 4, 1755.

[47] *Orme*, 355; Mackellar's sketch No. 2, *loc. cit.*

[48] *Orme,* 355; 1 *Sharpe,* 253.

[49] Shirley probably had been killed before this time by a bullet through his head (1 *Sharpe* 253; Orme, P.R.O., C.O. 5: 46, p. 68–73), and Morris and Orme in all likelihood had received their disabling wounds, but all that is known of the time of these casualties is that they occurred "early in the engagement" (Washington to his mother [July 18, 1755], 1 *G. W.,* 151). Robert Dobson, senior Captain of the 48th, and a favorite of Braddock's, was assigned as temporary aide after Orme was wounded (*Pargellis,* 119; Sargent, *op. cit.,* 211; 2 *Shirley,* 321).

fire and had halted the column. Then, as the continued rattle of muskets had convinced him the action was serious, he had started for the front. At first he was half paralyzed by the indescribable confusion and the unfamiliar ground. Instead of a line, he found a mass of men, ten or twelve deep, who were firing at random and were shooting many of their comrades in the back.[50] "They kept," said Adam Stephen afterward, "in a mere huddle . . ." [51] Braddock could not decide, on the instant, what to do or how to do it. While he hesitated, St. Clair made his way through the mad, milling press of men and called to the General for God's sake to take the northern hill in order to keep the army from being surrounded. Before the Quartermaster could say more to explain the situation, he lost consciousness because of his wound.[52]

Capt. Thomas Waggener, a veteran of Fort Necessity, had kept his men together and now he undertook to lead them up the hill to the trunk of a great fallen tree that he thought he could use as a parapet. He succeeded in getting there with the loss of three men only, but to his amazement he found himself subjected to the fire of British who mistook his Company for French. Some of the regular officers, seeing his movement, concluded that he and his soldiers were attempting to run away, and they discouraged those who were willing to reenforce him. In getting back under fire, the Captain lost all except thirty of his men.[53] George, like Waggener, felt that the high ground could be taken and the enemy driven off, and he appealed to the General to permit him to collect the provincial troops and to send them against the hill in the Indian manner. Braddock merely shook his bewildered head.[54]

The British of the advanced force and of the van crowded more and more closely together by this time, and they fired, for the most part, in aimless confusion. Here and there, a courageous officer was

[50] Washington thought this responsible for two-thirds of the casualties (1 G. W., 150).

[51] Stephen-Hardwicke.

[52] Pargellis, 103.

[53] This is one of the few incidents of the battle concerning which some reservation has to be made. Waggener is identified as commander by Thomas Burd in a letter of July 25, 1755, printed in Watson's Annals of Philadelphia and Penn. in the Olden Time, v. 2, p. 139, but the letter echoes much rumor along with some fact. Burd's statement manifestly is incorrect in crediting Waggener with eighty men. None of the Virginia Companies had an enlisted strength above fifty. Cf. Orme, 327-29. Washington, writing in 1786, mentioned an advance of "some of the irregulars (as they were called) without direction . . ." (29 G. W., 43). While it is altogether probable that this was Waggener's effort, there is the possibility of error in the confusion of this and some unrecorded attempt to storm the hill.

[54] Washington's restrained later language (1786) was "the propriety of it was not seen until it was too late for execution." (29 G. W., 43.)

able to keep a grip on a few score men and to give direction to their fire. Presently, too, some of Halkett's troops pushed up the road, but in a few minutes these reenforcements lost heart and added new disorder on the right.[55] Sir Peter Halkett himself was killed early;[56] his junior officers and his soldiers, like those already engaged, could do nothing but load and fire, load and fire. The maddening thing about it was that while man after man dropped with a groan or a dying gasp, most of the troops still could not tell where their enemies were. To this moment of the fight, some British soldiers had not seen a single Frenchman or Indian. If a redman showed himself at all, he might dash out, scalp some dead or wounded soldier, and leap back behind a tree or drop into the concealing grass.[57] This hideous sight and the baffling, futile character of the battle were beginning to demoralize the British. Some, but by no means all, the provincials tried to fight the Indians in their own way.[58]

Braddock at last realized that the hill must be wrested from the savages and that the two six-pounders must be recaptured before they were turned against the bleeding British crowded in the road. He sent George off to find officers and to tell them to organize one party of 150 to charge up the hill and another party of like size to recover the cannon. In delivering these orders, George managed to stay in his saddle despite his weakness. During the action, he had two horses shot under him, but he found another and skillfully made his way through the woods. His tall figure was a mark for hidden riflemen. One of them sent a bullet through his hat; another, a third, and still another slit his uniform with hot lead.[59] He was conspicuous, in the generous words of the wounded Orme, for "the greatest courage and resolution"[60] and, happily, thus far was unscathed.

While George was trying to find Company officers and to get them to attack the hill and to recover the guns, Braddock was doing the same thing. Again and again he undertook to rally the men, to form a line and to lead them against the hidden enemy and the high ground North of the road. Nothing could be done. The survivors would not budge from the huddle.[61] At last, in desperation, Braddock decided to withdraw to the right and East in order to cover his wagons and

---

[55] 29 G. W., 43.

[56] 1 Sharpe, 253.

[57] 1 Sharpe, 263, 268; Pargellis, 111, 117; Seaman, Sargent, 386.

[58] 1 G. W., 151; 1 Entick, 147; Stephen-Hardwicke.

[59] 1 G. W., 151; 29 G. W., 43.

[60] 1 Sharpe, 253.

[61] Cf. 1 Sharpe, 253.

to take from them provisions for use in event he had to leave the field altogether.[62] The General did not proceed far with this shift. Already five bullets had struck one or another of the horses he had ridden; now it was his turn. A missile crashed through his right arm and penetrated his lungs.[63] After he was placed on the ground by the men near him, he remained conscious, but, of course, could not attempt to direct the withdrawal to the wagons which were strung out along the road.

Few of the officers received the order to cover the vehicles, and consequently they continued to exhort the men to attack from the ground where they were crowded together. Lieutenant Colonel Burton, with much spirit, succeeded in getting about 100 soldiers of the 48th Regiment to form in line, and then he gave command for a charge up the hill. He led it gallantly, his men followed courageously part of the way to the crest—and then drifted to the right and fell back to the road. The reason was that Burton had received a wound. Without him, the men would not advance.[64] Other officers undertook to do what Burton, for all his effort, had been unable to accomplish. Sometimes in small groups, they started up the grade in the hope their men would attend, but they could not induce the dazed infantry to venture from the road.[65] Other leaders individually stepped out and appealed to their soldiers—all to no purpose. Officers, said Orme, were "absolutely sacrificed." [66]

The situation now was desperate but not altogether hopeless. Two hundred men were held together by uninjured commanders and by officers returning from the surgeons with bandaged wounds. These troops, keeping their heads, still were able to hold the enemy at a distance, though they were deaf to every order to mount the eminence or to rush out and put the six-pounders into action.[67] On the extreme right, also, there was organized resistance without any attempt at a

---

[62] *Orme*, 356; Report of Dunbar and Gage on the Court of Inquiry, 2 *Shirley*, 312. This incident of the battle cannot be timed precisely. Orme placed it before the events presently to be described in the text. Dunbar and Gage did not relate it to any occurrence prior to the climax of the battle. Almost certainly the order was given by Braddock himself and was not distributed generally, but a caveat is necessary.

[63] 1 *Sharpe*, 253. The absurd, familiar story has often been printed that he was shot deliberately by an American, who was infuriated when Braddock killed the man's brother with a sword stroke for alleged skulking. Lowdermilk (*op. cit.*, 187–88) was inclined uncritically to accept this yarn, though Sargent (*op. cit.*, 245 ff) wholly discredited it. Another tradition of the wounding of Braddock (cited in *Lowdermilk*, 162) was that Orme vainly offered sixty guineas to anyone who would carry Braddock from the field. Captain Robert Stewart of the Virginia Troop of light horse, with another officer and Braddock's servant, are said to have taken him off in his own sash, which they unwrapped from around his waist.

[64] *Orme*, 356. Burton was listed in Sargent, *op. cit.*, 362, as slightly wounded.

[65] 1 *Sharpe*, 253.   [66] *Ibid.*   [67] *Pargellis*, 107.

counter-stroke. The Captain on this flank, which had been the rear-guard, had time to dispose his men carefully before the redmen appeared. By posting the troops behind trees, he beat off the scattered savages with some loss. No large number of Indians penetrated that far eastward.[68]

While these centres of resistance remained, those officers who had received the order to withdraw to the wagons undertook to do so and to carry their commands with them. They were powerless. The men in the road stayed where they were and continued their blind fire. Orders no longer meant anything. Bewildered though they were and close to exhaustion, the troops seemed to realize, as Adam Stephen put it, that "you might as well send a cow in pursuit of a hare as an English soldier loaded in their way . . . after Canadians in their shirts . . . or naked Indians accustomed to the woods."[69] Nor had these English soldiers in the wilderness failed to notice that when any of their comrades made an attempt to assail the high ground, the fire of the enemy became more rapid.[70] Counter-action was suicide. Hopelessly the men continued to ram home their charges and to level their pieces aimlessly. Ammunition was almost exhausted;[71] few officers remained on their feet; most of the Lieutenants and Ensigns who kept with the confused mass in the road did not know to whom to look for orders.[72] The cannon were deserted;[73] the rain of bullets from hidden marksmen did not cease or even diminish. That same paralyzing, fiendish whoop of the savages rang through woods carpeted with dead and dying men. Now, as the sun was descending, more and more of the soldiers began to collect around the wagons. "They stood about . . . for some little time without any fire," their senior officers later reported,[74] and then, from their front and rear,[75] they heard a heavier fire. This was more than could be endured by wagoners who had held their teams for hours. Most of the men in charge of the vehicles cut loose the horses, mounted and made off as fast as they could for the

---

[68] *Orme*, 355; *Pargellis*, 117. This rear Company almost certainly was provincial but has not been identified satisfactorily.

[69] *Stephen-Hardwicke*.   [70] *Pargellis*, 107.

[71] *Orme*, 356; 1 *Sharpe*, 253. Gage's men had gone into action with twenty-five rounds (*Halkett's Orderly Book*, July 8, 1755); the amount of ammunition carried by the other troops is not established, but probably was the same (*ibid.*, May 27, 1755).

[72] 29 *G. W.*, 43.   [73] *Pargellis*, 107.

[74] Dunbar and Gage in 2 *Shirley*, 312–13.

[75] Dunbar and Gage (*loc. cit.*) said "front and left flank" and Gordon (*Pargellis*, 107) said "left." They used these terms as they applied at the opening of the action. "Left" now had become more than ever the "rear" of troops who faced North.

ford.[76] Frightened soldiers plunged past comrades of stouter heart and gave themselves to mad panic. "They behaved," said George indignantly, "with more cowardice than it is possible to conceive; . . . they broke and ran as sheep pursued by dogs." [77] Many of the troops threw away arms, even parts of their clothing to speed their flight down to the river [78] through a shallow ravine. Efforts to halt them met—again the words are George's—"with as much success as if we had attempted to have stopped the wild boars of the mountains." [79] Soon the struggling men were crowding and choking the passageway that led down to the crossing.[80]

When all hope of rallying the soldiers on the right bank was gone, George's first duty was to get safely across the river the wounded General whom Robert Stewart had brought from the front. By good fortune, Washington found a little cart that had not lost its team, and into this he and Stewart put Braddock, who still was master of himself. Carefully, too, George loaded on the vehicle some of the General's equipage. In the company of the best of the troops,[81] Washington then descended to the bank and, under fire, conveyed the hard-breathing commander over the ford.[82] Had George looked back while he was crossing, he would have seen some battle-maddened Indians plunge into the water and kill exhausted fugitives there. Otherwise, there was no immediate pursuit. Most of the savages remained on the battlefield to plunder the wagons, to rob the dead and, above all, to scalp the wounded and the slain.[83] Among these victims were eight women.[84] George shuddered to think that this massacre might include all the wounded among the 300 persons or more, dead included, he subsequently estimated the army had left behind on the field of slaughter.[85] Had all the wounded been brought off, George could have reconciled himself to the looting of the wagons and even to the scalping of the slain. He told himself then and many times afterward that if the savages had not stopped to pillage, they might have pressed through the Narrows and might have confronted the survivors from the right

[76] Franklin, *Autobiography* (Bigelow ed.), 191.   [77] 1 *G. W.*, 151.
[78] *Orme*, 356.   **[79] 1 *G. W.*, 149.**
[80] *Pargellis*, 108.
[81] They probably were the 200 who had kept together.
[82] 29 *G. W.*, 43.   [83] *Orme*, 356; 1 *Sharpe*, 269.
[84] They had remained with the advanced detachment, for one reason and another, after the other women, twenty-four in number, had been sent to Eastern Pennsylvania (*Pargellis*, 108; P.R.O., 98 Chatham Papers, 12 ff). For the order that the soldiers' wives leave the army, June 9, 1755, see *Lowdermilk*, 135–36.
[85] 1 *G. W.*, 149–50. For the difference between Washington's estimate (July 18, 1755) and the actual loss, see *infra*, p. 86.

bank at the upper ford. Had the French and their savage allies done that, then all the British who had escaped from the battleground might have been starved or slaughtered.[86]

With Burton and Orme, who kept afield in spite of their wounds, George now shared the task of trying to restore order among the survivors who were panting on the left bank or were wandering around in a daze. High ground was chosen, about a quarter of a mile from the river and some 200 yards from the road—a position strong enough to be held indefinitely by courageous troops. George and the others reasoned that if the men could be induced to occupy this eminence, they could beat off all attacks till Colonel Dunbar came up.[87] Burton made an appeal to the soldiers and prevailed upon the least shaken of them to serve as outposts.[88] Braddock observed this, approved it, and directed George to ride farther back along the line of the morning advance and to rally the men who had fled in that direction.

Obediently, George turned his horse's head. Beyond the upper ford,[89] he found Lieutenant Colonel Gage. How the commander of the advance party got that far to the rear, George did not ascertain, or if he learned, he did not record.[90] Gage had with him eighty men, whom he apparently had rallied and now had under some discipline.[91] George felt that the officer was doing all that the situation required; so, about sundown, he recrossed the upper ford to return to Braddock. On the way back to the hill the officers had agreed to make their stronghold, George met a grim cavalcade—Braddock and such of the troops as had held to their duty after the first panic was overcome.[92] The other soldiers had slipped away from the eminence and singly or in small groups were trying to put more distance between them and the enemy.[93]

Manifestly it was futile to talk after that of standing fast, of rallying, of getting the men into the ranks, and of recovering the wagons. Nothing remained to do except to organize a retreat and to execute it as quickly as possible without further loss.[94] Colonel Dunbar with the remainder of the second Brigade was supposed to be advancing and at no great distance; he could cover the retreat and could forward provisions and liquor to the hungry and exhausted men.[95]

[86] 29 G. W., 45. [87] Orme, 356.

[88] Pargellis, 107; Orme, 356–57.

[89] Most of the participants referred to this as the first ford in writing of the advance and, in describing the retreat, they termed it the second. This is apt to confuse a reader.

[90] Gage subsequently was accused of cowardice in quitting the field. See William Findlay in 14 Niles Register, 179. [91] Orme, 357.

[92] 29 G. W., 44; Orme, 356. [93] Pargellis, 107; Orme, 356–57.

[94] 29 G. W., 44 [95] 29 G. W., 44; Orme, 356–57.

For sending orders to Dunbar, a mission of darkness and distance, the wounded Braddock looked again to young Washington: there was no one else who both knew the country and could speak in the General's name.[96] Forty-eight hours previously, George had bumped over that road, a weak convalescent in a wagon. Now, having been on horseback for more than twelve mad hours of incredible strain, he had to set out again. He did, though he had to muster all his moral courage to undertake it. With two guides he crossed the upper ford for the fourth time that day and passed the first fugitives.

A different and even more hideous scene was being enacted in front of Fort DuQuesne at that hour. The victors were returning then with their booty—"soldiers' caps, British canteens, bayonets" and, most cherished of all, scores on scores of bloody scalps. A young Pennsylvanian, a prisoner at the fort, shuddered as he heard their scalp hallos, their triumphant whoops, the fire of their small arms and the boom of saluting cannon. Then, "about sundown," according to the same horrified witness, "I beheld a small party coming in with about a dozen prisoners, stripped naked, with their hands tied behind their backs, and their faces and parts of their bodies blackened—these prisoners they burned to death on the bank of the Allegheny River opposite to the fort. I stood on the fort wall until I beheld them begin to burn one of these men: they had tied him to a stake and kept touching him with firebrands, hot irons &c and he screaming . . . the Indians in the meantime yelling like infernal spirits."[97]

By that time, night and the forest had engulfed George and his two companions. When he and Gist, half-frozen, had tramped from Murthering Town to the Allegheny River, they had at least the light of the snow. Now the blackness was so overwhelming that if the movement of the horses or the snapping of bushes under their hoofs indicated that the animals had gone off the trail, the guides had to stop, dismount, and feel long stretches of the ground until they reached the powdered earth, the ruts and the tree-stumps of the road. Guides once previously had done that for George, the night he had gone to Half King's camp to surprise Jumonville; this time the escape of the remnant of the army might depend on holding to the road or finding it when lost. On every night ride, the silence had been op-

[96] Robert Dobson, temporary aide (see *supra*, n. 49) knew nothing of the country, except for what he had observed during the march to the Monongahela.

[97] James Smith, in J. Pritts, *Mirror of Olden Time Border Life,* 2nd ed., 388. Smith was so sickened by the sight that he climbed down from the wall and went to his quarters.

pressive; this evening the woods were vocal with the misery of men.
Now a horse would stumble over the body of a soldier who had died in
the road while crawling toward the rear. Again the animal, seeing a
corpse invisible to the rider, would step carefully over. It was amazing
how far into the woods some of the soldiers wounded early in the
battle had made their way. Hearing horsemen, a dying private might
scream for help. Another, passed by, might pray for the vengeance of
God on hardhearted brutes who would leave a man to perish in that
pit of hell. George had to go on—to stop to succor one man was to be
false to hundreds—but he never forgot that ride. "The shocking
scenes . . ." he said almost thirty years afterward, "are not to be
described." He remembered: "The dead, the dying, the groans, lamenta-
tion and cries along the road of the wounded for help . . . were enough
to pierce a heart of adamant." [98]

This nightmare lasted for hours. Then the cries ceased, because the
horses had passed beyond the point reached by the most resolute and
the fleetest of the fugitives. The weird silence of the forest returned, as
if the whole army had perished and the three horsemen themselves were
ghosts. At last, when mind began to wander in the affrighting realm
between delirium and sleep, there was another sound than that of the
clomp-clomp of the dragging feet of half-dead horses: the creatures of
the forest were awakening. Ahead, the woods were as black as ever;
overhead, there was a sheen of gray. Dawn was approaching. When,
finally, there was light enough to see plainly the other men on the
trail, the three doubtless went through the ceremony that nearly always
is observed at such a time: each must have greeted his companions as if
they had ridden separately all night and had just come together again.

The weariest miles lay ahead, miles so long and so gloomy that it
seemed impossible for any human being to keep his saddle after twenty-
four hours and more of riding, of fighting, and of witnessing the
horrors of the battlefield. George gripped his saddle with exhausted
knees and held fast to his bridle-rein. He must reach Dunbar's camp!
The resolution that had carried him through the snow-covered wilderness and over the floating ice of the Allegheny did not fail him now.
Late in the morning of the 10th of July,[99] George's horse staggered

98 29 G. W., 44.
99 Washington (29 G. W., 44) recorded only that his ride "took up the whole night and
part of the next morning"; but if the writer in the Penn. Gazette of Aug. 28, 1755, was correct
in saying that orders came after noon to send wagons and refreshment to Gist's, manifestly
George, who brought those orders, could not then have been long in camp.

into the area of Dunbar's wagons, near "Rock Fort" as the British called Jumonville's hiding place,[100] seven miles Northwest of Great Meadows.[101] The young Virginian was so fatigued and overwrought that he scarcely was able to discharge his mission [102] or, probably, even to observe intelligently the excitement around him.

Rumor of bad news had spread through the camp after 9 o'clock that day.[103] A youthful drover who had left with cattle for Braddock had returned with his animals and had given no satisfactory explanation of his reason for doing so.[104] The whisper was that Braddock's force had been wiped out.[105] After that, the earliest of the surviving wounded and the first of the fugitives from the battlefield had arrived with their tales of carnage.[106] Now, about noon,[107] Colonel Dunbar lost his head and ordered the drummers to beat "To arms." Instead of bringing the men to their places, this spread panic among cowardly soldiers and teamsters. Some of them broke for the rear as if the enemy were about to open fire. Sentries stopped as many as they could, but guards were overrun.[108] The impulse to retreat gripped even officers. Fortunately, an increasing number of the lightly wounded who reached camp from the scene of action told of men in the rear whose presence was at once a screen and an assurance that the slaughter on the Monongahela had not been complete. Dunbar recovered sufficient self-command to resolve to hold his position at least for the next night.[109] The wagons for which George brought orders were hitched, were loaded with supplies, and were sent forward during the afternoon under a strong guard.[110]

George did not go with the convoy; even his powerful will could not drive his exhausted body any longer. He had to remain at Dunbar's to rest,[111] but, when he awakened on the morning of the 11th, he found new anxiety in the confusion of the camp and in the virtual disappearance of all discipline.[112] Wounded and fugitives continued to limp in; wild tales of every sort were told and credited; demoralization was so general that Dunbar probably deserved credit for being able to

---

[100] Orme, 357. On many maps this is marked "Dunbar's Camp."
[101] 6 Penn. Col. Rec., 482.   [102] 29 G. W., 44.
[103] The time is given as 5 A.M. in Penn. Gazette, Aug. 28, 1755; but the statements of wagoners who ran away would indicate an hour between 9 and 11 that morning. See 6 Penn. Col. Rec., 482.
[104] Ibid., 483.   [105] Penn. Gazette, Aug. 28, 1755.
[106] 6 Penn. Col. Rec., 480.   [107] Ibid., 482, 484.
[108] Ibid., 480, 482.   [109] Penn. Gazette, Aug. 28, 1755.
[110] Ibid.   [111] 29 G. W., 44.
[112] So Orme reported, op. cit., 357. While Orme wrote specifically of conditions in the evening, there is every reason to assume like conditions prevailed during the forenoon.

comply with a further order from Braddock to send to him additional wagons and two Companies of infantry.[113]

In the evening, Braddock and the main body of wounded and unhurt survivors arrived at Dunbar's Camp,[114] from Gist's settlement, which most of them had reached on the night of the 10th after a continuous and unpursued retreat.[115] The General himself had been transferred from the cart to a hand-litter and, when soldiers refused to carry him, he had been forced about 3 P.M. on the 10th to mount a horse.[116] How he endured the agony of his wound on the long ride over the rocky mountain road, none could understand; but he retained consciousness and undertook to give orders. He seemed to realize that the wounded at Dunbar's Camp and those with him were too far from any shelter to be transported on litters, even if he had the bearers. The feeble horses left to the expedition could not convey all the wounded and all the supplies. Braddock therefore directed that available teams be assigned for the wounded, for the two six-pounder cannon that had been left with Dunbar, and for such indispensable provisions as could be conveyed by the remaining animals. Everything else was to be destroyed—ammunition, surplus powder, flour, wagons, equipment—so that it would not fall into hostile hands. Then the position near Rock Fort was to be abandoned. The demoralized, crippled army was to be removed farther from the victorious enemy. Dunbar marveled that the General felt able to give orders of this magnitude and importance, but he neither protested nor disregarded them as the instructions of a man no longer qualified to exercise command.[117]

In ordering a retreat, Braddock directed that it begin the next day,[118] but so many wounded men and stragglers arrived on the 12th,[119] that even the most essential arrangements could not be completed before sunset.[120] As reported to Governor Sharpe: "Nearly 150 wagons were burnt, the powder casks staved in a spring, the cohorns broke or buried and the shell bursted. The provisions were scattered abroad on the ground, or the barrels broke and thrown into the water." [121] Completion of the work of destruction was left on the morning of the 13th to rear-

[113] *Penn. Gazette*, Aug. 28, 1755.
[114] *Ibid.*; *Orme*, 357.
[115] *Orme*, 357.
[116] 2 *Din.*, 221–22.
[117] 1 *Sharpe*, 254, 269, letter of William Johnston, Sept. 23, 1755; 11 *Penn. Mag.*, 94; Dunbar quoted in St. Clair to Thomas Robinson, Sept. 3, 1755; P.R.O., C.O. 5: 46, p. 51–54.
[118] *Penn. Gazette*, Aug. 28, 1755.
[119] Dunbar, *Pargellis*, 110.
[120] *Ibid.*
[121] 1 *Sharpe*, 269. Dunbar subsequently denied the oft-repeated charge that cannon were buried. See *Lowdermilk*, 169–70. The confusion doubtless arose from the fact that eight cohorns were destroyed or hidden underground by Braddock's order (*Pargellis*, 97, 119).

AN OLD BATTLE ON MODERN STREETS

After the incredible defeat of Braddock, July 9, 1755, Governor Shirley of Massachusetts, Governor Dinwiddie of Virginia, and others of like station refused at first to credit reports of the disaster; and when they had at length to admit that Braddock had been overwhelmed, their question of course was, Why? In England, the question was the same.

Answers were not of the wisest nor of the fullest. Braddock and Halkett, the two senior officers, were dead. Most of the survivors saw only what occurred directly around them. A subsequent court of inquiry was hampered by the fact that one of its members was under popular condemnation for his abandonment of Fort Cumberland after the troops from the Monongahela had returned to that outpost.

Patrick MacKellar was one of those who had learned enough about the action to give testimony of enduring historical value. As senior of the three engineers with Braddock, he knew the line of march and the order of battle and he promptly prepared several excellent maps of the expedition.

The most valuable of these are the two here repro-

(Continued on third page following)

duced. One shows the situation of the British at the moment the advancing French and Indians were discovered; the other exhibits the confusion that existed when Gage's and St. Clair's men had been hurled back on the vanguard and the flanks of the British had been turned. Careful scrutiny of these maps greatly facilitates an understanding of an engagement which, if described in too much detail, is apt to bewilder.

The scene of Braddock's defeat now lies completely within the Borough of Braddock of the Pittsburgh metropolitan area. A student seeking to identify the various positions finds himself looking at roof-tops and narrow streets. Fortunately, in 1909, Sydney Dillon, Chief Engineer of the Edgar Thomson Works of the Carnegie Steel Company, took pains to superimpose MacKellar's drawings on a map of the town of Braddock as it then was. The visitor who avails himself of Mr. Dillon's labor is able to ascertain precisely at what points on the streets of Braddock the various scenes in the tragedy of July 9, 1755 were enacted.

Through the courtesy of G. M. Dillon, Superintendent of Public Works in Braddock, and a brother of Sydney Dillon, these maps now are reproduced with the permission of the United States Steel Corporation.

guards, who were instructed to burn what they could not demolish.[122] The main body of survivors started for the Great Meadows, but apparently the men left at Rock Fort did not wait long to follow them. When the French subsequently visited the site they found that some of the wagons had not been reduced to ashes,[123] presumably because a heavy rain had fallen shortly after the torch had been applied to the vehicles by hurried guards who did not wish to take any chance of being cut off.[124]

Braddock of course went along with the main force.[125] He had not been talkative at any time after he left the Monongahela, but his orders and his few remarks indicated that he had suffered no loss of memory through shock and that he knew what was happening around him. "Who would have thought it?" he asked, in manifest reference to the defeat.[126] On the night of the 11th he had stated clearly what he wished to be done, and he had not forgotten that cannon had been left with Dunbar and must be saved, if possible.[127] He had continued to give orders,[128] but now, after he had traversed approximately one mile of the road between Rock Fort and Great Meadows, he received an inquiry from Dunbar concerning some doubtful question. This seemed to make Braddock realize that he should not attempt to direct the retreat. He called Dunbar to him and in a few words turned over the command to the Colonel.[129] Then or later in the day he said, as if to himself, "We shall better know how to deal with them another time."[130] About two miles West of Great Meadows, he called a halt.[131] Close by was Orme, his aide and his favorite, wounded but with every prospect of full recovery. To the young Lieutenant, Braddock gave new instructions: Orme must acquaint Keppel promptly with what had happened, and must tell him that "nothing could equal the gallantry and good conduct of the officers nor the bad behavior of the men."[132] In that pride of

---

[122] *Penn. Gazette*, Aug. 28, 1755.

[123] See *Relation* of the Battle of Fort DuQuesne, "come from Canada on the *Louisburg*"; Paris, Aff. Etr., Mém. et Docts. France, 535, 110–13. This account states that the scene of destruction was at Fort Necessity, and that four mortars and two culverines were found there—mistakes that tend to discredit the entire narrative.

[124] *Ibid.*   [125] Cf. 1 *G. W.*, 148.

[126] *Orme*, quoted in Franklin, *Autobiography*, 192. The memory of Franklin or of Orme played the traitor in this brief, familiar account. Other records show that Braddock was not so nearly silent as Orme's narrative would indicate.

[127] *Penn. Gazette*, Aug. 28, 1755.

[128] *Pargellis*, 120.

[129] Gage, quoted in Shirley to Thomas Robinson, Nov. 5, 1755; 2 *Shirley*, 321.

[130] Franklin, *Autobiography* (Bigelow ed.), 192.

[131] See *infra*, n. 136.

[132] Orme to Keppel, July 18, 1755; P.R.O., C.O. 5: 46, p. 43–46.

his corps and with that shame of his troops, the general died about 9 o'clock on the evening of the 13th of July.[133]

Of Braddock's "family," George was the one best charged with responsibility for the burial of the defeated General. Shirley was dead and doubtless had been scalped on the field of battle; Morris and Orme were incapacitated by their wounds; Dobson [134] was inexperienced in staff work. Although George had by no means recovered from the strain of the 9th–10th, he had strength enough to perform the last services for a man who had admired him and had given him coveted opportunity. As soon as practicable on the morning of the 14th, George selected a place in the road near the head of the column, and there he had a squad dig a short, deep trench. He chose that spot because the French Indians might hear of the death of Braddock and might seek to find the grave in order that they might disinter and maltreat the body. When the ground was ready, George had the General's corpse brought forward with such honors of war as the condition of the troops permitted.[135] Then, when the column began to move eastward again, George had all the wagons pass over the grave and all the footmen tramp the earth down, so that no mark of the burial should remain.[136] The device was successful. French and Indians learned that Braddock had expired but they did not find his grave.[137]

On the brief remainder of the march to Fort Cumberland, George's particular care was for the comfort of his fellow staff-officers, Morris and Orme, and of their traveling-companion, Colonel Burton. All

[133] *Orme*, 357; *Pargellis*, 120. "Seaman" (Sargent, *op. cit.*, 388) gave the hour of death as 8 P.M., but as he misdated that event, the narratives of Orme and of the unidentified author in Pargellis of course are preferred. The French subsequently had a story that Braddock had called his officers to him and had said at some unspecified stage of the retreat: "Tell me, I beg you, by whom are we now defeated and can you know of a parallel rout? We have been crushed without knowing by whom we were defeated: it must be a supernatural force that has reduced us to this state. What will they say of us in England? That we have been butchered! As for me, I would rather die than be forced to give an account" (*Relation* via *Louisburg*, cited *supra*, n. 123).

[134] See *supra*, p. 17, 71, 78.

[135] In normal circumstances, as a Major General, Braddock would have been entitled to the attendance of two Battalions and three Squadrons, and to a salute of three rounds of seven pieces of cannon.

[136] 29 *G. W.*, 45. The location of Braddock's grave and the fact that the men and wagons could pass over it without a countermarch, is the basis of the statement made earlier in the text that the halting place of the army was about two miles West of Fort Necessity. See *Lowdermilk*, 188. When Washington wrote in 1786 he added the familiar appraisal of Braddock that may or may not have represented his feeling in 1755: "Thus died a man whose good and bad qualities were intimately blended. He was brave even to a fault and in regular service would have done honor to his profession. His attachments were warm, his enmities were strong, and having no disguise, both appeared in full force. He was generous and disinterested, but plain and blunt in his manner even to rudeness" (29 *G. W.*, 45).

[137] Workmen, repairing the road about 1824, unearthed a skeleton which, from the insignia of rank, was believed to be that of Braddock (*Lowdermilk*, 189).

three of these were on horse-litters,[138] and by the evening of the 15th or the morning of the 16th, they were safe at the fort without any molestation on the way.[139] Back at Wills Creek, George heard that he had been reported dead and had been credited with a farewell speech.[140] This diverted him and, at the same time, confirmed his belief that he was—to quote his words to his brother John Augustine—"in the land of the living by the miraculous care of Providence that protected me beyond all human expectation." [141] As soon as his strength permitted he wrote to assure his mother [142] and his household on the Potomac [143] of his safety. Danger and death had made him mindful of those around him who were not of his own circle. He added to his mother's letter a postscript to inform a humble woman of the neighborhood that her son had escaped with a minor wound of the foot.[144] In his first report to the Governor, he said, "I tremble at the consequences that this defeat may have upon our back settlers, who I suppose will all leave their habitations unless there are proper measures taken for their security." [145]

Even before George could write this to the Governor, he doubtless had heard of the manner in which the news of the disaster on the Monongahela had reached Fort Cumberland. About noon of the 11th [146] a boy had arrived from the West with a report that Braddock had been killed and that Sir Peter Halkett's Regiment had been cut off by French and Indians. The soldiers' wives and the few other women at the camp had been thrown into a frenzy. "I packed up my things to send," wrote Mrs. Browne, "for we expected the Indians every hour." [147] Other wagoners confirmed or exaggerated the first story. As some of the frightened drivers told it, not more than 100 men had been saved from the slaughter.[148]

Colonel Innes, commanding at Fort Cumberland, had not waited for further intelligence, nor, indeed, had he even written down all that was known. He had dashed off this and had given it to an express:

Sir: I have this minute received the melancholy account of the Defeat of our Troops, the General killed and Numbers of our Officers, our whole Artillery

---

138 See *supra*, p. 81.
139 1 *G. W.*, 148; 29 *ibid.*, 45. *Halkett's Orderly Book* shows that the wounded were transported in wagons until the 16th when those slightly injured were sent forward, with surgeons, on foot. An issue of fresh meat was made the sick on the 14th. Batmen and the women of the Regiment were required to march in the rear of the column (*ibid.*, July 13).
140 1 *G. W.*, 152.
141 Letter of July 18, 1755; 1 *G. W.*, 152.　142 1 *G. W.*, 150-52.
143 *Ibid.*, 152.　　　　　　　　　　　144 1 *G. W.*, 152.
145 Letter of July 18, 1755; 1 *G. W.*, 150.　146 6 *Penn. Col. Rec.*, 479.
147 32 *V* 317-18.　　　　　　　　　148 1 *Sharpe*, 248; 2 *Penn. Arch.*, 379.

taken; in short the Account I have Received is so very bad, that, as please God I intend to make a stand here, it's highly necessary to raise the Militia everywhere to defend the Frontiers.

Your humble servant,

James Innes

Fort Cumberland July 11th 1755
  To all to whom this may Concern.[149]

This message was carried to Lord Fairfax, who forwarded it at once to Dinwiddie and apparently made copies for the Governors of nearby Colonies.[150] In this form the frightful news reached Williamsburg, where, on the 9th, the very day of Braddock's defeat, the Governor had prorogued the General Assembly with the statement, among others, that he was "in great hopes, before this, that General Braddock is in possession of the fort on the Ohio that the French took from us last summer . . ." [151] Dinwiddie had never doubted the ability of Braddock to do this. The Governor had predicted, in fact, that the French would surrender Fort DuQuesne on sight of the English forces.[152] When, therefore, Innes's crude dispatch came into the hands of Dinwiddie on the 14th of July, the Governor could not believe the report correct. He complained that it was "entirely general" [153] and, though he at once dispatched an express for details,[154] he concluded—or persuaded himself—that the story received by Innes was nothing more than the yarn of a mendacious deserter.[155]

To procure additional information, Colonel Innes, meantime, had sent a youth westward, astride one of the best and freshest horses at the fort, but the lad had returned the next day, July 13, with a tale that the animal had broken down and that he had learned nothing further concerning the defeat. This negative report was forwarded to the Governor with an expression of Innes's hope that "things cannot be so very bad with us." [156] An extensive and authentic account of the disaster, with humiliating detail of rout and loss, was not to reach Dinwiddie until July 24.[157] Governor Shirley was to hear on July 22

---

149 Verbatim, according to the text in 1 *Sharpe,* 246, except that abbreviated words in the original are spelled out here. The text in 6 *Penn. Col. Rec.,* 478, is slightly different. The open address may have been intended by Innes primarily for the County Lieutenants who would be the men to "raise the militia."

150 *Ibid.*

151 *Journ. H. B.,* 1752–58, p. 294.

152 2 *Din.,* 48. See *ibid.,* 49, 52, 63, 98, 99.

153 2 *Din.,* 99.

154 *Ibid.,* 114.

155 *Ibid.,* 102.

156 Innes to Dinwiddie, July 13, 1755; 31 *Md. Arch.,* 70.

157 2 *Din.,* 116.

of the ruin of Braddock's expedition, and was then to believe that the facts were swollen by rumor. This was serious news for Shirley, who, as ranking officer in North America, had to assume temporary general command.[158]

George, at Fort Cumberland, soon learned that the wounded who reached Wills Creek numbered twenty-three officers and 364 men.[159] The final list of casualties was to show sixty-three officers and 914 men killed or wounded, a total of 977 in a force of 1459.[160] Virginians had sustained losses that almost destroyed the three participating Companies. Of the twelve Virginia company officers in the fight, Adam Stephen wrote that six were killed.[161] In La Peyroney's command, the Captain and all officers and non-commissioned officers down to a Corporal were slain; one only of Captain Polson's officers remained alive. Washington estimated that in the three Companies not more than thirty men were left.[162]

These Virginia casualties became the more serious in the face of what George heard of future plans, though he apparently was not in the councils of Col. Thomas Dunbar, the senior surviving officer. As early as July 18, perhaps before that time, George learned that Dunbar intended to leave Fort Cumberland, as soon as he collected all his men, and that he planned to proceed to Philadelphia and to go into winter quarters there. This meant, as George wrote Governor Dinwiddie, "there will be no men left here unless it is the poor remains of the Virginia troops who survive and will be too small to guard our frontiers." [163] More than that Washington did not say at the time concerning Dunbar's decision, which was based on the belief that the situation was hopeless. As the artillery was lost, the Colonel reasoned that Regi-

[158] Shirley to Richard Peters, July 23, 1755; 2 *Shirley*, 209; Shirley to Thomas Dunbar, Aug. 6, 1755; *ibid.*, 216.

[159] *Pargellis*, 126. *Halkett's Orderly Book* (July 15, 19, 1755) shows that the extent of the casualties was not known during the first days of the retreat from Rock Fort.

[160] Casualty list in P.R.O., C.O. 5: p. 46, quoted in 6 *Gipson*, 96. George's own estimate as of July 18 was that nearly sixty officers had been killed or wounded, that about 300 men had been killed, and that a like number, or more, had been wounded (1 *G. W.*, 151, 152). Later (1786) Washington thought that of a total of 1200 to 1300, some 800 or 900 were casualties (29 *G. W.*, 45). The "Seaman's" figure, doubtless heard at Fort Cumberland, was 896. See Sargent, *op. cit.*, 388. The list in 15 *V* 258, is worthless. In Halkett's 44th the loss between June 1 and July 23, 1755, exclusive of commissioned officers, was 195—from 822 to 627 (*Cumberland Papers*, Windsor Castle, 46, 39).

[161] *Stephen-Hardwicke* loc. cit.

[162] 1 *G. W.*, 151. Waggener's loss is not reported. Captains Polson and Stewart had distinguished themselves particularly. See Orme to Dinwiddie, July 18, 1755; P.R.O., C.O. 5: 46, p. 68–73.

[163] Letter of July 18, 1755; 1 *G. W.*, 150. As of July 21, 1755, the reported strength of the regular troops at Fort Cumberland was 110 officers and 1613 privates. The n.c.o's. were not listed on the return (*Cumberland Papers*, Windsor Castle, 46, 166).

ments weakened by death, wounds and sickness could accomplish nothing more that year.[164] Dunbar's plan raised a storm; George did not have any part in brewing it. His relations with Dunbar never had been intimate: he neither volunteered advice nor received any request for his opinion. Besides, on the death of Braddock, his appointment as a volunteer aide had come officially to an end. He still was willing to work to redeem the disaster, but he felt that as the little army, in his own words, had been "drove in thus far"—to Wills Creek—he was at liberty to go home when his strength permitted. After the manner of young men anxious to return to their kin, he set specific dates—in this case July 27 or 28—for his arrival at Mount Vernon.[165]

By the 22nd, approximately, George felt himself able to undertake the journey homeward. Returning via McCracken's and over the mountains at Vestal's Gap, he stopped at Thompson's [166] and then at Alexandria, where he undertook to procure passage for Orme aboard some comfortable vessel.[167] On Saturday, July 26, he had the joy of drawing rein on his own lawn and of surveying on the broad-bosomed Potomac a scene incredibly different from that which he had witnessed a fortnight previously on the Monongahela.[168]

George knew that his Belvoir neighbors of course wished to hear the news he brought as much as he wanted to see them, and he accordingly sent an invitation for Colonel Fairfax and the ladies to visit him, inasmuch as he was too weary to make the journey to the nearby plantation that day. Colonel Fairfax replied immediately with an affectionate welcome home. To the Colonel's letter, Sally Fairfax and the other young ladies at Belvoir added this saucy note:

Dear Sir—After thanking Heaven for your safe return I must accuse you of great unkindness in refusing us the pleasure of seeing you this night. I do assure you nothing but our being satisfied that our Company would be disagreeable should prevent us from trying if our legs would not carry us to Mount Virnon this night but if you will not come to us tomorrow morning very early we shall be at Mount Virnon

> S. Fairfax
> Ann Spearing [Spears?]
> Eliz[th] Dent [169]

[164] See 1 *Sharpe*, 254, 278.   [165] 1 *G. W.*, 153.
[166] He was at McCracken's on the 23rd, at Winchester on the 24th and probably at Thompson's on the 25th, though his entry of expenses at Thompson's is undated (*Ledger A*, folio 22).
[167] 1 *G. W.*, 153. Orme wished to go to Philadelphia and thence back to England. Cf. 1 *Sharpe*, 254. George found virtually all the shipping engaged for the transport of tobacco.
[168] Cf. 1 *G. W.*, 153.   [169] 1 *Hamilton*, 74.

Whether the meeting on Sunday the 27th of July was at Belvoir or at Mount Vernon, it doubtless was one of pleasantness and of long conversation in which there must have been more questioning of Washington than there was narration by him. Even among those close friends, George did not possess ease in telling of his experiences, certainly not the grim story of the manner in which, as he wrote John Augustine, "we have been most scandalously beaten by a trifling body of men." [170]

After he said goodbye to the Fairfaxes, George on the 28th wrote Orme of his efforts to find a suitable vessel at Alexandria, and then he added: "It is impossible to relate the different accounts that was given [in the town] of our late unhappy engagement; but all tended greatly to the disadvantage of the poor deceased General, who is censured on all hands." [171] Indeed, all the way back to Fort Cumberland and to Mount Vernon, George had heard the complaints of soldiers who felt they had been led into the wilderness to be slaughtered. Officers who survived the battle had praise for the members of their corps and contempt for the alleged cowardice of the men in the ranks. Criticism from other sources now became audible. George soon began to discover what colonial Governors and public men thought of the campaign, and for many months afterward he read the comment of England on a defeat so overwhelming that it stunned the strongest.[172] To the credit of the home country and of the Colonies, there was no disposition to take one inclusive view in England and another in America. On either side of the Atlantic, different men emphasized different mistakes of strategy and of tactics, but geography did not shape the critique except in two particulars. One of these concerned blame of the provincials for failing to furnish a sufficient number of horses and wagons; the other had to do with the superior attitude most of the British officers assumed in dealing with the colonials. Criticism naturally dealt first with Braddock's approach, then with his conduct of the battle and, third, with the situation his retention of command created for Dunbar after the retreat to Rock Fort.

Seven specific criticisms were made of Braddock's advance to Fort DuQuesne. These were:

---

170 i G. W., 153.
171 i G. W., 154.
172 Cecilius Calvert to Sharpe, Sept. 9, 1755; 31 Md. Arch., 489. See also Orme to Washington, March 2, 1756; i Hamilton, 199. Horace Walpole's later comments will be found in his Memoirs, v. i, p. 390–92.

1. He erred in choosing Alexandria rather than Philadelphia as his seaboard base.

2. The commander invited disaster by attempting to proceed directly from Fort Cumberland to his objective without organizing depots and magazines at each stage of his advance.

3. In the movement of his troops he was culpably slow.

4. Transport was inadequate for the demands made on it.

5. Braddock's artillery was too heavy for the route he had to pursue.

6. In the final stages of the advance, the General should not have ventured ahead until Dunbar's arrival gave him the power to strike with his full force.

7. Fundamentally, Braddock's whole management of the campaign displayed overconfidence in a type of warfare with which he was unfamiliar.

The alleged unwisdom of choosing the small new town of Alexandria as a seaboard base, rather than the old and well-stocked city of Philadelphia, was in part a matter of colonial jealousy, and was to be argued again and more vehemently; [173] but it likewise was a question of roads and grades and elevations, concerning some of which even the most intelligent frontiersmen did not have accurate information.

Braddock's attempt to carry forward his whole expedition from Fort Cumberland all the way to the Ohio, without the establishment of any large advance base or magazine, was condemned somewhat widely and for the obvious reason: If defeated far to the westward, he might be compelled to retreat a great distance with many attendant risks.[174] This criticism was connected, in the mind of Governor Sharpe, with the "impatience of the young men" who surrounded Braddock and rashly urged him to push on.[175] Other colonials rightly associated the danger of a self-contained advance with the feebleness of Braddock's transport. He had too few horses and wagons, they said, to attempt to carry so heavy a train of artillery and all the provisions, supplies and ammunition he felt he must have with him after he left Fort Cumberland. Responsibility for this shortage of transportation was appraised, in most instances, according to the sympathy or the prejudices of the speaker.[176]

173 1 *Entick*, 142. The reader who wishes a brief epitome of the detailed critique that begins at this point will find it in a single paragraph, p. 99, *infra*.

174 Cf. Dulany's News Letter, Dec. 9, 1755; 3 *Penn. Mag.*, 15.

175 Sharpe to William Sharpe, Sept. 15, 1755; 1 *Sharpe*, 284.

176 See R. H. Morris to Sharpe, July 20, 1755; same to Dinwiddie, Aug. 19, 1755; 2 *Penn. Arch.*, 380, 390; 2 *Din.*, 180. Dinwiddie stated that he urged Braddock to move at the end of

Inadequate transport was regarded as a factor, also, in Braddock's decision to leave Dunbar behind him and to push on with the stronger horses and a small force of men. Dunbar contended that Braddock had imposed on him by failing to leave him a sufficient number of horses to move his entire force simultaneously. As one of Dunbar's officers somewhat quaintly put it, "the horses were too tired to come at once." [177] St. Clair maintained that the final advance without Dunbar was a mistake and, in reporting later to the home government, the Quartermaster asserted that he had sought to have Braddock halt, thirty miles from Fort DuQuesne and to remain there until Dunbar could arrive. [178] Dinwiddie was of opinion that Braddock should have waited on the bank of the Monongahela until Dunbar arrived to strengthen him.

The most general contemporary complaint was of Braddock's over-confidence in an unfamiliar country where warfare was different in almost every way from that for which he had been trained; [179] and this criticism carried the argument from what might be termed the strategy of approach [180] to the tactics of the battle. Nearly everyone who wrote about the campaign agreed that Braddock should have heeded the warnings of the provincial officers. They told him, as plainly as they dared, that stand-up fighting and line fire would not avail in a heavily wooded country, where the men scattered and hid themselves completely while firing from the shelter of rocks or trees or logs. Instead of changing his tactics, "General Braddock," as Adam Stephen said in accurate epitome, "unhappily placed his confidence and whole dependence on the Regiments." [181]

Step by step, Braddock was denounced for the mistakes he made on the 9th of July. He failed, observers said, to use his irregular troops for reconnaissance as he approached the enemy. Had he done so, it was asserted, he might have "sprung" the Indians and might have mown them down with his volleys. [182] Again, critics said, when Braddock de-

---

April or the beginning of May with a half or even a third of the artillery but that the General refused to advance without the whole of it (*ibid.*, 313). No record of this exhortation has been found elsewhere.

[177] 14 Peters Papers., *Hist. Soc. Penn.*, p. 20.

[178] St. Clair to Thomas Robinson, *loc. cit.*

[179] *Annual Register*, 1756, p. 3–5. Cf. 6 *Penn. Col. Rec.*, 496.

[180] This is an instance where the terminology of eighteenth-century war proves inadequate. Criticism was not directed against Braddock's strategy, strictly speaking, but against what now would be styled his logistics. Unfortunately that word was not used in its present sense during Washington's lifetime.

[181] *Stephen-Hardwicke.*

cided to proceed past Frazier's trading-post with the troops in his immediate command, he should have given specific orders to Gage. Actually, it was alleged, Gage received no orders.[183] Beyond these matters, criticism of the engagement became a contest in denunciation of the cowardice attributed to the regulars. Washington's own words [184] were typical. The General's blunders were forgotten in the flight of his men. An anonymous poet wrote:

> Beneath some Indian shrub if chance you spy
> The brave remains of murder'd Braddock lie,
> Soldiers, with shame the guilty place survey,
> And weep that here your comrades fled away.
> Then with his brother-chiefs encircled round,
> Possess the hero's bones of hostile ground,
> And plant the English oak that gave his name,
> Fit emblem of his valour and his fame!
> Broad o'er this stream shall thus his honours grow
> And last as long as e'er its waters flow! [185]

Particular reasons assigned for the panic that disgraced British arms were the fire of an invisible adversary,[186] who had all the advantage of ground,[187] the loss of officers, and the depletion of the supply of ammunition.[188] There was disagreement whether the panic began with Gage's men and spread to the main force, or whether Burton's troops were already in confusion when the soldiers in front of them fell back.[189]

However this might be settled, some critics held that the disaster might have been redeemed had not Dunbar retreated from Rock Fort in what was regarded as a panic that rivaled Braddock's.[190] Dinwiddie,

182 31 *Md. Arch.,* 489. Here again Stephen spoke wisely: "[Braddock] found to his woeful experience what had been frequently told him, that formal attacks and platoon firing never would answer against the savages and Canadians. It ought to be laid down as a maxim to attack them first, to fight them in their own way and go against them light and naked as they came against us . . ." (*loc. cit.*).
183 Dulany's News Letter, Dec. 9, 1755; 3 *Penn. Mag.,* 17. This was not precisely correct. Gage had orders to halt at 3 P.M.
184 *Supra,* p. 76.
185 *Gentleman's Mag.,* August, 1755, p. 383. These lines are said to have appeared first as a broadside. In the next issue of the magazine, p. 421, is a less good "Apology for the men who deserted Braddock."
186 See *supra,* p. 70.
187 Cf. William Shirley to Sir Thomas Robinson, Aug. 11, 1755; 2 *Shirley,* 217.
188 Orme to Keppel, July 18, 1755; P.R.O., C.O. 5: 46, p. 43–46.
189 Dulany's News Letter, Dec. 9, 1755; 3 *Penn. Mag.,* 17; *Penn. Gazette,* Sept. 5, 1755; Chauncey, *Letter to a Friend.*
190 Dulany's News Letter, Dec. 9, 1755; 3 *Penn. Mag.,* 15.

in particular, contended that Braddock was in no condition to give orders for the destruction of provisions and supplies, and that Dunbar should have taken command and should have entrenched and remained where he was when the wounded General arrived.[191]

Later, when an official inquiry was made by Dunbar and Gage, they were careful to avoid all personalities. Their conclusion was that "the bad behavior was general," but that this was attributable "in some measure . . . to the following reasons: 1st, [the troops] were greatly harassed by duties unequal to their numbers, dispirited by want of sufficient provisions and not being allowed time to dress the little they had, with nothing to drink but water and that scarce and bad. 2nd, the frequent conversations of the provincial troops and country people that if they engaged the Indians in the European manner of fighting they would be beat, and this some of the officers declared as their opinion . . . 3rd, the want of Indians or of other irregulars to give timely notice of the enemy's approach, having only three or four guides to go out as scouts." The last finding was the familiar one that the British had to fight an invisible enemy in a forest.[192]

Evidence disclosed at a later time shifts some of the emphasis previously given two or three factors in the campaign.[193] First of all was the fundamental fact that Braddock operated in a country concerning which he knew nothing at the outset and accumulated information slowly. St. Clair's assumption, without close reconnaissance, that he easily could open a short route over the mountain to the mouth of Savage River [194] was typical of the attitude of the General and his higher officers. Braddock himself was of the belief for months after his arrival in Virginia that only fifteen miles of rough country would be encountered between Wills Creek and Fort DuQuesne.[195] Apparently,

---

191 2 *Din.*, 215, 222. See *supra*, p. 81.

192 2 *Shirley*, 313. The original of this "Inquiry as to the Behavior of the Troops at Monongahela," dated Nov. 21, 1755, and signed by Dunbar and Gage is P.R.O., C.O. 5: 46, p. 271–74, LC Trans. Available orders seem to bear out the statement that the men of the advanced force had scarcely anything to drink except water. The only issue of rum mentioned in *Halkett's Orderly Book* was an unspecified amount on June 27.

193 Osgood (*op. cit.*, v. 4, p. 342) concluded that Braddock's mission was out of proportion to the small forces assigned him. Fortesque (*History of the British Army*, v. 2, p. 270) thought that a blunder was made in starting from Alexandria instead of from Philadelphia. Braddock's "domineering temper and the insolent superiority he affected as an Englishman over Americans could not tend to ease the general friction between the British and Provincials." Beer (*British Colonial Policy*, 19) was of opinion that the inadequate support given by certain of the Colonies showed the necessity of some form of union. Otherwise Britain must be prepared to bear a disproportionate share of the cost of defence. Pargellis's tactical criticisms, together with those of Sargent, are considered *infra*.

194 See *supra*, p. 22.

195 See *supra*, p. 25–26.

during the whole time at Fort Cumberland he made no effort to determine if the grade of the old road over the mountain was the easiest that existed. Lieutenant Spendelowe was acting on his own initiative, with no orders, when he discovered the route that was used always thereafter to the great relief of the troops and the teams. Mapmaking seems to have received no attention. Whether this be charged against indolence or against the belief that a British army could go anywhere, the result was costly. Among other things, it contributed to the slowly gathering apprehension in the mind of observant colonials that the General was not qualified for the type of warfare in which he was engaged. Lack of confidence developed.

In another sense, unfamiliarity with the country and its resources was one reason for the bitterness of the controversy over the delay of the Colonies in providing transport and supplies. Doubtless to his last hour, Braddock believed that the provincials' failure to provide promptly the wagons, the horses, the flour and the meat needed for the expedition denied him an early start that would have assured the easy capture of Fort DuQuesne. Governor Dinwiddie was of the same mind, though he blamed Braddock, not the Colonies, for the delay.[196]

That the teams and the supplies were not placed at the disposal of Braddock when he expected them, none could deny; but so far as the colonial governments were responsible, the reason was inexperience, not rascality. In their pride and their desire to help, most of the provincial authorities undertook more than they could perform. Besides, a few private contractors, as in every war, doubtless sought deliberately to cheat the royal government. Had the Governors been informed accurately of what they could do, through contractors above the average in honesty, Braddock would have known what was practicable and what was not. It does not follow that he would have been sufficiently wise to use his wagons to establish, first of all, a series of advance bases to one of which he might have withdrawn, after a disaster, without having to abandon the entire country West of the Alleghany mountains.[197] In war, good transportation never was a satisfactory substitute for good sense.

This, too, must be remembered: Vexatious as was the delayed arrival of the wagons, the nature of the country was such that, regardless of supplies, advance was not possible until the roads had been dried by the

196 See *supra*, p. 89, n. 176.
197 The difference between this campaign and that of 1758, as respects advance depots, will be apparent when Grant's defeat and the retreat of his forces to Loyal Hannon are considered.

sun of May. St. Clair had discovered to his grief that in the mountains the snow did not vanish until the 15th of April.[198] At least three weeks had then to elapse, and preferably a month, before any new, poorly drained road could be made passable for wagons. Braddock at Fort Cumberland consequently did not have to chafe in idleness crying for more vehicles, much more than a fortnight longer than he would have had to wait, in the best of conditions, for General Mud to retreat. Moreover, if the French figures of their own strength are correct Braddock stood on the defensive with something over 1400 men, speaking one language, to receive the attack of not more than 900 French, Canadians and Indians, a majority of whom could not communicate with one another. The average capable commander in Braddock's place would not have felt, in those circumstances, that delay had crippled him. He would have felt satisfaction that he had overcome it. Delay, then, did not give Braddock inferiority of force on the day of battle, though this was circumstantial. Had the delay been longer and his military judgment no better than it was, he would have been compelled to take the risk of meeting all the French reenforcements that then were moving to the Ohio. If that had happened, the British force might have been destroyed. Whether Braddock should have used so large a part of his limited transport for a small advanced force in the final days of the campaign is a related question best discussed in another connection.[199]

On the day of battle, what Braddock lacked primarily, in approaching the field, was not more wagons but more Indians. This was the first of the three most important reasons for the outcome of the action. Before he started his advance, Braddock understood something of the value of Indians in scouting and reconnaissance, but he did not appreciate the use of these warriors as the French employed them in woodland combat. Failure on the part of Braddock to have these indispensable allies was due in some measure, but by no means exclusively, to his own lack of experience in dealing with them. When he permitted Bright Lightning and the other Indian girls to come into the English camp at Fort Cumberland, he invited debauches he later had to forbid, much to the dissatisfaction of the troops. At the same time, his decision to send the Indian women into Eastern Pennsylvania prompted nearly all the red warriors to follow their wives and thereby to leave Braddock almost without native guides and scouts.

[198] *Pargellis*, 93.

[199] See *infra*, p. 100–01.

It is easy to exaggerate this failure of Braddock. Had he been diplomatic instead of blunt, and skillful instead of inept, he scarcely could have been expected to overcome the advantage the French had gained before he reached America. Although the evidence is meagre, everything indicates that the defeat of Washington at Fort Necessity in 1754 led the Shawnees and the Mingoes to conclude that the French would win the war. In much the same belief, even those tribes of the Six Nations that had long and friendly ties with England found it prudent to remain neutral if not openly to espouse the cause of Britain's adversary. Braddock's country thus had lost temporarily the support of the Indians before he so much as had a chance to woo them. He needed allies in order to win a victory; he could not hope to regain the allies until he had won the victory. It was an impossible situation.

Braddock's failure to have Indian contingents in his advance on Fort DuQuesne has to be charged in part to friction between the Governor of Virginia and his colleague of South Carolina. Dinwiddie had an exalted opinion of his skill in dealing with the Indians and he felt confident that if he could not array the Six Nations quickly on the side of Britain, he could bring into the Ohio Valley a large force of Catawbas and Cherokees. The readiness of these powerful Southern natives to fight the battles of England at his instance was one of the Governor's illusions. His relations with the tribes had been confined to the reception of a few visitors and the exchange of perfunctory "speeches," but his early interest in the Cherokees and their neighbors had been increased thereby, and his faith in their prowess had deepened.[200] In soliciting the support of these Indians, Dinwiddie on occasion ignored the fact that much the larger number of them resided in the Carolinas. Instead of dealing with them through the Governors of those Colonies, Dinwiddie undertook direct negotiations on his own account.[201] By the time Braddock had arrived, Dinwiddie had persuaded himself that 1000 Catawba and Cherokee warriors were ready to move northward and to accompany the British expedition.[202] If he ever had any stronger foundation for this than hope, he destroyed it by arousing the antagonism of Gov. James Glen of South Carolina, who regarded him as both an interloper and a bungler in dealing with the natives of that domain.[203]

[200] See Koontz, *Dinwiddie*, 167–68, 255.   [201] Cf. *ibid.*, 267 ff.
[202] See *supra*, p. 8, 48.
[203] *Ibid.*, 317–18, 324. The *Dinwiddie Papers* echo much of the quarrelsome exchange between the two Governors. See, in particular, Dinwiddie to Glen, Sept. 25, 1775; 2 *Din.*, 212–14.

Braddock expected the help of these Indians, but none of them had put in an appearance. Dinwiddie had continued to believe they would. As late as June 26 the Governor had called on them to proceed to the Ohio, whither "a great General . . . from your Father, the King of Great Britain" had marched "to defeat the designs of the French in taking your lands without your consent." [204] To the last, Dinwiddie remained of opinion that his reliance on the Southern Indians was justified. After the battle of July 9 he wrote: "If Mr. Glen, agreeable to promise, had prevailed upon a number of the Cherokee and Catawba warriors to join our forces, we should not in all probability have been defeated, as they would have attacked the Indians in their bush way of fighting, which the regulars are strangers to; but by your letter . . . [Glen] had a meeting with those two nations of Indians at the very time they should have joined our forces. He has all along, I think, done everything contrary to his duty and the service of the expedition." [205] The Governors might continue to wrangle; the dark truth remained that the absence of Indians acquainted with forest fighting was a decisive factor on the bank of the Monongahela that bloody July day.

The second such factor was the one the colonials stressed—Braddock's unshakable faith in British tactics and in British troops. He was not alone in this. For months before the expedition was sent from England, Dinwiddie had been insisting that two Regiments of British troops of the regular establishment could save the English Colonies. The Governor's appeal was based in part on his disappointment in procuring volunteers to replace a militia he knew to be worthless. He wanted trained soldiers in adequate number, men who could be counted upon to muster and to march when ordered to do so. It never occurred to him that their tactics would make them well-nigh defenceless against Indians and Canadians. He was satisfied that British troops under commanders "from home" were invincible.

Braddock, of course, was entirely ignorant of the type of combat that prevailed in America. What was worse, he was not a man to learn. He lacked all originality of mind and exemplified the system that produced and schooled him, a system traditional, methodical and inflexible.

For Glen's side of the case, see J. R. Alden, *John Stuart and the Southern Colonial Frontier*, 24 ff. An earlier account is that of B. R. Carroll, *Historical Collections of South Carolina*, v. 1, p. 434 ff. In Edward McCrady, *The History of South Carolina under the Royal Government, 1719–1776*, p. 302 ff, is the allegation that Dinwiddie sought to "entice" the Indians "from their allegiance with" South Carolina.

204 2 *Din.*, 76. Cf. *ibid.*, 55, and *Orme*, 314.

205 Dinwiddie to Gov. Arthur Dobbs, 2 *Din.*, 123–24.

A man of his training was not apt to fail to do everything the regulations and the accepted tactics prescribed. It was still less likely he would do anything more. Trained for war on the continent of Europe, where the masters employed their art, Braddock believed that the tactics in which he had been drilled for forty years were close to perfection. Were British who had fought against Marshal Saxe to heed men who never had fought a battle or even seen an army? It was as if the child were essaying to instruct the teacher! As a matter of fact, few of the political elders who had the temerity to talk to Braddock about his chosen art of war had any personal experience in frontier fighting. Young men like Washington scarcely counted until they proved themselves: Braddock's associations were with the official class, English-reared and English in military creed.

Braddock did not even apply well the tactics in which he and his troops were trained.[206] He was, moreover, inexcusably careless in not making certain that Gage had reconnoitred thoroughly, some miles in advance, before proceeding toward Fort DuQuesne from the lower ford. The General had been alert on the 8th,[207] but apparently he had been satisfied on the 9th, after returning to the right bank, that as the French had not attacked him while crossing, they would not offer resistance outside the fort. The result contained a warning to every soldier: Great dangers often are rendered small by vigilance; lesser dangers always are enlarged by negligence.

Contact with the French might loosely be termed a "meeting engagement" in that the opposing forces came together where neither expected to encounter the other. Through their Indian scouts, the French had kept themselves informed of Braddock's advance, day by day and stage by stage.[208] When the column moved within striking distance, the garrison of Fort DuQuesne made ready to ambush it; but when the time came to start the march on the 8th, the Indians refused to go. Action had to be deferred until the next morning. Then Capt. Daniel Beaujeu marched his white troops from the fort, halted them in line and appealed to the Indians to join him. "Je suis déterminé à

[206] Those who care to study how Braddock is believed to have erred in his march and probably in spacing his troops are referred to Stanley Pargellis's "Braddock's Defeat," 41 *A. H. R.*, 253.

[207] *Pargellis*, 105. In St. Clair's report of Sept. 3, 1755 to Thomas Robinson (*loc. cit.*), the statement is made that when the column was sixteen miles from the fort, St. Clair vainly asked Braddock for permission to take 400 men and to post them in advance to deal with any sortie. This evidently is a different version of the incident described in the text, *supra*, p. 62.

[208] James Smith in Pritts, *op. cit.*

aller au devant des ennemies," he shouted, and paused for a minute. "Quoi—laisserez-vous aller votre [209] père seul? Je suis sur de les vaincre!" That decided them.[210] Even after this late start, the French commander may have hoped that the British could be caught at the lower ford.[211] He certainly did not ambush them, as some survivors thought. When the French actually sighted the head of the British column, the quick thinking of Beaujeu and his prompt deployment of his troops gave him initial advantage.[212]

In a few minutes the contest took on the nature of a surprise because of the third important factor, the nature of the ground. On either side of Braddock's advanced parties, at the time Gage met the enemy, there chanced to be ravines sufficiently deep to serve as natural trenches for the French and Indians. These ravines, moreover, were close enough to afford the enemy a perfect field of fire against the head and flanks of the British column.[213] Braddock's guides and engineers had not discovered these ravines or else, finding them empty, had disregarded them. Once the French and their savage allies had occupied the gullies without being observed, the question was whether the British would charge and clear the ground. If they did not, the only other question was that of the slaughter the British would endure before they broke and ran. Braddock and his officers realized the damage being done by the French fire from the hill, and they attempted to storm the high ground. They apparently knew nothing of the ravines at the time of the battle. Later, as survivors reflected on the lines of fire, some of them concluded that the French had "cast an entrenchment across the road before our army." [214] Actually, Nature built the defences. When Braddock's column had been caught in motion, strung out along a woods road, twelve feet in width, he was trapped. His troops were in hopeless confusion and incapable of maneuvering or even of forming to charge. If any hope of escape remained after Gage and St. Clair fell back on Burton, it was that of getting the guns and wagons back across

---

[209] The original reads *notre*.

[210] Relation depuis le Départ des Trouppes de Québec, *loc. cit.*

[211] The Indians who had been seen by Gage doubtless reported the first crossing. Beaujeu's haste on the march would indicate that he wished to flush his prey on the river bank or close to it (Sargent, *op. cit.*, 225); but concerning this there is no positive contemporary record. Beaujeu was killed; none of his companions seems to have filed a report.

[212] Cf. 2 *Frontier Forts of Western Penn.*, 64.

[213] The best-known description is in 16 Hazard's *His. Reg.*, 97, but the accompanying narrative of the battle will not be found trustworthy.

[214] H. Alricks to Governor Morris, July 22, 1754; 2 *Penn. Arch.*, 383. Cf. Morris to Governor Shirley, 6 *Penn. Col. Rec.*, 496.

the river quickly and then of having the infantry break in the same direction. That probably was impossible.[215]

In general summary, then, it may be said that part of the contemporary criticism of Braddock was unjust, some of it well-founded and some of it, on review, subject to change of emphasis. The colonials' zeal and ignorance of their own resources led them to promise more in the way of transportation than they could deliver. Braddock was not delayed on this account more than a fortnight beyond the time the weather permitted an advance. Nor was he deprived of superiority of force on the day of battle because of lack of wagons. At the same time, shortage of transportation compelled Braddock to take risks and would have made it impossible for him, as the roads then were, to establish advance bases even if he had planned to do so. Other fundamental factors in Braddock's defeat were the absence of Indian help, which was in a small way only his fault; his unfamiliarity with distance and difficulties; and his unshakable faith in British troops and tactics. On the field itself, his approach was overconfident, with the result that his foe skillfully made the most of the nature of the ground and turned a meeting engagement into an overwhelming surprise attack. The wonder was not that Braddock's men ran but that they stood as long as they did.

Washington's responsibility at the time of the débâcle was limited by his position. As a voluntary aide-de-camp, he had no troops under his command. According to the strict letter of military usage, he had discharged his full duty when he had delivered the General's orders and had set an example of courage and of diligence in action. Any analysis that goes beyond this would exaggerate his position and his obligations. There remains the moral question whether he did all he should have done in making his experience available to Braddock. Obviously, the three matters that related most directly to the lessons George had learned in 1754 were, first, the employment of pack horses instead of wagons; second, the necessity of fighting the French Indians in their own way, and, third, the wisdom or unwisdom of making the final advance with a part only of the small army, in light order.

The first of these three matters, involving the delay and inadequacy of transportation, has been shown to have been the subject of much

[215] In Sargent, *op. cit.*, 225, is a detailed statement of the tactics and maneuver Braddock might theoretically have employed to repulse the enemy and to extricate himself. In the confusion that existed, no troops could be expected to do what Sargent prescribed.

angry recrimination during the early stages of the campaign. Through all of this, the record of Washington had been consistent and explicit. As early as June 14, it will be remembered, he had written his brother John Augustine: ". . . the difficulties arising in our march from having a number of wagons will, I fear, prove insurmountable unless some scheme can be fallen upon to retrench the wagons and increase the number of bat horses, which is what I recommended at first, and, I believe, is now found to be the most salutary means of transporting our provisions and stores to Ohio." [216] To that view he held in full appreciation of the problems of transportation.[217]

In warning Braddock that frontier warfare called for changed tactics, George had of necessity been discreet. He had protested freely and warmly when Braddock had blamed all the provincials for the dereliction of a few contractors and public men; [218] but on so delicate and sacred a subject as the tactics of the regular military establishment of Great Britain, a young colonial guest in the "family" of the commanding General had of course to be careful and scarcely could have hoped for a hearing had he been vigorously outspoken. Years afterward, with much care and deliberate underlining, Washington was to explain how he had employed every "proper occasion" to tell Braddock and the other officers as fully as he should that the French and the Indians had to be fought in their own way.[219] Washington was to add: ". . . so prepossessed were [the British officers] in favor of *regularity* and *discipline,* and in such contempt were *these people held,* that the admonition was suggested in vain." [220] All that could be done in this, George believed he had done.

Concerning the third matter of his larger responsibility, the decision to use an advance force, George never said so in plain words, but manifestly he believed that the choice was between getting to Fort DuQuesne with part of the army or not getting there at all before the French were reenforced heavily. At first, as of May 14, he thought the contemplated English advances farther northward, on Lake Ontario and at Crown Point, would prevent large additions to the garrison of the main French outpost on the Ohio; [221] but later on, vague intelligence reports convinced him, as he put it, that "we shall have more

---

216 1 *G. W.,* 140
218 See 1 *G. W.,* 133 and *supra,* p. 48.
217 See *ibid.,* 142, 145.
219 His words are quoted *supra,* p. 57.
220 29 *G. W.,* 41–42. In this quotation, the punctuation is somewhat radically revised to make the meaning clear.
221 1 *G. W.,* 125.

to do than go up the hills to come down again." [222] By June 7 he was
satisfied "we shall not take possession of Fort DuQuesne so quietly as
was imagined." [223] When he advised, about June 16, that the force be
divided and the advanced column be hurried forward, he had reasoned
that low water between Lake Erie and Venango would delay the dispatch of reenforcements to the Ohio,[224] and that if Braddock moved
forward rapidly, the British could reach the fort before the French
were strengthened substantially. Were Braddock to advance slowly, the
French would be more numerous when he arrived.

In the greater part of this argument, George was correct. The French
garrison at Fort DuQuesne during the winter of 1754–55 apparently had
been 465 regulars and Canadians and approximately 100 French Indians. As early as March 6, 1755, a detachment of fifty-one officers and
men had gone to Fort Frontenac to get six cannon for delivery to the
Ohio. After that, beginning April 23, detachments were sent forward
to a total of 540 by May 6. Later in May, four mixed detachments, ag-
gregating slightly over 100 French, Canadians and Indians, were started.
Villiers was dispatched with 200 men to destroy any buildings at
Oswego and then to proceed to the Ohio. By no means all these men
were destined for Fort DuQuesne. They were intended "for all posts
on the Ohio," [225] though Vaudreuil extravagantly calculated that about
1600 men, Indians included, would be available when the English
reached the forks.[226] Had it not been for the very condition on which
George based his recommendation to Braddock for a rapid advance, the
French certainly would have had at Fort DuQuesne approximately 817
white soldiers, 170 French Indians and an undeterminable number of
savages from the Ohio.[227] The low water made it necessary to employ,
as Vaudreuil wrote, "the major part of [the] men in making journeys
to and fro for the purpose of transporting those provisions and muni-
tions which cannot even then reach [the Ohio] because of the delay at
Presq'ile portage and the lowness of the water in the River au Boeuf." [228]

Young Washington, therefore, was not greatly at fault in his advice
to Braddock: Reenforcements were not actually delayed in reaching the
Ohio, but, because of the low water, most of them had to be employed
in bringing up provisions and supplies. A proper question in this con-

222 1 G. W., 134.   223 Ibid., 137.
224 Ibid., 143, and supra, p. 52.
225 DuQuesne to the Ministry, June 25, 1755; Can. Arch., C. ii, A 100, p. 10–15, Cor. Gen.
226 Vaudreuil to Machault, July 24, 1755; 10 Col. Docs. N.Y., 307, cited in 6 Gipson, 88.
227 DuQuesne to Ministry, loc. cit.   228 Vaudreuil to Machault, loc. cit.

nection is: If George had not advised that the force be divided, would Braddock, by slower approaches with his entire force, have won the battle he lost with part of his men? Apart from the matter of French reenforcement, was it a mistake to advance with 1450 men instead of using approximately 2200? Nine times in ten the answer would be that so long as an army is not unwieldy, the greater the superiority of force, the less the loss. In the battle of the Monongahela, it scarcely could have been so if the same mistakes of overconfidence had been made. Orme was of opinion that division of force and of supplies saved more than it cost. He wrote Keppel: "It was extremely happy the General had made this disposition, for as the provision was taken [by the French in the battle], we must have starved or fallen into the enemy's hands, and the addition of numbers could not have served us as the panic was so general." [229] That probably was a correct estimate. It is difficult to see how additional troops, handled as was the smaller force, could have served any other purpose than to add to confusion and to casualties. The fate of the whole would have been that of the part.

George, then, was correct in urging pack animals, though shortage of transport was not decisive. He did all that a volunteer young aide-de-camp could do in warning his seniors concerning the dangerous tactics of their forest foe. In advising Braddock to divide the army and to hasten forward with a small, light column, George was incorrect in some of his reasoning; but Braddock's acceptance of George's plan did not give him inferiority of force on the day of battle; nor, probably, would rejection by Braddock of the advice of Washington, and the consequent employment of the entire army, have changed the outcome.

George's military conscience was clear.

[229] Letter of July 18; P.R.O., C.O. 5: p. 43–46.

CHAPTER VI

WASHINGTON PONDERS THE "HONOR" OF SERVICE
(Aug. 1–Sept. 3, 1755)

AT THE TIME, George was not of mind nor of mood to consider Braddock's strategy. The nearer realities of fatigue and humiliation absorbed the young Virginian. Defeat on the Monongahela by an inferior force was so disgraceful, "so scandalous," as he phrased it, "that I hate to have it mentioned." [1] He felt that those held responsible for the disaster would be censured, and he resented particularly the notorious dispatch that Innes had dashed off, "without having any better confirmation of the truth than an affrighted wagoner's story." [2] Old resentments rose again; George's military experience seemed to be a succession of unregarded sacrifices: "I was employed to go a journey in the winter (when I believe few or none would have undertaken it) and what did I get by it? My expenses borne! I then was appointed with trifling pay to conduct a handful of men to the Ohio. What did I get by this? Why, after putting myself to a considerable expense by equipping and providing necessaries for the campaign, I went out, was soundly beaten, lost them all—came in, and had my commission taken from me or, in other words, my command reduced, under pretence of an order from home." [3] He had in honesty to admit that he had gone voluntarily with Braddock, and that he could not hold the Colony liable for the loss of his horses and belongings, but, he insisted, "I have been on the losing order ever since I entered the service . . ." [4]

He would not have it so another time! Never would he engage on the same terms. He did not expect to profit; he had resolved he would not lose. [5] Command must be his, "something certain," [6] and under conditions he would himself impose. [7] Even then, if he reentered the

[1] To Augustine Washington, Aug. 2, 1755; 1 *G. W.*, 157.
[2] To Robert Jackson, Aug. 2, 1755; 1 *G. W.*, 155.
[3] To Augustine Washington, Aug. 2, 1755; 1 *G. W.*, 157.
[4] *Ibid.*   [5] *Ibid.*, 156, 157.
[6] To Warner Lewis, Aug. 14, 1755; 1 *G. W.*, 160.
[7] *Ibid.*, 160–61.

service, he suspected he would lose such reputation as he had won,[8] because he did not believe an offensive possible without an artillery train.[9] It might be practicable to build a few small forts for the storage of provisions;[10] but after the losses the frontier farmers had sustained of wagons and of teams, a long time would be required to accumulate sufficient transportation to carry food and supplies over the mountains.[11]

Every obstacle anticipated by Washington was rendered worse by an incredible succession of events. After Dunbar retreated to Fort Cumberland, Governor Dinwiddie had not been willing to believe that the army had lost all offensive power. On July 26, Dinwiddie asked Dunbar: "Are you not able, after a proper refreshment of your men, to make a second attempt to recover the loss we have sustained?" In a long letter the Governor listed the resources left at Dunbar's disposal, and then he reminded the commander that the four months immediately ahead were the best of the year for military operations. The French, he reasoned, would reduce force on the Ohio in order to increase their troops on the Lakes.[12] "Why cannot we recover the train in the same manner as the enemy took them? . . . Recover the train of artillery and the honor of the British forces. If you cannot attack their fort in form, you may be able to besiege them, and by preventing any supplies of provisions, starve them out . . ."[13] In support of his argument for an offensive, the Governor explained: "You must still have remaining upwards of 1600 men, and I have called the Assembly of this Dominion to meet [August 5] when I think I can promise you a reenforcement of at least 400 men."[14]

This appeal, which of course required the approval of Shirley as acting Commander-in-Chief, Dinwiddie sent express to Dunbar. The Colonel received it August 1, at Fort Cumberland, whither Governor Sharpe of Maryland had gone as soon as possible after receipt of the news of the disaster on the Monongahela. As Sharpe was still there when Dinwiddie's letter arrived, Dunbar invited him to attend a council of war[15] to which the paper from Dinwiddie was read. Following

---

[8] *Ibid.*, 162.

[9] To Augustine Washington, Aug. 2, 1755; 1 *G. W.*, 157.

[10] *Ibid.* 157.   [11] To Warner Lewis, Aug. 14, 1755; 1 *G. W.*, 162.

[12] 2 *Din.*, 118–19. Dinwiddie elaborated this in a letter to Gov. William Shirley, July 29, 1755 (2 *Shirley*, 212).

[13] Letter of July 26, 1755; 2 *Din.*, 118–19.

[14] *Ibid.* In a letter of July 29, 1755, to Governor Shirley, acting Commander-in-Chief of the British forces, Dinwiddie's language was: "Our Assembly meets next Tuesday, when I have no doubt of their qualifying me to reenforce [Dunbar] with 4 or 500 men if you approve of my plan," i.e., the plan submitted to Dunbar (2 *Shirley*, 212).

[15] 1 *Sharpe*, 266.

that, Dunbar reviewed his situation: All the artillery of the expedition except four six-pounders and four cohorns had been lost; officers, men and equipage were lacking; the troops were dispirited; above all, Dunbar had no money with which to meet the cost of another expedition. Because of these conditions, both Dunbar and Sharpe considered a westward advance impractical and they tacitly declined Dinwiddie's proposal. Sharpe subsequently wrote his Virginia colleague: "I believe the other members, as I did myself, apprehended your meaning in general to be that if the particular modes of reducing Fort DuQuesne land and proceed to Philadelphia.[17] Sharpe had been prepared for this. . . . specified [in your letter] could not be followed, any other step should be taken whereby the enemy might be most offended and His Majesty's service best advanced."[16]

With no argument and no consideration of alternatives, Colonel Dunbar then had the council of war approve a resolution, formulated in advance, which recommended that the troops leave Fort Cumber- because he had learned on his arrival at Fort Cumberland that the officers had been told to make ready for the road.[18] Dinwiddie had heard of no such plan and when he received the letter in which Dunbar acquainted him with the decision,[19] he could not believe what he read. Soon he had the details of Dunbar's march, via Winchester. The Colonel left on August 2, the day after the council,[20] and took with him the uninjured survivors of Braddock's force, the three Independent Companies, one of which he had said he would leave at the fort,[21] and such guns and artillerists as had been saved from the débâcle—a total of 1516 men of all arms."[22] Dunbar even required the remnant of the Virginia Troop of light horse to escort him to Winchester.[23] "He ap- pears," said Dinwiddie wrathfully, "to have determined to leave our frontiers as defenceless as possible."[24] The three Independent Com- panies, the Governor protested, had been sent him to protect Western Virginia and had been under his command: Dunbar had no authority whatsoever for carrying them to Philadelphia—to go into "winter quar-

[16] Letter of Sept. 2, 1755; 1 *Sharpe*, 278.

[17] 1 *Sharpe*, 264–65.

[18] *Ibid.*

[19] In 2 *Din.*, 139, reference is made to the receipt of this letter, but the text has not been found.

[20] 2 *Din.*, 164.   [21] 2 *Din.*, 223; cf. *ibid.*, 139.

[22] P.R.O., C.O. 5: 16, f. 355. Dinwiddie concluded that Dunbar carried off four six-pounders and four cohorns, but he was in doubt concerning the fate of the cannon that had not been lost on the field of Braddock's defeat (2 *Din.*, 173, 206, 209).

[23] 2 *Din.*, 223.   [24] 2 *Din.*, 170.

ters" in the middle of August! [25] As Dinwiddie saw it, the British had opened an easy road of French advance from the Ohio to the Virginia frontier and then had left that road to be defended by the surviving provincial troops and 400 sick and wounded regulars at Fort Cumberland.[26] "I must confess," Dinwiddie wrote Sharpe, "the whole conduct of Colonel Dunbar appears to me monstrous." [27]

The worst seemed to be in prospect when Indians appeared in Maryland and on the northwestern frontier of Virginia and began to murder isolated families. At the moment, all that Dinwiddie could do for the protection of the farmers was to organize five temporary Companies of rangers [28] and to call out militiamen. In an early movement to supply ammunition to a detachment, one of the most valuable leaders of Augusta County, Col. James Patton, rode incautiously from a convoy to visit friends and fell victim to marauding savages.[29] Elsewhere in Augusta, the settlers abandoned their homes, fled eastward and refused to assemble in any number for common defence.[30] Large parts of Frederick and Hampshire were almost without defenders. Lord Fairfax, the County Lieutenant, was completely ineffective in dealing with reluctant militiamen. In denouncing them, Dinwiddie was forced to tell his Lordship, "They appear to be under no command." [31]

It was manifest from the hour the General Assembly met on the 5th of August that what was left of the Virginia Regiment must be augmented, equipped and assigned the task of dealing with the savages and with any French who might descend on the frontier. This prospect of course aroused George's interest and led him to consider a journey to Williamsburg, but he was discouraged by his continued physical weakness and by his conviction that he could not get a new command on terms he would care to accept.[32] In that mood he abandoned the

---

[25] 2 *Din.*, 170, 193, 209; Dinwiddie to Innes, Aug. 25, 1755; *Sparks Transcripts*, No. 55, VSL. For Dinwiddie's efforts to get Shirley to countermand Dunbar's movement and for Governor Morris's action to continue the march to Philadelphia, see 2 *Shirley*, 211 ff, with C. H. Lincoln's valuable notes, and 6 *Penn. Col. Rec.*, 563–64.

[26] 2 *Din.*, 139, 147 ff, 170.

[27] *Ibid.*, 170.

[28] 2 *Din.*, 177, 179. For the appearance of the savages, see 3 *Penn. Mag.*, 22 and *Va. Gazette*, Oct. 10, 1755.

[29] *Gentleman's Mag.*, Sept. 1755, p. 475. For Patton, who died without male issue, see 1 *Din.*, 8 n; 2 *Din.*, 152. Cf. *Preston MSS*, Wis. HS. (microfilm VSL), v. 1, Apr. 24, 1742; v. 2, Oct. 25, 1743; 2 *W. Va. Mag.*, 7; 1 *C* 249.

[30] 2 *Din.*, 155. The Governor seems to have developed a special grudge against the Augusta militia.

[31] Letter of Aug. 14, 1755; 2 *Din.*, 155. The one bright spot in Virginia was Lunenburg County, where planters had raised a fund to pay a Company of fifty men for six months. See 2 *Din.*, 164.

[32] Letter to Warner Lewis, Aug. 14, 1755; 1 *G. W.*, 160.

idea of visiting the capital during the session of the General Assembly,[33] and he began to devote such energies as he possessed to his private affairs and to the musters he was expected to hold as District Adjutant. He felt he would be strong enough by the end of August to look after Fairfax and nearby Prince William. For service in seven other Counties he undertook to bargain with Colin Campbell at a figure of £40.[34]

As August days slipped by and the complete exposure of the frontier to attack became apparent, George underwent a slight change of mind. He still was so weak that he thought "one of the best of constitutions" impaired,[35] but he was gaining strength with consequent rise in spirits. The news that reached him from Fort Cumberland was of a sort to stir his fighting blood. When, at length, his mother wrote him one of her usual exhortations against exposing himself to danger in another expedition, he replied with patience but with less of a "never, never" than in the letters he had written earlier that month. In a single confused sentence he replied: "Honored Madam: If it is in my power to avoid going to the Ohio again, I shall, but if the command is pressed upon me by the general voice of the country, and offered on such terms as cannot be objected against, it would reflect eternal dishonor on me to refuse it; and that, I am sure, must, or ought, to give you greater cause of uneasiness than my going in an honorable command; for upon no other terms I will accept of it if I do at all; at present I have no proposals or any mention made about it, only from private hands." [36]

That "only from private hands" was exciting. The previous evening George had received by special messenger a letter from his friend and cousin, Warner Lewis, who had been in Williamsburg the previous week. Lewis had important information to communicate: The General Assembly had voted £40,000 for the defence of the Colony; there was talk of raising as many as 4000 men to repel the French and the Indians. "I believe, were you present," said Lewis, "that the greatest regard would be shown any proposals you should think proper with regard to the expedition." George's other friends, including Speaker Robinson, were said to be impatient to see him. "Everyone of my acquaintance," Lewis wrote down, "profess[es] a fondness for your having the command of the men now to be raised." [37] The Assembly probably would adjourn late in the week. If George's health permitted, he

[33] *Ibid.*
[34] 1 *G. W.*, 158–59.
[35] 1 *G. W.*, 156.
[36] Letter of Aug. 14, 1755; 1 *G. W.*, 159.
[37] In the original, this sentence is a dependent clause that begins with "as."

should come to Williamsburg by the 14th. Lewis would meet him there.[38]

The time of course was too short! Even if George sought to get there by the 16th, the day of probable adjournment, he could not do so in his enfeebled condition, and he scarcely could have done it in full vigor. All that George could attempt the evening he received the letter was to have the messenger rest while he thought carefully and deliberately of the answer he would return. The next morning—the same day on which he wrote his mother—he explained in a letter to Lewis why he had not undertaken to go to Williamsburg sooner. This gave George an opportunity of stating some of the things on which he would insist if he took command. They were, he said, matters which "ignorance and inexperience made me overlook before." Officers should be appointed with his advice and concurrence; the number of men with commission should be increased; provision should be made for a military chest.

Then George listed the circumstances that made him think the next campaign would be difficult and delayed. His pride showed itself in the confession he added: "Seeing these things . . . had no small influence upon me, as I was pretty much assured I should lose what at present constitutes the chief part of my happiness, i.e., the esteem and notice the country has been pleased to honor me with."

George's sound judgment must have admonished him that these words might be regarded by Lewis and his other friends as notice that he was resolved to stand aside. Washington therefore hastened to say: "It is possible you may infer from what I have said that my intention's is to decline at all events, but my meaning is entirely different: I was determined not to offer, because to solicit the command and at the same time to make my proposals I thought would look a little incongruous, and to carry a face of too much self-sufficiency, as if I imagined there were none others equally (if not more) capable of conducting the affair than myself. But if the command should be offered, the case is then altered, as I am at liberty to make such objections as my reason and my small experience have pointed out." [39]

In all this was self-conscious regard for the effect his future conduct of operations might have on the reputation he already had acquired; but he wrote as he felt and he remained of that state of mind: whether

---

[38] Warner Lewis to G. W., MS, Aug. n.d. [9], 1755; *Thom Collection,* Mount Vernon.
[39] 1 *G. W.,* 162–63.

he accepted or declined any command that might be offered him would depend on the terms.

He could not be sure at the moment how strong was the probability that an offer would be forthcoming. Charles Lewis, Warner's brother, wrote to ask a place in George's establishment, as if everything were settled; [40] but Philip Ludwell spoke in a letter of "another warm solicitation" of the command,[41] though the Governor seemed favorable to George. "If we could be so happy," Ludwell wrote, "as to have you here at this time, and . . . it were known you were willing to take such command, I believe it would greatly promote the success of our endeavors with the Assembly." [42]

Within a week George had more positive information: He learned that Dinwiddie was willing to name him commander of the forces that were to be raised. A continuance of military life was open to him; but if he then ascertained the details of the commission tendered him, he still was uncertain whether he would accept them.[43] He felt that, at the least, he should go to Williamsburg and hear what Dinwiddie might have to propose. That much was due George's friends, the Governor and "the country" as George usually styled Virginia.

By the 27th of August,[44] he reached the capital. He found that the General Assembly had voted him £300 to cover his loss of property in the campaign, and had done the same thing in less amount for other officers who had joined in a petition for relief, a document to which he had not subscribed.[45] On the 23rd, the Assembly had been prorogued with the thanks and commendation of the Governor,[46] but Dinwiddie

---

40 See George's reply, Aug. 14, 1755; 1 *G. W.*, 163.

41 This may have been in the interest of William Fitzhugh, who offered on the 22nd of August, in a letter to Dinwiddie, to lead a force against Fort DuQuesne, Dinwiddie replied, August 30, that he considered Fitzhugh the "most proper person for a desperate attack" (see 2 *Din.*, 180) but that the time for preparation was too short. William Byrd III and Col. James Innes likewise may have been recommended to the Governor.

42 Letter of Aug. 8, 1755; 1 *Hamilton*, 77.

43 Dinwiddie's commission and instructions to Washington are dated Aug. 14, 1755; but they are entered in the Governor's Letter Book between papers of September 2nd and 5th. (2 *Din.*, 184–87). As noted *infra*, George paid for the commission on the 3rd. In none of Dinwiddie's published correspondence prior to Sept. 6, 1755 is there mention of the appointment of Washington to the command (cf. 2 *Din.*, 191). George Mason's letter of August 21 to Washington (1 *Hamilton*, 82), makes it plain that the position had been offered George by that date. Mason then expressed the hope that the young Colonel would "find the new regulations of our military affairs agreeable" to George's wishes. The inference from all this is that the commission was drafted August 14 but was not issued until the Governor had conferred with George.

44 The exact date has not been established. George was en route August 24 and on the 27th was in the chair of the French barber in Williamsburg (*Ledger A*, folio 23).

45 6 *H* 528; 15 *V* 251.

46 *Journ. H. B.*, 1752–58, p. 314–15.

himself continued in profound dejection.[47] Along with the news of
massacre on the frontier, he had dark reports of the situation on Wills
Creek. After Dunbar had marched away from Fort Cumberland, provincials had begun to desert because, as Dinwiddie explained, they
thought "they were left by the regulars to be destroyed by the barbarous enemy."[48] As many as ten or twelve men had slipped away
during a single day.[49] The Governor estimated that the Virginians and
Marylanders had numbered 200 or 250 at the date of Dunbar's departure.[50] Dinwiddie had no accurate later figures, but by September 6
he was to doubt whether as many as 100 effectives remained at the fort
to resist attack and to guard the supplies.[51]

There were no arms for the men who were to recruit these shadowy
ranks. That was the second dark fact added to the grim situation the
French and Indians had created. In the magazine at Williamsburg, the
Governor previously had approximately 1700 reserve muskets, but he
had sent these northward, on order, to equip the New Yorkers and the
Jerseymen who were to share in the operations against Niagara and
Crown Point.[52] They were poor weapons, of the worst Dutch manufacture, with weak locks and some with hammers that had not been
steeled,[53] but they had been better, obviously, than no muskets at all.
Now, when volunteers were found, weapons must be found also, and
powder and shot besides. The magazine was empty.[54]

In struggling with all these difficulties, Dinwiddie increasingly was
disposed to blame Dunbar for the worst of them.[55] Soon the Governor
was to convince himself that his provisional tender to Dunbar of 400
or 500 recruits, subject to the approval of General Shirley and of the
General Assembly, had been a firm offer. The acceptance of it, Dinwiddie ere long was telling his friends, would have made possible an
offensive of some sort beyond the mountains.[56] Now that this was im-

47 Cf. Dinwiddie, Aug. 7, 1755: "I never was so much dejected" (2 *Din.*, 145).

48 Dinwiddie to Henry Fox. Aug. 20, 1755; 2 *Din.*, 164. When Washington wrote his
memoranda for Humphreys in October, 1786, Washington was under the impression that he
had brought Dinwiddie the first news of what had happened at Fort Cumberland and elsewhere on the northwestern frontier (29 *G. W.*, 46); but the records show plainly that Dinwiddie's information, as of August 27, was measurably complete.

49 2 *Din.*, 172.   50 2 *Din.*, 164, 193.   51 2 *Din.*, 191, 193.

52 2 *Din.*, 163, 182. Dinwiddie may not have been accurate in giving the number of these
arms.

53 Peter Schuyler to William Shirley, Sept. 20, 1755; 2 *Shirley*, 277.

54 2 *Din.*, loc. cit.

55 Cf. Dinwiddie to James Abercromby, July 24, 1756: "All our misfortunes are owing to
Colonel Dunbar" (2 *Din.*, 467).

56 The development of Dinwiddie's *idée fixe* on this subject may be traced in 2 *Din.*, 118–19,
169, 223. Apparently the Governor never was aware of discrepancy in his statements on this
subject.

possible, the Governor was hoping to prevail on Maryland and Pennsylvania to join Virginia in building beyond the Alleghenies a fort that could be a base of future operations.[57]

Still more was the Governor intent on executing the new military laws the General Assembly of Virginia had enacted at the session concluded a few days before George's arrival in Williamsburg. Two of these statutes had been designed to cure defects in the militia laws; [58] a third had levied taxes for defence of the Colony and for the pay of troops.[59] All three of these acts built as many stumbling blocks as they cleared away, but this was not apparent immediately.

Largest discussion and first labor were centred on the law to provide funds for keeping an armed force continuously on the frontier. In the drafting of this measure, the hopes of Warner Lewis and others for a force of 4000 had been overridden. Fiscal caution and the rivalry of members had compromised on provision of 1200 men only, which figure was to include three Companies of previously authorized rangers and a contingent of fifty men for the garrison of Fort Cumberland.[60] This meant that approximately 1000 men had to be recruited by volunteering or by a draft of unmarried militiamen, or by both methods.

Before George had reached Williamsburg, Dinwiddie had issued commissions to Captains of most of the sixteen Companies that were to be formed into a Regiment. Some of the surviving Captains of Washington's former Regiment had been continued in commission; other young Virginians who had been confident of their ability in recruiting had been named Captain, Lieutenant or Ensign. Some of these new officers already had come to Williamsburg or were on their way there to receive instructions.[61]

Discovery of this must have been a great disappointment to George. When he had written Warner Lewis of the conditions under which he might accept command, he had put first "having the officers in some measure appointed with *my* advice, and with my concurrence." He had argued for this on the traditional grounds of responsible command and, in particular, because officers often were detached and were afforded opportunities of misbehavior in the type of fighting that had to

---

57 2 *Din.*, 171. Cf. *ibid.*, 207 for one of Dinwiddie's numerous statements that Dunbar could and should have built such a fort after Braddock's defeat. The original of this letter of Sept. 20, 1755, to Horatio Sharpe is among the *Emmett MSS*, 13445, in NYPL. Dinwiddie had soon to abandon this plan because the Assemblies of the other Colonies did not look with favor on it (*ibid.*, and 1 *Sharpe*, 290).

58 6 *H* 530–34, 544–50.   59 6 *H* 521.
60 6 *H* 525.   61 2 *Din.*, 185; 1 *G. W.*, 165, 198.

prevail on the frontier. "Should not [the appointment of officers] be left," George had asked, "to a man whose powers and, what is dearer, whose honor depends upon their good examples?" [62]

These arguments must have been in Washington's mind when, at the proper time and doubtless with becoming formality, Dinwiddie offered him the command of the greatly enlarged Regiment. In advance or in subsequent negotiation, the Governor met the other conditions George had imposed—that he have a military chest and two needed assistants, one an aide-de-camp and the other a secretary. If Commissary Charles Dick resigned, as he had indicated he would, Colonel Washington would be free to name his successor. [63] Finally, there was a new distinction: George would not only be in charge of the Regiment but also "commander of all the forces that now are or may be employed in the country's service." [64] Everything was offered, in short, except that which George considered most essential, a voice in the selection of his subordinate officers.

Would Colonel Washington accept? With all thanks to the Governor for the compliment paid him, he would *not*. He did not believe, in the existing conditions, that he could serve without losing the honor he had won. To that decision he would adhere.

Apparently Dinwiddie was not prepared for George's refusal. Nor did Washington's other friends in Williamsburg expect him to decline, in spite of all that he had said in his letter to Warner Lewis. Together, the Governor and those at the capital who had the largest measure of the Colonel's respect united in trying to persuade him to change his mind. [65] George continued to see more of risk than of gain, more of difficulty than of advantage, in the position offered him. He held fast to what he had told Augustine—"I am always ready and always willing, to do my country any service I am capable of, but never upon the terms I have done." [66] In the face of all the arguments the Governor advanced, George continued to believe acceptance would cost him what, as he had said to Warner Lewis, "constitutes the chief part of my happiness, i.e., the esteem and notice the country has been pleased to honor me with." [67]

[62] 1 *G. W.*, 161–62.   [63] 2 *Din.*, 185–86.
[64] *Ibid.*, 185.
[65] It is entirely possible that during these negotiations the draft of the commission was revised to meet Washington's demands. Dinwiddie may have made a new promise, which he subsequently fulfilled without particular enthusiasm (2 *Din.*, 224), to solicit for George the King's commission.
[66] 1 *G. W.*, 156.   [67] *Ibid.*, 162 and *supra*, p. 108.

The Scotch Governor was not to be downed. He argued, he exhorted; doubtless he called in all nearby members of House and of Council who might influence the young officer so anxious to preserve his reputation. At length, he probably offered a compromise: As he had named the Captains, George might select the field officers.[68] This meant much, not only as the vindication of a principle but also because it assured George the continuing service of Adam Stephen and of Andrew Lewis, whom he had tested. Probably, also, at some stage of the negotiations, and without the Governor's knowledge, members of the committee charged with the expenditure of funds made a financial proposal that appealed to Washington: he could have pay of 30 shillings a day, £100 yearly for his table, an allowance for batmen and a commission of 2 per cent on all funds he handled.[69] When all the considerations were weighed, George concluded that if he stood to lose reputation by assuming a difficult command, he might lose still more in public esteem by persistent refusal. His final judgment was written down, about a year and a half later, for the information of another commander: "I have long been satisfied of the impossibility of continuing in this service, without loss of honor. Indeed, I was fully convinced of it before I accepted the command the second time (seeing the cloudy prospect that stood before me;) and did for this reason reject the offer, (until I was ashamed any longer to refuse), not caring to expose my character to public censure. But the solicitations of the country overcame my objections, and induced me to accept it." [70]

Once he said "Yes," Aug. 13, 1755, all his energies were given to his new duties. He issued recruiting orders promptly to the officers in

[68] This seems almost certain, but the only direct evidence is in the statement of Washington to Andrew Lewis, Sept. 6, 1755 (1 G. W., 167), that "the country . . . were kind enough to allow me the liberty of appointing my field officers."

[69] First mention of this in Washington's extant correspondence, under date of Apr. 29, 1757 (2 G. W., 34), may be interpreted to indicate that this financial arrangement was then of comparatively recent date; but in his Ledger A, folio 45, a credit of £814, as of May 1, 1757, covers £40,709, which is a larger amount than he would have handled in a period of one year. The sum would appear to be about as much as he would have disbursed in approximately twenty or twenty-one months. A caveat is in order. The fact is not established beyond challenge. An entry on the same folio of Ledger A shows that he drew £100 per annum for his "table," that is, for the cost of his food, from Aug. 13, 1755. It is not certain, though it is reasonable to assume, that this arrangement dated from the time he accepted command and was not a post-dated grant of funds. Washington stated in April, 1757, of the financial arrangement as a whole, "The committee first gave it, and the Assembly afterwards allowed it as a recompense for my services and the extraordinary trouble and confinement I should meet with . . ." (2 G. W., 34).

[70] Letter to Lord Loudoun, [January n.d.], 1757; 2 G. W., 17. In 1786, Washington wrote in the third person that "a very enlarged and dignified commission, to command all the troops now raised, or to be raised in the colony, was given to him [in 1755] with very extensive powers, and blank commissions to appoint all new officers" (29 G. W., 46); but in this he demonstrably had a lapse of memory.

Williamsburg and set their rendezvous.[71]   Then he paid the Governor's clerk the stout fee of £2, 12*s* 9*d* for his commission, settled his bill at Doncastle's, and left on the 3rd of September with a small amount of public funds to resume active duty.[72]

Commander-in-Chief . . . twenty-three and a half years old.

[71] 1 *G. W.*, 163; *Va. Gazette*, Sept 5, 1755.
[72] *Ledger A*, folio 23.

CHAPTER VII

First Discouragements of a New Command

(Sept. 4–Oct. 7, 1755)

THE NEW COMMANDER-IN-CHIEF found trouble at the first town he reached after he left Williamsburg with his fresh commission. When he arrived in Fredericksburg on the 5th of September, he learned that as volunteers had not been forthcoming, some vagrants had been drafted.[1] These unwilling recruits had protested so violently that it had been necessary to lock them in the county jail to prevent their desertion. This action, in turn, had incensed friends of the prisoners, who, with little ado, had broken into the building, had released the mutineers, and had defied the militia officers.[2]

A more ominous beginning to the campaign for new troops George scarcely could have experienced. It convinced him that drafted men would be worthless as soldiers, unless they were under strong officers, who would have the weapon of positive and punitive law. Love of country would not of itself induce the average young man to volunteer to meet the savage on the frontier. To be sure that force would effect what patriotism would not, George dispatched an express to Fort Dinwiddie, Augusta County, for Maj. Andrew Lewis, then in charge of that part of the frontier.[3] Lewis, as Washington knew, had the firmness and the vigor to control the men who would rendezvous at Fredericksburg voluntarily or under compulsion. The Major accordingly was directed to come to Fredericksburg and to assume command there. Then he was to instruct the men in the new platoon exercises, and to train them in shooting at targets—an essential of preparation for the grim gamble of hitting or being hit by the Indian who some day in the woods beyond Wills Creek might show his hideous face and his leveled gun barrel for an instant.[4]

---

[1] This was done under the act, passed at the session of the General Assembly in October, 1754, "for raising levies and recruits to serve in the present expedition against the French, on the Ohio" (6 H 438).

[2] 1 G. W., 174; the date of George's arrival is apparent from a reference in *ibid.*, 168.

[3] Capt. Peter Hog was directed to relieve Lewis. See 1 *Hamilton*, 94, and *infra*, p. 120.

[4] Cf. 1 G. W., 167–68, 170–71; 304 *Papers of G. W.*, 181; LC.

Besides encountering mutiny and public resistance in his first discharge of his new duties, George had another disillusioning experience in Fredericksburg. Just before he had set out from Williamsburg, he had been told by Governor Dinwiddie that it would be well, if possible, to retain in the public service Charles Dick, who had threatened to cancel an agreement he had made to purchase and to deliver provisions and supplies at Wills Creek.[5] Dick was a man of means, a trader as well as a planter. He had seen a chance of profit in army contracts and on occasion had shown enterprise; but, like many other individuals who had served the colonial government, he had found it easier to get a contract than the pay for it. George vainly undertook to see Dick the evening he reached Fredericksburg, and on the morning of September 6, he talked fully with him. Dick was in a yes-and-no state of mind. He would be glad to serve the country, of course, but he did not know whether he could. The Colony owed him for provisions he had purchased; he had not been able to collect what was due him. It might even be necessary for him to stop the delivery of supplies already in hand unless he was compensated for what he had laid out.

George could not believe Dick really meant what he said, but it was necessary to ascertain whether the agent really would act. Carefully, therefore, George prepared a formal letter of inquiry and had it delivered to the merchant. The reply, none too gracious, was that Dick might continue to discharge his official duties if "thoroughly satisfied by a certain agreement," but that he could not go to Williamsburg to settle his accounts and at the same time perform the tasks assigned him.[6] George advanced Dick as much as he could spare of the sum placed at his disposal by the Governor, and he doubtless encouraged the merchant to remain active. More than that he could not accomplish.[7] Nor was Washington satisfied that Dick's heart was in the enterprise. Thus, the old difficulty of provisioning the Army, the old problem of getting food to the frontier, was rising once more. It seemed to be one of the essential things that somehow never were well done.[8]

From these discouragements at Fredericksburg, George rode on to Alexandria[9] where he found a situation scarcely better. John Carlyle could furnish some clothing for the survivors of the Virginia Regiment,

[5] 1 *Ford*, 187.

[6] Charles Dick to Washington, Sept. 6, 1755; 1 *Hamilton*, 87–88.

[7] 1 *G. W.*, 169, 173–74.

[8] See 1 *G. W.*, 171; 1 *Ford*, 187.

[9] He left, apparently, on September 7 and probably arrived on the 9th. He certainly was there on the 11th (cf. 1 *G. W.*, 171).

who were ragged and soon would be barefooted. Contracts might be let for shoes and shirts and stockings.[10] That was the extent of the good news. The rest was bad. At the regular muster of the militia,[11] an effort had been made to get recruits for the Regiment. Not a man stepped forward.[12] The new officers who so confidently had accepted commissions to raise troops began to express apprehension of failure as soon as they had the coveted papers in their hands.[13] Recruiting, George had to admit, undoubtedly would be slow. All else might be delayed, too, because in so feeble an organization he had to do many things that should have been the care of others. "The making of contracts myself is foreign to my duty," he wrote Speaker Robinson after he had been at the task a few days, "neither have I the time; and to see the service suffer will give me infinite uneasiness, as I would gladly conduct everything, as far as I am capable, with life and spirit, which never can be done without a fund of money is lodged in camp for defraying the contingent charges." [14] No men, no discipline, no clothing, no organization, no money—within a week after Washington had taken command, more and more of the story of the spring of 1754 was repeating itself.

By the 12th of September, George had done all he could to get the affairs of the Regiment in decent, temporary order at Alexandria. Then, by the familiar route,[15] he hurried to Winchester, where he paused on the 14th and 15th long enough only to prepare a few orders [16] and to direct that accounting be made of supplies.[17] On the 17th he reached Wills Creek and Fort Cumberland. This badly placed defence was not yet complete and still was exposed to easy rifle-fire from woods that had been left standing across the creek.[18] The garrison consisted of the survivors of the Virginia Regiment, together with the Maryland Company of Capt. John Dagworthy, who had been with Braddock's army. Governor Sharpe mistakenly had assumed that not more than 100 provincials had remained after the departure of Dunbar's men, be-

---

10 1 *G. W.*, 172. Clothing issued in March, 1754, had been scandalously poor (2 *G. W.*, 15).

11 This had been set for August 31–September 1, and presumably had been held at that time, when George was in Williamsburg. See 1 *G. W.*, 158.

12 At least this seems the logical inference from George's statement, "[recruiting] was attempted at the general muster in this county, without success" (1 *G. W.*, 174).

13 *Ibid.*

14 Letter of Sept. 11, 1755; 1 *Ford*, 187–88.

15 Cf. *Ledger* A, folio 23, for his expenditures at Coleman's Ordinary, located at the crossing of Sugarland Run (*Landmarks*, 481).

16 1 *G. W.*, 175.

17 G. W. to John Johns, Sept. 15, 1755; 3 03 *G. W. Papers*, 196, LC.

18 See 1 *G. W.*, 181.

cause, as he understood it, the Virginians, North Carolinians and Marylanders had discovered they could not be tried under the mutiny act when they no longer were attached to regulars.[19] Many had deserted, but 198 rank and file remained.[20] Approximately a dozen officers from the three provinces were present; more than fifty were absent, most of them on recruiting duty.[21] George's companion of 1754, Adam Stephen, was nominally in command [22] and probably was the best choice among available officers, but he did not have the men under a firm discipline. One of the privates, John Stewart, was selling liquor almost openly to the other soldiers and was maintaining around him constantly what Washington denounced promptly as a "disorderly and riotous assembly." Drunkenness was common. Soldiers in Flanders, soon to be described by an irreverent British cleric, could not outswear the provincials of Fort Cumberland.[23]

These were conditions with which George knew how to deal. On the day of his arrival he formally announced that "George Washington, Esquire, is by His Honor Governor Dinwiddie, appointed Colonel of the Virginia Regiment, and Commander-in-Chief of all the forces that now are, and shall be raised &c, &c." [24] He proceeded to list the other officers of the Virginia Regiment and to prescribe a uniform for them. Every officer was required, also, to "provide himself with a common soldier's dress for detachments and duty in the woods." [25] More immediately—and in strict conformity with the example set by Braddock— "all officers of the Virginia Regiment" were directed "to attend Colonel Washington at 5 o'clock this evening . . ."

Doubtless they came, all of them. Adam Stephen, reappointed Lieutenant Colonel, was the most conspicuous. Capt. Charles Mercer appeared officially for the first time as aide-de-camp, a position to which his seniority among company commanders entitled him.[26] Absent, but already rated high, was Maj. Andrew Lewis, who had been named

---

19 1 *Sharpe*, 284. Officers did not accept this interpretation but they could do nothing to punish desertion because they lacked authority to convene a general court martial (*Ibid*).

20 As the term "rank and file" was used in the returns, it included all those who stood in line with the firelock in their hands. Corporals would be counted; Sergeants would not be.

21 This MS return, covering all the provincial troops, is signed by Adam Stephen and is dated Sept. 27, 1755, ten days after Washington arrived. Officers probably came and went during that interval, but it is not believed the rank and file changed substantially in number (2 *Washington Papers*, unpaged, LC).

22 For the status of Col. James Innes, see *infra*, p. 134, 174.

23 Cf. the orders of Sept. 19, 1755 in 1 *G. W.*, 179.

24 1 *G. W.*, 175.   25 1 *G. W.*, 176.

26 1 *G. W.*, 176, 208. John Kirkpatrick, a young businessman of Alexandria, was to be the Colonel's secretary (*ibid.*, 208), but the date of his appointment is not known, except that it was prior to October 11.

and later reappointed to the vacancy created by George Muse's resignation. Lewis was then 35, tall, powerful and silent, happier in the woods, stalking Indians, than ever he could be in camp, a businessman of much shrewdness and of soundness in his judgment of the savages.

With his usual amiability in his treatment of officers, Washington set his subordinates to their duties. After that, orders were issued in steady flow—to deal with drunkenness, swearing and obscene language, to terminate John Stewart's traffic in liquor, to complete the work on the fort and, in general, to improve discipline. With equal energy George set out to procure the support of Andrew Montour, in the hope that the strange Indian leader would bring to Fort Cumberland friendly savages who might be organized into a separate command. Rumor had it that Montour was at Great Island, on the Holston River, with 300 natives.[27] George admitted that his letter to Montour savored "a little of flattery" but he consoled himself with the reflection that this was "justifiable on such occasions." [28]

The most serious early task before the new Commander-in-Chief was, of course, that of recruiting. George organized two new Companies among the Virginians at Fort Cumberland, doubtless as an incentive to filling the ranks, and he ordered additional officers to seek volunteers in the back country of Maryland and of Pennsylvania and at public places not previously visited.[29] Much had to be left to the ingenuity of the Captain, the Lieutenant or the Ensign sent in quest of men.

Washington turned next to an unfamiliar duty. During the confusing days that followed Braddock's defeat, Indian raids had been murderous in Augusta County, South and Southwest of that part of Frederick County in which Lord Fairfax resided.[30] Governor Dinwiddie had undertaken to cope with these attacks by calling out the militia and by organizing Companies of rangers.[31] The militia, it will be remembered, had proved worse than useless, but there seemed to be a prospect that the rangers might afford some protection if they were stationed in small forts suitably spaced, fifteen or twenty miles apart, in the country most exposed to incursion. One such stockade, named after the Governor,

---

[27] 1 *G. W.*, 180, 182, 206, *infra*, p. 126. The place later was called "Big Island."
[28] 1 *G. W.*, 206.
[29] 1 *G. W.*, 178; 303 *Papers of G. W.*, 203–04, LC.
[30] Cf. 2 *Din.*, 132.
[31] As typical, note the entry in *Journ. H.B.*, 1752–58, p. 292, concerning recruitment of rangers in Frederick and Hampshire. See also *supra*, p. 106.

had been erected on Jackson's River, West Augusta.[32] This place, a number of "private forts" erected by the settlers themselves, the discipline of the ranger companies—in a word, responsibility for protection of the entire region—was primarily Washington's. He thought it necessary to see for himself a situation that had alarmed the settlers on a long stretch of rich, newly-developed country.[33]

As soon, therefore, as he had put affairs in order at Fort Cumberland, Washington started up the Shenandoah Valley, past Winchester, and beyond the farthest point he had reached in his surveys of Augusta lands in 1749.[34] By swift, hard riding he reached Augusta Court House on the 22nd of September [35] and turned westward. Soon he was on a new trail, scarcely yet fit to be termed a road, that led over the Allegheny Mountains. As he crossed the narrow valleys or looked down into the coves where the settlers had built their huts, he found nearly all the farms deserted. Fear of the Indians had driven eastward the families that had been subduing the wilderness.[36]

By the 25th, George reached Fort Dinwiddie. He found that Capt. Peter Hog had arrived five days previously, in accordance with orders George had issued at Fredericksburg, when the Colonel had decided that Andrew Lewis was needed on the Rappahannock.[37] Hog, consequently, could not be blamed for the condition which George found, but it was bad enough to dishearten. Troops who had erected the stockade had answered so many alarms that they had not had time to build the bastions. Tools and tents and arms were few. Ammunition was low. There was no salt for fresh meat, even, and no prospect of pickling any beef for winter unless salt, tools and implements were sent. Hog explained that Lewis had made contracts for about twenty-four days' provisions but that the Major, on his departure, had not been able to leave any money with which to buy food for later delivery.[38]

Far worse were conditions to the westward. On the Greenbrier River, about twenty miles over the mountains, the approach of Indian raiders late in August had caused settlers to hurry to a feeble little fort erected

[32] In terms of modern geography, the site is about five miles West of Warm Springs, Bath County, Virginia (1 *G. W.*, 182 n and Koontz, *Frontier*, 118). Koontz noted that the fort was known, also, at different periods, as Warwick's, Hog's, and Byrd's Fort.

[33] 1 *G. W.*, 206.

[34] The date of his departure from Fort Cumberland is not known, but his orders of September 20 to Lieut. Col. Adam Stephen indicate that he was then preparing to leave the Potomac.

[35] *Ledger A,* folio 23. It may be permissible to note again that Augusta Court House is the present-day Staunton.

[36] See Dinwiddie's proclamation, *Va. Gazette*, Sept. 26, 1755.

[37] See *supra*, p. 115, n. 3, and 304 *Papers of G. W.*, LC.

[38] 1 *Hamilton*, 92–94.

by neighbors. About sixty persons, armed and unarmed, adult and children, had been huddling there when the Indians descended on them. Through cowardice, panic or negligence, the defenders in four days lost thirteen and perhaps more before the savages made off on receipt of news that Andrew Lewis was near at hand with his troops. The savages, in addition, took perhaps a dozen lives, carried off two girls, burned eleven houses and slaughtered or drove with them horses and cattle estimated to number 500.[39]

In reporting this gruesome affair, Captain Hog maintained that the corn crops of the fleeing or murdered settlers were the best in the Colony. Left unharvested, this corn would subsist marauding Indians all winter. To assure the retreat of the redmen, a sufficient force must be assembled at Fort Dinwiddie to assist in gathering the crop and placing it beyond the reach of the Indians. Moreover, said Hog, if the settlers were to be prevailed upon to return, new forts must be built upon the western rivers.[40]

George listened and gave a few orders and suggestions. Hog was authorized to make contracts for grain and meat, and to draw on the commissary. Salt doubtless could be forwarded and meat prepared for the winter if Hog could find coopers to make casks for storing the beef. The bastions must be constructed, barracks built and timber within musket shot removed. That was all that could be done.[41] Reenforcement was contingent on recruiting and on the need of men elsewhere on the frontier.[42] The security of the fort depended on continued vigilance and on daily discipline. For the time being, the Greenbrier must be disregarded. In this conviction, Washington said farewell and started back toward Augusta Court House as soon as he could.[43] Thence he shaped his journey to Alexandria, where he drew rein on the 2nd of October.[44]

This hurried tour of inspection dramatized the impossibility of

---

[39] *Va. Gazette*, Sept. 19, 1755: *Md. Gazette*, Sept. 25, Oct. 2, 1755. In the *Preston Papers*, Wis. HS, is a "register" of those killed at Greenbrier. This covers twenty names, exclusive of those of the two captured Landis[?] girls; but some of those killed at the fort may be included. Dinwiddie almost certainly was misinformed when he was told that the Indians did not number a fourth as many as were at the fort (2 *Din.*, 218; cf. *ibid.*, 198).

[40] 1 *Hamilton*, 93–94. This is a letter written by Hog to Washington before the Captain knew his superior officer was about to pay him a visit. It is safe to assume Stephen repeated in person the arguments he had made in his written communication.

[41] 1 *G. W.*, 182–84.

[42] Governor Dinwiddie considered the danger past in Augusta. See *Va. Gazette*, Sept. 26, 1755.

[43] He was at the Court House on the 26th (*Ledger A*, folio 23).

[44] *Ibid.*, and 1 *G. W.*, 184.

George's task in defending a long, long frontier with a handful of men. Recruiting had to be expedited by every legitimate device. Lives depended on it. So did the security of the Colony, and, in part, the recovery of the Ohio. That was the first lesson of the journey to Fort Dinwiddie. The second was the realization that George could not rely, as yet, on the existing commissary system to supply the remote forces. Whatever Charles Dick might or might not do in the future, he was not sending food to the outposts and he was not accumulating beef on the hoof. George had to act where others failed. It was another responsibility outside his commission, but it was one he could not and would not evade. In Augusta, where he found many fine cattle, he contracted for 620 beeves to be delivered at Fort Cumberland by November 1.[45] Incidentally, in that same Garden of Eden for livestock, he found two horses, a gray and a black, which appealed so much to his trained eye that he bargained for them at £11, 5s 9d each, colonial currency in hand.[46]

Taken together, the experience of his first month in command convinced George that he had a multitude of perplexities some of which must be discussed with the Governor and with the Burgesses' committee on expenditures. Washington lingered at Alexandria only long enough to issue some essential orders,[47] and then he took the road again, this time for Fredericksburg, on the first stage of the ride of 160 miles to the colonial capital.

At Alexandria, he had found only twenty-five recruits, a most disappointing number.[48] On arrival in Fredericksburg he counted a less discouraging total of about seventy;[49] but he learned that some of the officers had not reported at that rendezvous by the designated date, October 1. One new Captain, Carter Harrison, had neither arrived nor sent any explanation of his delay.[50]

To begin at once the training of the few who were ready to put on the coat of the Colony, George decided to dispatch sixty or more of them to Fort Cumberland.[51] Painstakingly he drafted the orders and then, in the role of Quartermaster, made the best provision he could for the recruits' clothing and shoes.[52] Unemployed officers were told to

---

[45] 1 G. W., 206.   [46] Ledger A, folio 23.

[47] 1 G. W., 184-85, and instructions of Oct. 3, 1755, to Capt. David Bell at Winchester to march the recruits at that rendezvous to Fort Cumberland, 303 Papers of G. W., 212, LC.

[48] 1 G. W., 189.   [49] Ibid.

[50] Ibid., with the mistaken note that this was Henry Harrison. The correct name is given ibid., 176.

[51] 1 G. W., 186; 303 Papers of G. W., 215, 218-20, LC.

[52] 303 Papers of G. W., 215, LC.

scatter in search of additional men and to report again on the 20th of October.[53]

It could have been in no exalted mood that George discharged these drab, time-consuming duties and, on the 7th of October, started for Williamsburg, via Todd's Ordinary. He might have been comforted had he known then that Landon Carter that same day was writing him: "Tread the same path that you first cut out to your own glory, that your country may in the end feel the good effects that she promises herself from your singular virtues and fortune."[54] On that "same path" George had proceeded as far as the familiar and friendly plantation of his friend Col. John Baylor on the 7th[55] when an express pushed up the lane with a dispatch from Col. Adam Stephen. This bore date of Winchester, October 4, and began as follows:

Sir: Matters are in the most deplorable situation at Fort Cumberland. Our communication with the inhabitants is cut off. By the best judges of Indian affairs it's thought there are at least 150 Indians about us. They divided into small parties, have cut off the settlement of Patterson Creek [and] Potomac, above Cresaps, and the people on Town Creek about four miles below his house. They go about and commit their outrages at all hours of the day, and nothing is to be seen or heard of, but desolation and murder heightened with all barbarous circumstances, and unheard of instances of cruelty. They spare the lives of the young women, and carry them away to gratify the brutal passions of lawless savages. The smoke of the burning plantations darken the day, and hide the neighboring mountains from our sight.[56]

There followed some information about matters of less importance at the fort and then: "Unless relief is sent to the back inhabitants immediately none will stay on this side Monocasy or Winchester." George read on: "The magazine is secured and a well set about on the fort. So many alarms prevented the work going on with dispatch. I

---

[53] 1 *G. W.*, 186.　　　　[54] 1 *Hamilton*, 108.

[55] For Baylor, see 6 *V* 197, 305.

[56] 1 *Hamilton*, 103. The punctuation of the reference to the settlements cut off by the Indians is erratic and uncertain, but is believed to have been revised correctly here. Washington subsequently stated that Colonel Stephen gave personally a "worse account than he related in his letter" (1 *G. W.*, 188)—a remark that raises a question whether the dispatch received by Washington at Colonel Baylor's on the 7th was the one Stephen wrote at Winchester on the 4th, or a message of earlier date. It could not have been that of September 25 or that of September 27, as printed in 1 *Hamilton*, 95–97 and 99–100, because neither of these described a situation serious enough to justify the action Washington took. The possibility exists, of course, that Stephen penned and dispatched a letter subsequent to that of September 27 and prior to that of October 4; but there is no reason why a paper sent express from Winchester on the 4th should not have reached Colonel Baylor's late on the 7th.

have reason to believe Captain Dagworthy will look upon himself as commanding officer after you have joined the troops." [57]

That last sentence [58] may or may not have stuck in Washington's mind at the moment. The rest of the letter shaped instant duty: he must report the situation to the Governor; he must tell His Honor he could not proceed to Williamsburg; and he must turn his horse around and go back full speed to Fredericksburg and thence to the frontier.

[57] 1 *Hamilton*, 103–04.
[58] It is not the last sentence of the letter.

CHAPTER VIII

The Hard Schooling of Stubborn Minds
(October, 1755–January, 1756)

WITHIN LESS than three hours after he wrote the Governor from Colonel Baylor's house, George rode into Fredericksburg[1] where, by the best of luck, he met Adam Stephen, who, like himself, had started for Williamsburg.[2] The Lieutenant Colonel had an even worse situation to report than he had described in the letter George had received earlier that day.[3] George Washington listened, put the new information in focus, and decided to let Stephen continue to the capital, in the hope of procuring funds there,[4] while he drafted orders on the basis of what Stephen told him. Lord Fairfax, said Stephen, already had called out the militia of Frederick County, with a very poor response,[5] and had appealed to Prince William County for 100 men.[6] George wrote immediately to urge that these reenforcements proceed on horseback.[7] He requested, also, that a militia Troop of light horse be put on the alert in Fairfax.[8] All the recruits still in Fredericksburg were ordered to start for Winchester as soon as practicable;[9] Captain Thomas Waggener was directed to hasten to Alexandria, to assemble the recruits at that rendezvous, and to march them to the Valley town. He and the officers advancing from Fredericksburg were to take with them all the ammunition they could collect.[10] George believed that if these movements were made promptly they would give him sufficient strength to drive off the Indians, who, he told himself, might retreat before he could strike them.[11]

Orders dispatched,[12] Washington left Fredericksburg late on the 8th with impressed horses, and hurried to the Shenandoah. Early on the

---

[1] 1 *G. W.*, 188.
[2] Apparently to settle his accounts. Stephen never explained, so far as is known, why he left Winchester when so critical a situation prevailed.
[3] 1 *G. W.*, 188. [4] *Ibid.*, 189.
[5] 1 *Hamilton*, 105. [6] 1 *G. W.*, 188, 191, 201.
[7] 1 *G. W.*, 192. [8] 1 *G. W.*, 188, 192.
[9] 1 *G. W.*, 190. [10] 1 *G. W.*, 190–91.
[11] 1 *G. W.*, 188, 190. [12] 1 *G. W.*, 188, 193.

10th, he paused at Greenway Court, but, as Lord Fairfax was away from home,[13] he proceeded to Winchester. When he arrived there about noon,[14] he found a madhouse. Farmers were coming into the town as a refuge from the enemy and were bringing with them their wagons and most valued belongings; residents were leaving Winchester in the belief that the only road to safety was the one over the Blue Ridge.[15] An armorer who had been engaged to repair muskets was setting off with his vehicles and had to be halted forcibly and returned to his task.[16] Col. Thomas Martin, Lord Fairfax's nephew, was on duty but had the grimmest of reports to make: Frederick militiamen who had been mustered by Lord Fairfax and sent to the South Branch of the Potomac were preparing to quit their station.[17] It did not seem probable that more than twenty or twenty-five additional men from the County would report. The others had sent word that they intended to die with their families.[18] Two ranger Companies were said to be under siege in stockades on the South Branch.[19] There was no armed force in Winchester other than a few recruits for Capt. David Bell's rangers.[20] This handful of raw newcomers had no ammunition.[21]

Except at Fort Necessity and on the dreadful day of Braddock's defeat, George never had encountered so much confusion and panic. Facing it, he kept his head and went instantly to work. First of all, as nobody had any information about the Indians, George hired two scouts and gave them dispatches to the officers who commanded the stockades on the South Branch. George doubted whether these men would reach their destination, because one of the men had all the marks of a greater love of his cups than of his country; but as they were the only persons available, George engaged them and started them on their way to notify the officers what to do and where to go if forced to evacuate the posts.[22] Next he sent for ammunition.[23] Another letter was addressed to Montour and one to Gist, who was offered a commission as Captain of a Company of scouts. Gist was urged to do what he could to prevail on the influential Montour to join Washington. "Never," George wrote, "were Indians more wanted than at this

[13] 1 G. W., 200.   [14] 1 G. W., 193, 200.
[15] 1 G. W., 200, 206; Dulany's News Letter, 3 Penn. Mag., 22.
[16] 1 G. W., 201.   [17] 1 G. W., 194, 205.
[18] 1 G. W., 201.   [19] Ibid.
[20] 1 G. W., 204, 205.
[21] Charles Mercer to John Carlyle, Oct. 10, 1755; 303 Papers of G. W.; LC.
[22] 1 G. W., 194, 196.
[23] 1 G. W., 196, and Mercer to Carlyle, supra.

time." [24] The appeal to Montour was written most deliberately in spite of all the stresses of the crowded hours, and it was phrased as if it were addressed to some British comrade whose help was needed in an emergency.

Montour, of course, could not arrive for days if, indeed, he came at all. Until the recruits from Alexandria and Fredericksburg were at hand, the only reenforcements George could hope to receive from any quarter would be the militia of Frederick and the adjoining Counties, on whom Lord Fairfax had called before George had heard of the Indian attack. Washington sharply admonished the Captain of the wavering, disaffected Company on the South Branch not to retreat beyond Edwards's. The officers must undertake, moreover, to prevail on the settlers to remove their families to a place of safety and themselves to join in driving off the Indians. "They will be under no disagreeable command," George assured the militiaman, William Vance, "nor will they be confined an hour longer than this particular service requires, should that be only one week." [25] Washington wrote, probably, with more confidence than he actually had in the militia. What faith he had in them waned before the day was out: From the whole of the County of Frederick there arrived only twenty militiamen, who were brought in by a diligent Captain, John Harden.[26]

These men and the few recruits of the detached ranger Companies were all on whom George could count. Earlier in the day, when he had heard that Harden's militia were on their way and that others were expected, he had hoped that something should be undertaken.[27] After the reenforcement proved so small, George had to wait.

As the morning and the afternoon of the 11th brought nothing sensational, George had time in which to write the Governor of his situation and of his inability, under existing statutes, to compel the obedience of the militia. Less than six weeks after his appointment to command, he was so discouraged that he talked of quitting. He told Dinwiddie: "Unless the Assembly will enact a law to enforce the military law in all its parts . . . I must with great regret decline the honor that has been so generously intended me; and for this only reason I do it—the foreknowledge I have of failing in every point

24 1 G. W., 198–99.
25 Letter of Oct. 10, 1755; 1 G. W., 194–95. This information was included in the dispatches sent by the two messengers.
26 Harden thought he could count on seventeen, but he mustered twenty, or else three others came on their own account. See 1 G. W., 196, 205.
27 1 G. W., 196.

that might justly be expected from a person invested with full power to exert his authority. I see the growing insolence of the soldiers, the indolence and inactivity of the officers, who are sensible how confined their punishments are, in regard to what they ought to be. In fine, I can plainly see that under our present establishment, we shall become a nuisance, an insupportable charge to our country, and never answer any one expectation of the Assembly." [28]

George did not finish the letter that day. About 8 P.M., a fatigued and fear-stricken express staggered into Winchester with a report that Indians had reached a plantation about twelve miles from the town and that the settlers in that neighborhood were fleeing. George strengthened the guard and sent two scouts to ascertain how numerous the Indians were and in what direction they were moving. Trivial as his force was numerically, Washington felt he had to use it and he accordingly directed Captain Harden to prepare to move out early the next morning and to scour the woods.[29] In all these measures of safety, from the very hour of arrival, George had been encountering stubborn opposition. "No orders are obeyed," he reported, "but what a party of soldiers, or my own drawn sword enforces." It was not passive or even silently sullen antagonism. Threats were made that the people would "blow out the brains" of the young Colonel who presumed to send them to die under the war-hatchet of scalping parties.[30]

On the morning of the 12th of October, before Harden could start the march, another express dashed into Winchester, "ten times more terrified," as George judged him, than the man who had arrived the previous evening.[31] The newcomer reported that the Indians were within four miles of town. He himself had heard constant firing and the shrieks of those whom the savages were murdering. George could not endure that. His two scouts had not returned; he knew nothing of the position of the Indians; but if they were that close to Winchester, scalping and killing, he would meet them. Forty-one men answered his call, twenty-two of them recruits for the rangers and the remaining nineteen militiamen.

With these, George proceeded in the direction of the firing. A march of an hour or two brought him and his party where, at irregular intervals, they could hear the sound of firearms. Soon, yells were audible. Quickly George deployed his little force, closed in, and found

[28] 1 G. W., 202.
[30] 1 G. W., 201.
[29] 1 G. W., 200, 202.
[31] 1 G. W., 203.

the aggressors—three members of the Troop of Virginia light horse, drunk and carousing. The shots had come from their pistols; the shouts had been their defiance of the world and all its law. George put them under arrest, of course, and marched them back to Winchester. There he met the scouts who had been dispatched to the scene of the earlier disturbance. The trouble in that neighborhood, they told George, had been nothing more than the movements of a Negro and a mulatto, who had been sent out to look for cattle.

That was not the only fiasco. Colonel Martin had arrived in Winchester while Washington and his force of forty-two were on their march. In the belief that reenforcements might be needed at any moment, Martin had sent orders to the Captain of a Company of militia, resident no great distance from the town, to muster his men and bring them up. Word came back that the Captain said his wife, his family and his corn were at stake, as were the crops and households of his men: they could not answer the call. "These circumstances," George wrote the Governor, "are related only to show what a panic prevails among the people, how much they are alarmed at the most usual and customary cries, and yet how impossible it is to get them to act in any respect for their common safety." [32]

The next day, October 13, brought a change for the better. Although George received information that the militia on the South Branch still intended to leave their post, reports from the scouts sent out on the 10th were to the effect that the Indians were leaving that stream. Besides, Maj. Andrew Lewis with the recruits from Fredericksburg was within one day's march of Winchester. Captain Waggener arrived on the morning of the 13th with thirty men after a rapid three-day advance from Alexandria. He "informed me," George recorded, "that it was with difficulty he passed the [Blue] Ridge for the crowds of people who were flying as if every minute was death." Waggener had done his utmost to stop them, but to no purpose. They believed that Winchester was in flames.[33] George, in his turn, now sent out expresses on all the roads to assure the fleeing farmers that the danger was past,[34] and he posted public notice that the Indians were believed to have returned home and that the frontiers soon would be well guarded.[35] Recruits were started for the Potomac; preparations were made, also, for Washington himself to proceed to Fort Cumberland to strengthen its

[32] 1 G. W., 203–04.
[34] 1 G. W., 206.
[33] 1 G. W., 205–06.
[35] 1 G. W., 208–09.

garrison.[36] As it was, mischief enough had been done! An estimated 150 Indians had killed about seventy persons.

The whole alarm had been a bitter, disillusioning experience that accorded with all that had preceded it in George's brief new period of command. Militia seemed indifferent at best and, at worst, cowardly and disdainful of law and discipline. George felt, in addition, that some of his officers were inexcusably and intolerably slothful. Nobody seemed to care whether the most important duty was performed on time or performed at all. Charles Dick had sent no flour to Winchester and had made no provision for feeding the recruits at Fredericksburg, though given notice of their needs. "I must beg," George wrote the Governor, almost despairingly, "that if Mr. Dick will not act, some person may be appointed that will." [37] Capt. Carter Harrison still was absent and unreporting. Another Captain, one Lieutenant and two Ensigns had failed to send a single individual to the rendezvous on the designated date. Indignantly George wrote: "If these practices are allowed of, we might as well quit altogether, for no duty can ever be carried on, if there is not the greatest punctuality observed, one thing always depending so immediately upon another." [38] As for volunteers, they were enlisted so slowly—only six in Alexandria and nine in Prince William, for example [39]—that the time in which officers were to seek new men had to be extended to November 15.[40] Of the few recruits sent to the frontier, a considerable number usually got drunk on the road. When Andrew Lewis started from Fredericksburg on the 10th of October, so many of his eighty men were intoxicated that he could cover only seven miles the first day.[41]

So it was with one perplexity after another. George felt that his threat to resign was wholly justified on the ground that he could get no support; but along with his desire to abandon what seemed a hopeless enterprise, he was firm in his resolution to do, meanwhile, whatever the situation demanded of him. Under authorization given when Washington accepted his commission, Capt. George Mercer worked diligently as his aide and John Kirkpatrick of Alexandria as his clerk; but his own duties were burdensome every hour of the day and often during anxious nights. There was more than military self-righteousness in his assurance to the Governor: "I have been obliged to do duties quite

36 *Ibid.*, 205.
37 1 *G. W.*, 207.
38 *Ibid.*
39 1 *Hamilton*, 111.
40 1 *G. W.*, 212.
41 Journal of Capt. Charles Lewis, 4 *W. Va. His. Mag.*, 109–10.

foreign from my own, but that I shall never hesitate about when others do and the good of the service requires the contrary." [42]

The most vexing of these duties, when the time came to carry re-enforcements to Fort Cumberland, was the old one of procuring wagons. Reconciled to staying longer in Winchester than he originally had intended,[43] George had hoped to start on the 16th of October,[44] but he met disappointment in finding vehicles.[45] He finally had to authorize impressment [46] and he did not get under way until the 21st or 22nd.[47] At 9 P.M., on the 22nd, he and Capt. George Mercer stopped on the Little Cacapon, where they found Maj. Andrew Lewis's command encamped at the end of its third day's march from Winchester toward Fort Cumberland. Here, for the first time, George saw what the panic of the settlers meant in misery and in loss of property. As far as could be observed, nobody had been killed on the farm, but all the residents had been impelled to flee. The place was deserted. Corn and oats were in the barn; livestock was wandering about; the household effects remained in place. Had pestilence swept the plantation, it could not have been more desolate.[48] In a knowledge that these conditions were a temptation, George issued a strict order under which any soldier who pillaged or plundered anywhere would receive 500 lashes.[49]

The next morning, October 23, Washington rode on with Mercer under a protesting sky. Rain and snow swept the countryside and slowed the march. Nine miles only could be covered before a halt had to be made at a farm. Although the residents must have realized that troops were security, they were surly and ill-natured.[50] Another wet day made the march of October 24 disagreeable, but progress was somewhat better.[51] In his haste, George probably did not pause beyond Patterson's Creek to see the horrifying evidence of what the Indians had done there. On one tract, the master had been killed, the house sacked and burned, and the cornfield overrun. After neighbors had buried the settler, wolves had dug up the body and had devoured part of it. Washington may have shuddered at this. He certainly would

[42] 1 G. W., 206. For first references to the appointment of Mercer and Kirkpatrick, see *supra*, p. 118, n. 26.
[43] 1 G. W., 199. [44] 1 G. W., 215.
[45] 1 G. W., 216. [46] 1 G. W., 218.
[47] If he waited until the morning of the 22nd, he covered thirty-eight miles that day by 9 P.M., a long but not an impossible ride.
[48] Charles Lewis's journal, *op. cit.*, 111.
[49] The order was issued on the 23rd (1 G. W., 222).
[50] Lewis's journal, *loc. cit.* [51] *Ibid.*

have been angered had he known that even in the midst of this woe, two of the women attending Lewis's little column had been caught in the act of robbing deserted houses. These creatures could not be punished under the orders George had issued for the troops, but they were ducked promptly by direction of Major Lewis.[52]

Wills Creek was reached on the 25th of October.[53] Fort Cumberland was intact, though Indians had come almost within gunshot during their raid.[54] Families of nearby settlements had been victims of a cruelty that made survivors blanch. On one farm, the unburied bodies of a scalped woman, a small boy and a young man lay near a burned house.[55] A party of soldiers, sent out to harvest a fabulous crop of corn, subsequently found three persons who had been brained with stakes, scalped and thrown into a fire that had half consumed the victims.[56] George promptly directed that in all such instances the grain be saved.[57] Where the owners survived but feared to go into the fields because Indians might surprise them, the Colonel provided guards to stand by while the farmers pulled the corn.[58] Adequate security, in Washington's opinion, depended on four things—the recruiting of the Regiment to full strength, the strengthening of the militia law, a successful effort to procure the services of friendly Indians,[59] and the erection of a few small, temporary forts to serve as cover for rangers and their provisions.[60]

Superlative judgment was not required to see these needs; utmost pains might not suffice to overcome the unreasoning indifference of the people or the inclination of the Indians to sell their services over and over again to the highest bidder. George had no personal access to any savages except those who might rally to Monakatoocha or to Montour; but when it came to adding white men to his ranks, he could and did prod negligent officers. Those who had as yet no regular duties on the frontier were told to go on recruiting tours at once and to appear at the assigned rendezvous by December 1 or face court-martial. These orders were made sternly emphatic for one Captain whose disregard of orders angered the Colonel.[61]

In settling such of these matters as had to be arranged North of the

---

52 Lewis's journal, loc. cit.
53 Possibly during the evening of the 24th (cf. ibid).
54 Cf. Stephen in 1 Hamilton, 99.   55 Lewis's journal, op. cit., 115.
56 Lewis's journal, op. cit., 115.   57 1 G. W., 225.
58 Ibid.   59 1 G. W., 215, 217, 225.
60 1 G. W., 222.
61 1 G. W., 227, 229, orders issued on the return to Winchester.

Potomac, Washington moved fast because he had encountered a stubborn man who had raised a contentious issue. John Dagworthy,[62] Captain of the Maryland Company at Fort Cumberland, belonged to a family that had resided as early as 1716 in Middlesex County, New Jersey, and thereafter in Somerset and Hunterdon Counties, also.[63] He was said to have been "in good business" when, in 1746, he received a royal commission as Captain and undertook to raise a Company to share in the Canadian expedition. A desire to remain in the regular army [64] sharpened Dagworthy's industry. He worked hard and, first and last, had 103 officers and men in his Company,[65] which was one of five raised in New Jersey and placed on transports in September, 1746, for a rendezvous at Albany.[66] These troops saw no active service. After they were brought home and discharged, Dagworthy and another Captain went to England, with the endorsement of the Council of New Jersey, to see if they could not continue as officers of the regular establishment.[67] They did not succeed in this ambition, but Dagworthy effected an arrangement whereby he received a sum of money in lieu of half pay or further service. Apparently, he was not required to return the document by which he had been commissioned in 1746.

Sometime after his return to America, Dagworthy removed to Maryland and bought a property in Worcester County. He was residing there when, in August, 1754, Governor Sharpe undertook to raise a Company to share in the defence of the frontier. Command of this small force was given to Dagworthy,[68] who subsequently was criticized by the auditing committee for the "very extraordinary cost" of recruiting.[69] His Company participated in Braddock's campaign, during the course of which Dagworthy asserted that his royal commission of 1746–48 still ran and therefore gave him seniority over provincial officers. Braddock had to sustain this contention and, indeed, had to admit that Dagworthy, by date of commission, outranked all except two Captains of the Regiments from England.[70]

[62] He is wrongly entered as Eli Dagworthy in the index to *Sharpe*. Eli, whose name seldom appears in the records, may have been a brother of John.

[63] The first Dagworthy appears to have been named John. He was described as an "honest, bold man" and he more than once was recommended for office. Although everything indicates that he was the father of Captain Dagworthy, no positive record has been found. See *N. J. Arch.*, 1st ser., v. 5, p. 317; v. 15, p. 98; *Penn. Gaz.*, Sept. 16, 1756; Monette, *First Settlers of Piscataway*, pt. iv, p. 540–64; *ibid.*, pt. v, p. 774.

[64] *N. J. Arch.*, 1st ser., v. 7, p. 102.

[65] *Ibid.*, v. 6, p. 425.

[66] *Penn. Gazette*, Sept. 11, 1746.

[67] *N. J. Arch.*, 1st ser., v. 7, p. 102.

[68] 1 *Sharpe*, 95.

[69] 52 *Md. Arch.*, 84–85.

[70] 1 *G. W.*, 290.

With the defeat of Braddock and the scattering of the forces, Dagworthy's contention temporarily was forgotten, but about Oct. 1, 1755, he returned to Fort Cumberland, where some thirty survivors of his Maryland Company were included in the garrison.[71] Command of the fort had been vested by Dinwiddie and then by Braddock in Col. James Innes,[72] who, on leaving the post to attend to private business in North Carolina, had assigned the command to Adam Stephen as senior officer present. Dagworthy would not have it so: as the holder of the King's commission, he insisted that he outranked Stephen and had authority to direct affairs at the fort. He did not push his argument to the point where he actually gave orders to the Virginia Regiment, but he contrived to take over the fort itself from Stephen, and he demanded and received all the honors due the commander.

There was no disposition on the part of George or of Dinwiddie to discredit Dagworthy. In his place as a Captain, he was admitted to be a "very good officer," but, as the Governor put it, "he produces his commission, by which he sets up a right to command over the field officers in the pay of this Dominion, which creates a great uneasiness among our officers and troops." [73]

Neither Dinwiddie nor Washington would admit the validity of Dagworthy's assertion of the right of command. There was a question in their minds whether his royal commission had not lapsed when he was given a flat sum on expiration of service instead of being put on half pay. However that might be decided, Dagworthy, as the Virginians saw it, would have been entitled to command if, but only if, he had been sent to Fort Cumberland by the King's order to serve where regular and provincial troops were stationed together. He had not come to the fort under orders "from home" but by direction of the Governor of Maryland. Besides, there were no regulars at the fort, joined with the provincials, to warrant any distinction between royal and colonial officers. Dagworthy, in George's eyes, was the provincial Captain of thirty Maryland soldiers—that and no more.

So firmly was Washington convinced of this, and so fully determined to maintain his seniority, that he had resolved he would surrender his commission before he would accept Dagworthy's pretensions to command. At the same time, George remembered that Braddock had

---

[71] 1 *Hamilton*, 104.
[72] In *Halkett's Orderly Book* this is entered as of June 2, 1755.
[73] Dinwiddie to Shirley, Nov. 4, 1755; 2 *Din.*, 261.

recognized Dagworthy's commission and he reasoned that on this basis he might have to accept the Captain's orders so long as he was at Fort Cumberland.[74] In the circumstances, it was desirable to leave the fort before this issue came to a test.

Another reason for finishing as speedily as possible all official business on Wills Creek was a letter from Dinwiddie concerning the imperative question of better regulation of the Virginia troops. The Governor wrote that he realized the defects of the existing military statutes and that he had called the General Assembly to meet on October 27 and to correct them. He hoped George would be in attendance to explain the need of stronger laws.[75] Washington could not possibly get to Williamsburg by the date the session opened, but he determined to go there as fast as he might, and he lost not an hour he could win from the clock. By steady work and rapid preparation of orders, the Colonel was able to leave Fort Cumberland in the early dawn of October 27, probably, and by the hardest galloping to reach Winchester on the 28th.[76] He spurred on to Neville's October 30.[77] Then on the 31st he was in Fredericksburg.[78] When he rode into Williamsburg,[79] the session of the General Assembly was well advanced.

The Governor had asked the two Houses to put the provincial troops under the "military law" but had been vague in his proposals.[80] In recommending higher rewards for the scalps of hostile Indians and stiff penalties for those who obstructed recruiting or sheltered deserters, the Governor spoke in closer understanding of actualities.[81] The House had proceeded with little delay to revise the act that imposed judicial punishment, and, on the day of George's arrival, it had settled differences with the Council and had passed the measure.[82] This new law therefore reflected Washington's views only in so far as these had been expressed to the Governor and to Speaker Robinson in the letters George previously had written.

From the first, Washington had been compelled to draw a distinction between the discipline he could impose, through punishment, on the militia and that which he could hope to maintain with the volunteers of

---

[74] The case against Dagworthy, given in numerous scattered references, was conveniently summarized by the Governor of Virginia in 2 *Din.*, 329, and by Washington in 1 *G. W.*, 290.

[75] Letter of Oct. 18, 1755; 1 *Hamilton*, 113.

[76] His orders of the 27th certainly read as if he were at Fort Cumberland; those of the 28th are dated at Winchester (1 *G. W.*, 225, 227).

[77] *Ledger A*, folio 23.

[78] 2 *G. W.*, 233.   [79] After nightfall on the 3rd of November.

[80] *Journ. H. B.*, 1752–58, p. 319–20.   [81] *Ibid.*, 320.

[82] *Journ. H. B.*, 1752–58, p. 321, 324, 326–27.

the Virginia Regiment, the light horse and the rangers.[83] In looking back on the expedition of 1754 that ended in the capitulation at Fort Necessity, Washington felt that there probably had been no law in existence under which he then could have compelled obedience and prevented desertion.[84] His weapon had been the men's ignorance. After the Virginia Regiment had joined Braddock, it was subject to British military law,[85] which bristled with threats of the death penalty. Then, from the time Dunbar marched away in August and took all the regulars with him, the Virginians were not under the general military law of Parliament. Their discovery of this had been regarded by Washington and by Dinwiddie as the chief reason for the desertions that left at Fort Cumberland nothing more than the bones of an organization.[86]

The General Assembly at its session that same month, August, 1755, had not considered separate legislation necessary to prevent desertion, and it had shaped the recruiting act primarily to encourage enlistment by the grant of immunity from civil process for debt. In the same statute the legislative body provided for the draft of unmarried men, if sufficient volunteers were not recruited within three months; [87] but this part of the law contained a ruinous proviso: any man drafted from the militia for service with the Regiment or the rangers could provide a substitute; and if he did not offer another in his place or appear in person, he could not be jailed nor could he be fined more than £10. As George wrathfully pointed out, this was equivalent to permitting a man of means to purchase exemption by paying this fine, which went, moreover, into the colonial treasury, not into a recruiting fund. If a penniless man was drafted, and was unwilling to serve, it was easy for him to run away.[88] As for desertion, even if there had been adequate penalties, the public sympathized with men who told tall tales about their mistreatment at the hands of their officers. Deserters frequently were hidden by farmers or left undisturbed by constables.[89] In those instances where deserters were apprehended and returned, George probably had no legal authority to do anything more to them than

---

[83] See G. W. to Lord Loudoun [Jan. n.d., 1757], 2 G. W., 6.

[84] A reader not interested in military organization may skip this analysis of the law and, if he so desires, may resume the general narrative *infra*, p. 138.

[85] 2 *Din.*, 251.

[86] See *supra*, p. 118. Apparently the applicable modern term *cadre* was not used in eighteenth-century British military literature.

[87] 6 H 527.

[88] 2 G. W., 9.

[89] 2 G. W., 8; *Journ. H. B.*, 1752–58, p. 320.

to lock them up and subsequently to have them whipped by order of courtmartial. He had no way of disciplining any of his Regiment otherwise than under the provisions of the revised militia act.[90]

This amended militia law of August, 1755, though better than the old statute, was weak in critical provisions. Upon conviction by courtmartial, a man could be subject to corporal punishment for desertion and incitation to mutiny. The death penalty could not be inflicted for any offence except communication with the enemy and then only after trial before the General Court of the Colony.[91] For disobedience to orders, profanity, drunkenness and the like, no soldier could be fined in excess of £5 or given more than twenty lashes for one offence.[92] Another hampering provision of the militia act, as amended in August, 1755, was that the militia could not be employed "more than five miles beyond where the inhabitants of this Colony shall be settled on the western frontiers."[93]

These, then, were the feeble terms of the law of the previous August that the General Assembly had been called to strengthen in October, 1755. As the revised bill stood when George arrived from the frontier, it provided the death penalty for mutiny, for desertion, for the refusal of an officer to obey his superior, and for any act of violence by such an officer against the person of a senior. Lesser punishment might be meted out at the discretion of the courtmartial.[94] If such a court decreed death, two-thirds of the members had to concur. Execution could not be carried out until the Governor had reviewed and approved the sentence[95]—a condition to which George objected from the first.[96] Provision was made, also, for the apprehension of deserters and for the reward of persons who captured the culprits and returned them to their command.[97]

Some of the defects of this act may have been apparent to George when he first read its terms. Others were to be brought to light by test. Foremost among the faults were three words in a stipulation, readily overlooked, that the Governor might grant a commission to a field officer "for the holding of a general court martial *within this Colony.*"[98] This meant that when Washington's troops were at Fort Cumber-

---

[90] 6 H 546, sec. v.
[92] *Ibid.*, 547–58, sec. vii.
[94] 6 H 560, sec. ii.
[96] 2 G. W., 250.
[98] *Ibid.*, 560, sec. iii. The italics are not in the original.

[91] *Ibid.*, sec. iv.
[93] *Ibid.*, 548, sec. x.
[95] *Ibid.*, 562, sec. vi.
[97] 6 H 562–63, sec. vii–ix.

land or anywhere else beyond the boundaries of Virginia, offenders could not be tried there but must be brought back into the Old Dominion.

Another serious weakness of the revised act of October, 1755, was the omission from it of any reference to large categories of offences less serious than desertion or mutiny.[99] These delinquencies remained punishable only under the militia law, which prescribed trivial penalties for them. Omitted from the law, also, was any arrangement whereby an officer could pay immediately for the return of a deserter. Finally, the law was operative for one year and no more. If hostilities continued, Governor and Commander-in-Chief would have to ask the General Assembly in the autumn of 1756 to pass a new and drastic statute. With all these imperfections, the October act "for making provision against invasions and insurrections"[100] was so much stronger than the law it replaced that Washington was encouraged. "We now have it in our power to enforce obedience," he was soon to tell Adam Stephen, "and obedience will be expected from us."[101]

Encouragement there was, also, in dealing with the second pressing matter that had brought George to Williamsburg, the pretentions of Captain Dagworthy to command over all the troops at Fort Cumberland. As soon as possible after reaching the colonial capital, George explained more fully to the Governor this revival of the issue of the seniority of royal commissions that had plagued his pride from the time Captain Mackay had refused to accept the countersign from him.[102] Dinwiddie was irritated by the fresh details. He could not see the slightest basis for Dagworthy's argument, nor could Col. William Fitzhugh, then in Williamsburg. Both men agreed that Dagworthy commanded only a provincial Company, under a Governor's commission. He should be arrested, they said, for his presumption. Even if Dagworthy's commission still was valid, he was not at Fort Cumberland, the Virginians reiterated, under any orders from the King. Both in the nature of his duties and in the circumstances existing at the fort, the Captain had no more right to assume the command than any visiting half-pay officer would have.[103] The Governor felt he must renew to his home government his request that the officers of the Vir-

99 2 G. W., 12.
100 Its full title was "An act to amend an act, entitled an act for amending an act, entitled an act for making provisions against invasions and insurrections" (6 H 559 ff).
101 Letter of Nov. 18, 1755; 1 G. W., 235.
102 See *supra*, Vol. 1, p. 389.   103 1 G. W., 262.

ginia Regiment be given the King's commissions.[104] Meantime, Dinwiddie said, he would write General Shirley and ask that the acting British commander issue brevet [105] commissions to Washington, Stephen and Lewis at the rank they held in Virginia service. This would give them a status Dagworthy could not challenge.[106] Until Shirley passed on this request, there could be no settlement of the dispute over seniority unless the Maryland officer receded from his position.

George accepted this as the sensible procedure and turned to discussion of other matters on which he asked decision. He pointed out to Colonel Corbin and to other members of the Council that it might be impossible, when the Regiment was at some remote station, to comply with a provision of the new law and to dispatch quickly to the Governor the papers in the case of a deserter found guilty and sentenced to death by a court martial. At all times, said Washington, it would be costly, troublesome and inconvenient to have to await the Governor's assent to hanging or shooting a culprit who had been condemned lawfully. The response of Corbin and the others was that this defect of the new law could be rendered harmless by the simple dispatch to Washington of death warrants signed in blank by the Governor. Neither George nor the Councillors seemed to regard this as evasion of the spirit of the act.[107]

Other troublesome matters were settled readily: George was to be allowed a military chest of £10,000; [108] servants and apprentices were not to be enlisted; [109] the Maryland and North Carolina troops at Fort Cumberland—only some fifty in the aggregate [110]—were no longer to be fed at the expense of Virginia.[111] Toward the friendly Indian tribes, the attitude of the Colony was to be generous. Dinwiddie still believed

---

104 Almost at that very time, as it chanced, Orme wrote Washington: "If you can get confirmed I shall think it very lucky you accepted of the commission[.] If you are not I think Mount Vernon would offer you more happiness" (Letter of Nov. 10, 1755; 1 *Hamilton*, 125). Dinwiddie's new appeal for the issuance of the King's commissions to the Virginia officers was in his letter of Nov. 15, 1755 to Sir Thomas Robinson (2 *Din.*, 267).

105 Misreading of Dinwiddie to Shirley, Nov. 4, 1755 and Jan. 24, 1756 (2 *Din.*, 261 and 330), made out this word to be "private," which is meaningless in the context. The correct reading is given in 1 *Hamilton*, 173, and in an extract from Dinwiddie's second letter, sent Sharpe by Shirley and printed in 1 *Sharpe*, 349.

106 The letter to Shirley bore date of November 4. See 2 *Din.*, 261. Dinwiddie's proposals for dealing with Dagworthy are here inferred from the letters the Governor wrote.

107 2 *G. W.*, 250. The records of this period show an interesting contrast between the attitude of the Council and that of the House of Burgesses toward the armed forces. In general, the Council's sympathies were with the officers, the Burgesses' with the men in the ranks.

108 Acts of the Committee of the Assembly; 2 *Papers of G. W.*; unpaged, LC.

109 1 *G. W.*, 238.   110 1 *Hamilton*, 128.

111 1 *G. W.*, 236. This was a decision of the committee in charge of expenditures. Dinwiddie approved (*Ibid*).

Governor Glen of South Carolina was responsible for the failure of the Cherokees to assist in the expedition of 1755 against Fort Du-Quesne,[112] but he continued his efforts to win their aid [113] and he soon was to send two conspicuous Virginians, Peter Randolph and William Byrd III, to negotiate a treaty with them.[114] George was in absolute accord with the Governor's view and was apprehensive that the French might undertake to win over the powerful Southern tribes if Virginia delayed.[115] This was one reason for discussion of a plan to aid the Cherokees in an expedition against the Shawnee towns.[116]

George could review these developments with reasonable hope that vigorous action would follow, though there was an unhappy renewal of bad feeling between Dinwiddie and the House of Burgesses in one matter that was not George's particular concern: The Governor and Council disagreed violently with the lower branch of the Assembly over a bill to establish a "loan office" through which paper currency might be issued to a total of £200,000, presumably on the security of needy debtors' lands. This proposal of the House was regarded by Dinwiddie as so serious a threat to the public credit that he prevailed on the Council to reject it. Then, for fear that some compromise might be reached, he dissolved the Burgesses on the 8th of November.[117] Privately, Dinwiddie explained that the lower branch intended, also, to set up a secret committee. Besides, he said, members were not attending regularly the sittings of the House; Burgesses were beginning to be "troublesome and factious," [118] and were "very mutinous and unmannerly." [119] It was best, the Governor confided, to get rid of them and to "take my chance of new members, who, I hope, will meet when called on in a body with more good temper and inclination for the public good . . ." [120] This meant new elections and, incidentally, a chance, if George so desired, to become a candidate for the House.

With hope raised and ambition perhaps stirred anew, George allowed himself a few days of pleasure in the society of Williamsburg and Yorktown. It was the second time he had been there after Braddock's defeat, but when he had come briefly to see the Governor in August,

112 2 *Din.,* 188, 212, 216–17, and, in detail, 224–25. Adam Stephen blamed the Indian trader "Capt" Richard Pearis (1 *Hamilton,* 121).

113 2 *Din.,* 270.   114 2 *Din.,* 285.

115 Cf. 1 *G. W.,* 215.

116 For the development of this plan, see *infra,* p. 202; 2 Din., 278, 296–97, 298–99 ff, and 1 *Hamilton,* 147, 149.

117 *Journ. H. B.,* 1752–58, xxiv, 328–32; 2 *Din.,* 269, 274, 277.

118 2 *Din.,* 269.

119 *Ibid.,* 274.   120 *Ibid.,* 269.

the capital was at its worst season of heat and flies and mosquitoes. Now some of the town houses of the rich planters were open; well-to-do residents who fled before "chills and fever" were back at home; Williamsburg had about it, too, the excitement that always prevailed when Burgesses and Councillors were there to converse, to entertain, to dance, to drink, to toast the ladies, and to gamble heavily with cards and dice.

George found new pleasure in the balls and assemblies, no doubt, because he was a more considerable figure on any floor. Ever since he had carried Dinwiddie's message to Fort Le Boeuf in the winter of 1753–54, he had attracted attention. Now he represented the troops whom colonial pride had exalted as the heroes of Braddock's defeat, the men who were credited with having saved British honor from the panic of the regulars. Magazines printed in England after the receipt of the news of the disaster on the Monongahela had been received in Williamsburg, along with London newspapers and letters from merchants, agents and friends. In some of these communications, as George wrote Adam Stephen a little later, "the behavior of the Virginia troops is greatly extolled and meets with public praises in all the coffee houses in London." [121] Some of these reports, to George's regret, went far beyond the facts. A London magazine, for example, told shamefaced readers that 300 Virginians—again to quote Washington's epitome for Stephen's benefit—"maintained an unequal fight against 1600 French and Indians for three hours after the regulars fled." [122]

This was embarrassing, to be sure, but if it was credited in England it might accomplish the result for which George was hoping, the early grant of King's commissions to the officers of the Virginia Regiment. [123] Meantime, there was amusement among the Virginia veterans of the Monongahela over the exaltation of their conduct and, along with it, a resolution on the part of some to justify the praise given them. Said Adam Stephen: "The accounts of our behavior is much exaggerated; we must give them credit and pay the public the balance next campaign." [124] There was no stopping the applause. By the autumn of 1756, a colonial notable was to be writing: "The Virginians . . . fought like lions and behaved with prodigious valor; they bravely stood the severest fire from the enemy; and after the flight of the

121 1 *G. W.*, 237; letter of Nov. 18, 1755.
122 *Ibid.*
123 *Ibid.*, 237.
124 Letter of Nov. 22, 1755 to Washington; 1 *Hamilton*, 129.

British regulars, brought off the wounded General, who would other-wise have fallen into the most barbarous and savage hands." [125]

Be that as it might be, a most flattering reception was accorded every-where in the autumn of 1755 to the Virginia Colonel who had been conspicuous on the field of Braddock's disgrace. George was a proper guest and prompt to return the hospitality shown him. For a ball held about the 11th of November, he purchased tickets to a total of £4, a sufficient price to cover the admission of several of his hosts and hostesses.[126]

It was close to the middle of November [127] when George bade fare-well to the Governor and to Williamsburg friends and set out for Winchester and perhaps for Fort Cumberland via Fredericksburg.[128] At the Rappahannock town, which he reached on the 16th, George re-ceived reports from Adam Stephen and others of quiet conditions on the frontiers. The greatest need, according to these letters, was a large supply of salt for pickling beef then awaiting slaughter. George rea-soned that he would do better to get the salt than to proceed in person to the Valley. He purchased what he could in Fredericksburg and then went on to Alexandria, where it was more abundant and cheaper.[129] If all went well, George told himself, he could remain near home, en-couraging recruiting, until Dinwiddie received an answer from Shirley on brevet commissions, unless, meanwhile, a vessel brought the Vir-ginians the King's notice of their admission to the regular military establishment. By waiting on the lower Potomac George, moreover, could avoid a clash of authority with Captain Dagworthy.[130]

At his new station, as in Fredericksburg,[131] Washington had un-pleasant evidence that recruiting would be slow among the older settle-ments.[132] A diligent officer, Capt. Robert Stewart, and one of his

---

[125] 1 *Hamilton*, 389; endorsed by Washington: "Written, it is supposed by Col. Richard Bland, 1756."

[126] *Ledger A,* folio 24.

[127] A reference in 2 *G. W.*, 240, suggests that Washington may have been in Williamsburg that day; he was in Fredericksburg on the 16th. See *ibid.*, 235.

[128] For his avowed intention of proceeding "immediately up," see G. W. to Adam Stephen, 1 *G. W.*, 235. The reason for doubting whether he included Fort Cumberland in "up" will appear in a later sentence.

[129] 1 *G. W.*, 240, 241–42, 245, 249.

[130] 1 *G. W.*, 235, 237. See, also, *infra,* p. 168.

[131] Washington's last known letter at Fredericksburg bears date of November 18. The first one definitely marked Alexandria was written on November 28 and indicates that George had been there the previous night (1 *G. W.*, 239, 240), but the background of the letter of November 22 to Dennis McCarty suggests at least the possibility that the writer was in Westmoreland or Fairfax, where McCarty was most apt to be recruiting.

[132] 1 *G. W.*, 236.

subordinates of the light horse, had worked for almost two weeks and had enlisted only five.[133] "There are several officers," George indignantly recorded, "who have been out six weeks and two months, without getting a man, spending their time in all the gayety of pleasurable mirth, with their relations and friends, not attempting or having a possible chance of recruiting any but those who, out of their inclination to the service, will proffer themselves." [134] One Ensign, Dennis McCarty, had gone to the other extreme and, according to the tale told George, had forcibly seized, confined and tortured several men who would not volunteer.[135] Washington sharply warned McCarty, but, for the rest, he decided to wait until the officers on recruiting duty came to Alexandria on the designated date, December 1. Then each would be assigned the men enlisted by him and by other officers of his Company, and would be told to complete the number required of him—or to surrender his commission.[136]

When December arrived and the officers obediently reported, there was another disappointment. "Yesterday," George wrote on the 3rd of December, "being the day to rendezvous here, came in ten officers, with twenty recruits, which make up the number at this place, twenty-five Great!" [137] The entire contingent brought in by these officers exceeded by one man only the recruits Christopher Gist already had sent to Fort Cumberland for his Company of scouts.[138] Washington was disgusted but not dismayed. He knew from his own struggle with the snow in December, 1753, that winter was a trusty guard of the passes of the Alleghenies. It was costly and troublesome to have recruiting so protracted but, if it were completed before the spring thaws opened the road from the Ohio, no great risk would meantime be run. In this belief, George sent out most of his recruiting officers again, under slightly changed instructions.[139] Not even reports of continued desertion from Fort Cumberland could destroy his temporary cheerfulness. He blamed the officers more than the men. "Surely," he wrote Stephen, "they do not pursue them with proper resolution, or [the deserters] might be taken." [140] George's attitude had been much the same toward a reported mutiny in Captain Hog's company at Fort Dinwiddie on account of the Colony's failure to pay the men. This, Washington wrote the responsible officer, "must be attributed entirely to your neglect,

133 1 Hamilton, 143.
135 1 G. W., 240.
137 1 G. W., 247.
139 1 G. W., 243–44.

134 1 G. W., 241.
136 1 G. W., 241.
138 1 Hamilton, 139.
140 1 G. W., 247.

as I gave you orders in my last, to go, or send to that fort, with the money for that Company." [141]

Never before had Washington been so much inclined as during the late autumn at Alexandria to leave the performance of duty to subordinates whom he was quick to rebuke. This was all the more remarkable because it was in sharpest contrast to the assurance he had given the Governor in October that he would "never hesitate" about doing duties foreign to his own, when others were reluctant.[142] Washington was changing his mind, too, about his next move. From Fredericksburg he had written Stephen that he would go to Alexandria and wait a short time in hopes of receiving the express from Shirley concerning Dagworthy's pretentions.[143] More than a week later, from the Potomac, George assured Stephen he would "come up very shortly, my stay here being only for a few days, in order to receive recruits and hurry up the stores to Winchester." [144] He stated at the time that he was awaiting the arrival of the express from Shirley.[145] Next his explanation was, "I wait here in hourly expectation of seeing a vessel from Hampton with sundries for the use of the Regiment. [As] soon as she arrives and I have sent off the contents, I shall set out for Winchester"—he did not say for Fort Cumberland also.[146]

On the 5th of December, George sat down to write the Governor for the first time since he had left Williamsburg three weeks previously. He explained that he had come to Alexandria to get salt and to procure recruits and supplies, and then, without any sort of transition, he blurted: "I have impatiently expected to hear the result of your Honor's letter to General Shirley and wish that the delays may not prove ominous. In that case, I shall not know how to act, for I can never submit to the command of Captain Dagworthy, since you have honored me with the command of the Virginia Regiment &c." [147]

George went on to discuss some vexations in supplying the troops and next, as if conscious his absence from Wills Creek might be criticized, he wrote: "As I cannot now conceive that any great danger can be apprehended at Fort Cumberland this winter, I am sensible that my constant attendance there cannot be so serviceable as riding from place to place, making the proper dispositions and seeing that all our necessaries

141 Letter of Nov. 18, 1755, to Paymaster Alexander Boyd, 1 G. W., 239.
142 The letter is in 1 G. W., 206.
143 See *supra*, p. 142.
144 1 G. W., 241.
145 *Ibid.*
146 Letter of Dec. 3, 1755; 1 G. W., 247.
147 1 G. W., 249.

are forwarded up with dispatch. I therefore think it advisable to inform your Honor of it, hoping that it will correspond with your own opinion." [148] In other words, so long as quiet prevailed and there was any risk of having to be subordinate to Dagworthy at Fort Cumberland, George could not bring himself to go there. Perhaps without being aware of it, he was inventing reasons why he should not go.

No news came from Shirley. Such information concerning Dagworthy as reached George from Fort Cumberland was an added blow to the pride of the Virginia Colonel. Adam Stephen still had not formally surrendered command of the fort or of the troops to Dagworthy, but he had not resisted with vigor the exercise of authority by the Maryland Captain. Jealousies had been aroused among idle officers at the post; factions had been formed; tales were being carried; every officer seemed ready to credit any rumor. The story to which Stephen gave most serious ear was to the effect that Dagworthy had said no troops could leave the fort unless he gave the order. In a letter to his chief in Alexandria,[149] Stephen threatened to defy this boast by sending men from Cumberland to relieve militiamen who were being disbanded on the South Branch,[150] but actually Stephen was circumspect when he might have put the issue to the test.

Like him, George's friends elsewhere were indignant that the commander of thirty Marylanders should presume to tell 500 Virginians [151] what they should and should not do. "It astonished me," wrote Speaker Robinson, "to hear that a petty officer should pretend to command the forces raised by this Colony and a fort erected at our expense." [152] More than that the Speaker could not say, except to encourage George to hope for a King's commission; but day after day passed without receipt of such a paper.

While George waited, the elections for the new House of Burgesses were held in Fairfax and in the other constituencies of Northern Virginia. Washington's own County had been represented in the previous House by John West and Gerrard Alexander.[153] At the next election, West was again a candidate; Alexander was not. George William

---

[148] 1 *G. W.*, 251. [149] 1 *Hamilton*, 145.
[150] Cf. 1 *G. W.*, 269. [151] For the number, see 2 *Din.*, 329.
[152] Letter of Dec. 16, 1775 to Washington; 1 *Hamilton*, 151. The original text reads "this colony and its a fort . . ."
[153] Hugh West, Sr. had been elected but had died prior to Aug. 30, 1754 (*Journ. H. B.*, 1752–58, p. 197). While the given name "John" is not applied to the "Mr. West" mentioned in the journal of 1755 as a successor to Hugh West, the fact that he carried to the Council the act for dividing Fairfax County (*ibid.*, 272) is almost proof-positive that he represented Fairfax after Hugh West's death, and was the same John mentioned in the next sentence of the text.

Fairfax, who had represented Frederick in 1752–55,[154] stood this time in the County that bore his name. A third candidate appeared in the person of William Ellzey.[155]

The contest, which was to be decided on the 11th of December, proved to be close and exciting. To assure the choice of their favorite, many of the electors decided to vote for one candidate only. Washington of course was the enthusiastic supporter of his friend and neighbor, George William Fairfax. Soliciting in Fairfax's behalf, Washington clashed with William Payne. Hot words passed. Payne, much smaller than Washington, struck the Colonel with a stick and felled him. Washington was not seriously hurt, and, when on his feet again, was escorted to his quarters by angry and excited friends. The Colonel of the Virginia Regiment, the Colony's most distinguished soldier, publicly knocked down in a personal encounter—surely that meant a duel. Alone in his room, Washington did what he was learning always to do when in danger of going to extremes: he got a grip on his temper and asked himself whether he or Payne was at fault. When he had fought this out, he sat down and wrote a note in which he asked Payne to meet him the next day at a specified place and hour. Payne came; the town waited. Instead of renewing the argument or demanding satisfaction, Washington kept his pride under leash and frankly apologized because, he said, he was in the wrong. Payne was as much impressed by this display of character as he was surprised to avoid a duel.[156] The impelling motive behind this apology was to be set forth, more than a year and a half later, in this avowal of one of the "principles" by which Washington was shaping his life: ". . . it is with pleasure I receive reproof, when reproof is due, because no man can be readier to accuse me than I am to acknowledge an error when I am guilty of one, nor

154 *Journ. H. B.*, 1752–58, p. vii.
155 The name sometimes has been printed erroneously as Lewis Ellzey, a different individual.
156 *McGuire*, 330; *Weems*, ed., 1918, Chap. XIV, p. 243. This is one of the Washington traditions that appears to be well founded. It was credited by McGuire, who was not uncritical. Bishop Meade (2 *op. cit.*, 165) found it still current and unadorned among Payne's descendants. All the relevant circumstances fit the story: Washington was in Alexandria; Payne participated in the election (for his family, see 29 *V* 498); his vote and that of his father are of record. The only demonstrable major error in the tradition is that Payne is said to have been a supporter of Ellzey's when, in fact, he and his father voted for John West and for West only. Minor details, of course, are inaccurate—as, for example, that Washington's troops were in Alexandria at the time. A letter from Adam Stephen to Washington, written Dec. 23, 1755, is strong confirmatory evidence. Stephen mentioned the indignation prevailing at Fort Cumberland "upon hearing you were insulted at the Fairfax election . . ." (1 *Hamilton*, 158). Perhaps an equally good reason for crediting the tradition is the fact that Washington's reported action accords absolutely with the standard of conduct he avowed in his letter to Dinwiddie, quoted in the text.

more desirous for atoning for a crime when I am guilty of one . . ." [157]

As for the elections, they brought surprises. In Fairfax, the result was exceedingly close. Twelve votes only separated John West, at the head of the poll, from William Ellzey at the bottom. George William Fairfax defeated Ellzey by two.[158] Soon Washington heard less pleasant news of the outcome in Frederick. To the previous House of Burgesses, George William Fairfax and Gabriel Jones had been elected, but Jones later accepted the office of Coroner and had to resign. In his place, Perkins was named,[159] but was not again an aspirant for the office. As George William Fairfax had vacated his seat to become a candidate in Fairfax, the field was open. Hugh West declared himself; [160] so did Thomas Swearingen. The day of the election,[161] December 10, some of Colonel Washington's friends presented his name, but as they had made no previous canvass, they could not muster many votes for him. West received 271, Swearingen, 270, and Washington forty.[162]

Whether or not Washington knew that his candidacy was to be announced in this manner, he took good pains to copy the list of his supporters [163] when, about a week before Christmas, he journeyed from Alexandria to Winchester.[164] There, on the 27th, he received a letter Dinwiddie had written him almost a fortnight previously.[165] It was a paper to deepen depression. The Governor stated that the express had returned from New York, but that General Shirley had not reached

[157] Letter of Aug. 27, 1757, to Dinwiddie; 2 *G. W.*, 122. For the circumstances in which this letter was written, see *infra*, p. 261.

[158] The poll stood: West, 232; Fairfax, 222; Ellzey, 220. See 1 *Papers of G. W.*; LC. This is in Washington's autograph. A later copy in 2 *ibid.*, 97 ff, gives the totals as: West, 252; Fairfax, 232; Ellzey, 224. This contains many errors and does not appear to be in the handwriting of Washington, though endorsed by him.

[159] *Journ. H. B.*, 1752–58, vii, 167. Perkins's name appears once only in the journal, and then in favorable action by the House on his application to be excused from attendance for the remainder of the session (*ibid.*, 261). His given name is not known.

[160] He doubtless was the son of the Hugh West who died while a Burgess from Fairfax.

[161] 1 *Hamilton*, 158.

[162] Toner transcript in 816 *Papers of G. W.*; LC. Judge Robert Barton (*Proceedings VHS*, 1891, p. 113–27) wrongly gave the date of this election as 1757. He repeated the interesting Winchester tradition that antagonism to Washington originated with an ordinary keeper, Lindsay by name, whose renewal of license the Colonel had opposed. If this hostility did exist, it could not have shown itself until election-day because the candidacy of the commander was not known till then. Stephen doubtless was acquainted with the facts when he wrote Washington: ". . . I think your poll was not despicable, as the people were a stranger to your purpose until the election began" (1 *Hamilton*, 158). Apropos of Thomas Swearingen, in 7 *Frederick Orders*, Nov. 3, 1756, is an entry for the payment to him of £20, 14s 6d for attending the General Assembly in March, 1756. Nowhere else, in the course of this study, has it been observed that this conditional requirement of the election law was met.

[163] 816 *Papers of G. W.*; LC.

[164] He was in the Valley town by Dec. 20, 1755; 1 *G. W.*, 256.

[165] It was dated December 14 and was sent by Capt. John Mercer (1 *G. W.*, 261), who may have stopped, en route, to spend Christmas at home.

the city when the messenger left. An answer from Shirley concerning Dagworthy's status might be expected soon by another hand. Dinwiddie hoped the reply would be favorable to Washington and to the other Virginia field officers, but he went on somewhat querulously to say: "I am of opinion you might have obviated the inconsistent dispute with Captain Dagworthy by asking him if he did not command by virtue of Governor Sharpe's commission, as that he had formerly from His Majesty now ceases, as he is not on the half-pay list . . ."[166]

George did not take horse, on receipt of this, and start for Fort Cumberland to have a settlement with Captain Dagworthy, man to man. Instead, Washington the next day sent Adam Stephen a long quotation from Dinwiddie's letter and reviewed the arguments advanced at Williamsburg to show that the Marylander had no right to command. The case was stated vigorously; the conclusion was a mild request to Adam: "I wish you would sound [Captain Dagworthy] on this head, and hear how he will answer these things, and let me know when you come down, which I desire may be immediately, as I want much to consult you upon several accounts."[167]

Stephen's answer was much briefer and less enthusiastic than his letters to Washington usually were. The Lieutenant Colonel merely acknowledged George's communication, promised to report in Winchester as soon as he could make up desired accounts, and then he added: "I will likewise sound out C. D. on the topics you mention, and am with great respect, your most obedient."[168] When George duly received and read this, he scarcely could flatter himself that Stephen had any zeal for "sounding" the Captain who virtually had wrested command from him.

Stephen came to Winchester shortly after New Year's Day, 1756,[169] and he brought word that Dagworthy held to the position previously taken. The Captain said he had stipulated when accepting command of the Maryland Company that he should proceed under his royal commission and not under one from the Colony. Sharpe and Sir John St.

---

[166] 1 *Hamilton*, 147.   [167] 1 *G. W.*, 262.

[168] 1 *Hamilton*, 157. This is dated December 20, but from the internal evidence manifestly was written after the receipt of Washington's letter of the 28th. The correct date may be the 30th as the communication from Winchester had been carried by Jenkins, the fast-riding, dependable express.

[169] The date is not established but the gap after December 30 in Stephen's letters to Washington indicates that he made the journey, as promised, and in accordance with Washington's orders. Stephen must have been at Winchester prior to January 11, because, as the text makes plain, Washington was there as late as January 10 but was in Alexandria on the 13th (1 *G. W.*, 283, 285).

Clair had told him not to give up his rights; the Governor had instructed him specifically to keep the command.

Dagworthy also had made a new move, Stephen said. When told that Virginia had decided not to feed Maryland and North Carolina troops from the provisions she had accumulated at Fort Cumberland,[170] Dagworthy had given orders to the Virginia commissary not to touch provisions without his permission. The food, he asserted, was in the King's fort; [171] all the troops had equal right to draw provisions on his orders; the Virginians might have placed the flour and meat there, but they could not remove anything without his consent.[172] He was so positive and so confident of his authority that Stephen had not challenged him. Washington, hearing his subordinate's report, was equally reluctant to act otherwise than on direct orders from Dinwiddie. In the memory of Braddock's action in upholding Dagworthy the previous summer, George continued cautious. "I should not by any means choose to act," he soon was to tell the Governor, with respect to the suggestion of sounding Dagworthy in person, "lest I should be called to an account myself." [173]

Doubtless Washington heard from Stephen of other developments at Fort Cumberland—of a renewed petition by Virginia officers to be put on the regular establishment, and of a discussion among them of the honors to which their own commanders were or were not entitled if Dagworthy actually had the authority for which he contended. On these matters George did not pass anticipatory judgment, and, as he felt he had done everything he could on the frontier for the time being, he started back to Alexandria during the second week of January.[174]

He would have been compelled in honesty to confess to himself as he rode over the Blue Ridge that he had permitted his avoidance of the humiliating controversy over the seniority of a King's Captain to keep him from Fort Cumberland. At the same time he could have maintained that he had not failed to discharge other duties that had been exasperating even if instructive. First of all, the men had been kept from hunger. In spite of the difficulties of procuring salt and of pro-

170 Washington had written Adam Stephen on November 18 (1 G. W., 236) to notify the Maryland and North Carolina Companies. At that time, Washington apparently anticipated no trouble beyond the possibility that the commands might disband. In that event, Stephen was told to enlist as many of them as he could in the Virginia Regiment.

171 Washington (1 G. W., 289) said "in the King's garrison," a term still valid, in the eighteenth century, for the place as well as for the men occupying it.

172 Ibid. and 2 Din., 329.

173 Letter of Jan. 14, 1756; 1 G. W., 290.

174 See supra, n. 169.

viding feed for the cattle until slaughtered, meat in sufficient quantity for winter and for spring had been pickled and put in casks.[175] Next, a beginning had been made, roughly but effectively, in establishing discipline. Much prodding had been necessary in getting officers to provide themselves with uniforms [176] and to make daily returns.[177] One Lieutenant had to be suspended for cheating at cards.[178] The Captain of a ranger Company had to be told bluntly to send his meddlesome wife from camp at once, or, said Washington, "I shall take care to drive her out myself, and suspend you." [179] Trouble had repeatedly to be endured with Captain Hog, who was proving incompetent on detached service at Fort Dinwiddie.[180]

Progress was made with nearly all the other officers. Their confidence was won. "Remember," George told them, "that it is the actions, and not the commission, that make the officer, and that there is more expected from him than the title." He went on: "Do not forget that there ought to be a time appropriated to attain this knowledge as well as to indulge pleasure. And as we now have no opportunities to improve from example, let us read for this desirable ends. There is Bland's and other treatises which will give this wished-for information." Washington doubtless was unaware of it as he wrote down this reference to Humphrey Bland's *Treatise of Military Discipline,* but he then was making the first entry on the list of books American soldiers were to be called upon to read. Although devoted exclusively to tactics and discipline, it was the best English work of its generation, written by an able, high-minded British officer and published in 1727. Washington was to have a copy on the way to him in April, 1756, and he was to keep it by him.[181]

With this exhortation to study, Washington had combined assurance that in the observance of the "strictest discipline" there would be "the strictest justice administered to all." He concluded: "I assure you, gentlemen, that partiality shall never bias my conduct, nor shall prejudice injure any; but throughout the whole tenor of my proceed-

---

[175] See *supra,* p. 142, for salt. The reports of Commissary Thomas Walker are in 1 *Hamilton,* 132, 140, 152, 153, 161. Cf. 1 *G. W.,* 245.

[176] 1 *G. W.,* 266.   [177] 1 *G. W.,* 257.

[178] 1 *G. W.,* 269, 270.   [179] 1 *G. W.,* 264.

[180] 1 *Hamilton,* 137; 1 *G. W.,* 259, 284; 303 *Papers of G. W.;* LC; cf. 2 *G. W.,* 152.

[181] A copy, with the imprint "London, 1727," but probably of a later date, was listed in the inventory of Washington's library. See Boston Athenaeum, *Catalogue of the Washington Collection,* 537. The last edition, printed in 1762, was styled the ninth, but, so far as is known, no comprehensive bibliography of this classic, the "basic text" of the American Army, has been prepared. The National War College has two editions; William and Mary the eighth.

ings, I shall endeavor, as far as I am able, to reward and punish without the least diminution."[182] It was the same with the soldiers in the ranks, but always at a distance and with the sternest line drawn between officer and enlisted man. As far as feeble colonial industry allowed, Washington exerted himself to get the troops everything they required from kettles to clothing[183] and he lamented the fact that winter found some of the Regiment so ill-clad they soon would be unfit for duty.[184] He undertook, too, to provide a hospital,[185] precisely as he saw to it that his men were acquainted with the wiles of Indian warfare[186] in order to save them from the possibility of another such massacre as that of the preceding July 9. For the rest, it was discipline, discipline, discipline— and the constant threat of death for deserters.[187]

Recruiting, always slow, was nearly halted in wintry weather.[188] Temporary loss of numbers was sustained when part of Hog's Company and a draft of the rangers[189] were sent to join the Cherokees in execution of the plan, which had been deferred and then renewed, for an attack under Maj. Andrew Lewis's direction on the Shawnee towns,[190] an enterprise for which George did not anticipate success.[191] Detachment and desertion did not keep Washington from forming the Regiment into sixteen Companies, Jan. 9, 1756; but this was in large part a paper organization, far below authorized strength. Some of the Companies were so thin that officers who had been appointed on promise to recruit a specified number were told once again they would be held to punctual compliance.[192]

Finally, the Virginians had built two forts on the South Branch of the Potomac and were to construct two more. As the Colonel explained to the Governor,[193] these defences would protect nearly 100 miles of the frontier, to say nothing of the cover that might be afforded by the work in Hog's care on Jackson's River. When this final item was entered to Washington's credit, and the Indian raids of the early autumn were charged against him—though he was not to blame for

---

[182] 1 *G. W.*, 271.

[183] 1 *G. W.*, 250, 263; 2 *Din.*, 291. This subject is treated topically, *infra*, p. 374.

[184] 1 *G. W.*, 287.   [185] 1 *G. W.*, 255.

[186] 1 *G. W.*, 286.   [187] 1 *G. W.*, 257–58, 287.

[188] For its various aspects in November, 1755–January, 1756, see 1 *G. W.*, 243–44, 267, 269, 284; 1 *Hamilton*, 160.

[189] 2 *Din.*, 320.

[190] See 2 *Din.*, 278, 296–97, 319 ff; 2 *G. W.*, 285. Lewis received his orders from Dinwiddie Jan. 23, 1756; Andrew Lewis to Captain Preston, Jan. 28, 1756—*Preston Papers*, loc. cit.

[191] 1 *G. W.*, 286.   [192] 1 *G. W.*, 272 ff.

[193] For the location of these works, see *infra*, p. 176, 181.

them—there was a favorable balance to his account for the last four months of 1755. It was not a large balance, but George might justly have said that he had made the best of an evil hour in Virginia's life.

There was not, he thought, any substantial prospect that he could do more in 1756 than guard the northwestern frontier unless he had a greater increment of force than recruiting was apt to yield. He believed a defensive had to be maintained in the New Year. If the Governor decided on a different policy, George wished instructions so that he might begin forthwith to prepare.[194] Dinwiddie was not of a mind to undertake the impossible. "Our people," he had said in December, "want a martial spirit, and what to do for the next campaign, I know not, for our militia law restrains me from marching them out of the confines of this government, and without forces from Britain and good officers, we shall, I fear, make a bad figure against the enemy . . ."[195]

Better prospects for bolder plans seemed to be offered farther northward. During the campaign of 1755,[196] William Johnson had not been able to execute his part of the ambitious operations and to reach Crown Point; but he had struck a hard blow September 8 on the shores of Lake George, and thereby, in the judgment of his admirers, had kept the French and Indians from pouring down the valley of the Hudson.[197] Shirley, for his part, did not reach Oswego till August 17. He then constructed across the river a new work which he called Fort Ontario, and he planned to attack Fort Niagara swiftly with part of his forces; but adverse weather, the non-arrival of provisions, sickness and the defection of Indians prevented. Thereafter Shirley had to content himself with an elaborate design for offensives in 1756 that would cut off the French from the Great Lakes and from the upper watershed of the Ohio.[198] On Dec. 12, 1755, in New York he met with Dunbar, St. Clair and the Governors of nearby Colonies and won approval for nearly the whole of a quadruple attack designed to compel the French to disperse their forces and to remain on the defensive. One column, with vessels for quick transportation, was to destroy the French forts from La Galette on the St. Lawrence to Presque Isle, Lake Erie. Another column was to essay the capture of Crown Point; a third was

---

[194] 1 *G. W.*, 286–87. Reconnaissance to choose the location of new forts is mentioned in *ibid.*, 276, 278.

[195] Letter of Dec. 24, 1755, to Sir Thomas Robinson, 2 *Din.*, 307.

[196] For the original plan of these operations, see *supra*, p. 23.

[197] The operation is treated fully in 6 *Gipson*, 165–77.

[198] 6 *Gipson*, 135–60. The concluding sentence of the summary in the text is merely a paraphrase of one of Gipson's, p. 160.

to make a feint on Quebec. To the South, the Cherokees were to be rallied to assist the English in redeeming Braddock's defeat by pushing victoriously to Fort DuQuesne.[199]

These were the continental plans when George left the Shenandoah Valley and rode to Alexandria in January, 1756. His resolution now was fixed: he wanted to have a share in any campaign that might be undertaken, but he would not accept Dagworthy as his superior officer. If he did not receive a favorable answer from Shirley, he was willing to do something he had not contemplated until after he had left Winchester: [200] He would go to Boston in order to ask for a ruling on Dagworthy's status and to lay before the General a petition his officers had drawn up for inclusion in the regular establishment. If this were done, Washington's Captains would have commissions as good as Dagworthy's, and George himself would have one that would make him outrank the Marylander. In event this appeal was vain, George had made up his mind he would resign from the service of Virginia rather than, in his own words, "submit to the command of a person who, I think, has not such superlative merit to balance the inequality of rank." [201]

The controversy took a new turn soon after Washington returned to Alexandria. Lieut. William Stark of Capt. Thomas Cocke's Company of the Virginia Regiment had concluded that Captain Dagworthy was lawfully in command at Fort Cumberland and he said so without reserve. Getting down to cases, Stark stated that as the command was with Dagworthy, he would not turn out the guard or have them "rest their arms" in honor of their own Colonel or of any other field officer of the Virginia Regiment, unless Dagworthy so ordered. This incensed Washington's other subordinates to such a flame of resentment that Stephen on the 16th of January brought Stark before a court of inquiry. The Lieutenant admitted the charge and pleaded the justification of orders. On that plea, reluctantly, the court had to find for him.[202] Stephen was furious and, after abusing the accused man roundly in a letter to Washington, was disposed to bring Stark to trial again for asking the dismissal of an officer who had called the Lieutenant a coward.[203] Washington was angry, also, but on two different grounds— that Stark had not been tried under any article of war, and that even if

199 6 *Gipson*, 178. The proceedings of this council appear in 1 *Sharpe*, 315.
200 1 *G. W.*, 295.
201 Letter of Jan. 14, 1756, to Dinwiddie, 1 *G. W.*, 289–90.
202 1 *Hamilton*, 188.   203 *Ibid.*, 167–68.

Dagworthy had been commander, troops were required to pay "certain compliments. . . to their own field officers." [204]

Some days after this provoking affair was reported to George, he gradually learned what Shirley had done in answer to Dinwiddie's appeal of the 4th of November. [205] The New England Governor and acting Commander-in-Chief wrote Dinwiddie, December 4 that he had instructed Governor Sharpe to settle the dispute between Washington and Dagworthy. At the New York conference on plans for the campaign of 1756, Shirley had repeated these instructions. Sharpe had promised compliance, [206] and, on his return to Annapolis, he wrote Dagworthy to confine himself to the command of the fort and not to interfere with any troops in the barracks or to assume any authority over the Virginians who might be posted there. [207] Apparently, before Dinwiddie received information to this effect, Dagworthy boasted at the fort that Sharpe had told him to keep the command. [208] The Captain took care, at the same time, to obey the remainder of Sharpe's orders, [209] but he said nothing about his orders to leave the Virginia troops to their own officers—that was Dagworthy's only statement. Dinwiddie and Washington concluded that Sharpe had not carried out the instructions of Shirley but, on the contrary, as George thought, had written Dagworthy to retain the command previously exercised. [210]

When, therefore, Dinwiddie gave his approval to a personal appeal by Washington to Shirley, [211] the Colonel did not permit the weather of midwinter to deter him. He would go to Boston to establish his seniority as readily as he had ridden to Fort Le Boeuf two years previously to deliver the message of the Governor. The appeal to Shirley was to be on definite grounds—that the public service was obstructed by the stand Dagworthy had taken and that the transfer of the Vir-

[204] Under Dagworthy's order, of which George took the trouble to procure a copy, guards and sentries were directed to show honors to their Colonel and other field officers, though not the same honors as to the commander of the fort. See 1 *Hamilton*, 188, 189 and n.; 1 *G. W.*, 291.

[205] See *supra*, p. 139 and 2 *Din.*, 261.

[206] 2 *Din.*, 309–11; 1 *Sharpe*, 347.

[207] See Sharpe to Dinwiddie, Jan. 4, 1756, 1 *Sharpe*, 334–35. In this letter Sharpe avoided with some skill any admission that Dagworthy had been acting without authority.

[208] 1 *G. W.*, 289.

[209] This is manifest from Stephen's account (1 *Hamilton*, 194) of the duties the Virginia Lieutenant Colonel was discharging unhampered.

[210] 1 *G. W.*, 289. As the time required for the transmission of these letters in winter cannot be determined, it is impossible to say when all the details became known to Washington. He had not learned on January 14 of Shirley's reply of December 4 to Dinwiddie; by the 1st of February, Washington knew of the orders Shirley had given Sharpe.

[211] 2 *Din.*, 327. Speaker Robinson had seconded George's application (1 *Hamilton*, 178; cf. *ibid.*, 151).

ginia Regiment to the regular establishment, as requested by the officers, would be in the public interest. "This," said George, "would at once put an end to contention, which is the root of evil and destructive to the best of operations . . ." [212] Dinwiddie did not dispute the validity of the argument, but he doubted whether Shirley had power to put on the regular establishment a Regiment with provincial officers already chosen. "His Majesty," Dinwiddie reminded George, "sends over officers to the various Regiments that are to be raised." [213]

Lack of belief in the success of the appeal to Shirley did not keep Dinwiddie from supporting it heartily. Like the Virginia officers, he was affronted by Dagworthy's pretensions, and, being tenacious in his own views, he was anxious to demolish the Captain's argument. With much care Dinwiddie wrote George of the special circumstances involved. Particular stress was placed on the fact that "His Majesty's commission takes place of [214] any Governor's commission when the regulars are joined with the provincials, but this is not the case in this dispute." George must urge that point on Shirley.[215]

In a letter of his own to the General, Dinwiddie repeated this analysis and enlarged upon the effect Dagworthy's use of Virginia provisions would have on the Burgesses who had levied the taxes to buy the food Dagworthy insisted on distributing to the entire garrison. "If," said Dinwiddie, "I would call the Assembly now, I know this affair has raised the rancor of the people so much that they would go into extreme of resentment and do no business for the service." He elaborated briefly and drove his point home: "As Commander-in-Chief of the forces, this is in your power only, and without some regulation in regard to this unhappy dispute, I shall not be able to do anything with our Assembly." [216] Then Dinwiddie renewed his application that the General issue brevet commissions to the Virginia field officers, and he asked, too, a direct order for the reinstatement of Stephen as commander at Fort Cumberland during the absence of Colonel Innes.[217]

This was as much ammunition as George could hope to carry in support of the officers' memorial. Washington remembered, too, the fine impression that Shirley had made on him at the Alexandria council—"every word and every action discovers the gentleman and great politician" [218]—but he left nothing to chance. He would make his best

212 I G. W., 289.
214 That is, "precedence over."
216 Letter of Jan. 24, 1756; 2 Din., 330.
218 See supra, p. 23.

213 2 Din., 327.
215 2 Din., 327.
217 Ibid. See, also, supra, p. 134.

approach. Officially he wrote his Commissary, in tones of composure: "As the contention about the command is risen to the disagreeable height it now is, and would probably, if not timely prevented, be attended with very bad consequences to the public, I solicited leave, which is obtained, to visit the General and represent all those matters to him . . ."[219] Personally, George planned to appear in a style that befitted the "Colonel of the Virginia Regiment and the Commander-in-Chief of all the forces that now are, and shall be raised &c &c."[220] He arranged for Capt. George Mercer, his aide, to accompany him and to act as paymaster. Capt. Robert Stewart, also, was to ride with his chief. Of course George's body servant was to be in attendance. A second servant, Thomas Bishop, would be useful. To provide funds for a journey of 1100 miles by five men and their mounts, George made ready to place in Mercer's hands a sum equivalent to approximately the accumulated pay he had drawn on the 1st of December.[221] With equal, customary care he perfected his other arrangements and, during the first days of February, 1756,[222] set out from Alexandria. He *must* establish his position: he would *not* be subordinate.

[219] Letter of Feb. 1, 1756, to Thomas Walker; 1 *G. W.*, 293.
[220] From the opening paragraph of his initial orders at Fort Cumberland, Sept. 17, 1755. See *supra*, p. 118.
[221] *Ledger A*, folio 25. The later entries, covering the journey, are on folios 25-28, printed in 1 *G. W.*, 298 ff.
[222] The exact date is not known. Payments to Captain Mercer are entered in Washington's *Ledger A*, folio 26, under date of February 4, but these were not made, necessarily, on the date of departure. In writing Dinwiddie, February 1, Washington stated that he would "set out on Monday next," which was the next day (1 *G. W.*, 293). George's last letter from Alexandria before departure bears date of February 2 (*ibid.*, 296). As he almost certainly was in Philadelphia by the evening of February 7, the assumption that he left home on the 4th would mean that he covered 180 miles in three and a half or four days' travel in midwinter.

CHAPTER IX

PRIDE SPURS A LONG JOURNEY
(February–March, 1756)

As FAR AS ANNAPOLIS, distant thirty miles, the route across the Potomac and over Londontown Ferry was one that Washington knew.[1] Beyond the little Maryland capital of about 150 houses and a pleasant society,[2] George and his companions traversed a way unfamiliar to him. He crossed the Patapsco, the Gunpowder and the Susquehanna ferries— none too pleasant in the forbidding weather of February—and he perhaps stopped briefly for a glance at the Principio Iron Works, in which his family still had an interest.[3]

Thence the road ran as the easier grades invited, from Elk River to New Castle, to Brandywine Ferry and to Chester. Had the season been that of bloom or of harvest, the young Virginians would have observed that they were entering now a country of better cultivation. Orchards lined the road and spread over the rolling hills.[4] Farming was not of the wasteful abuse-it-and-move-on sort that prevailed in large parts of Virginia. Ferries, too, were better.[5]

On the seventeen miles of road North of Chester, the last of these ferries crossed the Schuylkill and brought George to the largest city he

[1] *Va. Almanac*, 1756; Lewis Evans, "A General Map of the Middle British Colonies in America."

[2] *Burnaby*, 65. The archdeacon, who made his tour in 1759, and Lord Adam Gordon, visiting in 1765, are the only foreign travelers of approximately the same period who followed substantially the route that Washington pursued. The principal divergence, from Philadelphia to New York, is noted in the text. Burnaby's descriptions are applicable to the time of Washington's journey, except for the completion in 1756–58 of a few important buildings. Lord Adam Gordon's narrative, reprinted in Mereness, *op. cit.*, must be read more critically because, needless to say, the changes of the nine years intervening between George's journey and Gordon's were important, particularly as respects the attitude of the people to the government of Britain.

[3] Vol. I, p. 74, 264. This interest was retained until sold, presumably in 1773 by Anne Aylett Washington, Austin's widow. See account of Augustine Washington, 1769; Anne Washington to Thomas Russell, May 28, 1772; Thomas Russell to Anne Washington, June 15, 1772; extract from letter of Thomas Russell to Messrs. Wightwick, Dec. 24, 1774, *Principio Papers*, Br. Mus., Add. MS 29600, f. 16, 20, 31. It is stated in 18 *T* 135 that the sale was Mch. 28, 1773, but the correspondence here quoted, of later day, shows the sale not then consummated.

[4] *Burnaby*, 75; Gordon in *Mereness*, 410. The route is given in *Va. Almanac*, 1756, and may be traced on Evans's map.

[5] Gordon in *Mereness*, 410.

ever had seen.[6] Philadelphia then counted more than 3000 houses [7]
and had regular, well-paved streets with a sidewalk on either side.[8]
Nearly all the larger buildings were of brick. There were eight or ten
churches, a college, a hospital that made provision for lunatics, a large
if awkward state house, and two libraries. A good market was held
twice a week. At night, the streets were lighted and patrolled. Public
order was good even if public spirit was not high. Money-making
manifestly was the chief concern of a quiet population, which included
some thousands of Quakers.[9]

George was interested in the town and its people but, most of all, in
its shops. During 1754–55 he had been so long on the frontier that he
could not gratify to the fullest his undiminished love of fine dress.
Now, in a city that boasted good tailors and hatters, he could buy
clothing and headgear appropriate for a Virginia gentleman of fashion
who was about to wait on the Commander-in-Chief.[10] Probably to
have his new garments fitted and finished,[11] George spent four or five
days in Philadelphia. His presence aroused curiosity which he did not
relieve by any statement of his plans. One guess, duly transmitted to
England, was that he was engaged in preparations for an early surprise
attack on Fort DuQuesne.[12]

Courteously but silently, with his new clothes duly protected against
the mud of the road, George left Philadelphia for New York about the
13th of February.[13] Had he turned his horse's head toward the little
town of Trenton, he might have ridden on to the new college of Nassau
Hall at a place some of the mapmakers wrote as Prince Town. Thence
he would have passed New Brunswick, which was said to have women
whose beauty was rivaled by that of Philadelphia maidens only. From
New Brunswick, a road led to Newark, a sprawling town, almost two

---

[6] His arrival probably was on February 7, but the only positive evidence is that of entries of
the 8th in *Ledger A*, folio 26. The *Penn. Gazette* of February 12 noted his arrival "last week."
If this statement was accurate, it fixes the time of George's coming as prior to Sunday, February 8.

[7] Gordon was told in 1765 that the number was in excess of 3600 (*Mereness*, 410–11).

[8] Peter Kalm, quoted in Faris, *Old Philadelphia*, 141, made reservation concerning their
reputed excellence.

[9] *Burnaby*, 75; Gordon in *Mereness*, 410–11; Faris, *op. cit.*, 62, 156; for the London Coffee
House, a favored resort, see Watson, *Annals of Philadelphia*, 339.

[10] *Ledger A*, folio 26, reproduced in 1 *G. W.*, 298. His bills were in excess of £26, Pennsylvania curency.

[11] Adverse weather may of course have been another explanation.

[12] P.R.O., C.O. 5: 52, p. 73, LC Trans.

[13] As the text explains, he arrived in New York on the night of February 15. The journey
of ninety-eight miles, by land and water, scarcely could have been made in two days of wintry
weather even if, as the evidence suggests, the horses were overridden. Lord Loudoun, proceeding
in the opposite direction, March, 1757, required three days. See his *Memorandum Begun at
New York*, entries of Mch. 12–14, 1757; Huntington Library.

miles in length, that reminded visitors from England of a village in the home country.[14]

Instead of following this route, George and his four companions crossed the Delaware at Burlington and proceeded by Allentown and Cranberry Brook,[15] to Perth Amboy.[16] The pace at which the party pushed on had begun by this time to wear down the horses, but it was not moderated. Time, in George's opinion, was more valuable than horseflesh.[17] Animals and riders alike went aboard a small vessel at Perth Amboy, whence with favoring wind they reached the Narrows. A journey of five miles carried Washington to Flat Bush, and another of like distance introduced him to New York City[18] on the night of February 15.[19] His first resting place may have been a tavern[20] but the next day, perhaps, he found Beverley Robinson[21] and went to that Virginian's residence.[22] Robinson had been fortunate. He was a son of John Robinson, former President of the Colony, and was a brother of George's correspondent, Treasurer John Robinson, Speaker of the House of Burgesses. Beverley had raised a Company in Virginia for the Canadian expedition in King George's War but, like Capt. John Dagworthy, had fought no battles. Being attracted by the growth of New York City, he had remained there and had achieved a shining conquest —no less than the heart of Susannah Philipse, the elder of the two sisters of Frederick Philipse, third and last Lord of the Manor of Philipsboro.[23] Susannah was one of the richest heiresses of New York[24]

14 *Burnaby,* 94–97.   15 The present Cranbury.

16 Except for the inclusion of Allentown, this route is substantially that of the division of the Pennsylvania Railroad from Burlington to Perth Amboy. The alternative route, needless to say, is that of the main line of the same railroad from Philadelphia to New York.

17 See *supra,* p. 27 for an earlier instance in which, apparently, he exhausted his mounts on a rapid journey from Alexandria to Winchester.

18 On the assumption that he followed the shortest, recommended route, *Va. Almanac,* 1756. Faris, *op. cit.,* 248, noted that from 1706 and perhaps before that date, packet boats ran between Perth Amboy and Manhattan. See also 13 *N. J. Arch.,* 1st. ser., 237; 14 *ibid.,* 42. Washington and his party may have used one of these vessels and perhaps disembarked at the lower end of Manhattan.

19 *Ledger A,* folio 26; *Boston News Letter,* Feb. 20, 1756.

20 Cf. *Ledger A,* folio 26, "By cash for my club at Tavern, 5s 1d." This is undated but is the first entry of New York expenses.   21 See *infra,* n. 25.

22 Henry Strippel, specialist of the New York Public Library on the history of that city, states that no satisfactory evidence has been brought to light regarding the location of Robinson's house at this period. In fact, no documentary proof that Robinson had a New York City residence in 1756 is available, though the assumption appears to be justified. Mr. Strippel points out that Robert Gilder in *The Battery, the Story of . . . Manhattan Island's Tip,* 56, spoke of the house "occupied by Captain [Beverley] Robinson on Stone Street" but gave no date or reference.

23 Harold D. Eberlein, *The Manors and Historic Homes of the Hudson Valley,* 157 ff.

24 For the Philipse estate, see Thomas A. Glenn, *Some Colonial Mansions,* 245 ff. Frederick Philipse, first of that name to attain wealth in America, is sketched in *DAB.* His fortune was built on shipping, the acquisition of good land, the importation of slaves and the manufacture of wampum.

and had a place in New York society equal to that of Beverley Robinson in Virginia.

It was, of course, a satisfaction to George to hear a familiar name in a strange city.[25] No less satisfaction was there, and of a more exciting nature, in introduction to Mary Philipse, who was residing at the time with Mrs. Robinson, her older sister. Mary Eliza Philipse, familiarly Polly Philipse, was then in her twenty-sixth year.[26] In person she was erect and deep bosomed with a neck that had some indication of goitre. Her eyes were clear and confident, her nose was large and her mouth broad, with a half-dimple at either end.[27] If she showed then what later was her most marked characteristic, she was of a nature to dominate and to shape others to her will,[28] a feminine quality with which George had been unhappily familiar at Ferry Farm. Still, any unmarried girl who owned 51,000 acres of valuable New York land [29] was interesting, even if she might wish to have her own way.[30] George doubtless looked and bowed and concluded that, at the least, he should return to his hostess and her sister some of the courtesy shown him. New Yorkers were talking, at the moment, of an exhibit offered in the city at the News Exchange under the alluring title of "The Microcosm, or World in Miniature." This had been advertised in Williamsburg the previous autumn; George may have seen it then.[31] In any event, he thought a visit with the ladies to the News Exchange would be appropriate, especially as there was assurance that a "fire is kept going in the Exhibition Hall during the whole time." [32] To the "World in Minia-

[25] There is no evidence, one way or the other, that George had known Beverley in Virginia, but as Robinson had left the Colony not later than 1746 and had married in July, 1748, the chances are that the two men had never met.

[26] Born July 3, 1730, according to the thirteenth annual report, 1908, of the American Scenic and Historic Preservation Society, 206.

[27] Her portrait is reproduced in Glenn, op. cit., 245.

[28] Cf. the quotation in thirteenth report, supra, p. 206, from Lorenzo Sabine's Loyalists of the American Revolution, of the tradition that she "had immense influence over everybody."

[29] Shelton, Jumel Mansion, 13; Hufeland, Westchester County, v. 2, p. 3–4.

[30] In all that pertains to George's relations with Mary Philipse, there is an element of unverifiable tradition. The fact that George had only a small tavern bill in New York is not of itself proof positive that he was entertained privately for the duration of the visit to the city. His account at a tavern might have been covered by Captain Mercer's unitemized expenditures. On the other hand, George's action later in borrowing money from Beverley Robinson suggests close social relations that might readily have included entertainment at Robinson's home. The convincing evidence that Washington was there, however briefly, and was introduced to Mary Philipse, is represented, first, by George's entry in his ledger of £1, 8s 6d for "Mr. Robinson's servants," and second, by the letter of Joseph Chew, July 13, 1757, 2 Hamilton, 139. This letter leaves no doubt whatever that George had met Mary Philipse and that a match between them had been considered a possibility.

[31] Va. Gazette, Oct. 24, 1755. It was not "reviewed" or advertised in the next issue, at a time when it should have been on display if the engagement was kept. George, it will be remembered, was in Williamsburg during the first days of November, 1755.

[32] N. Y. Mercury, Feb. 16, 1756.

ture" they accordingly went, and in style, too, because the expense was
£1, 8s.[33] What they saw was a structure of scenery in the form of a
Roman temple, within which were mechanical devices that ranged
from "Orpheus . . . in the forest, playing a lyre" to a "carpenter's yard
with men busily and accurately at work." Nine Muses played "a con-
cert on harp, hautboy, etc." In a simulated grove, birds flew about and
sang. Over the scene, "coaches, chariots and chaises" passed "before the
eye, all moving easily and gracefully." If the operation of a "gunpowder mill" did not interest, then "ships" sailed "across the waves,
with speed . . . adapted to the distance from which they [were]
seen." At least, all this was the promise of the exhibitors,[34] a promise
that could not have been altogether misleading because George took
the ladies back to the News Exchange for a second viewing.[35]

Other social attractions there were for Washington, with or without
the ladies. He attended "Mr. Baron's rout" at the moderate outlay of six
shillings, and he bore his "club" of four shillings, tuppence at Willet's.
The town's merchants, who were not then as celebrated as those of
Philadelphia and Boston, did not extract much money from George.
He bought a pair of shoes and he left with the tailors something less
than £4. At cards, he lost no more than eight shillings.[36] His heavy
expenditure was for horses to replace those that had been exhausted by
hard service on the way to New York. After hiring a man to find him
good animals, George purchased two for himself and one still finer for
Captain Mercer. As the total bill for these was almost £75 and had
not been anticipated, George was compelled to dig deeply into the
funds he had entrusted to his aide and paymaster.

Except for this transaction, Washington's experiences in New York
were chiefly social, and they did not absorb his practical eyes so completely that he failed to observe the bustling city itself. The number
of houses in New York was then and later a subject of debate and
widely varying estimate. Proud residents insisted that 4000 buildings
could be counted on Manhattan Island; detractors refused to admit
that the total exceeded 2000.[37] Most of these structures were of brick
and were set pleasantly on streets which, if not as regular as those of
Philadelphia, were paved and extensive. The most spacious of these

[33] *Ledger A,* folio 26.
[34] *N. Y. Mercury,* Feb. 16, 1756. To judge from the miscellaneous character of this exhibition it probably was a collection of German mechanical toys.
[35] *Ledger A,* folio 26.   [36] *Ledger A,* folio 26.
[37] Barck, *New York,* 12; Burnaby, 104; Gordon in *Mereness,* 414; letter of Edward Thompson, Aug. 15, 1756, in Wilson, *Memorial History of the City of New York,* v. 2, p. 314.

streets, appropriately called the Broad Way, was lined with shade trees. It was bare of foliage, of course, at the time of George's visit but even then attractive and impressive.[38] Public buildings and churches, while not numerous, gave promise of a large future. Among others, the Middle Dutch Church, Trinity and St. George's Churches already had been reared.[39] The fort at the tip of the island occupied a glorious site,[40] but all agreed that when the newly begun King's College was erected, it, too, would have a noble and commanding view.[41] Among buildings less formal, several of the taverns were excellent; the City Arms, more properly the New York or Province Arms, had high reputation;[42] Burns's Coffee House, on the Broad Way, opposite a neglected bowling green, was of two floors and attic with a garden in rear.[43]

The town had its problems. Industry had made scant progress, except for shipbuilding; there was little fresh water on the lower part of the island;[44] fear of an uprising had dictated severe restrictions on the city's share of the largest Negro population that any Northern province reckoned;[45] castes had persisted and had drawn sharp lines—officials, landed proprietors, merchants and traders, lawyers and, less regarded, small owners, clerks, journeymen and mechanics.[46] Nine years later, when most of these classes were disturbed by new British taxation, a visitor was to say of New York, "People here live to a good old age and very comfortably did they choose to be contented." [47]

Washington saw much of this interesting panorama and was himself the object of some curiosity. Just as there had been conjecture in Philadelphia regarding his visit, so in New York there was speculation concerning his reason for going—as he now admitted he was—to see Governor Shirley in Boston. In conversation with James Pitcher, the Virginia Colonel remarked that seventy Cherokees already had joined the Virginia forces and that others were expected shortly.[48] This led

---

[38] *Burnaby,* 104.

[39] Andrews in *Views of . . . old New York,* 97; *Burnaby,* 104. Lord Adam Gordon, six years later, put the number at 12.

[40] Ullman, *Landmark History of New York,* 11; Wilson, *Memorial History of New York,* v. 1, p. 222.

[41] *Burnaby,* 104.

[42] See O'Coner, *Servant of the Crown,* 41.

[43] Figured, perhaps with some artistic license, in James Grant Wilson, *op. cit.,* v. 2, p. 368.

[44] *Burnaby,* 104.

[45] Gordon in *Mereness,* 414. Thompson (Wilson, *op. cit.,* v. 2, p. 314) was told that most of the Negroes of New York City were from Guinea.

[46] Barck, *New York,* 12.

[47] Gordon in *Mereness,* 414.

[48] James Pitcher to Henry Fox of London, Feb. 23, 1756; P.R.O., C.O. 5: 46, p. 780, LC Trans.

gossips to conclude that Washington intended to confer with Shirley regarding the employment of the Southern Indians as British allies.[49]

George left his New York friends to their own interpretation of his business and, on the 20th of February,[50] he and his companions started for Boston. At New London, where he left most or all of his horses,[51] he found a long-time friend of the Washingtons and of the Balls in the person of Joseph Chew.[52] From New London, George apparently went by vessel directly to Newport, Rhode Island, and had hearty welcome in the home of another Virginian, Godfrey Malbone.[53] Pushing on in the face of severe weather,[54] he probably went on a man-of-war from Newport to Boston, which he reached on the 27th of February, the eighth day after he left New York.[55] Quarters were taken at Cromwell's Head Tavern on School Street, a two-story wooden structure

[49] Penn. Gazette, Feb. 26; Boston Gazette, March 1, 1756.

[50] N. Y. Mercury, Feb. 23, 1756; Penn. Gazette, Feb. 26, 1756.

[51] 1 Hamilton, 200.

[52] Ibid.

[53] A description of Newport in 1759 will be found in Burnaby, 117. He did not form a high opinion of the town. Its churches, he said, were not worth looking at.

[54] 1 Hamilton, 200.

[55] Boston News Letter, Mch. 4, 1756. This part of the journey presents several fascinating and unsolved problems concerning the route pursued. A letter of Joseph Chew's, dated New London, Mch. 4, 1756, and addressed to Washington in Boston, is one of the two known documents that relate to Washington's movements Feb. 20–27. This is printed in 1 Hamilton, 200. The other document is folio 27 of Ledger A. Together, these papers show: (1) George was at New London between the 22nd and the 26th; (2) he left there two injured mounts and certain animals which Chew described vaguely as "all your other horses"; (3) at New London, George asked Chew to make arrangements to have him and his party taken across the Sound to Long Island on their return journey; (4) the weather was severe when George left New London or became bad soon after; (5) George on the 26th noted gifts to "Mr. Malbone's servants" in an amount of Rhode Island currency which would indicate that he had been a guest in Malbone's house; (6) on the 27th George paid in Massachusetts currency 11s 3d "to a man of war crew" (folio 27). There scarcely is a doubt that "Mr. Malbone" was Godfrey Malbone of Newport, father of John Malbone and grandfather of the painter, Francis Greene Malbone. These facts establish New London and Newport as on the route Washington followed, but they do not specify the means of conveyance beyond New London. The probability is this: Either George went to New London on the road up the north side of the Sound, disliked it and resolved to go back via the road on Long Island from the vicinity of the present East Marion to Brooklyn; or else George proceeded to New London by way of Long Island and the Sound ferry and determined to return by that route. At New London, George probably found the weather so forbidding that he decided to leave his horses there and continue to Boston by water. He must have sailed directly to Newport, because on a hurried journey he would not have taken time to leave the direct road at Providence and go down Providence River and Narragansett Bay to Newport in February to pay a social visit to a man nowhere mentioned as an intimate. If George came to Newport by vessel, he had of course to leave by water; and as he gave gratuities to Malbone's servants on the 26th and to the crew of a man-of-war on the 27th, which was the date of his arrival in Boston, he must have gone from Newport to Boston aboard a ship of that type. The only possible flaw in this explanation is the absence of proof that Malbone was at Newport in February, 1756; but, so far as is known, Malbone had no other home after he went from Virginia to Rhode Island. Besides, if Malbone had been living on the mainland, at some point on the road to Boston, why would Washington have been paying gratuities to sailors on the 27th? The tradition of his visit to Malbone is recorded (Alice G. B. Lockwood, ed., Gardens of Colony and State, v. 1, p. 210–11), but there is no certainty whether the tradition was continuous or was based on the late publication of parts of Ledger A.

the sign of which was hung so low that every tall passerby had to bow to the Protector.[56] George himself prepared to make his bow to Governor Shirley as soon as His Excellency could receive him.[57] Introduction to the town was somewhat belated but was complimentary. In its first issue after George's arrival, the *Boston Gazette* announced the visit of "the Hon. Col. Washington, a gentleman who has deservedly a high reputation for military skill and valor, though success has not always attended his undertakings." [58] On the basis of a dispatch from New York, the conjecture was repeated that he was promoting alliance with the Southern Indians.[59] His entertainment accorded with his introduction, except for the unhappy fact that the New Englanders trimmed him at cards. He lost a pound and two-and-six at the Governor's House, and in a bout with other celebrities he had to confess himself worsted for close to £4, though there was consolation in the fact that when he computed the sum in Virginia currency it was only an eighth of what it appeared to be in Massachusetts paper.[60]

The city itself was as good as its card players. Washington had no basis of comparison, but visitors from across the Atlantic said that Boston more resembled an English town than did any other American city.[61] Streets, like the houses, seemed spacious. One of them was at least two miles in length.[62] Stores were numerous and were opulent with such goods on their shelves as George had found nowhere else. His thrifty and mathematical mind showed him, too, that at the rate of exchange between Virginia and Massachusetts currency, prices were low. He made the most of the bargains. A new hat, an impressive delivery by a good tailor, a mass of silver lace and two pairs of gloves represented more than £200 in current paper money, but only £25 and a trifle in bills from the press in Williamsburg.[63] If George was certain to return with a flattened purse, he would have a swollen portmanteau.

Cards and fittings at the tailor's and exchanges of civility with Bostonians did not occupy all George's time of waiting on the decision

56 Crawford, *Old Boston*, 113; Porter, *Rambles in Old Boston*, 384, cited in 1 Ford, 234 n.; Drake, *Boston Taverns*, 43–44. The building stood till 1888.

57 The date of George's arrival, February 27, is established by Boston *Weekly News Letter*, Mch. 4, 1756.

58 Edition of Mch. 1, 1756.   59 *Ibid.*

60 *Ledger A*, folio 27.   61 Gordon, *Mereness*, 449.

62 *Ibid.* It later was to bear Washington's own name. For another description, see *Burnaby*, 133.

63 *Ledger A*, folio 27. George converted into Virginia currency all his expenditures in each colony where he stopped for any length of time on this visit to Boston.

of Governor Shirley. He visited Castle William, the fort on an island in the harbor.[64] He doubtless saw, also, Faneuil Hall, the Court House, King's Chapel, which was then out of use,[65] and the Province House at the head of Milk Street. Governor Shirley himself lived handsomely in Roxbury, but he received guests at the official building and from its balcony he addressed the people or had his proclamations read. The three-story building of Holland brick was adorned with a portico and with a cupola. Its finial was a metal Indian with outstretched bow who shifted position when the wind veered—as George, in starkest reality, had seen the Western Indians do when French outwitted British, or British outbid the French. Beneath the changeful Indian, the approach to the Province House was through iron gates and up twenty steps of red sandstone. A handsome lawn and stately trees set off the building.[66]

It was here, doubtless, that Governor Shirley received George with the courtesy and kindness that had impressed the young man at the Alexandria conference.[67] George delivered formally his officers' petition to be accepted on the regular establishment. Along with this he placed in Shirley's hands Dinwiddie's letter of the 24th of January,[68] and he doubtless stated his own opinion of Dagworthy's asserted right to command at Fort Cumberland. Shirley was surprised that the issue had arisen, because Sharpe had promised him months before to end the dispute.[69] Now the General listened and questioned Washington concerning recruitment, prospects and support of the war by the Southern Colonies. After a time Shirley said that he would consider the question of Dagworthy's status and would give George his decision later.[70]

Apparently the Governor concluded that he could do nothing about the award of brevet commissions and the inclusion of the Virginia troops

[64] *Ledger A,* folio 27. The fort, "Castle Island" and the harbor are described by Lord Adam Gordon in *Mereness,* 450, and, earlier, by Edward Johnson (1654) and Daniel Neal (1719) as quoted in Shurtleff, *Boston,* 60–61, 477. See also Snow, *Boston Harbour,* 109 ff, and Drake, *Antiquities of Boston,* 806.

[65] Drake, *Landmarks,* 30. For later mention by Burnaby as "very handsome," see his *Travels,* 133.

[66] Drake, *Landmarks of Boston,* 239. The gates alone remain, separated by a flight of steps from a grimy street.

[67] See *supra,* p. 23. There is no record of when or how often Shirley conferred with Washington, though the inference in the text appears to be justified completely.

[68] See *supra,* p. 155 and 2 *Din.,* 328 ff. When Shirley sent Sharpe an extract from this communication he gave the date as January 23, but the text is the same. See 1 *Sharpe,* 348.

[69] 1 *Sharpe,* 347.

[70] Cf. Shirley to Sharpe, Mch. 5, 1756: "I have taken some time to consider this point . . ." (1 *Sharpe,* 348).

in the regular establishment, but on the 5th of March, he called Washington to his office and gave him a paper that read thus:

Boston, 5 March, 1756

Governor Dinwiddie, at the instance of Colonel Washington, having referred to me concerning the right of command between him and Captain Dagworthy, and desiring that I should determine it, I do therefore give it as my opinion, that Captain Dagworthy, who now acts under a commission from the Governor of Maryland, and where there are no troops joined, can only take rank as a provincial Captain and of course is under the command of all field officers, and, in case it should happen, that Colonel Washington and Captain Dagworthy should join at Fort Cumberland, it is my order that Colonel Washington shall take the command.

W. Shirley.[71]

In a letter of even date to Sharpe, the General tactfully elaborated this and directed that Dagworthy either be removed from Fort Cumberland or else be informed that if he remained he had "put himself under the command of Colonel Washington." [72] This, Shirley repeated, was because Dagworthy was acting under a provincial commission. The only dispute that could arise over Dagworthy's right to command would be when provincial troops were joined with regulars—a situation that did not exist at Fort Cumberland. Furthermore, Shirley told the Governor of Maryland, Roger Morris had informed him that Braddock had received orders from the Duke of Cumberland to put the fort in condition to house a garrison of 200 men. Under these orders, Shirley was told, Braddock had named Colonel Innes to command at Fort Cumberland and had so announced officially. "If that be so," Shirley wrote, "the matter must remain on the same foot [Braddock] put it upon." [73]

It seemed a clear-cut victory for George—and on the very ground Governor Dinwiddie had told him to urge.[74] Armed with the paper Shirley gave him, Washington could go to Fort Cumberland and force Dagworthy to renounce pretended authority and either to accept orders from his superior or to quit the place. George's seniority was vindicated. He was Colonel and Commander-in-Chief of the Virginia forces and could take charge at Fort Cumberland, but . . . but . . . but there was one unhappy disclosure: On the 23rd of February, Shirley had appointed Governor Sharpe to head all the troops that were to

---

[71] 2 *Shirley*, 412–13; 1 *Hamilton*, 201.
[73] 1 *Sharpe*, 348.
[72] 1 *Sharpe*, 347.
[74] See *supra*, p. 155.

be raised in Pennsylvania, Maryland, Virginia and South Carolina. At the very minute Shirley was giving George seniority over Dagworthy, an express was spurring toward Maryland, with a commission under which the man whom George believed to be responsible for Dagworthy's stand would have control of him—and of the next expedition against Fort DuQuesne.[75] Always someone stood between young Washington and first place in public honor!

The vindicated senior of Captain Dagworthy and the new subordinate of Governor Sharpe wasted no time in Boston after he received Shirley's decision. By the 10th of March, Washington was back in New York, where he again was the guest of Beverley Robinson and, no doubt, likewise was an interested listener to the conversation of Miss Mary Philipse. Four days or a little more were spent there.[76] Before he left, he had to borrow £91 from Beverley Robinson to make good his unanticipated expenditures and to provide funds for the journey southward.[77] On the 17th he reached Philadelphia.[78] There or a little nearer home, he may have been detained several days by illness;[79] but as soon as he was well enough to do so, he pressed on to Annapolis, which he reached on the 23rd.[80] He delivered dispatches from Shirley and no doubt conferred briefly with Sharpe, whom he still suspected of continued sympathy with Dagworthy. Once across the Potomac again, George scarcely paused before setting off for Williamsburg to report to Governor Dinwiddie.

By the date George started to the capital, March 25,[81] it was known generally that Sharpe had received command of all the forces to be raised in the South for another march to the Ohio. Sharpe had himself notified both the Governor of Virginia[82] and Adam Stephen, who still had in his care the Virginia troops at Fort Cumberland.[83] Dinwiddie

[75] Shirley to Sharpe, Feb. 23, 1756; 2 *Shirley*, 396 ff; acknowledged in Sharpe to Shirley, Mch. 7, 1756; 1 *Sharpe*, 351 ff.

[76] The only established dates are those of his payments in New York currency, Mch. 10–14, *Ledger A*, folio 27.

[77] *Ledger A*, folio 26.

[78] *Penn. Gazette*, Mch. 18, 1756; cited in 1 *Ford*, 234.

[79] This is the only explanation of an entry in *Ledger A*, March 25, of an item of £1 "cash to my nurse." As will appear, George at that date was riding to Williamsburg. On the 23rd, as noted, he was at Annapolis. He scarcely would have paid a nurse as much as £1 for attention on the 23rd–24th, alone. As there is an interval of one week between George's arrival in Philadelphia and his appearance in the Maryland capital, he may have been stricken in Philadelphia or en route to Alexandria. His expenses "from Philadelphia to Alexandria" were somewhat high (*Ledger A*, folio 27).

[80] 1 *Sharpe*, 380.

[81] That is to say, he had small expenses at Dumfries on the 25th as if he were on the road to Fredericksburg (*Ledger A*, folio 27).

[82] 1 *Sharpe*, 350.   [83] 1 *Hamilton*, 201.

had been prompt to extend congratulations,[84] but Stephen was
chagrined. He wrote his Colonel that after receipt of the news of the
appointment of Sharpe, Captain Dagworthy boasted of influence with
the new commander and strutted more than ever. Dagworthy even
went so far as to announce that he intended to have the Virginia Regiment reduced to Independent Companies.[85] Actually, Sharpe undertook promptly to execute Shirley's instruction that the ambitious Captain either accept Washington's orders or leave the fort; but the Governor of Maryland believed George himself had created the tangle by
staying away from Fort Cumberland after Dagworthy had been instructed to confine himself to command of the fort and not to interfere with the Virginia troops.[86] Before many weeks were past, George
was to confess: "I know that the unhappy difference about the command . . . has kept me from Fort Cumberland . . ."[87] At the moment, he was in no mood to admit that he had evaded a direct test of
authority with Dagworthy. On the contrary, as he spurred toward
Williamsburg, he felt aggrieved anew that his rival's friend and patron,
Sharpe, had been put over him. It was futile to continue! When he
reached Williamsburg he would resign again.[88]

[84] And equally prompt to inquire how the expenses of the Cherokee contingent were to be
paid (2 *Din.,* 367).

[85] 1 *Hamilton,* 203 ff, 205 ff. Stephen's two letters were dated March 29, when George was
en route to Williamsburg.

[86] Sharpe to Shirley, Mch. 23, 1756; 1 *Sharpe,* 380.

[87] 1 *G. W.,* 317. See *infra,* p. 387 and Washington to Speaker Robinson [incorrectly dated
Dec. n.d., 1756], 1 *G. W.,* 532.

[88] "I went to Williamsburg fully resolved to resign my commission . . ." (Letter of Apr. 9,
1756, to Robert Hunter Morris; 1 *G. W.,* 310).

CHAPTER X

A Crisis with an Incredible Ending
(Mch. 30–May 16, 1756)

Washington arrived in Williamsburg on the 30th of March [1] and found the Governor in a somewhat complacent frame of mind regarding the peace that had prevailed on the frontier since rangers had been organized and Fort Cumberland had been reenforced.[2] No report had come of the progress of Andrew Lewis's expedition against the Shawnees, but silence was not regarded as indicative of disaster.

The General Assembly was in session and had been since March 25. An unusual number of new members had been elected, precisely as Dinwiddie had hoped,[3] though the old leaders still controlled all action.[4] Burgesses realized that the recruiting of volunteers had not filled the Virginia Regiment and would not. A draft consequently was unavoidable. Only the details of it were debatable. Sentiment was strong, also, for the construction of a long chain of small forts to protect the frontier, a policy which Washington then believed the Colony could not execute without a far larger number of men than there was any reason to believe Virginia would call to service.[5]

On one point the legislators approached unanimity. In Shirley's instructions of February 23 to Sharpe, the acting Commander-in-Chief had urged that the Southern colonies raise 7284 men, of whom 4000 would suffice, he thought, for the proposed advance on Fort DuQuesne. The remaining 3284 should be made available, Shirley said, for operations in Lake Ontario.[6] Sharpe had not believed these figures attainable,[7] but he had forwarded the request to Dinwiddie.[8] The Virginia executive thought his Colony should give financial aid to the campaign in the North;[9] he knew the lawmakers of the Old Dominion too well to believe they would look with favor on the dispatch of a

---

[1] See his entry for expenditures at Wedderburn's that date, *Ledger A*, folio 27.
[2] Dinwiddie to the Lords of Trade, Mch. 20, 1756; *Dinwiddie Papers*, VHS; 2 *Din.*, 374.
[3] See *supra*, p. 140. [4] *Journ. H. B.*, 1752–58, p. xxv and 355.
[5] 1 *G. W.*, 301. [6] 2 *Shirley*, 394.
[7] 1 *Sharpe*, 351. [8] *Ibid.*, 350.
[9] 2 *Din.*, 281.

large contingent. They did not surprise him. The day before Washington reached Williamsburg, the Burgesses passed resolutions in which they disapproved the detachment of "so great a proportion" of their troops as was demanded for the Canadian expedition.[10] The Council, for its part, already had pronounced impracticable the employment of Virginia soldiers in the North, but members were willing to use the resources of the Colony for another advance on Fort DuQuesne if Maryland and Pennsylvania would do their part.[11] In the foreground of all planning was, finally, the firm conviction that Indians had to be employed against Indians. As George himself described the need and the opportunity, in a letter to Dinwiddie, the Cherokees had it in "their power to be of infinite use to us; and without Indians we shall never be able to cope with those cruel foes to our country." [12]

Few hours were given Washington to discuss this or anything else at the capital. There was not time, in fact, to explain to the Governor why he once again had resolved to resign. When the Colonel had been in Williamsburg only a day or two, an express brought bloody news: French and Indians had broken into the frontier settlements of Frederick and Hampshire. Details were few; danger was acute. George postponed all his business with the Governor and, taking horse, started back to his command.[13]

On the long, familiar road via Fredericksburg and Ashby's Gap, George had time for reflection on the future. Immediately ahead of him there might be excitement and tragedy. After that, Virginia for a time probably would have to remain on the defensive. Then, sooner or later, there would be another offensive to the westward. With that in prospect, Washington's ambition triumphed over his pique and disappointment. Resignation seemed no longer to be demanded by his pride. If there was to be a march to Fort DuQuesne, he must share it— and, at the least, must be second in command, next to Sharpe himself. So, probably at one of his stopping places on the road, George did what more than once he had found effective—he asked for the position he wanted. He wrote a formal request to Shirley to commission him as second officer in the new enterprise, and this letter he sent under cover to Sharpe with a plea that the Governor of Maryland approve his

---

[10] *Journ. H. B.*, 1752–58, p. 345; 2 *Din.*, 380.
[11] See Address of the Council to the Governor, 2 *Din.*, 379–80.
[12] Letter of Apr. 7, 1756; 1 *G. W.*, 301–02.
[13] 1 *G. W.*, 309. He perhaps left early on April 2, but the weight of the evidence in *Ledger A*, folio 27, is that he departed on the 1st.

application. In due time he was to be told that Sharpe had obliged him. "As Mr. Washington is much esteemed in Virginia and really seems a gentleman of merit," the Governor of Maryland was to write, "I should be exceedingly glad to learn that your Excellency is not averse to favoring his application and request." [14]

New and strange tests of this "merit" confronted George beyond the mountains. He rode so hard that he was by his own admission "not a little fatigued" [15] when he reached Winchester on the 6th [16] and found the people in what he accurately reported to be "a general consternation." [17] Indians again had overrun most of the back settlements and had murdered an unreckoned number of persons with the cruelty of hell's own tortures. Nearly all the frontier families had abandoned their homes and had fled to Winchester or to the nearest of the few garrisoned stockades. Misery and fear overwhelmed the lovely countryside when the first transforming touch of spring was upon it. Many of the fugitive farmers had no food for their children and no ammunition for their rifles; and from the hour Washington drew rein, all of them looked to him to supply their wants and to recover their goods. [18]

George was almost helpless. In Winchester he could not muster more than forty armed men—and most of these new recruits for the Regiment or the rangers. [19] Gunpowder was low. [20] Much the greater part of all the supplies and provisions of the Regiment were at Fort Cumberland. From that base, Winchester virtually was cut off. Only hunters familiar with the country could hope to get from the town to the storehouse on Wills Creek, and they had to proceed at night. [21]

[14] Letter of Apr. 10, 1756; 1 *Sharpe*, 389. This is the only known document that gives an outline of the incident. Both Washington's letter to Sharpe and the one to Shirley appear to have been lost. Consequently, the place and date of Washington's decision are indeterminable. If Sharpe wrote promptly on receipt of George's letter, which probably was sent by express, the time of writing might have been as late as April 4, which suggests, of course, that the letters may have been prepared in Fredericksburg. This is mere conjecture.

[15] 1 *G. W.*, 304.   [16] *Ibid.*, 300, 304.

[17] *Ibid.*, 309. Minor raids and occasional murders by the Indians during Washington's northern journey are described in *Penn. Gazette*, Mch. 25, 1756 and *Md. Gazette*, Mch. 11, 1755.

[18] *Ibid.*, 300.

[19] Washington's first mention of the number at his disposal was made on the 19th, when he said he had fifty (1 *G. W.*, 321). As fifteen of these are known to have reported on the 15th (see *infra*, p. 174), it is possible that he could not have counted more than thirty-five on arrival. Fifty, all told, had been assembled by the 19th (see *infra*, p. 176). A dispatch of April 30 from Williamsburg stated that "there are not now more than forty men at Winchester," but did not specify when this was (*Md. Gazette*, May 13, 1756).

[20] Washington reported on the 22nd that he had only one or two barrels left (1 *G. W.*, 326).

[21] 1 *G. W.*, 300, 303, 312. The *Md. Gazette* of May 13, 1756, published an article dated Williamsburg, April 30, in which expresses from Winchester were quoted as saying communication with Fort Cumberland had been cut off for three weeks when they had left the Shenandoah Valley.

The sole immediate recourse was the old one—to the militia. Concerning that notoriously undependable force, George at once questioned Lord Fairfax, County Lieutenant, and other senior officers who had hurried to Winchester: Could they raise the militia? They shook their heads. The men would not obey orders to assemble as a body. Individual Captains might call their Companies together and appeal to them. Some of the members might respond.[22] This was all the officers could suggest. George had to accept their proposal, though the indifference of the militia outraged him. Later he set April 15 for the rendezvous of all those who would go with him and drive the Indians out of the Shenandoah Valley.[23]

Such were the acts and the reflections of the first day at Winchester. The situation was similar in almost every detail to the one that Washington had faced in October, 1755, after the express bearing evil tidings had found him at Colonel Baylor's.[24] He had endured and survived the raids of the previous autumn, but his experience then did not equip him to stop panic or deafen him to the horrible stories of murder and pillage.

Relief of a sort came suddenly. A short time after George had finished his first report to the Governor on the 7th, into his quarters strode Richard Pearis, the Indian trader and interpreter, whom Dinwiddie had blamed, along with Governor Glen, for the failure of the Cherokees to give the Virginians help the previous year. Pearis now made a redeeming report: He and some companions had run into a small party of Indians with whom they had exchanged fire for about half an hour. One of Pearis's men had been killed and two wounded, but the Virginians had hit several of the enemy and had slain the leader, a Frenchman. In proof, Pearis produced the gentleman's scalp and a bag taken from around the dead man's neck. This contained instructions from the commander at Fort DuQuesne and identified the slain officer as the Sieur Douville. The instructions, signed by Dumas— a well-known officer who had distinguished himself in the battle of the Monongahela—bade Douville conform to the usages of honor and humanity, and to restrain the savages. At the same time, he was to undertake to burn the magazines at Conococheague, far inside the settlements. The very boldness of this design made the outcome of the first skirmish all the more pleasing to Washington. He duly forwarded

[22] 1 *G. W.*, 300.
[23] 1 *G. W.*, 307, 311, 312.   [24] See *supra*, p. 124.

Douville's scalp to Dinwiddie, with the recommendation that the men who took it be rewarded as Indians would have been for the same feat.[25] The Colonel next proceeded to send out scouting parties and to direct such feeble defensive measures as his limited forces permitted,[26] but the killing of Douville appeared to have discouraged, and perhaps to have scattered, the hostile raiders. Although frightened settlers continued to flee, no additional murders were reported for several days.

George took advantage of this breathing spell to plan for the future: At the earliest possible date, he would bring 100 men down from Fort Cumberland and with these soldiers and men raised around Winchester, he would undertake a swift and sharp offensive.[27] To succeed in this, he must have the aid of courageous savages immediately. "Indians are the only match for Indians," Washington repeated, "and without these we shall ever fight upon unequal terms." [28] George had heard, on reaching Winchester, that Andrew Lewis's expedition against the Shawnee towns had failed and that the Cherokees who had accompanied the Major had returned to the Virginia settlements.[29] Washington at once urged that these red warriors be prevailed upon to join him.[30] Even if they were few in number, they would be invaluable.

Looking beyond the instant crisis to the adequate, continuous defence of the frontier, Washington reasoned that troops of the type of his own Virginia Regiment had to be the backbone of any permanent force. As he did not think it possible to procure volunteers, he reasoned that the new draft should be of able-bodied marksmen for a term of eighteen to twenty months. By the end of that period, George somewhat grimly observed, two campaigns would have brought "matters nearly to a crisis one way or other." [31] The General Assembly was expected to vote £20,000 and to authorize an increase of his command, by means of the draft, to 2000 men. All these troops George wished to incorporate into a single Regiment, under his own direction, rather than to see them organized into two Regiments, with someone else as Colonel of the second. "I had no other motive in proposing this scheme," Washington was careful to affirm, "than the pleasing hopes of serving my country." [32]

[25] 1 G. W., 302; 1 Sharpe, 409; 2 Sparks, 137 n; 2 Penn. Arch., 600; Penn. Gazette, Apr. 29, 1756; Md. Gazette, May 6, 1756.

[26] 1 G. W., 303, 306–07, 309, 310.   [27] 1 G. W., 300.

[28] To Speaker Robinson, April 7, 1756; 1 G. W., 305.

[29] For the expedition and the return, see 1 Hamilton, 208, 212, 227, 228; 2 Din., 383, 387–88, 389, 397, 413; Md. Gazette, May 6, 1756.

[30] 1 G. W., 301.   [31] 1 G. W., 305.

[32] Letter of April 16, 1756, to Dinwiddie; 1 G. W., 313.

While George was developing these plans, April 15 arrived, the day for the rendezvous of all who were willing to join him in driving the Indians away. It proved as disappointing as any previous dealings with the militia of Frederick could have led him in his gloomiest mood to expect. Fifteen men, fifteen only, appeared. Some of these haggled or insisted on conditions George could not possibly allow.[33] Murder might lurk outside every settler's door; panic might empty Frederick and drive across the Blue Ridge families that had to leave their herds and their household goods behind them. Even that prospect did not fire the farmers to make common cause for common safety. "The timidity of the inhabitants of this County," said Washington briefly, "is to be equalled by nothing but their perverseness." [34] Lacking help from Frederick, he would have to wait until men came from Fort Cumberland to escort him back to that post where he could command a few hundred soldiers who knew something, at least, of discipline and of duty.[35]

On the 18th, as George waited, Col. James Innes arrived from Williamsburg, which he had visited on his return after some months of attention to his private affairs in North Carolina.[36] Washington had no exalted opinion of the soldierly excellences of Innes, "the old Gentleman," as he was styled by his juniors.[37] There still was a possibility that Dinwiddie's known partiality for his fellow Scot might induce him to name Innes to command in event Washington carried out his threat to resign.[38] In spite of this, the Governor's favorite now was on the way to do what George long had striven to accomplish, namely, to put Dagworthy in his place. General Shirley specifically had said that if Braddock had designated Innes for the command of Fort Cumberland, the North Carolinian must have it.[39] Orders were orders until they were revoked.

Innes, then, was not unwelcome *per se* at Winchester, but he was the bearer of a letter from Dinwiddie that infuriated Washington. The Governor enclosed a commission to hold courts martial, and then, with no preliminaries, went brusquely on: "I hope the affairs of the Regiment are not in so bad a condition as represented here. The Assembly were greatly inflamed, being told that the greatest immoralities and drunkenness have been much countenanced, and proper discipline

---

[33] 1 *G. W.*, 311, 315.   [34] 1 *G. W.*, 314.

[35] 1 *G. W.*, 311–12.   [36] See *supra*, p. 134.

[37] Cf. Stephen in 1 *Hamilton*, 263.   [38] See Vol. I, p. 430.

[39] See *supra*, p. 166.

neglected; I am willing to think better of our officers and therefore suspend my judgment till I hear from you." [40]

George previously had heard nothing of this. He knew that he had some lazy officers [41] and some, doubtless, besides one young Captain he had admonished,[42] who lingered too long over their cups; but the charge that immoralities and drunkenness "had been countenanced"— that was a reflection on him personally! As soon as Washington could find time, he sat down and wrote the Governor a vigorous denial. He did not attempt to assert how much truth there might be in charges against individuals; "but *this* I am certain of, and can call my conscience, and what, I suppose, will still be a more demonstrable proof in the eyes of the world, my orders, to witness how much I have, both by threats and persuasive means, endeavored to discountenance gaming, drinking, swearing, and irregularities of every other kind; while I have, on the other hand, practiced every artifice to inspire a laudable emulation in the officers for the service of the country, and to encourage the soldiers in the unerring exercise of their duty." [43]

The earnestness of this long sentence—one of the longest that even he had ever written—scarcely was weakened by rhetorical overwriting. He meant every syllable of it. "How far I have failed in this desirable end," he continued, "I cannot pretend to say"; but he thought his effort should be taken into account before he was condemned. Then he made his indirect confession that pride and a desire to avoid possible humiliation at the hands of Dagworthy might have been responsible in part, for what now was alleged: "I . . . know that the unhappy difference about the command, which has kept me from Fort Cumberland, has consequently prevented me from *enforcing* the orders, which I never fail to *send*." His sense of justice now prevailed. "However, if I continue in the service"—that was half doubt, half threat—"I shall take care to act with a little more vigor than has hitherto been practiced, since I find it so absolutely necessary." [44]

George was in this state of mind—sensitive, humiliated and half convinced of error—when, on the 19th of April, a Sergeant of the Virginia Regiment brought a most alarming report from Lieut. William Stark at Edwards's Fort. Stark reported a losing engagement in which two officers and fifteen men had been left, some of them dead, in the hands

[40] Letter of Apr. 8, 1756; 1 *Hamilton*, 213; 2 *Din.*, 381.
[41] 1 *G. W.*, 319.   [42] 1 *G. W.*, 291–92.
[43] 1 *G. W.*, 317.   [44] *Ibid.*

of the enemy. The Sergeant added verbally even more exciting details —that the numbers of the attacking force probably were larger than Stark's letter indicated, that many French were participating, that the greater part of the assailants were mounted, and that they had surrounded and were preparing to storm the feeble defences.[45]

Edwards's Fort was on Cacapon River in Hampshire County,[46] distant not more than twenty miles from Winchester.[47] The first attack might be preliminary; the town itself might be the real objective of a powerful raid. In this belief, Washington called into council Colonel Innes and those officers of the Virginia Regiment who happened to be in Winchester. He told them of Stark's dispatch and of the Sergeant's verbal report. What did the council recommend? Judgment was unanimous. The militia of Frederick and adjoining Counties must be raised immediately; when a strong force was available, it should take the offensive; meantime, Colonel Washington should retain in Winchester for its defence the fifty recruits who had assembled there en route to various posts.[48]

Washington accepted these recommendations. He sent Capt. Henry Harrison to take command at Fort Edwards, if the place could be reached.[49] Ammunition was forwarded, also, in the hope that courageous men, carrying the powder and shot, could slip past the enemy.[50] Capt. William Peachey was hurried off to notify the Governor and to ask for a muster of the militia [51] over whom Washington could exercise no authority till they were brought to him. Lord Fairfax was urged to call on the militia of Frederick and the adjacent Counties to move to Winchester as rapidly as possible. "Nothing but dispatch," George wrote in some excitement, "can answer our present purposes, for unless I can throw some ammunition into Edwards's Fort tonight, the remainder of our party and the inhabitants that are there will more than probably fall a sacrifice to the Indians." [52] Washington did all that was recommended by his elders or suggested by his own resourcefulness, but he felt that reliance of any sort on the militia was worse than doubtful.

---

45 1 G. W., 319, 321.

46 The present-day village of Capon Bridge occupies approximately the site. See Koontz, Frontier, 120.

47 1 G. W., 319. The distance by air is barely seventeen miles.

48 1 G. W., 319.

49 1 G. W., 319–20.

50 1 G. W., 321, 322.

51 2 Din., 387. Peachey's name does not appear at the time, but the identification is made certain by events described infra. Cf. 2 Hamilton, 182.

52 1 G. W., 321.

It was, he wrote the Governor, "a poor resource, a very unhappy dependence, though our only one at present." [53]

Nothing further happened until 2 o'clock on the morning of the 20th of April. Then another express arrived from Stark: The fort still was undamaged; the enemy had not attacked; ammunition was much needed. Enclosed in Stark's dispatch [54] was a strange paper in which Capt. John Ashby reported from his fort on Patterson Creek [55] that savages, who said they numbered 400, had demanded the surrender of his stockade. Ashby described his "party"—he meant parley—with an Indian, and he concluded: "I give him a dram and so departed without one fire of a gun and in the evening I heard them attact the fort at the mouth of the creek and a number of guns fired but what is done I know not. I believe every word they told me was a lie. I seen a vast number but not four hundred." [56]

Washington had accepted the Sergeant's report that Edwards's Fort was surrounded, but he could not credit this new tale. An effort was being made, George thought, to intimidate Ashby into surrender; [57] it was necessary to stiffen his resistance. George wrote the commander at Edwards's Fort to ascertain where the Indians had their rendezvous and, if possible, to deliver a night attack on them; [58] Ashby was enjoined to hold his fort to the last extremity. Should he face the prospect of being overwhelmed, he was to blow up the stockade and was to retreat to Cumberland. [59]

Bad news followed bad. From several outposts George received expresses that informed him on the 21st and 22nd of isolation, threatened attack and shortage of provisions. [60] At the mouth of Patterson Creek, the officer and thirty men who were guarding supplies in a small fort successfully beat off attack. [61] Elsewhere the story was one of gloom, danger and murder. On the night of the 22nd, three families were slaughtered. Indians and French were believed to be prowling along almost every road; an attack on Winchester appeared to be imminent. [62] Even Col. James Wood, the most influential and wealthiest of the planters, left his estate and sought shelter—an action that made his tenants and adherents conclude the situation was hopeless. [63]

[53] 1 G. W., 319.   [54] 1 G. W., 321.
[55] Still called Ashby's Fort and located nine miles South of Cumberland, Maryland.
[56] 1 Hamilton, 220–21. For activities around Ashby's Fort, April 1, see Md. Gazette, May 6, 1756.
[57] 1 G. W., 321, 326.   [58] 1 G. W., 321.
[59] 1 G. W., 326.   [60] 1 G. W., 323, 324, 325.
[61] 1 G. W., 326. This doubtless was the firing Ashby heard.
[62] 1 G. W., 329.   [63] 1 Hamilton, 252, 264.

George authorized the evacuation of the fort at Enoch's, if that became necessary.[64] Another council reviewed and confirmed the decision that the small force at Winchester should remain there.[65] Washington repeated his urgent call for militia from Fairfax and Prince William.[66] He pleaded, too, for volunteers from the Valley—but in three days could prevail on twenty only to join him.[67] No word reached him that any reenforcements were on the march. George was almost frantic. He wrote the Governor, "I am too little acquainted, Sir, with pathetic language, to attempt a description of the people's distresses, though I have a generous soul, sensible of wrongs, and swelling for redress. But what can I do? If bleeding, dying! would glut their insatiate revenge, I would be a willing offering to savage fury, and die by inches to save a people! I *see* their situation, know their danger, and participate their sufferings, without having it in my power to give them further relief, than uncertain promises." [68]

It was acutely personal in another way, also. George explained wrathfully and with no attempt at concealment of his sensitiveness and his love of distinction: ". . . In fine, the melancholy situation of the people, the little prospect of assistance, the gross and scandalous abuses cast upon the officers in general, which is reflecting upon me in particular, for suffering misconducts of such extraordinary kinds, and the distant prospects, if any, that I can see, of gaining honor and reputation in the service are motives which cause me to lament the hour, that gave me a commission and would induce me, at any other time than this of imminent danger, to resign without one hesitating moment, a command, which I never expect to reap either honor or benefit from; but, on the contrary, have almost an absolute certainty of encouraging displeasure below,[69] while the murder of poor innocent babes and helpless families may be laid to my account here!" [70]

On the 23rd, while Washington was trying to draw exposed families to Winchester and was considering the evacuation of minor forts, his secretary returned from Williamsburg with a letter of John Robinson's. As always, the Speaker was a devoted and admiring friend, but this time he began less tactfully than usual with reference to the incursions

64 *Ibid.,* 322, 324. For the location of Enoch's on the Cacapon, see *infra,* p. 181.
65 I *G. W.,* 331 and n.   66 *Ibid.,* 323–24.
67 *Ibid.,* 322, 326, 327.
68 Letter of Apr. 22, 1756; I *G. W.,* 324–25.
69 "Below" was the term frequently employed for Williamsburg and the older settlements.
70 I *G. W.,* 325. The punctuation of these two quoted sentences has been left intact because it reflects the emotion with which Washington wrote.

of the French and Indians. These attacks were due, he thought, "in a great measure to the obstinacy and dastardliness of the people themselves, and, I am sorry to say it, I fear from the conduct of some of our officers, of whom there are terrible reports . . ." [71] Robinson added in the very next clause that he was sure Washington "would put a stop to [the officers'] irregularities"; but the words cut the bruised skin of the overwrought Colonel. It was precisely as he had said: "Below," at Williamsburg, they were assailing his officers and indirectly were blaming him—when the frontier was aflame and he was almost helpless for lack of men. If only the critics would name the offenders! [72]

Every day, every hour—almost every minute as it seemed to George—brought new alarms,[73] but still no report of reenforcements. One express after another was dispatched with appeals for help from other Counties.[74] George sent a second officer to Williamsburg to explain the situation and to ask for arms and ammunition. Provisions were required, also, even in that land of overflowing plenty, because panic had scattered herds, and the presence of hostile savages on the roads had made it impossible to collect supplies.[75] The Governor was exhorted once again by Washington to procure Indian assistance immediately. If possible, Dinwiddie must create a diversion by a secret expedition against the villages of the hostile savages.[76]

Stern measures of a different sort might be required directly on the Virginia frontier, from which, as George continued to assure the authorities in Williamsburg, nearly the whole population had been driven.[77] Shocking rumors were being repeated; treason was in the air. Some of the settlers, it was said, had despaired of help from their own government, and, as George reported, they talked of "capitulating and coming upon terms with the French and Indians, rather than lose their lives and fortunes through obstinacy." [78] Washington scarcely could believe this, but he promised himself and his Governor that as soon as he had men enough he would do his utmost, as he put it, "to detect and secure such pests of society." [79]

Rumored sedition, shortage of ammunition, continued murders on isolated farms,[80] the insecurity of the roads, the misery of the people,

[71] 1 *Hamilton*, 221.
[72] Washington to Robinson, Apr. 24, 1756; 1 *G. W.*, 331.
[73] 1 *G. W.*, 329.   [74] 1 *G. W.*, 341.
[75] 1 *G. W.*, 329.
[76] 1 *G. W.*, 330. For Dinwiddie's efforts to get Cherokees and Nottoways to go to Winchester, see 2 *Din.*, 389; 1 *Hamilton*, 227, 228; *Md. Gazette*, May 6, 1756.
[77] 1 *G. W.*, 329, 332.   [78] 1 *G. W.*, 330.
[79] *Ibid.*, 331.   [80] Cf. 1 *G. W.*, 337.

the criticism leveled at his officers, an aching tooth that had to be drawn,[81] the wretchedness of George himself in being unable to give help [82]—none of this denied him the exercise of his singular power to detach himself from many problems in order to concentrate on one.

He had learned from Williamsburg that the General Assembly was discussing and probably would pass a bill for the erection of a new and longer chain of forts. His most recent information was, also, that the total armed force to be authorized by the lawmakers was not to consist of 2000 but of 1500 men.[83] On the 24th, George sat down and wrote Robinson a letter in which he put these two probabilities together and discussed the defensive policy of Virginia with as much of calm logic as if he had been, on an untroubled day, at the Governor's palace or in the council chamber of the capitol.[84]

He did not muster all his arguments at the moment, to be sure, and he had to return to the subject three days later; [85] but in the two papers he disclosed ability to rid his eyes of the motes of the day and to fix them in clear, undeviating scrutiny of a single issue.[86] Usually, when he had completed his study of a subject, he was convinced and often was ready to fight hard for acceptance of his views; but he was careful, as a rule, to make it plain that he, a soldier, would obey orders. In repeating now to Dinwiddie the argument he had presented to Robinson, he affirmed that the "public safety and interest" had been "solely the object of all my thoughts, words and actions, and," he added—with his ever-sensitive regard for the good opinion of society—"in order to avoid censure in every part of my conduct, I make it a rule to obey the dictates of your Honor, the Assembly, and a good conscience." [87] His argument was not in vain. The bill for erecting the forts had been passed before his letters reached Williamsburg, but the measure was forthwith amended to authorize what he particularly recommended, a strong fort at Winchester.[88]

While George was submitting his views to his superiors, he had one piece of good news of the garrisons at the various stockades from which Winchester had been isolated. Adam Stephen sent word that all the men and all the defences were safe.[89] The only loss of soldiers,

81 *Ledger A*, folio 29; Apr. 27, 1756.   82 1 *G. W.*, 342.

83 1 *G. W.*, 330. Provision for the forts was in the supply bill signed May 1, *Journ. H. B.*, 1752–58, p. 392; text in 7 *H* 7 ff.

84 1 *G. W.*, 332–36.   85 *Ibid.*, 338–40.

86 For the argument over the chain of forts, see *infra*, p. 194.

87 1 *G. W.*, 344.

88 *Journ. H. B.*, 1752–58, p. 393, 396–97; 7 *H* 26 ff.

89 1 *G. W.*, 337. Stephen's dispatches were received on the 25th.

so far as either officer knew, was in the affair at Edwards's Fort on the 18th of April. Concerning this, information was accumulated gradually until, at length, the survivors came to Winchester and related substantially all the details. About the 15th of April, Capt. John Mercer had started with approximately 100 men to search for the Indians who were devastating the countryside. At Washington's instance, he had undertaken to scour the Warm Spring Mountain,[90] but, when heavy rains stopped him, he received new orders to proceed to Enoch's.[91] Apparently, Mercer with part of his troops halted at Edwards's Fort, en route to Enoch's, which was on the same stream, the Cacapon, ten miles or more to the northward. On the 18th, three of Mercer's men went out of the fort, ostensibly to look for horses, but after a time two of them came running back and reported that they had encountered Indians within sight of the stockade.

Mercer at once started after the savages with forty or fifty of his followers. He and his party had proceeded about a mile and a half when suddenly they were fired upon, probably from ambush. Answer was immediate. Soon, from behind trees and rock, a confused skirmish began on the mountainside. The sound of action reaching the fort, one detachment and then a second went to Mercer's aid; but the first of these parties was stripped quickly of half its strength by the cowardice of a Sergeant who led his men back to the fort.

Meanwhile, the skirmish continued. The Virginians could get few shots at the concealed savages who gradually worked their way around the white men. In a short time the contingent from the fort was so nearly surrounded that a retreat was ordered. Mercer, his Ensign and fifteen men, dead or crippled, were left behind to be scalped and perhaps to be mutilated. The unhurt survivors and two wounded reached the fort where they remained without further molestation.[92] After the savages left the vicinity, a scouting party found the body of one Indian thrust under some rocks and partly concealed. Bloodstains on the ground raised the hope that other redmen had been killed or carried away, mortally wounded, but no additional dead were discovered.[93] The affair thus had to be written down as a seventeen-to-one loss, an-

---

[90] 1 G. W., 315, 318.   [91] Ibid., 316.

[92] Lt. William Stark's MS dispatch of "Sunday night," Apr. 18, 1756, is the principal source of information. It is in 5 Papers of G. W., LC, and is supplemented by the court-martial proceedings in the case of Sergeant Nathan Lewis, May 3, 1756 (infra, p. 192). See also 1 Hamilton, 227, 246 ff; 1 Sharpe, 403; 2 Shirley, 395.

[93] 1 G. W., 354–55. Adam Long, a prisoner at Fort DuQuesne, was told by some of the returning Indians, engaged in this affair, that they lost nine of their number (Md. Gazette, Oct. 7, 1756).

other example of the inability of half-trained white men to cope with Indians in woodland fighting. It was tragic, even if it was a small disaster in comparison with the murder of settlers, but it appears to have been the only instance in which, to the 27th of April, the Regiment itself reported any casualties.[94]

That day, April 27, George had to write the Governor: "Desolation and murder still increase, and no prospects of relief. The Blue Ridge is now our frontier, no men being left in this County except a few that keep close with a number of women and children in forts, which they have erected for the purpose. There are now no militia in this County; when there were, they could not be brought to action." He had begun to fear that the same condition might prevail among the militia of the other Counties, because he had received no specific report that any men from any other part of Northern Virginia were moving to the Valley.[95]

The prospect now changed. Dinwiddie had not been idle. After Lord Fairfax's appeals for help had been sent out, the Governor had ordered the Lieutenants of Frederick and of the nine Counties East of the Blue Ridge and nearest the lower Shenandoah Valley to muster their militia, to draft one-half of them, and to have them rendezvous at Winchester.[96] The first to answer was Capt. John Dalton of Fairfax, who reached the town on the 29th of April with thirty-one volunteers and fifty-four of the militia of his County. Four Captains from the same familiar ground reported that they had about 100 militiamen in the gap of the Short Hills and wished to know whether to send forward the whole. After bringing Dalton into consultation on this, Washington learned that the commanding officer in Fairfax had assumed a complement of ten men would be taken from each Company. George approved this and ordered forty to be marched to Winchester. Almost to his surprise, as he admitted in his memoranda, they "actually came" two days later and gave him his first real acquisition of strength after he had reached the Valley—125 men.[97] They were followed at once by Capt. William Russell and twenty-three, and these, in turn, by an ad-

[94] One of the Troop of light horse had been killed and one was reported missing late in January (*Md. Gazette*, Apr. 15, 1756).

[95] 1 *G. W.,* 341.

[96] *Md. Gazette*, May 13, 1756; see the Preston Papers, 333, *loc. cit.* for a call on Augusta, April 24, for one-third of its militia. In 2 *Din.,* 392–93, under date of April 27, is a draft of the circular letter sent to the County Lieutenants. This probably was issued that day (cf. *Journ. H. B.,* 1752–58, p. 384) but the date of arrival of the Fairfax contingent in Winchester shows that it came in response to early appeals sent out by Washington and Fairfax and not in answer to the Governor's call. Cf. 1 *G. W.,* 323, 345.

[97] 1 *G. W.,* 345.

ditional twenty-five whom Washington on further consideration decided he should summon from the Short Hills.[98] George now had a total of 173 Fairfax militiamen. That is to say, he had them for a day. Thirteen deserted as soon as they could slip off.[99]

By most cruel chance, it now seemed probable that the invaders had begun to leave precisely when the militia commenced to reenforce the small Virginia Regiment. Information was scant and not convincing, but by the end of April it indicated that the raid was over and that the Indians had started back to Fort DuQuesne. Whether or not this proved true, George did not intend to permit the militia to remain in idleness any longer than it took him to prepare orders for them. One hundred were directed to march on May 4 for the South Branch; the others were to join a searching party of the Regiment, already told to search Back Creek for the presence of Indians. Here again, everything was done as the Colonel required, except for the fact that ten more men deserted—a disconcerting total of twenty-three in three days.[100]

Washington knew by the 3rd of May how widely the call from the Governor had been dispatched and from how many Counties he was at length to receive aid, such as it was. Indeed, the Colonel now had the embarrassing prospect of more militiamen than he could shelter or use or willingly would feed and pay at the expense of the Colony. In tones almost ludicrously different from those of his recent calls for help, George wrote the Governor "humbly to offer it to Your Honor's superior judgment if it would not be advisable to stop all the militia that are ordered from the ten Counties, save about five or six hundred from the adjacent ones?" This number, he said, would suffice until the receipt of the drafts and the completion of the forts, which he heard the Assembly had decided to authorize.[101] Besides, the employment of so many militia might hamper the draft which would provide men able to perform larger service at less cost.[102] Time would suffice for halting the militia because, George explained, "I never knew any yet to appear in ten days after they were expected." [103]

He soon found himself mistaken in his reckoning of time and unjust in his estimate of the diligence of some of the senior officers of the militia in mustering their forces. Consequently, he was too late in his representations to the Governor. On the 6th of May eight officers and

98 *Ibid.*, 346. The other men who remained in the Short Hills were dismissed.
99 *Ibid.*
100 *Ibid.*   101 1 *G. W.*, 355.
102 *Ibid.*   103 *Ibid.*

121 men arrived at Winchester from Prince William;[104] the next day brought Lt. Col. Henry Peyton and, separately, Capt. Joseph Murdock with two officers and twenty men, faithful survivors of a contingent of fifty from King George. Thirty had deserted on the road.[105]

To that date, the only violence charged by Valley folk against any of the soldiers had been laid at the door of some of Capt. Henry Woodward's men of the Virginia Regiment. They were alleged—George thought falsely—to have killed a farmer's fowls, to have torn down one of his houses for firewood, and to have turned horses into his corn.[106] In contrast, nearly all the militia had been most law-abiding in their idleness. The exception was the Prince William contingent. Militiamen from that County for some reason appeared to think themselves superior not only to the privates and n.c.o's. of the Virginia Regiment but to the officers also. On the 8th, one of the Prince William newcomers became so violently abusive that the guard seized him and locked him up. This insult the sons of Prince William would not endure. An officer of the detachment collected some of his militia, who proceeded to the guardhouse, released their comrade and then demolished the building to make sure it was not used again for the incarceration of free men.

The leader of this mutiny was not content with this achievement. He swore publicly that all the officers of the Virginia Regiments were scoundrels, whom he "could drive before him." This was a little too much, even where veterans had been praying for reenforcements. One of the Regiment took the fire-eater in hand and, in a manner left unexplained, so thoroughly acquainted him with military law and its enforcement that all the flames of threat died away in cold fright.[107]

Now another remarkable performance: Back to town during the evening of the 8th came Capt. John Dalton and Captain Russell with their Fairfax volunteers and such of their militiamen as had not deserted by that time. Dalton was asked, of course, why he had not carried out his orders to operate briefly with a scouting party of the Regiment and then to post the militia in a pass previously designated. He blandly replied that Captain Russell's volunteers—to quote George's own indignant words—"had got tired and must needs go home and that the militia, which were only thirteen, were too small to post at any pass . . ."

104 *Ibid.*, 346.
106 1 *G. W.*, 362.
105 *Ibid.*, 346–47.
107 1 *G. W.*, 347.

A volunteer being his own master, in the loose organization then existing, he could go as freely as he came and at the time of his own choosing. So, the next morning, Dalton and Russell and their volunteers set out for home. George let their militiamen return with them. When volunteers, unabashed, quit because they were tired, it was a trivial victory for discipline that the Prince William officer who had been responsible for the riot on the previous day came to headquarters and made his apologies. Washington did not punish him.[108]

After these experiences, Colonel Washington scarcely could have received with enthusiasm on the afternoon of that same 9th of May the news that Col. Thomas Slaughter was approaching with 200 Culpeper militiamen, who were said to carry an average of one firelock only for every four men. George had to send back instructions which Slaughter might have regarded as inhospitable, not to say uncivil: he was told to remain where he was, because the town already contained more militiamen than it could lodge, and had "many quarrelsome fellows amongst them." [109] The Culpeper militia stayed where they had halted; Colonel Slaughter himself felt impelled to ride into town to report an error: His count of arms had been mistaken. Among his men there were eighty firelocks.[110]

There was no stopping the flow of militia now. Like long-delayed rains, once they began to descend on the Valley, they poured down from the hills. On the 10th, a full corps of officers and 170 men of Caroline arrived under George's friend Col. John Baylor. The next day introduced the Spotsylvania contingent—148 strong. On their heels tramped the yeomanry and the gentry of Stafford, 114 of them.[111] Actually, too, nine of the deserters from the King George militia put in an appearance.

Three days had brought Washington about 670 militiamen. He did what he could to entertain the officers in such comfort as the little town could offer,[112] but he had to elaborate his plans for employing the men in the ranks. Otherwise the "quarrelsome fellows" would war among themselves. It was not easy to make them earn their keep, because there were few reports now of the presence of hostile savages near the

[108] 1 G. W., 347.
[109] 1 G. W., 347–48.
[110] 1 G. W., 348.
[111] Washington's memoranda do not specifically credit this contingent to Stafford, but its commander was Col. Henry Fitzhugh, and the presence of Stafford militia subsequently was mentioned and nowhere else explained.
[112] See, for example, in 3 Papers of G. W., LC, a gracious "thank-you" letter of June 7, 1756, from Col. John Baylor.

inner settlements. George therefore reasoned that if any of the out-posts needed strengthening, those on the western streams did, because they were nearest the enemy. As a thrifty engineer, he concluded, also, that if he could not dispatch the militia to pursue the redmen, he could use some of them to raise stockades and to build storehouses. Doubt-less in a desire to get the Prince William militia as far from other troops as possible, George assigned them to duty on the Little Cacapon and on Patterson Creek—ample punishment for all their rioting.[113]

Now came a surprise for which George was unprepared, in spite of his acquaintance with the mind of militia and the ambition of aristocrats. He had reasoned, with sound economy, that a Captain and four Subal-terns would be a sufficient number of officers to keep the Prince William contingent under such discipline as the men might be induced to respect. It was not to be as Washington planned it. Lieutenant Colonel Peyton had been in town five days and had been assigned no duties, an unpleasantly negative position for one who was Burgess, Justice and County Lieutenant.[114] He now stepped forward, tendered a special commission given him by the Governor, and insisted, as firmly as a gentleman should, that he be named to command the militia who were going to Patterson's Creek.

Washington was dumbfounded. "I expostulated with him on the absurdity of it," George later recorded, "and represented the unnecessary charge it would run the country to, employing of supernumerary offi-cers." He argued in vain. The Lieutenant Colonel with the special commission waved aside the question of pay. Peyton had no other motive, he said, than a desire to serve his country; he expected no re-ward or gratuity. Besides, unless he went with the men, he was sure they would desert.[115]

That was a poser for George. Before him was that special commission —and commissions seemed to have been drawn to plague him anyway. Because of that paper Peyton actually might have the legal right to demand that he head the contingent. Even if the right were debatable under military law, no leader wished to run the risk that the militia would desert. Soldiers should obey any commander put over them, of course, instead of obeying one man and defying another; but, as George was finding anew every day, militia were . . . different. He took the precaution of writing down the names of those present when

113 1 G. W., 348.   114 See 1 Va. Biography, 304; Hayden, 502.
115 1 G. W., 349.

Peyton made so extraordinary a request, but he named the Lieutenant Colonel to the command and sent the gentlemen off that same afternoon with a Captain, four Subalterns and ninety-six privates.[116] "I earnestly entreat," George wrote in Peyton's instructions, "that you will be careful to observe good order and discipline among your men, that you will ever be mindful of the charge you are entrusted with, and diligent in executing with the utmost dispatch, all these several orders."[117]

Detachment of the trouble-making sons of Prince William did not ease perceptibly the situation in Winchester. Other militiamen and their officers became restive and wondered how much longer they would have to await permission to return home and to attend to the delayed planting of a tobacco crop for which great preparation had been made.[118] The men seemed to think, as Washington recorded, that they had "performed a sufficient tour of duty by marching to Winchester."[119] With equal assurance they demanded more food. Soldiers of the Regiment received their allotted pound of meat and pound of flour a day, ate it or bartered it, and did not die of hunger. Militiamen insisted this food was not enough. Washington listened to their complaints, as reported by their superiors, and he frugally decided to give them the rations set aside for the officers but not drawn—an arrangement by which he could keep the total issue of provisions within the volume the troops were supposed to use. Hungry and idle militiamen continued to protest they were being half starved. Colonel Washington had reluctantly to raise the daily allowance to a pound and a quarter, but with no assurance that this would silence grumbling or contribute to content.[120]

Nor was there any certainty that militia ordered to a station would get there or stay there. While George still was puzzling over provisions, an express arrived from Lieutenant Colonel Peyton with a humiliating report: On the first night out, a Sergeant and fourteen of the Colonel's devoted private soldiers—the men over whom he had so much influence —had . . . had deserted. Those who had disappeared in the darkness were nearly a sixth of Peyton's enlisted strength. He called, therefore, for reenforcements. Washington had planned to send the small King George detachment to Mendenhall's Fort, and as these men were ready

---

116 1 *G. W.*, 348–49.   117 *Ibid.*, 368.
118 See Francis Jerdone's letter of May 15, 1756 in 16 *W* (1) p. 126.
119 1 *G. W.*, 349.   120 *Ibid.*

to march, he started them for Peyton's camp. That is, Washington undertook to dispatch them all, but of the number who had not deserted on the march to Winchester,[121] some were sick and others were admitted quickly to the list of deserters. Not more than twenty left with their Lieutenant. Four of these disappeared.[122]

It was difficult for even so correct a mathematician as Washington to avoid confusion over the strength of his troops, because new contingents were reporting while detachments marched off and desertion sapped every roster. On the 14th of May, Col. William Taliaferro [123] arrived with his officers and 100 privates from Orange County. The same day Col. Charles Barret of Louisa presented 130 of his County militia. It was hourly more difficult to find employment for so many. By inquiry, some carpenters could be identified and hired for special work at Winchester; [124] but after the garrisons were drafted and the artisans enlisted, the others either should be dismissed or else be sent to defend the exposed southern part of the western frontier. To make a wise choice, George called all the field officers into council on the evening of the 14th. They were unanimously against attempting to use the militia at a great distance, and they were equally of one mind in advising the discharge of all not "absolutely necessary to resist a second invasion upon this quarter." [125]

Washington accepted this decision, but when he came to compute the number of militiamen required at the ten places he had chosen as their posts, he found he would need at least 482 of the 877 men, or thereabout, who remained around Winchester and in the town.[126] Apportioning these ratably among the militia of the various Counties, choosing by lot those who were to remain, and then assigning a proper quota to each fort, took some hours. Promptly after that, the march of the detachments was set for May 16, but it had to be delayed a day because of desertions and lack of transport.[127] The discharged men

---

121 Nine of these deserters, it will be remembered, had returned. See *supra*, p. 185.

122 Washington's statement on this, 1 *G. W.*, 349, is not clear.

123 Washington spelled the name with two "ls," a usage that Fitzpatrick followed, but the distinguished Virginia family of this name used one "l." As pronounced in Virginia, it is Tarliver with the accent on the "a."

124 1 *G. W.*, 348.   125 1 *G. W.*, 369–70.

126 Cf. 1 *G. W.*, 350, 371. He had received approximately 1175 n.c.o.'s. and private soldiers, volunteers included, with their complement of officers, and he had detached or sent home 298 of these. This last total included deserters from the Fairfax contingent. Absolute accuracy is not attainable, because Washington failed to enter in his memoranda (1) the size of the proposed garrison at Mendenhall's Fort and (2) the exact strength of the Culpeper militia whom he mentioned as "about 200." Cf. 1 *G. W.*, 347, 348.

127 1 *G. W.*, 349–51.

were allowed to start home as soon as the draft had been completed and rations had been issued for their use on the road.

George had not then received a letter of May 13, in which Col. William Fairfax urged him to be patient with his "medley of undisciplined militia"; [128] but at sunset on the 16th of May, Washington could have told himself that patience already had been rewarded. Part of the militia were ready to march to their stations on the basis of a fair drawing of names; the others were going home; from among the whole number, seventy had been employed as carpenters to work in Winchester at 6d per day in addition to their regular pay and provisions. Those of the militia who had been ordered to the small forts on the South Branch and on the various creeks had been admonished that if any of them deserted, they would be drafted immediately into the Virginia Regiment.[129] The situation thus appeared to be better than at any time after the militia had engulfed Winchester.

That very night brought mockery, brought it suddenly and incredibly. An express rode into town with letters from Ashby's, Cocke's and Pearsall's forts, all to the same effect: a considerable body of Indians was said to be astir in the region of Patterson Creek and the South Branch. Incautiously, the express let the contents of his dispatches be known to some of the militia. He might as well have ridden down the street shouting that a thousand war-crazed savages were entering the town. Men under orders to go to the South Branch or to Patterson's Creek pictured themselves as scalped already. Regardless of officers and orders, they began to pour out of Winchester on the roads to the gaps of the Blue Ridge. With scarcely a pretense of concealment, they deserted en masse. Entire Companies disintegrated. Of the Louisa militia, who probably had numbered about seventy after part of them had been dismissed, only six could be found the next morning.[130] Stafford's fifty-eight had dwindled to eight. Probably 100 and more of the Caroline contingent had been in town at dusk; at dawn forty answered to their names. Col. John Spotswood had brought 130 from Spotsylvania and had told fifty-eight to go back to the Rappahannock and seventy-two to stay for garrison. Overnight he lost forty of his seventy-two.[131]

---

128 1 Hamilton, 256.   129 Orders of May 15; 1 G. W., 371.

130 This calculation of the strength of the contingent is based on the assumption that as George required about 482 of the 877 men, he kept 55 per cent of each contingent and let 45 per cent start for home.

131 1 G. W., 351.

So ruinous were the desertions, fired by reports of the return of the savages, that Colonel Washington had to revise his assignments for guarding the forts and had to reduce the number of places to be defended. He sent messengers off, also, to the militia officers who were marching men homeward. These leaders from Louisa, Orange and Culpeper were told to reverse their steps and to bring back their soldiers to take the place of those who had disappeared. In due time Colonel Barret and Colonel Taliaferro reported at headquarters but they had no men with them, absolutely none. The officers explained that their contingents had taken different roads home and had scattered. Some of the Orange militiamen had remained with Colonel Taliaferro, but, when they heard they were ordered back to Winchester, they deliberately charged their pieces and continued on their way, in defiant notice that they would fight Washington's patrols rather than go back and face the savages. Colonel Slaughter managed later to collect eight or nine Culpeper men, but that number was too small to justify recall.[132]

The militia had vanished as a fighting force; the curtain had fallen on the burlesque.

[132] 1 G. W., 351–52.

CHAPTER XI

PERPLEXITIES OF FRONTIER DEFENCE
(MAY 17–AUG. 15, 1756)

FORTUNATELY, the rumors that had produced the final panic of the militia May 16–17, 1756, were as untrue as the runaways. No additional murders were committed; no hostile Indians were seen. Washington sent forward the militiamen who had not deserted and he stationed them where they would encourage and assist the planters in reestablishing themselves.[1] With that, he ended one of the strangest chapters in his book of experience. If the price had not been the lives of farmers' wives and children, the futility of any reliance on untrained, unequipped militia would, in retrospect, have been ludicrous. The announcement of the Fairfax volunteers that they were tired, the superior tone of the men from Prince William, the insistence of Colonel Peyton on taking the field, the final dissolution of the force in unpursued flight before an unreal foe—all this would have been juicy meat for a satirical comedy.

To George, who had all of the responsibility of command and none of the blessing of humor, there had been nothing in the behavior of the militiamen to provoke laughter. He wasted no time in denouncing a system he had known to be worthless. A copy of his journal of those incredible two weeks of May was sent the Governor, but it was accompanied by no rhetorical tirade on the pusillanimity of the inexperienced, easily frightened defenders of Virginia firesides.

George put all his thought on two things. The improvement of the discipline of the Regiment was one of these. "The spirit of desertion was so remarkable in the militia," he told Dinwiddie, "that it had a surprising effect upon the Regiment and encouraged many of the soldiers to desert." He explained that he always sent out officers to pursue deserters and that he had caught two of the men who had gone

---

[1] 1 G. W., 351. For his appeal to the settlers to return, see his undated "Advertisement" in 1 G. W., 384. See also *Penn. Gazette*, May 27, 1756.

off. One had a previous good record that entitled him to consideration; the other was " a most atrocious villain." Washington insisted that this deserter and the Sergeant who had shown cowardice in the affair at Edward's Fort be put to death. Both had been condemned by court-martial. Execution of the Sergeant had been deferred in order to have him hanged or shot before the eyes of the drafted men who soon were expected and would be given this initial warning of what deser-tion and cowardice cost. "These examples and proper encouragement for good behavior," said Washington, "will, I hope, bring the soldiers under proper discipline." [2]

Immediate recruitment was George's second concern. After the fiasco of April and May had followed the failure of the recruiting of volun-teers for the Regiment, a draft [3] of able-bodied militiamen and prompt, careful training of them represented the only possible means of raising the strength of the Regiment to the 1500 authorized at the session of the General Assembly that had ended on the 5th of May. Washington had hoped the lawmakers would vote funds for 2000 men, as had been predicted,[4] but he did not indulge in excessive complaint when the total was set at three-fourths of that figure.[5] In several particulars, the law seemed to meet requirements: It provided for a new draft of un-married men, chosen by lot in the Counties and Cities, to bring up the Regiment to this required strength, and it so restricted exemption that only the man who produced £10 immediately after he was drafted, or found a willing substitute *instanter,* could escape service.[6]

Washington's chief criticisms of the statute were, first, that the General Assembly provided rightly enough for the incorporation of the drafted men into the Regiment [7] and then inconsistently stipulated that they could not be marched "out of this Colony." [8] In the second place,[9] the legislature limited the operation of the draft to Dec. 1, 1756, doubtless on the theory that the danger of Indian raids would end with snowfall and that money could be saved thereafter by releasing the drafted men. "By the time they shall have entered into the service,"

---

[2] Letter to Dinwiddie, May 23, 1756; 1 *G. W.,* 386. The trial of Sergeant Nathan Lewis, accused of cowardice, may be traced in 1 *Hamilton,* 246, 247, 249, and in 1 *G. W.,* 354, 357–58, 359, 386.
[3] Apparently the word "conscription," though employed early to describe enlistment, did not convey in English the idea of compulsion until almost 1800.
[4] See *supra,* p. 173.
[5] For the act, see 7 *H* 9–20. Washington's observations to Dinwiddie appear in 1 *G. W.,* 330, 332. A review of the legislative session will be found in *Journ. H. B.,* 1752–58, xxv.
[6] 7 *H* 15, sec. x.   [7] *Ibid.,* 16, sec. xi.
[8] Cf. 1 *G. W.,* 383.   [9] 7 *H* 16, sec. x.

Washington protested, "they will claim a discharge." He was seeking a force to serve for the duration of the war and he believed that if unwilling recruits were compelled to remain a sufficient time with the Regiment, all of them could be disciplined and some could be persuaded to enlist in the colonial counterpart of the "regular establishment." [10]

Every man who thus could be prevailed upon to join the Regiment was needed. In spite of all efforts to upbuild the force, the return for May showed that the Regiment had no more than 321 effectives.[11] An enemy of George's might have said that this low figure proved him devoid of ability as a military organizer. Friends could have retorted that the unwillingness of Virginians to enlist in the defence of their Colony was an indictment of them, not of their commander. Once again, and this time not sharply or against a background of hurt pride and thwarted ambition, George had to decide to make the best of what he had or else to give up the struggle and to return to civil life. Inherent persistence, a developing sense of duty, and a love of command held him to his task.

Perhaps the most unpalatable part of this task was acceptance of the inevitable limitations on what could be done. The decision of Governor Dinwiddie, a decision in which Washington concurred, reluctantly was for the maintenance of a defensive in Virginia during the summer and autumn of 1756.[12] To secure the frontiers and to protect the settlers, the long-discussed chain of forts was to be constructed and, by legislative enactment, was to be extended southward almost to the North Carolina boundary.

Over the size, number and location of these forts, conference and argument appeared to be endless. George's view, gradually taking form, was that it was impossible with scanty forces to maintain additional forts on the upper stretches of Patterson's Creek or of the South Branch of the Potomac[13] because of the distance from Winchester and the difficulties of supply. Fort Cumberland, on the other hand, was so isolated that its garrison neither could serve usefully in the defence of Virginia nor receive and forward promptly any information of the enemy's movements toward the region of the Shenandoah.[14] It

---

[10] See his argument in 1 *G. W.*, 387.   [11] 3 *Papers of G. W.*, LC.

[12] 2 *Din.*, 274; 1 *G. W.*, 333, 383; 1 *Sharpe*, 418, 430.

[13] Cf. 1 *Hamilton*, 302–03.

[14] Cf. Washington to Dinwiddie, Apr. 27, 1756: "Since the first murders were committed by the Indians, I have never missed of receiving intelligence of their motions; while Col. Stephen [at Fort Cumberland] has, in a manner, lived in total ignorance thereof" (1 *G. W.*, 343).

might be wise, George thought, to keep a small number of men on Wills Creek. Chief reliance must be on a fort at Winchester, large enough and strong enough to serve as a magazine and as a refuge for the settlers during Indian raids. Roads converged at Winchester; it was the starting point for an advance on Fort DuQuesne. That French stronghold was the supreme objective. Nothing was safe and nothing stable till the enemy was driven from the Ohio.

To connect Fort Cumberland and the new defences at Winchester, George thought another large work might advantageously be erected, but the line between the Valley town and Wills Creek, Washington kept insisting, was the most advanced that could be held in 1756. Indeed, as he had written Speaker Robinson, he believed Winchester "now the farthest boundary of this county—no inhabitants beyond it: and if measures are not taken to maintain it, we must retire below the Blue Ridge in a very short time." [15] Based on this line, which would run northwestward, the Companies of the Regiment not employed in the main forts could be placed "equidistant," in Washington's own words, "or at proper passes along our frontiers." [16] A sketch of these dispositions had been prepared in due form by Washington and had been forwarded late in April to the Speaker of the House.[17] George had been careful not to protest too vigorously against the extension of the chain of forts as far southward as the General Assembly desired, but he had been no less careful to point out that 1500 men could not cover the whole of the Virginia frontier.[18] It had been on the strength of these representations that the General Assembly had authorized the erection of a large fort at Winchester and had placed the building of it under his care.[19]

Washington's other argument, that of the inadequacy of his force, had not induced the Burgesses either to increase the troops or to reduce the number of forts to be established. As soon as he had learned the probable scope of the new laws, George had begun his combing of the militia [20] in search of carpenters, and by May 23, he could report that he had started work on the defence of Winchester.[21] After that, week

---

[15] 1 G. W., 339.   [16] 1 G. W., 335.

[17] Ibid., 335. Unfortunately, this paper has disappeared. It consequently is impossible to ascertain whether George intended to garrison new, small, semi-permanent forts or whether he purposed merely to use the existing outposts and to erect additional stockades which the soldiers could occupy when sent from the principal forts to meet an Indian raid.

[18] As noted supra, p. 180, Washington's views were set forth, though not with complete clarity, in letters of Apr. 24 and 27, 1756, to Speaker Robinson, and in one of Apr. 27, 1756, to Governor Dinwiddie. See 1 G. W., 331-96, 338-40, 340-44.

[19] See supra, p. 180, n.   [20] See supra, p. 188.   [21] 1 G. W., 388.

by week, he was burdened with it. Always there was a shortage of
tools;[22] usually the laborers were few, and, unless George watched
them, were indifferent.[23] The enterprise was much the largest construction George had undertaken. It was moderately instructive and
consistently exasperating.

In other ways, too, those weeks of digging dirt after the departure
of the savages brought Washington some mild satisfaction and, as always, a measure of new distress, personal and official. On May 12, 1756,
the King proclaimed somewhat more liberal regulations on the thorny
old subject of regular and provincial rank. Recognition of a sort was
given provincial general and field officers. They remained the juniors
of all officers of like insignia and royal commission, but on duty in
North America they were to take rank as the "eldest Captains."[24]
This, of course, was not enough to satisfy a young colonial, ambitious
for fame, but it was far better than the situation that had existed under
the regulations in force at the time of Braddock's expedition.[25] It no
longer would be true of Washington as he had written William Fitzhugh in November, 1754, that "every Captain, bearing the King's commission, every half-pay officer, or other, appearing with such a commission, would rank before me."[26]

There was gratification, besides, in the assurances friends were giving
George that the charges of immorality and drunkenness in the Regiment were not leveled against him. Hints were made that Adam
Stephen, commanding the Virginia troops at Fort Cumberland, might
not have been diligent in his suppression of loose living;[27] Dinwiddie
grumbled that Washington should not express "great uneasiness of
mind for not having everything as [the Colonel] wished."[28] All other
letters from Williamsburg were written generously in manifest desire
to assure the sensitive Washington that he was not blamed for what
was alleged against some of his officers.

"Our hopes, dear George," said Speaker Robinson, "are all fixed on
you for bringing our affairs to a happy issue, and I am very sure if you
are properly assisted they won't be disappointed in their expectations."
He added a prayer for the young officer's safety.[29] "Your good health
and fortune is the toast at every table," William Fairfax pledged the

---

[22] Cf. 1 G. W., 392–93. What appears to be the first drawing for the fort will be found in
5 Papers of G. W., LC.

[23] 1 G. W., 388.

[24] 1 Sharpe, 412–13.

[25] See supra and 1 Hamilton, 56.

[26] 1 G. W., 105–06 and Vol. I, p. 440.

[27] See 1 Hamilton, 240, 262.

[28] 1 Hamilton, 231.

[29] 1 Hamilton, 240; May 3, 1756.

Colonel.[30] Landon Carter wrote, somewhat less tactfully, of the rumor of Washington's impending resignation: "Sir, merit begets envy, and should such a thing happen at this hour, it must glut the malice of those who wish you ill. Will they not then say, 'See your darling cloaking fear under the color of disgust'?" The charge of immorality in the Regiment, Carter went on, could not have been made by anyone who knew Washington; it might have been the artifice of someone who wished to induce Washington to resign in order that he might succeed to the command.[31] Charles Carter reported: ". . . from my constant attendance in the House I can with great truth say I never heard your conduct questioned. Whenever you are mentioned, 'tis with the greatest respect." [32] Later the same friend explained: ". . . all I can learn is that a few of your youths in the service have been at times imprudent and drank too freely, and in their cups have said what none of them in their sober moments would willingly own. I think, as you have never in the least been reflected on, you are too much affected." [33]

In spite of this, another development of the times made Washington feel "much affected" because his whole future as a soldier might be involved. In a communication received from Dinwiddie during the last week of April, George read: "Letters from Britain leave us still in uncertainty as to peace or war. Two Generals are appointed for America—Lord Loudoun and General Abercrombie [34]—and it's thought they will bring over two Battalions, but whether for this place or New York remains uncertain; but it's further said His Majesty intends to send blank commissions for the Americans. If so, I doubt not you will be taken care of." [35] Until he learned this, George had assumed that Shirley would remain in command and that he had to look to that gentleman for the position he sought as second in command to Governor Sharpe on the next expedition to the Ohio.

Actually, this was the situation: On the 16th of April, Shirley had learned through private letters from England that Lord Loudoun had been appointed Commander-in-Chief of His Majesty's forces in North America and that Gen. Daniel Webb was coming over at once to

[30] Letter of Apr. 26, 1756; 1 Hamilton, 232.

[31] 1 Hamilton, 223–24. No evidence has been found to support the statement frequently printed that an effort was made in the spring or summer of 1756 to oust Washington and to give the command to Innes, though, as noted already, Innes probably would have been named by Dinwiddie if Washington had resigned.

[32] Ibid., 225–26.   [33] 1 G. W., 233.

[34] The last syllable of the name properly was "by," but the form used by Dinwiddie was employed frequently by the colonials.

[35] Letter of Apr. 23, 1756; 2 Din., 388.

assume direction of military affairs until Loudoun arrived.[36] Shirley
had felt that as this notification was unofficial, he should go ahead
with all his preparations for the campaign of 1756.[37] In that spirit,
answering Sharpe, he was to write most politely on May 16 that he
would name Washington second in command of the Ohio expedition
"if there is nothing in the King's orders, which I am in continual expectation of, that interferes with it." [38] Shirley's formal recall was not
received until shortly before June 13; [39] his authority as commanding
General was exercised until Gen. James Abercromby reached Albany
on the 25th of June.[40]

Washington waited for none of these developments. As soon as it
was apparent that Loudoun, not Shirley, was to be the man to decide
on operations and on the subordinates who were to participate in them,
Washington wrote Dinwiddie and asked the Governor to recommend
him to the new Commander-in-Chief. "His Honor" almost was
grieved that Washington had thought this necessary. "You need not
have wrote me," he said, "to recommend you to the Earl of Loudoun."
The Governor explained: "Colonel Ludwell leaves this [i.e., Williams-
burg] in a few days to compliment his Lordship on his arrival. By
him I wrote fully to General Abercrombie, who is second in command,
and my particular friend, in your favor, which I think much better
than writing to his Lordship, as I know the influence he has with
him." [41] In the letter to Abercromby, the Governor praised Washington as a "very deserving Gentleman," for whom, had Braddock lived,
he doubtless would "have provided . . . handsomely in the regulars."
With unusual warmth, Dinwiddie went on to say of Washington: "He
is a person much beloved here and has gone through many hardships
in the service, and I really think he has great merit, and believe he can
raise more men here than any one present that I know. If his Lordship
will be so kind as to promote him in the British establishment, I think
he will answer my recommendation." [42]

That was something for which to strive! Meantime, much had to be
done, much that was tedious and troublesome. Men drafted under the

---

36 2 *Shirley*, 428.   37 *Ibid.*
38 2 *Shirley*, 448; 1 *Sharpe*, 416.   39 *Ibid.*, 461.
40 Webb landed in New York on June 7, but, hearing that his senior, Abercromby, was
off the coast, he did nothing officially until that officer arrived. See Pargellis, *Lord Loudoun in
America* (cited hereafter as Pargellis, *Loudoun*), p. 83.
41 Letter of May 27, 1756; 2 *Din.*, 424. Washington's letter to Dinwiddie has disappeared,
but the reply of Dinwiddie leaves no doubt Washington asked the Governor's aid.
42 Letter of May 28, 1756; 2 *Din.*, 425.

new law soon would begin to arrive in Winchester.[43] Provision must be made for them. Indians, too, were expected. The owners of tippling houses must be warned against selling them strong drink; all other persons must be put on notice not to give the redmen liquor or money.[44] For a time, too, it looked as if George was to have guests and counsellors who were used to high living and to the fullest consideration. When the Indian raids had been at their height, a number of the leading men of the Colony had volunteered to procure followers and to hasten at their own expense to Winchester. These gentlemen, who styled themselves the "Associators," had not been able to organize and to reach their rendezvous at Fredericksburg in time to be of help, but they had suggested that they might ride along the entire frontier and advise concerning the proper location of the forts.[45] George awaited their coming with mingled expectancy and uneasiness, and with impatience because of their slowness.[46] He was spared embarrassment. If any of the visitors came as far as Winchester, they must have returned in a few days to their homes.[47]

As soon afterward as he could, June 4, Washington left Winchester [48] and rode rapidly to Williamsburg to settle his accounts and to discuss plans for the new forts and the garrisoning of them. Arriving on the 6th,[49] he found the Governor much gratified that his agents had succeeded in negotiating a treaty under which the Cherokees and Catawbas agreed to send warriors to Virginia to share in the operations against the French.[50] Personally, the Governor was ailing. Unless his health improved during the summer, said Dinwiddie, who now was 63, he would be compelled to ask permission to go home and to visit Bath for treatment.[51] There was another and a sure indication that the old Scot was failing: Even before George had started from the Valley, the Governor had been leaving to his discretion many things that previously

[43] 2 *Din.*, 406.

[44] 1 *G. W.*, 365. The first natives to arrive—a small contingent of Nottoways—were sent to Fort Cumberland (*ibid.*, 383).

[45] *Md. Gazette*, May 20, 1756; 1 *Hamilton*, 239, 241, 251, 268; 2 *Din.*, 406; 1 *G. W.*, 379, 382, 386; 10 *V* 108, with article from *Md. Gazette* of June 17, 1756. They expected to reach Winchester May 25.

[46] 1 *G. W.*, 382, 386.

[47] Washington made no mention of them after stating, May 23, that he was awaiting their arrival, but see 2 *Din.*, 439.   [48] 1 *G. W.*, 391; *Ledger A*, folio 29.

[49] He was at King William Court House on the 5th but was at Doncastle's on the 6th and apparently spent the night there (*Ledger A*, folio 29).

[50] For the details of relations with these tribes after Peter Randolph and William Byrd III were sent to open the negotiations, see 2 *Din.*, 367, 368, 387–88, 389, 413, 438. References to the treaty are in *ibid.*, 442, 445–46. See also *Md. Gazette*, Mch. 25, May 6, 1756.

[51] 2 *Din.*, 437.

had been determined in Williamsburg.[52] Now, he readily and wearily referred troublesome decisions to the young frontier commander.[53] When Washington rode away from the capital on June 10,[54] after an inexpensive visit, he had more authority and responsibility than ever had been assigned him officially. As respected fundamental strategy, Dinwiddie had been compelled to reiterate, and Washington to agree, that Virginia must remain on the defensive in 1756 unless regulars and artillery could be made available by Lord Loudoun.[55] At the same time, regardless of the delays and supineness of adjoining Colonies,[56] both the Governor and the Colonel felt that Virginia must do her part for her own people and, if possible, must make her advanced settlements secure: Washington's Regiment therefore was to be recruited to full strength by the draft; the chain of forts was to be completed along the whole of the frontier.

In this understanding, Washington rode swiftly to Fredericksburg, where he gave orders that additional tools for constructing the forts be collected and sent immediately by wagon to Winchester.[57] He paid, also, a brief visit to his mother, who nicked him for forty shillings,[58] and then he proceeded to the Valley by way of Mount Vernon.[59] In spite of the heavy cost of his journey to Boston, he was able, while in Fairfax, to pay the rent of 1755 for the estate,[60] which again was to be managed by "Jack" Washington, newly married to Hannah Bushrod.[61]

On his arrival at Winchester, about June 19,[62] George reopened his rented house, where he apparently had been faring well in the care of Thomas Bishop as caterer.[63] Washington intended to remain for a few days only in Winchester and then to proceed to Fort Cumberland for a council on the building of the forts, but the non-arrival of the wagon with tools from Fredericksburg delayed him.[64] It was July 1, or later, when once again he established his headquarters temporarily on Wills Creek [65] and received full verbal reports of what had happened while

[52] Cf. 2 *Din.*, 406, and Washington's earlier complaints of lack of instructions, 1 *G. W.*, 356.
[53] Cf. 1 *Hamilton*, 274.   [54] *Ledger A*, folio 29.
[55] 2 *Din.*, 455.
[56] Cf. 1 *Sharpe*, 444; 5 *N. C. Col. Records*, 657.
[57] 1 *G. W.*, 392.   [58] *Ledger A*, folio 29.
[59] *Ibid.*, expenses at West's and Snicker's.   [60] *Ibid.*, £93, 15s.
[61] Cf. 1 *Hamilton*, 217, 232, 265; *Ledger A*, folio 29.
[62] Cf. 1 *Hamilton*, 280.
[63] Ledger entries of the summer of 1756 show that Bishop procured for Washington whatever luxuries Frederick County offered. Washington's first entry of rent for Capt. William Cocke's house in Winchester, £40, was made in *Ledger A*, folio 32, Dec. 4, 1756. Presumably this was for one year's rent then due.   [64] 1 *G. W.*, 392, 393.
[65] He expected to leave Winchester June 29 (1 *Hamilton*, 294). His first published orders at Fort Cumberland were dated July 6. See 1 *G. W.*, 395.

he was "below." The Indians had made no new raids of any magnitude on the northern frontier during his absence,[66] though the prospect of their return at any time could not be disregarded.[67] Washington doubtless was told, also, that Governor Sharpe had visited some of the outposts and had announced that he was going to build a strong fort in Maryland, East of Cumberland.[68] At this new Maryland defence, the Virginians probably assumed that Captain Dagworthy would be employed, but they gave him little further thought. He already had been subdued.[69]

When Washington had heard the little there was to tell at Fort Cumberland, he held a council of war on plans for the forts, and he put into effect the first of a series of orders for stiffer discipline. Then, shortly after the 13th of July, he returned to Winchester,[70] and, amid recurring alarms but without serious Indian attack,[71] proceeded to work on the three heavy tasks that were his lot that summer—recruitment, discipline and fort building.

As always for Washington on the frontier, recruitment was a problem in subtraction as well as in addition. He felt that he had to keep the militia, if he could, until he received the draft. It proved a labor not worth the effort, because whenever there was a brush with the Indians, or even the prospect of one, the conduct of the militia was worse than disgraceful. While Washington was at Fort Cumberland, a typical instance of cowardice had occurred. Capt. John Rutherford, of the rangers, was escorting an express from Winchester to the Commander-in-Chief and, for that purpose, was employing some of the militia stationed at Ashby's Fort. Rutherford proceeded carefully, with his flanking parties in the woods on either side of the road. Soon word

[66] He doubtless had heard before he left on June 4 of a successful skirmish in which one of Nathaniel Gist's sons and a party of the Virginia Regiment had been engaged, May 29, on the mountain West of Fort Cumberland. See 1 Hamilton, 270, 272.

[67] Cf. Dinwiddie's observations, May 8, 1756, that the Indians might carry their plunder westward and come back to Virginia with reenforcements (1 Hamilton, 243–44).

[68] Cf. 1 Hamilton, 282–83. This was the later Fort Frederick.

[69] Washington did not record any further controversy with him. Dagworthy's name occurs in a letter to John Robinson, entered in 1 G. W., 533, as of "December, 1756"; but infra, p. 231, n. 107, it is explained that this letter manifestly was written in the spring of 1756.

[70] He was at Fort Cumberland on the 13th and in Winchester by the 21st. See 1 G. W., 399, 400. His ledger shows no entries for the dates between these two.

[71] Western Maryland was the object of murderous Indian raids during the summer of 1756 and was evacuated by most of the settlers as far to the eastward as Frederick. Cf. 1 G. W., 463. For the various reports that reached Washington, see 1 Hamilton, 309, 320, 325, 326. See also 1 G. W., 444–45, 447, 475, and Md. Gazette, Sept. 9, 1756. One of these affairs involved a young Virginia Lieutenant who was brought before a court martial but given no heavier sentence than a reprimand, because of his inexperience (Md. Gazette, Aug. 12, 1756; 1 G. W., 395). Murders in Augusta are mentioned in 1 Hamilton, 313 and 1 G. W., 423.

was sent back that ambushed Indians were lying in wait. Warning was shouted; the men were told to deploy. Instead, when the Indians opened fire, about half the escort did not even wait to give shot for shot. They ran away and would not halt until they were safely within their stockade.[72] It manifestly was a waste of time and of money to keep such cravens on the frontier. If they were left alone, they would do nothing; and if they were exposed, they would desert. The Governor authorized their dismissal as soon as the crops were harvested; Washington gleaned from them as many carpenters and as many volunteers as he could, and acquiesced cheerfully in the orders of Dinwiddie.[73] By the middle of August, all except thirty were to depart. These men of Culpeper County remained willingly under a devoted Captain, John Field, who had great influence over them.[74]

The draft was the positive phase of recruitment but it was not all that Washington had hoped it would be. In the very teeth of the statute that made action compulsory in every County except desolate Hampshire, many of the commanding officers of the militia delayed their prescribed council and the drawing of names. By the 25th of June, the increment reporting at Winchester numbered 264 only,[75] a figure that Dinwiddie considered most disappointing.[76] While forced enlistment continued to lag in the southern Counties[77] and even in Fairfax,[78] many deserted en route to their rendezvous or after arrival there.[79]

Too much was expected of ignorant men. Low pay, fatiguing service and severe hardships were discouragements that vigilance could not overcome.[80] Three ranger Companies on the frontier of Augusta dwindled to not more than thirty rank and file. When an effort was made to incorporate these into the Regiment, the officers covertly resisted the transfer and nearly all the privates deserted.[81] The Regiment suffered, too. Besides individual deserters, sixteen went off in a body.[82] As late as August 1, the total of Regiment, rangers and scouts was not more than 926[83] of an authorized 1500 and a needed 2000.[84] In the hope of raising this total, Washington procured the Governor's consent

[72] 1 G. W., 415–17.
[73] 1 Hamilton, 297; 1 G. W., 400, 405.
[74] 1 G. W., 445.
[75] 1 G. W., 394.
[76] 1 Hamilton, 295.
[77] See William Fairfax to Bryan Fairfax, Aug. 1, 1756; 1 Ford, 326 n.
[78] 1 Hamilton, 361.
[79] 1 G. W., 417.
[80] Ibid., 444.
[81] 1 Hamilton, 343 ff; 1 G. W., 459, 462, 475.
[82] 1 G. W., 444. In Va. Gazette, Aug. 26, 1756, the number is given as seventeen, of whom fifteen were said to be Marylanders.
[83] 1 G. W., 437.
[84] 1 G. W., 464, 469.

to enlist servants who in many instances previously had shown themselves willing to trade masters and to accept the Colony in place of the
farmer. Some of these men were procured,[85] but a better prospect
of reenforcement was offered by the Cherokees. The arrival of 150
of their toughened warriors was predicted by the Governor.[86]

These fighters were experienced in their own arts of war, however
difficult they might be to satisfy. Washington's white recruits could
not be trained, or held to their duties when trained, otherwise than by
his success in his second task, the thorough inculcation of sound discipline. Clamor in the General Assembly had prompted Washington
to transmit to Adam Stephen in May a general warning that good conduct would be rewarded and crime punished.[87] After Washington
went in person to the Maryland post he turned from sermons to
severity. Swearing was made punishable with twenty-five lashes.[88]
Drunkenness, in which most of the men indulged until they spent all
their pay,[89] was combated with direct punishment of fifty lashes,[90] with
rewards for those who reported comrades guilty of this offence,[91] and
with fresh attempts in the regulation of tippling houses.[92] A rum ration
for men working on the forts,[93] an increase in pay, and an allowance
of clothing somewhat improved conditions but did not modify George's
belief that the penalties of all articles of war applicable in Virginia had
to be applied with vigor.[94] As for desertion—the ultimate in the defiance of all discipline—the old condition still prevailed: Desertion
could not be prevented, Washington thought, until the farmers ceased
sheltering runaways and constables did their duty in arresting those
who left their command.[95] Discipline, in a word, remained grim business for the Virginia commander, always a challenge and often a
defeat.

The attempted performance of Washington's third task, that of
building forts, was hampered from the outset by lack of faith. Both
Dinwiddie and Washington did what they could to execute the will of
the General Assembly, but the Governor did not believe George had
sufficient men to construct the forts,[96] and the Colonel did not think

85 1 G. W., 417, 453, 471; 1 Hamilton, 365; 2 Din., 479.
86 2 Din., 490 ff. Cf. 1 G. W., 435. For developments subsequent to those listed on p. 140,
n. 116 supra, see 1 Hamilton, 353; 2 Din., 495, 508; 7 H 62; Md. Gazette, Sept. 9, 1756; 1
G. W., 464.
87 1 G. W., 381.   88 1 G. W., 396.
89 1 G. W., 470.   90 1 G. W., 440.
91 1 G. W., 451.   92 1 G. W., 409, 440, 470.
93 1 G. W., 441.   94 1 G. W., 467.
95 1 G. W., 461, 465.   96 1 Hamilton, 297.

they were worth building as the lawmakers planned them.[97] Although it was improbable that small garrisons at scattered, weak forts could offer effective resistance, Washington complied with the terms of the law and had asked the council at Fort Cumberland on July 10[98] to decide on the location of those from the Potomac to the head of the South Branch. Agreement had been reached with minor change in the original plan. For the frontier below the South Branch, the council accepted Dinwiddie's view[99] that the choice of sites and the building of forts should be left to Capt. Peter Hog,[100] who was supposed to know the country well. With the assistance of Col. William Fairfax,[101] plans and orders were drawn and were dispatched promptly to the other officers in charge, along with as many of the necessary tools as could be collected.[102]

Before work on any considerable number of these stockades could be undertaken, the ripening of the crops in Hampshire and in Frederick created a dilemma for Washington: On some of the rich fields abandoned by their owners, the grain awaited the scythe; elsewhere, the farmers remained in nearby forts and of course clamored to save their harvest but could not do so without the help and the protection of the troops. Which should come first, the defences or the grain? Washington decided to save the food and to delay the forts.[103] As for the work in Augusta and farther southward, two episodes had made it uncertain whether all the stockades and blockhouses would be defended properly after hard labor was spent in constructing them. At Peter Hog's Fort Dinwiddie, conditions of virtual mutiny existed late in June.[104] Vause's Fort, a blockhouse in Augusta, had been surrendered and the survivors murdered or carried off as captives, though details were uncertain.[105] If these affairs were typical of what was to be expected in Augusta, defence there would be futile until the people themselves resisted stubbornly. To Governor Dinwiddie's way of thinking, they were more interested in personal gain than in common effort.[106]

One of Washington's substantial conclusions during the summer of

---

97 1 *G. W.*, 468–69, 474.   98 See *supra*, p. 200.
99 1 *G. W.*, 393, 444.   100 1 *Hamilton*, 301 ff; 1 *G. W.*, 416, 444.
101 1 *Hamilton*, 310.
102 1 *G. W.*, 407–08, 409, 415. For Hog's instructions, see 1 *G. W.*, 400; 2 *Din.*, 460. See also Koontz, *Frontier*, 118 ff. Minutes of the subsequent council of July 27, 1756, at Augusta Court House, a meeting not attended by Washington, appear in 1 *Hamilton*, 305–07. Included are a few references to the size of the proposed forts—most of them sixty feet square—for which see also *Penn. Journal*, Feb. 5, 1756. Cf. 15 *V* 247.
103 1 *G. W.*, 412, 438, 443.   104 1 *Hamilton*, 286.
105 For the details, see *infra*, p. 212–13.
106 For some of Dinwiddie's criticisms of Augusta, see 2 *Din.*, 483, 551, 557.

1756, in all that related to the new "chain," was that Fort Cumberland should not remain in the care and charge of Virginia, which was to centre her frontier defences on Winchester. As Maryland was to build a new fort far to the East of Wills Creek, George could see no reason for maintaining troops and keeping stores on that remote stream. When Washington paid a visit to Governor Sharpe while the Governor was on the frontier during July, he explained this to the Maryland commander, who made no objection.[107] Dinwiddie would not have it so. Cumberland, he said, was a "King's fort" which could not be abandoned without the consent of the home government or of the new Commander-in-Chief for North America.[108]

Undeniably, then, recruitment, discipline and fort building were hard classes in the school of experience that George Washington was attending. Sometimes the lessons were almost too difficult for him. "As the case now stands," he wrote Treasurer Robinson, "we are upon such odd establishment, under such uncertain regulations, and subject to so much inconvenience that I am wandering in a wilderness of difficulties, and am ignorant of the ways to extricate myself, and to steer for the satisfaction of the country, the soldiers or myself." Then he confessed: "Having no certain rules for the direction of my conduct, I am afraid to turn to this hand or to that, lest it should be censured." [109]

It was not always burdensome. That fear of public criticism, "loss of honor," was constant; but his energy kept him alert and his ambition, as always, made him look to new enterprises. Fencing, for example, had never been among his accomplishments, though it was regarded as a social grace of gentlemen even if it was losing its eminence in the code duello. At Winchester, as it chanced, was a Sergeant Wood, who knew enough about fencing to be willing to give instruction in it. George became his pupil and worked so steadily and so long that he accumulated by August 7 a bill of £1, 1s 6d, which he paid.[110]

This was diversion. Preparation for larger adventure was of more serious sort and was undertaken amid the realities of formal war and new English defeat. By orders "from home," proclamation was made in Williamsburg on August 7 [111] of the official declaration of war by

---

107 1 *Sharpe*, 468, 485.
108 1 *G. W.*, 419, 427, 428, 443, 453; 1 *Hamilton*, 350.
109 Letter of Aug. 5, 1756; 1 *G. W.*, 432–33.
110 *Ledger A*, folio 30. As explained in Vol. I, p. 277, the tradition that van Braam was Washington's "old fencing master" is without supporting evidence. Certainly the adjective "old" has to be discarded, because the Dutchman was a young man.
111 See 1 *Hamilton*, 333, 348; 2 *Din.*, 471.

Britain against France on the 17th of May, 1756.[112] This was repeated in Winchester on August 15 [113] and, most appropriately, by the young soldier whose skirmish with a French youth in May, 1754, had been the "first shot" of a war that was to shape the lines of empire on the richest of continents. With the leading citizens of the town, Washington marched his available three Companies of the Virginia Regiment to the fort, where the declaration was read aloud. Toasts then were drunk, the cannon were thrice discharged, and three rounds of musketry were fired. The little column next made the circuit of the cross-streets, proclaiming the war, and returned to the "great parade." Once again the declaration was read.

Colonel Washington thereupon spoke to this effect: "You see, gentle-men soldiers, that it hath pleased our most gracious sovereign to declare war in form against the French King, and (for divers good causes, but more particularly for their ambitious usurpations and encroachments on his American dominions) to pronounce all the said French King, subjects and vassals, to be enemies to his crown and dignity; and hath willed and declared all his subjects and people, and in a more especial manner commanded his captain-general of his forces, his governors, and all others his commanders and officers, to do and execute all acts of hostility in the prosecution of this just and honorable war; and though our utmost endeavors can contribute but little to the advance-ment of his Majesty's honor, and the interest of his governments, yet let us show our willing obedience to the best of kings, and by a strict attachment to his royal commands, demonstrate the love and loyalty we bear his sacred person; let us by rules of unerring bravery strive to merit his royal favor, and a better establishment as a reward for our services." [114]

This deliverance, which George doubtless read from a manuscript, contained more of fervent adjectives and professions than he usually employed, but the final clause voiced the personal sentiment he often had expressed as well as one military ideal he had pursued: The King's service should reward the subject.

---

[112] A copy of the declaration appears in 2 *Shirley,* 450–53.

[113] Washington wrote on the 14th for instructions regarding the ceremonies to be observed (1 *G. W.,* 446); but apparently he did not feel he should delay the proclamation until he received the Governor's directions, written on the 21st (2 *Din.,* 485).

[114] In 1 *G. W.,* 446–47, this is reprinted from 14 *Pro. M.H.S.,* 264, along with a note by Ford that he had been "unable to trace it in the gazettes at that time." It was published in *Va. Gazette* of Aug. 27, 1756 and was reprinted in 2 *V* 345–46. The text quoted above is that of the Virginia paper.

Harder service it now promised to be. A few days before Washington announced the proclamation of war, disaster had befallen the King's arms in Northern New York. After a winter of hideous suffering and hunger, the 1134 survivors of three Regiments and of detachments of the Royal Artillery had been trapped in the trio of feeble, badly located forts at Oswego, had been subjected to serious casualties, and had been compelled to surrender to a force of French and Indians on the 14th–15th of August. It was a defeat difficult to retrieve because of distance and the loss of British vessels on Lake Ontario.[115] An Albany correspondent of Beverley Robinson's had summed it up with accuracy when he said: "Oswego, scandalously gone, provincial army very low spirited and sick, very small hopes of any good." [116]

This was an unhappy introduction to the new Commander-in-Chief, Lord Loudoun, who had landed in New York on the 23rd of July, 1756.[117] As Loudoun had been named titular Governor of Virginia in succession to the Earl of Albemarle,[118] it had been wholly in order for Washington to prepare an "Address" to the General on behalf of the Virginia Regiment. Washington had forwarded this paper to Beverley Robinson, who transmitted it to Loudoun's principal aide.[119] In addition, the young Colonel had Dinwiddie's recommendation to Loudoun through Abercromby and probably a final, generous endorsement by Shirley, who had told Sharpe he would urge Loudoun to make Washington second in command of the next expedition to the Ohio, precisely as he himself had planned to do.[120] Not content with all this, Washington wished to impress the General as a vigilant commander.[121] Word that the new Commander-in-Chief was coming to Virginia inspired a candid paragraph to Adam Stephen at Fort Cumberland. Washington wrote: "Let all your leisure hours be employed in disciplining the men; for as Lord Loudoun is to be here, and probably will see them, I would willingly have them make the best appearance possible." [122]

In thus appealing for the consideration of Loudoun, the prime aim of

[115] Shirley's responsibility is probed in Pargellis, *Loudoun*, 148 ff; the results of a full study of the French and English sources appear in 6 *Gipson*, 196 ff; the best known account is Parkman, *Montcalm and Wolfe*, v. 1, p. 422 ff.

[116] Quoted by Robinson in 1 *Hamilton*, 361.

[117] Pargellis, *Loudoun*, 82; *Md. Gazette*, Aug. 5, 1756.

[118] Pargellis, *Loudoun*, 60–61. Albemarle had died Dec. 22, 1754.

[119] 1 *Hamilton*, 360. No copy of the address has been found.

[120] Shirley's letter of July 13, 1756, in 1 *Sharpe*, 447.

[121] The new fort at Winchester was to be named after Loudoun, but there is as much probability that the name originated with Dinwiddie as there is that Washington was responsible for it.

[122] Letter of Sept. 6, 1756; 1 *G. W.*, 454.

Washington remained the one he had expressed to all those who had preceded his Lordship in command. Dinwiddie had urged in a letter to Loudoun that the neighboring Colonies collect provisions and raise men "to march to the Ohio and attack Fort DuQuesne." [123] Everything in the young soldier's heart echoed that appeal. A strong, sustained offensive held out the only promise of victory, but all that Washington had learned on the hard trail from Fort Cumberland to Fort LeBoeuf warned him now of the necessity of the largest preparation. Resolved as he was to go to the Ohio, he wanted to be sure an army advancing with ordnance and heavy supplies would have provisions and feed sufficient for the long journey. In writing Dinwiddie, he spoke his whole mind thus: "I observe your Honor's proposal to Lord Loudoun of carrying on an expedition to the Ohio. I have always thought it the best and *only* method to put a stop to the incursions of the enemy, as they would *then* be obliged to stay at home to defend their own possessions. But we are quite unprepared for such an undertaking. If it is fixed upon, *now* is the time for buying up provisions, and laying them in at the most convenient place." [124]

A teacher of war, reading that, might have said it was a good examination paper to be written by a young commander whose men had been brought close to starvation on their first attempt to reach the Ohio in 1754.

[123] Letter of July 1, 1756; 1 *Din.*, 456.
[124] Letter of Aug. 4, 1756; 1 *G. W.*, 423.

ORIGINAL OF "VIRGINIA-CENTINEL NO. X"

In September, 1756, Washington and the officers of his Regiment were subjected to an abusive attack by a pseudo-erudite writer in the *Virginia Gazette,* who usually has been styled "Centinel X." The most violent charge of the "Centinel" was that the men in command of the troops of the Old Dominion pursued their ease to the neglect of their duty. They were "drunken debauchees," he said.

For many years the "Centinel's" indictment could be reconstructed in the vaguest way only from references to it in the letters of the outraged officers. Finally, Worthington C. Ford found a reprint of the article in a Philadelphia journal of the times; but no copy of the *Virginia Gazette* containing the original tirade was known to be in existence until the issue of Sept. 3, 1756, reproduced on the opposite page, was found among photostats made for Colonial Williamsburg from documents in the Huntington Library. As explained in the text, this particular *Gazette* was sent Lord Loudoun by Governor Dinwiddie because it contained proclamations the Governor had issued.

It becomes manifest from this original and from other documents, that the anonymous writer styled himself "the Virginia-Centinel," and that the "X" was not part of his pseudonym but was the number of the article in a series that ran to "XVI" and perhaps beyond that number.

THE VIRGINIA GAZETTE.

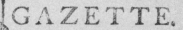

With the freshest ADVICES, *FOREIGN and* DOMESTIC.

The VIRGINIA-CENTINEL. N°. X.

Quit metus, ò nunquam dol'turi, ò semper inertes
Tyrrheni, quæ tanta animi i ignavia cessit?
Qui ferrum? quid be here geritur tela invita dextris?
At non in Venerem segnes, nocturnaque ossla,
Aut, ubi curva chore indixit tibia Bacchi,
Expectate dapes, et plenæ pocula mensæ;
Hic amor, hoc studium —————— VIRG.

THE Profession of Soldiers, especially of such a Time as this, is not only noble but prevalent; and to the at once of universal Honour and Gratitude. They are the Guardians of their Country, and all that is dear to us that honour our Word. And therefore their Fame should not be too easily depreciated; their Foibles or the most extravagent, or ill conduct censured, by Chimney corner Politicians, who sit breaking of Ease, in inglorious Ease, and know not the Greatness or the Realities of their Toils they eld. While their Character is tolerable, and they in any Measure answer the End of their Profession, their Names should be treated with the utmost Tenderness and Respect.

    But Soldiers differ; some will shoot their *Fleet*,
    And some drink *Bumbo* —for their Country's Good,
    Some in the Field will nobly risque their *Lives*,
    Some *Hero-like*, will *favour*, or play at *Filler*,
    Some shew themselves the genuine Sons of *Mars*,
    Some, brave in *Venus'* or in *Bacchus'* Wars,
    Can shew their *Leburous* and *drunken* Scars.

No Profession in the World can secure from Contempt and Indignation a Character made up of Vice and Debauchery; and to Man only can give such a Character as forced. When men would express Knaves, Speed thrifts and Bank-rupt, who have ever been never used to command or know what has been found infufficient to the Management of their own private affairs; are honoured with Commissions in the Army, and are advanced to send in, to seniority, the Interests and indolence of Friends, & c and not after lying to Merit, where the Character soldiers are robbed, to a Post of Honour or Passion, or through War or such a sort of Authority; and at the mean Time, perhaps, others of Merit have been cashiered, or sent to a work of Correction, which the Military sort as below beaming scorn. Of ever winking his Merit, a continuing a He, wherein the soldier in that any Republican History, when the Officer by the next degrees, a Full-stature of Diladelphia, Vice and Luxury were the Disgraces in Peace; and their common in Enduring, hit they may Expert, who would expect to show it in such a cheerful mind of Colluding on the fatal way, lying and encouraging, or the regular Mixture, and preventing their best that, per temper has by his more subject, Landers to the me in Quest of men, an such has of such Profit ——When there is the Cafe how wretchedly perish until a Nation's [...]. What idle Lumber, what an Encumbrance, are such Soldiers.

I would by no Means in the leaft be the Standard by which to judge of the Military taken, there is but the sobriety, the least of the Coward. Successful Richness will never arise from popula Applause, and enfortunate good Counsel with a few stripe scars in. But we should give brave to so much as disrespect, but very ready to be Abroad, or for necessary Self defence; while Men who will Proffanor or into culture Hardships, and encounter Dangers, continue thus them, and their Country to be ravaged in their very easy Business. Such, very any Country cannot be either; nor can that Country receive much Advantage from a Regiment of such dastardly Debauchees.

    "Shew me one Scar character'd on their Skin,
    "Man's blood follows for a Slave put off their own win. " SHAK.

Men of Virtue, and true Courage, even have no Heart to build, and mingle in such a Crowd. And the few of that Character, that may be among them, are in Danger of being the general Contagion, or of being dragg'd and mortified at the Sight of the Scene of Vice that is organ'd old Oppression.

Horace, who by the Effects of the Debauching *Roman* Times, in the Period of its height of Glory, and most illustrious Victories, will teach at the Discipline proper for Soldiers.

* Francis's Translation.

PARIS, *May* 10.

AS the Court does not yet judge it proper to publish what has been done at Minorca since the Landing of our Troops, the Public knows nothing of what passes in that Island but from private Letters, which do not even agree in the Particulars we are not concerned to know. So far say that the French are opposed the 2d in the Night before Fort St. Philip's own make it two Days after; and there are some who affirm that our Troops had no broke Ground on the 2th, by Reason of the Badness of the Roads, which had prevented the coming up of the Artillery, and other Things necessary in the Operations of a Siege. All that we positively know, is, that our Troops were in full siege of the Town of Mahon.

A Camp is to be formed immediately at Boulogne, in Order to cover the French Works for repairing the Harbour of Dunkirk.

May 14. The Report of the Trenches being opened before Fort St. Philip the 20th of this Month was premature, and we learn by a Courier, which the Duke de Richieu dispatched from thence the 19th, they had that Day only begun to make their Approaches; that the necessary preparations for the Siege took up a Deal of Time, and particularly that the bringing up the Artillery was attended with extreme difficulty, neither Horses nor Carts being to be found in the Island; and besides, as they advanced, to repair the Roads which the English had done up, that they were likewise obliged to use all their Art to cover the Men as they worked,

fax was at Belvoir,[6] had not George found himself unexpectedly involved in a matter that seemed to him to concern his character as a man and his reputation as an officer. For some months the *Virginia Gazette* had been publishing at irregular intervals a series of numbered articles, signed "L. & V.," and printed under the heading "The Virginia Centinel."[7] The author may have been inspired by a publication in *The Gazetteer and London Daily Advertiser* that had attracted some interest in America,[8] or he may have been fired by the danger of a French victory. It was his belief, in any event, that the days were evil, that men had become effete, and that the Church of Rome was allied with France to overthrow British right in America. Although these obsessions dominated his writing, he spoke in one of his articles[9] of the practical problems of recruiting in Virginia. Even "such an acceptable and popular officer as Colonel Washington," he had said, "has not been able to enlist a sufficient number of men in such a populous Colony as this without compulsion." On August 20, in his ninth article, "The Virginia Centinel" had written: "At length matters are come to a crisis. The controversy that was long in suspense has issued in a declaration of war." There followed a justification of British resistance as necessary.[10]

Republication of the articles of "The Virginia Centinel" showed that they had attracted some attention, though they had not been the theme of wide discussion in private letters.[11] Nothing in the articles had forecast the spirit displayed in "The Virginia Centinel. No. X" that occupied nearly the whole of the front page of the *Virginia Gazette* of Sept. 3, 1756.[12] Bombast and pseudo-scholarship ran through it. Nowhere

---

[7] As No. IX was printed August 12 and No. X September 3, it is manifest that the "Centinel" did not deliver himself weekly.

[8] The *Pennsylvania Gazette* had reprinted in its issue of July 1, 1756, an article from the London paper of Mch. 23, 1756, signed "Philo-patriae." In the *Md. Gazette* of August 12, an author had emulated or employed the same style in an article signed "Philopatris."

[9] Reprinted in part, without number, in the *Md. Gazette* of August 12.

[10] Reprinted in the *Penn. Gazette*, Sept. 16, 1756.

[11] For an interesting letter of June 7, 1755, in which Richard Bland announced his intention of writing "to wipe off all reflections from my country and the several persons concerned in the conduct of our military enterprises, so far as they can be justified," see 22 *Penn. Mag.*, 437.

[12] The text usually has been quoted from the version Worthington C. Ford found in the *Penn. Journal and Weekly Advertiser* of Nov. 4, 1756. Another reprint is in the *Md. Gazette* of Nov. 25, 1756. The only original discovered thus far is in the Huntington Library. On the front page, opposite the left of the name plate is written "Enclosed in Gov. Dinwiddie's of 8 September, 1756." Dinwiddie wrote Loudoun on that date and referred to proclamations issued after hearing that Oswego had fallen. The proclamations, he said, "you may observe in the enclosed News-Paper" (2 *Din.*, 498). As the paper contains the documents, it is safe to say that the copy is the one sent Lord Loudoun, whose correspondence, diary, etc., are in the Huntington collection.

did the anonymous author give a hint of his identity or of his grievance unless it was in a line that suggested as author some militia officer who had been to Winchester the previous spring and had not been treated acceptably there.[13] His indignant paragraphs groaned with Latin quotations and frowned with historical allusions. The profession of the soldier was declared noble, but "no profession in the world can secure from contempt and indignation a character made up of vice and debauchery."

There followed this long rhetorical flourish: "When raw novices and rakes, spendthrifts and bankrupts, who have never been used to command, or who have been found insufficient for the management of their own affairs, are honored with commissions in the army; when men are advanced according to seniority, the interests and influence of friends, &c. and not according to merit; when the common soldiers are abused, in a fit of humor or passion, or through an ostentation of authority; and in the meantime, perhaps, tolerated or connived at, in practices really worthy of correction; when the militia men are browbeat and discouraged in every noble achievement as claiming a share with the soldiery in their monopoly of honor; when the officers give the men an example of all manner of debauchery, vice and idleness; when they lie skulking in forts, and there dissolving in pleasure, till alarmed by the approach of the enemy, who could expect to find them nowhere else; when instead of searching out the enemy, waylaying and surprising them, obstructing their marches and preventing their incursions, they tempt them by their security and laziness, to come in quest of them and attack them in their fortifications—when this is the case how wretchedly helpless must a nation be?"

After another Latin quotation and a few commonplaces on military boldness, the "Centinel" left no doubt that he was speaking of the Virginia Regiment, even if he did not call it by name: ". . . when nothing brave is so much as attempted, but very rarely, or by accident, or for necessary self defence; when men whose profession it is to endure hardships and dangers cautiously shun them, and suffer their country to be ravaged in their very neighborhood; then, certainly, censure cannot be silent; nor can the public receive much advantage from a Regiment of such dastardly debauchees." The attack trailed off into a

13 Washington's subsequent disfavor in the eyes of Richard Corbin inevitably raises the question whether Corbin may not have been the author, but there is no confirmatory evidence of any sort in his *MS Letter Book* and no indication that he was thinking particularly at the time of the subjects discussed by "The Virginia Centinel."

quotation from Horace and a list of those rulers whose luxury, effeminacy, cruelty and sensuality had "unmanned many an army and enslaved or ruined many flourishing cities and kingdoms."

In his usual sensitiveness, Washington took every word of this to himself, but with one difference: Previously, he would have ridden forthwith to Williamsburg and would have returned his commission, or he would have written Dinwiddie and Robinson that he would not continue to serve when he was subjected to such censure. This time, instead of resolving he would resign, he asked himself whether he should; and, in seeking an answer, he addressed immediately his intelligent secretary, John Kirkpatrick, who then was in Alexandria. Would Kirkpatrick inquire of George's friends and ascertain what they would think of his resignation? [14] A reply came quickly from the alert secretary, who was a most devoted friend. He echoed Washington's own indignation but advised that the Colonel meet with silent contempt the accusations of the "Centinel." Said Kirkpatrick: ". . . to regard his ill natured slander by vindication of facts would be a condescension, arguing a consciousness of the crime, which is all his spite aims at." Those with whom he had talked in Alexandria, Kirkpatrick went on, looked with disapproval on the thought of Washington's resignation. That action might inspire further attack. Thoughtful Councillors and Burgesses were mindful of George's interests and were pleased with his conduct of the defence of Virginia. Candidly Kirkpatrick added: "How far you have missed in the design cannot be laid to your charge, on a single review of the circumstances, difficulties and extent of frontier. Might I be allowed to offer my opinion, I would overlook the scurrility of the Centinel, continue to serve my country with the usual zeal, remark the determination of this Assembly and their future behavior, wait upon his Excellency Lord Loudoun, and take my measures in consequence of their issues. For as Pope says:

"'Envy, will merit like a shade pursue
And like a shadow prove the substance true.'" [15]

Kirkpatrick showed Washington's letter to William Ramsay, a longtime friend, who wrote to the same effect. The "Centinel," said Ramsay,

[14] Washington's letter to Kirkpatrick is not believed to be in existence, but the reply of the secretary and that of William Ramsay, mentioned *infra*, make it plain that Washington did not write of his resignation as determined.

[15] 1 *Hamilton*, 370–71. The quotation, slightly incorrect in the second line, is from the "Essay on Criticism," lines 466–67.

seemed to reflect on the Governor and on those who sought commissions for friends, more than he slurred Washington. Other allegations, which Ramsay analyzed briefly, could not apply to the Colonel. "Upon the whole, sir," Ramsay wrote, "triumph in your innocency." He continued: "Your disinterestedness, your unwearied application and zeal for your country's good determine you to continue in its service at a time there may be the greatest call for you and when probably some signal day may mark you the bravest (as hitherto you have been) of persons. Show your contempt of the scribbler by your silence, your watchfulness and care, and thereby disappoint him." [16] This counsel did not convince George completely, but it deterred him from any immediate action to vindicate himself. Nor did he become so absorbed in the controversy or so depressed by it that he neglected other things [17] or sulked at Mount Vernon. Either there or at Winchester, soon after his return,[18] he wrote "Austin" a letter in which he answered the charges of "The Virginia Centinel." This communication he forwarded to his half-brother and, with it, money to pay for its insertion in the *Virginia Gazette* if "Austin" considered publication desirable.[19] As yet there was nothing from any of the officers at Fort Cumberland to indicate what they thought of the aspersions of their anonymous critic.

Still in uncertainty of mind concerning their probable action and his own, Washington received at Winchester bad news from the southern part of the Virginia frontier. That region had been subjected to Indian raids at intervals from as long previously as June 25, when a force of French and Indians under de Belestre had appeared at the palisade Ephraim Vause had erected near the Roanoke River for the protection of his family and his neighbors.[20] The invaders affirmed afterward that they had marched for a month "through fearful mountains" and past

[16] I *Hamilton*, 368–69. Ramsay's punctuation is so confused that the first two of these quoted sentences do not make sense unless they are separated, but this interpretation of his meaning may be mistaken.

[17] As always, he was careful about his dress. In need of new shirts, he had bought some Irish linen and some cambric, and when he heard through John Alton that Sally Fairfax had said Nancy West was to be at Belvoir, he sent over the materials and an old shirt to serve as a pattern by which that skilled seamstress could replenish his supply. "The shirt fits tolerably well," he explained, "yet I would have the others made with somewhat narrower wrist bands, ruffles deeper by half an inch and the collars by three-quarters of an inch . . ." This information concerning the requirements of a fastidious gentleman was addressed as formally to Mrs. Fairfax as if she were no nearer or dearer than any other woman (1 G. W., 473).

[18] He stated, September 23, that he intended to leave Mount Vernon that evening (1 G. W., 467), but he must have been delayed. He was at West's Ordinary on the 26th (*Ledger A* folio 31), and he did not reach Winchester until the 27th (1 G. W., 473).

[19] The letter itself has disappeared, but "Austin" mentioned its receipt in his answer of October 16, which is quoted *infra*, p. 221.

[20] See note to the map, p. 229.

300 abandoned homes, but they had abundant fighting vigor when they reached Vause's fort. Its defenders were a handful of ill-disciplined rangers under a newly commissioned Captain John Smith, who negligently permitted men to leave the place until the French commander realized that those who remained in the stockade were too few to defend it. He closed in and, when two of the garrison had been killed and five wounded, he offered the survivors terms, which they accepted. De Belestre, himself wounded, did what he could to save the twelve males and the thirteen women and children, and he successfully protected them from immediate massacre, but later he had to give them into the hands of the savages, who started back home with them. The Indians were said, also, to have carried off 120 horses.[21] Washington had heard in July of this disaster, though details had been vague. Now, late in September, came word of new raids in Augusta. They were not quite so destructive as those of June, but they were driving the settlers from their homes.[22]

The situation was one that Washington felt he must examine in person, especially as a new fort of the proposed chain was to be erected near Vause's; so, on September 29, in the company of Capt. John McNeill [23] he rode up the Shenandoah Valley again. At Augusta Court House, which he probably reached on the 30th,[24] he was told that the Indians were not far distant and were continuing their depredations, though with less boldness. Here was opportunity. If a party of militia could be brought together, Washington said, he would lead them westward and would scour the forest as far as Jackson's River. By doing this, it might be possible to "fall in" with the Indians, as he put it. Col. David Stewart,[25] the local militia commander, did not encourage Washington to hope for success in raising any of the militia for such an adventure, but he promised that if the Commander-in-Chief would remain until Monday, October 4, he would undertake to collect a force

[21] Dumas to Vaudreuil, Sept. 19, 1756; Canadian Archives Nationales, F-3, v. 4, p. 448–56; Koontz, Frontier, 144–45, with quotations from Andrew Lewis's comment. The French put their losses at one Canadian and one Indian killed and one officer and four Indians wounded. Some of the accounts of the attack on Vause's fort suggest that the details have been confused with those of the Greenbrier raid of the previous year. The account Smith gave of the affair in his petition of 1758 to the General Assembly (Journ. H. B., 1752–58, p. 499, 505; cf. 15 V 254) was greatly at variance with Washington's understanding of the facts. See 2 G. W., 166.
[22] 1 G. W., 509; Md. Gazette, Oct. 7, 1757, an inaccurate account.
[23] 1 G. W., 473, 476, 477.
[24] Perhaps on the morning of the 1st of October. He wrote (1 G. W., 477) of waiting four days to October 4 but it is not certain whether he meant to include that as the fourth day.
[25] Waddell noted (op. cit., 138) that the name originally was written Stewart but later was spelled Stuart by the well-known Valley family.

Together the three—Washington, Buchanan and the servant—rode from Luney's Ferry to Vause's Fort.[32] The country was ideal for ambuscade, with neither settlers nor patrols to give warning of the presence of savages; but, once again, George's good fortune attended him. The trio dismounted at their destination about October 8,[33] without having been compelled to fire a gun. They found Hog at his post, but scarcely more than that could be said of the Captain. His own Company had dwindled to eighteen men, too few to do much work on the fort which was to be erected near the one Ephraim Vause had built. Hog's men were supplemented numerically, but scarcely in any other way, by a Company of militiamen who were counting the days that would pass before their month of service ended and they could go home. They knew they could not be held longer than thirty days,[34] and they maintained, also, that they could not be made to labor on the fort unless they were paid forty pounds of tobacco per diem, the wage set by act of Assembly for militia carpenters.[35] Hog himself had degenerated as a commander during his long period of detached duty. His discipline was lax in some things and in others non-existent. Apparently he complied with most of the demands of his men,[36] and he had not tried to shake the militia from their insistence on the letter of the law, even though this meant that he could not hope to finish the little fort till Christmas.[37]

George did not argue with the militiamen, either. It was better, he reasoned, to endure them for their brief stay than to create discontent in Hog's Company by allowing the militia more than the men of the Regiment got. To put the Company on the same level of compensation as militia carpenters was impossible under the law. Eight pence per day was the soldiers' allotment; eight pence they should receive. "What-

[32] The location of this fort has been the subject of much argument and of some research, but no more substantial conclusion was reached by Koontz than that it was "about ten miles West of present Christiansburg" (*Virginia Frontier*, 144). An unidentified person has written in the VSL copy of Koontz's book that the site is ten miles East of Christiansburg and on part of the ground occupied by the present town of Shawsville. The same writer noted that land grants give the name as Vause. More recent inquiry by F. B. Kegley regarding this and other sites is embodied in the maps on p. 215 and 229.

[33] See n. 24 and 48, *infra.*

[34] 1 *G. W.*, 478–79. Apparently these men, thirty in number, had been mustered under a proclamation that fixed their tour of duty at thirty days. Nothing has been found in the militia law or in the act to repel invasions that limited the time militia could be employed. For references to this "thirty-day service," see 1 *G. W.*, 480, 500. It is possible, of course, that this Lunenburg Company was the one that citizens of that County had proposed in the summer of 1755 to raise and to pay for six months, but the interval of time and the form of the references to the troops render this improbable.

[35] 6 *H* 549; 1 *G. W.*, 478–79.   [36] Cf. 1 *Hamilton*, 289.
[37] 1 *G. W.*, 478–79.

ever expectation Your Honor may have had from the militia assistance," George was to write the Governor, "I am told they never lent a hand, save a few, that first came out with Captain Hog, whom he had paid after the same rates with our men . . ." [38]

Waste of manpower and feebleness of discipline were not all that shocked Washington at Hog's station. The pass at Vause's farm was of great importance, George saw, and if it were defended properly, it would protect all of Bedford and the greater part of Augusta. His disgust with what he saw of the misuse of the position led him to explode later with: "They have built three forts here, and *one* of them, if no more, erected in my opinion in a very out-of-the-way place. This they call Fort Trial." [39] He refrained from adding that it should have been named Fort Failure. Nor did he reflect, apparently, that the ground for the first stockade probably has been chosen by a farmer, not by an engineer.

Washington advanced Hog money for the current pay roll.[40] Then he bade the Captain good-bye and continued southward, because he now resolved to make his inspection of the Virginia defenses complete by going on to the forts in Halifax, next the North Carolina line. Colonel Buchanan could not attend on this ride but he promised to meet Washington at the headwaters of the Catawba on the return journey.[41] With this understanding, Washington, his servant and a new guide set out.

They had to pass in the rain through a forest that would shelter an army, but they saw not a single Indian nor observed even the movement of a pine sapling to suggest that a human arm had struck it by accident. Danger, though unnoticed, was close and murderous. Not long after George and his companions passed, a solitary traveler [42] was waylaid by ambuscaded Indians and was slain. Subsequently Washington was told that the leader of the savages had gone off for a few minutes and had directed his men not to fire in his absence on any persons traveling southward, as Washington was, because they must catch a party known to be moving in the opposite direction. It was to be certain his quarry

---

[38] *Ibid.*, 479.

[39] 1 *G. W.*, 479. Another Fort Trial appears near the North Carolina line on Kegley's map, see p. 229.

[40] 4 *Papers of G. W.*, LC. A copy of Washington's dispatch of June 2, 1756, covering £89, 10*s* pay roll, and giving certain instructions to Hog, is in the Boston Public Library.

[41] 1 *G. W.*, 481.

[42] Washington at first heard two were involved (1 *G. W.*, 479), but his later account (*ibid.*, 501) mentioned one only.

was near and his trap was well set that the Indian had left his riflemen for a short time. While he was off, they obediently withheld their bullets even from the tall white target. To George, this seemed one of the narrowest of his escapes from death, the narrowest certainly since the battle of the Monongahela.[43]

As soon as Captain McNeill heard of the killing on the road, he undertook to organize a pursuit of the murderers by the idle Company of Lunenburg militia at Fort Vause. Their commanding officer, Captain Hunt,[44] agreed to undertake this, and, with his men, easily followed the trail of the Indians to a stream where muddy water and wet rocks showed that savages, estimated to number twenty, had passed only a few minutes previously. Hunt stopped, pondered and evidently concluded that he was getting too close for safety. McNeill begged and exhorted him to proceed, but Hunt hesitated, conferred with his men and then went back the way he had come. This episode, George told himself, gave the measure of the "diligence and the resolution" of the militia "in pursuing the enemy." [45]

In Halifax County, which Washington soon reached, he found nothing to change his impression of the worthlessness of the militia and of the inadequacy of the chain of feeble forts; but he had one surprise. Like Governor Dinwiddie he had looked imploringly to the Cherokees for the help the English felt they must have against the French Indians after the friendly tribes of the Six Nations had deserted or had yielded to French threats, blandishments and bribes. Washington had awaited with eagerness the response the Cherokees would make under their new treaty [46] in sending warriors to Virginia. About five miles from the North Carolina line, on the 10th of October, he received the first answer. His own regimental Major, Andrew Lewis, had gone to the Cherokee country to bring the red fighters to Virginia. Cheerful reports of his success had been received.[47] Now Lewis returned along the trail while Washington was at a fort nearby. Instead of the large force Dinwiddie and Washington were hoping to receive, Lewis had in his care seven men, three squaws—and no more.[48]

---

43 He recalled it, though with some obscuration of detail, when he wrote in 1786 his comments on the Humphreys manuscript. See 29 *G. W.*, 47.

44 It has not been possible, as yet, to identify him positively. Memican Hunt of Lunenburg is mentioned in an electoral contest of 1759 as giving "a treat to a Company of militia he formerly had commanded." See Landon C. Bell, *The Old Free State*, v. 1, p. 144. The only other Hunt conspicuous in Lunenburg at the time was James, a Justice of the County Court in 1755–62 (*ibid.*, 330).

45 1 *G. W.*, 501.   46 See *supra*, p. 198.

47 *Md. Gazette*, Sept. 9, 30, 1756.   48 1 *G. W.*, 477; 2 *Din.*, 544.

This failure deepened a discontent, a half-despair, that Washington had been accumulating on the long, lonely road from Winchester to the North Carolina line. Militia were undependable; employment of them was wasteful; the Regiment was not strong enough, even when recruited fully, to do the work expected of it; there was censure and insinuation even in times of hardship and trial. Now, at the southern end of the projected long line of forts, all these things were an acute irritant. Washington's impulse to resign his command rose again; he interpreted the refusal of the General Assembly to provide 2000 men as proof of suspicion on the part of members that he sought an enlarged force in order to exalt his own authority.

With emotions confused and complicated, he sat down and wrote Dinwiddie by the express he directed Lewis to send to Williamsburg: [49] "I scorn to make unjust remarks on the behavior of the militia as much as I despise and condemn the persons who detract from mine and the character of the regiment . . . I only want to make the country sensible how ardently I have studied to promote her cause, and wish very sincerely my successor may fill my place more to their satisfaction in every respect than I have been able to do. I mentioned in my last to your Honor that I did not think a less number than 2,000 men would be sufficient to defend our extensive and much exposed frontier from the ravages of the enemy. I have not one reason yet to alter my opinion, but many to strengthen and confirm it. And I flatter myself the country will, when they know my determinations, be convinced that I have no sinister views, no vain motives of commanding a number of men, that urge me to recommend this number to your Honor, but that it proceeds from the knowledge I have acquired of the country, people, &c. to be defended." [50]

In this state of mind Washington reversed his direction on the 10th of October and started for his rendezvous with Colonel Buchanan at the head of the Catawba.[51] Without incident he returned to Fort William, a little stockade on the upper stretch of that watercourse.[52] True to promise, Colonel Buchanan met Washington there and brought with him about thirty men, a majority of whom were militia officers.

[49] Lewis to Dinwiddie, Oct. 11, 1756; P.R.O., C.O. 5: 48, p. 69. There is a difference of one day between Washington and Lewis concerning the date of their meeting.

[50] Letter of Oct. 10, 1756; 1 G. W., 480.

[51] 1 G. W., 481.

[52] The Catawba rises about twelve miles West of Salem, Virginia, and flows northeastward until it empties into James River. As the waters of the North Fork of the Roanoke and those of the Catawba are almost coterminous, it is impossible to state precisely where the fort stood.

The Commander-in-Chief was gratified that Buchanan had been able to assemble so many, but to a man who knew the necessity of silence in dealing with hostile savages, the next week brought experiences of a sort Washington never had known in all the months he had spent on forest trails and roads. "With this small company of irregulars," Washington wrote afterward, "with whom order, regularity, circumspection and vigilance were matters of derision and contempt, we set out . . ." In circumstances of less danger, it would have been ludicrous. The gentlemen-adventurers shouted ceaselessly to one another, as if they were on a fox-hunt; the dignified young Colonel was horrified at such disregard of military precautions but probably too considerate to put the riders under formal command and too polite to tell them to be silent.[53] George doubtless meant precisely what he said when he reported: ". . . by the protection of Providence, [we] reached Augusta Court House in seven days without meeting the enemy; otherwise we must have fallen a sacrifice, through the indiscretion of these whooping, hallooing *gentlemen* soldiers!"

At the forts, conditions scarcely were better. A few diligent officers, such as Thomas Bullett at Fort Dinwiddie, were on duty.[54] Elsewhere, most of the militia Captains were absent from their posts. Food was being wasted, and ammunition, too. "On our journey," Washington recorded, "as we approached one of their forts, we heard a quick fire for several minutes, and concluded for certain that they were attacked; so we marched in the best manner to their relief; but when we came up, we found they were diverting at marks." [55] Calls for militia to engage in scouts, to scour the country or to gather the crops of farmers who had fled to the stockades met with no response. On occasion, orders from Washington were not even acknowledged.[56]

George felt that he had seen all there was to see, and all of it discouraging. So, from Augusta Court House he spurred northward and,

[53] 1 *G. W.*, 492. The route of this part of the journey is not known and can be surmised only on the basis of the least difficult grades of a mountainous country. One guess would be that the party followed Catawba Creek to its mouth and then turned to the Northeast up the valley of the James, past the present Glen Wilton to the site of the modern Clifton Forge. Thence there was a choice of routes either via the pass now known as McGaw, and down Falling Spring Creek to Jackson River, or up the James to the site later that of Covington, and thence up the Jackson. When Washington turned East, he may have pursued substantially the present route of the Chesapeake & Ohio Railroad. As an alternative, he may have gone higher up Jackson River and then may have ridden more nearly on a direct line to Staunton. In any event, he must have passed through Buffalo Gap.

[54] 1 *G. W.*, 494. Washington was there October 18. Washington consistently spelled the name with an "e," in which form it is indexed in *G. W.*, but in *Hamilton* it is indexed Bullitt.

[55] 1 *G. W.*, 494. It is not known where this occurred.

[56] Cf 1 *G. W.*, 481–82, 494.

on the night of the 22nd of October, rode into Winchester.[57] He found
new distress there. Indians had resumed their raids on the South Branch
and elsewhere; farmers' appeals for help were reaching Winchester
daily; the whole situation was so alarming, in terms of resources, that
Washington had to confess himself deeply anxious.[58] Fortunately, the
alarm was of brief duration, with the result that Washington could turn
again, intently, to the personal question that had been gnawing both
his pride and his conscience from the hour he read the attack in the
tenth article of "The Virginia Centinel": Should he resign? He found
strong arguments against such a step in a letter from his brother
"Austin," who had gone to Williamsburg to ascertain what the effect
of the tirade had been on George's reputation and prospects. Augustine
was reassuring: "I am certain your character does not in the least suffer
here, for I do assure you as far as I can inform myself . . . you are in
as great esteem as ever with the Governor here and especially the
House of Burgesses." The effect of the attack could not be ascertained,
so far as other Colonies were concerned, Augustine admitted, but for
the time being George's friends thought he should make no answer. He
certainly should not resign his commission: "Your country never stood
more in need of your assistance." Besides, the brother observed, if
Washington resigned, Innes might be named.[59] Giving up the commission, the forthright Augustine continued, "will in some measure be
giving up your country." If George left the service, the other officers of
the Regiment would; the men would desert; and the country would
be left defenceless.[60]

Soon after the receipt of "Austin's" letter, the issue changed
abruptly. Virginia officers at Fort Cumberland did not see the tenth
article of the "Centinel" until October 5, while Washington was on his
tour of inspection. They met the next day and sent Lieutenant Colonel
Stephen a furious letter in which they insisted that the Governor must
have known and might have consented to the publication of the article.
Otherwise, they loosely reasoned, the printer "would never have dared
to insert such a paper in his *Gazette*." [61] Dinwiddie, in either event,

[57] *Ibid.*, 481–82, 482.
[58] 1 *G. W.*, 482.
[59] See *supra*, p. 174.
[60] Letter of Oct. 16, 1756; 1 *Hamilton*, 375–77.
[61] The charge against Dinwiddie was, of course, wholly illogical: he would not have as-
sailed his own appointees. As far as is known, the identity of "The Virginia Centinel" never
was established. The last reference found to him is a reprint in the *Penn. Gazette*, Mch. 17,
1757, of an article, No. XVI, on the necessity of an Indian alliance. The style is less stilted than
that of No. X.

"must have believed the censures therein to be just." The angry young Virginians then served notice: "We are resolved to obey as officers no longer than the twentieth day of November next, unless we have as public satisfaction as the injury received." [62]

That was serious business. In several past crises the extreme utterance of others had led George to draw back. This time, apparently, he perceived that what he had threatened to do himself was dangerous when done by others. His own wrath cooled. Cost what it might, he must keep the officers from leaving the service when their resignation would mean the disintegration of the Regiment and the further exposure of the Colony to attack. To make plain to the outraged officers the consequences of their ultimatum, he resolved to go to Fort Cumberland as soon as practicable, but before he could do this he had to bestir the soldiers and the laborers at Winchester, where work was lagging on the defence that now was styled officially Fort Loudoun. [63]

When he again had a grip on these men, he had to take time to prepare a report to the Governor on his inspection of the forts in Augusta and to the southward. Washington had written from Halifax; [64] he wished now to complete the narrative and to summarize his conclusions. Of the militia, he said only what he had abundant reason to believe—that "for want of proper laws . . . they are obstinate, self-willed, perverse, of little or no service to the people, and very burthensome to the country." [65] The garrisons "were weak for want of men, but more so by indolence and irregularity." He specified carefully and then went on to describe "the wretched and unhappy situation of the inhabitants." [66] Although he did not so state in any single sentence, he made it plain that the defensive system of the Colony was as futile as it was expensive. He concluded with a statement of current needs at Winchester and of the measures he had taken to supply them. "The other day," he said, without any thought of reflecting on his correspondent, "eleven Indians of the Catawba tribe came here, and we undoubtedly might have had more of them, had the proper means been used to send trusty guides to invite and conduct them to us; but this is neglected." [67]

This letter was completed on November 9. As soon as it was copied and signed and a few other essential duties were performed, George

[62] 4 *Papers of G. W.*, 181, LC.
[64] 1 *G. W.*, 477 ff.
[66] *Ibid.*, 494.
[63] Cf. 1 *G. W.*, 485.
[65] 1 *G. W.*, 493.
[67] *Ibid.*, 497.

hurried to Fort Cumberland [68] and undertook to convince the officers, first of all, that when they had set November 20 as the date of their resignation, they had allowed too little time for the Governor, the Council or the Burgesses to give them "satisfaction" in any form. Consequently, he asked them to defer all action until he could investigate and report to them. None too willingly they assented, but they insisted they must have the thanks of the General Assembly and an avowal of disbelief in the charges of the "Centinel." The alternative was set forth with deliberate sarcasm—that the Governor or the lawmakers must appoint in their place "a set of gentlemen who will more fully answer their and his expectation and perform that for their country which it seems their Governor, if not they, little hope for from a company of dastardly debauchees."

This was demanded in a joint letter that was not lacking in sharp references to the Governor. Dinwiddie was accused of ignoring the officers' grievances and, inferentially, of crediting the accusation. He or the Assembly, they said, might expect to "be answerable to Lord Loudoun, or to His Majesty for the consequences," if one or the other of their demands was not met. In all of this, the tone of the communication was deferential toward Washington, but his feelings were not spared. His subordinates addressed their revised ultimatum to him because, as they said, "we imagined that you were [as] particularly aimed at as any among us, we having acted in obedience to your commands." [69]

When this was subscribed, November 12, the offended officers apparently thought the General Assembly had met the previous day, but actually, though it had been prorogued to November 11, it had not been called back to Williamsburg.[70] If, then, the complainants were to have early redress, they had to look to the Governor and Council. Washington agreed that their appeal should be presented. To seek vindication and to transact an accumulation of army business, he prepared to start for Williamsburg.

A particular question to be decided at the capital was the tediously recurring one of the future of Fort Cumberland. Washington now was convinced that the defences there not only should be evacuated but

---

68 He was there about November 11–12. Cf. 1 *G. W.*, 514.

69 Letter of Nov. 12, 1756; 1 *Hamilton*, 383–84. Washington's appeal to the officers, if made in writing, has not been preserved, but its essential terms are reconstructed easily from the reply.

70 *Journ. H. B.*, 1752–58, p. 410, 413.

should be destroyed also, in order that the enemy might not use them. More than ever he was fixed in his judgment that Winchester should be the advance base of the Virginia forces. The Governor had been no less insistent that Fort Cumberland be garrisoned, but at length he had authorized Washington to hold a council of war [71] on the future of the defences at Wills Creek and to act as the majority voted. Washington, in turn, had instructed Stephen to convene the council and to have its members express their free choice, though he had reiterated his own opinion.[72] Not to be outdone in courtesy, the council, on October 30, had applied for a larger garrison temporarily and had concluded that Lord Loudoun or Governor Dinwiddie should speak the last word.[73]

Washington, reviewing the minutes, expressed some surprise that the officers had asked for a reenforcement they knew he could not supply. He said plainly that if he had attended the council he would have voted for demolition of the fort, but he, too, believed that the importance of the issue justified reference to the Governor and the General Assembly.[74] Finally, in ignorance of the outcome of the deliberations at Fort Cumberland, Dinwiddie had written that Lord Loudoun seemed to think the fort should be retained. Washington still was given discretion, with the further statement that if the officers decided the fort could be maintained, the Governor would be glad.[75] All those who had any measure of responsibility were agreed that some decision should be reached promptly; Washington alone was entirely convinced what that decision should be—and he was willing to pass the question back once more to the Governor for determination when he visited Williamsburg.

On this mission, the Colonel had reached Alexandria and had been there several days, enjoying some of the comforts of John Carlyle's home,[76] when he received an extraordinary letter from Dinwiddie. The Governor had been confined to his room for two weeks or more in October [77] and not been improved in body or in temper. He had taken offence at the reference Washington half casually had made, in the report of November 9, to the arrival in Winchester of the eleven

---

[71] 1 G. W., 482–83.   [72] Ibid., 483–84.
[73] 2 Hamilton, 6–9.   [74] 1 G. W., 487–90.
[75] Dinwiddie to Washington, Oct. 26, 1756; 1 Hamilton, 378.
[76] Apparently he reached Alexandria on the 16th, which would indicate that he stopped for a few hours only in Winchester on his return from Fort Cumberland. See Ledger A, folio 31 and 1 G. W., 507.
[77] 1 Hamilton, 379.

Catawba Indians whose number might have been increased by the use of responsible guides.[78] Dinwiddie for months had been humiliated by the failure of his efforts to procure substantial help from the Southern Indians and doubtless he had been shamed anew by the arrival of Andrew Lewis with the ludicrous reenforcement of seven Cherokee warriors and three squaws.[79] Hit where he was sore, the Governor struck back angrily at Washington: "You seem to charge neglect in me, not having proper conductors. This charge is unmannerly, as I did what I thought proper, though disappointed by the villainous traders." [80]

Temper colored the whole of Dinwiddie's letter, even in a retort to a suggestion Washington had made of the enlistment of Virginia regulars: "The establishing of regulars would be very agreeable to me, but where are the men to be got, when you have not been able in a twelve months to complete your Regiment?" [81] There was, also, a rebuke for Washington's failure to name the individual militia officers who had failed to do their duty on the southern part of the western frontier,[82] and further censure of the Colonel for choosing an acting commissary without getting the approbation of the Governor.[83]

Most startling of all was a succession of brief, concluding sentences in which Dinwiddie said that the proposals concerning the future of Fort Cumberland had been reviewed by himself and the Council: "In consequence thereof, I hereby order you immediately to march 100 men to Fort Cumberland from the forces you have at Winchester, which Captain Mercer says is 160 men. You are to remain at Fort Cumberland and make the place as strong as you can, in case of an attack. You are to send out parties from the fort to observe the motions of the enemy if they should march over the Allegheny Mountains. Any stores at the fort not absolutely necessary for its defense you are to send . . . to Winchester. You are to order one of your subaltern officers (in whom you confide) to command at Winchester and to oversee the finishing of the fort building at that place. These orders I expect you will give due obedience to, and I am with respect, sir, your most humble servant . . ." [84]

This was sharp, stern discipline for the young Colonel who was on

---

[78] 1 *G. W.*, 497.
[79] See *supra*, p. 218.
[80] 2 *Din.*, 552.
[81] *Ibid.*
[82] *Ibid.*, 551–52.
[83] *Ibid.*, 553.
[84] *Ibid.*, 553. For the circumstances attending this decision, which members of the Council told Robinson was made at the instance of Lord Loudoun, see Robinson to Washington, Dec. 31, 1756; 2 *Hamilton*, 30–31. Robinson intimated that Dinwiddie inspired Loudoun's action.

his way to Williamsburg to tell the Governor that the officers at Fort Cumberland demanded they be replaced unless the attack on them by "The Virginia Centinel" was disavowed! The Governor had said nothing about the officers or about the *Gazette* article, but if there was to be a war of words, Dinwiddie manifestly had the initiative. Washington was astonished and stunned. To dispatch 100 additional men to Fort Cumberland would be to leave Winchester undefended, the stores unprotected, and Fort Loudoun not only uncompleted but also exposed to the elements and to thieves who would carry off the building materials accumulated there at heavy expense and with cruel labor.

Of all the occasions on which Washington might have thought himself justified in throwing up his commission, this certainly was the most provoking and warrantable; but the effect on him of Dinwiddie's criticisms was exactly the reverse. He had talked of quitting the service on account of the article by "The Virginia Centinel" until his officers had threatened to do the same thing; he had been angry until he found from this newest letter that Dinwiddie was wrathful, too, and, in using his authority, was about to make a most dangerous blunder. The risk to the "country" and to the work he had taken in hand cooled Washington and calmed him.

If he had to move his troops from the fort he favored to the one he considered an incubus, he obviously had to be in the Valley and not at Williamsburg. He accordingly made his arrangements to return to Winchester and then, mastering himself completely, he sat down and replied to Dinwiddie's letter point by point. He apologized for what Dinwiddie had considered his "unmannerly" reference to the Indians' guides; he explained his vagueness concerning the incompetent militia officers encountered on an inspection tour which, he insisted, he undertook from a desire to serve his country. "[I] am sorry," he wrote, in unwonted simplicity of style, "to find that this and my best endeavors of late meet with unfavorable constructions." He went on: "What it proceeds from, I know not. If my open and disinterested way of writing and speaking has the *air* of pertness and freedom, I shall redress my error by acting reservedly, and shall take care to obey my orders without offering at more." [85] After a review of the other matters of which the Governor had complained, he returned to the proposal for the abandonment of Fort Loudoun, told Dinwiddie what this involved, and then wrote a final sentence that was apt to make the Governor

[85] Letter of Nov. 24, 1756; 1 *G. W.*, 509.

reconsider: "So, to comply with my order (which I shall do literally if I can) not a man will be left [at Winchester] to secure the works or defend the King's stores, which are almost wholly removed to that place." [86]

Three days later, November 27,[87] Washington left Alexandria for Winchester and, on arrival, called immediately for a return of the troops in the Valley town. Dinwiddie had understood Mercer to say they numbered 160, of whom the Governor had ordered 100 to Fort Cumberland. How many were actually there? Scattered among the forts were 120 drafted men, who were to be released December 1— almost immediately—because the law set that time limit. Of soldiers of the Regiment then in Winchester, counting the sick and the boys who were learning to be drummers, only eighty-one were on the roster of effectives.[88] If, then, Washington abandoned Winchester completely, he could not furnish the whole of the reenforcement ordered to Fort Cumberland.

By good chance, wagons and flour for the transfer of the troops and their equipment to the Maryland post were not available immediately.[89] Without disobedience of orders, time sufficed for an appeal to the Governor. George wrote it carefully and deferentially and set forth the loss that would attend the evacuation of Winchester. He prudently forwarded documentary proof of the shortages that delayed the movement, but when he came to explain the personal aspect of the change, his anger almost overflowed. In the state of mind he then was developing, he suspected that enemies were saying he had invented objections to going to Fort Cumberland because he wished to continue a comfortable life in the house he had rented of Capt. William Cocke.[90] Indignantly Washington asserted: "Some, sir, who are inclined to put an unfavorable construction upon this generous recital may say that I am loath to leave this. I declare upon my honor that I am not, but had rather be at Fort Cumberland (if I could do the duty there) a thousand times over: for I am tired of the place, the inhabitants, and the life I lead here." [91]

Vexations multiplied. On the 3rd of December, no less than eighteen men of the Regiment deserted. Washington pursued and fortunately

---

[86] *Ibid.,* 511.

[87] The date is proved by gratuities to John Carlyle's servants and by expenses on the road (*Ledger A,* folio 31).

[88] 305 *Papers of G. W.,* 73, LC; 1 *G. W.,* 511–12: 1 *Hamilton,* 17.

[89] 1 *G. W.,* 511, 516.   [90] See *supra,* p. 119.

[91] 1 *G. W.,* 514.

caught sixteen of them. When questioned, they said they had been told by former Ensign Dennis McCarty that they could leave the service of Virginia without danger to themselves and could join the Company Dinwiddie had authorized McCarty to raise for a new Royal American Regiment then being recruited. McCarty's record as an officer had not been good; [92] his conduct now was denounced by Washington as "base and villainous," the scheme of a man "with whom all his ties of honor and morality are of no force." [93] McCarty himself could be dealt with, but there was danger that he might "scandalously and underhandedly," in George's words, have "seduced" others besides the eighteen.[94] While this depletion of the feeble Regiment still was an immediate possibility, Washington had to enlist indentured servants to guard the stores at Winchester and by so doing provoked another complicated, though not a wrathful, discussion with the Governor.[95]

Dinwiddie and the Council perforce had a change of heart when they learned from Washington that the reenforcement of Fort Cumberland would necessitate the abandonment of the unfinished and insecure fort at Winchester. On the 15th of December,[96] Washington received the Governor's instructions to evacuate all the smaller forts except Waggener's on the South Branch and to divide all the available men between the garrisons of Winchester and of Wills Creek, so that Fort Cumberland might be strengthened and Fort Loudoun still be held.

This meant, of course, that Indian raiders could penetrate easily the abandoned area between the two main forts, but, at that, the danger to the settlers during the winter season would not be great. It was less bad to take that risk than to abandon Fort Loudoun and its supplies to plunderers.[97] The puzzling phase of the compromise was this: If all the stockades except Waggener's were abandoned, more men would be released than the Governor had instructed Washington to employ at Fort Cumberland and at Fort Loudoun. What should be done with them? ". . . I mean nothing more by asking the question," George

[92] For the accusation that he had imprisoned men who would not volunteer for service in the Virginia Regiment, see *supra*, p. 143.

[93] 1 *G. W.*, 515–16.

[94] For the cancellation of McCarty's commission and the denunciation of him, see 1 *G. W.*, 515–16, 518, 524; 2 *Hamilton*, 22, 40; 2 *Din.*, 562.

[95] This aspect of the enlistment of servants may be followed in 1 *G. W.*, 417, 497, 517; 1 *Hamilton*, 343, 365; 2 *ibid.*, 21, 43; 2 *Din.*, 571, 586. Captain McNeill enlisted forty-one servants (1 *G. W.*, 524).

[96] 1 *G. W.*, 522.

[97] 2 *Hamilton*, 16; 1 *G. W.*, 522–23.

APPROXIMATE LOCATION OF THE VIRGINIA FRONTIER FORTS

Redrawn by permission from F. G. Kegley's *Virginia Frontier*, page 244, this sketch records the
conclusions of Mr. Kegley concerning the location of frontier forts, some of which are mentioned
once or twice only. In numerous instances, it is impossible to determine exactly where stockades
were erected by farmers.

hastened to write, "than to know your Honor's intentions, which I
would willingly pay strict obedience to." [98]

Even with that unanswered, Washington had won a partial victory.
Fort Loudoun had been saved. Besides, John Robinson had written a
comforting letter from Williamsburg. In his usual friendly spirit, the

[98] 1 *G. W.*, 523.

Speaker had repeated "Austin's" argument that Washington's resignation would provoke those of the other officers and thus would leave the frontiers exposed. Robinson wrote: "I hope you will allow your ruling passion, the love of your country, to stifle your resentments at least till the arrival of Lord Loudoun or the meeting of the Assembly when you may be sure of having justice done you ... I have never heard any man of honor or of reputation speak the least disrespectfully of you or censure your conduct in the least, and I am sure there is no well wisher to his country that would not be greatly concerned to hear of your resigning . . ." [99]

That would have been convincing as well as comforting if Dinwiddie had not put in doubt the very assurance Robinson had given—that Lord Loudoun would appreciate Washington's service. In his letter ordering the abandonment of the stockades, the Governor had quoted a paragraph from a communication in which Lord Loudoun had said of the proposed evacuation of the small forts: "If [Colonel Washington] leaves any of the great quantity of stores behind, it will be very unfortunate; and he ought to consider that it must lie at his own door." Then Loudoun had added: "This proceeding, I am afraid, will have a bad effect as to the Dominion and will not have a good appearance at home." [100]

That was alarming. George felt that Loudoun had been prejudiced against him [101] and that he had been the victim of "pretended friends." [102] He could perceive, of course, that Loudoun wrote in misconception of the facts, if not in ignorance of them; but misconception and ignorance were a source of prejudice, not a cure of it. The one recourse that occurred to George at the time was to wait in person on the new Commander-in-Chief, and to present the reasons for what he had proposed. In accordance with his usual practice of meeting personally his official superiors as soon as possible, George already had procured Dinwiddie's permission to pay his respects to Lord Loudoun when the peer came to Virginia. Washington pressed now for early information of the General's arrival and frankly told the Governor: "I hope nothing has intervened to alter this indulgence" of explaining the situation on the frontier. [103]

Until this opportunity was offered, Washington would wait and of

99 Letter of Nov. 16, 1756; 2 *Hamilton*, 1–2.
100 2 *Hamilton*, 19. 101 1 *G. W.*, 525.
102 2 *Hamilton*, 2. 103 1 *G. W.*, 526.

course would carry out his orders. The garrisons at the small forts were instructed to proceed to Pearsall's and to stay there until the arrival of the provisions they were to escort to Fort Cumberland; [104] Capt. George Mercer was directed to remain at Fort Loudoun and to exercise "particular diligence and care" in the continued discipline of the men and in the further construction of the fort.[105] Then, on December 20 or 21, Washington took all his wardrobe, his camp equipment, his horses and the new puppy he had bought that month [106] and set out for Fort Cumberland. The controversy over the accusation of "The Virginia Centinel" was not forgotten, but it had been put into the background till Lord Loudoun was on the ground and wrongs were righted and justice done the Virginia Regiment.[107] Washington spoke from the heart when he said, almost on the eve of his departure: ". . . my strongest representations of matters relative to the peace of the frontiers are disregarded as idle and frivolous; my propositions and measures as partial and selfish; and all my sincerest endeavors for the service of my country perverted to the worst purpose. My orders are dark, doubtful and uncertain; today approved, tomorrow condemned. Left to act and proceed at hazard, accountable for the consequence, and blamed without the benefit of defence . . . However, I am determined to bear up under all the embarrassments some time longer, in hope of better regulation on the arrival of Lord Loudoun, to whom I look for the future fate of Virginia." [108]

[104] 1 *G. W.*, 522–23.
[105] 1 *G. W.*, 530–31.
[106] He paid 2*s* 6*d* for it (*Ledger A*, folio 32).
[107] The letter to John Robinson in 1 *G. W.*, 530, dated "December, 1756," would create the impression that the controversy was much alive as the year was closing; but the absence from this letter of any reference to the "Centinel" and the close similarity of the language to that of the letter to Dinwiddie, Apr. 18, 1756 (1 *G. W.*, 317), make it almost certain that the communication to Robinson was part of the dispute in the spring over the first charge of immorality at Fort Cumberland. Reference to the fact that the Assembly was "incensed against the Virginia Regiment" would have been apropos in April but pointless in December. If, therefore, the date of the letter was supplied later by Washington, he probably confused two episodes that had several features in common.
[108] Letter of Dec. 19, 1756, to John Robinson, 1 *G. W.*, 528–29.

CHAPTER XIII

Under Suspicion of Treason
(January–March, 1757)

The weeks of waiting for the visit of Lord Loudoun to Virginia could not be for Washington a time of idleness even at Fort Cumberland in winter. After the Christmas holidays, which some of the men sought to enliven with theatrical performances of a sort,[1] George had to find clothing for the half-naked troops, who had been expecting it since October,[2] and he had to submit to another controversy with the Governor over the appointment of a commissary. Dinwiddie accused George of not giving "proper countenance" to Thomas Walker, the disgruntled official; Washington's reply was that in like circumstances he would have treated his own brother the same way.[3] It was not a vain dispute because, at its close, Washington virtually disclaimed all responsibility for provisioning the men.[4] More serious was a mutiny on the South Branch. This was put down promptly and sternly, with the arrest of the ringleaders, though Washington was in the embarrassing position of not being able to punish them adequately because the pertinent and punitive act of October, 1755, had expired.[5]

These unpleasant matters having been faced and endured, Washington turned to the preparation of a report to Loudoun on the condition of the Virginia forces and the situation on the frontier. Washington wrote this paper with much care because he intended to use it as an introduction to the new Commander-in-Chief, who had been compelled to go to New England and to defer plans for visiting Virginia.[6] This

---

[1] Washington paid the players £2 from his own funds on the 10th of January, 1757. See *Ledger A*, folio 32.

[2] 1 *G. W.*, 527; 2 *ibid.*, 15; 2 *Hamilton*, 29, 31–32, 39.

[3] 2 *Din.*, 572, 574; 2 *G. W.*, 1–2; 2 *Hamilton*, 42–43.

[4] 2 *G. W.*, 3–4.

[5] 2 *G. W.*, 1. Cf. 1 *G. W.*, 504 and 2 *Din.*, 584. The amended mutiny act, see *supra*, p. 138, and 6 *H* 559–64, had been effective for one year only.

[6] 2 *G. W.*, 4. Loudoun was in New York Jan. 2, 1757. See his *Memorandum*, the MS of which is in the Huntington Library. It virtually is a diary. The General reached Boston Jan. 19, 1757 (*Penn. Gazette*, Feb. 17, 1757) and arrived in New York again February 20 (*ibid.*, Feb. 24, 1757).

meant longer waiting but it did not discourage the young Colonel. He was resolved to make the best possible impression by his report and later to call on Lord Loudoun in order to present a welcoming address by his officers. As it happened, almost simultaneously, the Marquis de Vaudreuil, Governor General of New France,[7] was reporting optimistically to his government on the state of His Christian Majesty's cause on the Ohio. The troops were making continuous progress, the Marquis reported; they had taken two stockades by assault; if statements of prisoners were to be credited, the English had abandoned Fort Cumberland.[8]

Washington began a covering letter to Loudoun's senior aide in precisely the opposite strain, with the assertion that a British offensive, if practicable, was necessary: "Our all in a manner depends upon it. The French grow more and more formidable by their alliances, while our friendly Indians are deserting our interest. Our treasury is exhausting, and our country depopulating . . ." At the same time, Washington assured Lord Loudoun that 3000 men could cut communications between Fort DuQuesne and the Lakes and, with artillery, could destroy the fort on the Ohio.[9] The difficulties that weakened the Virginia Regiment and hampered all its operations were the principal theme of the report itself. Almost every point of previous complaint to Governor Dinwiddie was reviewed, from the worthlessness of the militia to the difficulty of paying rewards for the return of deserters.

Then, without abashment or apology, Washington became personal: "This . . . is at present my situation. Therefore it is not to be wondered at if, under such peculiar circumstances, I should be sickened in a service which promises so little of a soldier's reward. I have long been satisfied of the impossibility of continuing in this service, without loss of honor." The Virginia Colonel then explained how reluctant he had been to resume command after his retirement in 1754, and he proceeded somewhat in the manner of a courtier to explain that one reason for his continuance with the Virginia forces was the appointment of Loudoun. "Hence it was that I drew my hopes and fondly pronounced your Lordship our patron . . . Do not think, my Lord, that I am going to flatter; notwithstanding I have exalted sentiments of your Lordship's character and respect your rank, it is not my intention to adulate.

[7] For his habitual boastfulness, see Parkman, *Montcalm and Wolfe,* v. 2, p. 178.
[8] Vaudreuil to Drucor, Jan. 13, 1757; *Col. des MSS relatif à la Nouvelle France,* v. 4, p. 29.
[9] 2 *G. W.,* 5.

My nature is open and honest and free from guile." [10] With like frankness George avowed the ambition of the Virginia Regiment to have a "better establishment," and he informed Loudoun that Braddock had promised to advance him: "General Shirley was not unkind in his promises, but he has gone to England. I do not know, my Lord, in what light this short and disinterested relation may be received by your Lordship; but with the utmost candor and submission it is offered. It contains no misrepresentations, nor aggravated relation of facts, nor unjust reflections."

At the end, George returned to praise of the gentleman whom he hoped, as he said, to make his patron: "Virginia is a country young in war and, till the breaking out of these disturbances, has remained in the most profound and tranquil peace, ne'er studying war or warfare. It is not, therefore, to be imagined that she can fall into proper measures at once. All that can be expected at her hands she cheerfully offers, the sinews of war, and these want only your Lordship's ability and experience to be properly applied and directed." There was more of this and then, in a final flourish, expression of the hope of an "opportunity of testifying how much I admire your Lordship's character, and with what profound respect I have the honor to be, &c." [11]

Washington held to his purpose to find the earliest possible opportunity of "testifying" to the qualities of the man who could advance him quickly. When the Colonel learned that Loudoun had deferred a second time the visit to Virginia but had called a conference of provincial Governors to meet in Philadelphia,[12] he warmly solicited Dinwiddie's permission to attend. "I cannot conceive," the Governor testily replied, "what service you can be of in going there, as the plan concerted will of course be communicated to you and the other officers: however, as you seem so earnest to go, I now give you leave . . ." [13] Washington departed promptly, stopped at home on his way to the city,[14] left on the 13th with Capt. Robert Stewart and Thomas Bishop, and reached the place of conference about the 21st [15]—only to be told

---

[10] 2 *G. W.*, 17–18. Cf. his first letter to Gov. Francis Fauquier, June 17, 1758, which began: "Although but a poor hand at complimenting, but permit me, nevertheless to offer your Honor my congratulations . . ." (2 *G. W.*, 213).   [11] 2 *G. W.*, 18–19.

[12] He may not have known at the time that the designated date was February 17. See 2 *Hamilton*, 44.   [13] Letter of Feb. 2, 1757; 2 *Hamilton*, 45.

[14] As evidenced by the fact that he carried a letter from William Fairfax to Dinwiddie. See 2 *Din.*, 595.

[15] *Ledger A*, folio 33. It is impossible to state positively whether the expenditures of the 21st–22nd were made in Philadelphia, but apparently they were and those of the 23rd most certainly were.

that the new Commander-in-Chief had not made his appearance.[16]
Governor Dinwiddie was there,[17] as were his colleagues Sharpe of
Maryland and Dobbs of North Carolina. William Denny, Governor of
Pennsylvania, was in residence [18] and would be available, of course,
the hour His Excellency arrived.

Pending that gratifying event, Washington had to make the most
of such accommodations as a Philadelphia inn could offer in midwinter.
He found the shops as well-stocked as formerly with finery for gentlemen,[19] but he did not patronize them as he had in 1756. His indulgences
were less expensive. He saw much of Governor Sharpe and probably
had the company of that gentleman several times when he dined and
then sat over a bottle of wine, the cost of which was divided accurately
among the drinkers.[20] Cards, too, were a diversion, with the companions of Colonel Washington somewhat on the winning side.[21]
Once, at least, he attended the assembly at the invitation of some resident member, but he carefully paid the cost of his ticket, five-and-nine,
Virginia money.[22] It was customary at these affairs to arrange sets of
ten couples, formed in order of arrival, and to devote the evening to
dancing and to card-playing. Rum punch was supplied freely to sustain
the enthusiasm of the members and guests for six hours of festivity.[23]

Of serious work, there was little that Washington could do. He
probably had brought with him the rough draft of a semiformal
"remonstrance," in substance another appeal by the officers of his Regiment to Governor Dinwiddie to redress their grievances. The Colonel
spent some time in trying to improve this document. In doing so, he
dwelt on the long, difficult service of the officers and men, who had
never been dismissed, as other troops were, at the end of a year's campaign: "As to those idle arguments which are sometimes used, namely,
you are defending your own properties, I look upon to be whimsical
and absurd; we are defending the King's Dominions and although the
inhabitants of Great Britain are removed from danger, they are yet

---

[16] 2 Din., 591, 602.

[17] He had left Williamsburg February 10 (2 Din., 594).

[18] At the Shippen house, used in 1699 by William Penn. See Watson, Annals of Philadelphia (1st ed.), 315.

[19] See, for example, John Ord's advertisement in the Penn. Gazette of February 10.

[20] There are eight, perhaps nine, "club" entries of this type in Washington's Philadelphia
expenses (Ledger A, folios 33–34).

[21] Ibid., folio 33, shows losses of £4, 16s, Pennsylvania currency.

[22] Presumably the price still was 7/6, as set in 1748/49. See Balch, Philadelphia Assemblies, 39.

[23] Ibid. The names of the ladies of the assembly of 1757 are published ibid., 58, but those
who formed Washington's "set" are not identified.

with us equally concerned and interested in the fate of the country, and there can be no sufficient reason given why we who spend our blood and treasure in defence of the country are not entitled to equal preferment."

After further arguments, there followed a half-apology for boasting of the performance of the Regiment's officers; "but we are compelled thereto by the little notice taken of us—it being the general opinion that our services are slighted, or have not been properly represented to His Majesty: otherwise the best of Kings would have graciously taken notice of us in turn, while there are now six Battalions raised in America and not an officer of the Virginia Regiment provided for, notwithstanding many of them had distinguished themselves in the service before orders were issued for raising one of the Battalions above mentioned." [24] This protest, for some reason, was not put in final form and presented forthwith to Governor Dinwiddie.

Besides recreation and the restatement of his grievance, Washington had at least one other experience of interest during his weeks of waiting for the Commander-in-Chief. About ten days after the Virginian reached Philadelphia he found in the *Pennsylvania Gazette* an unusual advertisement of a forthcoming book. Aboard a French vessel captured at sea, British naval officers had found a volume published in Paris by royal order the previous year. This was a "Mémoire contenant le Précis des Faits, avec leur Pièces Justificatives pour Servir de Résponse aux Observations Envoyées par les Ministres d'Angleterre dans les Cours de l'Europe," and it was described accurately by the title. It was a collection of documents designed to show that blame for the existing war rested on Britain, not on France—just such a volume, in short, as a printer might seize upon and print quickly in order to satisfy public curiosity of what "the other side" was saying. More than one such printer, it would appear, soon had the same resolution to translate and issue the Mémoire. There may, indeed, have been something of a race between two of the disciples of Cadmus, one in New York and the other in Philadelphia.

The advertisement in the Pennsylvania paper was exciting to Washington because it listed among the contents a "Journal" attributed to him.[25] Washington at once investigated, because the publisher an-

---

[24] *Wigan Collection from Sulgrave Manor;* copy at Mount Vernon. It is instructive to compare this paper with the remonstrance published in 2 *G. W.*, 25, and provisionally dated April 16. That document is summarized *infra*, p. 245.

[25] Issue of Mch. 3, 1757.

nounced that the book would be put to press on the 20th of March and would be issued in six weeks. The Virginian found that the translation had not been completed and that what had been put into English was awkward and poorly expressed.[26] For his own protection, doubtless, he had a translation of his own made of some of the passages that related to himself.[27] The "Journal" proved to be a French elaboration of notes he had kept in varying form, sometimes *in extenso* and sometimes in little more than outline, from Mch. 31 to June 27, 1754; that is, from the time he was commissioned to start for the Ohio, to protect the building of the fort at the Junction, until the eve of the retreat to the Great Meadows. Many things that he had jotted down the French editor of his captured notes had eliminated, and some things of which he had not even thought at the time were attributed to him.[28] He corrected as much of this as he could, in the short time that remained before publication, but apparently the Philadelphia printer decided to adhere to the English text already available.[29] George did not fail to subscribe to it.[30]

At last the dull diversions of idle days were relieved: Loudoun was coming! On the 14th of March, the guns of the Association Battery and of ships in the harbor announced his arrival. The bells of the city bade him welcome.[31] As the waiting Governors had become impatient, they sat down eagerly to confer with him and to hear the little he had to say about his military plans.[32] There were some ceremonials, notably a dinner given March 18 by the corporation of Philadelphia at the State House;[33] but, in the main, there was solid discussion, which soon turned to the state of affairs in Pennsylvania and to the means by which the people could be aroused to support the war with vigor.[34]

Washington found Lord Loudoun a bachelor, aged fifty-two, stout and somewhat below middle height, but strongly muscled and apparently fit for the field.[35] The General had the marks of high station

[26] See his undated letter to the printer or editor in 2 *Sparks*, 463.
[27] See *Ledger A*, folio 34: "By cash to a French translator 21/6."
[28] 2 *Sparks*, 263.
[29] There are no more than the normal typographical differences between the New York and Philadelphia editions.
[30] *Ledger A*, folio 35. Apparently he did not purchase then nor is there any record that he later owned a publication that William Bradford advertised in the *Penn. Gazette* of Feb. 3, 1757, just before his arrival in Philadelphia—"A Brief View of the Conduct of Pennsylvania for 1755 so Far as it Affected the General service of the British Colonies, particularly the Expedition under General Braddock." The author was William Smith. [31] *Penn. Gazette*, Mch. 17, 1757.
[32] See Governor Denny in 3 *Penn. Arch.*, 117 ff.
[33] *Penn. Gazette*, Mch. 24, 1757; Watson, *Annals of Philadelphia*, 347.
[34] See Denny, *loc. cit.* A copy of part of the minutes is in *Br. Mus. Add MS* 21632, f. 38.
[35] Philip Wraxall, quoted in Pargellis, *Loudoun*, 82.

and of good living and he displayed an interest in administration that doubtless brightened the eyes of the methodical Washington. Had the younger man known his new commander's habits, he would have felt still another tie, because Loudoun was as much disposed as Washington was to do his own "paper work" and not to leave to an assistant the drafting of dispatches.[36] From Loudoun's senior aide, Washington soon learned something both personal and pleasing: the General had been much pleased with Washington's report on the situation in Virginia.[37] Loudoun doubtless was equally pleased when he met the young Virginian who succeeded in nothing more certainly than in winning the good-will of his seniors. George was not invited to all meetings of the conference, which began March 15, but he was called in March 20 [38] when a choice was to be made concerning the forts to be held in western Virginia [39] and the garrisons to be employed there.

Washington seems to have shared fully in the other activities of the conference in blank ignorance of the fact that he had been under suspicion in one of the mysteries of the year. The British ministry had received in 1756 four letters, one after another, signed "Filius Gallicae" and addressed to the Duc de Mirepoix. These had been intercepted en route from America to France, though an effort had been made to have them sent through Ireland or Holland. They were written ostensibly by a British officer in America who was of French Catholic stock and sympathy and was ready to betray the King to whom he had sworn allegiance. The "officer" disclosed, or pretended, in discussing various subjects, that he was to share in an expedition against Fort DuQuesne, that he was unmarried and thirty-eight years of age, and that he had an aide-de-camp.[40] Evidently the anonymous correspondent had access to information concerning military operations that were being planned in America and in one instance he communicated facts that were not then known in London.

The correspondence smelled of treason and inspired a sweeping search for the guilty man.[41] He had asked that instructions be sent him under cover to "Pierre Fidel" [42] at the Post Office in New York. Acting on this, the British authorities sent a decoy package to that name and address, but it was not claimed. Thereupon first General Webb and

---

36 Cf. Pargellis, *Loudoun*, 168.
37 James Cunningham to G. W., Feb. 27, 1757; 2 *Hamilton*, 49.
38 Loudoun's *Memorandum*, loc. cit.   39 2 *G. W.*, 34.
40 *Report A.H.A.*, 1896, v. 1, p. 673, 676.
41 Henry Fox to Newcastle, Mch. 27, 1756; Br. Mus. 179 *Newcastle Papers*, f. 12.
42 In another letter he spelt it Fidell. See *Report A.H.A.*, 1896, v. 1, p. 669, 684.

then Lord Loudoun undertook to sift suspects. They found nobody who seemed to have the position the anonymous writer asserted to be his. At length, on Jan. 1, 1757, Samuel Vanhorne, a New York merchant, residing on Wall Street, came to Sir Charles Hardy, Governor of New York, and explained that business often took him to Philadelphia where friends frequently asked him to inquire if there were letters for them in the New York Post Office and, if so, to forward the communications. During a visit from which he had just returned, said Vanhorne, a man dressed like an officer had accosted him and had asked if there was in the New York office a letter for Pierre Fidel. Doubtless having been informed of the decoy, Vanhorne answered that such a letter was awaiting its addressee. The man in military dress replied that he wished he had it, as "the man for whom it was intended was on the frontier." [43]

Sir Charles immediately notified Lord Loudoun, who went that same evening with Colonel Stanwix to the Governor's quarters to interview Vanhorne. The merchant repeated his story. With some difficulty and much persuasion, Loudoun won Vanhorne's promise to go back to Philadelphia with Colonel Stanwix. The Colonel was ordered to arrest the suspect, if Vanhorne pointed him out, and to secure all his papers.[44] Vanhorne's description was fairly specific and might be useful: the man who inquired about the letter was tall, dark, with a red coat and a sword and appeared to be a stranger.[45]

Search by the Colonel and the merchant was to no purpose; the man had disappeared. Loudoun had then to attempt to identify "Pierre Fidel" on the basis of Vanhorne's description, added to what the traitor had said casually in his letter of himself and of his military position: What tall, dark officer was there in America, thirty-eight years of age, unmarried, who had an aide-de-camp and was going to participate in the expedition against Fort DuQuesne?

The only officer who was known to Lord Loudoun's informants as in any way answering to this description was Colonel Washington. He was single; he had an aide; he was to share in the next march to the Ohio. As it chanced, Lord Loudoun had close at hand Capt. David Kennedy, who had seen Washington in New York in March, 1756,

---

[43] So Dr. Douglas Brymner transcribed Loudoun's dispatch of Jan. 4, 1757, in *Report A.H.A.*, 1896, v. 1, p. 700; the execrably written entry in Loudoun's *Memorandum* may with like probability be read as "the man it is from is now on the Front'r."

[44] Loudoun's *Memorandum*, Jan. 1, 1757.

[45] Pargellis, *Loudoun*, 77n.

when the Colonel was returning from the visit to General Shirley in Boston. Loudoun consequently asked Kennedy for a description of the Virginian. Washington, said the Captain, was "a man about six feet high of a black complexion, [with] black hair which he then wore in a bag—looks like a foreigner, a strong man." Kennedy remembered Washington's companions, Mercer and Stewart, and recalled that Washington's uniform was "blue, faced with red and laced." [46]

Loudoun was not sufficiently impressed by this to order Washington's arrest, but he was eager, no doubt, to see the man who perhaps in some vengeful, incredible madness, had turned traitor. When the Colonel at length stood before the General, Loudoun must have observed at once how far Washington failed to fit Kennedy's description, with brown, not black hair, in his twenties and not thirty-eight, having none of the "foreigner" in his countenance—and pockmarked besides, which certainly would have been observed if Washington had been the officer Vanhorne had seen in Philadelphia. Washington was eliminated; "Pierre Fidel" continued to be a mystery. [47]

George may not have known then or thereafter of a suspicion he would have regarded as the worst of disgraces; but he heard of some of the decisions made by the council of Governors, who sat with Lord Loudoun through March 23. Loudoun told the council virtually nothing concerning his plan of operations in the North—he was "very reserved and secret" Dinwiddie said, in half praise and half grumble [48]— but he and the Governors agreed confidentially that no offensive could be undertaken in Pennsylvania or to the southward during 1757. A defensive must be maintained there, by an enlarged force, and particularly in South Carolina where a French attack from Santo Domingo or from the Alabama fort in the Creek country was apprehended. Contingents from North Carolina, Virginia and Pennsylvania must be sent to Charleston to strengthen the regulars and the South Carolina forces. [49] This plan had the endorsement of the Governors, and, in particular, of Dinwiddie, who regarded the defence of South Carolina as an idea almost his own [50]—in sharpest contrast to his feelings about that Colony when James Glen was Governor.

Washington knew nothing of the situation in South Carolina and

---

46 Loudoun's *Memorandum*, Feb. 27, 1757.

47 Loudoun made no mention in his *Memorandum* of exculpating Washington. References to him in connection with the traitorous correspondence merely cease.

48 2 *Din.*, 603.   49 Council Minutes, 2 *Hamilton*, 51 ff.

50 2 *Din.*, 602–03.

expressed no opinion of it. He was not admitted at the moment to the secret that no attempt was to be made in 1757 against Fort DuQuesne, which he still believed 3000 men, properly equipped and well-led, could capture without excessive hardship or losses.[51] From his point of view, the single gratifying decision of the Council of Governors was a minor one of which Dinwiddie took pains to inform him [52]—that Maryland was to assume responsibility for Fort Cumberland.[53] This meant relief for the Virginia Regiment, but nothing was said by Lord Loudoun to indicate that any other change was apt to come in the fortunes of the command. In the "address" Washington presented on behalf of the Virginia troops, and in the report he submitted Loudoun, he had refrained from making direct application to have the Regiment placed on the regular establishment; [54] but that of course remained the reward he and his brother officers most desired. Loudoun no doubt was gratified by the Regiment's assurance that "We are ready to testify with the greatest cheerfulness and resolution, whenever we are so happy as to be honored with the execution of your Lordship's command." [55] Doubtless, too, he thanked Washington. Beyond that, Loudoun did nothing. His thought was of Great Lakes, not of the Allegheny Mountains.[56]

[51] See *supra*, p. 233. Washington's lack of precise information is shown in his letter of April 5 to Governor Dinwiddie; 2 *G. W.*, 20.

[52] *Ibid.*

[53] Council Minutes, *op. cit.*, 53.

[54] 2 *G. W.*, 19–20. Washington had spoken only of a "better establishment." See *supra*, p. 234.

[55] 2 *G. W.*, 20.

[56] For the departure of the General from Philadelphia, see *Penn. Gazette*, Mch. 21, 1757. The Governors' return, via Annapolis, is described in Ridgely, *Annals of Annapolis*, 130.

CHAPTER XIV

CAPTAIN DAGWORTHY GETS LAUGHED AT
(APRIL–JULY, 1757)

WASHINGTON already regarded himself as a fatalist.[1] He always was disposed now to take a gloomy view of the future, in so far as his own military future was concerned; and when he reached Alexandria early in April, 1757,[2] he had added another to the long list of disappointments that had been his in pursuit of military fame. His initial command had been hampered by Mackay and then by defeat at Fort Necessity; Braddock had been good enough to promise advancement but Braddock had been killed; after George had been named Commander-in-Chief of Virginia troops under his second commission, first Dagworthy and then Sharpe had stood in his way; when Dagworthy had been eliminated and Sharpe had been won over to ask for him as second in command, Shirley had promised to give him that post—and then Shirley had been recalled; now Loudoun was favorable, but, as Washington quickly learned, there was to be no offensive against the Ohio in 1757. For months that were running to years, Washington had been seeking to get on the regular establishment and, once again, encountered silence that might signify "No." Ahead was the dull life of Winchester, the continued vagueness and contradiction of orders, and after that, what?

The first of many answers was not long delayed. At Alexandria, he found a letter in which Captain George Mercer, commanding at Winchester, said that ninety-five Catawba Indians had arrived in the Valley town. This presented possibilities of a sort that revived Washington. Perhaps these savages could be used in an expedition toward Fort DuQuesne. If that was not possible, they could be employed in

---

1 Cf. his letter of Sept. 12, 1758, to Sally Fairfax: ". . . evinces an opinion which I have long entertained, that there is a Destiny which has the control of our actions, not to be resisted by the strongest efforts of human nature" (2 *G. W.*, 288).
2 Ledger entries from March 17 to April 5 lack dates but they indicate Washington was in the town a few days before writing on the 5th to Governor Dinwiddie.

small scalping parties to harass the enemy. Besides, in the transfer of Fort Cumberland to the custody of Maryland, someone must see to it that all Virginia property, except provisions, was removed to Winchester. Further, George suspected that Dinwiddie might take from the feeble Regiment on the frontier the men for the Virginia contingent that was to strengthen South Carolina. This weakening of the Regiment must be resisted, at least until the General Assembly met and decided on the size of the armed force Virginia was to maintain. Still again, the evacuation of Fort Cumberland would release some troops for garrisoning the stockades between that post and Winchester. These men must be posted wisely. Finally, the Governor had directed George to come to Williamsburg during the session of the General Assembly beginning April 14, and to report on arrearages of pay.[3] If the most pressing of these immediate tasks were to be discharged, Washington must be off to the Valley. So, once more, he put aside his grievance in order to do his duty.

Busy days followed. The Governor was as anxious to get the contingent for South Carolina on its way to its new station as George was to hold it.[4] Transfer of Fort Cumberland involved delays as well as formalities.[5] Much had to be done in anticipation of the coming of a larger force of Cherokees and Catawbas,[6] in whose behalf a new "association" was being organized for a second attempt to reach and to destroy the Shawnee villages.[7] Meantime, the French Indians were appearing again almost under the stockade of Fort Cumberland and were waylaying small parties of men on the road.[8] Officers at that fort were renewing their appeal for the King's commissions. Everything was happening at once! George visited Wills Creek briefly, received the officers' remonstrance over their status, presided at a council that opposed the detachment of men for service in South Carolina— and then started at his usual speed for Williamsburg.[9] He was in Fredericksburg on the 24th,[10] and by the 27th was in the capital.[11]

[3] 2 *Din.*, 611; *Journ. H.B.*, 1752–58, p. 415.

[4] 2 *Din.*, 606; 2 *G. W.*, 20, 27; 2 *Hamilton*, 60, 64–65. Stephen's instructions bore date of May 26, 1757. See 2 *Din.*, 634–35. Dinwiddie wrote June 20, 1757 (2 *Din.*, 650) that Stephen "sailed from this the 20th ulto.", but a letter of May 23, 1757 (2 *Hamilton*, 76), stated that Stephen had not then reached Williamsburg. It is possible that "20th ulto." should read "30th."

[5] 1 *Sharpe*, 536, 542; 2 *ibid.*, 16–17; 2 *Din.*, 636–37, 638, 659; 2 *Hamilton*, 62; 2 *G. W.*, 24–25; *Lowdermilk*, 229; Washington to Doctor Ross, Sept. 6, 1757; *Papers of G. W.*, Toner Transcripts, LC.

[6] Cf. 2 *Hamilton*, 56.

[7] 2 *Din.*, 584, 589, 592.

[8] 2 *G. W.*, 24–25.

[9] 2 *G. W.*, 24–29.

[10] *Ledger A*, folio 34.

[11] *Ibid.*

As anticipated, he found the General Assembly in session and at work on a program of military legislation and of general lawmaking as well, in order to offset the neglect of needed civil enactments during the preceding brief sessions.[12] Indications were that the session would be long and that it probably would be Governor Dinwiddie's last. He had applied to the ministry in March for leave to go home in the hope of restoring his health. At that time he had spoken in a letter of resigning and, in a later paragraph, of procuring leave of absence;[13] but when he addressed the General Assembly on the 14th of April, he spoke as if his departure were final.[14]

For the Governor's decision on the policy involved, Washington wrote out promptly a statement of the condition of his command. He dwelt on its needs and deficiencies, putting first the acceptance by Virginia of the British military law, and at the end he came—as frequently he did—to personal considerations. The Assembly was about to make changes in the regulation of troops; Washington "must beg leave to know . . . upon what terms your Honor purposes to keep me, and what may be my certain dependence."

This question was addressed to the Governor, not to the committee of Council and Burgesses, because Washington understood that the committee was to abandon the audit of accounts and was to transfer to the Governor all financial arrangements provided for the Regiment by statute. Speaker Robinson had explained to Dinwiddie that Washington was receiving 30s per diem pay and 2 per cent commission on all funds he handled for the troops.[15] The Governor was reported to have regarded this as high compensation. George now earnestly asked the Governor not to lower either pay or commission: "For the committee first gave it and the Assembly afterwards allowed it as a recompense for my services and extraordinary trouble and confinement I should meet with in the prosecution of such complicated duties, as the nature of this service would oblige me to engage in. I also hope that your Honor will not, after the repeated assurances given of your good inclination to better my command, render it *worse* by taking away the only perquisite I have, and the only thing that enables me to support the expense which unavoidably attends my *Table* and removing about from place to place on our frontiers where every kind of neces-

12 *Journ. H.B.*, 1752–58, xxvii.
13 Dinwiddie to William Pitt, Mch. 22, 1757; 2 *Din.*, 599–600.
14 *Ibid.*, 612, 614.
15 See *supra*, p. 113.

saries is accompanied with incredible expense from the distresses which exist there." [16]

It was not altogether a vain plea. The General Assembly heard Washington's statement of the arrearages due the Regiment and, as always, gave him good will and admiration; but members did not change the plan to entrust financial administration to the Governor, nor did any of them prevail upon the Governor, if even they tried, to continue the commission of 2 per cent. Dinwiddie consequently kept George's salary at 30s, agreed to provide for the men who attended his horses, and allowed him a flat £200 per annum for his table and expenses.[17] Later there was to be a dispute between the Governor and the Colonel over the batmen;[18] but the major terms were accepted by Washington. At the time he said nothing more about resigning.

The remonstrance of the officers was unavailing. This document, which Washington doubtless brought with him to Williamsburg, was a new and more tactful version of the paper on which he had worked in Philadelphia while waiting for Lord Loudoun. The blunt assertion "we are defending the King's dominions" became "we are defending part of the domain of Great Britain." Nothing was left of the allegation that the service of the Virginia Regiment had "not been properly represented to His Majesty." There remained: "We cannot conceive that because we are Americans we should therefor be deprived of the benefits common to British subjects, nor that it should lessen our claim to preferment." There was complaint, even, of the treatment of the militia compared with that accorded the Regiment; but the main grievance itself implied a tribute to the Colonel in this particular: It showed that two years and more of discipline had given the regimental officers a sense of unity, of confidence and of pride in their own organization: ". . . we want nothing but commissions from His Majesty to make us as regular a corps as any upon the continent. Because we were regularly enlisted, attested and bound, during the King's or Colony's pleasure.[19] We have been regularly regimented and trained; and have done as regular duty for upwards of three years as any Regi-

---

[16] 2 G. W., 34-35.

[17] 2 Hamilton, 73. His previous allowance for his table, it will be remembered, was £100. See supra, p. 113.

[18] See ibid., 84; 2 G. W., 49, 61. It is interesting, perhaps, to note that in an entry of Mch. 31, 1755, wrongly entered as 1756, Daniel Disney, in "writing up" Halkett's Orderly Book spelt batmen baughmen.

[19] This sentence is printed as in the original but it may have been meant as a part either of the one that precedes it or of the one that follows.

ment in His Majesty's service . . . And, in a word, we labor under
every disadvantage, without receiving a single benefit which the regulars do." [20]

All this was admitted as readily in Williamsburg as it was asserted
at Fort Cumberland, but relief and recognition must come from the
Crown, not from Burgesses who were conscious of the Colony's financial distress. They were well-inclined, if powerless, and as always, they
were sociable. George accepted entertainment and gave it. Perhaps he
extended it the more gladly because Sally Fairfax was in town with her
husband and her father-in-law.[21] Colonel Fairfax was wretched for
part of the session because of the disappearance of an unstable son,
Bryan Fairfax, but after the young man was found in Annapolis, he
was relieved and was able to resume his place in the Council and at the
board of the tavern. Washington himself was not always there.[22]

Conferences came at last to an end. Washington completed all his
business by the 17th of May but left the General Assembly still in
dispute [23] over the size of the forces to be employed for the operations
to be undertaken that year and in 1758.[24] Return was by Fredericksburg, with a visit to his mother, who borrowed £5.[25] From Ferry Farm
he went to Alexandria and then along the oft-traveled road to Winchester, which he reached on the 24th of May.[26]

In the Valley town and nearby, Washington found a larger number
of Indians than ever he had seen together previously. On the day of
Braddock's defeat, more of them—mad, screaming enemies—had surrounded him, but he had not caught even a glimpse of many of them.
Now he could not escape the presence or the importunity of Cherokees,
Catawbas,[27] Nottaways and Tuscaroras.[28] Negotiation, treaties, presents
and promises had brought Washington and his officers more savages
than they could hope to employ advantageously while Virginia remained on the defensive. Some of the Cherokees had been westward
on a raid while Washington was East of the Blue Ridge and they now

---

[20] 2 *G. W.*, 26–27.   [21] Cf. 2 *Hamilton*, 70.
[22] See Appendix II–1.   [23] 2 *Din.*, 628, 631, 632.
[24] His instructions, sketched on p. 248, are dated May 16, but some of the entries in *Ledger A*,
folio 35, suggest that Washington did not leave the capital until the 17th.
[25] *Ledger A*, folio 35.
[26] There apparently is an error of one day or perhaps of two in an entry of expenses, May 25,
at West's Ordinary. The correct date probably was May 23.
[27] Most of these Catawbas had started home (2 *G. W.*, 38).
[28] These four tribes were listed in Washington to Dinwiddie, May 29, 1757 (2 *G. W.*, 39).
Dinwiddie wrote, May 2, that "nearly 400 Indians" had gone to Fort Loudoun, but Atkin, June
8, listed only 329 Catawbas, Cherokees and Tuscaroras (3 *Penn. Arch.*, 175–76).

had returned with four scalps, two prisoners and an eager-handed demand for presents that had not arrived in Winchester. "They are," said Washington in disgust, "the most insolent, most avaricious and most dissatisfied wretches I have ever had to deal with." [29]

The nuisance was immediate; the benefit *in futuro;* the danger that the Indians would march off in dudgeon could not be blinked. Responsibility of conciliating them was not long to be Washington's. He had learned that he was to be relieved of it, because the home government had named Edmund Atkin Superintendent of Indian Affairs in the Southern Colonies. This appointment had been made in recognition of a long report on the Southern natives, written by Atkin, who was a native of Exeter and later a merchant in Charleston and a member of the Council of South Carolina. He attached great importance to the Office of Indian Affairs, which he had sought in his paper to have Britain create, and he had proposed that, in addition to large emoluments, the agent have at his disposal a Regiment of regulars and a Company of rangers. After he had received the appointment, without the troops, he had returned to America and had undertaken to get from Lord Loudoun an expense fund of £2000.[30] Loudoun had agreed to a salary of £600 a year and—more to get rid of Atkin than to use him—had sent him to the Southern Colonies to make such financial arrangements as the Governors would accept.[31]

Atkin did nothing in haste and preferably did nothing at all. He had come to Williamsburg on April 9, 1757,[32] but he resisted all prodding to go to Winchester. It was too expensive a journey, he said.[33] Finally, when Dinwiddie promised to pay him £100 to £150 for expenses on the frontier, Atkin started slowly and with much groaning of spirit for the Valley.[34] Some of the peculiarities of the fifty-year-old Scot had been ascertained by Washington; but if the management of the Indians was the affair of Atkin, as Dinwiddie had told him it was,[35] then George wanted to be relieved of the Indians and wished the new official to be present to look after them. Meantime, the natives daily demanded more and more, and professed to believe that talk of Atkin's coming was de-

---

[29] Letter of May 24, 1757; 2 *G. W.,* 36. A larger party of Cherokees still was "out" (*ibid.,* 38).

[30] Atkin is mentioned frequently in the "Memorandum" entries Loudoun made at Philadelphia during March, 1757.

[31] See J. R. Alden, *John Stuart and the Southern Colonial Frontier,* 60, 70, 71; Pargellis, *Loudoun,* 258–59.

[32] 2 *Din.,* 628.

[33] *Ibid.,* 617, 618, 628.

[34] Alden, *op. cit.,* 71.

[35] 2 *Din.,* 623.

signed to deceive them.[36] To placate them, Washington had to send an express with a request that the Governor speed the agent.[37]

It was not until late on the 2nd of June [38] that Atkin arrived and, after some diplomatic delays and pretended indifference, began a council with the savages. This was long and complicated [39] and resulted, among other things, in a decision to send part of the Cherokees under escort to the North Carolina border on their way homeward, in order to prevent any more such crimes as had been committed by certain warriors of the same tribe on their march North.[40] Atkin professed to act in superior knowledge of the Indians, but he did not impress Washington.[41] It would be far better, the Colonel thought, if Virginia had a single agent of her own—Christopher Gist, for example—who would transact all business with the Indians, under the supervision of Dinwiddie or of Atkin.[42] "Nothing ought ever to be promised [the Indians]," Washington argued, "but what is performed; and only one person be empowered to do either." [43]

Competent or complacent, sagacious or stupid, Atkin had the responsibility. George was relieved of it. The Colonel likewise had been told that the Governor would handle financial matters that previously had been his care. Moreover, prior to his departure from Williamsburg on the 16th of May, George had been given explicit orders: In the interest of economy, the Regiment was to consist of ten Companies of 100 men; seven specified Captains were to be retained; the others, if they chose to remain in the service, were to be reduced to Lieutenants; troops were to be stationed in prescribed number at seven designated forts; Washington himself must maintain his headquarters at Winchester and must see that work on the fort was pushed; he should continue the assistant commissaries in service till the pleasure of the General Assembly was known.[44] That was the scope of his revised and restricted duties. Washington did not know whether the changes in his orders had been made to simplify his task or to reduce his authority. He was convinced only that Dinwiddie would find pleasure in hearing—to quote his own words—"that I was involved in trouble, however undeservedly; such are his dispositions toward me." [45] Before

36 Cf. 2 *G. W.*, 39.
37 2 *G. W.*, 40.
38 Or perhaps the morning of the 3rd. Cf. 2 *G. W.*, 44. He left Williamsburg about May 23. See 2 *Hamilton*, 75.
39 3 *Penn. Arch.*, 175 ff.
40 *Ibid.*, 176; 2 *G. W.*, 48.
41 2 *G. W.*, 52.
42 2 *G. W.*, 41, 43, 44.
43 *Ibid.*, 41.
44 2 *Din.*, 622–23.
45 2 *G. W.*, 53.

going to Williamsburg, the Colonel had spoken of himself as having "become in a manner an exile." [46] If quiet prevailed, he now might be condemned to a dozing life away from home, though he yearned for action and believed there never had been and never would be such another opportunity as was offered of capturing Fort DuQuesne. [47]

No leg of the course was run as the needle pointed. Circumstance for some weeks saved Washington from the tedium of administrative routine. He had, first of all, to deal with the desertion of eleven men at Fort Maidstone. [48] Next was the diplomacy of placating the Captains who were regarded as supernumerary and were to be released unless they accepted recommission as Lieutenant. At the moment, it looked as if Christopher Gist was the only Captain willing to remain in service at lower rank. [49]

Another delicate negotiation was that of determining the military relationship Washington was to bear to Col. John Stanwix of the Sixtieth Infantry, whom Loudoun had named to command five Companies of regulars assigned to support provincials in the defence of the western frontiers of Virginia, Maryland and Pennsylvania. [50] First orders to Washington from Stanwix were for the delivery of ammunition from the royal stores at Winchester. [51] Compliance of course was proper and was prompt; [52] but Washington took pains to inquire of the Governor, "If I should meet with anything from [Stanwix] at any time that may clash with your instructions to me, how I am to conduct myself in the affair." [53] The reply was to be, "You are to follow such orders [as] Colonel Stanwix may send you from time to time, without any regard to any orders you may have received from me." [54]

This answer from the Governor referred specifically to a situation that developed in mid-June. When Washington had returned to Winchester from Williamsburg he had found that several raids to the westward had been undertaken by the Virginians and their new Indian allies. One such thrust had been made by the natives who had brought in four scalps and two prisoners. [55] Major Andrew Lewis later had led toward the Ohio a scalping party of considerable size, but as he had not been

[46] *Ibid.*, 22.
[47] 2 *G. W.*, 38–39.
[48] See 2 *G. W.*, 50, 92.
[49] *Ibid.*, 55.
[50] Pargellis, *Loudoun*, 344.
[51] 2 *Hamilton*, 74–75.
[52] 2 *G. W.*, 37; Edward Shippen to James Burd, June 16, 1757; *Shippen Papers*, 84; receipt of John Spour, May 28, 1757; *Washington Papers*, Penn. His. Soc.
[53] 2 *G. W.*, 50–51.
[54] Dinwiddie to Washington, June 20, 1757; 2 *Din.*, 643.
[55] See *supra*, p. 247 and 2 *G. W.*, 36.

able to prevail on the savages to take more than eight days' provisions with them, he soon was back, with no scalps on any warrior's belt. Two parties remained out, one of twenty Indians and ten soldiers with whom Capt. Robert Spotswood had started in the direction of Fort DuQuesne, and another under Lieut. James Baker, who had taken fifteen Indians and five white men toward Logstown. With Baker had gone a renowned Indian fighter, known as Swallow Warrior.[56]

An express from Fort Cumberland brought news, June 12, 1757, that Baker had returned on the 9th with five French scalps and one French prisoner. Washington was provoked that Baker apparently had failed to report directly to him and at once,[57] but after he found that Baker duly had forwarded a dispatch, which in some manner was delayed, his satisfaction was unqualified.

It developed that on the 5th of June, near the head of Turtle Creek, about twenty miles from Fort DuQuesne, Baker and his men had come upon ten French soldiers, including three Ensigns, who had separated the previous day from a company of raiding Shawnees. The English and their Indians were naked when they flushed the enemy, and consequently could not be identified immediately. While the French hesitated for a few seconds, the Virginians and the Indians fired. Swallow Warrior, seeing his target fall, sprang forward to scalp the man and, at that instant, received a bullet through the head. The other French broke and ran, but some of them found their pursuers fleet and cunning. Two of the fugitives surrendered. The Indians brought them triumphantly back to Baker—only to turn on them furiously when they found that Swallow Warrior was dead. One prisoner they killed in spite of Baker; the other he was able to save. Two wounded Frenchmen were scalped and slain; two adversaries already were dead.

Besides Swallow Warrior, there had been another casualty on the English side in the person of his son, who was shot through both thighs. The young Indian had to be removed, of course, because the escaping Frenchmen would sound an alarm that might bring an avenging force to the scene of the skirmish. Mercifully, one of Baker's men took the wounded warrior on a stout pair of shoulders and bore him until exhausted. Then another and another carried the youth. This continued for the four days of the return journey, during which none of the party had any food except wild onions.[58]

[56] 2 G. W., 51.
[57] 2 G. W., 59.
[58] 2 Hamilton, 89–90; 2 G. W., 57, 60; 1 Ford, 448n.

The return of Baker left only Robert Spotswood and his party afield. Washington was beginning to feel concern for them [59] when, during the night of the 15th–16th of June, an express rode into town with this dispatch:

Fort Cumberland June 14, 1757

Sir,

Six Cherokee Indians who just now came from Fort DuQuesne, say that six days ago they saw a large body of troops march from that garrison with a number of wagons and a train of artillery, and by their route, must intend an attack on this garrison.

I am, sir, your most humble servant,

Jno. Dagworthy.[60]

Accompanying this was a letter from James Livingston, Major of the Maryland forces at Fort Cumberland, who explained that the six returning Indians had belonged to Spotswood's party and had been for some days close to Fort DuQuesne. They said they had heard a great gun fired near the battlefield of Monongahela. The French, according to the Cherokees, had "numbers of wheeled carriages and men innumerable and had marched two days before they quit the Monongahela waters." Major Livingston took pains to point out that this intelligence came from Indians and that not one white man had brought like information, but he expressed belief that the story was true.[61]

Washington, too, credited the news [62] which seemed to point to a larger expedition than the French ever had sent eastward from Fort DuQuesne. If the information was correct, it probably recorded the doom of Captain Spotswood and his men [63] and it called for immediate consideration by a council of all the commissioned officers then in Winchester—four Captains, two Lieutenants and three Ensigns. At 2 A.M. on the 16th, Washington opened the discussion with two questions: Should the Virginia Regiment proceed at once to the relief of Fort Cumberland, or should the effort be made to assemble a sufficient force to make Fort Loudoun defensible, and to await further orders? Second,

---

[59] 2 G. W., 61.

[60] 2 Hamilton, 91. A similar dispatch to Governor Sharpe is printed in 31 Md. Arch., 227. Dagworthy did not sign with his rank. As he had a Major under him, it would be assumed that he was a Lieutenant Colonel in 1757. He held that rank in 1758, but nowhere, in records prior to that year, is he mentioned otherwise than as Captain Dagworthy. Perhaps he still had faith in the magic of rank under the King's commission.

[61] Ibid., 91–92.   [62] 2 G. W., 67; 37 ibid., 478.

[63] 2 G. W., 68.

should the scattered garrisons be concentrated in one fort on the South Branch, or should all of them be brought to Winchester? [64] The decision, which was made promptly, was shaped in part by the form of the questions: Unanimously the council voted to recall the garrisons to Winchester and to hold them there, working on the fort, till more was known about the French advance.[65]

The orders issued by Washington during the next few hours showed that he was acquiring experience: Maj. Andrew Lewis was directed to undertake a scout at once. If he found the French numerous, he was to march the smaller garrisons to Winchester.[66] Copies of the messages from Fort Cumberland were forwarded, of course, by express to Governor Dinwiddie, to Governor Sharpe and to Colonel Stanwix.[67] Other expresses carried to the County Lieutenants of Fairfax, Prince William and Culpeper a plea that they assemble their militia and move the whole or a part to Winchester without waiting for formal orders from the Governor.[68] Washington expected no material reenforcement from this appeal,[69] but he thought he should make it. Next, he directed that construction of the fort, which had been progressing with slowness,[70] should be pressed by night as well as by day.[71]

When these things had been arranged, Washington sent Dagworthy an account of the steps that had been taken. "So," Washington went on, ". . . I have no doubt that a very considerable force will be with you in a very short time." Then he added: "I have dispatched the bearer to inform you of this, that it may inspirit your garrison. I heartily wish you all the success your *merit* may deserve"—a final remark that Dagworthy may have thought susceptible of two interpretations.[72]

For three days thereafter, June 17, 18, 19, if George had further word from Fort Cumberland, it merely repeated rumor and echoed suspense.[73] On the 20th, still uncertain, Washington examined with Atkin the French Ensign who had been captured by Baker's contingent and subsequently had been brought to Winchester along with the Indian scouts of Spotswood's party. The young Frenchman was

---

[64] Minutes of the council, 2 *Hamilton*, 94–95.
[65] *Ibid.*
[66] 2 *G. W.*, 65–66.
[67] 2 *G. W.*, 66; 37 *ibid.*, 478.
[68] 2 *G. W.*, 66–67.
[69] 2 *G. W.*, 69.
[70] 2 *G. W.*, 42.
[71] 2 *G. W.*, 66.
[72] *Ibid.*
[73] The reason for qualifying this sentence is that the undated fragment of a letter from Major Livingston in 2 *Hamilton*, 93, suggests that Washington may have received a second express during these three days.

clever in diluting deceit with a drop or two of fact and consequently he did more to confuse than to inform his inquisitors. The Indians' testimony left Washington of opinion that the French were advancing in strength, with howitzers, on the road to Fort Cumberland; but he awaited reports from Lewis, who presumably was now fifty miles in advance.[74]

That same day, June 20, Washington received from one of the Maryland officers an appeal for the services of Indian warriors, who doubtless were to be sent out to scout the trails the French would follow. Washington urged the few savages he could find in Winchester to go to the Potomac, but he might as well have asked the river to reverse its course. Each Indian seemed to regard Washington's request as an attempt to sacrifice him. "They positively refused marching," George had to reply, "until they saw such numbers as would give some probability of success against the formidable force of the enemy."[75] Washington added on his own account, "I have endeavored all in my power to raise the militia, but have only a small prospect for success."[76] It was a strange experience for him to stand in reversed military position, and to be the man to say "No" to entreaties of the same frantic note he had himself so often shaped. For once, moreover, he was mistaken about the response of the militia. Two Companies from Fairfax arrived on the 21st, the sixth day after he had dispatched his call to the County Lieutenant.[77] Never had the militia done so well.

The day prior to their arrival,[78] Washington received a somewhat embarrassed letter from Dagworthy. Six other Indians, said the Maryland commander, had arrived from the vicinity of Fort DuQuesne and had asserted that previous reports of a French advance with artillery and wagons were untrue. A large scouting party had left the Ohio and was moving in the direction of Fort Cumberland, but, the veterans admitted, the tale about vehicles and heavy guns was the imagining of badly scared young warriors who had hurried eastward after a glimpse of the enemy.[79]

These more experienced natives of the second party Dagworthy sent to Winchester, along with his explanation, in order that the Virginians might question them. Washington did so and concluded that they had not actually been close to Fort DuQuesne, but that they had

[74] 2 G. W., 68.
[75] 2 G. W., 69.
[76] Ibid.
[77] 2 G. W., 70.
[78] It was written on the 17th and consequently was at least three days on the road.
[79] 2 Hamilton, 97.

CHAPTER XV

REBUILDING THE REGIMENT

(SUMMER OF 1757)

THE LAST ECHO of Captain Dagworthy's false alarm was not pleasant to the ears of Virginians. If the men at Winchester and on the South Branch could mock the Marylanders for creating foes through tales told by friends, Dagworthy's men soon could say that Washington's advisers would make enemies by misusing friends. In blundering confidence that he knew how to punish as well as to reward the savages, Edmund Atkin locked up ten of them for some infraction and thereby created a turmoil so serious that Washington had to act quickly to placate the offended natives before they set out in wrath for their own country.[1]

Fortunately, Washington was able to smooth out the sensibilities of the Indians, but he was finding now that one trouble was merely a link with another. While doing what he could to counteract the mistakes of Atkin, the Colonel had the doleful duty of relieving of command one of his earliest officers. Capt. Peter Hog had failed to maintain discipline and to build economically in reasonable time a properly situated fort at Vause's.[2] There was no alternative to getting rid of him. After Hog was sent home, the supervision of the southern end of the western defences was placed in the competent hands of Andrew Lewis.

Some shifts were made, also, in the disposition of the detached Companies, but the greatest change was[3] the absence of Adam Stephen in South Carolina. Frontier garrison duty had not carried Stephen, as it had Peter Hog, in a gradual descent to incompetence; but where Stephen was, trouble was. His acceptance of Dagworthy's seniority never had been explained, though Stephen's letters often contained sharp criticisms of the Marylander. It was against Stephen, however

---

[1] 2 *Hamilton,* 147, 153, 156, 165, 167, 169; 2 *G. W.,* 98.
[2] 2 *G. W.,* 101–04. Cf. *ibid.,* 152.   [3] 2 *G. W.,* 104–06.

unjustly, that some of the charges of drunkenness and immorality at Fort Cumberland had been directed.[4] He had been loyal to Washington but he had been too prone to repeat gossip and to share in factional quarrels. Besides, Washington was compelled to report to Dinwiddie that Stephen had failed to take with him to South Carolina certain officers whom the Governor had designated for that service. ". . . This," Washington added, "is not the only instance in which he has used such liberties [in dispensing with orders]."[5] Later, Dinwiddie was disposed to think Stephen's negligence had been responsible for the loss of twelve deserters en route to Williamsburg.[6] The Governor suspected, further, that Stephen had placed on the transports more women than the six per 100 men allowed in the regular army.[7] Finally, Washington found, after resuming command of all his troops, that Stephen so often had given orders contrary to those he had received that, said Washington, "it will be with great difficulty, if it is even possible, to extricate the officers and myself from the dilemma and trouble they have occasioned."[8]

These occurrences were incidental to the main task, which was that of rebuilding the Virginia Regiment in conformity to the new legislation of the General Assembly. The lawmakers had adjourned on June 8,[9] after a session of almost nine weeks, and had passed no less than six acts that concerned Washington and his men. Long debate had been indulged and much difference of opinion had been aroused before the decision had been reached to send two Companies of the Virginia Regiment to South Carolina in accordance with the plan endorsed at the Philadelphia conference of the Governors.[10] The bill that finally met with the Burgesses' approval authorized a total force of 1272, including non-commissioned officers,[11] organized into twelve Companies. Two of those to be recruited, in addition to two already in existence, could be dispatched to South Carolina if the commanding officer of His Majesty's forces in North America thought necessary. One Company was to garrison the fort in the Cherokee country; the remaining seven were to be employed for the general defence of the Colony. Further-

[4] See *supra*, p. 174–75, 195.   [5] Letter of May 24, 1757; 2 *G. W.*, 37.
[6] 2 *Din.*, 635–36.
[7] 2 *Din.*, 636, 674. Washington took pains to specify in his instructions of July 29 to the Captains in command of the small fort that "no more women draw rations than in the proportion as six to 100 men" (2 *G. W.*, 111). These females, it will be remembered, were washerwomen.
[8] Washington to Robert McKenzie, July 29, 1757; 2 *G. W.*, 108–09.
[9] *Journ. H. B.*, 1752–58, p. 492.   [10] See *supra*, p. 240.
[11] Strangely, the statute, 7 *H* 70, gave the number as 1270 and, p. 74, correctly as 1272.

more, three Companies of rangers, each of 100 men, were to be enlisted for the protection of the southwestern Counties, with the proviso that these men were not to be sent out of the Colony or incorporated with the Regiment.[12]

To raise this force, all vagrants were first to be drafted. Then the same thing was to be done with one in forty of the able-bodied militia-men "not being free-holders or house-keepers qualified to vote at an election of Burgesses." [13] A County with 400 such militiamen would supply ten; a County with 200 would provide five, and so on. If this double draft did not suffice, a bounty of £5 per man was to be offered volunteers.[14] To cover the pay and expenses of this force, outstanding treasury notes were to be called in and fresh notes issued, to a total not exceeding £80,000.[15] By a separate measure, the mutiny act, which carried the death penalty for desertion, was renewed for one year in substantially the form of the expired law.[16] The militia act was extended for three years,[17] and the invasion statute, which covered the power of impressment, was made effective for two years more.[18]

These enactments gave Washington the firmest military code he ever had been able to employ, and apparently they offered the best prospect of filling the Regiment which had shrunk by June 16 to 384 rank and file.[19] Most of the recruits might be vagrants, but under the law they could be whipped for disobedience and threatened with death if they deserted. By these means, and by reasonable rewards, they could be made good soldiers.

Such was the prevailing, undisputed doctrine of discipline. It did not vindicate its champions in the summer of 1757, nor did the new draft law serve its purpose fully. The first of these unwilling recruits had been delivered before the end of June,[20] but they had been numeri-cally below the assigned county quotas and physically some of them had been unfit for duty.[21] Washington became concerned. Anxious to complete the Regiment and to avoid any future dependence on the militia,[22] he knew that desertions would occur en route to Winchester

12 7 H 75, 76.

13 7 H 70–71.

14 7 H 74.

15 7 H 81.

16 7 H 87–92.

17 7 H 93–106.

18 7 H 106–16. Further measures dealt with Indian trade and with rewards for scalps (7 H 116 ff).

19 Exclusive of the two Companies sent to South Carolina (2 G. W., 65).

20 Cf. 2 G. W., 83.   21 Ibid.

22 Cf. Washington to Henry Fitzhugh, July 2, 1757; 305 Papers of G. W., 228, LC.

and he urged the County Lieutenants to make allowance for this in fixing the total number of men they drafted.[23]

The returns were shocking. Ninety men were sent in one body from Fredericksburg; twenty deserted on the road.[24] By July 9, a total of 210 had reported but more than a fourth of these had disappeared.[25] Then, after the assembled recruits had been paid and clothed, twenty-four slipped away in a single night.[26] Washington had regretfully to inform Colonel Stanwix that of 400 received at Fredericksburg and Winchester, 114 had deserted.[27] All of the thirty who had quit Winchester had been recaptured, but it had been necessary to use weapons. One of the deserters was killed; one pursuing soldier was wounded.

Washington had felt for months that he could not stop desertion until, once again, he executed some notorious offenders.[28] Now, entirely convinced and ready, he wrote Stanwix: "I have a gallows near forty foot high erected (which has terrified the *rest* exceedingly) and I am determined if I can be justified in the proceeding, to hang two or three on it, as an example to others."[29]

He did. Among the men in arrest was Ignatius Edwards, thrice a deserter, and William Smith, who, said Washington, "was accounted one of the greatest villains upon the continent." Both had been tried by court-martial and condemned to death by shooting. Washington thought hemp carried a sterner warning than lead and, accordingly, on the 28th of July, just as the newly recruited companies were leaving Winchester for their posts, he staged a spectacle the drafted men were not apt to forget: Edwards and Smith were carried to the platform of the tall gallows and were hanged before the eyes of all beholders. Washington reported this to Dinwiddie and added: "Your Honor will, I hope, excuse my hanging instead of shooting them. It conveyed much more terror to others; and it was for example sake we did it."[30]

The immediate warning was not in vain, but the quotas still did not suffice to fill the Regiment. Eight Companies could not count more than 90 rank and file each. Dinwiddie was so discouraged that he

23 Cf. Washington to Charles Carter, July 2, 1757; 305 *Papers of G. W.*, 225, LC.
24 2 *G. W.*, 92.
25 2 *G. W.*, 85.   26 2 *G. W.*, 92.
27 These totals were from the returns of July 15, 1757.
28 Cf. 2 *G. W.*, 89, 93.   29 Letter of July 15, 1757; 2 *G. W.*, 97.
30 Letter of Aug. 3, 1757; 2 *G. W.*, 118. In the letter that announced the hangings, Washington enclosed the court-martial proceedings against Edwards, Smith and other men. As the law still required (7 *H* 90) that execution of sentences be suspended until the Governor had reviewed the case, it would appear that the Governor had accepted Richard Corbin's suggestion, see *supra*, p. 139, and had sent Washington death-warrants in blank for execution by shooting.

doubted whether it even was worth while to undertake to recruit the men needed to reach the authorized total.[31] Washington himself believed that recruiting would take much time to little purpose unless he had authority to enlist servants.[32] He had soon to conclude, also, in spite of all British theories of discipline, that punishment was of "little weight" in reducing desertion.[33]

A regimental roster continuously below authorized strength represented the principal failure of an exasperating year on the defensive. Washington did not blame himself for this weakness, nor did his superiors charge him with it. Governor, Council and Commander-in-Chief alike attributed the thin ranks of the Regiment to the pusillanimity of the people. The only different opinion was expressed by Crown officials and soldiers of the regular establishment who censured the House of Burgesses for the restrictions it had placed on the use of the militia and for the term and conditions of enlistment it had imposed for the Regiment.

Washington had distress, also, though no sense of blame, over the apparent loss of Captain Robert Spotswood and some of the soldiers who had gone with him on the scout toward Logstown. Survivors who made their way back to the English settlements told of Indian pursuit of the party and of orders from the Captain for the men to separate. After that came the silence of the concealing woods.[34] Another distress was over the continuing slow progress of work on Fort Loudoun,[35] and still another—more an annoyance than a distress—was the dispute with Dinwiddie concerning the allowance for batmen.[36]

Overtopping all the unhappiness of the service was the feeling of Washington that he had been treated unfairly by the Governor, that he and his officers had been maligned, and that they had been denied the right they believed they had earned of inclusion in the regular establishment. Again and again, it seemed to Washington, critics sought to drag him down and to deprive him of the honor in which he was held by the people of the Colony. A new instance of this occurred during August. Ignatius Edwards, one of the men hanged for desertion, was reported to have said that William Brent had visited the prison and had promised him £100 with which to buy his discharge from Colonel

[31] 2 *G. W.*, 117; 2 *Hamilton*, 171. There apparently was no foundation for the report Sharpe mentioned on the 14th of August that Washington had lost 100 men by desertion in a week and had recovered none of them (2 *Sharpe*, 74).

[32] 2 *G. W.*, 121.   [33] 2 *G. W.*, 122.

[34] 2 *G. W.*, 86, 93, 134; 2 *Hamilton*, 127.

[35] 2 *G. W.*, 78, 79; 2 *Din.*, 644.   [36] 2 *G. W.*, 89.

Washington. This was thought a charge of sufficient gravity to justify a call on Brent for affirmation or denial. He promptly made oath to the falsity of the allegation and he swore, further, that he never suggested to Edwards anything which, if carried out, would "reflect dishonor on the conduct and character" of Washington.[37]

Matters far less serious were taken almost as seriously by Washington. In a letter of August 13, the sick and rapidly ageing Governor [38] rebuked him mildly for not being specific in reporting: "You must allow this is a loose way of writing, and it's your duty to be more particular to me." [39] George, sensitive as always, took this to be condemnation against which he could not fail to defend himself, and he answered formally: "I must beg leave . . . to observe in justification of my own conduct, that it is with pleasure I receive reproof, when reproof is due, because no person can be readier to accuse me than I am to acknowledge an error, when I am guilty of one; nor more desirous for atoning for a crime, when I am sensible of having committed it. But, on the other hand, it is with concern I remark, that my best endeavors lose their reward, and that my conduct, although I have uniformly studied to make it as unexceptionable as I could, does not appear to you in a favorable light." With this introduction he proceeded to elucidate the matters about which Dinwiddie had complained and then, after some 300 earnest words, he concluded: "However, if I have erred in these points, I am sorry for it, and shall endeavor for the future to be as particular and satisfactory, in my account of these things, as possible." [40]

Had Washington been of vengeful nature, he would have found satisfaction, not to say compensation for past slights, in the fact that Dinwiddie himself now was in difficulties. While His Honor had been in Philadelphia early in March, Lord Loudoun by circular letter had directed all the Governors to impose an embargo on outgoing vessels in order, first, that bottoms might be available for the transport of soldiers, and, second, that information of proposed military movements might be kept from the enemy.[41]

Dinwiddie had complied at once,[42] but after his return to Virginia, the House of Burgesses presented him an address in which it asked him

37 Affidavit of William Brent, subscribed and sworn to, before John Carlyle, Aug. 16, 1757; 6 *Papers of G. W.*, LC.
38 Dinwiddie had, in addition, an attack of malaria in the summer of 1757 (2 *Din.*, 691).
39 2 *Din.*, 684.
40 2 *G. W.*, 122–24.
41 Pargellis, *Loudoun*, 265.
42 2 *Din.*, 597.

to lift the embargo. The legislators asserted that 50,000 bushels of wheat already were aboard ship, destined for regions that were short of bread. This grain would be lost if the embargo were continued.[43] Most of the tobacco likewise had to be sent to England for goods and credit. If this leaf were held in Virginia, without a market, the people could not pay their taxes.[44] Dinwiddie took this as a warning that the Burgesses would not vote money for the war unless he ended the embargo. He consequently asked the Council for its advice and, on its unanimous statement that the raising of the embargo was necessary, Dinwiddie on the 8th of May authorized waiting vessels to put to sea.[45]

Loudoun was furious when he heard that the first rupture of his embargo was in the Colony of which he was titular Governor. Knowing that Dinwiddie wished to resign, Loudoun wanted to have him recalled, instead, as punishment. The old Scot, greatly disturbed, made the best defence he could; [46] but, for a time, he had the frown of his principal. Not until September, 1757, was Loudoun to relieve Dinwiddie's mind with the generous assurance that "it is now all over, and I have forgot it." [47] To a man less deliberately just than Washington undertook to be, the manifest discomfiture of the Governor would have been amusing, perhaps pleasant. As it was, Washington's letters contained not one line of satisfaction or, indeed, of comment.

Such were the events that relieved or rendered more tiresome the routine of the early summer of 1757; such the balance of satisfaction and of disappointment of compensation and of distress—the Regiment still below strength but gradually becoming efficient in spite of desertion, Spotswood dead, Stephen agreeably dispatched to South Carolina, Fort Loudoun taking shape slowly, Dagworthy somewhat discredited, Dinwiddie still quick to argue about batmen or anything else that involved economy, but sick, anxious, and soon to pass off the stage.

Washington himself was depressed and perhaps was bored, but he was not disheartened. Pride, anticipation and experience all were echoed in the closing words of the letter of instruction he wrote the Captains who were about to take their Companies to the more remote forts. ". . . devote some part of your leisure hours to the study of your profession, a knowledge in which cannot be attained without applica-

[43] 2 *Din.*, 665.   [44] *Journ. H. B.*, 1752–58, p. 448.
[45] 2 *Din.*, 618, 664–65; 2 *Sharpe*, 10.   [46] 2 *Din.*, 621, 664–65.
[47] Koontz, *Dinwiddie*, 385. The course of the controversy is followed briefly in *ibid.*, and is summarized in Pargellis, *Loudoun*, 265–67.

tion; nor any merit or applause to be achieved without a certain knowledge thereof. Discipline is the soul of an army. It makes small numbers formidable; procures success to the weak, and esteem to all; and may, in a peculiar manner to us, who are in the way to be joined to regulars in a very short time, and of distinguishing through this means from other Provincials." [48]

That last was an awkward, unimpressive sentence, but the spirit and the ideals of the writer shone in the seven words that preceded it: "Discipline is the soul of an army."

[48] Letter of July 29, 1757; 2 *G. W.,* 114.

CHAPTER XVI

A SEASON OF SLANDER, ILLNESS AND CHANGE

(AUG. 1–NOV. 9, 1757)

BEFORE ONE perplexity vanished another mocked. About the 1st of August, 1757, George developed a mild dysentery, which he ignored to the extent that he did not reduce his activities in the least.[1] Among compelling personal duties was that of going to Alexandria for another attempt at a settlement of Lawrence's estate. On the 4th of August he set out [2] and, on arrival, found few questions to be discussed. The books were in order. When all the adjustments with George Lee had been made—as far as these concerned the estate as distinguished from the lease of Mount Vernon—there was no credit to Washington to offset the debts of £125, 12s 9d contracted in 1753–55 and represented by purchases from the estate. This sum he duly paid.[3] Almost half of it was for livestock, the survivors and issue of which doubtless were at Mount Vernon.

A fine crop of tobacco was growing on the land and was especially encouraging because Washington had decided that he would undertake to raise the best leaf in considerable quantities.[4] From his salary and allowances he had saved money with which he soon was to buy 500 additional acres on Dogue Run for £350,[5] and he had invested £300 in additional slaves from November, 1756, through May, 1757.[6] Thus would he have more "hands" for more work. Some of his tobacco of 1756 had been shipped, but there remained eight hogsheads that should be put aboard a waiting vessel. Washington had to decide to whom to consign and whether to insure this leaf, but as these questions did not press, they were not answered until he returned to Winchester. His conclusion then was to take no insurance on the tobacco,

[1] 2 *Hamilton*, 231, 242.
[2] Possibly on the 5th, but the amount of his payment at Thompson's suggests that he spent the night of August 4–5 at the ordinary (*Ledger A*, folio 36).
[3] *Ledger A*, folio 4.   [4] 2 *G. W.*, 124, 125.
[5] *Ledger A*, folio 49, Dec. 19, 1757.
[6] *Ledger A*, folio 31, 33, 34. The number does not appear.

as it was to go in several bottoms, but to insure the goods purchased with the proceeds of the crop and sent back to America.[7]

Nothing specific could be undertaken immediately for the repair and furnishing of Mount Vernon, but much had to be pondered and planned, doubtless with the assistance of "Jack" Washington and his young wife, who were residing on the estate that year.[8] A marble chimney piece, needed window glass, wallpaper, papier-mâché ceiling for two rooms, and various articles of hardware and furnishing had been ordered in April,[9] but, of course, would not be received for months. One added requirement had now to be considered: George owned a dozen Virginia chairs that had good bottoms but lacked strength for what he called "common sitting." He had to devise some plan by which he could utilize the bottoms and strengthen or replace the chairs.[10] After reflecting on the involvements of taste and of shillings, he ordered strong new chairs from England at approximately 15s each. These were to be so made that the old bottoms could be used on them and the new bottoms on the old chairs, which would suffice for service in the bedrooms.[11]

All business was completed as far as it could be by the beginning of the last week in August, when Washington went back to Winchester.[12] There he found three troublesome situations: New Indian raids had occurred on the upper part of the South Branch, but all effort to overtake the enemy had failed;[13] second, from the arriving new drafts and from the old Companies, men deserted so frequently that the effective strength of the Regiment was not rising above approximately 700;[14] third, Edmund Atkin appeared to be handling Indian affairs with arrogance and ineptitude.[15]

Washington had not made more than his initial approach to the second and third of these perplexities when a messenger brought sad

---

[7] 2 G. W., 124.

[8] George Washington's letters to "Jack" during 1757 have disappeared, but occasional entries in Ledger A indicate payments to the younger brother at Mount Vernon or nearby. In a letter of Sept. 2, 1758, Humphrey Knight remarked that he thought Washington would like to hear frequently from the estate "especially this year as Mr. John Washington is absent" (3 Hamilton, 72).   [9] 2 G. W., 23.

[10] 2 G. W., 138.   [11] 2 G. W., 138.

[12] As usual, the dates in the ledger are subject to two interpretations but they indicate the start probably was on the 24th. See folio 36.

[13] 2 G. W., 121.

[14] 2 G. W., 120, 126, 127. Cf. ibid., 143. Colonel Stanwix was to write from Carlisle, Penn., on September 19, that he had lost nearly fifty men from his five Companies. He retook twelve, hanged two, and felt it would be "right and for the good of the service to have hanged the other eight" (2 Hamilton, 196).

[15] 2 G. W., 123.

news: On September 3, death had taken Col. William Fairfax,[16] the man who had done more than any other single individual to counsel and to advance young George Washington. Because of the glamour of a title and the weight of wealth, it may have been assumed by some of Washington's friends that Lord Fairfax had given the strongest momentum to George's own effort; but, actually, the peer had done little for Washington as a boy and nothing material for him as a young man. Colonel Fairfax, on the other hand, had transferred to George the moral assistance he had given to Lawrence. He could not have been kinder to the son-in-law than to the dead man's younger brother.

As a member of the Council of State for thirteen years, 1744–57, William Fairfax had served during the whole of George's military duty from the time of the journey to Fort Le Bœuf. There scarcely had been a session of the General Assembly from 1753 onward during which Fairfax had not sat in the upper house, to see, among other things, that Washington was informed of every move that would help or hurt. Fairfax enjoyed the confidence of Dinwiddie and doubtless smoothed some of the roughness that developed on the road of communication between Williamsburg and Winchester. Although there was perhaps something pompous in the manner of Colonel Fairfax, there always was sound counsel, accurate information and intelligent restraint in his letters to his young friend up the river at Mount Vernon.

Washington appreciated the advantage of his proximity and association and in this spirit he had admonished his brother John: "It is in their power," he said of the family at Belvoir, "to be very serviceable upon many occasions to us, as young beginners." He acknowledged: ". . . for to that family I am under many obligations, particularly to the old gentleman." [17] Doubtless from Colonel Fairfax, who was widely traveled and used to genteel life and manners, George learned more of the arts of society than from any other person except Lawrence. It was, therefore, as much a personal duty as it was a neighborly social obligation to make plans to ride over the mountain to Colonel Fairfax's formal funeral, later in the month,[18] even though the continuance of the bloody flux would make the journey difficult and perhaps painful.[19]

---

[16] *Gentleman's Mag.*, November, 1757, p. 531; 16 *V* 208. For his will, see 4 *V* 102–04.
[17] Letter of May 28, 1755; 1 *G. W.*, 129.
[18] For the postponement of funerals, see Vol. I, p. 114.
[19] The dates of extant letters show Washington at Fort Loudoun as late as September 24. See 2 *G. W.*, 135.

Those days between the news of Colonel Fairfax's passing and the time of the obsequies were among the unhappiest of Washington's whole period of command. About the 14th of September, he received a letter written by William Peachey, one of the Captains of the Regiment who had been discharged when the number of officers had been reduced. Captain Peachey described with great particularity how Charles Carter had quoted William Claiborne as saying Richard Corbin had quoted him, Peachey, as affirming in the spring of 1756, when sent to Williamsburg for aid, "that the whole business at that time was to execute a scheme of [Washington's] to cause the Assembly to levy largely both in money and men, and that there was not an Indian in that neighborhood, that the frontiers or even Winchester and the adjacent county did not appear to be in any more danger at that time than any other . . ." By the same chain of "he-told-him," Peachey reported that this "piece of deceit or imposition of yours (as they term it) has lessened the Governor's and some of the leading men's esteem for you; or at least they make use of it as a reason for the worse opinion (they say) they have than formerly of you." Peachey added that he would try to "find the scoundrel that dares make himself the author of such a scandalous report." [20]

In Washington's eyes, few things could be so calamitous to him personally as to lose the good opinion of the outstanding men of the Colony, the "honor" of which he often had written; but the absurdity of the charge, or his own weakened physical condition, or the necessity of dealing coldly and decisively with so infamous a slander kept him from blazing with wrath. He was conscious that he had lost favor with Dinwiddie, and he was inclined to believe that Corbin had spoken as Claiborne and Charles Carter had reported. For this reason Washington wanted to know, first of all, whether the Governor had heard the accusation and knew its source.

So, on the 17th, George copied in a letter to Dinwiddie what Peachey had written and then he asked: "I should take it infinitely kind if your Honor would please to inform me whether a report of this nature was ever made to you, and, in that case, who was the author of it?" Most carefully, Washington explained that he realized from the change in Dinwiddie's attitude to him that some person had maligned him, but he could not believe that such malice as this was credited by the Governor. In some detail he dwelt on the panic of the spring of 1756 and

[20] Letter of Aug. 22, 1757; 2 *Hamilton*, 182.

on the impossibility that so many settlers, at great loss to themselves, would have been party to imposition. With his characteristic and self-revelatory candor he admitted that he might have made military mistakes through lack of experience. "I think it would be more generous," he said, "to charge me with my faults, and let me stand or fall according to the evidence, than to stigmatize me behind my back."

He continued: "It is uncertain in what light my services may have appeared to your Honor; but this I know, and it is the highest consolation I am capable of feeling, that no man, that ever was employed in a public capacity, has endeavored to discharge the trust reposed in him with greater honesty and more zeal for the country's interest than I have done . . ." If there was one who could say he had offered intentional wrong to the public, he would accept any punishment. "On the other hand, it is hard to have my character araigned and my actions condemned without a hearing." Wherefore, he asked specifically, Had Colonel Corbin told Dinwiddie what the Councillor was said to have communicated to Claiborne? [21] In a brief letter to Peachey, the aggrieved Washington assumed the truth of the statement that the charge originated with Corbin and he dismissed it in fewer words as "little less than a comic entertainment." [22] The second scene, which might not be laughable, depended on Dinwiddie's answer.

A new succession of Indian raids followed in this unhappy period of death and illness and slander. Savages returned to the upper stretches of the South Branch and penetrated within twelve miles of Winchester to murder and to steal.[23] First reports of no less than twenty deaths [24] prompted immediate orders for pursuit, with the usual result. ". . . It is next to impossible," Washington wrote, "that any of our parties should ever see the enemy." [25] More in detail he told Colonel Stanwix: "I exert every means in my power to protect a much distressed country, but it is a task too arduous. To think of defending a frontier as ours is, of more than three hundred and fifty miles' extent, with only seven hundred men, is vain and idle, especially when that frontier lies more contiguous to the enemy than any other. I am, and have for a long time been, fully convinced that, if we continue to pursue a defensive plan, the country must be inevitably lost." [26]

Ten of the twenty persons supposed to have been killed or carried off

[21] Letter of Sept. 17, 1757; 2 G. W., 131–33.
[22] Letter of Sept. 18, 1757; ibid., 134.
[23] 2 G. W., 129; Md. Gazette, Oct. 13, 1757.
[24] 2 G. W., 144.
[25] Letter of Sept. 24, 1757 to Governor Dinwiddie; 2 G. W., 135.
[26] Letter of Oct. 8, 1757; 2 G. W., 144.

by the enemy emerged at length from hiding places,[27] but the frightened and discouraged settlers continued to flee from their farms. Washington repeated his warning: "If there is no expedition to the westward . . . nor a force more considerable than Virginia can support posted on our frontiers . . . there will not, next campaign I dare affirm, be one soul living on this side the Blue Ridge the ensuing autumn" outside garrisons and perhaps a few residents of Winchester.[28] The hope of protecting the frontier with the reorganized Regiment and a chain of forts had proved as vain as all the previous plans. Nothing would save Virginia except an offensive that would drive the enemy from the Ohio. Washington was determined to convince Colonel Stanwix of this necessity if, as he apprehended, the General Assembly could not itself provide a much larger force with which to combat the Indians.[29]

It probably was while this resoluton was taking form that George went to Belvoir for the funeral of Colonel Fairfax.[30] On the road, Washington received from his mother a letter in which she explained that his brother Charles, who was still a minor, was anxious to marry Mildred Thornton but had encountered a difficulty. The girl's mother knew the terms of Augustine Washington's will and reasoned that if Charles died while still under age, his inheritance from his father would go, under the law of descent, to George, his oldest full brother. Mrs. Thornton, wishing to protect Mildred's interests, asked that the heirs of Augustine waive their rights and permit Charles's estate to pass to his widow in event he died before he reached his twenty-first birthday. George's answer was: "Mrs. Thornton, if she believes I am capable of taking these ungenerous advantages, knows little of the principles which govern my conduct. However, I suppose [she] is actuated by prudent motives and therefore would be safe. If she will get any instrument of writing drawn I will sign it provided it does not effect me in other respects than her daughter's fortune if my brother dies under age."[31]

In this letter, Washington mentioned that he had come to attend Colonel Fairfax's funeral, but he gave no details. It was not his habit, at 25, to look wistfully backward and it never was his nature to lament what he had not caused and could not change, but he did not forget

[27] *Ibid.,* 148.
[28] Letter to Dinwiddie, Oct. 24, 1757; 2 *G. W.,* 151. Cf. *ibid.,* 155.
[29] *Ibid.,* 155.
[30] Washington left Winchester prior to September 27 (cf. 2 *Hamilton,* 205–07) and was at Mount Vernon until the afternoon of September 30 (2 *G. W.,* 137).
[31] 2 *G. W.,* 137.

Colonel Fairfax or his debt to that gentleman. Writing shortly afterward of a favor Fairfax had sought for a son, Washington told the Governor: ". . . I esteem him greatly on account of his father, for whose memory and friendship I shall ever retain a most grateful sense." [32]

When the last tribute had been paid at the church, Washington hurried back to the Valley, where he had to cope immediately and vigorously with an affair that had developed while he was in Fairfax. A private who was waiting on the Quartermaster, John Hamilton, had a quarrel in Hamilton's absence with a girl the Quartermaster was keeping. In spiteful temper, the private reported to his superior that Hamilton had gone off and had no intention of returning. Then it developed that Hamilton, who had been a Sergeant in a British Regiment before enlisting in Virginia, had stolen quartermaster supplies and had sold them in Winchester. When called to a routine accounting, while nothing was suspected, he had devised a scheme of getting safely away before his embezzlement could be discovered. The circumstances were a particular humiliation to Washington, because he had made Hamilton Quartermaster as a reward for three years of courageous, good service in the Regiment.[33]

With this ugly incident behind him, Washington renewed his plea for an offensive in 1758. He wrestled, too, over the meaning of Governor Dinwiddie's reply to his letter concerning the preposterous charges Richard Corbin was alleged to have made. The Governor said: "I would gladly hope there is no truth in it. I never heard of it before, nor did I ever conceive you'd have sent down any alarms without proper foundation. However, I shall show it to Col. Corbin when he comes to town, but I'd advise you not to credit every idle story you hear, for if I was to notice reports of different kinds, I should be constantly perplexed. My conduct to you from the beginning was always friendly, but you know I had good reason to suspect you of ingratitude, which I am convinced your own conscience and reflection must allow I had reason to be angry, but this I endeavor to forget; but I can't think Col. Corbin guilty of what is reported. However as I've his Majesty's leave to go for England, propose leaving this November, and I wish my successor may show you as much friendship as I've done." [34]

---

[32] 2 *G. W.*, 130. For a later, casual reference, see *ibid.*, 136. The solicitation for the sons is reviewed in Appendix II-3.

[33] 2 *G. W.*, 141, 142, 144, 146; 2 *Hamilton*, 205; 305 *Papers of G. W.*, 317, 319, 321, LC.

[34] Letter of Sept. 24, 1757; 2 *Din.*, 703.

This letter caused Washington as much pain as it relieved. He was glad, of course, to know that Dinwiddie had not heard previously and did not now credit the slander, but that charge of ingratitude! Did it mean that Dinwiddie felt he had been too critical, too lacking in support of what the Governor had done? George answered almost despairingly: "I do not know that I ever gave your Honor cause to suspect me of ingratitude, a crime I detest and would most carefully avoid. If an open, disinterested behavior carries offence, I may have offended, because I have always laid it down as a maxim to represent facts freely and impartially, but no more to others than I have to you, sir. If instances of my ungrateful behavior had been particularized, I would have answered to them. But I have long been convinced that my actions and their motives have been maliciously aggravated." [35]

There the matter had unhappily to rest, but if Dinwiddie soon was to leave in November, Washington felt it was desirable to go to Williamsburg and to settle accounts. Otherwise there might be confusion afterward. The Colonel asked permission to do this, in the same letter in which he made his disclaimer,[36] and then he turned to the routine once more and particularly to the endless difficulties created by the policy of the Indian agent, Edmund Atkin. That gentleman had left the frontier and had given assurance that he had arranged all Indian affairs acceptably. At the time he had filed what Dinwiddie termed "a monstrous account of expenses," to a total of £809, but he had attempted to justify himself by a glowing report.[37] Indian goods worth £800 were in store at Fort Loudoun, Atkin had asserted; [38] Captain Gist was in charge. Actually, if Indian goods were at hand, they had been set aside for Catawbas, with none available for Cherokees, even when they brought in scalps. The only interpreter had been sent by Atkin through Augusta and had disappeared for the time being.[39] Gist did his best but he could accomplish nothing with the Indians when he could give them nothing. Washington provided what he might and then, once again in desperation, he had to appeal to the Governor for better management of dealings with the savages whose help must be available in the campaign of 1758.[40]

[35] Letter of Oct. 5, 1757; 2 G. W., 141.
[36] Ibid., 142.
[37] 2 Din., 707. Cf. ibid., 694, 700, 710; Alden, op. cit., 73.
[38] 2 Din., 713, 715.   [39] Ibid.
[40] Letter of Nov. 7, 1757; 2 G. W., 156–58. Dinwiddie compromised with Atkin for £459 and promised to keep the office at Winchester in operation until October, 1758. Atkin then went to South Carolina. See Alden, op. cit., 73.

When Washington sealed this letter on the 5th of November, he already had been told he was not to be permitted to go to Williamsburg to settle his accounts. The Governor snappishly had met his request with this refusal: "You have been frequently indulged with leave of absence. You know the fort is to be finished, and I fear in your absence little will be done, and surely the commanding officer should not be absent when daily alarmed with the enemy's intentions to invade our frontiers." [41] Thus rebuffed, George had to await a more favorable time when the Governor's humor was better or his successor had come. How soon that might be, George could not guess. He certainly did not anticipate the reality—that his letter of November 5 contained the last words he ever was to address to "His Honor."

Robert Dinwiddie did not possess either vast or quick intellect. The things he had not learned before he came to Virginia he was slow to acquire afterward. He felt himself hampered by his lack of knowledge of military matters, and he was honest in saying so, even if he had cherished ambitions to have a Colonel's commission and to wear the King's coat.[42]

From the outset, the Governor had sensed two of the fundamental realities of the situation on the frontier—that the French had to be driven from the Ohio and that the help of friendly Indians in large number was necessary to the success of any expedition into a wilderness occupied by the enemy. Dinwiddie, moreover, had stood squarely with the commanders on the frontier in advocacy of a large armed force, in the application of the draft, and in conviction that reliance on the militia was futile. If he had seemed on occasion to go to extremes of economy, it was because he knew the difficulty of getting supply from the General Assembly.

His first loyalty was to the home government; his yardstick for lawmakers was their display of that same quality. If they did the will of the King, most of their shortcomings could be forgiven; but if they disputed any order from England or acted otherwise than as the obedient, unquestioning subjects of an inerrant monarch, they were insolent and rebellious. At the same time that Dinwiddie advocated a general tax of all provincials by act of Parliament, he displayed no enthusiasm

[41] 2 *Din.*, 707–08.
[42] Cf. William Fairfax to Washington, May 20, 1756: "You have heard the Governor sometimes and I often, say that his being unacquainted with military operations, gives him much trouble in the requisite instructions and directions, which are consequently liable to mistakes" (1 *Hamilton*, 264).

for any other conference of the Colonies than one to discuss war. In administration he had been diligent and methodical, as well as frugal. His letters were long and sometimes obscure, but they seldom failed to answer all of a correspondent's questions and they left no doubt of his own stand.

Weaknesses Dinwiddie had, weaknesses that fortunately were on the surface, discernible and of a sort against which any associate could guard. The Governor was partial to Scots; he was easily deceived by the promises of Indians and much too optimistic in his estimate of what he could prevail on them to do. Because he was insistent on his prerogatives, he was quick to repel any infringement. Always petulant, he was apt, if angry, to issue sharp, peremptory orders. When he had done his best, he did not like to be rebuked for mistake or for failure. Criticism by his subordinates he considered to be disloyalty or ingratitude.

After the event, he easily persuaded himself that he had been right from the first and had foreseen what occurred. At least once, in discussing the possibility of renewing the offensive after Braddock's defeat, he made a suggestion, and, when it was not adopted, he subsequently represented it to have been a firm and patriotic promise, the acceptance of which would have been the assurance of victory. In dealing with the other Governors, both pride and prejudice occasionally marred his acts. He despised Glen of South Carolina and sometimes he hectored Sharpe. With the other Governors, except Dobbs of North Carolina, his relations were not intimate. He had no trouble with Dobbs but apparently he concluded in 1755 that little help was to be had from North Carolina.

Nearer home, Dinwiddie usually lived in amity with his Council and found its members of one mind with him. In spite of occasional quarrels with the Burgesses, he was not unappreciative of their loyalty. When he drew the final balance, he wrote Pitt, "I must remark this Dominion have given a testimony of their obedience to His Majesty's royal orders more than any one Colony on this continent." [43]

In his personal friendships, Dinwiddie was hearty, cordial and kindly, and never unmindful of the social amenities. It was the more to be regretted, for this reason, that the last months of his relations with Washington were clouded with misunderstanding, after almost four years of pleasant association. Dinwiddie had given George his first opportunity as a soldier, and had called him again to command after

[43] Letter of Sept. 12, 1757; 1 *Pitt,* 104.

Braddock's defeat. If the Governor had employed Washington in 1755 because the young man was popular, that was creditable to his political judgment; and if he acted because he regarded Washington as the most promising of the few soldiers of an unmartial Colony, that was discernment.

The only possible ground for charging the Governor with duplicity toward the young Colonel was that Dinwiddie alleged "orders from home" as a reason for reducing the Virginia Regiment to Independent Companies in 1755 at a time when Dinwiddie was hoping to be made a Colonel. Washington believed that the inspiration of this successful effort to reduce his rank came from Wills Creek, not from Whitehall, and in this he may have been correct, but he did not make out a case against the Governor. Other differences, prior to the summer of 1757, were such only as would have occurred between any two men of like sensitiveness and responsibility.

Part of the final ill-feeling perhaps had its origin, as George suspected, in the hostility and venom of some secret enemy or jealous rival; but Dinwiddie's specific disclaimer of belief in the story about Richard Corbin indicates that the Governor did not listen readily or gullibly to such slander. The probability is that Dinwiddie's illness aggravated the infirmities of his sixty-four years and shook his judgment and his temper. Had he recovered, he might have been reconciled. Washington was younger than Dinwiddie by thirty-nine years and had, in addition to his respect for age and office, the ability to exercise his largest self-restraint where the issue was most serious. So long as he could control himself at all, he was coolest in words when hottest in wrath. In the last exchanges with Dinwiddie, even though he thought the Governor's mind was poisoned against him, Washington did not write an insubordinate line or one he could later have wished he had erased.

At the same time, a certain complaint and contention ran through Washington's letters of the summer of 1757 and for the same reason that Dinwiddie was bad-tempered: he was sick. The dysentery that had begun late in July persisted relentlessly; and as Washington would not lessen his pace,[44] the malady reduced his strength day by day. About the 1st of November this "bloody flux" became more violent. Soon George was so weak that he scarcely could walk.[45] On the 7th he was

[44] See Robert Stewart in 2 *Hamilton*, 242.
[45] *Ibid.*

in such violent pain that the physicians had to give him warning: If he did not suspend all activity and seek a "change of air," they could not be responsible for him; and even if he went away, he could not hope for early recovery.[46] That decided him. Without so much as attempting to write either Dinwiddie or Colonel Stanwix, he turned over the command to Capt. Robert Stewart, instructed that officer to notify his superiors of his illness, and without a day's further delay he started for Alexandria.[47]

[46] *Ibid.*, 231, 243.

[47] He probably left Winchester November 9 (cf. 2 *Hamilton*, 231). Dinwiddie wrote in answer to Stewart's letter: "The violent complaint Colonel Washington labors under gives me great concern. It was unknown to me or he should have had leave of absence sooner, and I am glad he did not delay following the doctor's advice to try a change of air. I sincerely wish him a speedy recovery" (letter of Nov. 15, 1757; 2 *Hamilton*, 239–40).

CHAPTER XVII

Courtship with Legal Entanglements
(November, 1757–March, 1758)

On arrival in Alexandria, Colonel Washington went to the home of John Carlyle and there he remained long enough to consult Dr. Charles Green, who retained a reputation for medical skill though devoted primarily to the cure of souls.[1] Washington sought, also, to have Dr. Gustavus Brown visit him, but that distinguished Maryland practitioner did not cross the Potomac.[2] For a time, the patient grew worse;[3] then, after he went to Mount Vernon,[4] he gained slightly in his battle with his malady. At Christmas, he was strong enough to transact some personal business,[5] and subsequent to New Year's Day, he talked of going to Williamsburg, though at least one friendly neighbor discouraged the effort.[6] Perhaps the most hopeful indication was George's state of mind. In preparing an invoice of goods from England, he included almonds, raisins, currants and "two dozen packs of playing cards." He ordered six dozen plates, also, and enjoined his agent, "pray let them to be neat and fashionable or send none."[7] His thought was not of dying, but of living and perhaps of bringing a bride to Mount Vernon if all went well.

For some weeks after this period of partial activity, his condition fluctuated. Toward the end of January, he undertook the journey to Williamsburg, but pain and renewed symptoms compelled him to return home[8] in so much discouragement that he talked once more

[1] 2 *G. W.*, 159. For Green, see *supra*, Vol. I, p. 54, 204.
[2] Dr. Craik (2 *Hamilton*, 247) spoke only of "Doctor Brown's neglect in not coming to see you," and he did not specify to which of the Doctors Brown he referred, but the eminence of Gustavus Brown of Charles County, Maryland, makes it virtually certain he was the man.
[3] Craik, *ibid.*
[4] Craik wrote November 25 (*loc. cit.*) as if Washington already were there.
[5] 2 *G. W.*, 159–60; *Ledger A*, folio 37.
[6] 2 *Hamilton*, 255. Cf. *ibid.*, 256.
[7] 2 *G. W.*, 162.
[8] *Ledger A*, folio 37. Apparently he got as far southward as Colonel Baylor's or Col. John Spotswood's estate. See also 2 *G. W.*, 162–63, 164.

the ocean, and my wife on the other. I do not know your young gentleman, nor have you or he thought fit to send me an account of his real
and personal effects; however, if my daughter likes him, I will give her
upon her marriage to him, half as much as he can make appear he is
worth." [29]

At the end of this letter, Col. Daniel Parke wrote: "I have no one
else to give my estate to but my daughters." That was not a covenant,
or even a promise; it simply was a statement of the law of descent, but
of course it was regarded as a certainty. John Custis and William Byrd
consequently would be, with their wives' and their own estates, among
the Colony's most secure heirs. This appeared to be put beyond all
doubt, save that of an "act of God." Custis, in particular, seemed to be
assured of a swelling fortune because Parke, hearing good reports of
the business skill of John, decided to utilize it by offering his son-in-law
a fifth of the entire yield of his estate in Virginia if Custis would move
from the Eastern Shore and manage the family plantations. Custis was
loath to do this both because he did not wish to neglect his own property
by absence from it and also because he even then was quarreling with
Frances over their respective interests.[30] At length Custis stifled his
doubts and undertook the management of the far-spreading tobacco
lands that Colonel Parke had inherited.[31] They were good lands; Custis
diligently kept them so.

In 1711, Custis had startling news from the Leeward Islands: After
a turbulent administration,[32] Colonel Parke had been murdered Dec.
9, 1710, in a riot on Antigua.[33] Later Custis and all the Parke connection learned of a series of scandalous occurrences that were said to have
been responsible for some of the resentments that frothed in the killing
of the Governor. Parke was alleged to have taken as his mistress
Catherine Chester, the wife of a somewhat notorious resident of
Antigua,[34] and by her it was asserted that he had an illegitimate

---

[29] Daniel Parke to John Custis, Aug. 25, 1705; *G. W. P. Custis,* 16 n.

[30] See *infra,* p. 285.

[31] See "The Several Pleas and Answer of John Custis . . . to the bill of complaint of Thomas
Dunbar Parke" . . . , n.d., VHS (cited hereafter as *Custis's Pleas*).

[32] See P.R.O., C.O. 152: 6, No. 63; *ibid.,* 7, Nos. 28, 43, 52; *ibid.,* 8, No. 40; *ibid.,* 9; *ibid.,*
42, No. 17; *Journal Commiss. Trade and Plantations,* 1704–09, p. 299, 485, 561, 562–63.

[33] The whole course of this cruel affair is traced in George French, *The History of Col.
Parke's Administration, while He was Captain General and Chief Governor of the Leeward
Islands.* Three dates are given for Parke's death—Dec. 7, 9 and 10, 1710. The 9th is the
date mentioned in a contemporary semi-official report, P.R.O., C.O. 152: 8. With much
difficulty, permission was procured to bury Parke in a church (*ibid.,* 153: 11, p. 314–20).

[34] This may have been the Chester whom Parke accused of causing the death of Sawyer,
"a Gentleman's son from Virginia," whom Chester hit behind the ear with a tankard; P.R.O.,
C.O. 152: 8, No. 40.

daughter, who was about a year old at the time of his death.[35] Parke's apologists denied that Mrs. Chester was his mistress. His kindness to her, it was maintained, sprang from pity.[36] Parke himself had said that Catherine Chester acquired the ill-will of residents of Antigua because she had sent him information of a plot to murder him. "This poor woman," he wrote, "is in a deep consumption and has been so for two years and wants a nurse more than a gallant and has the fate to be married to a cruel madman and a fool who turned her out of doors twice before I arrived." Parke added: "She was an orphan and had no relations to protect her, which is the reason she is made a sacrifice in order to throw dirt on me." [37]

Other scandals, too, were brought to light. In the looting of Parke's effects, his most confidential letters were found and read. Among them were some from girls and young matrons on the island with whom it was manifest that Parke had been intimate. "How far they design peace," one official said of the rioters, "is evident by their showing several letters from the women in the island that, if concealed, might not further differences in families." [38] Another resident said in a deposition: ". . . the only thing they can charge [Parke] with is his debauching many of their wives and daughters (which was indeed very dishonorable) but that can be no pretence when rightly considered, for that was not known until they had rifled his papers, which gave them more disturbance in their private families than they had met with before in their zeal for the public." [39]

In due time, Parke's Virginia heirs received a copy of his startling will of Jan. 29, 1709, which had been probated in Antigua.[40] Parke had no less than £30,000 of property in the Leeward Islands and he bequeathed the whole of it to the infant Lucy, the youngest daughter of Mrs. Catherine Chester, regardless of the name that might later be given her by her mother. If the daughter lived to marry and to have children, the property was to pass to her eldest son, provided she, her husband and their issue took the name Parke and used the Parke coat

[35] Sir Edward Northey's opinion, dated Oct. 1, 1711, and cited *infra*, n. 66, mentioned the child as then "about two years old."

[36] See George French, *Answer to a Scurrilous Libel entitled a Letter to Mr. George French*, 46.

[37] Parke to the Commissioners of Trade and Plantations, Mch. 21, 1710; P.R.O., C.O. 152: No. 18.

[38] P.R.O., C.O. 152: 42, No. 54.

[39] Thomas Morris, Feb. 27, 1711; P.R.O., C.O. 153: No. 11, p. 312–20.

[40] Copy in *Byrd Title Book*, 195; VHS; a summary, with the date correctly given, appears in P.R.O., P.C. 2: 105, f 531 ff.

of arms. In event this daughter of Catherine Chester died before she was twenty-one years of age, the estate passed for life to Mrs. Chester and on her demise to Julius Caesar Parke, who lived in England. That young man likewise was to receive the estate in the Leeward Islands if Lucy Chester and her issue declined the name and arms of Parke. Should Julius Caesar Parke die without direct heirs, then, but only then, would the property in the West Indies go to Frances Custis and her heirs at law. Frances was to inherit immediately the estate in England and in Virginia. If she had no surviving children, first Lucy Byrd and then Julius Caesar Parke would succeed. Frances was to pay Lucy Byrd £1000, was to remit £50 a year to Julius Caesar and was to provide the money for several minor legacies. Separate executors were named for the estate in the Leeward Islands and for the property in Virginia and England, as if there had been two Daniel Parkes, whose lives and fortunes were not to be mingled unless there were a failure of direct heirs.[41] The supreme humiliation and injustice of this testament were in the partiality shown the illegitimate daughter of Parke. He seemed to be pursued by an ambition to have his name perpetuated by all who were of his blood, whether by lawful or by wayward descent. Lucy Chester was required, in fact, and not merely permitted, to take the proud name of Parke if she was to enjoy the large estate, which was worth far more than the Virginia property of her father.[42] This was a bitter potion for a family that already had been compelled to swallow hard because of Colonel Parke's disdain of them and of their society.

Under date of May 12, 1711, the London merchant Micajah Perry wrote Custis in disgusted surprise that Parke had penned a document that left "a stain upon [his] name forever." Perry went on to say: ". . . early as it is, we are threatened with trouble." Colonel Parke's sister, Evelyn, and her husband, Gilbert Pepper, were coming to London from Ireland for an undisclosed purpose.[43] Mrs. Sherrard,[44] in addition, "pretends that she will try for an estate in Virginia for her son, who she hath called Parke." Further, Mrs. Rebecca Goodart raised a question concerning a matter of some £500, or a part thereof, due

[41] Abstract of will, Jan. 29, 1709/10; 20 V 372. A complete copy is in the *Byrd Title Book*.
[42] *Custis's Pleas.*
[43] *Ibid.* The two individuals are identified in a petition to the Commissioners of Trade and Plantations (P.R.O., C.O. 152: 9, nos. 157–58). Through this paper, they sought to acquaint the Queen with the details of Parke's death.
[44] Perry did not explain who she was, an omission which may be construed to mean that Perry was sure Custis already knew of her.

by her to the Parke estate. The one cheerful note in Perry's letter concerned Parke's "godson," Julius Caesar: "He is like to shift for himself for us; hath thought himself a God of great quality, hath been a proud and ostentatious fellow and lived accordingly. We think he is in prison now and there let him be. We see no reason to look further upon him, so let him cut his own way as he pleases." [45]

In a grim postscript, Perry added a list of Parke's known debts—about £2400 to Perry himself, a mortgage of £2200 on a property owned by Parke at White Church in Hampshire,[46] and some lesser items to a total of £6680. If White Church brought £4000, as Perry estimated it might, the debts of the estate in England would be £2680 net, before any legacies were paid.[47] To this total of English liabilities and legacies, the bequest of £1000 to Lucy Byrd in Virginia had to be added.

On the subject of Frances Custis's payment of these debts of the estate, the precise language of Parke's testament was this: "My will is that my daughter Frances Custis pay out of my estate in Virginia and Hampshire, all my legal debts and bequests, i.e., to pay the bequest of £1,000 to my daughter Lucy." [48] Parke had agreed prior to Lucy's marriage to settle £1000 on her and apparently had never paid it.[49] Byrd naturally was anxious to have this long-delayed promise fulfilled, but there was no way of raising in Virginia the sum of approximately £3680 estimated to cover English debts and the Virginia legacy to Lucy Byrd. In this situation Custis and Byrd joined their interests, went to the General Assembly of 1711, and procured a special act under which John Custis and his wife were authorized to sell a mill and certain lands and slaves, in order to apply the proceeds to the payment of the debts.[50] This done, William Byrd, who had large credit

[45] Quoted in full in *Byrd Title Book*. A somewhat similar letter was addressed to William Byrd on the same day. Accompanying this was the list of Colonel Parke's known debts and further reference to Julius Caesar Parke: "We have cast him off, he hath spent the Colonel no small sum and had we followed the Colonel's order, it would have been more, but let him go a Bastard as he is, and see who will regard him . . ." (*Byrd Title Book*, 208).

[46] The village is on the border of Chute Forest, fifty-eight miles from London and twenty-three from Salisbury.

[47] *Custis's Pleas*. A copy is preserved, also, in *Byrd Title Book*.

[48] Digest of the Parke estate, n.d. (*Custis Papers*, VHS). The confusing remainder of this part of the will is described in a later paragraph.

[49] See *ibid*. and John Custis to William Byrd, n.d., *Custis Letter Book*, No. 28.

[50] The plantations of Mount Folly and Taskenask were included, but unfortunately the act was published by title only in 4 *H* 29. The original is not in the archives of Virginia. An amendatory act of 1752 in 6 *H* 319 mentions a tract of 1678 acres as part of this entail. In P.R.O., C.O. 5: 1316, f 321 ff, are the Perry's petition of August, 1712, for the confirmation of the Virginia act of November, 1711, and the opinion of Atty. Gen. Edward Northey, Sept. 13, 1712, that the Virginia statute was unobjectionable at law.

"at home," agreed to assume the obligations and legacies in return for the Parke assets in England and the property the Custises were to sell in Virginia.[51] Custis duly proceeded to get an act of Parliament passed to permit the sale of most of Parke's estate in England. An equitable bargain appeared to have been struck, but, unfortunately, further debts were discovered in unexpected amounts and places, until the total approached £10,000.[52]

There was nothing for William Byrd to do except to make the best of a bad bargain and to try to pay off the debts in the hope that the increment in the value of the Virginia property would offset the loss. With diminished estate but still rich, Frances and John Custis renewed their quarrels. They now had a daughter, Frances, born in 1709,[53] and a son, Daniel Parke Custis, born Oct. 15, 1711,[54] and at the instance of friends they undertook in June, 1714, to reconcile their differences, but the formal agreement reached at that time [55] did not long survive pride and temper, contention and love of money. Nor did Frances herself live to defend or to extend her rights. She died Mch. 13, 1714/15 and, as the event was to show, to the definite satisfaction of her husband.[56]

If John Custis found relief in being free of a wife with the Parke blood, he still had to untangle the affairs of the family which, as he subsequently wrote, he "unfortunately married into." [57] His resentment was deepened by the discovery that the father of the spendthrift Daniel Parke had entailed certain tracts that had not been known to be in fee-tail at the time of the agreement with William Byrd. In ignorance of this, Custis had transferred to William Byrd in 1712 more of Frances Parke Custis's property than could have been held liable for her father's debts. Custis figured, in fact, that he had paid out, in one way and another, a larger sum than his wife's share of the Parke estate was worth.[58]

---

[51] Text of agreement of Feb. 11, 1711 in 55 V 377 ff. See also Byrd to Custis, Feb. 7, 1711 in Custis Papers, VHS. Various additions and changes in this agreement are mentioned in the Digest of the Parke Estate, loc. cit., but none of these is important in this review.

[52] John Custis to Dunbar Parke, Jan. 15, 1724; Custis Letter Book, No. 25. Custis gave various estimates of debts paid. Sometimes he put the figure above and sometimes below £10,000.

[53] 20 V 379. They probably had two other children, who died young, 3 W (1) p. 258.

[54] D. P. Custis Invoice Book, LC.

[55] 4 V 64–66. This is the document quoted in Vol. I, p. 115.

[56] For her death, see 32 V 239 n. Custis's sentiments are recorded infra, p. 285, 295.

[57] John Custis to [Robert] Cary, 1733, n.d., Custis Letter Book, No. 83. This important summary of the later litigation will be cited hereafter as Cary Letter.

[58] He wrote in 1724 that he had expended "several hundred pounds" more than could have been exacted of him. Nine years later, in the Cary Letter, he said he had parted with "several thousand pounds more" than he ever had received from the estate.

HE FATHERED THE "DUNBAR SUIT"

Sir Godfrey Kneller probably painted Col. Daniel Parke as he portrayed nearly all his later sitters—with good drawing and brilliant color but with a tired brush and a complete absence of enthusiasm. Even so, if Kneller presented it accurately, he must have been interested in Parke's hand, with a broad palm and long fingers almost as thin and as delicate as those of a fashionable woman.

Further, having painted ten sovereigns, Kneller took pains to make distinct the miniature of Queen Anne, set in diamonds, that had been one of the presents Her Majesty gave the Colonel for bringing her the news of Marlborough's victory at Blenheim.

Perhaps, too, the artist who had painted many portraits of Charles II knew how to interpret the turn of the lips and the half-abstracted, half-intent gaze in the eyes of Colonel Parke.

Certain it is that if Kneller remembered Parke and learned subsequently of what happened on Antigua before Parke was murdered, the artist would have flattered himself that the arch he had given the Colonel's mouth was sensual and that the look was lustful.

The scandal ran a long way and for a long time. Few stories of Washington's life were more remarkable than that of how his fortunes became entangled with the complicated chancery suit that grew out of Colonel Parke's amours in the Leeward Islands.

The reproduction on the opposite page is from a photograph made by the Frick Art Reference Library of the original owned by the late Dr. George Bolling Lee, who gave his permission for its use here.

MARTHA, RICH AND WIDOWED AT TWENTY-SIX

Martha Dandridge Custis had too much common sense and lived in too realistic a society to have assumed for an hour that her person and her property would not attract the eyes of planters in search of ease and beauty.

Her husband had died intestate. She consequently had her full dower right and not some agreed sum in lieu of dower. Besides, her two children were quite young. Their large inheritance probably would be for a long term of years under the care of whomsoever she made her second husband. To style her "The Widow Custis" might be to imply erroneously that she sat at the White House, "a-weeping and a-crying for a nice young man."

As Custis died in July, 1757, and Washington did not begin his wooing until March, 1758, at earliest, it is highly probable that other young Virginians had been ahead of him on the same mission.

If it was so, then the rejection of their suit was another evidence that common sense was the outstanding characteristic of Martha. She held to "No" until the right man came to receive her "Yes."

The poor portrait of her on the opposite page was made by John Wollaston before her first husband's death and when she was about twenty-six years old. The original is owned by Washington and Lee University, which has given permission for its reproduction here.

Because Colonel Parke's children by his wife had paid his debts in England, they probably were not distressed to hear that Edward Chester, husband of Catherine, had attempted to get control of the infant Lucy's real estate, as guardian of her body, after litigation with Caesar Rodney, one of the executors of Parke's estate in the Leeward Islands.[59] Learning of this, Custis wrote at length to inquire in more detail of Perry what had befallen the estate in the islands, because, he said, "several gentlemen has informed me that it is squandered almost away, or that if Rodney was to be called to account he could not account for one-third of it." [60]

Nearly seven years later, Custis doubtless learned more than he wished to know. An individual signing himself "Dunbar Parke" sent by a ship captain from Antigua a letter that was the beginning of new plagues for Custis. It developed that the writer had been christened Thomas Dunbar, but, on marrying Lucy Chester, had been prompted to change his name to Parke in order to qualify for the estate by conforming to Colonel Parke's will.[61] The communication of this stranger was to the effect that in acquiring land and slaves in the Leeward Islands, Colonel Parke had contracted debts that amounted to £4000 or £5000 at the time of his death.[62] Creditors had procured judgments against the legatees there, who had been compelled to satisfy them by selling part of the estate.[63] Dunbar Parke next asserted that Colonel Parke's will made plain the wish of the testator to leave his insular property free of all encumbrance. That was why Parke had charged all debts against the English and Virginia properties. Dunbar went on to say that he looked to Mrs. Custis to reimburse the Antigua estate. He desired a friendly settlement, but he was coming to Virginia in the spring of 1724, with Caesar Rodney, and, if necessary, he then would file a bill in chancery for the repayment from the Virginia property of the amounts by which the estate in the Leeward Islands had been depleted to meet the judgments entered there.[64]

This letter aroused every stubborn impulse of Custis's spirit. He consulted his lawyer and probably deferred an answer until he cooled down somewhat. If he had kept all the earlier papers in the case and

---

59 Cf. opinion of Sir Edward Northey on Parke's will, Oct. 1, 1711; *Byrd Title Book,* 198.

60 Letter of Mch. 28, 1717; *Custis Letter Book,* No. 2.

61 4 *Acts Privy Council,* Col. Ser., 288–90; P.R.O., P.C. 2: 105, f 531.

62 This is the figure given in the *Cary Letter,* but as will appear from the text the amount ultimately involved was £6000.

63 *Acts Privy Council,* 2 George I., p. 216.

64 Parke's letter is not among the *Custis Papers* but Custis's answer of Jan. 14, 1724, in his *Letter Book,* makes plain the substance of Dunbar Parke's demand. Additional information appears in the Digest, *loc. cit.,* and in the summary of Dunbar Parke's bill, *infra.*

consulted them after the receipt of Dunbar Parke's letter, he found at least two items to alarm him. One was confusion in the language of the section of Daniel Parke's will relating to legacies: One version of this part of the will read that Frances was to pay "all my legal debts and bequests, i.e."—as if it were the only one—"to pay the bequest of £1000 to my daughter Lucy." Another version stipulated that Frances was to pay out of the estate in Hampshire "the following legacies and all my debts." That was the language: "*All* my debts," with no reservation as to amount or place where due.[65] Further, after Micajah Perry reluctantly had undertaken to serve as executor of Parke's estate, he had consulted Sir Edward Northey, the King's Attorney General and a lawyer of much ability. Among Perry's questions had been one concerning procedure for the payment of Parke's debts to him and "to several persons in Antigua." Must not the executors recover these debts "against the personal estate in the four islands as well as against the estate in Virginia and England . . . ?" Northey's answer had been: "I am of opinion that the executor may retain out of any part of the personal estate that shall come to his hands to pay his debt, and if what's retained happen to belong to a legatee not intended to be charged with debts, such legatee must have satisfaction from the other who ought to pay it by will."[66] Adherence to this opinion had cost much, even before Dunbar Parke made his claim. Now, if Northey and Dunbar Parke both were correct, still more of the property of Parke's legitimate children might be taken from them.

Custis consequently took the strongest ground he could. He maintained in answer to Dunbar Parke that if the full extent of the entail of Col. Daniel Parke's Virginia property had been known sooner, the estate would not have been liable for as much as already had been paid out for Parke's debts. No assets remained. In fact, he said, Dunbar Parke's demand was "for more than [Parke's] estate in Virginia was ever worth before it was torn to pieces." Costly as his experience with the estate had been, Custis wrote, he would "go on to the end of the chapter." "[I] do assure you, Sir," he said, "I would go to law the . . . whole course of my life; spend the last penny I have in the world, rather than I will pay one farthing of your unjust and unreasonable demand; and must beg leave to tell you that you shall not repair your over-sights [in the mismanagement of the Antigua estate] at my cost. I must confess you may give me some trouble and put me to some

---

[65] *Byrd Title Book,* 195.
[66] Text of opinion in *Byrd Title Book,* 198.

charge; but depend on it; where you put me to one penny worth, you will put yourself to a pound . . ." [67]

To Dunbar Parke's attorney, Caesar Rodney, whom he apparently knew, Custis wrote in even stiffer strain: "When Colonel Parke made that scandalous will, he could never dream that anything from the islands could in reason be demanded from this estate, he having left such great effects there. Neither can you or [sic] anyone believe that knew the General [68] that he ever designed to die with that will, but made it purely to please that adulterous strumpet who so unfortunately intoxicated him. I took Mr. Rodney to be a man of more honesty and honor than to attempt (if it were in his power which God be thanked it is not) to rob the lawful posterity of his deceased friend to enrich a kennel of whores and bastards; and if you had the least respect for the memory of Colonel Parke you would not suffer his dead ashes to be so exposed by exhibiting such a scandalous will in any court where he was so well known as in Virginia. I am very well prepared for any attempt you design on me . . ." [69]

After this defiant declaration, the maneuver of litigants and counsel was delayed often and sometimes was stalled.[70] In the winter of 1729–30, Custis undertook a new move. A copy of the will of Daniel Parke, father of the slain Governor of the Leeward Islands, was forwarded by Custis to Antigua. "You will find," he wrote, "the son had but an estate for life and consequently had no power to dispose of anything at his death." Custis went on: "I have had the opinion of most of the eminent lawyers here and of some learned men in England and they seem to make a wonder anyone should make a question that the late Colonel Parke could burden an estate of which he had no right longer than life. All the favor I desire of you is that you will show this will . . . to your lawyer, and [I] must think they will advise you that this estate can no ways be liable for the late Colonel Parke's debts. This may prevent a troublesome, long and chargeable lawsuit. Could I see you, I believe all things would be easy." [71]

This had no more effect than Custis's previous assurances that he

---

[67] John Custis to Dunbar Parke, Jan. 15, 1724; *Custis Letter Book,* No. 25.

[68] Custis styled Daniel Parke as "Colonel" or as "General" with equal frequency. When he referred to Colonel Parke's father it usually was as "old Colonel Parke." The distinction between father and son seldom is difficult to make but reference to the "General" may be deceptive.

[69] John Custis to "Mr. Rodny," n.d. but next to the letter of Jan. 15, 1724, to Dunbar Parke in the *Custis Letter Book* and manifestly of corresponding date. The letter to Rodney is No. 26.

[70] Some of the executors or attorneys may have died.

[71] Letter to unnamed correspondent, Jan. 25, 1729/30; *Custis Letter Book,* No. 57.

would contest the suit to the last penny of his fortune. By the spring of 1731, Custis heard Dunbar Parke had gone to England and had consulted counsel that included Sir Robert Raymond, Lord Chief Justice.[72] Custis countered by sending across the Atlantic no less a person than Sir John Randolph, probably the most distinguished member of the Virginia bar.[73] In due time Randolph saw Dunbar Parke [74] who professed high confidence in the outcome of the suit. So did his chief counsel, William Hopkins of Virginia.[75]

By the autumn of 1732, the plaintiff's bill at last was ready, or nearly so.[76] It asserted that the Antiguan estate was not liable for any of Parke's debts, there or elsewhere, that the English and Virginia properties were liable, and that what had been paid in settlement of other debts of Parke did not absolve the Virginia heirs of liability in the Leeward Islands. All lands that had been purchased in Virginia or in Great Britain by Colonel Parke were alleged to be subject to sale for the dead man's debts. Further, Hopkins maintained that Custis was not entitled in reality to any part of Colonel Parke's estate because Custis had not carried out a testamentary requirement that the son of Frances Parke Custis and John Custis take the name Parke. On this foundation, Hopkins asked an accounting of the estate of Colonel Parke and judgment in the sum of £6000 with which to reimburse the estate in Antigua for the debts paid there. In event this was not done, an order of court for the sale of Parke's Virginia lands was asked.[77]

This bill shook Custis. He professed complete confidence in the outcome,[78] but he leaned heavily on Randolph and, for the first time, hinted at a compromise: "[I] leave all to your prudent management," he wrote, "assuring myself that you will do your utmost for me; but

[72] Actually, by that time, Sir Robert had been raised to the peerage as Baron Raymond of Abbot's Langley. For Custis's information concerning the plaintiff's action, see John Custis to Charles Higgs, Apr. 4, 1731; *Custis Letter Book*, No. 67. Among other reasons for going to England, Dunbar Parke hoped to collect a claim of Colonel Parke's estate against the island of Antigua. *Journal Trade and Plantations*, 1728–34, p. 386; entry of May 6, 1729.

[73] See John Custis to Micajah Perry, 1732, n.d.; *Custis Letter Book*, No. 74.

[74] The Virginia heirs and their counsel usually styled him Thomas Dunbar. Unless this is remembered, personalities become hopelessly confused.

[75] John Randolph to John Custis, Dec. 29, 1732; *Custis Papers*, VHS. For Hopkins, see 1 R 122 ff and 32 V 351.

[76] John Randolph wrote Custis, Dec. 29, 1732, *loc. cit.*, in a manner to indicate that the bill was to be filed with the General Court at the session in April, 1733; but Custis wrote Randolph, Sept. 5, 1732, as if he either had seen "Mr. Hopkins' most dreadful bill" or knew part of its contents.

[77] The amount is given in Custis to [Mrs. Pepper?], n.d., *Custis Letter Book*, No. 71. A summary of part of the bill is in Dunbar's petition, n.d., 1755; P.R.O., P.C. 2: 105, f 531 ff. Remaining parts of the bill have been reconstructed from Custis's letters.

[78] Letter to "Fitchwilliams," 1732, n.d.; *Custis Letter Book*, No. 73.

if you meet Dunbar and can make the matter up so secure that I shall never have farther trouble, I will go as far as £500 rather than take a voyage to England which I cannot see how I can avoid, let it go how it will here." [79]

"[The case]," he subsequently wrote "has been ripe for trial several times, and then some of the parties have died, which abated the suit." [80] William Hopkins and Dunbar Parke both came to their end in 1734, [81] but the plaintiff left issue and a belligerent brother in the person of Charles Dunbar, Surveyor General of the Leeward Islands. This worthy prepared to renew the suit ostensibly to protect the interest of his brother's children but actually, the Virginia heirs thought, to see if he could recover anything on a debt the estate of Thomas Dunbar owed him. [82] This was all the more vicious, in the eyes of Parke's legitimate family, because Charles Dunbar was believed to be one of those responsible for the murder of Colonel Parke. "I am no prophet nor the son of a prophet," William Byrd wrote, "and yet I have a very strong impression that whosoever brings so cruel a suit as this would be against Colonel Parke's children (who would not gain one farthing by their father's will if they must pay his West India debt), will never live to see the end of it." So determined were Byrd and Custis to settle the issue that Byrd wondered whether Mrs. Dunbar Parke might not be "prevailed upon" to oppose the suit of her brother-in-law. [83]

Revival of the suit was delayed by the failure of some of the Dunbar executors to qualify. [84] Another postponement doubtless was caused in 1737 by the death of Custis's chief counsel, Sir John Randolph. He was succeeded, at length, by John Mercer, [85] who believed he could win the case but found apparently that the combination of chancery procedure and distant opponents was one that defied all attempts to get an early decision from a General Court that met twice a year and twice only. John Custis wrote in 1741: "I am so crazy that I never expect to live to see the end of it. Chancery lawsuits are not determined in a hurry, though the suit is carried on as fast as the rules of law will

[79] Letter of Sept. 5, 1732; *Custis Letter Book*, No. 75.

[80] Letter to Peter Collinson, 1741, n.d.; *Custis Letter Book*, No. 129.

[81] For Hopkins's death, see 1 R 123. Dunbar Parke's will was dated Nov. 27, 1734 (P.R.O., P.C. 2: 105, f 534); his demise was prior to February, 1735 (9 V 245).

[82] John Custis to unnamed correspondent, 1741, n.d.; *Custis Letter Book*, No. 129.

[83] Byrd to "Captain Parke," Feb. 3, 1735; 9 V 245.

[84] P.R.O., P.C. 2: 105, f 534.

[85] In his letter of Jan. 4, 1758 to Martha Custis, he mentioned "the trouble I was at during the sixteen years I was concerned with the cause." At the time he wrote, he was negotiating the fee that was to be paid him.

permit. I hope providence will protect my son when I am gone to my long silence." [86]

Pending that, John Custis continued to lead a singular life in Williamsburg. He owned a tract of about four acres on Francis Street,[87] which later was described as "one of the most retired and agreeable situations" in the little town.[88] There he occupied a brick residence with two rooms and a passage on its main floor, "as strong and high a house," Custis maintained, "as any in the government." [89] He had the usual outbuildings,[90] but his delight was in the shrubs and evergreens of his garden, the hobby of an erratic life.[91]

Along with his flowers and his trees, he was mindful of the prospective marriages of his daughter Frances and his son Daniel Parke. The father was not averse to a gamble by his children in the game he had lost, but he was ambitious and fastidious. Frances had many offers and at length accepted a merchant to whom her father promised and then refused to pay £1000.[92] The husband so resented this that he left Frances and cut her off completely when he died within the year.[93] This was a blow to the father who had said some years previously that his children were "all the comfort [he] had in the world." [94]

[86] Letter to Peter Collinson, 1741, n.d.; *Custis Letter Book*, No. 129.

[87] Then often styled merely the "back street." Cf. *Va. Gazette*, Sept. 12, 1755.

[88] *Va. Gazette*, Dixon and Hunter, Nov. 27, 1778. Had Nassau Street been continued southward through what later was the property of the Eastern State Hospital, the Custis tract would lie at the southeast corner of Francis and Nassau Streets. The Custis House subsequently was known as "Six Chimneys" or the "Six-Chimney House" (see Williamsburg tax records of 1818, and *Southall Papers*, 179; *Colonial Williamsburg Papers*). Often confused with this residence was the "Custis Tenement," at the northeast corner of Palace Green and Duke of Gloucester Street. John Custis's deed for this, Apr. 9, 1714, is in the library of the College of William and Mary; a floor plan is among the *Custis Papers*, VHS; a copy of a lease for the three years, executed May 24, 1746, to John Wheatley, is included in the records of Colonial Williamsburg, Inc., after an original owned by Mrs. Hunter de Butts. According to a floor plan in the *Custis Papers*, VHS, this building provided one room, a loft and a yard for each of four families. The tenement stood until January, 1776. Then, while occupied by American troops, it caught fire, through the negligence of the men, and burned to the ground. See Edmund Randolph to Washington, Jan. 26, 1776; *Emmett Col.*, NYPL.

[89] This was apropos of a storm in the summer of 1724 so severe that Custis had to put on high boots to get, as he said, to the leeward side of his dwelling. See John Custis to unknown correspondent, Aug. 12, 1724; *Custis Letter Book*, No. 23.

[90] One of which has survived as "Martha Custis's Kitchen." The house was used in 1773 as the shop of a coach and chair maker. See *Va. Gazette*, Rind's, Apr. 29, 1773, and *Va. Gazette*, Purdie and Dixon's, Aug. 19, 1773. A brief description of the property is given in the advertisement of an approaching sale, *Va. Gazette*, Dixon and Hunter, Nov. 27, 1778.

[91] Many references to his importations occur in his Letter Book. See *supra*, Vol. I, p. 95. In his MS *Recollections of Williamsburg*, John S. Charles noted that as late as approximately 1861, many holly and cedar trees remained on the property and attracted great flocks of birds. Records of Colonial Williamsburg, Inc.

[92] Her husband, to whom she was united in January, 1739, was William Winch. See *Va. Gazette*, June 29, 1739, quoted in 15 V 303.

[93] See his will in 15 V 302–03.

[94] John Custis to Mrs. Parke Pepper, 1731, n.d.; *G. W. P. Custis*, 18–19 n.

Frances married again but died in 1744 without issue by either of her husbands.[95]

His daughter's misadventure made the elder Custis all the more cautious about the marriage of his son, Daniel Parke. If the young man thought his affection so nearly fixed on any young lady that a settlement was properly to be discussed with the girl's father, Colonel Custis always drew back. He did this even in the case of a prospective match between Daniel and a daughter of William Byrd.[96] Haggling and hesitation went so far that William Byrd had finally to dismiss the young man with the unpleasant statement that while Daniel was preferred to all the suitors, the Byrds could not trust to "such a phantom as Colonel Custis's generosity." [97] The peculiarities of the senior Custis went so far that for years he would not entrust his son with the management of a farm. When at last he did so, he became infuriated because Daniel asked him to provide some clothing and shoes for the Negroes on White House plantation, New Kent County, where, of course, the young man had no money until he could raise and sell a crop of tobacco.[98] Daniel proved to be a careful and observant farm manager,[99] and he won the sympathy and support of those of his elders who had influence—if any did—with his father. John Blair had written earlier to Daniel: ". . . I will not yet despair to see you blest in a sweet companion for life with all the endearments that attend the estate when most happy. But—patience yet awhile." [100]

Obediently Daniel deferred to his father's prejudices, parsimony and alternate displays of affection and of wrath. His thirty-seventh birthday found him still a bachelor, though some of his contemporaries then had sons old enough to be thinking of matrimony. In 1749, Daniel Parke Custis fell in love with Martha Dandridge, aged 18, daughter of John and Frances Jones Dandridge of New Kent. The father of Martha was one of the four sons of an immigrant merchant.[101]

[95] See the deposition of Edward Randolph; P.R.O., C.O. 5: 1328, f 181. Her second husband may have been the "Captain Dausie," actually Dansie, mentioned by Mrs. R. E. Lee in G. W. P. Custis, 18.

[96] Mrs. Lee in G. W. P. Custis, 18–19. [97] Ibid., p. 19.

[98] John Blair, evidently to D. P. Custis, n.d., Penn. HS, Autograph Letters, Elting Coll., 60. This letter evidently is of 1737 or earlier, because Va. Gazette, Aug. 19, 1737 contained description of a monster cucumber—" a yard in length and nearly 14 inches round the thickest part"—grown "in the garden of Mr. Daniel Parke Custis in New Kent County."

[99] See D. P. Custis to Coleburn, June 15, 1756; Gratz MSS, Penn. HS, concerning axes and other iron ware.

[100] Letter probably of Mch. 13, 1744, but the last numeral is not certain. Penn. HS. Autograph Letters, Elting Coll., 60.

[101] The first name of the immigrant Dandridge is believed to have been William. See 15 V 430–31; 32 V 237–38, 400; 5 W (1) p. 31. The date of Martha Dandridge's birth often is given as May 2, 1732, but the family Bible fixes it as "June 2, 1731, between 12 and 1 o'clock." 5 W (1) p. 30.

Martha's mother, Frances Jones, was a daughter of Orlando Jones and of his wife Martha, daughter of Gideon Macon.[102] The girl was one of the fairest and most amiable of her society, but by no means one of the wealthiest.

Daniel knew that his father was acquainted with Martha, but he did not know what would be the attitude of Colonel Custis, whose eccentricities were daily more marked and, in some ways, alarming. The head of the house had developed, in particular, an inexplicable fancy for a little slave boy named Jack, and once, after a madly unreasoning outburst of temper against Daniel, actually was believed to have made a will in which he left nothing to his children and his entire estate to the small Negro. With much difficulty—at least it was so whispered—he had been prevailed upon to revoke the will, but he manumitted Jack [103] and kept him the household favorite.

As Daniel had been unintentionally the cause of this episode, he did not think it prudent to face his father with a request for approval to marry Martha Dandridge; so he called again on John Blair, who was Deputy Auditor General and a member of the Council. Blair, in turn, invoked the aid of Thomas Lee.[104] Both these celebrities found the senior Custis wholly opposed to the marriage one day and at another time not altogether averse to it. His chief complaints were that Daniel did not discuss the subject with him fully, and, second, that he did not intend to do anything for the Dandridges, to whom he patently felt himself superior.[105] The advice of Blair and of Lee was that Daniel either tell his father frankly that he wished to make Martha Dandridge his wife or else that he marry her and take the chances the father would accept what could not be undone.

Daniel was afraid to try this. He awaited what seemed to be an auspicious hour and then he entrusted the delicate mission to his friend and attorney, James Power.[106] That gentleman proved himself a skilled if a somewhat expensive diplomatist. When he opened the subject of his negotiations to Colonel Custis, who doubtless was then in Williamsburg,[107] he found the father not only sympathetic but en-

---

[102] 10 V 412.

[103] Mrs. Lee (G. W. P. Custis, 20 n) stated that Jack's mother, Alice, also was set free, but Custis's will, infra, n. 114, does not so indicate. Jack's manumission is recorded in 6 York Records, 63; the date is Feb. 15, 1747/48.

[104] That is to say, the dates and the tone of Blair's references to "Colonel Lee" appear to fit Thomas Lee better than any other member of the family.

[105] See Blair to D. P. Custis, Apr. 9, 1749, Elting Coll., loc. cit., 59; same to same, ibid., 60. See also the answer of Matthew and Anne Moody to D. P. Custis, infra, p. 296.

[106] Power's letter, mentioned infra, is signed merely J. Power, but the emissary could scarcely have been any other than James, Burgess from New Kent County.

[107] See 23 V 369.

thusiastic also. He had rather have Daniel marry Martha, the Colonel affirmed, that any other young lady in Virginia. Her character, he maintained, enamoured him as much as her person attracted Daniel. This, Custis explained, was because of a prudent speech she had made.

Power was relieved, of course, and scarcely less pleased when the old gentleman invited him to spend the night, apparently an honor the Colonel did not extend to many guests. The emissary took no chances. Playing on Custis's notorious weakness for the Negro boy, Power explicitly and ceremoniously in Daniel's name gave Jack a horse, saddle and bridle that belonged, in actual fact, to Power's own son. This regal present seemed to confirm Custis's good humor and doubtless entranced Jack. What was said by Master Power Jr. on his father's return the next day is not a matter of record, but Power Sr. survived the interview, wrote Daniel a note conveying the good news and advised: "Hurry down immediately for fear [your father] should change the strong inclination he has to your marrying directly." [108]

Daniel proceeded, received full confirmation of his father's assent, and in due time married Martha.[109] He took her to the White House plantation, which was on the Pamunkey River, and there in spite of lawsuit and the crotchets of Father Custis, he led with her a happy and opulent life. It was distinctly easier in almost every way after John Custis made a new will on Nov. 14, 1749, and then obligingly died before he changed his mind again.[110] His death, November 22, may have been hastened by worry over the Dunbar suit, which had been set for hearing in April, 1750.[111]

Colonel Custis provided most bountifully for the Negro boy Jack. The executors were to build for the lad a "handsome, strong convenient dwelling house," near the head of Queens Creek. This was to be constructed according to plans that were to be drawn under Custis's direction by John Blair, and was to be furnished with two dozen Russian leather chairs, a couch, "good and strong" feather beds,[112] furniture and a black walnut table. Fencing was to be kept up and the property and appurtenances maintained in good order. Until Jack was seventeen,

---

[108] J. Power to D. P. Custis, n.d.; *G. W. P. Custis,* 20.

[109] The year was 1749 but the date is not known.

[110] The letter of R. Cary to D. P. Custis, Mch. 1, 1749, *Custis Papers,* VHS, might leave the impression that Custis died in 1748, but Cary evidently failed to write "1749/50." Custis resigned from the Council, Aug. 25, 1749, on account of ill-health (5 *E. J.,* 299, 312; *Journ. Commrs. Trade and Plantations,* 1750–53, p. 35, 106).

[111] For the date of the proposed hearing, see P.R.O., P.C. 2: 105, f 534.

[112] It is possible that "good and strong" was meant to apply to the couch and not to the beds. Punctuation is almost completely lacking.

he was to live under the supervision of Daniel Parke Custis, with liberal provision from the estate left Jack. At twenty, the boy was to take direction of his house and farm,[113] which was to be stocked adequately. Jack was to have a free life interest in this property, which, on his death, was to revert to Daniel Parke Custis. With a final, mocking touch, the old man provided that Jack's portrait be preserved. No provision was made for the boy's mother, who was mentioned only as "my slave Alice." [114]

To another favorite of Custis's, the wife of a nearby farmer, Matthew Moody, £20 were bequeathed, to be paid "annually during her natural life." [115] The residue of the estate was left in fee simple [116] to Daniel Parke Custis.

John Custis revenged himself, also, in a strange manner on the long-dead wife with whom he so often and so violently had quarreled. In his will, he provided that his tombstone be erected at Arlington, his Eastern Shore plantation, and that the inscription should be precisely in the language he set forth. Failure to comply with the letter of his instructions would involve forfeiture of the estate. This was the inscription:

UNDER THIS MARBLE TOMB LIES THE BODY
OF THE HON. JOHN CUSTIS, ESQ.,
OF THE CITY OF WILLIAMSBURG
AND PARISH OF BRUTON.
FORMERLY OF HUNGAR'S PARISH ON THE
EASTERN SHORE
OF VIRGINIA, AND COUNTY OF NORTHAMPTON,
AGED 71 YEARS, AND YET LIVED BUT SEVEN YEARS,
WHICH WAS THE SPACE OF TIME HE KEPT
A BACHELOR'S HOME AT ARLINGTON
ON THE EASTERN SHORE OF VIRGINIA

[113] Part of the will, in fragments, is among the *Custis Papers*, VHS; the full text is in H. F. Waters, *Genealogical Gleanings in England*, v. 1, p. 393–95.

[114] There is a possibility, of course, that by some transaction of which no record survives he made provision for her during his lifetime.

[115] In view of the suit that D. P. Custis subsequently brought against Matthew and Anne Moody (see next page), it seems likely that Custis had ordered for Mrs. Moody certain goods from England, "chiefly millinery" which the merchant Robert Cary Sr. considerately wrote D. P. Custis, Mch. 11, 1749/50, he was not including in a shipment made according to instructions previously received from the elder Custis. The letter of Cary is in *Custis Papers*, VHS.

[116] Barring this item: "I give and devise unto John Cavendish, for the many services he has done me, the house and lot where he now lives to hold the same rent free during his natural life."

On the opposite or rear panel of the tomb was to be:

THIS INSCRIPTION PUT ON HIS TOMB WAS BY HIS OWN POSITIVE ORDERS

Daniel Parke Custis had to execute this order, with the ugly implied slur upon the memory of his mother; but in the amplitude of his fortune he did not have to reside where he had to look at the scornful words. Other phases of the settlement of the estate [117] were troublesome enough. Suits had to be entered against those indebted to John Custis at the time of his death.[118] Examination of the contents of the house in Williamsburg showed, moreover, that much of John Custis's plate and some of his jewelry were missing—a pair of gold shoe buckles, some buttons and rings, a silver pint can, a marrow spoon, two silver dishes and six silver plates.

If he did not know it already, Daniel Parke Custis soon learned that his father had made many presents to Matthew and Anne Moody, and, after inquiry, he found that the articles which had disappeared from the silver closet were in their possession. They asserted vigorously that Custis had given them all these and many things besides, and that the gold buckles had been engraved by Custis's order as presented to Mrs. Moody in his memory. In spite of this, Daniel Parke Custis decided to sue for the return of the silver and jewelry.

For his pains, he received an answer in the course of which Mrs. Moody explained that John Custis had called her to his house and, before two witnesses, had presented her with the silver dishes and the six plates. She had demurred and had told him he had better give them to his son, as they were articles for which she would have little or no use. Thereupon, Mrs. Moody set forth:

John Custis told her she was an old fool and that unless she would take them he would throw them into the street for anybody to pick up that had a mind for them; that if they were his own he could dispose of them as he pleased; that he had rather this defendant should have them than any Dandridge's daughter or any Dandridge that ever wore a head. He said he had not been at work all his lifetime for Dandridge's daughter, illuding, as this defendant thought to the daughter of Mr. John Dandridge of New Kent

---

117 No appraisal or inventory has been found.
118 See, e.g., the judgment against Augustus Claiborne, July 20, 1752; *York Orders*, 1752–54, p. 76.

county to whom the complainant, as this defendant heard about that time, was making his addresses by way of courtship, for which match this defendant had at several times heard the said John Custis express a very great dislike, imagining, as this defendant has understood, that the said Mr. Dandridge's daughter was much inferior to his son, the complainant, in point of fortune . . .[119]

In dealing with a litigant of this temper, it was better to compromise than to contend. Daniel Parke Custis consequently agreed through counsel to settle Mrs. Moody's bequest by paying her regularly the sum of £20 per annum.[120]

Besides litigation, Daniel Parke Custis had the usual vexations over runaway Negroes [121] and probably something less than the average planter's troubles with managers and overseers.[122] One difficulty he was spared—that of making provision of bed and board and later of house and farm for Jack. The little Negro died suddenly in September, 1751, of "a pain in the back of the neck, for which he was blooded." [123] For this and numerous other reasons, Daniel Parke Custis now found life more pleasant than ever with his good-tempered young wife in the fertile valley of the Pamunkey. The heir of Parkes and Custises held no less than 17,438 acres on modest quit rents,[124] and he undertook to raise superior tobacco and to bundle and to prize it with care.[125] He operated fisheries; [126] he drained his marshes [127] and leased swamp land for the run of horses; he rented farms to tenants and he shared crops.[128] Custis never became a Burgess but he had another of the usual honors of a great planter, that of being a warden of his parish,[129] with which, as it chanced, Parkes and Custises and Dandridges had all been con-

119 Fragment of what evidently was the written answer of Matthew and Anne Moody to the bill of complaint of Daniel Parke Custis, in the *Custis Papers*, VHS. No judgment in this case has been found.

120 The last of these payments was receipted June 8, 1751 (*Custis Papers*, VHS).

121 See his advertisement in *Va. Gazette*, Dec. 12, 1755.

122 His contract of Nov. 4, 1755 with Joseph Valentine, in *Custis Papers*, VHS, is mentioned in Vol I, p. 140.

123 Blair's diary, 7 *W* (1) p. 152.

124 See John Blair's receipt of May 8, 1758; *Custis Papers*, VHS. This total doubtless included the Custis plantation of 3300 acres near Williamsburg. For its acreage, see *Md. Journal*. Sept. 22, 1778, copied by Colonial Williamsburg, Inc. See also Blair's diary, 8 *W* (1) p. 6.

125 See his letters of May 5, 1755 and June 16, 1756 to Cary & Co., and of July 13, 1756 to Gildart (Penn. Hist. Soc., Autograph Letters, *Elting Coll.*, 29, 30, 33).

126 Cf. John Case's receipt to Martha Custis, May 20, 1758, of payment for mending and hanging seine (*Custis Papers*, VHS).

127 Cf. agreement of May 10, 1756, with Edward Lovely, *Elting Coll., loc cit.*, 32.

128 See receipt of a share-cropper, Charles Whitlock, Dec. 12, 1758; see also a fragment of a somewhat inclusive account of "profits received by Mrs. Custis," n.d. (*Custis Papers*, VHS).

129 He was elected to the vestry of St. Peter's Church in 1740 and became warden that same year (*Vestry Book* of St. Peter's, New Kent, 261–62).

nected.[130] The good looks which even his father had conceded he possessed [131] he set off with fine clothes from a Williamsburg tailor,[132] and with furnishings from London, where, of course, Martha bought freely of the market's best ribbons and laces and silks and stomachers.[133] Besides fine horses, Custis kept a chair and a chariot,[134] and visited often in Williamsburg.[135]

His funds, though large, did not suffice for him to meet all the applications of his friends for loans. To John Mercer he wrote: "I thought or at least hoped, that I had satisfied you that I had not near the quantity of money as you and others imagine. I am sure I have not increased my stock very much since, and I have the same complaint to make as you have, having a great sum of money out and cannot get any in. There are several gentlemen that have lately applied to me for money, one of which is of the Council, which made me make a very solemn determination that I would never meddle with a farthing I have in England until my lawsuit there was over, which, if it should go against me, all that I have in the whole world would scarcely do . . ." [136]

That was the possibility that sometimes darkened life for Daniel Parke Custis. Children had been born to Martha. The first and the second babies, Daniel Parke and Frances, had died in childhood. A second son, John Parke, born early in 1754, was making friends with the horses; the fourth child, a dark-haired girl, had been born in 1755 and had been named Martha. Other daughters and sons might be added, because the young mother was healthy. Everything would be well for another and still another generation of Parke-Custises in Virginia if . . . if . . . that Dunbar suit was decided in favor of the legitimate issue of Daniel Parke. To lose that case would be to lose all!

So far as the litigation could be decided in Virginia, trial was delayed by the death of John Custis, against whom, as chief defendant, the bill

---

130 John Parke was a vestryman in 1685, and John Dandridge in 1735. Custis's servants had been baptized there in 1709–13 (ibid., 2, 241, 348). Daniel Parke Custis was active in providing a steeple for the church in 1742. See receipt of Rev. D. Mossom, Sept. 29, 1742; Custis Papers, VHS.

131 See John Custis to Mrs. Pepper, 1734, n.d.: ". . . you never saw any two persons more alike than he is like his grandfather Parke . . ." (Custis Letter Book, No. 87). The portraits of D. P. Custis, of his wife and of their two children by John Wollaston were paid for Oct. 11, 1757 (Custis Papers, VHS).

132 See George Heath's account of 1756; Custis Papers, VHS.

133 See her invoices of Jan. 25, 1753; Dec. 7, 15, 1754; Elting Coll., loc. cit., 40, 41, 43.

134 Tax receipt of Sam Jones, Apr. 7, 1758; Custis Papers, VHS.

135 Cf. Blair's diary, 7 W (1) p. 137, 138, 141, 149; 8 ibid., 6, 12, 14.

136 Letter of Nov. 2, 1754, to John Mercer, copied in John Mercer to Martha Custis, Jan. 4, 1758; Custis Papers, VHS.

had been drawn. In October, 1750, the Dunbar heirs renewed the suit against all those whose interests seemed to be affected. In accordance with the usual deliberation in chancery causes, Custis did not file his answer until Nov. 3, 1753. Then he denied liability in general terms and specifically demurred on the ground that the parties to the action were not correctly and fully named.[137] Hearing was set for November 3 but was postponed. At last, on April 10, 1754, the General Court sustained the demurrer, dismissed the bill and entered the charges against the Dunbar heirs—a triumph for Parke's legitimate issue, twenty-five years after Dunbar Parke first had threatened suit.[138] Appeal to England was promptly made by the Antiguan plaintiffs. Sometime in the early summer of 1755, Custis heard that the Privy Council had allowed the petition, as of April 3, and had referred the case to the Lords of Council for hearing appeals from the plantations.[139] The motion specifically was that the Virginia decree be reversed, with costs charged against Custis, that the demurrer be overruled, and that Custis be ordered to answer Dunbar's demand for payment.[140] This, of course, involved more delay and prolonged uncertainty.

Nothing decisive had been heard about the case when June, 1757, ended and the rich month of July opened. About the 4th, Daniel Parke Custis fell ill and developed symptoms that defied home medication. Dr. James Carter of Williamsburg, one of the best-known physicians and apothecaries of the town,[141] was summoned and was at Custis's bedside on the 5th. Effort and vigil were vain. Custis died on July 8, 1757, at the age of 45 years and nine months.[142] His widow, who was only 26, proceeded in a methodical way to make the arrangements for his funeral, though her boy John was sick at the time.[143] She had Charles Crump provide a black walnut coffin, which he brought to the White House and lined appropriately;[144] a seamstress hastily altered a

---

[137] P.R.O., P.C. 2: 105, f 534.
[138] *Ibid* and 4 *Acts Privy Council*, Col. ser. XVI, p. 288–90, 531.
[139] *Ibid.*
[140] *Ibid.*
[141] He is mentioned many times in Blanton and was much commended, in particular, for treating smallpox patients at the college in an outbreak there in 1768 (*op. cit.*, 63).
[142] The suddenness of the attack is indicated by the absence of bills for medical attendance prior to July 5. Dr. Carter's entries for two days' service and the inscription that Martha carefully prepared for her husband's tombstone fix the date of death (*Custis Invoices*, LC). Dr. Wyndham Blanton and Dr. Allen W. Freeman, reviewing the medication and the known facts, agree that no "cause of death" can be established; but both think a heart attack the most likely explanation of the death at that season, after so brief an illness, of a man of 45. See n. 147, *infra.*
[143] See Carter's bill, *supra.*
[144] See his receipt, Mch. 6, 1758 in *Custis Papers*, VHS.

WASHINGTON'S READY–MADE FAMILY

Col. Daniel Parke was so proud of his name that he wanted all his issue to bear it—his illegitimate as well as his lawful children.

He may have been facetious when he called a natural son "Julius Cæsar" but he wrote "Parke" after that name in his will. In the same document he insisted that his Antiguan daughter, born out of wedlock, take the name Parke or else forfeit the fortune he left her.

It was to be the same with the descendants of his wife: They must all be Parke. The men who married his daughters were too proud to do this; but John Custis, who had lived unhappily with Frances Parke, became a bit uneasy after the probate of Colonel Parke's will. Although he did not change Custis to Parke, he probably communicated his fears to his son Daniel Parke Custis, who gave all four of his children the middle name Parke.

So, on the opposite page, are John *Parke* Custis and Martha *Parke* Custis, the surviving children, as John Wollaston painted them in 1757. They were not much older than they here appear when, in 1758, they became Washington's ready-made family. Their short lives became a part of his; their portrait hangs on a wall of one of the institutions that bears his name, Washington and Lee University, by permission of which the picture is reproduced here.

An invoice to ordering a Coting ghting for the year 1758
one suit of Cloths for my self

one Genteel suit of Cloths for my self to be grave but
not Extravagent not to mourning

I have sent a suit of y pound to be dide of and I have not
Cloths fitt for me to ware and to you would have
it dide better then that I send you a bitt it was very
oddly don this gound is of a woolden that for
one p^r Toby stays for my self I have sent a measure
and beg they may be well shaped and of stiff Bone
& that will keep a there shape I would have my
gounds made to my stays as I had a buff last year
I have no ocation for one now the more to make
I can tell the time to make my Cloths by
also Too of the best Indian gounds to make
one Darke ground thigh leags
one fine white Callaco gound to be made of my fine call
one handsome suit of Dresdon worked head Cloth
Dresdon worked hankerchief one p^r of plain lawn
4 Indean worked hankerchief to cost 5s 10 shilling a peice
one peice of fine plain Lawn half doz not in Best
one peice of fine Cambrick no stf
2 frocks to fitt a girl of three years old
p^o 2 p^r fine paced shoes stays & gon Do to be covered with Red Leather
and a coat to them a handsome stiff quffes and tucker
p^o 2 p^r silk shoes for Do to be Laced
p^o 4 p^r Calla manca for Do & others for Do
p^o 2 fans for Do 2 necklaces for Do
p^o the yeard of Ribbon for Do
p^o 6 p^r white kid mittens for Do

MARTHA SENDS A SOMEWHAT INTIMATE INVOICE

Martha Dandridge Custis "loved clothes." There was no denying that and, within somewhat wide limits of pounds and shillings, no reason for curbing it. So long as the rich Custis estates continued to yield large crops of tobacco, she assuredly could have what she wanted in the way of dress.

This did not mean that she failed to make the most of what she bought. On the contrary, if the color of a good garment wearied the eye after a season, the article could be packed, sent back to England to be dyed, and the second year received again in Virginia virtually as new.

All this was in Martha's mind when she drew up the invoice of which the rough draft appears on the opposite page. It was not a task a lady usually performed, but Martha was a widow now and had to handle her own affairs.

First things of interest came first in the invoice: "One genteel suite of clothes for my self to be grave but not extravagent and not mourning." Next—somewhat intimately—"I have sent a night gown to be dide of an fashionable couler fitt for me to ware and beg you wont [will?] have it dide better than that I sent you last year but was very badly done This gown is of a good length for me."

There is no date on this other than that it is "an invoice . . . for the year 1758," the year Washington came to court. Had he "made his addresses"? Was that the reason the "genteel suite" was not to be "mourning" and the night-gown was to be "dide"?

The original is among the Custis Papers of the Virginia Historical Society. Reproduction is by permission of the Executive Committee of that organization.

gown to serve for mourning.[145] Custis then was buried by friends and servants.[146]

He died without a will[147] and thereby of course put upon Martha the full responsibility of administering the estate and of serving as guardian for her two children, John and Martha. She undertook the task with little experience but with abundant common sense. On affairs of law, she promptly consulted attorneys she knew to be competent and trustworthy because her husband had relied on them. In many matters, she followed the forms her husband had used, and she painstakingly drafted and revised her letters to merchants and other correspondents until they were explicit and adequate.[148] She was careful, too, in taking receipts even for small sums paid out on account of the estate,[149] though she soon found she could entrust this detail to her husband's manager, Joseph Valentine.[150]

Returns from Custis's merchants showed that Robert Cary & Co. of London had £3697 to the credit of the estate.[151] The Hanburys, another London firm, had by the spring of 1758 balances and new credits that amounted to at least £1800,[152] but this second sum Martha soon was to exhaust in paying accumulated obligations and some of the legal costs of the Dunbar case.[153] The estate as a whole was appraised tentatively at £23,632.[154]

That is to say, this was the net of the estate without regard to the

145 Receipt of Elizabeth Vaughan, Aug. n.d., 1757 (ibid.). The receipt does not state that the alterations were for mourning, but the date and the circumstance make that certain.

146 The place of interment has not been established. Daniel Parke Custis's mother and two of his children were buried in the graveyard of the Custis estate in York County, near Williamsburg, which graveyard probably was on or close to the site of old Marston Church. See 4 W (1) p. 66, for a note on the removal of the gravestones and remains of these three to Bruton churchyard. For Marston Church and parish, see 1 H 381, 387, 388; 3 W (1) p. 171; 3 T 300. There is, of course, a possibility that he may have been buried in Northampton County (see 3 W (1) p. 258 and supra, n. 53); but Dr. E. G. Swem, who has made a detailed study of the question, is satisfied that Custis was interred with his mother and two small children in the graveyard of the Custis estate.

147 Martha Custis to Robert Cary, Aug. 20, 1757; draft in Custis Papers, VHS. For the appraisal order in James City County, Aug. 11, Sept. 15, 1757, see Elting Coll., loc. cit., 31. As D. P. Custis manifestly was mindful of his family, the fact that he died intestate is collateral evidence that his last illness was sudden and so severe that he could not make a will.

148 See, for example, her letter of Aug. 20, 1757, to Robert Cary & Co., a much-corrected draft; Custis Papers, VHS.

149 E.g., her receipt from John Rone, Aug. 12, 1757, for 3s 6d; Custis Papers, VHS.

150 Cf. account of Robert Stephenson. Mch. 8, 1758; Custis Papers, VHS.

151 Their letter of Nov. 26, 1757, to Martha Custis is in the Custis Papers, VHS.

152 This estimate is based on a tattered draft of Martha Custis's letter of June 1, 1758, to Hanbury, in which she listed the bills of exchange she had drawn. It is not known how much of the total represented the tobacco crop of 1757. She had shipped seventeen hogsheads of this in April.

153 Ibid. She paid £500 in a bill of exchange to John Mercer, her chief counsel in Virginia.

154 See "Summary of the Account of D. P. Custis" in the handwriting of John Mercer. This is marked "1757" but the date is not in Mercer's autograph; Custis Papers, VHS.

Dunbar case; but the London mail that reached Virginia in the late summer brought dire news to the young widow and her children. Under date of July 16, 1757, Hanbury wrote that a final order in Council at last had been entered: After a committee hearing on June 24, the Privy Council on July 3 reversed the Virginia decision and, in effect, remanded the case to the Colony for a hearing on the determina- of the proper plaintiffs.[155] Martha's lawyers were outraged but still were disposed to urge that Lucy Chester's interest be bought out, or that suit be entered in Antigua.[156] Of course, Martha accepted their assurances on a question she did not begin to comprehend, but still . . . the case might drag out for another thirty years, while interest would be accumulating on an adverse judgment. Even the White House and the servants and the horses and chariot might not certainly be Martha's and her children's.

That was one view of it. Another was that the estate still was worth £23,000, that Martha was then in her twenty-seventh year, that one-third of all the Custis estate was hers, and that the expenses of her children during their minority were chargeable against their share of the large property their father had left.

Dunbar or no Dunbar, the young widow was among the wealthiest and most desirable in Virginia when the tall young Col. George Washington bowed low to her on the 16th of March, 1758.[157] Washington did not stay more than a day or a day and a half,[158] but as he looked at the lovely Martha and across the broad, rich fields of level land, he resolved to come again. He did so the next week,[159] and when he went back to Williamsburg after that second visit he had either the promise of Martha to marry him or her assurance that she would consider the proposal he made her. Then he finished his business at the capital, rode to Fredericksburg and to Alexandria, paused briefly, and rushed on to Winchester.[160] There he spent his earliest spare hour in ordering from London "by the first ship bound to any part of Virginia . . . as

155 P.R.O., P.C. 2: 105, f 534. Hanbury's letter has disappeared from the *Custis Papers,* VHS, but the reply of Martha Custis, Dec. 20, 1757 (*ibid*), and John Mercer to Martha Custis, Oct. 11, 1758 (*ibid*), make the facts plain.

156 See Mercer to Martha Custis, Oct. 11, 1758; John Mercer to James Power, Nov. 29, 1757, *Custis Papers,* VHS.

157 The date is fixed, with a margin of perhaps twenty-four hours on either side, by the entries of *Ledger A,* folio 38. For a discussion of the probability of an earlier meeting of George Washington and Martha Custis, see Appendix II-1.

158 He was in Williamsburg on the 18th. See 2 *G. W.,* 167.

159 *Ledger A,* folio 38. He probably was there March 25.

160 He may have been in Fredericksburg on the 30th (*Ledger A,* folio 38), and he certainly was at Mount Vernon April 1. See 2 *G. W.,* 168-69.

much of the best superfine blue cotton velvet as will make a coat, waist-coat and breeches for a tall man, with a fine silk button to suit it . . . six pairs of the very neatest shoes . . . [and] six pair gloves . . ."[161] In New Kent, perhaps about the same time, a certain lady was ordering from the same capital of fashion "one genteel suite of cloathes for myself to be grave but not to be extravagant and not to be mourning."[162]

161 Letter to Richard Washington, Apr. 5, 1758; 2 G. W., 170–71.

162 Martha Custis to Cary and Co., 1758, n.d., draft of letter; Custis Papers, VHS, reproduced here.

CHAPTER XVIII

Still Another New Commander

(April–June, 1758)

Much had changed during the five months of Washington's absence from Winchester. First and most conspicuous was the presence of the largest body of Southern Indians that ever had come to support the English in their war against the French. These savages had arrived so early in the year that Washington had feared they would prove an embarrassment. If they were sent against the French Indians soon after they reached the Valley, they would expect to go home when they returned from their raid; and if they could be prevailed upon to stay, the cumulative expense to the Colony would be great.[1] At the time of the Colonel's reopening of his headquarters in Winchester, some 400 savages still were in the town or were roving the country West of the English settlements; an additional 140 were on the way northward from their villages. In spite of the cost, these contingents were to be encouraged to remain, of course; but, once again, Washington was almost as uneasy when he had Indian warriors as he was when he lacked them.

He had lost some of his earlier confidence that he knew how to deal with the natives. Actually, he was more adept than ever he had been in keeping them in tractable temper, but in his heart he was disgusted with them and always was uncertain what their next act would be. Aside from their own unpredictable inclination to leave in a huff when no white man could understand why, there now was a situation which, if known, would provoke them: The powerful Tedyuskung[2] and other Delaware chiefs had proposed a treaty of peace to Governor Denny of Pennsylvania and had so informed the commanding officer at Fort Loudoun, with the request that he notify the Cherokees there.

[1] 2 G. W., 164.
[2] The name is spelled in many ways. This is the form used in the *Handbook of American Indians*.

A council of war, held a few days before Washington's arrival, had concluded that this information would stir the jealousy of the Southern natives and would prompt them to assert suspiciously that England was coming to terms with an enemy who would turn on them and destroy them.[3] This official silence might be wise; there was no assurance it would be effective: The Cherokees might get the news and decamp in anger. Nothing would be sure to hold them, Washington thought, except an early offensive, of which there seemed to be slight prospect.[4]

The second great change Washington found on his return to active duty was in the British command. About the time he had been taken sick in the summer of 1757, Lord Loudoun's proposed expedition against Louisburg had failed so completely that no attempt could be made even to land troops.[5] While Loudoun was at sea, returning to New York, the French under the Marquis de Montcalm had attacked and destroyed Fort William Henry at the lower end of Lake George. Almost the entire garrison had been captured. Several score had been murdered by the Indians after they had surrendered. It was a disaster as humiliating as any that British arms had sustained on the continent in a war that had included already the defeat of Braddock and the loss of Oswego.[6]

Loudoun's plan of campaign manifestly had failed in 1757. What was to be done in 1758? While Washington had been at Mount Vernon, struggling with his malady, the question had been debated on both sides of the Atlantic. William Pitt had been recalled to office June 29, 1757, as a Secretary of State and had been given supreme control of the war and of foreign affairs. When he received the news of failure at Louisburg and of the loss of Fort William Henry, he began to formulate his own plan and awaited critically the proposals of Lord Loudoun, for whom he had no kindly feeling because the General was a supporter of the Duke of Cumberland. Loudoun, for his part, felt that he had not received proper aid from home in the execution of his military designs in 1757, and he resolved to submit no general scheme of operations for the next year.[7] When, therefore, Pitt found no plan set forth in any of Loudoun's dispatches of the early autumn,[8] the Secretary concluded there was truth to rumors he previously had re-

---

[3] Minutes of council of war, Mch. 30, 1758; 3 *Penn. Arch.*, 367–69; 19 *V* 65–68.
[4] 2 *G. W.*, 171–72.
[5] Parkman, *Montcalm and Wolfe*, v. I, p. 485–86.
[6] *Ibid.*, 511 ff. The surrender was on Aug. 9, 1757.
[7] Pargellis, *Loudoun*, 252.
[8] For a summary of what Loudoun actually had in contemplation, see Pargellis, *Loudoun*, 356.

ceived that the General had resolved not to communicate with the ministry. As Pitt subsequently told Loudoun, the situation was one in which he either had to surrender his own duties or relieve the commander in America.[9]

About the middle of December, Pitt decided to make the change. He approved at first the suggestion of Newcastle that the operations in America be under the direction of Sir John Ligonier, who had succeeded the Duke of Cumberland as Commander-in-Chief,[10] but objection was made to this on several grounds.[11] In the end, Pitt left Maj. Gen. James Abercromby as titular head of the forces in America. Nominally in the care of Abercromby but actually under Pitt himself, were to be three expeditions, one against Louisburg as a preliminary to an advance on Quebec, the second against Fort Ticonderoga, and the third against Fort DuQuesne. To command the new attack on Louisburg, Pitt named Jeffrey Amherst, whom he promoted forthwith from Colonel to Major General. With Amherst were to serve three Brigadiers of promise. The thrust for Ticonderoga was to be Abercromby's own particular charge, though Pitt probably hoped it actually would be directed by Lord Howe,[12] a soldier he held in high esteem.[13] For the operation against Fort DuQuesne, Pitt's choice fell on Col. John Forbes, of the 17th Foot, who was made Brigadier General.

Incomplete news of these appointments reached New York on the 4th of March [14] and quickly spread up and down the coast. Colonel Stanwix heard some of the details before the 10th, but he, along with many others, understood the new Commander-in-Chief was to be Lord George Sackville.[15] To Stanwix himself came a step upward to the rank of Brigadier, with orders to share in the campaign on the Lakes.[16] This transfer of Stanwix and the recall of Loudoun meant to Washington that he had to repeat the process of winning the good opinion of new officers who replaced those whose esteem he had acquired. There seemed to be no end to the succession—Fry, Innes, Braddock, Shirley, Sharpe, Loudoun, and now Forbes.

In all these changes, Washington himself had received no recognition

[9] In Loudoun's own words, "either he must not be minister or I could not be General" (Pargellis, *Loudoun,* 347).

[10] Ligonier, a most picturesque French Huguenot, had not then been raised to the peerage.

[11] Pargellis, *Loudoun,* 340–41.

[12] This was George Augustus, third Viscount Howe, one of three brothers who often are confused.

[13] This is merely a paraphrase of Parkman, *Montcalm and Wolfe,* v. 2, p. 51.

[14] See A. P. James, ed., *Writings of General John Forbes* (cited hereafter as *Forbes*), 54.

[15] 2 *Hamilton,* 273.   [16] Cf. 2 *G. W.,* 172 n.

from the home government. So far as Whitehall was concerned, he might as well not exist. There had been no word of official praise, no fulfilment of the hope, long cherished and long frustrated, of a royal commission. Discouraged by this experience, Washington expected no advancement in the new organization, but as always, if he was to serve, he wished distinction, "honor" as he so often had termed it.

He proceeded once again to have himself recommended to the new General—and to have it done promptly. Forbes had assumed command about March 21.[17] In a letter of congratulation that Washington wrote Stanwix on the 10th of April, less than a week after his return to Winchester, he said with complete candor: ". . . I should have thought myself happy in serving this campaign under your immediate command. But everything, I hope, is ordered for the best; and it is our duty to submit to the will of our superior. I must, nevertheless, beg that you will add one more kindness to the many I have experienced, and that is, to mention me in favorable terms to General Forbes (if you are acquainted with that gentleman) and not as a person who would depend upon him for further recommendation to military preferment, for I have long conquered all such expectancies (and serve this campaign merely for the purpose of affording my best endeavors to bring matters to a conclusion) but as a person who would gladly be distinguished in some measure from the *common run* of provincial officers, as I understand there will be a motley herd of us." [18]

Had Washington known more at the time of John Forbes, he would not have been content merely to hope that his new commander would "distinguish him" from "the common run of provincial officers." The Virginian would have realized that whether or not he continued in the profession of arms, he could learn much from Forbes. That officer was 50 years of age, a Scot, born of good blood and first schooled for medicine but drawn to a military career by love of it. He had served with energy in the War of the Austrian Succession and in the Scottish campaign of 1745–46. His special distinction had been as a Quartermaster, a service in which, as Washington well knew, there had been much backwardness and lack of skill throughout the operations in Virginia. Forbes had sought the post of Quartermaster General in Braddock's army and had felt some disappointment when Sir John St. Clair re-

---

[17] *Forbes,* 59, 61.
[18] Letter of Apr. 10, 1758; 2 *G. W.,* 172–73. Washington himself underlined "common run."

ceived it.[19] Then, in March, 1757, Forbes had been given the 17th Foot, which was one of the Regiments sent to reenforce Loudoun for the Louisburg expedition. That officer quickly came to an appreciation of the ability of Forbes and made him Adjutant General. In that position, though not conspicuous, Forbes probably had a hand in the numerous and admirable reforms that Loudoun instituted.[20]

Washington could not have found in America a better instructor in the art of army administration. Nor could he have been associated with a man of greater patience, cheer and cordiality in relations with officers and with men. Forbes was cautious in not wishing to advance a yard until his troops were equipped and supplied, but he was tireless in effort to prepare them. While he never had been proclaimed brilliant, he was able, courageous and thorough.[21] Benjamin Franklin credited a messenger with saying of Lord Loudoun, "He is like St. George on the signs, always on horseback, but never rides on." [22] It could have been said of Forbes that he was not apt to mount till he was ready to move.

Transfer of command to this interesting man was, to repeat, the second new condition Washington found on his return to Winchester in April, 1758, and manifestly it had importance at least equal that of the first new condition, the presence of a large force of friendly Indian warriors. A third change was in Washington's military status. When he had served in Braddock's campaign, he had acted as a staff officer, not as a commander of infantry, though he had to rush in and try to direct troops on the dreadful field of the Monongahela. As chief of the Virginia Regiment in 1755–57, he had been subject in theory to British officers and in reality to Dinwiddie's direction, but most of the time, and both to his gratification and distress of mind, he had been Commander-in-Chief. Now he was to have a Regiment of infantry, as previously, but he was to serve "in the line" under any Colonel or Brigadier of the regular establishment who might be designated.

Nor was Washington to be Virginia's sole Colonel, at the head of her only Regiment. The General Assembly had met almost on the eve of

---

[19] See John Forbes to Hugh Forbes, Oct. 19, 1754; Forbes, 1. Those who are interested in the "might-have-beens" of history may find this a theme for mental speculation: Would the outcome of the campaign of 1755 have been different if Forbes, rather than the bungling, ill-tempered St. Clair, had been Quartermaster?

[20] A considerable part of Pargellis's valuable Lord Loudoun in America is devoted to an analysis of these reforms.

[21] The fullest sketch of a life concerning which there is singularly little information is that of A. P. James in Forbes.

[22] 1 Franklin's Writings (Bigelow), 299.

his departure for Winchester, and, in a session that ended April 12,[23] had passed a bill to raise the armed forces of the Colony to 2000 men, exclusive of the previously created ranger Companies. The additional 1000 volunteers were to be allowed a bounty of £10 each,[24] and were to be enlisted for service to Dec. 1, 1758, and no longer.[25] This new Regiment was to have its own field and company officers, precisely as Washington's Regiment had.[26] In the new law, there was some un-intended vagueness concerning the authority of Washington over these troops as Commander-in-Chief,[27] though, of course, when the two units were operating together and were not under a regular, Washington, as senior officer, would be authorized to issue orders to the other Colonel.

Choice of that officer was the prerogative of John Blair, the President of the Council and acting Governor, who accepted an offer William Byrd III of Westover made to recruit and to lead the new troops. Byrd at the time had been distinguished as one of the negotiators of the treaty with the Catawbas and Cherokees.[28] Previously, he had lived in Eng-land as a member of the household of his uncle-in-law, Col. Francis Otway, and there perhaps had developed taste for a military life. When Loudoun came to America, Byrd joined him as a volunteer [29] and won much praise. "[He] accompanied the army to Halifax last year," Forbes was soon to write of Byrd, "and set a noble example to all the gentlemen of the continent who have either inclination or abilities to serve the King and their country." [30] Byrd, who was in his twenty-ninth year,[31] possessed marked skill in dealing with the Indians and had won a measure of their confidence. He was, too, of a family much more distinguished in Virginia than that of Washington, but in public reputation at this time he did not rival his senior Colonel. Socially he might outshine the tall young officer from the Potomac; he had yet to win "honor" comparable to that which Washington had gained.[32]

[23] *Journ. H. B.*, 1752-58, p. 506.   [24] 7 H 164, sec. i.
[25] *Ibid.*, 168, sec. xvi.   [26] *Ibid.*, 168, sec. xiv.
[27] Sections i and ii of the act provided for the enlistment and the employment of the troops "by the president *or* commander in chief," but section xvi spoke of action by "the president *and* commander in chief for the time being" (7 H 164, 169). While it seems reasonable to assume that Washington is the Commander-in-Chief to whom reference is made in the one instance and that the president is titular Commander-in-Chief in the later section, the language is not as explicit as it should have been.
[28] See John Blair to William Byrd III, Mch. 8, 1758; *Emmett Coll.*, NYPL, No. 13471.
[29] Pargellis, *Loudoun*, 310, 311 n.   [30] Forbes to Pitt, July 10, 1758; 1 *Pitt*, 294.
[31] Born at Westover, Sept. 9, 1729, son of William Byrd II and Maria Taylor Byrd. (See 37 *V* 302.)
[32] For rejection by Washington and his council of a proposal to incorporate some of his officers in the Second Regiment, see 2 *Hamilton*, 281-82.

The law that created Byrd's Regiment had gone further than any of the earlier statutes in providing for the use of the Virginia troops. All except the rangers could be united, "by direction of the Governor or Commander-in-Chief . . . to the forces that shall be sent to our assistance by his Majesty or any of the neighhboring Colonies, and may be marched to annoy or attack the enemy in such manner as shall be thought proper by the commanding officer of his Majesty's forces in North America." [33] Emergency and unhappy experience thus had combined at last to sweep away all restrictions, save those of time, on the employment of the two Regiments: They were to be Virginia's contribution to the common cause. Furthermore, the General Assembly authorized a draft of such militia as might be needed to garrison the frontier forts until December 20, if it should be necessary to send the two Regiments outside Virginia. [34]

These three developments—the presence of Indians, the change of command, and the recruiting and equipment of the larger force—set Washington's task for the two months that followed his return to the Valley. Recruiting proved less difficult than in the past. [35] Although Forbes did not believe he would receive more than half the 2000 troops Virginia had authorized, [36] Washington's Regiment numbered 950 or more by May 28, and Byrd, with 900, was so close to authorized strength that the official formation of the Regiment was set for May 29. [37] Even St. Clair, who had found no words too furiously contemptuous for describing the Virginia troops of 1755, had to admit now that their successors were "a fine body of men." [38] The high bounty and short term of enlistment had accomplished what never had been achieved previously. [39]

The drafting of militiamen in anticipation of the departure of the garrisons of the frontier forts might be another and a sadder tale. When President Blair undertook to pass the issue to Washington, with

[33] 7 H 164, sec. ii.   [34] 7 H 169, sec. xvi.

[35] Except as respects the payment of recruiting expenses, for which see minutes of a council of officers at Fort Loudoun, May 9, 1758, and Washington to Robinson, May 10, 1758; 305 Papers of G. W., 14, 15, LC.

[36] Forbes, 77, 87, 91.

[37] See 2 G. W., 202; St. Clair to Col. Henry Bouquet, May 27, 28, June 9, 1758; Brit. Mus. Add. MS 21639, p. 1, 3, 5. Virginia's new Governor, Francis Fauquier, writing Washington, June 25, 1758, remarked that French regimentals from a prize-ship had been purchased for the Regiment (8 Papers of G. W., LC).

[38] St. Clair to Bouquet, May 27, loc. cit. For Sharpe's similar commendation, see infra, p. 317.

[39] For the echo of some of the difficulties of even this successful recruiting effort, see John Blair to unnamed correspondent (either George Mercer or Thomas Walker), June 3, 1758, and Francis Fauquier to William Byrd, June 19, 1758; Journ. H. B., 1758–61, p. 261–63.

authority to call some of the militia of nearby Counties to the forts, the Colonel carefully avoided the responsibility: "I could by no means think of executing (willingly) that discretionary power with which you were pleased to invest me, of ordering out the militia. It is an affair, Sir, of too important and delicate a nature for me to have the management of; for much discontent will be the inevitable consequence of this draft." [40] Washington spoke from experience; Blair was guided by hope that the logic of replacing the Regiments with militia would prevail over the reluctance of individuals. There, for the time, the matter rested.[41]

Savage allies raised new problems daily. Raids of hostile scalping parties took heavy toll in West Augusta.[42] From Bedford and from Halifax came reports of much misbehavior by Cherokees returning South from Winchester.[43] The need of Indians with whom to fight Indians was as manifest as ever; diplomacy, firmness and understanding of them were the imperatives. In full knowledge of this, Forbes, St. Clair and Washington all were doubtful whether the redmen would remain away from home and with the Virginia forces [44] or, contrarily, would wander into Pennsylvania and make trouble while Forbes was negotiating with the Delawares and Shawnees.[45] On May 27, Colonel Byrd arrived at Winchester with fifty-seven Indian warriors, but he had to report that he had met on the trail many who were going back to the Carolinas and that he had not been able to prevail on any of them to return with him.[46]

By the third week in June, all the Indians had departed except for those with Byrd.[47] Lamenting this, Washington once again had to insist that Indians were the "only troops fit to cope with Indians" in forest warfare.[48] In the Cherokee country itself, some of the headmen had promised to be ready to start for Virginia on the 21st of June, but on the day they were to depart, they said their conjurers had warned them that much sickness and death would attend them, for which reason they had decided not to go northward until autumn.[49] In the

[40] Washington to John Blair, Apr. 24, 1758; 2 G. W., 183–84. See also minutes of council, 2 Hamilton, 282.

[41] 1 Pitt, 229; 2 Hamilton, 289.   [42] 2 G. W., 192–93.

[43] Williamsburg report of May 26, 1758; Md. Gazette, June 29, 1758.

[44] 2 G. W., 179, 182–83; Forbes, 65, 77, 88.

[45] 2 Hamilton, 285; 2 G. W., 198–201.

[46] St. Clair to Bouquet, May 27, 1758; Br. Mus. Add MS 21639, p. 1.

[47] Ibid., p. 3, 5; Forbes, 108, 109, 113.

[48] Letter to Forbes, June 19, 1758; 2 G. W., 216.

[49] Certificate of Paul Demeré et al., June 22, 1758; Journ. H. B., 1758–61, p. 263–64.

face of this discouragement, it might have appeared that such hope as the English had of overcoming the adverse odds in the struggle for the frontier might depend on winning over some of the Indians who were said to be dissatisfied with their French allies. To this end, Forbes and the Pennsylvania authorities already were maneuvering with some skill.[50]

Throughout this recruiting, this adjustment to new commanders, and this humiliating effort to satisfy the insatiable Indians, preparations were being made hourly to move the Virginia Regiments—the "Virginia Brigade" as St. Clair once styled the force—across the Potomac and then, in due time, to Pennsylvania for the advance on Fort Duquesne. At the outset the questions that most concerned Washington, Sir John St. Clair and others had to do with wagons, tents, cartridge boxes, powder horns, blankets, hatchets and varied items of equipment relatively unimportant in themselves but essential to such an orderly advance as Forbes proposed to make.[51] The General had given Governor Sharpe [52] and Col. Henry Bouquet [53] authority to move the Virginians; Sir John St. Clair himself came to Winchester and undertook to equip the troops.[54] Before St. Clair could put Washington's troops under marching orders,[55] he determined to procure such equipment as he could from the Colony and accordingly directed Washington to go to Williamsburg to ask for arms and tentage and to "settle the affairs of the two Virginia Regiments." [56]

For a manifest personal reason, Washington was glad to go to the vicinity of the White House, but he was hurried and was anxious to

[50] The background is conveniently sketched in Parkman, *Montcalm and Wolfe*, v. 2, p. 149. Fredrich Post's journal of his remarkable missions, mentioned *infra*, p. 355, will be found among the most interesting documents of the French and Indian War.

[51] See St. Clair to Bouquet, May 31, 1758; Br. Mus. Add. MS 21639, p. 5. Bouquet, in his letter of June 3, 1758 to St. Clair, announced that he would forward hatchets, because the men "cannot encamp or get fuel without"—a reminder of the density of the woodland through which the army had to advance (*ibid.*, p. 9).

[52] *Forbes*, 90.   [53] *Ibid.*, 95, 96.

[54] Cf. 2 *G. W.*, 203.   [55] *Ibid.*

[56] *Ibid.* It doubtless is possible to interpret the language of Washington's orders to Adam Stephen as an intimation that St. Clair desired to take into his own hands the direction of everything and, to that end, wished to send Washington off. The instructions to Stephen began: "Sir John St. Clair having, by virtue of a power from the Commander-in-Chief for the Southern District, put the troops of this Colony under marching orders; and at the same time thought it necessary that I wait upon the President to settle" etc. St. Clair's own explanation was: "Mr. President Blair has laid me under many inconveniences by his not coming here, so that I was obliged to send Colonel Washington to him" (St. Clair to Bouquet, May 27, 1758; Br. Mus. Add MS 21639, p. 1). Taken with St. Clair's subsequent expression of satisfaction on the result of Washington's visit, these quotations made it appear improbable that St. Clair sent Washington off because he wished to be rid of the Virginia Colonel. St. Clair did not have to resort to this expedient to exercise command; it was his by seniority. Service as Quartermaster did not disqualify him for line duty.

get back to the frontier in time to share in an offensive he so long had been urging. Leaving Winchester on the 24th of May,[57] he was in Williamsburg on the 28th with a long succession of written questions, to which he asked the President to make early and explicit reply. These inquiries concerned not only equipment but also pay, promotion, recruiting and the future of Fort Loudoun,[58] and, in some instances, they called for more study than Washington's impatience allowed. As soon as the acting Governor had reached a decision, George rode over to the Pamunkey and paid homage to Martha Custis, and then, June 5, he started for Winchester.[59] To the satisfaction of St. Clair, he was back at his post on the 9th. The Britisher wrote: "Mr. President Blair has been graciously pleased to grant everything I asked except a careful officer at [Fort] Loudoun to take care of the valuable stores, lest they be embezzled."[60] It would be necessary, St. Clair thought, to move these supplies to Fort Cumberland or to some other post where he could keep an eye on them. To settle this and other questions, St. Clair rode over to Conococheague and took Washington with him for a conference on the 13th of June with Governor Sharpe and Col. Henry Bouquet.[61]

Although Washington had exchanged letters frequently with Bouquet, this apparently was the first time he ever had met the man who was to be Forbes's most trusted lieutenant and Washington's immediate superior. Henry Bouquet, Swiss-born and thirty-nine years of age, was portly and undistinguished in appearance, but of attractive and friendly manners. He had received careful schooling before he entered the Dutch army as a cadet in 1736, and subsequently he extended his training by service with the Sardinian forces in the War of the Austrian Succession. So admirable was his performance in every test that the Prince of Orange in 1748 made him Captain-Commandant of the newly organized Swiss Guards, with rank of Lieutenant Colonel. As

[57] That is to say, his orders of that date suggest that he was on the point of leaving. See 2 G. W., 203–05.

[58] 2 G. W., 205–09.

[59] His entries in *Ledger A*, folio 39, suggest that he may have spent some of his time in Williamsburg at the residence of Colonel Bassett, to whose servants he gave 12 shillings. His gratuity to Mrs. Custis's servants was 14s 6d, compared with 30s on each of his two previous visits. This indicates either that his visit was brief or, less probably, that he thought he need not be overgenerous with Negroes who soon were to be, in effect, his own. Later expenditures on the road show that Washington proceeded directly from the White House toward Winchester and that he did not return via Williamsburg.

[60] St. Clair to Bouquet, June 9, 1758; *Br. Mus. Add. MS* 21639, p. 17.

[61] See Bouquet to Forbes, June 14, 1758; *Br. Mus. Add. MS* 21640, p. 61. Conococheague, it will be remembered, was the site of Maidstone Fort.

circumstance led Bouquet afterward to close and pleasant contact with the British army, he accepted in the autumn of 1755 an invitation to become Lieutenant Colonel of the proposed new Royal American Regiment. In recruiting his Battalion, he showed a most notable combination of energy, patience, and firmness. Pennsylvania farmers denounced him for enlisting their indentured servants; the Assembly protested sternly when he marched 547 men to Philadelphia in December, 1756, and asked that quarters be provided for them. In these and in virtually all his other controversies, he ultimately won his point with a minimum of ill-will.[62]

Next to his definite ability and rounded training as a soldier, Bouquet's greatest quality was his freedom from the binding tradition of the British and German armies. In Charleston, South Carolina, where he had commanded during the months a French attack was anticipated, he had amazed the holders of colonial commission by his considerate treatment of them and their troops. "We are looked upon in quite another light by all the officers," George Mercer had written Washington, "than we were by General Braddock or Mr. Orme, and do our duty equally without any partiality or particular notice taken of one more than the other." Incredibly, the regular officers had made no demand "for necessaries for their own troops in which ours are not joined." [63] This was due to Bouquet. With like understanding, after he returned to Pennsylvania, he had begun to study new, more flexible tactics for forest fighting by British regulars.[64] He was as careful as he was skillful and on matters he did not understand, such as dealings with the Indians, he sought the best counsel he could get.[65] By temperament as by training, Bouquet probably was second only to Forbes among all the soldiers in America from whom Washington could learn.

For the consideration of Colonel Bouquet, the Virginian had prepared in advance seven groups of questions concerning equipment, the garrisoning of Fort Loudoun and the March to Wills Creek. To all of these he received clear and immediate answers in an English at least as good as that of the average British or colonial officer of his rank.[66]

[62] Cf. Fisher in 3 *Penn. Mag.,* 125: "Few English commanders lived so long in America so free from censure of the people."

[63] Letter of Aug. 17, 1757; 2 Hamilton, 176, 177.

[64] Branch in 52 *Penn. Mag.,* 45; Joseph Shippen to his father, Aug. 15, 1758; *Shippen Papers.* See also Edward Hutton, *Henry Bouquet;* 2 Fortesque, *British Army,* 334. An excellent bibliography is attached to S. M. Pargellis's article on Bouquet in *DAB.*

[65] Cf. Bouquet to Forbes, May 22, 1758. "As I do not understand Indian affairs I have taken George McGee in my service to take over this" (Br. Mus. Add. MS. 21640, p. 36).

[66] Washington's questions are in Br. Mus. Add. MS 21658; Bouquet's reply is in 8 *Papers of G. W.,* LC.

At the conference where Washington became acquainted with this remarkable man, Bouquet did not give the Virginia troops their marching orders, but, instead left the duty to St. Clair. That officer prepared instructions in detail and handed them to Washington,[67] who returned that evening to Winchester.[68] The usual eleventh-hour difficulties were encountered but by hard, vexatious work on Washington's part, they finally were overcome.[69] On the 24th of June, Washington left Winchester for Fort Cumberland with five Companies of the First Virginia and a Company of artificers of the Second—close to 600 men, and probably more than George ever had commanded on the road in a single body.[70]

It was not a fast or a flawlessly managed march. The road had been almost impassable until repaired three days before the start;[71] three bullocks were lost as they were being driven with the column; at Pearsall's, for reasons with which Washington was unacquainted, he had to take over a convoy of wagons loaded with fodder.[72] Not until the afternoon of July 2 did the disgusted Virginian, his tired men and his twenty-eight wagons[73] reach Fort Cumberland. "My march," the Colonel had to report, "by bad teams and bad roads . . . was much delayed"[74]—not an auspicious introduction to the command of Colonel Bouquet.

By that time, the last of Forbes's artillery and supply ships had reached Philadelphia;[75] his cannon had been put in the road to catch up with his infantry;[76] he himself was on his way to Carlisle, where he was to arrive on the 4th.[77] The heads of his three columns then were at that post, at Raystown,[78] and at Fort Cumberland. His force was to number close to 7000, of whom about 1400 were Scotch Highlanders.[79] Operations were to be different from Braddock's in this fundamental: Braddock had established an advance base at Cumberland and had undertaken to proceed straight from that point, with his wagon train, to Fort DuQuesne. Forbes intended to establish successive depots as he

---

[67] 2 *Hamilton,* 320–21.　　　　　　　[68] 2 *G. W.,* 210.

[69] 2 *G. W.,* 221, 223, 227. For complaints over the small worth of the men left to guard Fort Loudoun and the country South of Winchester, see 2 *Hamilton,* 335, 337, 340, 373. The appearance of Indians between Cresap's and Fort Cumberland was reported by Cresap to Bouquet, June 19, 1758.

[70] 2 *G. W.,* 227.　　　　　　　　　[71] 2 *G. W.,* 221.
[72] *Ibid.,* 224–27.　　　　　　　　[73] *Ibid.,* 228.
[74] *Ibid.,* 227.　　　　　　　　　　[75] *Forbes,* 109, 113.
[76] *Ibid.,* 126.　　　　　　　　　　[77] *Ibid.,* 126, 128.
[78] The present Bedford, in the County of that name, thirty miles North and slightly East of Fort Cumberland.
[79] *Forbes,* xi.

advanced. Braddock had attempted a long jump; Forbes was to make a number of hops. Washington had seen the one method result in failure; he now was to share in a test of the other. An interesting opportunity was about to open for him—if he was of the temper to make the most of it.

CHAPTER XIX

"DEAR BURGESS"

(JULY, 1758)

IN ALL RESPECTS save one, the first few weeks at Fort Cumberland did not differ greatly from those that Washington had spent on Wills Creek under other Commanders-in-Chief. There were the usual alarms and murders by small parties of hostile Indians;[1] an old argument was renewed—whether a small, light force could reach and destroy the villages of hostile savages.[2] Ex-Governor James Glen of South Carolina paid a welcome visit;[3] after the arrival of Col. William Byrd with eight Companies of his Regiment on the 6th of July,[4] much effort had to be devoted to equipping troops for service they were expected to perform directly under Bouquet at Raystown.[5] The first contingents of 200 under Maj. Andrew Lewis marched away promptly[6] and arrived on the 10th of July at Raystown, where they won praise from Bouquet both for the "extraordinary dispatch" of their advance and for the utility of their dress.[7] Washington had taken pains to have the men procure hunting shirts and leggings, and he had satisfaction in the prompt decision of Bouquet and then of Forbes to make that garb "our pattern in this expedition."[8]

Lewis's contingent was followed by other Companies[9] until, by July 12, a total of 535 Virginians, six Companies,[10] were at the Pennsylvania post and were under the command of Adam Stephen, who believed the entire Regiment would soon be assembled there.[11] Discipline and the prospect of a final thrust at the enemy on the Ohio had

[1] 2 G. W., 234, 236, 237.
[2] 2 Hamilton, 361; 2 G. W., 237. [3] 2 Hamilton, 365.
[4] He left Winchester June 26; 2 G. W., 230, 233.
[5] For the arrival of tentage, see 2 Hamilton, 364.
[6] 2 G. W., 233. [7] 2 Hamilton, 354.
[8] 2 Hamilton, 354. See also ibid., 361, and 2 G. W., 229, 235, 239.
[9] For the opening of the Raystown road, see 2 G. W., 232.
[10] 2 Hamilton, 359; 8 Papers of G. W., LC.
[11] 2 Hamilton, 410. For camp gossip concerning the probability of an early advance, see Md. Gazette, Aug. 31, 1758.

made the Regiment more efficient than ever it had been. Washington had confidence in his soldiers. "I hope, without vanity," he wrote Bouquet, "I may be allowed to say that from long intimacy and frequent scouting in these woods, my men are as well acquainted with all the passes and difficulties, as any troops that will be employed, and therefore may answer any purpose intended by them, *as well* as any other body."[12] Washington himself doubted whether an early general advance would be ordered,[13] but he was physically restored and energetic. "Our Colonel," a new officer said of him, "is an example of fortitude in either danger or hardships, and by his easy, polite behavior, has gained not only the regard but affection of both officers and soldiers."[14]

The circumstance that made this tour of duty different was the fact that George was now a candidate for office. He wished to be a member of the House of Burgesses, from which he so often had received orders, and he had taken care this time to give early notice of his candidacy, so that he would not repeat the unhappy experience of 1755.[15] Before he had left Winchester, he had declared himself for one of the two seats of Frederick County, which then was represented by Hugh West and Thomas Swearingen.[16] Neither of these men had been conspicuous in the deliberations of the General Assembly. Swearingen, as an officer of the Frederick militia,[17] probably was suffering from the general discredit of that unorganized force.

Col. Thomas Bryan Martin, young nephew of Lord Fairfax, had served as a Burgess of Hampshire County in 1756–58, but he now decided to stand in Frederick County, where the peer had given him the 8840 acres styled Greenway Court.[18] Martin had decided to conduct his canvass primarily against Hugh West,[19] and, by so doing, he made Washington, in a sense, the challenger of Swearingen. As the two young men were arrayed against incumbents they were handicapped somewhat, of course, but were not without hope that the voters would endorse new representatives. Although Washington had good assurances of support,[20] he suffered because of this circumstance: The

---

[12] Letter of July 21, 1758, 2 *G. W.*, 243. Governor Sharpe already had echoed St. Clair's admission that the Virginia troops were "very good men" (2 *Sharpe*, 227).

[13] 2 *G. W.*, 234.

[14] Robert Munford to Theodorick Bland, Sr., July 6, 1758; 1 *Bland Papers*, 10.

[15] See *supra*, p. 147.

[16] *Journ. H. B.*, 1752–58, p. ix.   [17] Cf. *ibid.*, 458.

[18] For his career, will, etc., see 34 *V* 54–55. Various references to Greenway Court appear in Appendix I–1 and I–2, part II.

[19] 2 *Hamilton*, 343.   [20] 2 *Hamilton*, 343.

writs of election did not reach Winchester until July 4; as twenty days had to elapse before the election could be held, the poll could not be conducted until July 24.[21] Washington, therefore, might be absent at Fort Cumberland during the time the other aspirants were afield.

Friends did all they could to offset this disadvantage. George William Fairfax [22] and John Carlyle [23] agreed to visit the Valley and to assist in lining up their tenants. James Wood, the most influential man in the County, was wholeheartedly for Washington, though he preferred West to Martin.[24] Gabriel Jones, one of the Burgesses from Augusta, was so determined to have Washington chosen that he neglected his own solicitation of votes to assist the Colonel. Washington's officers in Frederick were as active in his behalf as the military proprieties admitted, perhaps more active than they should have been. Lieut. Charles Smith, then in command of Fort Loudoun,[25] assumed responsibility with innkeepers and merchants for the beverages that were to be served voters on the day of election.[26]

At first, Washington's success appeared certain, but after he left for Fort Cumberland, some of his adherents thought the tide turned to the incumbents.[27] Lord Fairfax feared the Colonel would be "very hard pushed." [28] John Kirkpatrick had to report that some of the voters "entertain a notion of the inconvenience you lie under of attending the Assembly and of defending them at the same time." [29] Kirkpatrick thought it desirable and Gabriel Jones considered it imperative that Washington return temporarily to Frederick and solicit votes.[30] At the very least, Jones admonished "you being elected absolutely depends on your presence [election] day . . ." [31] James Wood did not go quite that far. "I . . . cannot perceive your interest on the decline," he wrote, "though some try to persuade me to the contrary." Even he, the most experienced of Washington's friends in Frederick, felt impelled to add: "If the duty of your station will permit, come down and show your face. I think I can then promise success." [32]

On receipt of these letters, Washington wrote back for more information and, perhaps, for some joint advice from a political council of his

---

[21] Ibid.
[22] Ibid.
[23] Ibid., 360.
[24] See his vote in 2 Hamilton, 409.
[25] 2 G. W., 222–23.
[26] 2 Hamilton, 397 ff.
[27] 2 Hamilton, 343.
[28] Letter of July 5, 1758, to George William Fairfax; Neill's Fairfaxes, 98.
[29] Letter to Washington, July 6, 1758; 2 Hamilton, 346.
[30] Ibid., 344, 346.
[31] Ibid., 344.
[32] Letter of July 7, 1758; 2 Hamilton, 349.

friends. He of course realized that his presence at Winchester was important. Naturally, he wanted to go and, as always, to do his utmost to achieve what he had undertaken; but he could not get the full approval of his conscience. Marching orders might reach him; an emergency might develop; the service might suffer, and censure might fall on him if he were absent on personal business.

Reflection led to this decision: He would ask Bouquet's permission to return for a few days to Winchester, but he would not go unless it manifestly was necessary and the military front was quiet. As Adam Stephen was at Raystown, Washington wrote him for private word on the manner in which Bouquet received the request, which was transmitted formally. Bouquet's reply was, in Washington's own phrase, "very handsome and polite"; [33] Stephen's confidential observation was that Bouquet wished to oblige Washington but, at the same time, thought himself answerable for anything that might occur at Fort Cumberland during the absence of the commander. [34]

Washington made his acknowledgments to Bouquet on the 19th of July and explained: "Though being [at Winchester for the election] would, at any other time, be very agreeable to me, yet at this juncture I can hardly persuade myself to think of being absent from my more immediate duty, even for a few days. I will not, however, come to any absolute determination in this matter till I receive answers to some letters on that subject (which I expect this night or tomorrow) . . ." [35]

The answers must have been in a measure reassuring. By the 21st, when Adam Stephen came down from Raystown on business of some importance, Washington had decided not to attend the election. [36] He wrote Bouquet that he had chosen "rather to leave the management of [the polling] to the care of my friends than to be absent from my Regiment when there is a probability of its being called upon." [37] To this he held, though even so adept a politican as former Gov. James Glen wrote: "I wish Colonel Washington could be prevailed upon to think with me that his presence is more necessary in Winchester, for one day at least, than in Camp Cumberland." [38]

The resolution of Washington being fixed, he could do nothing

[33] 2 G. W., 241.   [34] 2 Hamilton, 366–67.
[35] 2 G. W., 241. This was written the day previous to the date assigned a letter in which Washington bids farewell to Martha Curtis with the statement, "We have begun our march for the Ohio." The reasons for regarding that letter as a forgery, or as "edited" beyond all possibility of recovering the original text, are given in Appendix II–2.
[36] 2 G. W., 242.   [37] 2 G. W., 242–43.
[38] Letter of July 19, 1758; 2 Hamilton, 365.

except to await the result. Late in the night of June 25, or on the morning of the 26th,[39] he had it: One of the first of a number of letters from Winchester began: "D'r. Burgess." [40] He had been elected. What was more, he had led the poll. It stood: Washington, 309; Martin, 239; West, 199; Swearingen, 45.[41] In Washington's stead, James Wood had sat on the bench while voters declared their preference and he had thanked those who had voted for the absent candidate. Afterward, Wood had been "carried round the town with a general applause, huzzaing Colonel Washington." [42] Similarly, Charles Smith, dispensing hospitality in the leading candidate's interest, had continued to "treat" all comers even after the poll was announced.[43]

Some of the letters of congratulation were especially pleasing because they were written by men who had served under Washington and had seen him in every test of raid and of routine. Robert Stewart with characteristic discernment pointed out that the vote itself was large, that the electors were residents of a county which Washington had commanded "in the worst of times"—and that in the face of all this the majority for an absent candidate was substantial.[44] Robert Rutherford, Captain of rangers, wrote in like spirit: "The punctual discharge of every trust in you reposed, your humane and equitable treatment of each individual, and your ardent zeal for the common cause (so obvious to every unprejudiced, rational person) has gained your point with credit . . ." [45]

The expense had been considerable, because the drinkables consumed by voters on a July day had been incredible. Three hundred and ninety-one voters and unnumbered hangers-on who possessed no franchise had accounted for:

Rum	28 gallons.	Wine	34 gallons.
Rum punch	50 gallons.	Beer	46 gallons.
	Cider Royal	2 gallons.[46]	

39 Capt. Robert Stewart had the news before 8 P.M. on the 25th and wrote Washington at that hour, but he may not have dispatched the messenger that night. See 2 *Hamilton*, 388.

40 *Ibid.*, 381.

41 2 *Hamilton*, 409. This is Washington's own careful tabulation. Lieutenant Smith's totals were slightly different (*ibid.*, 385).

42 Letter of Charles Smith, July 24, 1758; 2 *Hamilton*, 384.

43 *Ibid.*

44 2 *Hamilton*, 388.

45 This seems the most logical punctuation of a somewhat complicated sentence (2 *Hamilton*, 389).

46 Fractions of gallons are eliminated. So is a small entry of three and a half pints of brandy. The rum was made into a hogshead and a barrel of punch, roughly eighty-five gallons. See the various bills in 2 *Hamilton*, 398–400.

This was a total of 160 gallons, or something more than a quart and a half per voter. Washington's bills from the various inns and tippling-houses, including a dinner for his special friends, was £39, 6s.[47]

The winner did not complain. "I hope," he wrote, "no exception were taken to any that voted against me but that all were alike treated and all had enough; it is what I much desired; my only fear is that you spent with too sparing a hand"—something he never had written previously.[48] His gratitude was promptly voiced. To Gabriel Jones he wrote: "Permit me to return you my sincerest thanks for your great assistance at the late election, and to assure you that I shall ever return a lively sense of the favor. I am extreme sorry that you neglected your own election in Augusta by this means, but I hope you are secure in Hampshire," [49] which happily proved to be the case.[50] Along with this debt to Gabriel Jones, who in a measure had acted personally for him, Washington felt that he owed much to the County's bellwether, James Wood. "If," he began, "thanks flowing from a heart replete with joy and gratitude can in any measure compensate for the fatigue, anxiety and pain you had in my election, be assured you have them." With fervor and some of the rhetoric in which he still indulged occasionally, Washington pledged himself to "everything that lies in my little power for the honor and welfare of the County" and he promised this, he said "when promises may be regarded, before they might pass as words of course." [51]

Planter he was, not of the most opulent but of holdings that gave him full understanding of the difficulties of colonial agriculture and of dependence on England; soldier he was, learning to make the most of the least; and now he was to be a lawmaker and was to see how those who authorized the drafts and levied the taxes looked on the officers who spent the revenue in the bloody business of war.

[47] *Ibid.,* 400.
[48] To James Wood, n.d.; 2 *G. W.,* 251.
[49] 2 *G. W.,* 249.
[50] *Journ. H. B.,* 1758–61, p. vii.
[51] 2 *G. W.,* 251.

CHAPTER XX

RIVAL ROADS TO THE OHIO
(July—December, 1758)

IN THE LETTERS written to thank the friends who had managed his canvass, Washington had spoken gloomily of the military outlook: "Our expedition seems overcast with too many ills to give you any satisfaction in a transient relation of them. God knows what's intended; for nothing seems ripe for execution; backwardness, and I would (if I dared) say more, appears in all things." [1] This pessimism was not born of events in the northern provinces. He knew, as he wrote, that Lord Howe had been killed and that the advance on Ticonderoga had been a failure, though apparently he did not regard that reverse as the definite end of all offensive British operations on Lake Champlain in 1758.[2] His hope was high for the capture of Louisburg by General Amherst, Admiral Boscawen and their forces.[3]

What depressed and angered Washington was nearer and, as he thought, plainer—the slow progress of preparations for the advance to the Ohio. In this enterprise the support of Indians seemed almost as uncertain as ever.[4] Washington could not agree with Bouquet that where this was true, "I think it would be easier to make Indians of our white men than to coax that damned tawny [5] race." [6] The Virginian's answer was the familiar one: "I cannot conceive the best white men to be equal to them in the woods; but I fear they are too sensible of their high importance to us to render us any very acceptable service." [7] Apparently, when he wrote this, Washington did not know that Forbes

[1] Letter to Gabriel Jones, July 29, 1758; 2 *G. W.*, 249. See also his letter of n.d. to James Wood, *ibid.*, 252.

[2] 2 *G. W.*, 243, 269.　　　　　　　　　　　[3] *Ibid.*

[4] 2 *G. W.*, 234, 248; *Md. Gazette,* Aug. 3, 1758; Bouquet to Washington, July 23, 1758; Br. Mus. Add. MS. 21641, f 19 ff. Cf. Bouquet to Forbes, July 21, 1758: "Ten of Col. Byrd's Indians arrived yesterday evening to demand many things. They seem like feeble-minded children. Ours are doing very well and for a long time have given us no trouble. We have recruited sixteen who will join us on the expedition."

[5] This probably is the word Bouquet had in mind. He spelt it "tanny."

[6] 2 *Hamilton*, 362.　　　　　　　　　　[7] Letter of July 16, 1758; 2 *G. W.*, 238.

was seeking, and with good prospects of success, to detach the hostile Indians from their French allies.[8]

Ignorant of the fact that delay was justified on this ground, Washington was profoundly concerned over the selection of the best approach to the French stronghold on the Ohio. In June and during the first days of July, it had been reported widely that Forbes intended to follow the road used in 1755,[9] but now Washington feared that the General had been misled into choosing a line of advance through a country where a serviceable road did not exist and, as the Virginian believed, could not possibly be cut in time for the expedition to reach Fort DuQuesne before winter snows halted operations.

Advanced redcoats were at Raystown.[10] The question was whether the General should attempt to proceed from that point directly northwestward for eighty miles or should pursue Braddock's route across the Alleghenies and over Laurel Hill and Chestnut Ridge. If the advance were by a new road from Raystown, then the greater part of the troops at Fort Cumberland would be moved to the Pennsylvania base. This of course would involve the abandonment of the line of supply from Alexandria to Fort Cumberland for all purposes other than the victualling of the few men who might be left on Wills Creek. Conversely, if Braddock's Road were chosen as the route to the Ohio, then the line of supply from Philadelphia to Raystown might be less used and the line from the Potomac more generally employed.

Trade might follow the road the army smoothed. The rival interests of Pennsylvania and Virginia thus were at stake. Wrote James Young, "The Virginians are making great interest that our route may be by Fort Cumberland, but I hope they will not succeed."[11] Bouquet informed his commander: "The Virginia party by report of your route continue their clamors, and their secret motive I suspect is partiality. I must work with circumspection in order to reply to their clamors. If any accident should happen they would not hesitate to attribute it to the choice of the road."[12]

Washington did not admit and probably did not feel he had any

[8] See Parkman, *Montcalm and Wolfe,* v. 2, p. 149 ff.

[9] See John Armstrong to Bouquet, June 28, 1758, Br. Mus. Add. MS 21643; f. 130: "It is said Raestown is not to be the place of general rendezvous but Cumberland." Cf. James Glen, to Bouquet, July 5, 1758 (*ibid.,* 137): "I hear you have laid aside all thoughts of a road directly from where you are to Fort DuQuesne."

[10] For the preliminaries, see 2 *Ford,* 76–77n.

[11] Letter of July 23, 1758, to R. Peters; 3 *Penn. Arch.,* 489.

[12] Letter of July 21, 1758, to Forbes; Br. Mus. Add. MS 21640, f. 101.

selfish or personal interest in the continued use of a line of supply, via Fort Cumberland, that would make the Potomac the watergate to the Ohio. From the military point of view, he was so convinced of the superiority of Braddock's Road over any possible route from Raystown to Fort DuQuesne that he later was to attribute advocacy of a different policy to "Pennsylvanian artifice." [13] His argument was positive: From the time a road to the Ohio first was discussed, the Indians had said that the trail from Wills Creek was much the best. On the basis of their experience, the road had been built: it must be "firmer and better" than a new one could be. In the next place, circumstance demanded that a blow be struck on the Ohio in 1758 because the Central and Southern Colonies were making their maximum effort during the year and could not do as much again in 1759. The Indians would not remain friendly in the event the English continued inactive. If, then, a campaign was necessary in 1758, it could be pushed to success over Braddock's Road and not over the other route.

Gone from Washington's argument was any echo of the terrible experiences he had faced in reaching Gist's settlement. Only the memory of actually getting there seemed to be vivid. In retrospect, too, he believed that along Braddock's Road there was far better pasturage than probably could be found beyond Raystown. The streams were no barrier; small differences in distances were offset by the tested practicability of Braddock's Road and the certain badness of any other. It would be dangerous to divide force: everything must be concentrated on a road known to be passable.[14] Of all the reasons for using Braddock's Road, the one that Washington most emphasized was that of saving time. The season, he maintained, was too far advanced to permit of the construction of a new road that year through a rocky district of scant grass.[15]

At the date of the election in Frederick, neither Forbes nor Bouquet was committed irrevocably, though they tentatively had decided on the new route, northwestward from Raystown.[16] This line of advance had been recommended to them by responsible men in Philadelphia. The commanders had no reason to suppose they had been misled by provincial self-interest; doubtless they had heard the confident assertion

13 See *infra*, p. 331 and 2 *G. W.*, 277.
14 The full presentation of Washington's argument was in his letter of Aug. 2, 1758, to Colonel Bouquet, 2 *G. W.*, 252–60. Parts of the argument or summaries of it will be found in most of his letters on the general subject between July 7 and September 1, 1758.
15 Cf. 2 *G. W.*, 249.   16 Cf. *Md. Gazette*, Aug. 31, 1758.

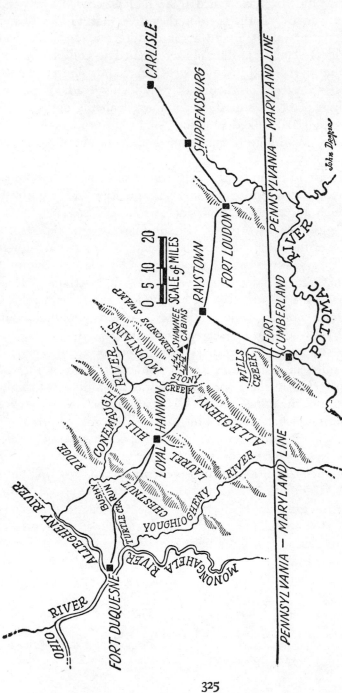

FORBES'S LINE OF ADVANCE, 1758

Some of the positions occupied by Washington's Regiment and by other troops under Forbes's command have been established from maps of Pennsylvania made during and immediately after the American Revolution; but between Loyal Hannon and Bushy Run, the descriptions given by the field commanders are so indefinite that the location of camp sites cannot be determined.

that Braddock would not have failed if he had proceeded westward through Pennsylvania.[17] Perhaps, too, they felt that ill omen and anticipation of defeat might attend a march along a road that had ended on a field of slaughter. The matter seemed so completely one of wise choice that Forbes and Bouquet were puzzled by the vehemence of the Virginians' insistence on the use of Braddock's Road. Washington, in the judgment of his superiors, minimized all the obstacles on the old route, which had balked Braddock many times in 1755. With equal confidence, Washington condemned a route he had never traveled.

Because of the stand taken by the men from South of the Potomac, Bouquet reviewed the provisional choice of the Raystown approach and collected such additional information as he could concerning the relative advantages of the two routes. In summarizing the reports, he took pains to say of the most conspicuous dissenter: "Colonel Washington is filled with a sincere zeal for the success of the expedition and will march wherever you determine with the same activity. He is sure that, with all the information he can gather, the route we have chosen is the most impracticable for horses; that the mountains are bad and that Braddock's Road is the only one to take." [18]

In this spirit, Bouquet had directed Washington to reconnoitre and to clear a few miles of Braddock's Road,[19] and at the end of July he arranged a conference in the hope, as he phrased it, "that we might all centre in one and the same opinion." [20] Washington had said twice that he would follow whatever route his superiors chose [21] but he went to the meeting with Bouquet resolved to urge speed and to get leave, in his own words, "to advance on with the Virginians to the crossing [of the Youghiogheny] at least, opening the road and constructing posts as we go." [22] All this and more he told Bouquet July 30—and all without convincing his immediate superior.[23] ". . . I said and did everything," Washington wrote, "to avert a mischief that seemed to forebode our manifest ruin; this is the light it appears to me." [24] Bouquet had kept an open mind and at the very time of his discussion with

17 See *supra,* p. 89 and Franklin, *Autobiography* (Bigelow ed.), 264.
18 Letter of July 26, 1758, to Forbes, Br. Mus. Add. MS 21640, f. 110.
19 2 *Hamilton,* 362; 2 *G. W.,* 243.
20 Bouquet to Washington, July 27, 1758; 2 *Hamilton,* 396.
21 Letters of July 7 and 25; 2 *G. W.,* 231, 246.
22 Letter of July 29, 1758, to Gabriel Jones; 2 *G. W.,* 249.
23 See his summary of his argument; Letter to Governor Fauquier, Aug. 5, 1758; 2 *G. W.,* 261–62.
24 *Ibid.,* 262.

Washington still was studying both the familiar deficiencies of Braddock's Road and some newly reported obstacles on the way from Raystown to Fort DuQuesne. Of the old route, he told Forbes: "We are in a cruel situation, being reduced to a single line of communication. It is sixty-four miles from Gist's to Fort Cumberland, and there are only three places where there is forage enough. The frost which destroys all vegetation comes in October and lasts until spring." Then he reported: "I have had an interview with Colonel Washington to see how he would surmount these difficulties. I gained no satisfaction. The most of these gentlemen have but one party and one army and they disregard all that does not support their ideas, never seeing the difficulties." [25]

Washington was profoundly disappointed. He went back to Fort Cumberland and wrote out his argument in full for Colonel Bouquet,[26] who had asked for such a paper in order that it might be placed before the General.[27] Then Washington did a dangerous thing. He mistakenly believed that Bouquet was the special advocate of the Raystown route, and that Forbes probably was being deceived regarding it. As it happened, Francis Halkett, a comrade of Braddock's army, was Brigade Major of the British forces in Pennsylvania and often was acting secretary to the commander.[28] Washington reasoned that if he explained the situation to Halkett, that officer might pass the information to the General. Without going over the head of Bouquet, it might be possible to appeal to Forbes in a matter concerning which Washington daily was more vehemently convinced he was correct. The Virginian accordingly addressed this letter to Halkett the day he completed the writing of the long argument he intended to send Bouquet:

My dear Halkett:
    I am just returned from a conference held with Colonel Bouquet. I find him fixed, I think I may say fixed, upon leading you a new way to the Ohio; through a road, every inch of it to cut, at this advanced season, when we have scarce time left to tread the beaten tract; universally confessed to be the best passage through the mountains.
    If Colonel Bouquet succeeds in this point with the General all is lost! All is lost by Heavens! Our enterprise ruined; and we stopped at the Laurel Hill this winter; not to gather laurels by the by, desirable in their effects.

[25] Letter of July 31, 1758; Br. Mus. Add. MS 21640, f. 112.
[26] 2 G. W., 252–60.
[27] Ibid., 260–61.   [28] Forbes, 21 n.

The Southern Indians turned against us, and these colonies become desolated by such an acquisition to the enemy's strength.

These are the consequences of a miscarriage; and a miscarriage the consequences of the attempt; I have drawn my reasons out at large and now send them to Colonel Bouquet. He desired I would do so, that he might forward them to the General; should this happen, you may judge of their weight.

I am uninfluenced by prejudice, having no hopes or fears but for the general good. That be assured of, and my sincere sentiments are spoken on this occasion. I am, dear Halkett,

Most affectionately yours,

George Washington.[29]

Three days later, and before his letter could reach Halkett, word came to Washington in a communication from Bouquet that the choice of the General was for the route directly from Raystown.[30] Virginia's spokesman replied with dignity and with just a touch of stiffness that he would obey orders, of course, but that he was of the same opinion still. If he were proved in error, he would acknowledge it as became "a gentleman, led astray from judgment, and not by prejudice"; and if he unfortunately were correct about the road, he would have done his duty in an affair "on the good success of which our all in a manner depends." [31]

This was by no means the end of it. Washington did more than adhere to his opinion. He continued to argue for advance along the old road, and he kept predicting calamity from the attempt to cut a new one during the brief remaining period of open weather. In a few days, he was on the black books of the commanding General. Forbes came accidentally upon Washington's letter to Halkett,[32] read it and felt that it explained the source of the Virginians' opposition to the Raystown route. "I am now at the bottom of their scheme against this new road," he told Bouquet, "a scheme that I think was a shame for

---

[29] 2 *G. W.*, 260–61. The unusual punctuation of this letter has been preserved in the belief that it perhaps reflects something of the emotion under which Washington wrote.

[30] 2 *G. W.*, 262. Cf. 3 *Penn. Mag.*, 127. Neither Forbes's announcement of this to Bouquet nor Bouquet's letter to Washington has been found. The period was one during which Forbes was acutely ill (*Forbes*, 169–70), and must have been giving most of his orders verbally. He noted August 9 that he again was able to write "after three weeks of a most violent and tormenting distemper . . ." (*ibid.*, 170).

[31] Letter of August 6, 1758; 2 *G. W.*, 263.

[32] Forbes stated in his letter of August 9 to Bouquet that the letter "accidentally fell into [his] hands"; but there remains, of course, the possibility that Halkett believed Washington wished Forbes to see the letter and that Halkett consequently put it where Forbes would find it.

any officer to be connected with . . ." [33] On the strength of this disclosure, Forbes began immediately to build up a distrust of the author of the communication. At first opportunity, he let it be known to Washington and to Byrd, whom he considered equally at fault, that "their judging and determining my actions and intentions before that I had communicated my opinion to them was so premature, and was taking the lead in so ridiculous a way that I could by no means suffer it." [34]

Even this neither changed Washington's opinion nor silenced him. Both he and Colonel Byrd had written Virginia's new Governor, Francis Fauquier,[35] that they did not expect large results from the advance in Pennsylvania. Fauquier replied that it might be too late to prevent the attempt to build the Raystown road, but that he hoped Washington and Byrd would explain to their commanding officers that Virginia's enlistment of troops and her supply of money had been based on the belief that a decisive effort would be made in 1758 to take Fort DuQuesne.[36]

Those officers needed no urging. The trial of their judgment was under way. Bouquet's men cut the road to the top of the Allegheny Mountains, got the first division of the artillery over the crest, and started work on the crossing of Laurel Hill. Beyond that barrier was the settlement of Loyal Hannon, which Bouquet intended to make his advanced base. "In three days," the Colonel wrote Washington on August 26, "Sir John [St. Clair] promises to be over to Loyal Hannon." Bouquet continued hopefully: "The second division will follow immediately and I expect with impatience the arrival of the General to move on myself: We must shortly enter upon action, and I know that we have time enough to carry our point, if we meet with no new difficulties." [37]

Washington's answer was grim: "We must doubtless expect to encounter many difficulties in opening a new road through bad grounds

---

[33] Letter of Aug. 9, 1758; *Forbes,* 171.

[34] Forbes to Abercromby, Aug. 11, 1758; *Forbes,* 173.

[35] Fauquier had arrived in Williamsburg June 5, 1758. See his letter of June 11 to the Lords of Trade, P.R.O., C.O. 5: 1329, f. 171.

[36] Fauquier to Byrd, Aug. 17, 1758; *Journ. H. B.,* 1758–61, p. 265; original in the *Draper MSS.* Cf. Fauquier to the Lords of Trade, June n.d., 1758, *loc. cit.,* f. 187. These letters of Fauquier's contain much of interest on Virginia during his administration and they deserve publication in full. The Corbin Letter Book, VHS, includes a letter of Richard Corbin to Dinwiddie, Apr. 20, 1758, and one to Governor Dinwiddie, Apr. 26, 1758, on the military situation and on the finances of the Colony. Both are worth consulting.

[37] 3 *Hamilton,* 57.

in a woody country, of which the enemy are possessed;[38] but since you hope our point may be carried, I would fain expect the surmounting these difficulties." He went on to assert that if Braddock's Road had been used, "in all human probability we might have been in full possession of the Ohio by now." Still he persisted: "Everyone knows what could have been done [on] the old road—few can guess what will be [done on] the new, there being not only the difficulties of the road to encounter but the chance of a French reenforcement also; but it is useless to add on this head; I should rather apologize for what I have said." The mail that prompted this letter brought one from General Forbes, who directed that Washington proceed westward from Fort Cumberland by the old road. These instructions were a triumph for the Virginian. He immediately wrote Bouquet a second letter in which he told of the orders from Forbes, described the good prospect ahead, and concluded with an expression of hope that Bouquet's advance from Raystown would be successful.[39] At the same time, Washington did not believe the Army should move westward in two columns. He wanted everything concentrated on Braddock's Road for an immediate start and he accordingly continued his criticism of the new route and of the delay in getting the troops on the march.

All the Virginians were of this mind. Byrd became ill and could take no further part in the controversy;[40] but other officers protested that delay would be fatal and that the new road could not be completed in time for an advance before frost destroyed pasturage and mud stalled wagons. " 'Tis a set of dirty Dutchmen, they say, that keep us here," Robert Munford wrote from Fort Cumberland, and after reciting details of a similar sort, concluded: "Thus are our officers in a manner ruined by persons whose souls scorn a thought that tends not immediately to their advantage."[41] William Ramsay, who was with the troops near Raystown lamented: "We [Virginians] have bled freely, yet are made hewers of wood and drawers of water . . . 'Tis generally thought Loyal Hannon[42] will be the ne plus ultra of our operations this campaign."[43]

---

[38] The text reads "possed."
[39] Letters of Aug. 28, 1758; 2 *G. W.*, 275; 37 *ibid.*, 481.
[40] See 2 *G. W.*, 278, 286.
[41] Letter of Aug. 4, 1758, to Theodorick Bland, Sr.; 1 *Bland Papers*, 13–14. Munford added a cheerful postscript to Mrs. Bland: "Honored Madam, I am well and lousie, but still your affectionate nephew, &c."
[42] He wrote "L. Hannin."
[43] Letter of Aug. 19, 1758, to Washington; 3 *Hamilton*, 36.

Washington outdid them all in extremes of language. Writing to Speaker Robinson, September 1, he said, after an opening rhetorical flourish: "The conduct of our leaders (if not actuated by superior orders) is tempered with something I don't care to give a name to, indeed I will go further, and say they are d—ps, or something else to P—s—v—n artifice, to whose selfish views I attribute the miscarriage of this expedition, for nothing now but a miracle can bring this campaign to a happy issue." He then reviewed the controversy over the road and described the reported weakness of the garrison of Fort DuQuesne: "See therefore how our time has been misspent; behold the golden opportunity lost; and perhaps never regained. How is it to be accounted for? Can G—l F—s have orders for this? Impossible: Will then our injured country pass by such abuses?"

The Virginian answered his own question by proposing that represensations be made directly to the King. "Let him know how grossly his honor and the public money have been prostituted." With this he coupled the wish that he might be sent as an aide to the person dispatched on the errand. "I think without vanity," he went on, "I could set the conduct of this expedition in its true colors, having taken some pains, perhaps more than any other to dive into the bottom of it." He added: "It has long been the luckless fate of poor Virginia to fall a victim to the views of her crafty neighbors, and yield her honest efforts to promote their common interest at the expense of much blood and treasure; while her sincerity justified her measures. We can now only bewail that blindness, and wish for happier times, which seem at so remote a distance that it is rather to be wished than expected." [44]

Writing this letter apparently relieved Washington's feelings. The next day, September 2, in a communication to the Governor, he was much more restrained. "I may be blamed possibly," he said, "for expressing my sentiments so freely; but never can be ashamed of the truth; and none but obvious facts are stated here." Then he wrote: "The General I dare say; from his good character; can account fully for these delays that surprise all that judge from appearances only, but I really cannot." [45]

There were, in plain fact, many troubles and some hopes at Forbes's headquarters, which had been moved on the 12th of August from Carlisle to Shippensburg.[46] The General himself was struggling with

---

[44] Letter of Sept. 1, 1758; 2 G. W., 276–78. The original punctuation is preserved for the reason given in n. 29, supra.

[45] 2 G. W., 282.   [46] Forbes, 176.

the bloody flux and was better one day and worse the next.[47] Besides, Forbes was having difficulty with Sir John St. Clair—"he is a very odd man, and I am sorry it has been my fate to have any concerns with him." [48] St. Clair on his own account had gotten into an altercation with Adam Stephen and had called the Virginians "mutineers." Stephen's reply was violent. "As I had not sufficient strength," St. Clair said later, "to take him by the neck from among his own men, I was obliged to let him have his own way, that I might not be the occasion of bloodshed," but he soon put the Virginian under arrest.[49] Probably on a hint from Forbes, who wrote Bouquet on the subject, Stephen ultimately was restored to his command. Even before this was done officially, he was given charge of a detachment.[50]

In this incident, Forbes's role was that of the conciliator and was favorable to Stephen, who had made a good impression on Bouquet; [51] but where Washington was concerned, Forbes still was on guard. ". . . Consult Colonel Washington," the General wrote Bouquet, a propos of a division of force, "although perhaps not follow his advice, as his behavior about the roads was no ways like a soldier." [52] Concerning the provincial officers in general, the seniors excepted, Forbes had been disillusioned. They were, he thought, "an extreme bad collection of broken inn-keepers, horse jockeys and Indian traders and . . . the men under them are a direct copy of their officers . . ." [53] If their lack of soldierly qualities disturbed him, their appetites amazed him.[54]

Forbes was conscious, also, that delay on his part was provoking comment. It was due primarily, he insisted, to the "horrible roguery and rascality" of the farmers who did not supply the promised vehicles and teams.[55] As the passing of September days reduced steadily the time

47 His letters contain a candid and courageous narrative of his illness.

48 Forbes to Bouquet, Sept. 4, 1758; *Forbes*, 199. General Abercromby had assigned St. Clair to Forbes. See 1 *Pitt*, 252. Bouquet felt that St. Clair was loading him down with details. See Bouquet to Forbes, Aug. 18, 1758, Br. Mus. Add. MS 21640, f. 145.

49 Parkman, *Montcalm and Wolfe*, v. 2, p. 145; 3 *Hamilton*, 81 and n.; 88.

50 3 *Hamilton*, 98. This was prior to September 14.

51 See Bouquet to Forbes, Aug. 20, 1758; Br. Mus. Add. MS. 21640, p. 147.

52 Letter of Sept. 4, 1758; *Forbes*, 199.

53 Letter of Sept. 6, 1757, to William Pitt; Forbes, 205; 1 *Pitt.*, 338. Cf. Bouquet to Forbes, May 29, 1758: "The civil government in the country is almost negligible" (Br. Mus. Add. MS 21640, f. 66).   54 Cf. *Forbes*, 201.

55 Forbes to Richard Peters, Aug. 28, 1758; *Forbes*, 191; Adam Hoops to Bouquet; Br. Mus. Add. MS 21643, f. 169. Cf. Edward Shippen to his father, Sept. 15, 1758 (misdated 1753): "We begin to be apprehensive that General Forbes does not mean to go in with the expedition as he talks of not getting wagons and of laying the fault of the failure to the Province" (*Shippen Papers*, 23). Governor Sharpe seems to have felt that Forbes's illness was one reason for delay. See 1 *Pitt*, 328.

during which the army could hope to advance on Fort DuQuesne, every new difficulty discovered along the route where the road was being cut by the soldiers was a test of the nerves of the commanders. A rain appeared to be a calamity, a day of warm sunshine an occasion of rejoicing. "Sir John went forward this morning," Bouquet wrote optimistically to Washington, "and sent me back word . . . that as far as he had gone he found the road good and every other thing answering our expectation." [56] Six days later, Harry Gordon—the same Gordon who had been with Braddock—had to report of a reconnaissance he had made: ". . . the road . . . was so bad as to be the very next thing to being impracticable for wagons . . . Bad weather made [the bridges] appear worse but pains enough had not been taken in the making of them." [57] Half in distress and half in grim satisfaction that the Virginians' prophecy of evil had been fulfilled, Adam Stephen wrote Washington: "You have no reason to alter your opinion of the route of the army." Stephen was then with the advanced force at Loyal Hannon and in position to pass judgment on every part of the road other than the stretch over Chestnut Ridge, which lay ahead.[58]

Such was the situation when Washington had the long-desired opportunity [59] of a personal conference with Forbes at Raystown, where there had been no buildings, according to Forbes, until he had sent 1500 provincials to construct storehouses and to erect a stockade.[60] Washington arrived at the new town on the evening of the 16th of September in some embarrassment because of the belated discovery of a dangerous shortage of flour at Fort Cumberland.[61] As the matter was explained to Forbes, he attributed it to contractors' failure in supplying vehicles, and to jealousy on the part of the Virginians because of the purchase in Pennsylvania of food for the army. ". . . I believe neither you nor I," he exploded in a letter to Bouquet, "values one farthing where we get our provisions from, provided we are supplied, or interest ourselves either with Virginia or Pennsylvania, which last I hope will be damned for their treatment of us with the wagons . . ." [62]

However that might be, Washington received in conference one clear order from his commander: He was to return to Fort Cumberland

[56] Letter of Sept. 4, 1758; Br. Mus. Add. MS 21641, f. 54.
[57] Letter of Sept. 10, 1758, to Bouquet; Br. Mus. Add. MS 21643, f. 208.
[58] Letter of Sept. 9, 1758; 3 Hamilton, 88.
[59] 2 G. W., 280, 284–85.   [60] 1 Pitt., 294.
[61] Forbes, 204, 209, 213; 2 G. W., 286; 2 Sharpe, 266. On July 6 there had been 10,400 lbs. of flour at the fort (8 Papers of G. W., LC).
[62] Letter of Sept. 17, 1758; Forbes, 212–13.

and was to move thence as promptly as possible to Raystown with his own and Byrd's troops.[63] This put an end to Washington's hope of an advance on Braddock's Road for at least part of the way to Fort DuQuesne—as Forbes had ordered August 28[64]—but it meant participation, which Washington had been craving. The expedition might and probably would end, he thought, at Loyal Hannon; he at least would have release from the tedium of a separate, immartial existence on Wills Creek where there was nothing to do except to regret, to drill the men, to look out for Indians, and to settle petty squabbles.

As it chanced, the controversy that might have disturbed Washington most personally and unpleasantly had been avoided before he paid his first visit to Forbes. When Washington had heard, approximately on the 20th of August, that Sharpe was coming to Fort Cumberland, he had written to inquire whether the Maryland executive had special seniority or would serve at his military rank, which was that of Lieutenant Colonel. "I should therefore be glad of your advice," Washington had written Bouquet, "being unwilling to dispute the point with him wrongfully, or to give up the command if I have a right to it; neither of which would I do knowingly." [65] Bouquet's answer had been prompt, clear and reassuring: In the circumstances that existed, Sharpe would have no military authority as Governor and as a Lieutenant Colonel of course would not rank Washington. "Therefore," Bouquet had said, "you are very right in keeping [the command]." [66] Now all this was behind Washington. He and Byrd and their officers were to rejoin the advanced contingents and were to mingle with the largest armed force of regulars and provincials that Washington ever had seen.

The Virginia Colonels were not to be received otherwise than as verbal prodigals, whose offence had been an excess of criticism. Soon after they reached Raystown, Adam Stephen informed them that he had been told by everyone that the road from Loyal Hannon to Fort DuQuesne was impracticable. One or another of the Virginians passed this information to Forbes, who took advantage of the occasion to speak his mind to Washington and to Byrd. The General felt that they actually would be glad, rather than sorry, that the new route could

[63] *Forbes,* 214.
[64] *Forbes,* 189; 3 *Hamilton,* 62–63; 37 *G. W.,* 481.
[65] 2 *G. W.,* 273.
[66] Letter of Aug. 23, 1758; 3 *Hamilton,* 46.

not be used, because they had so predicted in advocating Braddock's Road. "I told them plainly," Forbes said afterward, "that, whatever they thought, yet I did aver that, in our prosecuting the present road, we had proceeded from the best intelligence that could be got for the good and convenience of the army, without any views to oblige any one province or another; and added that those two gentlemen were the only people I had met with who had showed their weakness in their attachment to the province they belong to, by declaring so publicly in favor of one road without their knowing anything of the other, having never heard from any Pennsylvania person one word about the road . . ." [67]

It was a stern rebuke and it was not without warrant or repetition. A Pennsylvanian soon was to apply to Washington's tenacious advocacy of Braddock's Road a term that Forbes withheld. "Colonel Washington," a letter was to run, "has been a good deal sanguine and obstinate . . . but the presence of the General has been of great use on this as well as other accounts . . ." [68]

"Obstinate" was not a pretty word to apply to a sensitive man; but something besides the rebuke of his commanding General and something besides his belief that the wrong choice had been made by Forbes was troubling Washington when he came to Raystown. In August, he had written two letters to George William Fairfax about repairs under way at Mount Vernon. One of these letters had to do with a carpet and perhaps other furnishings for the house to which Washington was planning to bring his bride. On the 11th of September, Washington unsealed the replies, one of which explained the other. George William, who now was signing himself simply William Fairfax, wrote that he was answering one of the letters and Mrs. Fairfax the other, because they did not wish to detain the express. [69] The second letter was from Sally herself. It was brief but cordial. Mrs. Fairfax spoke of the carpet and jestingly attributed Washington's impatience with the management of affairs to his desire to possess his betrothed. [70]

Washington had seen Sally often on his visits home during the war and he probably had entertained her and her husband in Williamsburg

[67] Forbes to Bouquet, Sept. 23, 1758; *Forbes*, 219.

[68] John Armstrong to Richard Peters, Oct. 3, 1758; 3 *Penn. Arch.*, 552.

[69] William Fairfax to Washington, Sept. 1, 1758; 3 *Hamilton*, 67–68.

[70] Sally Cary Fairfax's letter of Sept. 1, 1758, has been lost along with the others she wrote Washington, but a part of the contents can be reconstructed readily from Washington's letter of the 12th, printed in the text.

when he was on official business there in the spring of 1757. He had received few letters, if any, from her since June, 1755. She wrote easily and well, in a tall, clear hand, and she had half promised, when he left home to join Braddock, that she would correspond with him.[71] Failure to do so had meant that she did not wish to exchange letters or else that she had not thought she should. Now he had a new opportunity. She knew he was going to marry Martha. What should he say to her of that prospect, especially when his letter might be opened by some curious person or might be read by her husband, with whom, as always, he was on friendly, unrestrained terms?

George decided that he would tell Sally how he felt about her and about the hopelessness of his relations with her. Perhaps he might even ask whether their many pleasant hours together had created in her heart any of the affection he had for her, even though he was going to marry another woman. He was about to depart for the front of action and he might not return. If he could, he would get her answer and take that with him. As she probably was going to be away from Belvoir, visiting at her old home,[72] he could write her with some freedom; at the same time, he must write her so carefully and so cryptically that if the letter were intercepted, it could be explained. On the 12th, before he left Fort Cumberland, he sent her this:[73]

Camp at Fort Cumberland, September 12, 1758.

Dear Madam:

Yesterday I was honored with your short but very agreeable favor of the first inst. How joyfully I catch at the happy occasion of renewing a correspondence which I feared was disrelished on your part, I leave to time, that never failing expositor of all things, and to a monitor equally faithful in my own breast, to testify. In silence I now express my joy; silence, which in some cases, I wish the present, speaks more intelligently than the sweetest eloquence.

If you allow that any honor can be derived from my opposition to our present system of management, you destroy the merit of it entirely in me by

---

[71] 1 G. W., 137.   [72] See infra, n. 79.

[73] The original has disappeared and, so far as is known, has not come under the scrutiny of any historical student who could apply the usual tests of handwriting, watermark, ink and age. Printed in the New York Herald of Mch. 30, 1877, and sold at an auction the next day, it has not even been verified for textual accuracy. One manifest error is corrected in the present reprint by the insertion of "[not]" in the fifth paragraph. Both Ford and Fitzpatrick hesitated to include this letter in their editions but decided to do so. In this they appear to have been justified. The style is essentially that which Washington used in other letters to Sally Fairfax, and it is a style so awkward and involved that forgery would not be easy. All the internal evidence is on the side of authenticity. No possible reason for rejecting it can be advanced other than the fact that the original has not been examined.

attributing my anxiety to the animating prospect of possessing Mrs. Custis, when—I need not tell you, guess yourself. Should not my own Honor and country's welfare be the excitement? 'Tis true, I profess myself a votary of love. I acknowledge that a lady is in the case, and further I confess that this lady is known to you. Yes, Madame, as well as she is to one who is too sensible of her charms to deny the Power whose influence he feels and must ever submit to. I feel the force of her amiable beauties in the recollection of a thousand tender passages that I could wish to obliterate, till I am bid to revive them. But experience, alas! sadly reminds me how impossible this is, and evinces an opinion which I have long entertained, that there is a Destiny which has the control of our actions, not to be resisted by the strongest efforts of Human Nature.

You have drawn me, dear Madam, or rather I have drawn myself, into an honest confession of a simple Fact. Misconstrue not my meaning; doubt it not, nor expose it. The world has no business to know the object of my Love, declared in this manner to you, when I want to conceal it. One thing above all things in this world I wish to know, and only one person of your acquaintance can solve me that, or guess my meaning. But adieu to this till happier times, if I ever shall see them. The hours at present are melancholy dull. Neither the rugged toils of war, nor the gentler conflict of A——— B———s,[74] is in my choice. I dare believe you are as happy as you say, I wish I was happy also. Mirth, good humor, ease of mind, and—what else?— cannot fail to render you so and consummate your wishes.

If one agreeable lady could almost wish herself a fine gentleman for the sake of another, I apprehend that many fine gentlemen will wish themselves finer e'er Mrs. Spotswood is possest. She has already become a reigning toast in this camp, and many there are in it who intend (fortune favoring) to make honorable scars speak the fullness of their merit, and be a messenger of their Love to Her.

I cannot easily forgive the unseasonable haste of my last express, if he deprived me thereby of a single word you intended to add. The time of the present messenger is, as the last might have been entirely at your disposal. I can't expect to hear from my friends more than this once before the fate of the expedition will some how or other be determined. I therefore beg to know when you set out for Hampton, and when you expect to return to Belvoir again. And I should be glad also to hear of your speedy departure, as I shall thereby hope for your return before I get down. The disappointment of [not] seeing your family would give me much concern. From any thing I can yet see 'tis hardly possible to say when we shall finish. I don't think there is a probability of it till the middle of November. Your letter to Captain Gist I forwarded by a safe hand the moment it came to me. His answer shall be carefully transmitted.

[74] Presumably, Assembly Balls.

Col. Mercer, to whom I delivered your message and compliments, joins me very heartily in wishing you and the Ladies of Belvoir the perfect enjoyment of every happiness this world affords. Be assured that I am, dear Madame, with the most unfeigned regard, your most obedient and most obliged humble servant.

N. B. Many accidents happening (to use a vulgar saying) between the cup and the lip, I choose to make the exchange of carpets myself, since I find you will not do me the honor to accept mine.

Now at Raystown, he was waiting for his answer, an answer that might contain the "one thing above all things in this world" that he wished to know. He was engaged to Martha; Sally was married and was happy, or, at least, she said so. Destiny, to his way of thinking controlled their fate. Still, he wished to know [75] . . . and did not find out. Sally replied promptly to his letter,[76] but she said nothing to disclose her state of mind toward him. Her letter was agreeable—that much he admitted. It gave details of what the young ladies of Sally's circle were doing and were intending. Washington was told, also, of plans for a performance of Addison's "Cato" in which Sally was to appear. Other neighborhood news there doubtless was, but nothing that dealt with the "one thing above all things" Washington desired to know.[77]

[75] It must be understood that this is an interpretation and not a statement of fact. Nothing lies behind the interpretation except the letter itself, the probabilities, the propinquity of residence in Fairfax, the eagerness of Washington to maintain a correspondence with Sally, and his subsequent statement that the happiest moments of his life had been enjoyed in her company (36 *G. W.*, 263). In putting this interpretation on events that extended over a number of years, there is no reason to assume any relationship that was not kept within the strictest proprieties. It scarcely could have escaped observation in a small society, having few subjects about which to gossip, that Washington admired Sally and that he displayed to her the measure of gallantry permissible on the part of a young bachelor and neighbor to the attractive wife of a close friend. On the other hand, scandal almost certainly would have been reported. Sally herself was of a prudent nature. Late in life she wrote that it had been her maxim "to go without what I wanted ever so much if I could not pay instantly, for I considered that I robbed the seller of the interest of his money by withholding the payment" (W. M. Cary, *Sally Cary*, 49). A woman guided by that principle might want the admiration of the tall master of Mount Vernon, who was already the most renowned young Virginian, but she would not take any chances with him. Washington, in turn, doubtless talked many times to her in those half-personal generalities that are indirect avowal of love. He never broke out, in any other surviving letter, as he did in this one, prompted by the receipt of a missive in her beautiful handwriting. Even if he was engaged and she was married, it was natural, it was youthfully human, for him to try to find out, before he went into the wilderness again, whether she really cared for him. Almost every man of 26 has at least that measure of vanity. The language of the letter is so involved and obscure that it best is interpreted as double entendre (see *infra, n.* 78), but whatever Washington's reason for writing as he did, no explanation is quite so unreasonable as one that would deny what he certainly meant to say—that he was going to marry Martha but was in hopeless love with Sally and wished above everything else to know whether she loved him. Any theory that he was writing throughout of Martha, rather than of Sally, leads to absurdities of misinterpretation.

[76] He received it on or prior to the 25th.

[77] Sally's letter is not in any of the known surviving records, but see Washington's reply of Sept. 25, 1758; 2 *G. W.*, 292 ff.

He was both puzzled and sobered by her tone. Answering her, he began: "Dear Madam, Do we still misunderstand each other's letters? I think it must appear so, though I would feign hope the contrary as I cannot speak plainer without, But I'll say no more, and leave you to guess the rest." [78] Then, admonished by her own restraint, he wrote much as Sally had, of the events occurring around him. Toward the end, he jested somewhat feebly on a few of the subjects mentioned in her letter, and he concluded: "Adieu dear Madam, you possibly will hear something of me or from me before we shall meet. I must beg the favor of you to make my compliments to Colonel Cary [79] and the ladies with you, and believe me that I am most unalterably. Your most obedient and obliged . . ." [80] He had not used in any earlier letter to her that adverb "unalterably."

It was not difficult for Washington to answer her in the spirit of her own news-filled letter, because he, too, had news to communicate. He had heard it on the 20th or 21st of September,[81] but probably had waited for details and had not even reported it to Governor Fauquier until the day he wrote to Sally of a strange and costly misadventure. Maj. James Grant of the 77th Regiment had gone westward over the Allegheny Mountains and Laurel Hill and, with his troops, had joined Colonel Bouquet at Loyal Hannon. Bouquet, senior officer there, had abundant force to beat off any surprise attack, but he was harassed by small bands of Indians who lurked around his camp, picked up stragglers and fired almost daily at the men sent to care for the horses in nearby woods. No effective tactics had been devised for keeping these savages at a distance. Having few Indians in his service at that time, Bouquet had not been able to use them to stalk or to ambush the marauders.

[78] *Ibid*. The punctuation is preserved and manifestly is difficult to interpret. Washington may have meant what would have been indicated readily enough by modern punctuation as: "I cannot speak plainer without—but I'll say no more and leave you to guess the rest." His use of this language here is confirmatory evidence that he intended his letter of September 12 to be vague: He could not write more plainly "without" disclosing his love in a paper that might be opened and read en route to her. Quite often, it will be recalled, curious persons did this with other persons' correspondence and then resealed it. Cf. Vol. I, p. 155.

[79] Her father. The fact that Washington sent these messages to Sally's "Cary kin" is the reason for saying she probably was at her "old home" when he wrote his previous letter. Evidence on this score, though strong, is not conclusive.

[80] 2 *G. W.*, 294. This letter was assumed by Edward Everett to have been directed to Martha Custis but this obviously is excluded by the reference to Colonel Cary and to young women of the Cary or Fairfax circle. Neill, in turn, thought the addressee was Sally's sister, Mary Cary. Here again the internal evidence explodes the theory. The opening sentences need not have been employed in a letter to Mary Cary: they fit perfectly into the letter previously written Sally Cary. Besides, a reference to "Miss Cary" near the end of the letter almost certainly concerned Mary.

[81] Forbes received the report on the evening of the 20th of September (*Forbes*, 215).

About the time of Grant's arrival, Bouquet had decided to send out a number of detachments to scour the country and, if possible, to waylay the French Indians and to recover the prisoners that had been carried off. Grant disapproved this. He was surprised, he said, that Bouquet was making ready to employ small parties when this had been found dangerous and futile. If Bouquet would give him 500 men, Grant stated, he would make a secret march to Fort DuQuesne, would ascertain conditions there, and, if circumstance favored him, he would make a night attack on the Indians who were supposed to be camped around the fort. No great danger would attend this reconnaissance; reports, said Grant, indicated that the French at the junction of the Allegheny and the Monongahela did not exceed 600.[82] Bouquet demurred. Grant pressed tenaciously and showed by his argument that he had given thought to his proposal, even to the detail of how his men were to distinguish one another in the event they delivered a night attack. At length Bouquet yielded and countermanded his orders for the march of the detachment, but he cautiously increased to about 750 the number of troops, exclusive of Indians, whom Grant was to take. Only when all the decisions had been made by Bouquet did he call in the officers who knew more than he, and immeasurably more than Grant had learned about woodland warfare—James Burd, who commanded the Pennsylvanians, and Andrew Lewis, in charge of the advanced Companies of Washington's Regiment.[83] Lewis's experience with British commanders in the American forest made him doubt their aptitude and training for this type of fight. His soldierly common sense warned him against the dispatch of so small a force as 750 white men, with a few native scouts, to reconnoitre close to the French fort and at so considerable a distance from his own base.[84] These objections being

[82] Intelligence reports on the strength of the French at Fort DuQuesne had varied much. In the late autumn of 1757, the French were not supposed to exceed 200 to 300, though 600 Indians were close by (Md. Gazette, Dec. 22, 1757). Deserters said in March, 1758, that the French numbered 230, with many Indians nearby and easily assembled (3 Penn. Arch., 363). Another report of the winter (Md. Gazette, Mch. 9, 1758), was that the Twightwees had been refused access to the French fort and had been so angered that they had made a treaty with the Six Nations against the French. Washington's information in the early summer was that the French garrison consisted of 400 or 500 who went across the river daily to work on a new fort (Fauquier to the Lords of Trade, July 24, 1758; P.R.O., CO: 5, 1329, f. 181). By Sept. 1, 1758, Washington estimated the total strength of the French to be not above 800, of whom 300 to 400 were Indians (2 G. W., 277). French information of English plans and movements, though meagre, was not inaccurate. Montcalm wrote the ministry, Apr. 18, 1758, that the English were preparing great movements on the Ohio and were seeking to draw the Indians from the French alliance. As of Oct. 21, 1758, Montcalm's report to his home government was to estimate Forbes's force as 8000 men. See Col. des MSS relatifs à la Nouvelle France, v. 4, p. 156, 201.

[83] Bouquet to Forbes, Sept. 17, 1758; Br. Mus. Add. MS 21640, f. 165. This is Bouquet's report to his immediate superior.

[84] The grounds of Lewis's protest were not set forth in Washington's reference to them (37 G. W., 483), but in the existing circumstances they were obvious.

overruled, Lewis was ready to obey orders but, silent and distant as he always appeared, he was insistent this time that it be remembered he had not approved the plan.[85]

Off, then, the column moved on the 9th of September—300 Highlanders of the 77th, 100 men of the new Royal American Regiment, about 175 of the First Virginia, 100 Pennsylvanians, 100 Marylanders, and a mixed Indian contingent of Nottoways, Tuscaroras and Catawbas.[86] No opposition was encountered anywhere along the line of march. At 3 P.M. on the 12th Grant was on what appeared to him to be advantageous ground at a distance, according to his guides, of ten or twelve miles from Fort DuQuesne.[87] There he halted, made preparations for the final stage of his advance, and at length shaped his plan to conform approximately to his orders from Bouquet, which were to this effect: He was to reconnoitre the route from Loyal Hannon to Fort DuQuesne and was to procure information concerning the garrison, the condition of the French defences and the number of Indians at hand. If he succeeded in reaching the vicinity of the fort without being detected, he would be free to occupy the adjacent hill and to open fire on the Indians camped outside the parapet. In the event he discovered the savages huddled around their fires after dark, he was authorized to have a detachment put on white shirts over their jackets and proceed to attack the Indians shortly after midnight.[88]

85 *Ibid.*

86 Bouquet reported (*loc. cit.*) that the Virginians numbered 150, but Washington stated (2 *G. W.,* 292) that eight officers and 168 men were engaged. Forbes wrote Pitt, October 20, that Grant's force consisted of 900 men (*Forbes,* 237). In the account given in the *Penn. Gazette,* October 12, Carolinians are mentioned, but this may have been the reporter's error. Troops from that Colony are mentioned nowhere else, in examined records, as participants in this phase of the expedition. North Carolina was having much difficulty in financing defence. See 5 *Col. Rec. N.C.,* 932.

87 Grant's report to Forbes, Br. Mus. Add. MS 21652, p. 24, reprinted in 2 *Frontier Forts of Western Penn.,* 83 ff, and in Sipe, *History of Fort Ligonier,* 57 ff, etc. This document, which bears no date in its present form, was written by Grant at Fort DuQuesne. Its emphasis is on events preceding those described contemporaneously in the other principal accounts of this expedition, Bouquet's letter of Sept. 17, 1758, to Forbes (Br. Mus. Add. MS 21640, f. 165 ff), and another letter of anonymous origin quoted indirectly in *Penn. Gazette,* Oct. 12, 1758. A report by Bouquet to Amherst sometimes is mentioned but apparently this was merely a copy, or perhaps an early draft of the report to Forbes. No such paper to Amherst appears among the originals in Br. Mus. Washington's own accounts, 2 *G. W.,* 290–91, 292–93, evidently were derived from the materials Bouquet used as the basis of his report. This information came from returning participants, who saw only a part of the action and knew little, if anything, of Grant's tactical plan. Moreover, Bouquet himself was confused regarding the sequence and relative importance of the events. In spite of the frailty of the foundation, most of the accepted versions of Grant's reconnaissance have been built on Bouquet's reports and Washington's letters. The result may be unfair to Grant, but as will appear presently, his own narrative is a sufficient basis for definite judgment on his conduct of the operation.

88 This is Bouquet's description of the plan, *loc. cit.* The Colonel did not state how many of the details concerning the attack were his and how many originated with Grant.

For the successful execution of this strange plan, Grant had, of course, to preserve the maximum possible secrecy during the final stage of his advance and had to regulate his march in such a manner that he would approach the fort after dark but with adequate information concerning the ground. Grant had been marked—not to say notorious—for what he frankly admitted was a "repugnance" to provincial officers, but he had announced sometime previously that he had overcome this.[89] He said after the expedition that on the way toward Fort DuQuesne he talked often to Andrew Lewis about the plan he intended to use, but he probably did not ask for counsel. Lewis was not the man to volunteer it. Like the regulars who had marched to the Monongahela under Braddock in 1755, Grant had confidence in his own military knowledge and faith in his men "from home" though neither he nor they had any larger experience in Indian warfare than that of a few patrols around Loyal Hannon.

Grant's troops rested on the night of the 12th–13th of September without challenge or alarm. At daybreak, the commander directed Lewis to take 200 soldiers and most of the Indians and to advance to a suitable position about five miles from the fort. There Lewis was to put his men in ambush. This was to be done on the theory that if the approach of the British had been observed, any party the French might send out would walk into the trap. Before French reenforcements could arrive from the fort, Grant would be able to join Lewis with the main body of troops.[90]

Grant then ordered one of the younger officers, Lieut. Colesby Chew,[91] to take a party of fifteen or twenty and with them—the words are Grant's own—"to reconnoitre the ground and to try, without exposing himself or the men, to draw a party of the enemy into the ambuscade." Chew either was told, or was expected without being instructed, to join Lewis about 10 A.M. Both parties moved off promptly. Grant waited at his bivouac until 3 P.M. that day, September 13, and then he resumed his march toward the fort. After he had proceeded four miles, he reached Lewis's ambuscade, which, he was told, was not seven miles from the walls of Fort DuQuesne. Somewhat to his surprise,

---

[89] Bouquet to Forbes, Aug. 20, 1758; Br. Mus. Add. MS 21640, f. 147. In April, 1775, a "gentleman in England" alleged to a correspondent in Virginia that Grant had told the House of Commons he always treated the colonials as beasts of burden and thought they deserved no better usage because they were fit for nothing else (Peter Force, *American Archives*, Ser. 4, v. 2, p. 319).

[90] Grant's report, *loc. cit.*

[91] Killed in the campaign; a brother of Washington's friend Joseph Chew of New London, Conn. (3 *Hamilton*, 113–14; *Journ. H. B.*, 1761–65, p. 122).

Grant did not find Chew with Lewis, nor did he get any news that the enemy was being lured toward the ambush. Everything was quiet; the position of Lewis appeared to be admirable. At 6 o'clock, Grant left Lewis's station and with that officer and all the troops except the contingent of Chew, he started for the hill that overlooked the Indian camps and the fort.

The reports of the guides concerning the distance proved to be erroneous. Instead of a stretch of less than seven miles from the ambuscade to the hill, there were twelve. When about ten of these were covered, Grant ordered Capt. Thomas Bullett and fifty men of the Virginia Regiment to halt and to remain at that point as a guard of the baggage. Once more on the way, Grant was joined by Chew, who reported that he had not had any luck. His three Indian scouts had left him soon after he moved from the bivouac that morning. In ignorance of the country, he had been forced to conceal himself until night permitted him to proceed in the direction he knew the column would follow.[92]

By 11 P.M. Grant reached the hill a few hundred yards from the fort and there he assembled 750 men or more, Indians included, almost within rifle-range of the French. So far as he knew, he still enjoyed all the advantage of surprise. How best to utilize that advantage, when he manifestly could not capture the fort by regular approaches, was the question Grant had to answer. His original plan had been to detail separate parties to attack the Indians around each of the fires, but as he looked down from the hill toward the fort, he saw only two or three fires close together. This might mean that few Indians were around the fort; it might indicate merely that the fires had burned out while the savages had slept; or it might be a warning that the natives had learned of the approach of the English and had withdrawn into the fort.

Grant sent for Lewis immediately and explained that the absence of Indian fires prevented the execution of the original plan. It still would be possible, he said, to remain a day in front of the fort without being discovered. The utmost should be made of that opportunity, and at once. Lewis must take 200 provincials and 200 Highlanders and, in Grant's words, "attack anything that was found about the fort." The commander explained afterwards: "I gave orders that no attention

---

92 Grant's report, *loc. cit.* Bouquet reported that Chew "did some reconnoitering and said that the Indians were in the blockhouses, easy to force." This was not mentioned by Grant.

should be paid to the sentries who would probably challenge and in case they were fired upon they were not to return it upon any account— but to march on as fast as possible and were not to fire a shot until they were close to the enemy; and that after they discharged their pieces they were to use their bayonets without loading a second time. I told the Major that I would order all our drums and pipes to beat the retreat, that I was indifferent what order they came back in, that it was the same thing to me if there were not three of them together, provided they did the business they were sent upon." [93] In spite of the midnight, Grant felt absolute confidence that these orders could be obeyed. The troops had on the prescribed white shirts and could distinguish one another a short distance apart; they did not have far to move; 400 seemed a sufficient number to deal with all adversaries who might be found outside the fort.

After the attacking force started down the hill, Grant disposed the other troops and placed the pipes and the drums immediately in front of the remaining Highlanders, who held the centre of the line spread across the high ground. Minutes passed. No sound of rifles came from the vicinity of the fort; no fires flared. Grant did not know what had happened to muffle or to engulf his attack. After a time of nervous waiting, Lewis came out of the darkness. It was impossible to proceed, he said; the road was bad, logs blocked it, the men were bewildered. They might fire into their own divided ranks and might not find their way back. Grant, surprised and angry, answered only that the sound of the drums and pipes would have told the men how to retreat, and then, with no further words, he hurried down from the hill to see conditions for himself. "I found the troops," he said later, "in the greatest confusion I ever saw men in, which in truth was not surprising for the Major had brought them back from the plain when he returned himself, and every man took a road of their own." [94] It was too late, Grant said in his official report, to attempt to re-form Lewis's command or to move forward the men who had been left on the hill. All he could think of doing, he wrote, was to move forward a detachment of fifty men toward the place where on arrival during the night he had seen two or three fires burning.

This was attempted, but no Indian camps were found. The detachment had to content itself with setting afire one of the storehouses,[95]

93 Grant's report, *loc. cit.*   94 *Ibid.*
95 The French report termed this a barn.

where the flames soon were extinguished.[96] About the time this party was mounting the hill again, in foggy dawn, Grant sent Lewis back with 250 men, of the Virginia and Royal American Regiments, to the point, two miles from the front, where Captain Bullett had been left with the baggage. This division of force was made because, as Grant phrased it, he thought the enemy might "possibly send a detachment to harass us in our march or perhaps to cut us off in case we were forced to make a retreat."[97] Lewis consequently was instructed to put his men in ambuscade so that he would have the advantage of any foe sent against him.

Now, with about 550 men at his command, Grant shifted some of his Highlanders to the left and put the Pennsylvanians on his right. Soon, when he learned that the position of the detachment on the left had been discovered by Indians, Grant directed his drums to beat the reveille. This he did "in order to put on a good countenance and to convince our men they had no reason to be afraid." He added later: "I must own I thought we had nothing to fear,"[98] but disillusionment was immediate. Out from the fort poured the French garrison, with their Indian allies in front. Small parties, working together, scattered among the trees, fired, loaded again and then dashed forward to like shelter. The Highlanders' officers, imprudently exposed, were shot down at once. Startled soldiers became bewildered and broke. On the other flank, according to Grant, the Pennsylvanians fell back without firing a shot. Grant resolved to continue the fight, but he promptly sent a message to Lewis to make the best dispositions possible until the advanced units retreated to the ground the Virginians and the detachment of the Royal Americans occupied.

Lewis never received the order. As soon as the swelling sound of the fire made it clear that Grant was attacked and was being compelled to give ground, Lewis yielded to the pleas of his officers and men that he go to the rescue. He pushed forward at once but could not establish

---

96 Grant's report, *loc. cit.*, and *Penn. Gazette*, Oct. 12, 1758.

97 Grant's report, *loc. cit.*

98 Grant's report, *loc. cit.* In all the printed versions of Grant's report occurs a singular passage to the effect that, in the event of such a situation as developed at this stage of the engagement, "Colonel Bouquet and I had settled that a plan should be taken 'a la barke de la Grisette'" which appears, on first reading, to contain some now forgotten illusion. The early copy of this report in the *Bouquet Papers*, Br. Mus. Add. MS 21652, f. 24, shows that the phrase has been misread. It is Italian, not French—de la barbe de la Garetta or, as the text is obscure, Garotta; but this does not aid in the interpretation. So distinguished an authority as Alberto Tarchiani, the Italian Ambassador to the United States, had to conclude that the phrase "does not make sense and corresponds to nothing in military parlance" (Letter of Nov. 7, 1747).

contact with Grant, whose men now were scattered and in hopeless confusion. While Grant vainly sought to rally the fugitives on any high ground they reached, Lewis tried to stop the French. The fire of the provincials delayed the enemy but did not halt him, because Lewis's line of advance was exposed and the flank was uncovered by the retreat of Grant's contingent.[99]

A few minutes more, and the situation was beyond repair. Panic gripped the men who had received the first attack. Even Lewis's veterans of forest warfare did not linger behind their trees for many shots at the enemy. Soon the survivors were flocking back to the baggage and to the guard under Capt. Thomas Bullett. That officer did not wait for refugees and pursuing French and Indians to engulf him. Although he could count only his fifty rifles, he attacked as furiously as if he had a Regiment. The fast and determined fire of this contingent made the enemy hesitate long enough for the surviving Highlanders and provincials to escape. "Fear had then got the better of every other passion," Grant later wrote. He personally had a chance to run to the rear but as long as he found one of his men still willing to stand ground, he would not leave. "My heart is broke," he told an officer who pleaded with him to retire; "I shall never outlive this day!" [100] Bullett's Virginians continued to load and to fire, but they were too few to turn a bad retreat into a drawn battle. They held on, with fine courage, until all the British and provincials who had escaped death or capture were behind them, on the way back to Loyal Hannon. Then Bullett's men, too, stubbornly and reluctantly withdrew. The enemy did not pursue far.

Losses were severe for the force engaged. Early reports put total casualties at 370,[101] though it was hoped that some of these were men who had crossed the river, had lost their way in the woods and ultimately would reach camp.[102] A subsequent list covered twenty-two officers and 278 men killed.[103] Of this number, the Virginians slain in Washington's Regiment numbered sixty-two. The wounded of that command were fifty-one.[104] At first it was feared that Lewis and Grant

[99] Perhaps both flanks were uncovered. In the absence of all information concerning the direction of Lewis's march, it is impossible to say.

[100] Bouquet to Forbes, *loc. cit.*   [101] Bouquet to Forbes, *loc. cit.*

[102] *Ibid.*

[103] The French maintained that their losses were eight killed and a like number wounded. See Daine to Maréchal de Belle Isle, Nov. 3, 1758; 2 *Frontier Forts of Western Penn.*, with quotation from 6 *Penn. Arch.*, 2nd ser., 423.

[104] 2 *G. W.*, 292; 37 *ibid.*, 482.

had been slain, but soon a flag of truce announced that both these officers, five of lesser rank, two Sergeants and thirty privates had been made prisoners of war.[105]

Disgust at headquarters was general. Forbes was sure "no man [could] justify" the affair, which he attributed primarily to Grant's acceptance of the story that the French forces at Fort DuQuesne were small. This belief, said Forbes, "I am afraid made the Major run headlong to grasp at a name and public applause . . ." [106] Forbes felt, too, that Bouquet was to blame for permitting Grant to advance with so few men.[107] Previously, said Forbes, the Major had applied to him for permission to reconnoitre in force and had offered to make formal pledge of what would and would not be undertaken, but Forbes, in spite of a high opinion of Grant's ability[108] had refused to give the Major detached command. Some of the Pennsylvanians had a clear impression of the man and of his aim. "Ye see," wrote William Peters, "Major Grant was spurred on by ambition and his meeting with no opposition till the action to exceed his orders." [109] Washington was not well-informed of the details but was convinced that the operation was poorly planned. Being himself ambitious, Washington did not denounce Grant's passion for distinction as a vice responsible for the defeat. All he said on that score was an echo of the universal conclusion that Grant must have gone beyond anything orders permitted.[110]

In the light of reports not then available to Washington, both Bouquet and Grant now appear to have been inexcusably at fault in planning the expedition without consulting in advance the provincial officers who had experience in woodland warfare. Grant was foolish in proposing tactics when he had only the vaguest knowledge of the ground or of the strength of his adversary. Bouquet did not live up to his reputation when, in like ignorance, he gave explicit orders. It availed Bouquet and Grant little to consult Andrew Lewis after the adoption of a plan that was basically defective and inflexible. If the purpose was to get information, twenty woodmen could have learned more in a shorter time and with immeasurably less risk. On the other hand, if

---

[105] 2 *G. W.*, 294; 3 *Hamilton,* 124. The circumstances of Grant's surrender are given in his report.

[106] *Forbes,* 225.   [107] *Ibid.,* 215.

[108] Cf. Forbes to Bouquet, Aug. 28, 1758, a propos of the command of a stronger guard: "I am afraid you must desist from the thoughts of it and turn the burden of the whole upon Major Grant, whose parts as a military man are inferior to few . . ." (*Forbes,* 189).

[109] Letter of Sept. 29, 1758, to R. Peters; 3 *Penn. Arch.,* 547.

[110] 2 *G. W.,* 294–95. He was more detailed but not well informed in a letter to his brother "Jack"; Sept. 25, 1758; 37 *G. W.,* 482.

the aim was to deliver a surprise attack on the Indians who were believed to be in camp around the fort, far more preparation and training
were called for than were allowed.

The operation in its final stage was a surprise night attack on a position with which the participating officers were unfamiliar. No more
difficult mission could have been assigned troops. It was an undertaking hopelessly beyond performance by such soldiers as Grant sent
down the hill in complete darkness to "attack anything that was
found about the fort." The Scots and the provincials did precisely as
any other body of like inexperience would have. That is to say, they
imagined the worst and did nothing. Grant found an anonymous
apologist who later attributed the disaster "to the absolute disobedience
of orders in a provincial officer the night they reached the Ohio and
by this man's quitting his post next A.M." [111] Had Lewis been free or
disposed to answer, he might have said that the orders of the night
of the 13th–14th were so manifestly impossible to execute that the
attempt would have led to the destruction of the entire force.

Grant's dispositions after the return of Lewis to the hill were reckless.
Even at that hour, close to daylight on the 14th, Grant had not been
discovered. Surprise was complete. Colonials later doubted this,[112]
but the French report is explicit: ". . . the vanguard of the English
. . . would have surprised M. de Lignery, commandant . . . the detachment having taken an unexpected route, had not some Englishmen
in advance made a noise and set fire to a barn at a distance." [113] The
French, in short, knew nothing of the presence of the English until,
after Lewis's return to the hill, Grant sent a few men in the general
direction of the place where, earlier in the night, he had seen two or
three fires. Grant was desperate when he disclosed his presence by
making this movement, in order, as he put it, "that something at least
might be attempted." He went on to explain: "I desired [the officers]
to kill a dozen of the Indians, if possible, and I would be satisfied." [114]
In other words, having marched up the hill and found his mission impossible, he risked his entire force rather than march down again and
admit that he could do nothing. His justification, in his own mind,

[111] *Gentleman's Mag.*, April, 1759, p. 171 ff.
[112] Cf. "A New Englandman" in *Gentleman's Mag.*, May, 1759, p. 223: "[The French and
Indians] knew every step of Grant's motions and had left their fires and hut in the field and
retired into the fort."
[113] Daine to Maréchal de Belle Isle, Nov. 3, 1758; 2 *Frontier Forts of Western Penn.*, 89, with
quotation from 6 *Penn. Arch.*, 2nd ser., 423. The correct name of the officer was not "de Lignery"
but François Marchand des Ligneris.   [114] Grant's report, *loc. cit.*

doubtless was that he could throw away the larger advantage of surprise, even for twelve Indians, because he believed the garrison of Fort DuQuesne to be too small to do him damage. That reason merely shifted blame from bad judgment in action to uncritical acceptance of poor military intelligence.

Grant's division of his little force, after the disclosure of his presence, was so manifestly reckless, so contrary to the rudiments of warfare, that criticism is unnecessary. At Forbes's headquarters, there was no disposition whatever to shield Grant or to deny the provincials full credit for what they had done to prevent a worse defeat. Too little was known at the time about the details of the action for Lewis's conduct to be appraised accurately,[115] though Bullett's defence was acclaimed.[116] Bouquet was inclusive, rather than discriminating, when he reported: "had it not been for the Virginians, all would have been cut to pieces." [117]

That was the judgment of the surviving Scottish regulars themselves. Washington wrote proudly: "The Highlanders and them [i.e., the Virginians] are become one people, shaking each other by the hand wherever they meet, though perfect strangers." [118] A somewhat contrary spirit in London was to be rebuked later by an anonymous "New Englander" in the Gentleman's Magazine: ". . . the surprise was indeed complete, but not the disgrace, for provincials were there to lay the blame on . . . unhappy provincials. If success attends where you are joined with the regulars they claim all the honor though not a tenth part of your number. If disgrace, it is all yours though you happen to be but a small part of the whole and have not the command; as if regulars were in their nature invincible, when not mixed with provincials and provincials of no kind of value without regulars." [119]

The tone of condemnation might differ on opposite sides of the Atlantic, but after Grant's defeat there was not at Raystown a touch

---

[115] This has held true ever since. Lewis filed no narrative and made no defence other than one included near the end of Grant's report, to the effect that when he went back to Grant to give notice that he could not execute orders for the night attack, he left his troops in good order. The only evidence at hand concerning his subsequent return to the assistance of Grant is a statement by Bouquet that Lewis heard the sound of Grant's battle and was "pressed by officers and men" to act as he did. Lewis's route and his action are so vaguely described that analysis is impossible.

[116] Cf. Washington to Sally Fairfax, Sept. 25, 1758: "Your old acquaintance, Captain Bullett . . . has acquired immortal honor in this engagement by his gallant behavior . . ." (2 G. W., 292–93. Cf. 37 ibid., 482–83).

[117] Bouquet to Forbes, loc. cit.

[118] Letter to J. A. Washington, Sept. 25, 1758; 37 G. W., 483.

[119] Issue of May, 1759, p. 223.

of the despair that prevailed at Fort Cumberland after the surrender of Fort Necessity or after the disaster to Braddock. The loss, though regrettable, was not considered serious enough to weaken materially a force that believed itself definitely superior.[120] In Forbes's mind, the only foe that could stop the British advance was continued bad weather.

To Washington, out of sympathy with the direction of the enterprise, "affairs in general" appeared to wear "a greater gloom than ever."[121] He echoed his old complaint: ". . . I see no probability of opening the road this campaign: How then can we expect a favorable issue to the expedition?"[122] In his letter to Sally Fairfax he said: "So miserably has the expedition been managed that I expect after a month's further trial, and the loss of many more men by the sword, cold and perhaps famine, we shall give the expedition over as impracticable this season, and retire to the inhabitants, condemned by the world and derided by our friends."[123] He was not reconciled or even mollified when General Forbes on the 24th of September publicly complimented him on the behavior of the Virginians in Grant's fight.[124] Privately, Washington admitted to his brother: "It is with infinite pleasure I tell you that the Virginians, officers and men distinguish[ed] themselves in the most eminent manner . . . every mouth resounds their praises."[125] Publicly, he carefully obeyed orders and continued to voice doubts.

Forbes daily was issuing prudent directions[126] of instructional value to a young officer who never had operated with so large a body of men as Forbes had under his command. There were lessons, also, in such matters as Forbes's arrangements for putting the army in condition to move on an hour's notice.[127] Equally informative was the General's careful explanation of the manner in which soldiers were to get themselves and their arms in order after exposure to a heavy rain.[128] As one of these well-fashioned orders followed another, Washington did not disdain them. On the contrary he doubtless read them carefully, and compared them with his own experience. Disappointed though he was, he was not disgruntled. Concerning the line of advance, he still differed from his chief but he did not sulk. Early in October, at the request of

120 Cf. Forbes to Bouquet, Sept. 23, 1758; *Forbes*, 218 ff.
121 To Governor Fauquier, Sept. 25, 1758; 2 *G. W.*, 291.
122 *Ibid.*
123 Letter of Sept. 25, 1758; 2 *G. W.*, 293.
124 Cf. 2 *G. W.*, 290.
125 To J. A. Washington, Sept. 25, 1758; 37 *G. W.*, 483.
126 *Forbes's Orderly Book*, Sept. 21, 22, 23 *et seq.*, 1758.
127 *Ibid.*, Sept. 28, 1758.   128 *Ibid.*, Oct. 11, 1758.

Forbes's Colonels, who met for discussion, Washington drafted two
diagrams to show how a column, moving through wooded country
and without wagons, could be formed quickly into an order of battle.
He took much pains to work out the tactical details and he illustrated
his dispositions by using a force of the size Forbes probably would
employ, namely 4000 men.[129] This evidenced cooperation, but neither
this nor anything else bespoke enthusiasm.

The chilly skepticism of the Virginians did not deter or even discourage Forbes. Resolute, though now too sick from bloody flux to
ride a horse, he battled with nearly all the usual perplexities of the field
and with some that were exceptional. The soldiers had to be notified
of a shortage of salt so serious that every man must find his own.
Women camp-followers were ordered to the hospital to be examined
for "the venial disease." If found to have it, they were to be detained
for curative treatment or else were to be turned out of camp.[130] Forbes
suffered, too, from a shortage of engineers. The one he esteemed most
had been killed or captured in Grant's disaster.[131] Harry Gordon, a
veteran of Braddock's campaign, had, in Forbes's grim figure, "either
gone off at the nail" or become dilatory. The General complained
of Gordon: "If a trifle is to be done he makes it a labor to man and
horse, and, if a work of consequence, makes slight of it." [132]

While all these and many like things were vexing the sick commander, the French became active. "Having a mind," in Forbes's
words, "to repay Major Grant's visit," the enemy sent a column against
Loyal Hannon. Its approach was discovered on the morning of the
12th by the firing of twelve guns Southwest of the camp. Col. James
Burd of the Pennsylvania troops, commanding in Bouquet's absence,
immediately sent out detachments to surround what he assumed to be
a marauding party. When he found the French and Indians were in
considerable strength, Burd dispatched a force of 500 to deal with them.
Soon these reenforcements and the survivors of the first detachments
were driven back to the earthwork that had been thrown up to protect
the camp. Thereupon the French boldly approached this defence and
opened a hot fire, but they did not make a direct assault. After about
two hours they reluctantly withdrew with many stolen horses—only

[129] The diagrams, explanation and bibliographical note will be found in 2 G. W., 295 ff.
See also Cal. N. J., Archives, No. 32.
[130] Forbes's Orderly Book, Oct. 4, 1758.
[131] This was Charles Rhor, of whose death Forbes was convinced by October 8. See Forbes
to Abercromby, Oct. 8, 1758; Forbes, 225.
[132] Ibid.

to return that night. Discouraged then, they disappeared. Although they had killed two officers and had slain or carried off sixty of the garrison, they scarcely had been repaid for an arduous march and a day's hard fighting. Forbes was disappointed that the French were not pursued, but he wrote cheerfully, "I fancy they will not visit soon again." [133]

It was now his turn, his last chance of 1758. In the knowledge that he had left only a brief period in which to strike at Fort DuQuesne, Forbes strained every man and every horse and every wheel in an effort to get close enough to deliver a swift and sudden blow. All troops were to be held in readiness for advance at the beat of a drum. Charges were to be drawn and arms reloaded; horses were to be well secured so that no time would be lost in getting the wagons started; officers were given permission to put on the garb they considered best for the woods. [134]

On October 15, Washington was directed to proceed by the road that had been opened through Shawnee Cabins, Edmond's Swamp, Stony Creek and Muddy Run to Laurel Ridge and thence over the mountain to Loyal Hannon. [135] Immediately, the objective of Washington and a Battalion of 200 was Stony Creek, which Bouquet, on inspection, had wished to render more secure after the fight with the enemy at Loyal Hannon on the 12th. [136] The first stages of this march were not a particular ordeal. Forbes himself went along in a swinging horse litter, [137] because he was too weak and too sore from his flux to use any other transportation. In the presence of their commander, the men probably were a little more diligent than normally they would have been. Veterans who had tramped from Winchester to Fort Cumberland and up and down the South Branch of the Potomac had nothing to fear from Pennsylvania mud as far along their road as the southeast side of Laurel Hill, which was reached on the 21st.

It was the road over the mountain that made Bouquet and Forbes wonder if, after all, they possibly could win the race with winter. As in the struggle with Allegheny Mountain, the odds changed almost daily. "I was in hopes fortune might have favored us with a little good

133 His letter of Oct. 16, 1758, to R. Peters is the best account of this so-called "Battle of Loyal Hannon." See *Forbes*, 236, and 1 *Pitt*, 372. Burd's early reports are in 2 *Frontier Forts of Western Penn.*, 201.

134 *Forbes's Orderly Book*, Oct. 14, 1757.

135 2 *G. W.*, 299 n.

136 *Forbes*, 229. For Bouquet's presence at Stony Creek on the 12th, see Bouquet to James Burd, that date; *Shippen Papers*, 143.   137 *Forbes*, 197, 202.

weather for our roads," Forbes had written on the 10th of October,[138] but hope seemed almost vain. Five days later, Bouquet's report of conditions was so unfavorable that Forbes acknowledged, "it pierces me to the very soul, yet still my hopes are that a few dry days would make things wear a more favorable aspect . . ."[139] The next day the road over Laurel Ridge was impassable, "so" the indomitable Forbes wrote, "we must wait some dry days to be able to go forward," and he added earnestly, "God grant them soon."[140] Actually, though he did not then know it, an alternative and easier pass over the mountain already had been discovered. When this could be opened by the mercy of the rain demons, it would offer a route four miles shorter than the one then in use.[141]

Along this newly cut road, Forbes painfully climbed on the 20th to the crest of the ridge. That was in itself a triumph, but when note of it was set down on the calendar it raised a doubt. Forbes had been told that October and November were the best months for a campaign because it then was possible to see a little way through the woods and thereby to avoid surprises. Instead, he found the season forbidding. "If the weather does not favor," he wrote, "I shall be absolutely locked up in the mountains, nor do I scarce see a possibility of recrossing the Alleganey Mountain."[142]

Every day that the weather permitted, Forbes pushed his men forward and at length, on the 23rd of October, he advanced Washington to Loyal Hannon.[143] The Virginian remained a non-convert on the road and a skeptic concerning the outcome of the campaign. He reported to Governor Fauquier: "My march to this post gave me an opportunity of forming a judgment of the road; and I can truly say, that it is indescribably bad. Had it not been for an accidental discovery of a new passage over the Laurel Hill, the carriages must inevitably have been stopped on the other side. This is a fact nobody here takes upon him to deny! The General and great part of the troops, &c. being yet behind, and the weather growing very inclement, must I apprehend terminate our expedition for this year, at this place. But as our affairs

[138] To Bouquet; *Forbes*, 228.
[139] *Ibid.*, Oct. 15, 1758.
[140] Letter to R. Peters, *ibid.*, 236.
[141] Bouquet to James Burd, Oct. 12, 1758; *Shippen Papers*, 143.
[142] Letter of Oct. 20–27, 1758; 1 *Pitt*, 373, 374.
[143] The itinerary was: October 14, Shawnee Cabins; 15th, Edmond's Swamp; 16th, Stony Creek; 17th–19th, Muddy Run; 20th, White Oak Ridge; 21st, S.E. side Laurel Ridge; 22nd, N.W side Laurel Ridge; 23rd, Loyal Hannon (*Forbes's Orderly Book,* summarized in 2 *G. W.,* 299 n).

are now drawing to a crisis, and a good or a bad opinion of them will shortly ensue, I choose to suspend my judgment, as well as a further account of the matter, to a future day." [144]

If the badness of roads was a matter of provincial jealousy, as well as one of success or failure in the campaign, a brave, unusual achievement now lighted the darkness of the rainy autumn and strengthened the heart of Forbes. He had been hourly mindful of the dangers he would face on the way to Fort DuQuesne if the Indians were his enemy [145] and he had been unwilling to acquiesce in the gloomy conclusion of some of the colonial leaders that the Indians of the Ohio country were now bound permanently to France. Instead, Forbes believed the Indians could be brought to see that Britain would win the war and that it was to their interest to be on the winning side. In soldierly conviction, he had undertaken to induce the government of Pennsylvania to negotiate for peace with France's savage allies.[146] Partly because of Forbes's persistence, Governor William Denny and the Council of Pennsylvania had asked Fredrich Post [147] to make a journey to the Ohio and to invite the Indians to renew their old treaties with England. Post, about forty-eight years of age, was a German lay missionary of the Moravian sect Unitas Fratrum, and for the whole of his sixteen years' residence in America he had been laboring among Indians [148] in whose language he had acquired proficiency. He demurred to the Governor's first appeal on the ground that such a service as was proposed for him did not become a missionary, but he was persuaded by the argument that, in Governor Denny's words, "bringing about a peace with the Indians would open the way for the servants of God to look for a future harvest." [149] Post left Philadelphia on the 15th of July and with a few companions went past Fort Augusta to Fort Venango and thence by way of Logstown to Fort DuQuesne. The French on the Ohio demanded of Post's Indian escort that he be surrendered, but the Indians refused, though they had not then decided whether they would accept his tender of peace. In spite of French machinations and the treachery of one of his companions, Post displayed so much courage, honesty and simple address that the Indians

---

[144] Letter of Oct. 30, 1758; 2 *G. W.*, 300.
[145] Forbes to Abercromby, Sept. 21, 1758; *Forbes*, 216.
[146] See *supra*, p. 310–11.
[147] He so signed his journal of July–September, 1758, though he usually is styled Frederick Post. See 3 *Penn. Arch.*, 544. He is entered in *DAB* as Christian Frederick Post.
[148] For the Moravians' work among the Indians, see 1 *Pennsylvania-Germania*, 499.
[149] See Post's passport of 1759, in 3 *Penn. Arch.*, 579.

agreed after some days to make peace if all the provincial Governors would join in it. With this assurance and the promise of some of the Indians to attend a conference soon to be held at Easton, Pennsylvania, Post succeeded in getting back to Fort Augusta on the 22nd of September, eight days after Grant's defeat. "Thirty-two days I did lay in the woods," he wrote gratefully; "the heavens was my covering, the dew came so hard sometimes that it pricked close to the skin . . . The Lord has preserved me through all danger and difficulties I have ever been under." [150]

While Post had been persuading the savages to end their war with England, Sir William Johnson and others, prodded by Forbes, had been inviting the Chiefs of many tribes to the meeting at Easton. Forbes had followed eagerly each step in this adventure of diplomacy and had countenanced military delays he otherwise would have rebuked, because he was afraid a premature blow against Fort DuQuesne might involve the death of some of the Indians who, by patience, might be prevailed upon to make peace and to desert the French.[151] At last, about October 27, Forbes heard that a treaty had been signed under which some of the Indians would make common cause with England but, as he reported to Pitt, "[they] require time, a thing at present so precious to me that I have none to spare." Then he stated his stark alternatives: "[I] must in a day or two choose either to risk everything and march to the enemy's fort, retreat across the Allegheny if the provincials leave me, or maintain myself where I am to the spring." [152]

These alternatives were not hypothetical. Apart from the paralyzing halt that might be caused by weather, there was danger the little army might be wrecked by discharge. The Second Virginia would cease to exist, under the terms of its enlistment, on December 1. Moreover, at a session of the General Assembly of Virginia recently adjourned,[153] it had been assumed that Fort DuQuesne would have been captured and the threat to the frontiers of Virginia ended by December 1. Provision accordingly had been made for the return of the First

---

[150] Fredrich Post's journal, a remarkable document, appears in 3 *Penn. Arch.,* 520–44. The quotation is from p. 543–54. His later journal, Nov. 27 ff, 1758, is in *ibid.,* 560 ff. Parkman's familiar account is in 2 *Montcalm and Wolfe,* 150 ff.

[151] See Forbes to Sharpe, Sept. 3, 1758, *Forbes,* 197; Forbes to Abercromby, Sept. 4, 1758, *ibid.,* 200; Forbes to Pitt, Oct. 20, 1758, *ibid.,* 238. His reports on the arrival of the natives and the prospects of the conference will be found in *ibid.,* 180–81, 183, 194, 203, 221, 230, 248.

[152] Letter of Oct. 20–27, 1758. For the minutes of the nineteen-day conference at Easton, Oct. 7–26, 1758, see 8 *Penn. Col. Rec.,* 175–223.

[153] It was convened September 14 and was prorogued October 12 (*Journ. H. B.,* 1758–62, p. 3, 45).

Regiment to Virginia at that date, and for its muster-out on May 1, 1759. The reason for continuing the life of the Regiment even to the next spring was that uncertainty might prevail for a time after Fort DuQuesne was taken and that the Regiment should prudently be kept in service to guard the frontier.[154] Now that there was doubt whether the campaign could be concluded victoriously before the end of November, Governor Fauquier had issued a call for the General Assembly to meet again on November 9 and to prolong the time the First Regiment might remain outside Virginia.[155] If the Assembly proved unwilling to do this, then, when one Virginia Regiment disbanded, the other would return to the old frontier. It was much the same with the Pennsylvania, Maryland and North Carolina troops. No pay beyond December 1 had been provided for them.[156] They might start home with the Virginians and leave the General no troops but the survivors of his 1500 Highlanders.

Forbes consequently had to work more vigorously than ever to put the troops in condition to go forward at maximum speed if November brought a sufficient number of clear days to dry the road. The grip of this emergency silenced the Virginia critics. Reporting to the Governor on November 5, Washington told of preparations for the advance: ". . . we expect to move on in a few days, encountering every hardship that an advanced season, want of clothing and indeed (no great stock of provisions) will expose us to. But it is no longer a time for pointing out difficulties; and I hope my next will run in a more agreeable strain." [157]

It still was most uncertain whether the "strain" actually would be better, but Forbes continued to improve his army and his communications. Effort was made to repair the badly washed road over the Allegheny Mountain; [158] a bakers' corps was established in order to reduce the number of small ovens used; the completion of eighty cartridges for each man was ordered; the sick were sent back to Raystown; [159] in the name of loyalty and of discipline the King's birthday was observed with salutes as formal and as numerous as if the little army were staging its ceremonials on a parade ground next an arsenal of England.[160] After this, and most regretfully, the ration was reduced

---

154 *Ibid.*, xiii; 7 H 171; 3 *Hamilton*, 117, 125.
155 3 *Hamilton*, 125–26; *Journ. H. B.*, 1758–62, p. 49.
156 Forbes to Amherst, Nov. 26–30, 1758; *Forbes*, 263.
157 2 *G. W.*, 301.   158 *Forbes*, 250.
159 *Forbes's Orderly Book*, Nov. 6–8, 1758.   160 *Ibid.*, Nov. 10, 1758.

in order that the men might have enough for the offensive or, if that failed, for a longer stay at Loyal Hannon in event mud choked the line of supply.

In these activities and in the regular drills and patrols, more than a third of the month dragged by. Skies remained dark. Uncertainty prevailed both as to the weather and as to the strength of the enemy. None of the Indians would undertake reconnaissance as far as Fort DuQuesne at that bleak and treacherous season. A solitary prisoner captured in the affair at Loyal Hannon had insisted there were 1000 white soldiers on the Ohio and abundant Indian support.[161] This was a higher figure than had been accepted in September, but it might be correct. The vigor of the reception given Grant and the boldness of the advance on Loyal Hannon had not indicated that the enemy lacked strength.

If, then, any less force than that of the entire command were thrown against the enemy's stronghold, the result with Forbes might be as ruinous as with Braddock. Daily there was grim subtraction; every day left one less of life for the force, one less of hope of victory. The whole army could not be counted upon now for more than three weeks. Another long period of wet weather assuredly would be a death warrant. A council of war, viewing all the contingencies, concluded "that it was not advisable" to go beyond Loyal Hannon until spring.[162]

The outlook was more discouraging than ever when, on the 12th of November, the outposts sent word that the enemy again was approaching Loyal Hannon. Forbes immediately had the drums beat the general assembly and, when the men formed ranks, he sent Washington off in person with 500 of the Virginia troops to pursue the French, who were assumed to be making another raid on the cattle and the horses of the British. Behind Washington, George Mercer was to proceed with another 500 men and was to try to surround the enemy. Washington proceeded briskly and in the late afternoon, at a point about three miles from camp, came upon a party of French and Indians around a fire. In a quick exchange of musketry, one of the alien soldiers was killed. By closing in quickly on the others, who undertook to flee, the Virginians captured a white prisoner and two Indians.

Washington held these prisoners near the fire and awaited develop-

---

[161] See Harry Gordon's interrogation, in French, of this prisoner, Oct. 14, 1758; *Shippen Papers*, 144.

[162] So wrote Washington (2 *G. W.*, 308–09). He is the only known witness on this point, but there is no reason to question the accuracy of his statement.

ments. Presently, through the growing darkness, a considerable force
was observed. Almost at the same instant, both sides delivered a
volley. Men fell; the wounded cried out. From the approaching troops
there likewise came shouts. Officers yelled their orders—and yelled
in English. The men were Mercer's own: Virginians were firing into
the ranks of their friends. Each side had mistaken the other for
French.

As soon as the grim mistake was realized, the men lowered their
guns and turned to the care of their wounded. The toll was heavier
than in any action Washington had witnessed after Braddock's defeat:
One lieutenant was dead; thirteen other soldiers had been killed;
twenty-six had been wounded.[163] The enemy, disappearing in the
darkness, might say mockingly that he did not need to attack the
English: they would kill one another. It was for Washington an experience so unhappy that he never wrote of it,[164] but some of his comrades remembered it. Twenty years later, a British officer was to record:
"The very first engagement in which he ever was concerned,[165] was
against his own countrymen." [166]

Washington's humiliation was not without balm. The white prisoner
taken by the Virginia Regiment proved to be a British subject, one
Johnson, who for some reason had thrown in his fortunes with the
French and had served in the garrison at Fort DuQuesne. If he could
be made to tell the truth, he could give Forbes the information most
desired, that of the strength of the enemy at Fort DuQuesne. Experienced officers [167] took Johnson in hand and informed him in stern
terms where he stood: For bearing arms against his King, he deserved
death. He would receive the extreme penalty, in some extraordinary
form, unless he divulged everything he knew about the French and
the situation on the Ohio. If he answered every question, and his information later was verified, he would receive a shining reward. Faced
with the promise of life and gold as the alternative to torture and
death, Johnson talked freely. The previous attack on Loyal Hannon,
he said, had been delivered by the French in an effort to make the
British think they were strong. Actually, the French at Fort DuQuesne

163 In Forbes to Abercromby, Nov. 17, 1758 (Forbes, 255), the total casualties are listed.
The Penn. Gazette of Nov. 30, 1758, reprinted in Md. Gazette of Dec. 7, 1758, is authority for
the statement that the killed were thirteen or fourteen.
164 At least in any letter that has survived.
165 The officer meant, of course, "as regimental commander."
166 "An Old Soldier," Gentleman's Mag., August, 1778, p. 368.
167 Their identity is not known.

were weak. The contingent that had made the raid on Loyal Hannon had quit the forks of the Allegheny and Monongahela; the Ohio Indians had gone home.[168] To this story, Johnson adhered. Similar information was given by the two captured Indians, who were examined separately and with much care.

Forbes believed his opportunity, his last opportunity, had come: he would gamble on the truth of this new intelligence; his advanced units must cut a road quickly over the last barrier of Chestnut Ridge; then with an unencumbered, fast-moving force he would march for Fort DuQuesne. Twenty-five hundred of the strongest men of the army must be selected. Each must take a blanket and a knapsack and nothing besides. Tentage and baggage were to be left behind. Only provisions, ammunition and some light artillery would be conveyed on wheels.[169]

To assure fullest mobility, Forbes divided his attacking force into three Brigades. One of these was to be commanded by Colonel Bouquet, and another by Lt. Col. Archibald Montgomery of the 77th. The third temporary Brigade, the only one entrusted to a provincial officer, was assigned to Washington.[170] He was not promoted and he could not be by Forbes, but in official papers and doubtless in formal salutation, he now was "Brigadier Washington." Even if he were merely acting at that rank, he had a standing to which many a Colonel of the regular establishment, twice his age, had aspired in vain. Brigadier . . . Brigadier . . . it had a pleasant, martial sound.

His command was to be his own Regiment, two Companies of artificers, and the Maryland, North Carolina and Delaware contingents,[171] whose joint first assignment was the unspectacular but indispensable one of helping to clear the projected road across Chestnut Ridge, the last great barrier on the way to the French stronghold. This stage of the advance was intended by Forbes to duplicate in miniature the system by which he had secured himself in traversing Eastern and Central Pennsylvania. Instead of attempting

---

168 *Penn. Gazette*, Nov. 30, 1758.

169 2 *G. W.*, 308–09; Capt. John Haslet to Rev. Dr. Alison, Nov. 26, 1758; 6 *Hazard's His. Reg.*, 227. Bouquet to Chief Justice William Allen, Nov. 25, 1758, *ibid.*, 226–27.

170 *Forbes's Orderly Book*, Nov. 14, 1758. In 2 *Ford*, 108, is a note between a letter of October 8 and one of October 30 to the effect that "on the 14th" the army was divided. This note was copied in 2 *G. W.*, 298. Casual reading would create the impression that this arrangement was made on the 14th of October, but Ford meant to give the date clearly set forth in the *Orderly Book*, November 14.

171 *Ibid.* The Delaware troops, as usual, were mentioned as the men from the "low counties."

to push steadily forward from a general base, Forbes, it will be remembered, had moved by stages and had established a succession of
storehouses on which he could draw. Now he sent out three forces.
One of Pennsylvanians under Col. John Armstrong was to proceed
through the woods ahead of the others and was to build redoubts one
or two days' marches apart. Washington was to follow and was to cut
a road; Montgomery was then to proceed, as a reenforcement of the
troops ahead and as a vanguard of the main body of infantry and
artillery. If Armstrong finished a given redoubt before the Virginians
reached him, then he was to work back on the road toward them.[172]

Into this labor Washington threw himself with tremendous energy.
As always, if he had a task to perform, he tried to do it superlatively.
On the 15th of November, the day after orders were issued him, he had
to wait several hours for the delivery of felling axes [173] and then he
received only forty-two; but with these he and his men set out and by
twilight, 4 P.M., were six miles from Loyal Hannon. There he met
Lieut. Thomas Bassett, who had thirty men and a like number of axes.
Washington immediately sent out his working parties. They found
the course of the projected road so faintly blazed that the Brigadier
had to request headquarters to assign him an engineer.

The next day at dawn, Washington began chopping down trees and
building bridges and causeways over rivulets and marshy ground. He
was resolved to do his full duty, but, even on the side of the last ridge
that barred the way, he could not forget the Potomac and the route
the Virginians were anxious to develop. In reporting to Forbes on the
day's work, which cleared six miles of the new trail, he raised the
question of the garrisoning and retention of Fort DuQuesne after it
was occupied. "I do not know so effectual a way of doing it," he wrote
his weary chief, "as by the communication of Fort Cumberland and
Genl. Braddock Road, which is in the first place good, and in the next,
fresh, affording good food if the weather keeps open which is more
than a road can do as much used as this one has been." [174]

More axes arrived that evening.[175] They were in such bad order, despite Forbes's regard for the care of all tools,[176] that some of the men
had to spend most of the night making them fit for use; [177] but the

---

172 This procedure nowhere is described in detail but it can be reconstructed easily from
Forbes, 254 ff and 2 *G. W.,* 301–08.
173 Washington used the other term, "falling axes."   174 2 *G. W.,* 303.
175 Bouquet wrote that he sent forty-two (3 *Hamilton,* 128).
176 Cf. *Forbes's Orderly Book,* Nov. 16, 1758.   177 2 *G. W.,* 304.

next day at dawn, all the axes were ringing in the forest on the mountainside. The result was that on the 17th of November—thirteen days
before the muster-out—he drove forward seven or eight miles.[178] Forbes,
meantime, was issuing new orders to expedite the march when the road
was ready: no women were to go forward with Washington's command;[179] new precautions were taken. Forbes even undertook to have
the men dress their food overnight, in order that they might lose no
time in the morning; but in this he could not overcome the provincials'
insistence on a hot breakfast, and he had to rescind the order.[180] Washington knew those habits better. He saw his men eat enormously in the
chill mountain air and he strained every resource to assure them sufficient fresh meat.[181]

November 18—twelve days and twelve only before the army would
begin to break up! The weather held fair.[182] There was a chance, if
still a gambler's chance, that the fort could be reached and taken. In
that assurance, Washington pushed forward on the morning of the
18th and at 11 o'clock reached Armstrong's camp.[183] His orders now
were to press to the head of Turtle Creek, through the woods,[184] and
to leave Armstrong as well as Montgomery behind him to work on
the road.[185]

Washington's prime anxiety that day was over the lack of exact
knowledge of the country ahead. He told Forbes: "I fear we have
been greatly deceived with regard to the distance from hence to Fort
DuQuesne. Most of the woodsmen that I have conversed with, seem
to think that we are still thirty miles from it."[186] If thirty miles remained to be covered, in what might be a rough, stream-cut region,
then . . . but Washington did not write of a risk as manifest to Forbes
as to him. Instead, Washington sent out scouts to determine the distance and to ascertain whether the country was one of easy or of difficult approach. Two other small detachments were told to scour the
country to the left and to the right and, in particular, to look for the
tracks of hostile savages or French.

[178] *Ibid.*, 304, 306.
[179] *Forbes's Orderly Book*, Nov. 16, 1758.
[180] *Ibid.*, Nov. 17, 18, 20, 1758.
[181] *2 G. W.*, 303 ff.
[182] That is to say, if there was any precipitation it was not heavy enough to be thought
worthy of mention in the somewhat abundant correspondence of these days.
[183] *2 G. W.*, 306.
[184] *3 Hamilton*, 129.
[185] Cf. *2 G. W.*, 306–07.
[186] Letter of Nov. 18, 1758; *2 G. W.*, 306. Cf. Richard Corbin to his son, Aug. 18, 1758:
". . . I believe if the wisest General the world ever saw was to command an army in the
deserts of America where he did not know or could not procure a geography of the country he
would hardly succeed against an enemy who had this knowledge" (*Corbin Letter Book*, VHS).

After Washington had finished his daily dispatch on the occurrences of the 18th, and was preparing to leave at 3 o'clock the next morning, one of his scouting parties returned. The commanding officer had news: Five miles in front of Armstrong's Camp, he and his men had found the trail of about forty persons, but they seemed to be pointing toward Kiskaminities,[187] and not toward the advancing English column.

Washington heard the news quietly. He felt that the precautions taken by him, through lieutenants experienced in Indian warfare, would suffice to give him ample notice of the approach of any considerable body of hostile warriors.[188] So, the next morning, November 19, he struck out through the woods with 1000 men for the head of Turtle Creek. The other Brigades followed. Nothing of importance occurred. No Indians, no fresh tracks were seen, but the Virginian took full precaution and, on the 20th, divided the command into half-platoons, each of which was to be under an officer or an n.c.o. Washington saw to it, also, that the men's arms were in order to greet any pale face or red that peered from behind a tree. Industriously the day was spent in cutting back through the woods to form junction with the troops in the rear.[189] On the 21st, the force having been reunited, new parties of axemen were sent out.[190]

The army now was close to Fort DuQuesne, exactly how close none could say with absolute certainty; but the English knew they were near enough to invite surprise attack. Vigilance already had been carried far beyond the care the average prudent commander would display; overnight it was made an absolute imperative for every man. With Bouquet's troops in advance on the 22nd, the columns made good progress and camped on the farther side of Turtle Creek. The men lay on their arms that night in complete silence.[191]

Before Forbes began the march on the 23rd—Montgomery opening the road and Washington escorting the artillery—the weapons of all soldiers were examined again. Warning was given that any man who fired his piece without an officer's order would receive 200 lashes on the spot.[192] Then the troops started through the woods and marched

187 The name is spelled in many ways. In *Hodge* the preferred spelling is Kiskiminetas. The town was on the creek of the same name, in the present Westmoreland County, Penn., about eight miles from the point where the creek empties into the Allegheny River.

188 Cf. his remarks to Forbes, 2 *G. W.*, 308.

189 Cf. Brigade Orders of Nov. 20, 1758, and General Orders of Nov. 21, 1758; *Forbes's Orderly Book.*

190 *Forbes's Orderly Book,* Nov. 21, 1758.

191 *Ibid.*, Nov. 22, 1758.

192 *Ibid.*, Nov. 23, 1758.

briskly in the cold weather. After they bivouacked, plans were drafted for another advance the next day, but, when distances were computed, it was found the column had come so far that Forbes concluded he should get new intelligence reports before venturing nearer. One estimate put the column fifteen miles from Fort DuQuesne;[193] another scout reckoned the distance at twelve miles.[194] The men once more were told precisely what they were to do in the event of a sudden attack. Flour for six days and meat for four were issued under the supervision of officers; all the felling axes were ground.[195] Most careful of all were the efforts to determine what the enemy was doing and whether his activities indicated that he knew the English were close enough to lunge. The usual patrols were sent to search the woods nearby. Reconnaissance to Fort DuQuesne itself was entrusted to Indians who went out separately.

The anxious 24th of November was spent in camp [196]—the beginning of the last week during which the army could be held together. If Forbes had only seven days, he was resolved to make the most of them. Again there was close supervision of everything that could make for victory. Dogs were too numerous and too noisy: those that were not tied up or sent back to Loyal Hannon were to be hanged. Methods of identifying friendly Indians were explained; officers were personally to inspect every firearm that evening; the advance was to be renewed in three columns on the morrow, with the spacing such that line of battle could be formed immediately.[197] In general orders Forbes wrote: "It is to be hoped that as our honor, interest, and in fine our all, depends on the happy issue of the service we are just going on, . . . the officers will in a particular manner exert themselves in getting everything in the best order and not be sparing of their pains at this critical juncture, and in case of action it is particularly recommended to each officer to keep their men calm and prevent their throwing away their fire, which they are apt to do when in a hurry." [198]

Night came early, a bleak night for thinly clad men in the chill, far-spreading, overpowering forest, a night of foreboding and of expect-

193 *Penn. Gazette,* Dec. 14, 1758, a letter based, apparently, on Haslet to Alison, Nov. 26, 1758; 6 *Hazard's His. Reg.,* 226–27.

194 Bouquet to Allen, Nov. 25, 1758; *ibid.,* 226.

195 *Forbes's Orderly Book,* Nov. 23, 1758.

196 Forbes's orders (*op. cit.*) would indicate the army moved on the 24th, but these instructions evidently were prepared overnight. Formal cancellation was not entered in the *Orderly Book.* Bouquet wrote specifically to Chief Justice William Allen, *loc. cit.* "The 23rd we took post at twelve miles [from Fort DuQuesne], and halted the 24th for intelligence."

197 *Forbes's Orderly Book,* Nov. 24, 1758.   198 *Ibid.*

ancy. The next day might bring, perhaps must bring, the battle to which Washington had been looking forward since that July day almost three and a half years previously, when he had been compelled to turn his back on the Monongahela and the ghastly field of Braddock's débâcle. Much of Washington's life had been devoted during those long, baffling months to persuading and preparing and making the utmost out of meagreness in order to ride to the Ohio at the head of an army that would hurl the French back to Canada . . . and now . . .

. . . Now a redman was going to headquarters—one of the scouts who had been sent out on the 23rd to ascertain what was happening at the fort. No great news was his. He had not been to the junction of the rivers, but he had been on ground whence he could look directly toward DuQuesne, and billowing there he had seen a great column of smoke.[199]

Smoke! Had the fort or some of the outbuildings caught fire, or could that rising cloud mean that the French had learned of the approach of the English, and, despairing of successful defence, had burned and abandoned their stronghold? It was a mystery of minutes only: another scout arrived. He had been to Fort DuQuesne—or rather where Fort DuQuesne had been. It was gone. So were the French. They had burned the fort and had abandoned the site!

No battle, then, was ahead—perhaps no flags, no surrendered arms, no booty—but the prize would be England's! As soon as the light horse could saddle and get off, they must ride to the junction and, if the fire still burned, they must put it out.[200] The infantry would follow the next morning.[201]

A long, long morning it must have been for Washington and a still longer afternoon. Twelve miles of unbroken woodland and all its little streams had to be crossed by men whose eager ambition had run far ahead of them. Darkness had fallen when, at 6 o'clock, the army reached its goal. There, at the junction, stood the wreck of the ramparts of the stout square fort, its ravelins and its gabions.[202] Two hundred

---

[199] Haslet to Allison; Bouquet to Allen, *loc. cit.; Penn. Gazette,* Dec. 14, 1758.

[200] Nearly all the accounts state that the light horse reached the site of the fort on the 24th. Sunset that day was at 4:37 P.M. local time. As cavalrymen would not have been reconnoitring after nightfall in an unfamiliar country, they must have been sent through the darkness from the camp to the fort and they could not have reached the rivers until 9 P.M. at earliest.   [201] *Forbes's Orderly Book,* Nov. 24, 1758.

[202] A ravelin is a small outwork of two faces that form an angle; gabions are wooden or, more recently, metal, open-end cylindrical baskets, designed to keep earth from sliding. In Thomas Forbes's journal of 1755 (4 *Md. His. Mag.,* 274) is one of the fullest and clearest descriptions of the fort as it then was.

yards away, on the bank of the Allegheny, was the shell of another burned fort, the deserted outworks of which manifestly had never been finished. Stark above the charred debris of walls and floors and roofs stood thirty chimneys in the fields and in the forts, as if to mock the half-frozen Englishmen who looked for shelter. One magazine of the fort had been exploded; the other contained sixteen barrels of powder, a great pile of rusted iron, some worthless gun barrels and, significantly, a large store of scalping knives. In the gathering darkness, this was a poor reward for so much of sickness and shivering, of muddy marches and long nights' misery—an ugly, disappointing scene to men who doubtless had pictured a frowning fort, its bastions crowded with stubborn French. No fort, no food, no booty the British found, but almost beneath them, full of movement, full of mystery, was the Ohio, the "Beautiful River" of French dispatches, the mighty stream that watered a valley of fabulous richness as it swept to the vast Mississippi.[203]

Indians in considerable number were on an island in the river, ready to make their peace with the victor. From some of those who remained nearer at hand, the British learned that the French had placed the cannon of the forts on boats and had carried them down the river. Then the garrison, reported to consist of about 500, had set fire to everything that would burn. By the light of the flames, the troops had departed, some by water, and some on foot down the bank of the Ohio. The troops were going, the Indians believed, to the Illinois country.[204]

Washington observed all this, which was in unbelievable contrast to what he had seen at the junction almost precisely five years previously,[205] but he did not admit, for so long as it took to blink his eyes, that the outcome disproved his assertion about the relative value of the two British routes to the Ohio. "The possession of this fort," he wrote Governor Fauquier, "has been a matter of great surprise to the whole army, and we cannot attribute it to more probable causes than weakness, want of provisions and the desertion of their Indians."

[203] All the letters and reports give much the same description of the scene. The most detailed are in Haslet to Alison, *loc. cit.*

[204] *Ibid.*, 2 *G. W.*, 308; *Gentleman's Mag.*, April 1759, p. 171–74. Vaudreuil in a dispatch of Jan. 20, 1759 (Paris Arch. Nat. C 11 A, v. 104, 12–21) explained that defence was hopeless and that the commander, des Ligneris, had taken a week's supply of provisions with him and had gone to Fort Machaud, which, said Vaudreuil, was "only a store house." The cannon from Fort DuQuesne were being "sent by canoe to the Illinois as the only means of saving them." The information given by the Indians led the British to believe that the French probably had gone to Venango (Fauquier to the Lords Commers. of Trade and Plantations, Jan. 30, 1759, P.R.O., C.O. 5: 1329, f. 247).

[205] Nov. 22, 1756; see *supra*, Vol. I, p. 288.

A plea that the Virginia troops be given "some little recess" from fatigue was followed by a statement that he would march his Regiment directly for Winchester. Then he returned again to the "fortunate and indeed unexpected success of our arms," and urged that goods be sent out immediately from the Old Dominion for trade with the Indians. Virginia and the other interested colonies, he said, should establish and maintain a strong garrison at the junction of the two rivers. Both his courtesy and his justice prompted him to add: "General Forbes is very assiduous in getting these matters settled upon a solid basis, and has great merit (which I hope will be rewarded) for the happy issue which he has brought our affairs to, infirm and worn down as he is." [206]

Bouquet went further in praise of the General, who now was on the eve of another prostrating and agonizing attack of his malady.[207] Forbes, said Bouquet, had deprived the French of their chief ally by what he had effected at the Easton conference. The General, indeed, had "procured a peace with those inveterate enemies more necessary and beneficial to the colonies than driving out the French." [208] In detail, Bouquet wrote Chief Justice William Allen: "After God, the success of this expedition is due entirely to the General, who, by bringing about the treaty with the Indians at Easton, has struck the blow, which has knocked the French on the head; in temporizing wisely to expect the effects of the treaty; in securing all his posts, and giving nothing to chance; and not yielding to the urging instances for taking Braddock's Road, which would have been our destruction." [209]

Forbes himself did not put it that strongly, but he knew he had made a great conquest at small cost in life, and he sought a soldier's rewards as frankly as Washington had solicited favor.[210] Neither ambition nor illness blinded Forbes to the possibilities of the land where, once again, the standard of Britain had been set. He would be compelled, he said, to keep a small force of provincials at the fort during the winter, after which he hoped Pennsylvania would give him support "to fix this noble, fine country, to all perpetuity, under the dominion of Great Britain." [211] Ceremonies attended so great an advance—a service of thanksgiving on the 26th with a sermon, a day of celebration on the

206 2 G. W., 310.
207 Cf. Forbes's description of his condition, in his letter of November 26–30 to Pitt (Forbes, 263).
208 Bouquet to Nancy Willing, Nov. 25, 1758; Shippen Papers.
209 Letter of Nov. 25, 1758; 6 Hazard's His. Reg., 226.
210 See his letter of Nov. 27, 1758–Jan. 21, 1759, to Pitt (Forbes, 267).
211 Letter of Nov. 26, 1758, to Governor Denny; Forbes, 265.

27th, and then a solemn march to Braddock's field, where the skulls of more than 450 men were buried. Their bones long before had been scattered by wolves.[212]

If Washington had a part in these events it probably was perfunctory because he was looking now to Williamsburg and to the White House on the Pamunkey. Reluctantly he obeyed the order of Forbes to assign some of the ragged men of the First Virginia Regiment to the garrison of Fort DuQuesne. Justice and gratitude prompted Washington to urge that arrangements be made for provisioning and for clothing these men more heavily during the bleak months they must remain on the icy Ohio. The entire Regiment, in fact, was worn and must be refitted: he would do his utmost for those who, in spite of ignorance and hardship and feeble transport, had performed their duty.[213] Assistance to them best could be rendered where his heart was calling him.

So, when Forbes reached the same conclusion and suggested that Washington might be able by personal representation to get early assistance from Virginia for the troops of the Colony, it was not necessary for the General to use persuasion. Washington was off, via Loyal Hannon, for Winchester. It was a typical wintertime journey through mud and wilderness, where hard plodding and scant feed broke down his horses in the very first stages of the return.[214] On arrival at Winchester during the night of December 8, Washington himself was both sick and exhausted.[215] As best he could, after brief efforts at recuperation, he made his way to Belvoir [216] and before the year's end he was in Williamsburg.[217]

[212] Cf. letter of Judge J. Yeates, Aug. 21, 1775; 6 *Hazard's His. Reg.*, 105.
[213] See his letter of Dec. 2, 1758, to Governor Fauquier; 2 *G. W.*, 312–15.
[214] *Ibid*. Washington was at Loyal Hannon December 2.
[215] *Ibid.*, 316.
[216] *Ledger A*, folio 52.
[217] A letter of Dec. 30, 1758, to Forbes would indicate that Washington already had been there at least one day (2 *G. W.*, 317).

CHAPTER XXI

THE MAN AND HIS TRAINING AT TWENTY-SEVEN

IT HAD NOW BEEN five years and two months since Washington had started for the Ohio to warn the French to leave that region. He had required fifty-two days only to reach in December, 1753, the "land in the Fork," which he had thought "extremely well situated for a fort"; [1] after that visit, nearly the whole of his energies for four years and a half had been devoted to getting there again.

Had he not been drawn to a military career by impulses he did not himself understand wholly, his life in 1754–58 doubtless would have been more nearly like that of the younger planters to whose class he belonged. He probably would have married, would have prospered as he opened new lands and bred more slaves, until, at 27, he might have been a vestryman, a Captain or possibly a Major of militia, and perhaps a Justice of the County or a member of the House of Burgesses. That might have been his maximum achievement, because he had none of the skill of public utterance that made for political distinction. As it was, he had fared no worse in purse and infinitely better in reputation than if he had turned his back on the call to serve his King and his country. It was at least doubtful, also, whether as George Washington, Esq., he could have made a marriage half so advantageous, from the standpoint of property, as the one soon to be solemnized with Martha Dandridge Custis.

That was not half the account of the years. While some of the young planters had gone to the dogs, and some almost daily had followed the hounds, and still others had crossed the Atlantic to the universities or to the Inns of Court, he had been attending the difficult school of the soldier. Often he had complained of the poverty of its resources and many times he had threatened to leave it; but he had adhered to its curriculum because he loved the life and because both its exactions and its rewards had challenged deep impulses of his soul.

[1] *Supra*, Vol. I, p. 288, and 1 *G. W.*, 23.

Now, he was looking to the future, to matrimony, to the management of a much-enlarged estate, and to service as a Burgess. He took pride in what he had done as a soldier, but he considered his years of military duty a closed chapter of his life, and, at the end of it, he did not write one retrospective line concerning the lessons he had learned or their possible value to him in the years ahead. Had he sat down to analyze the scope of his training, he would have found that the stern master, Experience, sometimes to the scourging of a sensitive skin, had taught him many fundamentals of command but had given him few of the higher qualifications. What he had learned on the frontier, what every officer had to learn in that school of experience, were the A B C's of leadership, commonplace but irreplaceable:

1. Washington had been able to assume responsibility. "I believe," he once wrote Governor Dinwiddie, ". . . that no person who regards his character will undertake a command without the means of preserving it, since his conduct is culpable for all misfortunes and never right but when successful." [2] With this his guiding principle, he often complained that he had to grope in the dark and that an express might bring condemnation for acts regarding which the previous one had conveyed no instructions from the Governor.[3] In spite of this, when occasion required, Washington did not hesitate to take responsibility. His various decisions on receipt of Dagworthy's warning of an anticipated French attack in June, 1757, proved to be no more than a drill in what should be done in an emergency; but Washington drafted his orders skillfully and promptly in the belief the advance was in force and the onslaught imminent. It was the same, later, when he was cutting the road for the advance of Forbes. He could not have acted as he did on a score of occasions if he had not seen clearly that a soldierly trust carries with it the obligation to make decisions and to take the consequences.

2. Washington learned that he often must deal with subordinates who were not men of his own choice or even of any special aptitude for arms.[4] He had to take the human material given him and had to ascertain its worth in order that he might use every officer at that individual's best. The good qualities of Adam Stephen and of Peter

[2] Letter of Sept. 23, 1756; 1 G. W., 469-70.

[3] See, as typical, 1 G. W., 474, and the comments of Landon Carter (1 Hamilton, 236) and of John Robinson (2 ibid., 230). In reality, Dinwiddie gave Washington discretion more frequently than the Colonel realized. Cf. 1 Hamilton, 245, 275, 277; 2 ibid., 119, 142.

[4] Forbes's estimate of them (supra, p. 332), was exaggerated, of course, but illustrative of this point.

Hog were discoverable before their weaknesses were; the reverse was true of several of the other officers. Some had lost their spirit at dull little frontier forts. Others regarded hardship and isolation as a challenge to make themselves better soldiers. Andrew Lewis, George Mercer, Robert Stewart,[5] John McNeill, James Baker, Thomas Bullett,[6] John Kirkpatrick, Washington's civilian clerk,[7] and several others had done well. One Ensign was suspended and denied access to the camp for cheating at cards;[8] a Lieutenant was accused of defrauding his men by forcing them to shoot, at a price, for shoddy prizes he purchased;[9] a few of the others who sent in their resignations probably did so to escape court-martial. There was no duplication by any officer of the violent defiance charged against Dennis McCarty.[10]

3. Washington learned in time how to gain the affectionate confidence and enthusiastic good will of most of these subordinate officers, though he did not succeed in winning a similar measure of personal esteem from many officers of his own rank in the regular establishment or in the service of other Colonies. Most of these men regarded him as competent, but they considered him ambitious and not particularly likeable or conspicuously able.[11]

4. Washington quickly learned the value of absolute justice in dealing with his officers and learned equally well the ensnaring danger of any sort of favoritism. Justice was instinctive with him. When he completed the organization of the Virginia Regiment into Companies, January, 1756, he included this pledge in his orders to the officers who, in some instances, were assuming command of troops for the first time: ". . . I am determined, as far as my small experience in service, my abilities and interest of the service dictate, to observe the strictest discipline . . . On the other hand, you may as certainly depend upon having the strictest justice administered to all . . . I assure you, gentlemen, that partiality shall never bias my conduct, nor shall prejudice injure any . . ."[12] To this binding promise he adhered. His somewhat

---

[5] For his efforts to get a regular commission with Lord Loudoun, see 2 *Hamilton,* 232, 240; 3 *ibid.,* 135. In May, 1756, Dinwiddie had recommended Stewart, along with Washington, to Gen. James Abercromby, and had said of the Captain: "He is a gentleman of good sense and great spirit. He behaved extremely well on the unlucky 9th of July . . ." (2 *Din.,* 425).

[6] He had experienced one period of doubt and difficulty and was to have another. See 1 *Hamilton,* 48; 3 *ibid.,* 160 ff.

[7] 2 *Hamilton,* 79, 222; 3 *ibid.,* 96–97. [8] 1 *G. W.,* 270, 288, 295.

[9] Thomas Waggener to unnamed correspondent, May 10, 20, 1758; William Woodford to Washington, May 20, 1758; 5 *Papers of G. W.,* 8 *ibid.,* LC.

[10] See *supra,* p. 227–28.

[11] See "An Old Soldier" in *Gentleman's Mag.,* August, 1778, p. 368.

[12] 1 *G. W.,* 271.

deliberate and formal courtesy was brightened by his amiability. He would counsel affectionately a young officer who drank too heavily;[13] he would aid with money those who needed it; he would recommend for higher rank or for the regular establishment those officers who merited his endorsement. If the issue was one of justice, he was inflexible. When he said in January, 1757, that he would have treated his own brother, in the same circumstances, precisely as he dealt with Commissary Walker,[14] he was applying a principle which he regarded as a guarantee to his officers that their efforts would be rewarded. Nor did he permit the influence of public men, in behalf of inexperienced applicants, to prevail over the record of service of junior officers and of volunteers who had performed the duty of private soldiers in the hope of winning commissions. The only instances in which Washington yielded ever so little to the importunity of friends were with two sons of Col. William Fairfax, his neighbor and counsellor.[15] Washington himself doubtless would have admitted these concessions to the Fairfaxes were not proper, and at the same time, he could have pointed to a considerable list of others whose candidates for commission he had not accepted.[16] To Dinwiddie's credit it could be said that he seldom undertook to influence Washington in the advancement of officers. If the Governor decided to appoint a Captain or to pick those who were to be retained when others were relieved, he chose the names and sent them to the Commander-in-Chief.[17] In other instances, he left Washington free to make his appointments from volunteers who showed zeal and ability. Promotion of Ensigns similarly was on a basis of merit as determined by Washington.

Much as Washington learned concerning the treatment and instruction of his comrades, he had this peculiarity in dealing with them: he scarcely ever praised any of them officially. Even in letters to the Governor, to whom he wrote often and on many themes, Washington seldom commended any subordinate. Andrew Lewis, for example, was the hardest-working officer of the Regiment and one of the most dependable. His frequent and exhausting scouting expeditions were reported by his Colonel and his journeys and assignments were mentioned, but in the whole of Washington's correspondence of 1755–57

[13] Cf. 1 *G. W.*, 291.   [14] Cf. *supra*, p. 232.
[15] This diverting example of the manner in which family influence was exerted for the advancement of "sons of the house" is elaborated briefly in Appendix II–3.
[16] See 2 *Hamilton*, 125, 195, 283, 287, 290, 292, 298.
[17] Note, as typical, 2 *Din.*, 622.

with Dinwiddie there was not one complimentary adjective nor a line of mildest approbation for the Major. Letters to Lewis himself contained only one perfunctory remark that, in a particular situation, his "diligence and punctuality" required "little or no spur."[18] If Washington promoted men or wished Dinwiddie to do so, he generally wrote a few words about their record when he put their names before the Governor, but praise in orders or praise before an officer's friends was not a part of Washington's code in dealing with his associates-in-arms.

5. Washington learned a different code for the men in the ranks, the traditional code of punishment as the basis of discipline. He accepted unquestioningly the dictum that the lash for small offences and the noose for cowardice, mutiny and desertion were indispensable. Orders sometimes dwelt on the reward of the good soldier[19] but they more often listed the penalties the offender might expect—twenty-five lashes with a cat-o'-nine-tails for profanity,[20] fifty for feigning sickness,[21] 100 for drunkenness, 500 for fighting with another soldier.[22] For desertion, 1000 lashes were administered one day in December, 1756, to each of five men.[23] Of another instance of extreme discipline, Adam Stephen wrote, ". . . and have whealed them till the spectators shed tears for them, which will I hope answer the end of punishment."[24]

6. Washington learned that drunkenness and desertion had ceaselessly to be combated with every weapon a commanding officer could fashion. Tippling-houses had to be under sternest regulation and had, if possible, to be suppressed.[25] So long as such places existed, Washington maintained that the soldiers would be drunk and unfit for duty until they spent the last tuppence of their pay. This would happen in spite of all the officers could do.[26] As for desertion, it was the nightmare of command. Washington tried all the expedients—warning, immediate pursuit, lashing, hanging, pardon,[27] rewards for the capture and return of runaways,[28] better pay and clothing. Nothing availed. Convinced,

---

18 Letter of Sept. 6, 1755; 1 *G. W.*, 167.
19 Cf. 1 *G. W.*, 381.
20 1 *G. W.*, 396.
21 1 *G. W.*, 451.
22 1 *G. W.*, 353.
23 Charles Lewis's journal in 4 *W. Va. His. Mag.*, 115.
24 Letter to Washington, July 25, 1756; 1 *Hamilton*, 321. Cf. Washington's instructions of Dec. 29, 1755, for officers to make certain the prison handcuffs were tight. 304 *Papers of G. W.*, 11, LC.
25 For the attempted control of places where strong drink was sold, see 1 *G. W.*, 179, 409, 440; 1 *Hamilton*, 280–81; 7 *Frederick Order Book*, 97. This last covers the dismissal, Aug. 4, 1756, of Washington's complaint against John Stewart (see also *ibid.*, 132, 159).
26 Letter of Sept. 23, 1756, to Dinwiddie; 1 *G. W.*, 470.
27 See 2 *Hamilton*, 119, 188.
28 Payment of rewards was a source of much trouble because, for a long period, the claims of persons who brought in deserters had to be referred to Williamsburg for payment. Cf. 304 *Papers of G. W.*; 1 *G. W.*, 235, 242, 287, 428, 497; 2 *ibid.*, 13–14.

at length, that "examples [were] of . . . little weight," [29] Washington returned to his earlier conclusion that desertion never would be controlled so long as citizens sheltered men who left the colors.[30]

7. Washington learned that as desertion steadily sapped his Regiment, he could not hope to raise it to full strength by the voluntary enlistment of free men. He was convinced of the futility of relying upon the militia,[31] but he did not attempt any longer to procure legislation for its reform. The only substantial resources of manpower were indentured servants, vagrants and such unmarried men as the county officers would be willing to draft. Many of these drafted individuals would desert, but some servants might find life in the army less arduous than labor for their masters. "I believe," Washington told the Governor, "unless we are permitted to enlist servants, we should spend much time to little purpose in [recruiting]." He added: "There is such a spirit of opposition prevailing in one sort of people, and so little spirit of any kind in another." [32] To the enlistment of servants, the two familiar barriers remained: Planters who held the indenture often were unwilling to release the men; Burgesses were aware of this reluctance and were loath to vote funds with which to pay for the unexpired time of the servants. Washington's lesson in recruiting was, for these reasons, largely negative: He knew where he could *not* get men; he did *not* know where he could.

8. Washington learned, among others, this fundamental of military administration: Transport and supply called for early planning and for constant, detailed attention; but if these qualities were displayed energetically, it was possible to provide food for troops in spite of the small number of wagons and the badness of roads. When Washington came to Winchester in the autumn of 1755, it will be remembered, he had to be his own commissary. He was compelled to take the personal receipts of those from whom provisions and supplies were bought and also to procure receipts from those to whom anything was delivered.[33] Even such matters as providing in advance for the feeding at a tavern of detachments on the march had, for a time, to be handled by Washington himself because he had neither clerk nor officer responsible for provisioning the men.[34] Later, after the commissary was reorganized,

---

[29] 2 *G. W.*, 122 and *supra*, p. 260.
[30] See 2 *G. W.*, 461, 465.
[31] For a few of the many denunciations of the militia by public men and soldiers, see 1 *Hamilton*, 296, 329, 342; 2 *Din.*, 489; 1 *G. W.*, 492; 21 *V* 438.
[32] Letter of Aug. 27, 1757; 2 *G. W.*, 121–22.
[33] A number of these appear in v. 303 of the *Papers of G. W.*, LC.
[34] *Ibid.*

its deficiencies were so marked that Washington often was at odds with the functionary in charge and was compelled to familiarize himself with the minutiae of operations so that he could make proper recommendations to Governor Dinwiddie.[35]

During the period Washington had the accounts of the Regiment in his care, he was responsible, also, for sheet on sheet of paper money that had to be counted and cut into bills.[36] He had, moreover, to see that vigilance was exercised to prevent the plundering of supplies,[37] to assure full weight and content of goods and of powder in casks,[38] and, as always, to seek wagons and teams that continued to be scarce and were rented unwillingly.[39] All this was further training for a young man who had schooled himself to be careful of his own affairs. It gave Washington a closer knowledge of the perplexities of the commissary and it showed him that if meat was to be provided for winter, purchase, slaughter and packing had to be arranged months previously.[40] The necessity of a large accumulation of flour and of meat was plainer than it had been in 1754. One of the most protective of all the lessons he learned was that of timing with reasonable accuracy the preparation and delivery of supplies and provisions.

9. Washington learned one other lesson in military administration—that shortages in clothing, in equipment and in tools, and deficiencies of medical care were inevitable and that the most had to be made of what was procurable. Clothing usually was inferior and always wore out before it could be replaced. The system of issue was changed repeatedly but never satisfactorily.[41] Axes were so difficult to get that in building a new fort Peter Hog's men had to borrow a few at the outset and then had to make some from iron sent him.[42] Everywhere on the frontier, the ill-equipped troops suffered daily from the failure of the iron industry in which Augustine Washington had been a pioneer. The first cooper who had come to Fort Cumberland to make casks for meat

[35] The course of the controversy over Thomas Walker may be traced in 2 *Din.*, 563, 565; 1 *Hamilton*, 87, 292; 2 *ibid.*, 25; 1 *G. W.*, 523; 2 *ibid.*, 1 ff.

[36] Memorandum of Dec. 16, 1755, for one such delivery is in 2 *Papers of G. W.*, LC. It covered 340 sheets and a single bill, to a total of £4000, but there was an error of £1 in the calculation, and one sheet of £16 was wanting.

[37] 304 *Papers of G. W.*, 307, LC.

[38] 6 *ibid.*, unpaged.

[39] 2 *Din.*, 258; 1 *G. W.*, 191, 218; 2 *Papers of G. W.*, LC.

[40] Somewhat full details of this aspect of commissary work will be found in Thomas Walker's letters to Washington in November–December, 1755; 1 *Hamilton*, 132, 140, 152, 153, 161.

[41] 1 *Hamilton*, 80, 148, 165, 171, 246; 2 *ibid.*, 29, 39, 217; 1 *G. W.*, 171, 263, 287, 297, 357, 419, 429, 441, 453, 527; 2 *ibid.*, 4; 2 *Din.*, 200.

[42] 1 *Hamilton*, 106.

found no tools there; [43] kettles were almost unprocurable; [44] drums were few; [45] it took Washington eight months to procure an armorer willing to go to Winchester. [46]

Medical care scarcely deserved the name, though the need of it was increased by the laxity of physical requirements. No men were disqualified except for age, fits, manifest debility, sores on the legs, or lack of height. [47] A hospital of a sort existed at Fort Cumberland, [48] but there and almost everywhere else competent surgeons were scarcely to be had. At one time, the commander of a remote detachment had to be advised by Washington to hire "some old woman from whom [the soldiers] have often relief." [49] In another instance, warning was given that the country had "great objection to those occasional quacks"; [50] still again, months passed before a financial arrangement was reached with an Ensign, who also was a surgeon, to look after the men at Captain Hog's fort. [51] Washington's reliance, as always, was upon Dr. James Craik, Surgeon of the Regiment, but even that devoted man had scant equipment and, sometimes, few medicines. [52] Efforts always were made by Washington to seek what his men lacked. If their needs could not be met, their commander expected them to get on as well as they might with what they had. Deprivation and shortage were taken for granted as hardships of war on the frontier.

10. Washington learned that the backwardness of American industry, the limitations on exports and the resulting scarcity of money made the sternest economy a sine qua non of military defence. "It's your duty as well as mine," Dinwiddie admonished Washington, "to make all prudent savings." [53] The Governor never relaxed in that determination to have the funds provided by the Assembly last as long and buy as much as any Scot's shilling. If a soldier died, his name was to be kept on the payroll four weeks to cover the cost of his coffin. [54] Allotment by Washington of some ammunition to poor, refugee set-

---

[43] Ibid., 99.

[44] 1 G. W., 250.

[45] Ibid., 461.

[46] 2 ibid., 90.

[47] 304 Papers of G. W., LC. The minimum height was five feet, four inches, unless the recruit was strong and active. Age limits were 16 to 50.

[48] Cf. 1 Hamilton, 162.

[49] Washington to Thomas Waggener, July 29, 1756; 1 G. W., 413.

[50] 1 G. W., 366; cf. ibid., 364, 411.

[51] 1 G. W., 228, 229, 284, 426, 506. In the late summer of 1758 a physician employed at Fort Loudoun was discharged for "being extravagant and knowing but little of physic" (3 Hamilton, 86).

[52] Cf. the situation that developed late in 1758; 3 Hamilton, 138.

[53] Letter of June 2, 1757; 2 Hamilton, 85.

[54] 2 Din., 185.

tlers in the summer of 1757 was approved by the Governor because, he wrote, "I doubt not your frugality on that head." [55]

The compliment was deserved. Washington was not far behind his chief, though sometimes he disagreed concerning particular items of expenditure. "If the carpenters are kept closely to their work," he told Peter Hog, "you may allow them a shilling a day, besides their soldiers' pay; but you are to be cautious how they are employed and not throw away the country's money idly . . ." [56] When Washington gave Dr. James Craik orders to procure medicines and stores for the hospitals, he admonished the Surgeon "to purchase no more than is absolutely necessary for the support and relief of the Regiment." [57] In almost every authorization to a subordinate to buy anything, Washington included similar exhortation to save the money of "the public." A circular to the Captains who were sent out to the smaller posts in July, 1757, contained no less than eleven admonitions to economy and regularity in specific acts. [58]

Such were the ten principal lessons Colonel Washington learned by the time Forbes reached the site of the burned and abandoned Fort DuQuesne. All, to repeat, were the most elementary lessons, but they were essentials of warfare that would be continued and might unhappily be renewed in America. War would be waged with ill-trained and sometimes reluctant and sullen soldiers who would be poorly supplied with transport, weapons, equipment and provisions by a feeble government that lacked solid financial resources. The only commanding officer who would have any prospect of success with such an army, under such a government, would be one who had learned how to make much of little, one who had above all other qualities that of resolute patience. In another generation a Frenchman was to cry, "Audacity, audacity, always audacity." Young Colonel Washington, returning from his campaign, might have submitted in advance a contrasting slogan: "Patience, patience, endless patience."

Washington had acquired that and some of the other essentials, but his training was deficient in seven disciplines of importance among the many an officer should master. He had not learned, in the first place, the art of dealing with the private soldier in a manner to arouse the individual's sense of responsibility for a cause. This was due in part to

---

[55] 2 *Hamilton,* 143.   [56] Letter of Dec. 27, 1755; 1 *G. W.,* 260.
[57] Letter of Dec. 16, 1755; 1 *G. W.,* 255.
[58] 2 *G. W.,* 109 ff. Cf. Washington to George Frazier, Nov. 18, 1755: "Be careful not to waste provision . . ." (303 *Papers of G. W.,* LC).

the average poor quality of man Washington received as a recruit, but the intelligence and training of some of these individuals was better than might have been thought. In a list of sixty-two drafts, for example, from six Counties, seven were regarded by Washington as "likely" or "very likely," six previously had been in the army, eleven were men with a trade, three were lawyers, one was a doctor, twenty-one were un-classified, twelve were unfit physically, and one only was written down, in words then of well-understood meaning, as "no good." [59] Of men of this type, Washington knew some for good conduct or for bad, and occasionally if a private soldier with a record for courage or fine be-havior got in trouble, Washington would help him. More than this he did not do because the prevailing, unchallenged English system of discipline prescribed that all dealings of the officer with the men in the ranks had to be through the Sergeant, unless an offender came before a court martial.

Perhaps this lack of contact with the private soldier was one reason for Washington's second deficiency, a deficiency so marked that it might be said to represent definite failure. This was continued non-success in recruiting. However his friends might praise him, proud as his subordinates might be of him, none could say that he ever had devised any plan by which young men would be attracted to the Regi-ment. The art, if art it was, undeniably was one in which he had no skill. He had shown that he could lead a Regiment; he had not dem-onstrated that he could raise one quickly.

Washington, in the third place, had learned scarcely anything about the utilization of militia and apparently he never made any allowance for their ignorance and their lack of weapons the law unreasonably expected them to provide. Their reluctance to serve, their readiness to desert, and the cowardice that many of them exhibited in the presence of the enemy created early in Washington's mind a disgust that soon became a prejudice. He had to call on them frequently, but he never did so with any confidence. Nor did he press his proposals for their training under sterner law and through longer service with the Regi-ment. This failure to strive continuously for better employment of better militia may have been attributable to a conviction that the Burgesses would not consent to any effective discipline of the men on

<hr>

59 Washington's *Note Book*, NYPL. This document is interesting chiefly because it contains brief memoranda on numerous subjects concerning which Washington subsequently wrote letters. In several instances it is easily possible to identify the letters in *G. W.* by the notes Washington jotted down for later elaboration.

whose vote their re-election in part depended. Whatever the future might hold, then, Washington would have no faith in the militia.

Washington's fourth deficiency in training was his limited acquaintance with officers from other Colonies. Most of his relations had been with Virginians or with regulars. Those who were closely associated with him usually were his friends; those at a distance might be rivals. His experience with Virginia's closest military neighbor, Maryland, had included the most unpleasant of all his *rencontres,* the Dagworthy affair. Washington had much to learn concerning the manner in which ambitious, self-important officers of the different Colonies could work together.

Akin to this was a fifth deficiency, that of failure to acquire precisely the right attitude toward his superior officers. In 1755, Washington had been quite humble in saying he wished to "attain a small degree of knowledge in the military art." He could not wish for a more favorable opportunity, he said, than that of serving under a General of Braddock's "known ability and experience." [60] Washington retained a certain affection for that blustering, blundering commander, but, after Braddock's defeat and Dunbar's withdrawal from Fort Cumberland, the more Washington dealt with the senior officers of the regular establishment, the less, in general, was his respect for their military accomplishments. He admired Shirley, but as an individual and a politician rather than as a soldier. Besides, in Washington's eyes, Shirley was more a provincial than a regular. Washington assiduously courted Loudoun: not one line of praise of that officer came from Washington's quill after they met in Philadelphia. The Virginian was openly critical, in fact, of Loudoun's failure to organize a campaign against Fort DuQuesne in 1757.[61] As for Forbes, that officer and Henry Bouquet were, all in all, the best soldiers with whom Washington had served. He could have learned much from them concerning many matters of military administration. Instead, he opposed so vehemently and so persistently the choice of the Raystown route that he probably became prejudiced against them and certainly, for a time, created suspicion in the mind of Forbes. There scarcely could be denial that, in contending for the use of Braddock's Road, Washington went beyond the bounds of what the military etiquette of the times allowed a subordinate. The tone of his correspondence creates a doubt whether he would have been altogether cooperative even if the issue of rival routes had not developed.

[60] 1 *G. W.,* 107.   [61] Cf. 2 *G. W.,* 22.

Washington's other deficiencies as a young commander were circumstantial. He had been given little opportunity of handling any large body of men on the road until the last weeks of the campaign under Forbes. Even then, he never directed the advance of more than 1000. That number he apparently commanded with ease, and he employed a road-building contingent with manifest success. Although a conscientious superior, in passing judgment on Washington, would have been compelled to point out the limited experience of the Virginian in troop movement, no fair-minded man could have said that Washington gave evidence of having reached the limit of his ability to command. He was not of the type that makes a good Colonel and at the same time demonstrates that he could not succeed in a more responsible position.

This applied, *mutatis mutandis,* to Washington's combat experience. He had not been in action from the time he recrossed the Monongahela with the wounded Braddock, July 9, 1755, until George Mercer's men fired on him and his contingent around the Frenchmen's fire in the twilight of Nov. 12, 1758. Washington had been within range of ambuscaded Indians after he left Hog's fort in October, 1756, and he probably had ridden at other times where lurking savages might have shot him, but none of this was schooling of the sort required of a man who might be called to command on a field as bewildering as that of Braddock's defeat. The Jumonville affair, Fort Necessity, service as aide in the battle of the Monongahela, the unhappy exchange of fire with his own men near Loyal Hannon—this was the measure of Washington's combat experience. At that, he had seen more of action than any soldier from the Southern provinces with the exception, perhaps, of Andrew Lewis and of a few of the company officers of his original command. Further, Washington seems never to have any misgiving of his ability to keep his head while engaged with the enemy. His baptism of fire had convinced him, apparently, that he could meet the challenge of conflict.

It was by chance, finally, and by reason of modest rank that Washington had been given no opportunity of employing in a strategic plan of his own design the tactics he had learned thoroughly. Always the larger plan of the campaigns was that of Washington's seniors. The one instance in which he had influenced substantially a decision on strategy was when he had advised Braddock to divide the army and to proceed without Dunbar to Fort DuQuesne. In opposition to a proposed strategic plan, Washington had been aggressively active once only. That had been when he had argued and protested and even had declaimed against the choice of the Raystown route, which was strategic in the sense that it might offer a surprise. Washington, in short, had witnessed a failure where he had hoped for success and he had witnessed a success where he had anticipated failure.

Even so, he had not been lacking in strategical study, nor had he been deficient in strategical sense, that refined, acute military judgment indispensable to the soldier. The absolute imperative of strategy on the Virginia frontier did not change from the day Fort Necessity was surrendered: an offensive in strength, pushed to the Ohio, was dictated by every consideration. Washington saw this early and urged it ceaselessly. Moreover, he had acquired a definite distaste for fixed positions, such as that at Fort Cumberland. He felt that reliance upon an ill-placed permanent defence destroyed offensive impulse and might deprive a commander of needed intelligence concerning the enemy. If, once again, a good soldier had made an estimate of young Washington in these fundamentals, he probably would have said that the Virginia commander, though displaying no genius in strategy, appeared to have sound conceptions and just appreciation of the value of the wisely timed offensive.

None of Washington's contemporaries made the effort, at the end of 1758, to weigh his military virtues against his shortcomings. For a reason presently to be explained, there seemed no reason for considering his potentialities as a provincial leader in the later campaigns of the war. The only man who might have been interested in doing this was Forbes, and he was close to death.[62] Washington's own officers did not look on him with the eyes of cold valuation as a soldier, but with something of the ardor of young men for a successful leader of their own age. They prepared and, on the last day of the year, signed a paper which, in spite of exuberant rhetoric, was solid proof of the progress he had made in one great essential of leadership, that of arousing the enthusiasm of his subordinates. The twenty-seven company officers who subscribed to this address spoke gratefully of the happiness they had enjoyed with their Colonel, of the honor they had won under him, and of the affection they felt for him. "In our earliest infancy," they wrote, "you took us under your tuition, trained us up in the practice

---

[62] He expired in Philadelphia, Mch. 11, 1759. See *Penn. Gazette,* Mch. 15, 1759, quoted in *Forbes,* 301.

of that discipline which alone can constitute good troops, from the punctual observance of which you never suffered the least deviation." There followed this elaborate tribute: "Your steady adherence to impartial justice, your quick discernment and invariable regard to merit, wisely intended to inculcate those genuine sentiments of true honor and passion for glory, from which the great military achievements have been derived, first heightened our natural emulation and our desire to excel. How much we improved by those regulations and your own example, with what cheerfulness we have encountered the several toils, especially while under your particular direction, we submit to yourself, and flatter ourselves that we have in a great measure answered your expectations." Assurance was added: "In you we place the most implicit confidence. Your presence only will cause a steady firmness and vigor to actuate in every breast, despising the greatest dangers and thinking light of toils and hardships, while led on by the man we know and love." [63]

Did Washington deserve these words? At the end of 1758, as he approached his twenty-seventh birthday, what manner of man was he? [64]

That his character was complicated, both his acts and his letters make plain; but his was not a contradictory character in the sense that he was one person today and another tomorrow. Rather was he complicated in character because he had developed rapidly through a succession of not less than ten emotional crises, some of them prolonged, in the five years of his military service. First came the affair of Jumonville, the contest with Mackay over seniority, and the humiliating surrender of Fort Necessity. Washington endured this with much self-mastery and with little apparent strain, but after he lost his commission as Colonel and resigned indignantly, he had acute resentment in August, 1755, and a feeling that he had been mistreated. After the débâcle of the Monongahela, his reappointment as Colonel, with the new distinction of Commander-in-Chief, restored his balance and good humor. There followed quickly the Indian raids of October, 1755, during which the inadequacy of the military law so nearly paralyzed his efforts that he threatened to resign. Almost before that test was behind him he had to pass through a remarkable period of half-evasion in the controversy with Captain Dagworthy over command at Fort Cumberland. In 1756

63 Address of Dec. 31, 1758; 3 *Hamilton,* 143–46.
64 The reader who may not care for so full an analysis of the character of young Washington as begins in the next sentence will find a brief summary at the end of this chapter.

the heartbreaking massacres in Frederick led to the severest emotional stress of which there is any record in his youth. It was then that he cried, "If bleeding, dying, would glut [the Indians'] revenge, I would be a willing offering to savage fury, and die by inches to save a people!" [65]

While he was agonizing on the frontier, some of the potentates in Williamsburg were whispering that his officers on Wills Creek were leading drunken, bawdy lives. Six months more, and young Washington had to swallow his rage as an anonymous critic denounced his men as a "Regiment of such dastardly debauchees." In comparison with that, the Governor's unwise orders of November, 1756, and Dagworthy's false alarm of June, 1757, represented minor emotional torsion; but there was venom in the allegation attributed to Richard Corbin that Washington had pretended in 1756 that Indian raids were threatened in order that he might frighten the General Assembly into voting more troops and more money. Well as he endured that test, the persistence, the positive obstinacy, of his struggle to have Forbes's line of supply run through Virginia, rather than through Pennsylvania, was evidence that emotion continued to battle with self-mastery.

In spite of Washington's emotional conflicts, his rise had been much more rapid than that of most of his contemporaries. At substantially the corresponding age, a young New England lawyer, John Adams, had been three years at the bar but had made little progress in upbuilding a practice. Samuel Adams, in his twenty-seventh year, had suffered a singularly unhappy business experience and recently had come into the control of his father's brewery. John Hancock, with a like moderate accumulation of years, was partner in the rich firm of Thomas Hancock & Co., though he would have been willing to admit that he had not overworked himself in gaining that distinction at the hands of his uncle. James Otis, when 26, had just begun pursuit of the law in Boston, whither he had removed from Plymouth County. Benjamin Franklin issued his first *Poor Richard's Almanac* in the year he reached that birthday. A struggling young man of 22, Patrick Henry, who was falling steadily in debt as a storekeeper in 1758, was more nearly to rival Washington in youthful achievement, but at 26 Henry was not to have been employed as counsel in the "Parson's cause," the first great case of his career. Horatio Gates, Captain of an Independent Company at 26, was not promoted Major until he was 34.

[65] Letter of Apr. 28, 1756, to Governor Dinwiddie; 1 *G. W.*, 325. See *supra*, p. 178.

In contrast, Washington, with all his complications of character, was Virginia's most distinguished soldier and might not extravagantly have been rated as the most conspicuous native-born American provincial who had followed a career of arms.[66]

The first impression he made on contemporaries was that of physical strength, vigor and nervous stability, qualities he doubtless inherited from his father. His straight six feet of height were the frame for an admirably proportioned body, of which only his very large hands and feet were out of scale. His energy and endurance matched his strength. Few men of his day worked as hard; probably none covered the road between Williamsburg and Winchester with more frequency and speed except for the express, William Jenkins, who was the *fliegende Holländer* of the Virginia forest trails.

These physical qualities may have been responsible, in large measure, for his extraordinary combination of amiability and determination. No characteristic was to appear more conspicuously in his first portrait than good temper; no adjective was applied more often to him in youth than "amiable." He might explode; he might display temperamental peculiarities, but his disposition, at bottom, was kindly. Along with a certain sweetness of spirit there was always and in all things a determination nothing could destroy and few things could deflect. Men took it for granted, if they knew him at all, that he would discharge the duty entrusted to him—would perform it amiably but would do it so certainly that doubt might be dismissed.

The next impression made by Washington was one of singular maturity of judgment and of character. From the time he brought to Williamsburg the dispatch from Fort Le Boeuf, his seniors regarded him as a man of experience that equalled their own. He seemed young when his elders looked at him, but not when they listened to him. This manifest dependability was the fruit of George Washington's early but deliberate decision to adhere to what he termed "the principles which govern my conduct," [67] certain "maxims" [68] that he accepted as permanently sound. It is futile to speculate when and how and why he reached a resolution to square his daily acts with a definite, if unwritten, code of honor. No evidence of any sort exists beyond that vaguely

---

[66] It will be remembered that neither William Shirley nor William Johnson had been born in the Colonies.

[67] Letter of Sept. 30, 1757, to his mother; 2 *G. W.*, 137. For the circumstances, see *supra*, p. 269.

[68] Cf. 2 *G. W.*, 141.

presented in the *Rules of Civility and Decent Behaviour* he copied as a boy. The essential fact, one of the two keys that unlock the character of the young man, is that these principles were adopted by him and were applied habitually and earnestly in his contest with all the hard realities of military life on the frontier.

Old, old principles they were, but principles disdained in every generation by so many that their rediscovery is a thrill and their application is an adventure: young Washington resolved to adhere absolutely to truth, to practice rigid honesty, to do his full duty, to put forth his largest effort, to maintain uniform courtesy and, above all, to deal justly. He made this a hard code of conduct in some of its exactions, but he did not put his ideals beyond attainment.[69] Truth telling, for example, might involve unpleasant candor. As he phrased it, "I may be blamed possibly for expressing my sentiments so freely; but never can be ashamed of the truth." Again, "I have always laid it down as a maxim," he said, "to represent facts freely and impartially."[70] If hurt, he would accept the consequences. Duty was sternly commanding; so was courtesy. Neither of them, in Washington's code, carried with it the obligation to love the unlovable. Self-control was to be distinguished from self-sacrifice.

Compliance with this severe code and the amiable display of a definite maturity of character increased, rather than diminished, young Washington's attractiveness. Powerful Virginia elders, who saw much loose living and indolence around them, found stimulation and reassurance in a young man of unassailed morals and of mature, sound judgment, who was full of energetic vigor and was devoted to the defence of a people slow and slothful in defending themselves. These qualities endeared young Washington to most of the potentates and explain in large part his success in dealing with them.

He did not rely on this alone to assure their support. Experience soon taught him that men in office love to be informed of events with which lesser persons are unacquainted. Usually, therefore, when Washington wrote Governor Dinwiddie, he transmitted the same information simultaneously to John Robinson, so long as the Speaker-Treasurer was on the committee that supervised and audited expenditures. The Colonel wrote often, too, to William Fairfax and less frequently to the influential Carters, Landon and Charles. In his letters, Washington was disposed to boast a little that his nature was "open and honest and

---

[69] 2 *G. W.*, 282.
[70] 2 *G. W.*, 141.

free from guile" [71] and that he did not flatter or know the art of complimenting. Perhaps in this he deceived himself or else he regarded flattery as praise completely unrestrained by taste or truth. Several of his letters, particularly those to Lord Loudoun, might have been written by a self-confessed eighteenth-century courtier. Washington was equally assiduous in seeking to employ policy as well as principle in winning the good will of Braddock, Shirley and Sharpe. Like early effort with Forbes was spoiled, in part, by the controversy over the Raystown route.

Washington's maturity, his energy, his high code of behavior and his skill in dealing with most of those in authority [72] were rendered more effective by his strong sense of order. Every task was performed as if it were a land survey—step by step, with the closest possible approach to absolute precision. As his memory was not especially strong, Washington relied on memoranda, the military equivalent of his surveyor's field notes. Whatever he undertook to do, he did thoroughly and methodically. That was his nature and that the process of his reasoning. He learned, too, so to respect the particular work he was doing, and so to devote himself to it, that he could concentrate on it in spite of distractions. Not even the proximity of hostile savages or the apparent imminence of attack in the spring of 1756 could keep him, for example, from writing deliberately and carefully about the forts that were to be constructed when the blood-covered raiders had gone home.[73]

Because Washington knew that he was thorough and conscientious in performing his duty according to his code, he had self-respect and, with it, a dignity of manner not derived solely from long-exercised military command. His gaze was direct and unflinching, eye to eye; the poise of his large head and the curve of his mouth were not arrogant, but neither were they ingratiating. He had undisguised pride in his station and in his achievements. On occasion, too, his sense of personal rectitude and of honest effort led to utterances that an enemy would have termed self-righteous. "I know this," he once said, "and it is the highest consolation I am capable of feeling, that no man that ever was employed in a public capacity has endeavored to discharge the trust reposed in him with greater honesty and more zeal for the public interest than I have done." [74] He had self-confidence, too, and

---

[71] Letter of Jan. n.d., 1757, to Lord Loudoun, 2 *G. W.*, 18.
[72] The major exception, Dinwiddie, is analyzed *supra*, p. 273.
[73] Cf. his letter of April 24, 1756, to Speaker Robinson, 1 *G. W.*, 331 ff.
[74] Letter of Sept. 17, 1757; 2 *G. W.*, 133. Precisely this sentiment, in almost the same language, was expressed again in December, 1756. See 1 *G. W.*, 525.

had it, among other reasons, because he believed he was right. When he urged a protest to the King, in the summer of 1758, against Forbes's choice of a line of advance to the Ohio, he expressed hope that he might go to England with the Colony's representative. "I think without vanity," said Washington, "I could set the conduct of this expedition in its true colors, having taken some pains, perhaps more than any other to dive into the bottom of it." [75]

This disposition to exalt his own rectitude and ability may have been a weakness in Washington's character as a young man. In addition, he had three deficiencies of temperament and aptitude that affected his way of living and influenced his career. The first of these was his lack of facility of speech. In conversation with his masculine friends, he was dignified and never loquacious but not under observable difficulty of finding words. If asked by a superior officer to state a case, he could do so, apparently, with logic and fair facility, at least to the extent that he neither experienced pain nor caused it by labored, halting utterance. Before a public body or on a formal occasion, he seems to have been almost inarticulate unless given time in which to prepare a manuscript which he would follow literatim.

Lack of facility of speech had important, hampering effects: It led Washington, in the first place, to attempt to express in letters what he could not promptly shape with ready words. At first, writing had been almost as laborious as speaking, because he must have followed the pompous models set forth in some poor book of the time. The "polite" letters of young Washington were wordy, vague and often were grammatically bad but, with practice on his part, they gradually were becoming better. Defects of style in his letters were less serious than the loss of time in drafting them. Although Washington frequently wrote memoranda for communications he was to forward, actual composition and the making of "fair copies" consumed hours, even though he wrote a swift, clear script and usually had a clerk. Washington was permitting himself, in short, to be entangled in too much "paper work."

Lack of facility of speech likewise made Washington somewhat awkward in his attention to ladies. Failure to shine in their company caused him to be, at 27, more than ever a "man's man." Moreover, his inability to find the smooth phrase might account for a silence that could be misinterpreted as hauteur or proud reserve. It is likely, too,

[75] Letter of Sept. 1, 1758, to Speaker Robinson, 2 *G. W.*, 278.

that a knowledge of his inferiority in verbal argument may have been one reason for Washington's avoidance of John Dagworthy during the time the Maryland Captain was asserting a right of command at Fort Cumberland. A man of Washington's strength and courage, who had seen battle and had ridden many dangerous trails, could not have been afraid of Dagworthy in any physical sense. When, therefore, the Virginian admitted that the "unhappy difference about the command" had "prevented" his going to Wills Creek [76] he could have meant only that, along with his desire to make no mistake on a question of rank, there was a disinclination to engage in a wrangle when a facile adversary might inflict on him a loss of dignity and standing. Beyond the line of unescapable duty, the young Colonel never willingly did anything he did not do well.

Washington's second lack was of humor. The intensity of his effort during the years of his rapid rise had made him serious and had led him to regard life as a contest. He would play cards occasionally and later he hunted often for diversion. If opportunity offered, he was not unwilling to back with a few pounds his judgment of a horse about to begin a race; when at home Washington found social pleasure in the company of Belvoir. At heart, his seriousness predominated and squeezed out whatever humor may have been born in him. No surviving record of his youth credits him with a laugh, even with a smile.

Another lack was that of the inspiration of family and of a strong religious belief. He remembered little of his father; he did not love his mother deeply; Lawrence was dead. George had affection for his other brothers and for Betty, but he possessed no great pride in his kin and had no interest in any of his ancestors except John the immigrant. That interest originated in the fact that the Indians had given him the native name bestowed long previously on the first American Washington. Religion, as distinguishing belief from moral principles, meant little at this period of the younger Washington's life. The church at that time "was more an institution than a means of grace" [77] in Virginia; Washington had not been at home frequently enough from his sixteenth year onward to enjoy often the benefits of public worship with his own people, in his own parish. He had believed in Providence and still did, but increasingly he felt, as he told Sally Fairfax,

[76] 1 G. W., 532. In a similar letter to Dinwiddie, the clause was "kept me from Fort Cumberland" (ibid., 317).

[77] This admirable statement is Dr. Gertrude Richards's.

that "There is a Destiny which has the control of our actions, not to be resisted by the strongest efforts of human nature."[78] In no surviving letter of his youth is the name of Jesus used; "Providence" appears more frequently than "God." The young man never had a positive religious experience, other than flashes of gratitude that an Unseen Hand had stayed the blows of an adversary.

Although there was no compelling faith in God, principles of right conduct prevailed: there is no echo of any scandal, no hint of a breach of accepted morals, no line of obscenity, no reference to any sex experience, no slur on any woman otherwise than in reference to those who might be demoralizing his troops. That he was in love with the wife of his nearest neighbor, even after his engagement to Martha Custis, scarcely can be denied; but his strange confession of that love was at the same time a confession that it was hopeless. Sally's letters to him were few and must have been reserved. She doubtless was interested in him, as almost any woman would be in the most conspicuous young man of her society. Nothing suggests that this interest ever passed the line of discretion. She may have flirted with him mildly. That was all.

His elemental and patent virtues might have been enlarged, his weaknesses might have been cancelled or offset, and, had there been no more to tell, he still might have been merely an able, honorable country gentleman, a citizen-soldier of modest achievement. The first chamber of his character might be entered and examined and might not be found more than creditably respectable and moderately interesting. It is when a second key is turned and the other chamber is opened that the full implications of his character and the driving power of his youthful career are seen.

His was the quenchless ambition of an ordered mind. Ambition was Washington through 1758; Washington was a synonym for ambition. If in repose his "principles" were the dominant of his life, in action ambition was. When first he emerged from boyhood, in a veritable explosion of energy, he had willingness to work ceaselessly in order to get what he wanted. As his ambition broadened, it compassed four things—wealth, "honor," eminence and military distinction. All these might be stated in terms of the infinitive of ambition, which is to excel.

So relentless was his ambition that it never burned out in enthusiasm

78 Letter of Sept. 12, 1758; 2 G. W., 288. For the circumstances in which this was written, see *supra*, p. 337.

or wasted itself in rash adventure. It was ambition that calculated every move coldly in terms of risk and gain and with a curious combination of self-consciousness and lack of it. A perfect example in all its parts was in a letter written one of his brothers soon after George, at the age of 23, joined Braddock: "The General has appointed me one of his aids de camps, in which character I shall serve this campaign, agreeably enough, as I am thereby freed from all commands but his, and give orders to all, which must be implicitly obeyed. I have now a good opportunity, and shall not neglect it, of forming an acquaintance, which may be serviceable hereafter, if I can find it worth while pushing my fortune in the military way." [79] Always he wished to be certain it was worth while. If he decided it was, and ambition led him to desire any position, he would ask for it from the men who could give it to him, and he would call on his friends to solicit it for him through the channels of largest influence. Modesty played no part in it, one way or the other: Honest ambition must be served.

Ambition for wealth made him acquisitive and sometimes contentious. After he had established himself he would spend freely, sometimes too freely, for the things that would make a good appearance; but even then he would insist upon the exact payment of every farthing due him. If he would lay down £94, 17s for silver lace in Boston, he would not forget an additional penny also was on the account, nor would he fail promptly to reduce this to a far less formidable sum in the currency of his own Colony. Back in Virginia he did not permit his pay or his commission to restrain him from conducting a long correspondence with Governor Dinwiddie over the number of batmen he was to have and the allowance that was to be made for them.[80]

Along with the determination to get everything that he honestly could, Washington had a weakness in another form of expenditure, a weakness that was, in part, a defect—or some would have it a grace—of his class and of his society. In a Colony that boasted no banks, every planter who needed money seemed to think himself entitled to borrow it from any friend who had it. There was less embarrassment in the asking than in the declining. Washington was from boyhood a victim of this practice. He even felt, on occasion, that he should not wait for his friends to make requests. When Robert Munford reported at Fort Cumberland as an officer in July, 1758, Washington invited the young

[79] Letter of May 14, 1755, to John Augustine Washington; 1 G. W., 124.
[80] See *supra*, p. 245.

man to eat at the headquarters table and tendered him, interest free, any money he might require.[81] In the case of "Billy" Fairfax, after that young gentle purchased a commission in the northern army, Washington sent him £50 and said cheerfully: "I beg that you will put yourself to no sort of inconvenience to return the money. Seven years hence will suit my purpose as well as at the present time."[82] Washington must have known that this was dangerous practice. Nothing but compliance with the social code of his day could have led a man of his natural acquisitiveness to lend so recklessly what he garnered so carefully.

His financial relations with members of his own family were different. Lack of attachment to his mother may have been due in part to her attitude toward money, but he felt that compliance with her calls was a matter of filial duty. He accepted the cost as part of his normal expenses. His brothers, too, might borrow, but they were expected to return; and if they made requests of him, he felt free to do the same of them, though when he asked anything of them, it was usually some personal service rather than money. Washington's charities at this period of his life did not interfere with his financial ambition. He did not give often or largely, and then generally to those who importuned him, crippled soldiers, "begging women," as he termed them, the victims of Indians and persons whose houses had been burned. Young Washington had no enthusiasm for the common man unless he was a good soldier, and no sympathy for him unless he was in trouble.

If Washington's ambition to acquire wealth always had a slow fire under it, his ambition for public reputation flamed in his youth. The word by which he usually described that which he sought for himself was "honor." He used the noun, its adjectives and its antonym not infrequently in familiar senses. To his mother in the summer of 1755, after he had accepted the direction of the Virginia troops, he wrote: "it would reflect eternal dishonor upon me to refuse it; and that, I am sure must, or ought to give you greater cause of uneasiness than my going in an honorable command . . ."[83] Again: "no sordid views have influenced my conduct, nor have the hopes of unlawful gains swerved me in any measure from the dictates of honor!"[84]

Sometimes Washington employed the word "honor" where modern readers may be puzzled to know whether the usual definition holds.

---

[81] Robert Munford to Theodorick Bland, Sr., July 6, 1758; 1 *Bland Papers*, 10.
[82] Letter of April 23, 1758; 2 *G. W.*, 182; *Ledger A*, folio 50. Bryan Fairfax gave bond in May, 1761, for repayment of this debt.
[83] 1 *G. W.*, 159.   [84] 1 *G. W.*, 533.

In his twenty-third year, he declined military office under Governor Sharpe, with the explanation that he did so "to obey the call of honor" and on the advice of friends.[85] More often he spoke of "honor" in what may have been its earliest English meaning as something to be "gained, held or enjoyed—Glory, renown, fame; credit, reputation, good name."[86] In intimating, for example, on Aug. 14, 1755, the conditions under which he would resume command of the Virginia Regiment, he said: "I believe our circumstances are now to that unhappy dilemma that no man can gain any honor by conducting our forces at this time, but rather lose[87] in his reputation."[88] He came back to it even more candidly in the same letter: "Seeing these things in the above light that I did had no small influence upon me, as I was pretty much assured I should lose what at present constitutes the chief part of my happiness, i.e., the esteem and notice the country has been pleased to honor me with."[89] During one of the most violent emotional upheavals of his youth, he repeated that sentiment the following spring: ". . . the distant prospects, if any, that I can see, of gaining honor and reputation in the service, are motives which cause me to lament the hour that gave me a commission . . ."[90] Still again, he wrote Loudoun: "I have long been satisfied of the impossibility of continuing in this service without loss of honor."[91] Other protests put his meaning beyond dispute: "If I can gain any credit," he told William Byrd just before joining Braddock, "or if I am entitled to the least countenance or esteem, it must be from serving my country with a free, voluntary will . . ."[92] In September, 1756, it was: ". . . no person who regards character will undertake a command without the means of preserving it, since his conduct is culpable for all misfortune and never right but when successful."[93] His first, amazingly frank letter to Lord Loudoun included the statement that for a time he had declined the second offer of the command of the Virginia troops because he did not care "to expose my character to public censure."[94]

Like confession of the fear of a loss of reputation he made repeatedly: As surely as he loved good opinion, he dreaded the sacrifice of it. Public censure was the nightmare of his ambition and, at the same

85 1 G. W., 106.
86 Modern English Dictionary.
87 Washington wrote "loose."
88 1 G. W., 162.
89 Ibid.
90 1 G. W., 325.
91 Letter of Jan. n.d., 1757; 2 G. W., 17.
92 1 G. W., 114. His letter of the same date, Apr. 20, 1755, to Speaker Robinson expressed the same feeling.
93 1 G. W., 469–70.
94 2 G. W., 17.

time, one of the reasons for discreet action: ". . . in order to avoid
censure in every part of my conduct, I make it a rule," he wrote the
Governor, "to obey the dictates of your Honor, the Assembly and a good
conscience." [95] Further: As he had no positive instructions, "I am
afraid to turn to this hand or to that, lest it should be censured." [96]
In the last year of his military service, he declined to exercise discretion
given him to call the militia into service. "It is an affair, Sir, of too
much importance and delicate nature for me to have the management
of, for much discontent will be the inevitable consequence of this
draft." [97]

Preferment, character, credit, esteem, honor—all these are synonyms
of the public reputation the supremely ambitious young Washington
desired and feared to lose. He never said as plainly as did a somewhat
older contemporary soldier, Frederick of Prussia, that he wanted to
"be talked about," but he desired precisely that.

The value his ambition attached to the good opinion of those in authority was one reason for his extreme sensitiveness, the canker of his
growth.[98] He believed himself willing to accept reproof, when he was
at fault, and on two important occasions, a sharp rebuke brought
promise of better performance. "If I continue in the service," he wrote
when the Governor complained of alleged drunkenness and loose
living in the Regiment, "I shall take care to act with a little more rigor
than has hitherto been practiced, since I find it so absolutely necessary." [99] Another time it was: "However, if I have erred in these
points, I am sorry for it, and shall endeavor for the future to be as
particular and satisfactory in my accounts of these things as possible." [100]
The more clearly the public interest was involved, the more sternly did
he curb his resentment of adverse comment. He cooled fastest where
danger was hottest. Usually he regarded criticism as likely to damage
him in public reputation, and, for that reason, he suffered cruelly in
pride.

Beyond doubt his sensitiveness had relation to his consciousness that
he was doing his full duty. Criticism similarly made him more unhappily aware of the limitations of force and equipment, and of the
impossibility of accomplishing what was expected of him with so few

---

[95] Letter of Apr. 27, 1756, to Governor Dinwiddie; 1 G. W., 344.
[96] Letter of Aug. 5, 1756, to Speaker Robinson, 1 G. W., 433.
[97] Letter of Apr. 24, 1758, to President John Blair, 2 G. W., 183–84.
[98] Cf. 385.   [99] Letter of Apr. 18, 1756; 1 G. W., 317.
[100] Letter of Aug. 27, 1757, to Governor Dinwiddie; 2 G. W., 120.

men. Once he resigned; [101] once he resolved to do so; [102] four times, at least, he threatened to return his commission. In one of these instances, he despaired of guarding the frontier with a thin Regiment under spineless military law; [103] the other threats [104] were connected with some criticism of his management of affairs or with some failure to get the rank or seniority his ambition coveted.

This ambition for eminence of rank and for seniority over men of like rank ran through four years of military career. He was willing to labor with all his energies and even beyond his physical endurance, but he wanted the reward of work. Nothing rankled more than subordination to officers of inferior title who happened to be on the regular establishment. The outburst of November, 1754, was: ". . . every Captain bearing the King's commission, every half-pay officer or other, appearing with such a commission, would rank before me . . ." [105] These words were not repeated; the sentiment was not changed till the regulations were revised to make a colonial Colonel rank a regular Captain. It was this resentment of being second, under absurd rules, that fired Washington to ride 1000 miles over wintry roads in 1756 and to pay from his own pocket the expenses of himself and four companions.

When Washington was 22, ambition for eminence and seniority was not divorced in his mind from his natural acquisitiveness. He would gain financially from military service if he could; he certainly must not lose. During the campaign of 1754, when he was burning with resentment over the seniority asserted by James Mackay, the commander of the Independent Company of regulars, he wrote of serving as a volunteer, without compensation, but he could not quite bring himself to do that. After he came home and indignantly resigned his commission because he was reduced in rank, he confessed frankly: "I never will quit my family, injure my fortune and (above all) impair my health to run the risk of such changes and vicissitudes as I have done, but shall now expect, if I am employed again, to have something certain . . ." [106] A letter of approximately the same date to his brother made it plain that "something certain" involved pay as well as security and distinction of rank. Washington wrote: ". . . I am always ready and always willing, to do my country any services that I am capable

---

[101] Autumn, 1754.
[102] March, 1756.
[103] October, 1755.
[104] October–December, 1755, over the Dagworthy affair; April, 1756, over criticism of the Regiment; October, 1756, over the article by "The Virginia Centinel."
[105] 1 G. W., 105–06.
[106] 1 G. W., 160.

SALLY FAIRFAX IN THE BELVOIR GUEST BOOK

Virginia Colonials learned early the art of makeshift. After they became prosperous, they imported from England everything they could afford—and much of what they could not—and they tried to procure the newest fashions in the wares and the clothing of "home." If they forgot to order a particular article, they got on well enough by making the most of what they had at hand.

The owners of Belvoir, for example, never thought to include a guest book in their frequent invoices from England; but when they wished to preserve the names of guests, they took down from a library shelf a copy of Thoresby's *Topography of . . . Leedes* (1715) in the back of which were a number of blank pages. At intervals, on one or another of these pages, visitors inscribed their "sentiments."

The first of the next two illustrations includes the signatures of Lawrence Washington and of John Carlyle, sons-in-law of Col. William Fairfax. Later, the young mistress of Belvoir added her name to those already in the book. She did so and—being more careful than any of the others—set down the date. It was Sept. 6, 1757, when a young neighbor who much admired her was going through one of his several controversies with Robert Dinwiddie. The Governor had accused him of

(Continued on third page following)

a "loose way of writing"; Washington somewhat laboriously, but with honest candor, was defending himself.

Sally knew nothing of this and, being a prudent young matron, could have done nothing had she known of her neighbor's troubles; but evidently she was herself in distress of spirit and in reflective mood, perhaps because of the death of her father-in-law, Col. William Fairfax, four days previously. She wrote in her best French, "Misfortunes never come singly," and "We never prize a blessing until we have lost it." These lines are among the few that remain in the pleasing autograph of this young woman who always will be interesting because Washington found her so.

The other autographs include that of Charles Green, rector of Truro Parish and a gentleman-planter besides, to say nothing of his familiarity with physic. He contributed a medley of Horace and of St. Augustine: "To have neither guilty secrets nor evil deeds to turn us pale" and "that rock stands unmoved in stormy seas, always the same, conscious virtue." William Fairfax wrote, "Love is full of anxious fears." Landon Carter, like Charles Green, quoted Horace: "Sustained in life by freedom from sin."

These autographs are reproduced from the "old guest book" at New Belvoir by permission of the heirs of Fairfax Harrison.

off; but never upon the terms I have done, having suffered much in my private fortune, besides impairing one of the best of constitutions. I was employed to go a journey in the Winter (when I believe few or none would have undertaken it) and what did I get by it? My expenses borne! I then was appointed with trifling pay to conduct an handful of men to the Ohio. What did I get by this? Why, after putting myself to a considerable expense in equipping and providing necessaries for the Campaign I went out, was soundly beaten, lost them all—came in, and had my commission taken from me or, in other words my command reduced, under pretence of an order from home. I then went out a volunteer with Genl. Braddock and lost all my horses and many other things, but this being a voluntary act, I should not have mentioned it, was it not to show that I have been upon the losing order ever since I entered the Service, which is now near two years; so that I think I can't be blamed, should I, if I leave my family again, endeavor to do it upon such terms as to prevent my suffering., (to gain by it, is the least of my expectation)." [107] Almost two years later, he stood on the same ground. "[I] must now beg leave to know," he wrote the Governor after a reorganization of the Regiment, "... upon what terms your Honor purposes to continue me, and what may be my certain dependence?" With that he proceeded to solicit in unabashed earnestness the continuance of his pay of 30s a day and his commission of 2 per cent on all the accounts he handled.[108] The command was, in fact, profitable. While he held it, he was able to purchase more land and to buy additional slaves.

This attitude toward military service appears to have sprung not only from Washington's ambition but also from his conception of King and country. At the outset, when he heard from Ensign Ward that the French had occupied the forks of the Ohio, there was an upsurge of patriotic impulse, "a glowing zeal," as Washington described it. He hoped the news of the disaster would arouse "The heroic spirit of every free-born Englishman to attest the rights and privileges of our King (if we don't consult the benefit of ourselves) and rescue from the invasions of a usurping enemy our Majesty's property, his dignity and land." [109] That spirit evaporated when, after the defeat at Fort Necessity, Washington's rank was reduced. Calculation succeeded ardor and subsequently gave place slowly to a more mature, less

[107] 1 *G. W.*, 156–57.   [108] 2 *G. W.*, 34.
[109] To Horatio Sharpe, Apr. 27, 1754; 1 *G. W.*, 44.

personal view. In a preliminary draft of the remonstrance to be filed by the officers of the Virginia Regiment, presumably during the spring of 1757, there was mention of the "idle arguments which [were] oftentimes used" that the Virginians were defending their own properties. These arguments were held to be "whimsical and absurd." Said the officers: "We are defending the King's dominions"—just that, the King's. When the address was presented, a more delicate and experienced hand had changed that to read: "We are defending part of the domain of Great Britain." The original language probably was Washington's; almost certainly it expressed his belief at the time. If the domain was the King's, it was his Majesty's to defend, and if his to defend, then his was the obligation to reward those who shared in protecting it. In England about that time, Bolingbroke was lamenting in his essay "On the Spirit of Patriotism" that "What passes among us for ambition is an odd mixture of avarice and vanity." [110] Perhaps it was so in Virginia; perhaps it was a belief in the wealth of the King, his possession of so vast a domain, which oiled the implicit argument that patriotism could be expected only where it was compensated.

As the remonstrance of 1757 made plain, young Colonel Washington did not feel that he had been compensated. A Virginia Colonel he was in 1754, after the death of Joshua Fry; a Virginia Colonel he was in the autumn of 1758, though Forbes styled him Brigadier for the fortnight of the final advance in November. All the addresses and petitions for inclusion in the regular establishment had gone unheeded, unnoticed. No word of praise had come "from home." Washington had lost all hope of receiving the King's commission which, had it been given him, might later have raised difficult questions of loyalty.

His loss was his exceeding profit. By the spring of 1758 a change was coming in the spirit of the young man who less than four years previously had lost his "glowing zeal" and had inquired in wrath and disappointment, "What did I get . . . ? My expenses borne." Old ambition and a new resignation to the performance of unrewarded duty were coupled now. ". . . I long ago despaired of any other reward for my services," he wrote Sir John St. Clair in April, 1758, "than the satisfaction arising from a consciousness of doing my duty, and from the esteem of my friends." [111]

The conjunction recorded the transition. As late as September "and" was to link defeated personal ambition with what he feared was lost

---

[110] *Works*, ed. of 1809, v. 4, p. 208.   [111] 2 *G. W.*, 189.

opportunity for the army. In alarm and chagrin over the choice of the Raystown route he wrote: "That appearance of glory once in view, that hope, that laudable ambition of serving our country and meriting its applause, is now no more!" [112] Less seriously he wrote Sally Fairfax, "Should not my own honor and country's welfare be the excitement?" [113] In the strange letter in which he asked to be distinguished from the "common run of provincial officers" he said honestly that he was serving in the campaign of 1758 "merely for the purpose of affording my best endeavors to bring matters to a conclusion." [114] Thus, gradually, were his ideals becoming clearer. Even in the matter of the Raystown route, he had defended his candor and freedom of utterance on the ground of "my duty . . . to his Majesty and to the Colony whose troops I have the honor to command." [115]

In summary, then, the company officers who subscribed their address on the last day of December, 1758, had seen their Colonel in many tests. A few of the ranking Captains had stood resolutely beside him in the flooded trench of feeble Fort Necessity. One or two of his subordinates had been where they could have observed the suppressed pain and perplexity in his honest eyes as he rode through the confused ranks in the woods near the bank of the Monongahela. His finely proportioned figure and his flawless horsemanship were the model of his juniors; his physical endurance had become a tradition in his Regiment. He was mature beyond his years with all the vigor of growth from the good earth of character. To officers who discharged their duties with courage, intelligence and spirit, he always was amiable and attractive and sometimes he was affectionate.

Slow to praise excellencies, he was equally slow to forget them. If he seldom applauded, he always remembered. He did not cross the gulf that regulations had fixed between officers and men, as if they had been the righteous and the damned; and he did not feign admiration of the ignorant, common man who was more apt, he thought, to be a coward than a hero. In his dealings with troops, Washington's reliance was not on human nature but on military discipline. The possibility of promotion for the diligent and of refreshment for the faithful was not disregarded; no substitute was offered for the performance of duty as duty. Daily practice exemplified what orders had proclaimed in historic words: "Discipline is the soul of an army."

112 2 G. W., 276.
114 2 G. W., 173.
113 2 G. W., 287.
115 2 G. W., 263.

Behind the flap of his own tent, the young commander sought the self-discipline he inculcated. This was not easy for a man of complicated emotional character. His ambition burned so steadily that it gave to all his efforts a concentration and a seriousness never relieved by the relaxing balm of humor. Even after he realized that high rank in his beloved profession of arms never would be his, he retained all the driving energy and all the instinctive planning required to press toward the goal of wealth, distinction and "honor"; but he could not laugh at his own relentless pursuit of pounds and epaulettes, and he could not smile at his own defeats. Instead, his consciousness of steadfast, wholehearted adherence to duty made him unhappily sensitive to criticism. Any scrutiny of his acts he was apt to regard as reflection on his integrity. He battled with this thinness of skin and, after five years in the field, he reached the state of mind in which he could grip his temper and repress his sensitiveness if his resentment of criticism was likely to injure the defence of the Colony in a day of danger. He had achieved that much; he had not conquered a pride that had on occasion the color of self-righteousness.

His principal weaknesses were superficial or circumstantial. Facility of speech never would be his. It would not be possible for him to move a multitude as young Patrick Henry soon was to do; but if Washington could not stir emotion he could accomplish something that might be less impermanent: he could win support by sound judgment and disinterested zeal. If, furthermore, he could not invoke the name and influence of a powerful family in an hour when pride was affronted or the armor of his self-reliance pierced, that was a weakness he counterbalanced by acquiring early and retaining permanantly the goodwill of members of the Council and of the House of Burgesses. He had, likewise, what many of his contemporaries would have regarded as a deficiency if he had spoken of it: there was for him no rock of refuge in religion. Not once in his letters had he quoted Holy Writ or the Prayer Book of the church into which he had been baptized. He believed in Providence but sometimes he thought the rightful name was Destiny. Instead of adhering to a creedal religion he held steadfastly, almost ostentatiously, to the principles of conduct he regarded as the code of gentlemen.

The foundations of that code were not love and mercy, faith and sacrifice, but honesty and duty, truth and justice, justice exact and inclusive, justice that never for an instant overlooked his own interests.

Justice demanded that he do his utmost and that, in return, he receive what he had earned, whether it was the public esteem he cherished or the last penny due him by "the country" for the food of every batman the letter of military regulations allowed him.

What he demanded for himself, he allowed with equal exactness to all his fellow men. Anything that any person deserved at his hands, that person must receive on balanced scales, whether in monetary payment, in reward, in courtesy, in candor or in truth-telling. Justice never could walk with Compromise. Nor did adherence to justice require that young Washington be a partisan of individuals. He espoused the cause of colonial officers who wished to be put on the regular establishment in order to gain prestige and to qualify for half pay, and in this he sought without abashment his own advantage. In 1758 he burned with indignation over what he conceived to be the cunning of Pennsylvanians in prevailing on General Forbes to choose the Raystown route. His justification for his obstinate wrath was his fixed belief that the common cause would suffer defeat through the delay the cutting of a new road would involve. If, again, injustice to any individual came under Washington's eye in his own command, he would correct it as a matter of course, but there he drew the line. He would do his part to relieve human misery and he might be the champion of public causes. Rarely did he become the advocate of any man, lest support of one be injustice to another.

Justice was not "the be all and the end all" of Washington's code of conduct, but it was as basic in that code as the development of patience was in his training. The officer who tapped on the tent-pole to make a report to his Colonel probably would not feel that he was in the presence of a great man, but he knew that Washington would hear him with sure patience and with dignified amiability, would reason logically and methodically, would concentrate on whatever duty the report imposed, would display sound judgment and cold, calm courage in the execution, would demand discipline and—always and inflexibly— would measure out exact justice.

Such was the soldier and the man. Some of his deeper characteristics were not known to the officers who addressed him at the end of December, 1758; but they wished to pay tribute to him as best they might, and they had now an occasion besides that of the conclusion of the campaign for expressing their affection for him: He had decided to resign—finally and without thought of reconsideration. His officers hoped against hope that he would remain with them, but if he would not, then those young Virginians wished to record that "as you have hitherto been the actuating soul of the whole corps, we shall at all times pay the most invariable regard to your will and pleasure . . ." [116]

This was "honor" of the sort he still loved, but there were other ambitions now. A new Fort Pitt was rising on the ruins of DuQuesne; the Virginia frontier would be secure. Washington felt he had done his part for the King's domain. Let the Northern Colonies take Quebec. For himself now, there was Mount Vernon and a seat in the House of Burgesses and Martha and the rich plantations of the Custises and the Parkes on slow-flowing, pleasant rivers! [117]

[116] 3 *Hamilton,* 145–46.
[117] The tradition is that Washington decided at the time of his engagement to Martha Custis, and at her instance, to resign at the end of 1758 or as long before that time as DuQuesne might be captured. While this tradition may be true, no supporting evidence exists, other than as the bolder tone of Washington's correspondence with Forbes and Bouquet may be regarded as that of a man who had no favors to ask in a service from which he soon was to retire. The address of his officers, December 31, would indicate that his decision had not long been made and was not regarded as irrevocable. Apparently he returned his commission as of the year's end. His resignation is mentioned as already in effect on Jan. 16, 1759. See 3 *Hamilton,* 151. According to his *Ledger A,* Washington drew no military pay from Virginia for service in 1759.

WASHINGTON'S FIRST ACQUAINTANCE WITH MARTHA CUSTIS

THE FIRST mention of Martha Dandridge Custis in the surviving correspondence of George Washington is assumed to have been a brief note to her on July 20, 1758, but this document either is a forgery or else has been so edited that even the date is doubtful.[1] It is prudent to disregard this paper altogether and to conclude, regretfully, that no correspondence that passed between them prior to their marriage is known to have survived. The only other documentary evidence of acquaintance prior to their union is represented by Washington's *Ledger A* and by the account G. W. P. Custis gave in his *Recollections* of the alleged circumstances of their first meeting. Such facts as appear in the ledger—and they are few—have been quoted in the text of the present work. Custis's account of Washington's introduction to Martha reads as follows:

"It was in 1758, that an officer, attired in a military undress, and attended by a body-servant, tall and *militaire* as his chief, crossed the ferry called Williams's, over the Pamunkey, a branch of the York river. On the boat touching the southern or New Kent side, the soldier's progress was arrested by one of those personages who give the beau ideal of the Virginia gentleman of the old *regime,* the very soul of kindliness and hospitality. It was in vain the soldier urged his business at Williamsburg, important communications to the governor, etc. Mr. Chamberlayne, on whose domain the *militaire* had just landed, would hear of no excuse. Colonel Washington (for the soldier was he) was a name and character so dear to all the Virginians, that his passing by one of the old castles of the commonwealth, without calling and partaking of the hospitalities of the host, was entirely out of the question. The colonel, however, did not surrender at discretion, but stoutly maintained his ground, till Chamberlayne bringing up his reserve, in the intimation that he would introduce his friend to a young and charming widow, then beneath his roof, the soldier capitulated, on condition that he should dine, 'only dine,' and then, by pressing his charger and borrowing of the night, he would reach Williamsburg before his excellency could shake off his morning slumbers. Orders were accordingly issued to Bishop, the colonel's body-servant and faithful follower, who, together with the fine English charger, had been

1 The note is in 2 *G. W.*, 242; a critique of it will be found in Appendix II-2.

bequeathed by the dying Braddock to Major Washington, on the famed and fatal field of the Monongahela. Bishop, bred in the school of European discipline, raised his hand to his cap, as much as to say, 'your honor's orders shall be obeyed.'

"The colonel now proceeded to the mansion, and was introduced to various guests (for when was a Virginia domicile of the olden time without guests?), and above all, to the charming widow. Tradition relates that they were mutually pleased on this their first interview, nor is it remarkable; they were of an age when impressions are strongest. The lady was fair to behold, of fascinating manners, and splendidly endowed with worldly benefits. The hero, fresh from his early fields, redolent of fame, and with a form on which 'every god did seem to set his seal, to give the world assurance of a man.'

"The morning passed pleasantly away. Evening came, with Bishop, true to his orders and firm at his post, holding his favorite charger with one hand, while the other was waiting to offer the ready stirrup. The sun sank in the horison, and yet the colonel appeared not. And then the old soldier marvelled at his chief's delay. ' 'Twas strange, 'twas passing strange'—surely he was not wont to be a single moment behind his appointments, for he was the most punctual of all men. Meantime, the host enjoyed the scene of the veteran on duty at the gate, while the colonel was so agreeably employed in the parlor; and proclaiming that no guest ever left his house after sunset, his military visitor was, without much difficulty, persuaded to order Bishop to put up the horses for the night. The sun rode high in the heavens in the ensuing day, when the enamored soldier pressed with his spur his charger's side, and speeded on his way to the seat of government, where, having despatched his public business, he retraced his steps, and, at the White House, the engagement took place, with preparations for the marriage." [2]

This, of course, is florid and is somewhat overwritten but it is the testimony of Mrs. Washington's grandson and it either must have come from her or must have been invented. It could not have been related before, say, 1791 at earliest, when the boy was 10 years old. In all probability it was told Parke Custis by Mrs. Washington at a later date, but, even if given him in 1791, the story then dealt with events that had occurred thirty-three years previously. Custis himself did not begin his *Recollections* until about 1826, or approximately sixty-eight years after the events under discussion here, and he did not complete them until almost thirty years afterward.[3] The chapter on Martha Washington was written originally for the *National Portrait Gallery of Distinguished Americans* and, being published in 1834, probably was written in 1833 or about seventy-five years after the courtship of Martha Custis.

This long lapse of time bars Custis's story as historical evidence of a sort

[2] G. W. P. Custis, 499–501.   [3] See *G. W. P. Custis*, 9, 120.

to be accepted in all detail but does not necessarily brand it as evidence to be disregarded altogether. Known facts are in part confirmatory: Washington went to Williamsburg early in 1758; a "Williams's Ferry" existed on the Pamunkey;[4] one of the Chamberlaynes was Daniel Custis's neighbor, with a home near Williams's Ferry.[5] All this proves that Custis's story had some foundation in fact.

The difficulty about accepting it is offered by the assigned date, 1758. Washington's only visits to Williamsburg that year, prior to the time he is known to have been betrothed to Martha Custis, were in March and in June. His itinerary on his first journey of 1758 is established as far as Speaker Robinson's home at Pleasant Hill. From that plantation, the normal route of travel would be across the Pamunkey at Eltham and thence southward by Chiswell's Ordinary to Williamsburg. If Washington had been in normal health, at a time when he was preparing to address Martha, he might readily enough have ridden fifteen miles out of his way to see her; but Washington, in reality, after a long, enervating illness was journeying to see a doctor from whom he thought he might receive a death sentence. In this condition, Washington certainly would not have taken the longer road from Robinson's, via the White House, if, as Custis's story indicates, he had no intention of calling on Martha and did not even know her.

It is entirely possible that Washington made the acquaintance of Martha substantially as her grandson said, but that he did this during the lifetime of Daniel Parke Custis. Further, in dealing with this, as with many other traditions, the probabilities of everyday life are not to be set aside arbitrarily in favor of a romantic explanation. John Custis was dead before George Washington became a public figure, but Custis's "six-chimney lot" passed to his son, who may have occupied it during sessions of the House of Burgesses, when the social life of the town was at its gayest. Even if sale of the property or unhappy association kept Daniel Parke Custis from residing there temporarily, he and his young wife were apt to have visited Williamsburg and to have attended some of the "assemblies." The distance from the White House to the capital was approximately thirty-three miles, a long road for most social affairs but scarcely too long for a man still in his forties with a wife under 25 years of age.

Washington, it will be remembered, was in Williamsburg from approximately Apr. 27 to May 17, 1757, while the General Assembly was in a long session and social activity was almost dizzy. During part of this time, his *Ledger A* shows no expenditure sufficiently large to cover board and lodging at prevailing prices and on the level of Washington's usual subsistence.

[4] 46 V 304.
[5] William Chamberlayne, immigrant, 1700–36, had three daughters and three sons—Edward Pye, Richard and Thomas. It was Richard who lived near the ferry. See 36 V 226 and 23 W (2) p. 495.

Either he failed to make the entries or else he received private entertainment. Of the alternatives, the second is the more probable. There is not a shred of evidence to show where he visited, and no more reason for asserting he was near the White House than at any other plantation. All that can be said with reasonable probability is that he was moving in the circle frequented by such persons as Daniel and Martha Custis. It would have been remarkable if, in so small a society, he had not met the Custises.

Putting together known fact and probability, this hypothesis may be advanced: Washington perhaps made the acquaintance of one or both of the Custises through an introduction by one or another of the sons of William Chamberlayne; this acquaintance may have created in Washington's mind so favorable an impression of Martha that when he heard of the death of her husband and learned that she had received a very large estate, he determined to make his addresses to her, if he recovered from his illness. The age was one of swift "marrying and giving in marriage" but in every other decision of his life, young Washington was deliberate. He would not have been apt to make hastily the most important of all the decisions of young manhood, the one that was to determine his companionship and to fix his fortune. There exists no positive proof that their engagement was made in March. It may have been effected on his visit in June; but the fact that he ordered so handsome an outfit immediately after his return from Williamsburg in April is almost an assurance that she had promised to marry him or had promised, at least, to consider it. The point to stress is the high improbability of his decision to seek her hand without acquaintance prior to March, 1758.

APPENDIX II–2

The First "Love Letter" to Martha Custis

In 2 *Ford,* 153, and in 2 *G. W.,* 242, appears a letter assumed to be one that George Washington addressed to Martha Custis. This reads in full as follows:

July 20, 1758

We have begun our march for the Ohio. A courier is starting for Williamsburg, and I embrace the opportunity to send a few words to one whose life is now inseparable from mine. Since that happy hour when we made our pledges to each other, my thoughts have been continually going to you as to another Self. That an all-powerful Providence may keep us both in safety is the prayer of your ever faithful and affectionate friend.

Ford did not state where the original of this document was, or whether he had examined it. Fitzgerald merely said: "The text is from Ford. The location of the original is not known." He then added a few sentences concerning the destruction by Mrs. Washington of her husband's letters "shortly before her death." Benjamin Lossing was the only writer who affirmed that he ever saw the paper. In his *Mother and Wife of Washington* he printed the letter, which, he said, was in autograph at Arlington.

For the subjoined reasons, the present writer believes this love-note either is a forgery or else has been edited to such an extent that the text is not to be trusted:

1. The letter bears a date but does not mention where it was written. Other instances of like omission occur, but nine times in ten Washington gave his address at the head of a letter.

2. No intitulation appears. In every other known letter to a woman, Washington began formally "Honored Madam," or "Dear Madam" or "Madam," or in some similar manner. A letter of June 18, 1775, to Mrs. Washington—one of the few extant—begins "My Dearest." [1]

3. The opening sentence reads: "We have begun our march for the Ohio." As will be plain from Chapter XX, this was not the fact. Washington was preparing, under orders, to clear a ten-mile stretch of Braddock's Road [2] and was asking that his troops be included in any force that might "move on." [3]

[1] 3 *G. W.,* 293. [2] 2 *G. W.,* 241, 243. [3] *Ibid.,* 243.

His great concern was that a "march for the Ohio" might *not* be begun.
More immediately, he had been perplexed in trying to decide whether he
should or should not go to Winchester for the election to be held there on
the 24th. Prior to the 21st he had decided not to do so [4] but nothing whatever was happening to justify the statement, "We have begun our march
for the Ohio."

4. Even if this opening sentence did not contain a statement at variance
with known fact, it is not in the style of Washington's correspondence. He
usually started his letters with a long, rhetorical compound sentence. This
general criticism applies to the entire document: Its style is much simpler and
more direct than Washington's was in 1758.

5. The writer of the letter stated that "a courier is starting for Williamsburg." Washington never used the word "courier" at this period. Always it
was "express."

6. ". . . and I embrace the opportunity to send a few words to one whose
life is now inseparable from mine." In this, the telltale word is "opportunity."
Washington consistently misspelled this word and usually wrote it "oppertunity."

7. The concluding sentence is not in the style Washington employed at
the close of his letters. He said farewell to his mother with a "and am,
Honored Madam, your most dutiful and affectionate son." [5] Less than two
months after the date of the letter alleged to have been written to Martha
in July, 1758, he ended one to Sally Fairfax: "Be asured that I am, dear
Madame, with the most unfeigned regard, your most obedient and most
obliged humble servant." [6]

8. It may be said in answer to some of the foregoing objections that the
letter has been stripped carelessly of intitulation and of mention of the place
where it was written. The spelling of "oppertunity" may have been corrected. Were all this true, the fact would remain that the letter is in a style
conspicuously unlike Washington's and that it is based on the beginning of a
march that had not begun and was not expected to start at an early date.
Few and precious as are Washington's letters to Martha, this is not entitled to
be counted among them. If ever the "original" is brought to light, it will be
found to be one of the forgeries or, at best, will be substantially different from
Lossing's alleged "copy."

[4] *Ibid.*, 242.
[5] Letter of Sept. 30, 1757; 2 *G. W.*, 137.
[6] Letter of Sept. 12, 1758; 2 *G. W.*, 289.

APPENDIX II–3

THE MILITARY ASPIRATIONS OF THE FAIRFAXES

COL. WILLIAM FAIRFAX's oldest son, George William, in October, 1755, "proposed an inclination to go out with Colonel Washington," as Dinwiddie put it,[1] and he probably visited headquarters in Winchester, but he did not seek a commission. Bryan, the third and youngest son of Col. William Fairfax, had some of the oddities of his great-uncle, Lord Fairfax of Greenway Court, and along with them he had an active, restless mind. In the spring of 1756, Bryan's expression of interest in a military life led his father to begin a campaign to procure from Washington a commission for him as Lieutenant.[2] This effort was pursued with so much vigor and detail that Washington was kept informed of Bryan's wishes, reservations and whims as if the fate of the frontier hung on the young gentleman.[3] Washington apparently explained that he had no vacancy and that he could not appoint an inexperienced recruit in preference to men who had been serving as volunteers. This, at least, was the answer he usually made in such cases, but it did not deter the father. Bryan himself was exhorted by Colonel Fairfax to remember the widow who gained her suit by troubling the judge till he avenged her, lest, as the judge said, "by her continual coming she weary me."[4] This counsel was heeded by the son and was applied by the sire. Bryan and his father persisted until, in the reorganization of the Regiment in the summer of 1757, Bryan not only procured commission as Lieutenant, but received it, also, in a Company that was to remain at Winchester, not in one that was to proceed to a remote fort on Patterson Creek or the South Branch.[5]

Washington yielded in doing this and soon had occasion to lament it. Bryan resigned his commission,[6] unsuccessfully sought the hand of one young lady and then of another, and soon disappeared from home. His father thought him dead, but, in a short time, Bryan wrote to say that he was in jail at Annapolis. He had gone off, presumably to enlist under an assumed name in one of the Northern Regiments, but apparently had overlooked the fact that a young man of military age, traveling in Maryland, had to provide

---

[1] 2 *Din.*, 249. [2] 1 *Hamilton*, 252.
[3] 1 *Hamilton*, 255, 257, 265, 311.
[4] William Fairfax to Bryan Fairfax, Aug. 1, 1756; 1 *Ford*, 326 n.
[5] 2 *Hamilton*, 297, 311, 334.
[6] First mention of this was in William Fairfax to Washington, Mch. 31, 1757; 2 *Hamilton*, 58.

himself with a pass. Lacking this, Bryan had been arrested on suspicion of being a deserter.[7] He had prompt succor, of course, and after he came back to Belvoir he received commission as a Captain of militia, "in hopes," his doting father wrote, "his courage and good conduct will give testimony of his capacity." [8] Washington had been so embarrassed by Bryan's disappearance that he had felt himself unable to write Colonel Fairfax a letter of sympathy [9] and he doubtless was somewhat mystified to have the father say of Bryan, "He has experienced your kindness, therefore need not repeat my desire in his behalf." [10]

This was not the end of Colonel Fairfax's campaigning. He had a middle son, William Henry—"Billy" for short—whose cause he took up almost as soon as he dropped Bryan's. This time the father wrote Washington [11] to solicit a Lieutenant's commission with the assurance, "I persuade myself Billy will be more steady than Bryan has proved, and give you more pleasure to encourage his improvement in military skill." [12] Shortly before his death, Colonel Fairfax appealed to the Governor, also,[13] and succeeded so readily, because of his position in the Council, that Dinwiddie virtually directed Washington to fill out a blank commission for "Billy" if a vacancy existed.[14]

New embarrassment thus was inflicted on Washington. He could provide the vacancy, but he presented his situation candidly to the Governor: "I should take it infinitely kind if you would oblige me so far as to send the commission immediately from yourself to that gentleman. For although I esteem him greatly on account of his father, for whose memory and friendship I shall ever retain a most grateful sense, yet, making him Lieutenant over so many old Ensigns will occasion great confusion in the corps and bring censure on me, for the officers will readily conceive that my friendship and partiality to the family were the causes of it. If Mr. Fairfax would accept of an ensigny, the matter might pretty easily be accomodated." [15] This broad hint of a compromise had no effect on the Governor, who doubtless reasoned that if Colonel Fairfax had insisted on a Lieutenant's commission for his third son he certainly would not have accepted less rank for his second son. Dinwiddie made out a Lieutenant's commission and sent it to Washington. "To please you," he grumbled, "I have ordered it to be filled up here, but I can see no difference if you had done it by my order." [16] This did not prove altogether acceptable to "Billy" Fairfax. He had ambition to serve in the regular establishment, not with the provincials, and in a field of active opera-

---

[7] 2 *Hamilton*, 69.
[8] William Fairfax to Washington, June 17, 1757; 2 *Hamilton*, 98.
[9] 2 *Hamilton*, 69.   [10] 2 *Hamilton*, 98.
[11] Letter of July 17, 1757; 2 *Hamilton*, 148.
[12] *Ibid.*
[13] *Ibid.*, 166.   [14] *Ibid.*, 187, 190.
[15] Letter of Sept. 17, 1757; 2 *G. W.*, 129–30.
[16] Letter of Sept. 24, 1757; 2 *Hamilton*, 203.

tions, not on frontier garrison duty. Procuring a letter of introduction from Washington, he went to Lord Loudoun's headquarters and, when he found about 100 other young men there, hoping to qualify for higher rank by serving as volunteers, he promptly bought himself a commission.[17] His final adventure is described in Volume III.

[17] 2 *Hamilton*, 253–54.

GENERAL BIBLIOGRAPHICAL NOTE

As a somewhat extensive Bibliography will appear in the final volume of this work, it has not been considered necessary to print a preliminary list of books and pamphlets here or in the volume that concludes the story of Washington's part in the American Revolution. Most of the titles are well known and are described in the footnotes with sufficient detail to make the identification of particular works easy. The Short-Title Index includes a number of those most frequently cited. Not listed there but of particular value for the years of the French and Indian War are the magazines of several State historical societies. These are not always well-indexed nor are even the tables of contents of some of them all that might be desired, but an examination of all issues of these periodicals is worth the time of any student of the period. In the case of the Colony in which young George Washington resided, the publication in 1934–36 of the matchless *Virginia Historical Index* of Earl G. Swem makes it possible to follow any lead and to identify hundreds of provincials who otherwise would be names only.

For the period of Washington's life covered by these volumes (1732–58), the principal manuscript collections are those of (1) the Virginia State Library, (2) the Virginia Land Office, (3) the Virginia Historical Society, (4) the Library of Congress, (5) the private library of Lloyd W. Smith, Madison, New Jersey, (6) the British Museum and (7) the Public Record Office.

The three principal Virginia depositories complement one another. In the State Library, the county court records are of particular importance. Some Counties have availed themselves of a State law that permits them to deposit early papers in the Library for safekeeping. In other instances, the Library Board, patriotic societies or interested persons have paid for photostating the contents of volumes that county pride retained. References to the records in the appended list, under the heading "Virginia, Colony of. County Records," calls attention to the diversity of titles given some of these records by early Clerks of Court. While this creates provoking uncertainty concerning the volume in which a document may be, an examination of the footnotes of Vol. I., Chap. IV will illustrate the extent and the diversity of the information these records contain. They are the treasure house of the social history of colonial Virginia. Much the same thing is to be said, *mutatis mutandis,* of the records of the Land Office, which fortunately include those of the Fairfax proprietary. It is a long labor to examine and to classify these grants according to the patentees, but if it is done, the land system described in Volume I takes clear form.

The resources of the Virginia Historical Society ought to be to every such organization an inspiration and a reproach, because they show how much can be done with little money by persons genuinely devoted to the preservation of valuable papers. As recently as 1927, the total annual income of the Virginia Historical Society did not exceed $9800. For many years it was less than that; but the scholarly secretaries of the society, each in his turn, collected source materials that otherwise would in many instances have been lost. Underpaid assistants painfully copied in longhand, sometimes even with a pencil, private documents lent the Society. There could be no better proof of the value of these fine services than the frequency with which "VHS" appears after the name of a particular collection in the appended list. Special note should be made of the Custis Papers which, with those in the Pennsylvania Historical Society, supply part of the background of the Dunbar case and disclose the condition of the Custis estate at the time Washington married Martha Dandridge Custis. A propos of the dispersion of the Custis records, a glance at the subjoined item on the Principio Papers will illustrate how manuscripts of a single connection sometimes are scattered without so much as a clue of the circumstances in which they originally were divided. In this instance, some of the unpublished papers came to light in the Maryland Historical Society files, some in the New York Public Library, others in the vault of Lloyd W. Smith, and still others in the British Museum.. By piecing all these together with the printed documents, it is possible to get a wearable fabric of fact, though there still are holes. All too often, where similar papers are neglected, the holes are beyond repair.

Fitzpatrick prefaced Volume I of his edition of *The Writings of George Washington* with so sound and so thorough a description of the great collection of papers in the Library of Congress that nothing need be added. It is of course to be regretted that so few of Washington's early letters survive; but those that escaped destruction are as self-revelatory, perhaps, as those of almost any other great person of history. Washington erred in "editing" his letters late in life to erase some of his clumsy writing of the seventeen-fifties. In nearly all other respects he was a faithful custodian of papers that are a heritage of the nation. It may be added that while some mistakes were made many years ago in handling, arranging and binding certain of the Washington Papers, the government has guarded them well.

Much of the information available in the Washington Papers of the Library of Congress has been available in letters and documents that never have been "wrung dry." This surprising condition is described in the Introduction of Volume I and need not be reviewed further. Second, a considerable amount of new and important fact is recoverable from letters to Washington which, like those from his hand, have not often been examined with fullest care. The third source of fresh information on Washington is represented by his account books. For 1747–58, no other records of his life contain as much that is unfamiliar or unknown. Parts of *Ledger A* have been used but, apparently, many of its items never have been analyzed. This will be equally apparent in Volume III, where most of the "gaps" in the life of Washington from 1759 to 1775 are filled with data from his ledger and his separate account books.

The collection of Lloyd W. Smith, Madison, N. J., is a notable example of what a patriotic private citizen can accomplish in bringing together just such papers as are most apt to be lost, to the impairment of historical truth. Besides giving safe custody to many records that would have been scattered, Mr. Smith built up gradually a store of books, pamphlets and manuscripts that is almost unique. His Revolutionary pamphlets are renowned but many of his other treasures are almost as rich.

In dealing with all archives outside the United States, time is saved by examining in advance the transcripts, if any, now in the Library of Congress. These collections are large and are apt to include much that a student would copy, at greater expense, in a European capital. For 1732–58, these "LC Transcripts" of official papers in the British Museum and in the Public Record Office are quite extensive, but the great English depositories include documents of high importance that have not yet been copied for the Library of Congress. Cases in point are parts of the Chatham Papers in the Public Record Office and of the Newcastle Papers in the British Museum. Besides these, the Colonial Office Papers from America and the West Indies, the files of the Board of Trade, the Privy Council and Chancery records, and the Close Rolls have repaid detailed examination. Among the Additional Manuscripts of the British Museum, the Bouquet Papers are of high interest; the Egerton Papers and the King's Manuscripts contain numerous gratifying surprises. Incidentally, the originals of the Bouquet Papers and of various other manuscripts are less difficult to read than are some of the LC photostats of these papers.

Many minor depositories in the United States have been visited. The directors of others have been generous in permitting members of their staffs to search for desired papers. None of these libraries contains much material on Washington prior to the American Revolution. This is true, also, of governmental archives in Ottawa, Montreal and Quebec. As it happens, some of the original papers in the Canadian archives are of extraordinary interest because of their association—witness the capitulation of Fort Necessity and the Stobo letter of July 28, 1755, reproduced in these volumes. Transcripts from the collections in Paris are numerous and representative, in some instances comprehensive even; but as the contents of French archives that relate to Washington are primarily those of 1777 and later, detailed report on them is deferred to Volume IV of the present work.

The wide dispersion of the letters of Washington is indicated by the references in *G.W.* Every paper printed in the thirty-seven volumes of that work is credited to its source and, if in Washington's autograph, is marked appropriately. Many well-stored and distinguished libraries have yielded not more than two or three folios from the pen of Washington. Some depositories have one only. As a result of this search, and other reasons, it may be said that probably few important, surviving personal papers of Washington remain unknown. Not many are unpublished. The tradition that Mrs. Washington destroyed all his letters to her must be accepted as correct, though the time and circumstances of this lamentable disservice to history are unknown. If there exists any considerable *cache* of Washington papers, it probably consists of the missing account books of the Custis estate, or of the papers listed in the Birch Catalogue 663 of the Washington relics offered for sale in 1891. Markings on the copy of that catalogue in the Library of Congress indicate that the items were auctioned one by one. No single individual is known to have bought any considerable number of them, nor have any of them been offered in recent years at any advertised sale. If they come to light, in whole or in part, they will be found to contain nothing that will change any major fact in the biography of Washington, but they may supply some needed details regarding the condition of Mount Vernon when Washington leased the property in December, 1754.

From the list that follows, most of the single manuscripts have been omitted in the belief that references to them in the footnotes will be found adequate.

PRINCIPAL MANUSCRIPT SOURCES

ALEXANDRIA (VA.) BOARD OF TRUSTEES. Proceedings, 1748 and after. Mount Vernon photostat of the original. Important for the connection of Lawrence and George Washington with the town.

BALL, JOSEPH. Letter Book, Jan. 12, 1743/44—Dec. 8, 1759. LC. Letters written from London to relatives and friends in Virginia, among whom were Mary and George Washington. The greater number of letters are to Ball's nephew and estate agent, Joseph Chinn, regarding the management of the Ball plantation in Lancaster County, Virginia.

BLATHWAYT. WM. Journal of Proceedings in Pursuance of Letters Patent dated the 11th of May, 1660. P.R.O., Treas., 64, 88–90. 2 vols. Documents regarding Culpeper and Arlington grants, Culpeper's administration as Governor of Virginia, quit rents, claims etc.

BOUQUET PAPERS, 1754–65. Br. Mus. Add. MSS 21631–21660. Correspondence, letter books, accounts, warrants, campaign notes, and regimental orders of Col. Henry Bouquet.

BRADDOCK, EDWARD. Letters from America, 1755. Br. Mus. Egerton MS. 2694, with other papers concerning the French encroachments, 1750–60.

BROWNE, MRS. CHARLOTTE. Journal, Nov. 17, 1754–Jan. 19, 1757. VHS photostat. Diary of an English woman with Braddock's army. The original manuscript was owned (1926) by S. A. Coulthard of Howe, Halstead, Essex, England. Sir Arthur Ponsonby Ponsonby published extracts from the journal in his *English Diaries from the 16th to the 20th Centuries* (London, 1922). Fairfax Harrison, who presented the photostat, edited in 32 *V* the part relating to Braddock's march.

BYRD TITLE BOOK. VHS. 1697–1715. Large folio volume of deeds etc., relating to the Byrd lands. Given to VHS in 1875 by John Esten Cooke. Several pages are devoted to the settlement of the estate of Daniel Parke, father-in-law of Wm. Byrd II, and of John Custis. Originals of three of the indentures, with pendant seals, are in VHS. The parts relating to land conveyances were edited by Mrs. Rebecca Johnston in 47–50 *V*.

CARTER, CHARLES, JOHN AND LANDON. Carter Plummer Letter Book. Copies of letters, for the most part addressed to English agents, from Charles, John and Landon Carter, executors of the estate of their father, Robert I, of Corotoman. These letters follow almost immediately those written by "King" Carter over a long term of years to practically the same agents, and they form an interesting supplement to the correspondence in the Carter Transcripts and in *Wright*. This manuscript, for some years on deposit in VHS, has recently been returned to its owner, Mrs. Fanny Minor Plummer of Mobile, Alabama.

CARTER, LANDON, of Sabine Hall. Diary of a leading planter. The original, privately owned, is being edited by T. Dabney Wellford. Parts of the diary have been published in *W* and in *T*.

CARTER, ROBERT. Letters to his agents, 1723–29. VHS Transcripts. Three are in L. B. Wright, ed., *Letters of Robert Carter*. The originals have not been located.

CARTHAGENA EXPEDITION, 1740–43. P.R.O., C.O. 5: 41–42. Official papers of no direct bearing on Lawrence Washington.

CORBIN, RICHARD. Letter Book, 1758–68. VHS. The letters, for the most part to British merchants, contain orders for clothing, household goods, and farm implements, as well as articles for the house Corbin was building to replace the one destroyed by fire in 1758.

CUMBERLAND PAPERS. Windsor Castle. Private papers of William Augustus, Duke of Cumberland, second son of George II and Captain-General of the British Army, 1745–57. Contain much material concerning American military operations. Many of the more important of these papers are printed in *Pargellis*.

CUSTIS, JOHN. Letter Book, 1717–42. LC. Important, diversified and contentious letters of the father-in-law of Mrs. George Washington by her first marriage.

CUSTIS, DANIEL PARKE AND MARTHA DANDRIDGE. Letters. Historical Society of Pennsylvania. The Martha Custis letters are nearly all printed in Mrs. Anne Hollingsworth Wharton's *Martha Washington*. Those to and from Daniel Parke Custis are unpublished.

CUSTIS, DANIEL PARKE. Invoice Book. LC. 1749–57. Restricted.

CUSTIS FAMILY. Miscellaneous Papers, 1637–1857. VHS. Papers of Col. John Custis, Daniel Parke Custis, and the wife and children of Daniel Parke Custis. Consist largely of orders, invoices and bills of lading for tobacco. A small but most important part deal with the settlement of Daniel Parke Custis's estate.

CUSTIS ESTATE. Account books, c. 1762–75. VHS. Two tattered books with the "marbled covers" ordered by Washington from London and used for the accounts of his stepchildren.

DABNEY PAPERS, 1708–97. VHS. Papers relating to Col. Charles Dabney during the Revolution. Also a few minor, miscellaneous papers in irrelevant insertion.

FAUNTLEROY FAMILY. Typescript. VSL. Col. Moore Fauntleroy, His Ancestors and Descendants. Two vols. paged continuously.

FILIUS GALLICAE. [Pseudonym.] Letters 1756–61. P.R.O., C.O. 5: 52. Addressed chiefly to the Duke of Mirepoix; concern treasonable correspondence described in Vol. II, Chap. XIII of this work.

FITZHUGH, WILLIAM. Letter Book, 1679–99. VHS. Manuscript copy of the original Letter Book now in possession of Benjamin T. Fitzhugh of Vicksburg, Miss. A photostat of the original is in LC. Practically the entire collection has been published in *V*.

FRENCH AND INDIAN WAR, 1755–58. P.R.O., C.O. 5: 46, 47. Correspondence of Braddock, Atkin, Loudoun, Shirley, Abercrombie etc. Mostly in print.

FRENCH AND INDIAN WAR. 1755. P.R.O., Special Collections. Chatham Papers, 98. A French account (translated into English) of Braddock's defeat.

FRENCH AND INDIAN WAR. 1754–65. French Narratives and Documents. Paris: Archives des Affaires Étrangères: Mémoires et Documents, Amérique. Vol. 3, 10, 11; Angleterre. vol. 438, 439, 441; Archives Nationales; C. 11. A. These last two include colonial records of 1750–60. As far as can be ascertained, all the more important of these papers are represented by transcripts in the Library of Congress or in the Public Archives in Ottawa. See the detailed analysis in Vol. IV.

FRENCH AND INDIAN WAR. Ordnance. P.R.O., C.O. 5: 166. Correspondence of the Secretary of State with the Ordnance Department. Relates to Virginia, for the most part after 1779. A few papers belong to the Indian War.

GOOCH, WILLIAM. Letters, 1727–51. VHS. Three volumes of typescripts of letters and reports addressed to the Lords of Trade and Plantations, to the Governor of the Colony and Ancient Dominion of Virginia, and to the Bishop of London. Contain much valuable information on the social, ecclesiastical and economic conditions in Virginia. Perhaps the most important of the correspondence deals with the contention between the planters and the home government over tobacco.

GOOCH, WILLIAM. Letters, 1727–44. Col. Williamsburg Inc. Thirteen letters written by William Gooch to his brother in England. Confidential comments on situations and personalities in Williamsburg.

HALKETT, SIR PETER. Orderly Book, Mch. 27–July 22, 1755. LC. Kept by Lt. Daniel Disney of the 44th Regiment. Supplements usefully the journals of Robert Orme and others in *Sargent.*

INSTRUCTIONS TO GEN. BRADDOCK. Nov. 25, 1754. P.R.O., C.O. 5: 6. Issued prior to his sailing for America.

LOUDOUN, LORD. Memorandum, January to March, 1757. Huntington Lib. Account of his arrival in America and of his conferences with the colonial governors in Philadelphia. Important for reference to his suspicion that Washington was author of the letters of *Filius Gallicae, q.v.*

NEWCASTLE PAPERS, 1667–1768. Br. Mus. Add. MSS 32686–33057. (Also catalogued as 1–307 Newcastle Papers.) Private and official papers and correspondence of Thomas Pelham Holles, Duke of Newcastle. They contain several volumes which are largely devoted to affairs in Virginia.

NORTHERN NECK PROPRIETARY. Original Grant, 1649. Br. Mus. Add. Charter, 13585. The face of this is reproduced in Vol. I.

NORTHERN NECK PROPRIETARY. Letters of Catherine Culpeper and of her husband, Thomas Lord Fairfax, 1694–95. P.R.O., C.O., 324: 26. Petitions, Royal Warrants, Grants and Letters.

NORTHERN NECK PROPRIETARY. Wilmington Papers. LC. Two volumes of transcripts with some original papers. Include public and private papers regarding Lady Culpeper's interest in the Northern Neck and abstract of the proceedings regarding the boundary, etc.

ORME, ROBERT. Journal. Br. Mus. King's MS 212. Journal of General Braddock's Expedition in 1755, prefaced by six colored maps. The journal was printed in *Sargent;* the maps have never been reproduced adequately.

PARKE, DANIEL. Official Papers, 1709–10. P.R.O., C.O., 7: 1. Antigua. Relate to Parke's administration as Governor of the Leeward Islands; throw little light on events that led to the Dunbar suit.

PETERS, RICHARD. Papers, 1697–1845. Penn. His. Soc. Especially useful for the campaigns in Pennsylvania during the French and Indian War and for the disturbances in Philadelphia.

PRESTON PAPERS. 1730–91. VHS. Relate largely to frontier conditions in the middle years of the eighteenth century in Virginia; useful for the study of the military problem of frontier defense which Washington had to solve, but otherwise contain little of definite bearing on his career. Another smaller mass of Preston papers is in the Draper Collection, Wis. His. Soc.

PRINCIPIO PAPERS. 1720 and later. Records of the Virginia and Maryland iron furnaces in which Augustine Washington and some of his descendants had a financial interest. These records are widely scattered, according to no determinable arrangement, among (1) the Emmett Collection, N. Y. Pub. Lib.; (2) the Lloyd W. Smith Collection, Madison, N. J.; (3) the Maryland His. Soc. and (4) the British Museum, Add. MS 29600.

RANDOLPH MANUSCRIPT. VHS. Three folio volumes containing eighteenth century copies of the Court Book of the Virginia Company of London, and other papers, from the transcript of these records owned by Wm. Byrd. The papers in vol. 3 refer to the proprietary of the Northen Neck in the time of Charles II.

STEPHEN, ADAM. "Life," 1775. Lib. Co. of Philadelphia. Biographical letter in the Rush Papers. Printed in 23 *Penn. Mag.* but cited in the present work from the original.

STEPHEN, ADAM. Papers. LC. A large folio volume of miscellaneous letters of Adam and Alexander Stephen. Those relating to Adam Stephen are of minor importance.

STEPHEN, ADAM. Br. Mus. Add. MS 35376, f. 127. Letter on Braddock's defeat in Hardwicke Papers.

THOM PAPERS. Mount Vernon. About five hundred letters retained by the Washington family when the Washington papers were bought by the Department of State. Few of these have ever been published. The collection takes its name from the donor, Mrs. DeCourcy Thom.

VIRGINIA, COLONY OF. Entry Acts, 1662–1758. P.R.O., C.O., 5: 276. A list of acts relating to Virginia with marginal notes telling whether or when the act was repealed.

VIRGINIA, COLONY OF. Assembly, 1660–1774. P.R.O., C.O., 5: 1423–27. Journals of Council, Assembly, and Council in Assembly, of Virginia. The collection has been used by VSL to fill the gaps in the records of the Assembly available in America.

VIRGINIA, COLONY OF. Church. VSL Photostat. Brydon, George MacLaren, Parish lines in the Diocese of Virginia.

VIRGINIA, COLONY OF. Church. Letters of the Clergy of Virginia to the Bishop of London. 1690 and after. VSL photostats. A miscellaneous collection from LC transcripts.

VIRGINIA, COLONY OF. Church. St. George (Spotsylvania) Vestry Book, 1726–45; 1746–1817. Lib. U. Va.

VIRGINIA, COLONY OF. Church. St. Paul's (King George) Register, 1716–98. VSL transcript and photostat.

VIRGINIA, COLONY OF. Church. Truro Parish Vestry Book, 1732–85. LC. Three generations of the Washington family (not in direct line) were vestrymen of the parish (Augustine, George and Lund).

VIRGINIA, COLONY OF. County Records, c. 1660–1760. Deeds, Wills, Inventories, Registers, Court Orders and Record Books of Westmoreland, Lancaster, Northumberland, Richmond, King George, Stafford, Prince William, York, Fairfax, Frederick, Augusta, Spotsylvania, Middlesex, Old Rappahannock, and Caroline Counties. Originals in VSL and in County offices; many photostats in VSL. It is believed that references in the footnotes are sufficiently explicit to guide a reader in consulting the original but there was no uniformity among County Clerks in designating particular records.

VIRGINIA, COLONY OF. De Jarnette Transcripts, 1606–96. VSL. Two volumes of copies of public papers made by D. C. DeJarnette, special commissioner appointed to ascertain the extent of original papers bearing on the Va.–N. C. boundary line. For details see VSL *Calendar of Transcripts*, 1905, p. 114, 119, 545.

VIRGINIA, COLONY OF. Governors. Letters to the Board of Trade. P.R.O., C.O. 5: 1316, 1328, 1329 cover the period of Washington's youth.

VIRGINIA, COLONY OF. Land Office. Records of the Colony and Ancient Dominion of Virginia. Warrants issued by the Governor. Books 2–6; Patent Books, 1–6.

VIRGINIA, COLONY OF. Land Office Records of the Proprietary of the Northern Neck. VSL. N.N. 1, 2, A, B, C, D, E, F, G, H, I. Warrants issued by the Proprietors and their agents.

VIRGINIA, COLONY OF. McDonald Transcripts, 1619–95 of P.R.O. Papers. VSL. 7 vols. (vols. 3 and 4 missing). See VSL *Calendar of Transcripts,* 1905, p. 114, 119, 603.

VIRGINIA, COLONY OF. Miscellaneous. VSL. Letters and Papers relating to the colonial history of Virginia, arranged chronologically. The greater part of these have been published in *C*.

VIRGINIA, COLONY OF. Miscellaneous. Letters and Papers relating to Virginia in P.R.O., C.O. 5: 1344. Letters from the Board of Trade with important enclosures: minutes of the meetings of the Privy Council, 1750; letters from Gov. Dinwiddie, most of which have been published; a copy of Washington's *Journal* of 1754; field notes taken in running the boundary of the proprietary, 1746.

VIRGINIA, COLONY OF. Quit Rent Rolls, 1704. VHS photostats from P.R.O. of lost originals. Returns are from the Tidewater Counties; most of them published in *V*.

VIRGINIA, COLONY OF. Sainsbury Transcripts, VSL. Twenty volumes of excerpts and abstracts of P.R.O. papers relating to Virginia. Few of these are for the period of Washington's youth. A rough outline of the contents of the collection will be found in VSL *Calendar of Transcripts,* 1905, p. 119 ff.

VIRGINIA, COLONY OF. The Sparks Transcripts, 1753–81. VSL. Two folio volumes collected by Jared Sparks. Include: Virginia Council Chamber papers, Board of Trade papers, private letters of Governor Dinwiddie. Many of the items are excerpts only; the most important are a few Dinwiddie letters not included in the Brock edition of *Din*. For a rough outline of the contents of the Sparks papers see VSL *Calendar of Transcripts,* 1905, p. 608 ff.

VIRGINIA, COLONY OF. Winder Transcripts, VSL. Two volumes of transcripts of papers in P.R.O. relating to Virginia history, 1607–79; about half of them deal with Bacon's Rebellion. See VSL *Calendar of Transcripts,* 1905, p. 534 ff.

WASHINGTON, GEORGE. Accounts, 1747–58. Washington's earliest account book is in the Lloyd W. Smith Collection; *Ledger A* (1749–72) is in LC along with numerous account books which are described in Vol. IV rather than here, because they relate principally to the period after the French and Indian War. In vol. 818 of the Washington Papers in LC are Toner Transcripts of papers regarding servants and quit rents.

WASHINGTON, GEORGE. Journals, 1748 and later. LC. Originals of the journals of 1748 (Journey across the Mountains) and of 1751 (to Barbados), Washington Papers, vols. 341 and 342. The journal of the voyage, as now extant, is printed in its entirety; minor entries of the journal of 1748, concerning boundaries etc., remain in manuscript. In the Toner Transcript, LC, vol. 733 of the Washington Papers, are parts of the journals now missing from the originals.

WASHINGTON, GEORGE. Letters, c. 1747–58. LC. Papers of Washington, vols. 1–10. This is part of the collection described fully in 1 G.W., xxxv ff. Fitzpatrick's edition lists all other depositories of letters available to him. Those of VHS for the early years are particularly important. Invoices and letters to merchants, 1756–65, are LC Washington Papers, vol. 385. In *ibid.*, vols. 674–75 are Toner Transcripts of unlocated letters of 1749–75. Most, though not all, of the letters to Washington for the period covered in these two volumes are printed in *Hamilton*. Specific reference is made in the text to those now used for the first time.

WASHINGTON, GEORGE. Memoranda, 1755. N. Y. Pub. Lib. A small book of jottings with notes of items to be included in letters to public officials and others. A photostat of the whole is in LC. Fragments in the Toner Transcripts, Washington Papers, vol. 733, and other references in various letters, indicate that Washington probably made many memoranda in other small blank books that were filled and later thrown away.

WASHINGTON, GEORGE. Military Papers, 1754–58. LC. Included are (1) general military papers, 1754–59, vols., 303–306; (2) military accounts, 1754–59, vols. 383–4, 386089; (3) Orderly Book of General Edward Braddock during the expedition against Fort DuQuesne in Washington's autograph, vol. 410. (4) Letter book of correspondence in the Braddock Expedition, vol. 411; (5) Orderly Book of Gen. John Forbes, Sept. 21–Nov. 27, 1758, vol. 414; (6) Letters to Col. Henry Bouquet, June 14–Sept. 18, 1758, vol. 413.

WASHINGTON, GEORGE. Miscellaneous Papers, 1745 and later. LC. For the period covered by these volumes, the more important of the miscellaneous papers are the familiar (1) Rules of Civility and miscellaneous notes in vol. 338; (2) the polls of votes in Frederick and Fairfax Counties, vol. 816 of Toner Transcripts; and (3) the list of freeholders in Fairfax County, *ibid*.

WASHINGTON, FAMILY. Papers, 1739–49. The Havemeyer Papers in the Lloyd W. Smith Collection. Letters relating to Augustine and Lawrence Washington. Several of these are printed in *Conway's Barons* but are quoted in this work from the originals.

SHORT-TITLE INDEX

SHORT-TITLE INDEX

The appended Short-Title Index includes those manuscripts and printed works frequently cited in this work and not always sufficiently identified by the title used in the footnotes. Books cited once only, or at long intervals in the footnotes, are not listed here. The depository of each manuscript collection carrying a short-title is given in the list of Principal Manuscript Sources that precedes this Index.

A.H.A. American Historical Association. Annual Reports.

A.H.R. American Historical Review.

Acts and Ord. Acts and Ordinances of the Interregnum.

Ambler. C. H. AMBLER. "George Washington and the West."

Anburey. THOMAS ANBUREY. "Travels through the Interior Parts of North America."

Ball Letter Book. JOSEPH BALL. MS Letter Book.

Baker-Crothers. HAYES BAKER-CROTHERS. "Virginia and the French and Indian War."

Beauchamp. WM. M. BEAUCHAMP. "Wampum and Shell Articles used by the Indians."

Beauchamp, Iroquois. WM. M. BEAUCHAMP. "The New York Iroquois."

Beauchamp, Iroquois Trail. WM. M. BEAUCHAMP. "The Iroquois Trail."

Beverley. ROBERT BEVERLEY. "History of Virginia."

Bienséance, etc. JEAN PIC. "Discours sur la bienséance de la conversation entre les hommes."

Biog. Hist. N. C. SAMUEL A. ASHE. "A Biographical History of North Carolina."

Birch Cat. 663. "Catalogue (No. 663) of the final sale of the relics of General Washington, compiled for Thomas Birch by S. V. Henkels."

Blair. MRS. EMMA H. BLAIR. "Indian Tribes of the Upper Mississippi Valley."

Blair, Bannister and Braxton. FREDERICK HORNER. "A History of the Blair, Bannister and Braxton Families."

Bland Papers. THEODORICK BLAND. "Selection of MSS of Col. Theodorick Bland jun."

Blanton. W. B. BLANTON. "Medicine in Virginia in the Eighteenth Century."

Blathwayt Journal. WM. BLATHWAYT. "Journal of Proceedings."

Boucher. JONATHAN BOUCHER. "Reminiscences of an American Loyalist."

Mrs. Browne. MRS. CHARLOTTE BROWNE. Diary, printed in 32 V.

Buck. S. J. and E. H. BUCK. "The Planting of Civilization in Western Pennsylvania."

Burnaby. REV. ANDREW BURNABY. "Travels through the Middle Settlements."

C. "Calendar of Virginia State Papers."

Cal. Am. & W. I. "Calendar of State Papers: Colonial, America and West Indies."

Cal. Clarendon Papers. "Calendar of the State Papers collected by Edward Hyde, Earl of Clarendon." Not to be confused with *Clarendon's State Papers.*

Carter Diary. LANDON CARTER. MS Diary.

Carter Transcripts. ROBERT CARTER. Letters. (VHS Transcripts.)

Carter-Plummer MS. Letters of John, Landon and Robert Carter to London agents.

Carver, Travels. JONATHAN CARVER. "Three Years Travel in America."

Cary Letter. Letter No. 83 in John Custis's MS Letter Book.

Chadwick. E. M. CHADWICK. "The People of the Long House."

Charles Parish. L. C. BELL. "Charles Parish, its History and Register."

CHASTELLUX. FRANÇOIS JEAN, MARQUIS DE CHASTELLUX. "Voyage dans l'Amérique."

Clarendon's Life. "The Life of Edward Hyde, Earl of Clarendon, Written by Himself."

Clarendon's Rebellion. EDWARD HYDE, EARL OF CLARENDON. "History of the Civil War."

Clarendon's State Papers. The Papers of Edward Hyde, Earl of Clarendon.

Coll. des MSS. Collection des Manuscrits relatifs à la Nouvelle France.

Conway's Barons. MONCURE D. CONWAY. "Barons of the Potomac and the Rappahannock."

Council Minutes. H. R. McILWAINE, ed. "Minutes of the Council and General Court of Virginia."

Corbin Letter Book. RICHARD CORBIN. MS Letter Book.

Cresap. KENNETH P. BAILEY. "Thomas Cresap."

Custis Letter Book. JOHN CUSTIS. MS Letter Book.

Custis Papers. MS Papers of John Custis, Daniel Parke Custis, etc.

Custis Pleas. "The Several Pleas and Answer of John Custis." MS.

Dab. "Dictionary of American Biography."

DNB. "Dictionary of National Biography."

Dabney Papers. "MS. Papers of Charles Dabney."

Darlington. WM. DARLINGTON, ed. "Christopher Gist's Journals."

Diaries. JOHN C. FITZPATRICK, ed. "The Diaries of George Washington."

Din. R. A. BROCK, ed. "The Official Papers of Robert Dinwiddie."

E.J. H. R. McILWAINE and (later) W. L. HALL, ed. "The Executive Journals of the Council of Colonial Virginia."

Eaton. DAVID EATON. "Historical Atlas of Westmoreland Co., Virginia."

Ellis Correspondence. GEORGE JAMES WETMORE, AGAR ELLIS, ed. "Letters written 1686–88 to John Ellis Esq."

Eubank. H. RAGLAND EUBANK. "The Northern Neck of Virginia."

Evans Analyses. In L. H. Gipson. "Lewis Evans."

Every Man his own Doctor. DR. JOHN TENNENT. "Every Man his Own Doctor."

Farish. H. D. FARISH, ed. HARTWELL, BLAIR, and CHILTON. "The Present State of Virginia."

Fauntleroy. THE FAUNTLEROY FAMILY. "VSL Typescript."

Fithian. PHILIP FITHIAN. "Journal and Letters."

Flippin. P. S. FLIPPIN. "The Royal Government in Virginia, 1624–1775."

Ford. W. C. FORD, ed. "George Washington. Writings."

Forbes. A. P. JAMES, ed. "Gen. John Forbes, Writings relating to America."

Frontier Forts. GEORGE DALLAS ALBERT. "Frontier Forts of Western Pennsylvania."

G. and H. EVARTS GREENE and VIRGINIA HARRINGTON. "American Population before 1790."

Morgan. H. LEWIS MORGAN. "The League of the Iroquois."

N. C. Col. Records. WM. L. SAUNDERS, ed. "Colonial Records of North Carolina."

N. C. Wills. J. BRYAN GRIMES. "North Carolina Wills and Inventories."

N. Y. Col. Docts. E. B. O'CALLAGHAN, ed. "Documents relating to the Colonial History of New York."

Newcastle Papers. BR. MUS. ADD. MSS 32683–33057. "Papers of the Duke of Newcastle." These are also catalogued separately as Newcastle Papers, vol. 1–307.

Nicholas Papers. SIR EDWARD NICHOLAS. "Correspondence."

Norris. J. E. NORRIS. "History of the lower Shenandoah Valley."

Olden Time. NEVILLE B. CRAIG. "The Olden Time."

Orme. ROBERT ORME, Journal in Sargent. "History of the Expeditions against Fort DuQuesne."

Osgood. HERBERT L. OSGOOD. "The American Colonies in the Seventeenth Century."

Pargellis. S. M. PARGELLIS, ed. "Military Affairs in North America."

Pargellis, Loudoun. S. M. PARGELLIS. "Lord Loudoun in America."

Peters Papers. RICHARD PETERS. MS Collection in the His. Soc. of Penn.

Preston Papers. PRESTON. MS. Papers relating to Western Virginia.

Preston MSS. DRAPER COLL. Preston Papers, Wis. His. Soc. relating to the French and Indian Wars.

Pitt. GERTRUDE S. KIMBALL, ed. "Wm. Pitt, Lord Chatham." Correspondence.

Mrs. Powell. MRS. MARY POWELL. "History of Alexander, Virginia."

Pritts. JOSEPH PRITTS. "Mirror of Olden Time Border Life."

R. "Virginia Historical Register."

Reichel. W. C. REICHEL. "Memorials of the Moravian Church."

Sally Cary. W. M. CARY. "Sally Cary."

Sargent. WINTHROP SARGENT. "History of an Expedition to Fort DuQuesne."

Seaman, Sargent. "Narrative of a Seaman" in Winthrop Sargent, *supra.*

Sharpe. HORATIO SHARPE. "Correspondence." (Archives of Maryland, vols. 6, 9, 14, 31.)

Shippen Papers. JOSEPH BALCH. "Letters and Papers Relating to Pennsylvania."

Shirley. C. H. LINCOLN, ed. "Correspondence of William Shirley."

Smyth. J. F. D. SMYTH. "A Tour in the United States of America."

Snowden, Historic Landmarks. W. H. SNOWDEN. "Some Historic Landmarks of Virginia and Maryland."

Sparks. JARED SPARKS, ed. "George Washington Writings."

Spotswood's Letters. R. A. BROCK, ed. "The Official Letters of Alexander Spotswood."

Stephen's "Life", Rush Papers. Adam Stephen's autobiographical letter in the Papers of Benjamin Rush.

Stephen Papers. MS. collection of the Papers of Adam and Alexander Stephen. LC.

Stobo. [Anon.] "Memoirs of Major Robert Stobo."

Sutherland. STELLA H. SUTHERLAND. "Population Distribution in Colonial America."

T. "Tyler's Quarterly."

Thwaites. REUBEN G. THWAITES. "Early Western Travels."

V. "Virginia Magazine of History and Biography."

INDEX

INDEX

Abbingdon grant, the, I, 35 *n.*

Abercromby, Major General James, II, 8, 196, 197, 305, 332 *n.*; name also spelled Abercrombie, II, 196 *n.*

Acadians, in Hampton, Va., I, 159

Accidence to the English Tongue, I, 131 *n.*

Accokeek Creek, I, 38, 39, 42, 205

Accokeek Farm, I, 57 *n.*

Accokeek furnace, the, I, 48, 52 *n.,* 55–57, 67, 73, 145

Accotick, I, 39 *n.*

Accotink, I, 39 *n.*

"Act for Amending the Staple of Tobacco, An," I, 141

Act, militia, I, 330ff., II, 137ff; for the encouragement and protection of the settlers upon the Mississippi, I, 333 *n.*; for making provision against invasions and insurrections, I, 347 *n.*; for the conscription of vagrants, I, 442; "to amend an act," II, 138 *n*; the mutiny, II, 232 and *n.,* 258; authorizing sale of Parke property, II, 284

Adams, John, II, 382

Adams, Samuel, II, 382

Adams, Thomas, I, 263 *n.*

Addison, Somerset Co., Penn., II, 46 *n.*

Addison, Joseph I, 46

Aix-la-Chapelle, Treaty of, *see* Treaty of Aix-la-Chapelle

Albany, Treaty of, *see* Treaty of Albany

Albemarle, Earl of, I, 170, 423, 424; II, 206

Albemarle County, I, 72

Albion, estate of the Townsends, I, 226

Alexander, Anne, I, 226

Alexander, Frances, I, 260, 261

Alexander, Gerrard, II, 145

Alexander, Major John, I, 21, 232

Alexander, Philip, I, 232

Alexander, Col. Robert, I, 226

Alexandria, Va. (also known as Belhaven), I, 120 *n.,* 161, 278, 401, 418; II, 14, 15, 26, 27, 87, 116, 117, 121, 142, 144, 224, 242, 264, 276; semi-annual fairs at, I, 122; establishment of, I, 232, 233; Lawrence Washington a trustee of, I, 329; training of militia in, I, 329; Washington's recruiting in, I, 335; Carlyle's residence in, I, 336; distance between Winchester and, I, 349 *n.*; Washington's troops in, I, 424; Braddock's reception at, II, 15, 18; Washington visits, II, 19, 20; Braddock's base, II, 89

Alice, John Custis's slave, II, 293 *n.,* 295

Aliquippa, Queen, I, 323

All Saints, Purleigh Parish, Essex, I, 528

Allegheny Mountains, the, II, 21, 22, 46, 120, 323, 329, 352, 356

Allegheny River, the, I, 281, 287, 310 *n.,* 321

Allen, Ensign, II, 44

Allen, Capt. John, I, 24, 25 *n.*

Allen, Chief Justice William, Bouquet to, II, 366

Allentown, Pa., II, 159

Allerton, Major Isaac (later Col.), I, 2, 3, 23–25, 129, 468

Allerton, Willoughby, I, 526

Allertons, the, I, 526

Alton, John, II, 55, 58, 212 *n.*

Ambridge, Pa., I, 271 *n.*

Amelia County, missionaries in, I, 105

American Instructor, The, I, 125

"American Regiment," the, in war with Spain, I, 65, 66, 69

American Regiment, Royal, *see* Royal American Regiment

American, the, first to be made a baronet, II, 10; books for army, II, 150

Amherst, General, II, 322

Amson, Dr. John, II, 278

Andros, Governor, I, 180

Annapolis, Md., II, 20, 21, 23, 167; George Washington's first recorded journey to, I, 247

Anne, Queen, I, 490; II, 280

Antigua, II, 280, 281, 282, 286, 289, 301

Appleby School, Westmoreland, I, 32, 46, 53, 56 *n.,* 70

Appleton, Frances (Mrs. John), I, 18, 19, 25, *see also* Washington, Frances Appleton

Appleton, Capt. John, I, 18, 21 *n.,* 25

Appomattox, the, I, 147 *n.,* 161

Appomattox Parish, I, 17 *n.*

Apprenticeships, I, 146

Aquia Creek, I, 39, 225

Arbuckle, Mrs. Margaret, I, 89

Aretkin, William, I, 470

Arlington, John Custis's plantation at, II, 295

Arlington, Henry Bennet, Earl of, I, 6, 462, 463, 471

Arlington-Culpeper Grant, I, 462, 479, 480

Armes, Ethel, I, 50 *n.*

Armiger, William, I, 27, 28 and *n.*

Armistead, Robert, I, 96

Armistead's Ordinary, I, 441 *n.*

Arms and ammunition, shortage of, and poor quality, II, 110, 126, 171, 179

Armstrong, Col. John, II, 360, 361; quoted, II, 323 *n.*

Armstrong's Camp, II, 361, 362

Artisan, the, in Virginia society, I, 84

433